1966

may be kept

SPAIN AND THE WESTERN TRADITION

The Castilian Mind in Literature from *El Cid* to Calderón

SPAIN AND THE WESTERN TRADITION

The Castilian Mind in Literature
from *El Cid* to Calderón

Volume III

Otis H. Green

Madison and Milwaukee, 1965
The University of Wisconsin Press

Published by the University of Wisconsin Press
P.O. Box 1379, Madison, Wisconsin 53701

Printed in the United States of America
by North Central Publishing Company

Library of Congress Catalog Number 63–13745

Preface

It seems appropriate for a mountain climber to apply — with the reader's kind indulgence — imagery taken from his sport to elucidate his intention in the present volume. Taking that indulgence for granted, he invites the reader to accompany him as he breasts the ridge that separates, in Spanish intellectual history, the generations of struggle toward fully realized nationhood from those other generations — complex and difficult to understand — in which we perceive both the enhancement of Spain's success in her effort at self-expression and the progressive failure of her policies in the age of the baroque. From the top of the ridge we shall see how we arrived at our vantage point and what sort of terrain we shall encounter on the other side.

As promised in the Preface of Volume I, the present book is divided into two Parts. The first, entitled "Self-Realization," traces in six chapters the development of the national culture — primarily literary culture — from an unsatisfactory state in the fifteenth century to the point where the sense of inferiority to nations ancient or modern has been overcome. The six chapters of Part II study important aspects of the Spanish Renaissance as a whole: its non-pagan and Christian character (VII); the preference of the nation's intellectuals for religious, ethical, and legal problems, as against those of science or of technical philosophy (VIII); the insistence by Spaniards that Spain is not inferior to more pragmatic and more practical nations (IX); the impressive power of assimilation of often opposing philosophical currents (X); the essentially optimistic belief that right makes might in a God-governed universe (XI); the conception of the relation of literature to society (XII).

This leaves important matters to be studied in the fourth and final volume, which will concern itself with the problem of how Spain achieved full self-expression in literature while she was retreating from utopia, yielding frontier after frontier as her political — and eventually her intellectual — energies waned after their long and prodigal expenditure in an attempt to achieve the impossible.

I would again express my thanks to the generous friends mentioned in earlier prefaces; to the Committee on the Advancement of Research of the University of Pennsylvania for grants covering the mechanical costs of producing the typescript; and to the John Simon Guggenheim Foundation for the award of a fellowship which has given me free time to see the present volume through the press while Volume IV is being composed. Finally, I renew my expression of gratitude to Mrs. Isobel Korbel of the University of Wisconsin Press for her ever competent and devoted efforts as *aide d'auteur,* and to Mrs. Augusta Espantoso de Foley, who generously read the page proofs.

OTIS H. GREEN

Philadelphia, Pennsylvania
May, 1964

Contents

PART I

Self-realization

A feeling of national euphoria and a sense of boundless optimism filled the Spain of the Catholic Monarchs. How would this spirit respond to the inexperienced rule of a foreign prince?

. . . .

In a reckless accumulation of commitments, Philip II had brought himself to war with three powers — England, the United Provinces, and France. . . . Given the forces at his disposal, the problem was insuperable.

JOHN LYNCH

NOTE TO PART I QUOTATION: *Spain under the Habsburgs, I: Empire and Absolutism, 1576–1589* (New York, 1964), 34, 334–35.

I · Symbols of Change

On September 8, 1517, Charles I of Spain — soon to become Charles V of the Holy Roman Empire — set sail from Middelburg in Zeeland on his first visit to his newly inherited Spanish kingdoms. "It was a proud fleet that weighed anchor at five o'clock on Tuesday morning," writes Hayward Keniston in his account of the voyage, "forty ships large and small. The King's ship, the largest of all, was gaily painted green and red, with gold trimmings; the sails, too, bore paintings of the Crucifixion between the columns of Hercules with the device *Plus Oultre*, the Trinity, Our Lady with the Christ Child, and the saints — Santiago, St. Nicholas, St. Christopher with his feet in the sea. To keep the fleet together there was an elaborate set of sailing orders regarding lights and cannon shots." [1]

As we set forth — reader and author — on our own voyage of exploration in search of the differentiating factors that gave to the Spanish Renaissance its special character within the greater European movement, we may well pause to consider the symbols painted on those sails. The emblem of the Pillars of Hercules and the device *Plus Oultre* (the Burgundian form of the Latin *Plus Ultra*) were invented, according to tradition, by the humanist Luigi Marliano, the King's physician, who accompanied him on this voyage; [2] we may assume that the decorations were considered appropriate by

1. *Francisco de los Cobos, Secretary to the Emperor Charles V* (Pittsburgh, ca. 1959), p. 36.
2. Marcel Bataillon, "Plus Oultre: la cour découvre le Nouveau Monde," in Jean Jacquot (ed.), *Fêtes et cérémonies au temps de Charles Quint* (Paris, 1960), p. 13. Bataillon reviews the evidence suggesting that the device *Plus Oultre* was at first adopted by Charles without reference to the Indies, the meaning being simply that Charles had gone, or would go, beyond all others in knightly excellence and virtues. Bataillon observes, however, that the importance of the new discoveries in time came to give a geographical significance to *Plus Oultre*. I believe that it is possible to go farther: the presence of St. Christopher depicted on the sails of the fleet of 1517 — *St. Christopher with his feet in the sea* — is an indication that already in 1517 the association of *Plus Oultre* with the idea of new realms beyond the Atlantic had taken place.

the young King's advisers, both Spanish and Burgundian, and that they were intended to impress favorably the leaders of his new subjects in the Peninsula.[3]

The ideals of the House of Burgundy have been convincingly analyzed by Carlos Clavería.[4] They included an attachment to a type of chivalry already somewhat anachronistic, and they kept alive, in the waning Middle Ages, a style of life and a pattern of conduct which Johan Huizinga has called "a renaissance of a fantastic Middle Ages."[5] Yet there was also an awareness of future expansion, of future greatness in a New World unknown to the Middle Ages. The motto on the sails is *Plus Oultre* — Sail on! And, besides the Pillars of Hercules, St. Christopher — the saint whose task it was to carry travelers across the waters — stands with his feet in the sea.

We shall return in later chapters to the two basic ideas symbolized by the painted sails of the King's flagship: the Spanish Renaissance[6] is an age of expansion, but under Christian banners; the sea is to be crossed by a saint.[7] Before we do so, it will be well

3. Santiago was, of course, the sword-wielding patron saint of Spain. St. Nicholas (Pope Nicholas I) was a great defender of the rights of the church and a valiant protector of the weak. The former could suggest the Virgilian (and imperial) idea of "striking down the proud"; the latter, that of sparing and defending the humble (*Aeneid*, VI, 853: *parcere subiectis et debellare superbos*). In 1611 Covarrubias, in his *Tesoro de la lengua castellana*, gives a two-line entry under *Nicolas*: it means almost the same as Nicodemus, from νικος (sic) victory, and λαος (sic) people. Under *Nicodemus* the etyma given are νικος and δημος people, signifying "victory through the people." Similar associations may have helped to determine the choice of this saint along with St. Christopher. The other symbols — the Trinity, the holy Mother and Child — add to the general religious tone and correspond to the King's idea of his mission.

4. *Le chevalier délibéré de Olivier de la Marche y sus versiones españolas del siglo XVI* (Zaragoza, 1950), p. 37.

5. "Burgund: Eine Krise des romanisch-germanischen Verhältnisses," *Historische Zeitschrift*, CXLVIII (1933), 19 (cited by Clavería).

6. Though I have learned much since I compiled it, I must refer — as a general and still useful survey of the problem of the Spanish Renaissance — to my article, "A Critical Survey of Scholarship in the Field of Spanish Renaissance Literature, 1914–1944," *SP*, XLIV (1947), 228–64.

7. This stressing of the religious note, necessary as it is, does not imply that the Spanish (or European) Renaissance was all saintliness, or even all sweetness and light: Jules Michelet was excessively optimistic in his interpretation of history when he wrote of the budding Renaissance: "Un monde d'humanité commence, de sympathie universelle" (*Histoire de France*, IX: *La Renaissance* [Paris, 1879], 387). Although Ulrich von Hutten, just one year after Charles set sail from Middelburg, was inspired to write Willibald Pirckheimer (Oct. 25, 1518): *O seculum! o litterae! juvat vivere* — "Oh century! Oh flourishing studies! It is good to be alive" — the *seculum* was more cruel, more bloody, than golden, as the wars of religion became the *misère de ce*

to suggest certain dates that may serve us as symbols of the changing attitudes of the Spaniards as they move forward into modern times.

1380 AND 1399

Though in the present work we are studying the Castilian mind in literature, we must again, as in the preceding volumes, give some attention to Catalonia, the northeastern region of Spain which served as a bridge to Renaissance Italy. Ten years before Dante's death, seven years after Petrarch's birth, the Catalans took possession of the Greek Duchy of Athens. This was in 1311; in 1319 they took over also the Duchy of Neopatras, modern Hypate. Their connections with Byzantium and Greece were thus very close. The classical age of Catalan literature begins with Bernat Metge (1350–1410).[8]

In September of 1380, King Pedro of Aragon and Catalonia described the Acropolis of Athens as "the richest jewel in all the world, the like of which no other king of Christendom could match." The jewel was rich, a king's treasure; but it was also beautiful, and Don Pedro gives a strong aesthetic tone to his description. "It is . . . , as Gregorovius and Rubió y Lluch have stated, the first aesthetic recognition of the Acropolis, after almost a thousand years of silence, to appear on the lips of anyone in western Europe."[9] The Catalan Metge is one of the first of modern European writers to utilize the myth of Orpheus in a work composed in the vernacular — his *Lo somni* of 1399. With an aesthetic appreciation

temps (Ronsard). Very soon after 1518 the Emperor Charles (Defender of the Faith) would have to bear the opprobrium caused by the sack of the Eternal City by his troops (1527), as well as the shock of finding himself branded a heretic by the Pope. In Spain, the bulwark of orthodoxy, the sixteenth century was, so to speak, "conceived in sin": very early (*ca.* 1507) the Inquisition was used to further political ends. See the section "Fray Hernando y los orígenes de la Inquisición" in the *Estudio Preliminar* by Francisco Márquez which prefaces the edition by Francisco Martín Hernández of Fray Hernando de Talavera's *Católica impugnación* . . . (Barcelona, 1961), pp. 17–22, especially p. 18, n. 16; for a more general view, see pp. 5–53.

8. Metge's early use of Latinisms is in the medieval tradition in tone, style, and vocabulary (*Libre de fortuna e prudencia*, 1381); in *Lo somni* (1399) he uses Latinisms as a humanist. See Martín de Riquer's edition of his *Obras* (Barcelona, 1959), pp. 29, 164, of the *Prólogo*.

9. Kenneth M. Setton, "The Byzantine Background to the Italian Renaissance," *Proceedings of the American Philosophical Society*, C (1956), 64–65; see also references in n. 19.

not unlike that of King Pedro, he sees in the tale of the Greek musician's descent to Hades not a theme for ethical contemplation or moral edification but a beautiful fable, a symbol of the power of poetry to move beasts and rocks and trees.[10] In this he anticipates the Italian Angelo Poliziano by nearly a hundred years.

This sense of the beauty, the elegance and brillance, and the attraction of the ancient world, and the desire to adapt and assimilate, to equal and even to surpass the life style of the Greeks and Romans, and, at the same time, "to work the pagan marble with Christian hands"—or, as others put it, "to spoil the Egyptians" (Exod. 12:35–36)—was one of the compelling impulses felt by the Spaniards in their suddenly accelerated march toward national self-realization. When Spaniards pass from the apologetic attitude—*Pro adserenda Hispanorum eruditione*[11]—to the proud affirmation that Spain's achievements surpass those of the ancients, as in Tirso de Molina's defense of the national drama, the Renaissance in Spain has reached its end. It will be necessary to revert to this theme in a later chapter.

1456

This is the date of the death of Juan de Mena, pioneer of the Spanish literary renaissance.[12] Mena, like his friend and contemporary the Marqués de Santillana, sought to create for Spain a literature of increased culture, more worthy of learned men.[13] Mena's writing is characterized by "the complex superposition of various classical suggestions and their fusion in the creative imagination of the poet, a quotation from one source, a reminiscence

10. *Obras, ed. cit.*, p. 159 (*Prólogo*).

11. This is the title of a work by Alfonso García de Matamoros (Alcalá, 1553); see the modern edition with translation by J. López de Toro (Madrid, 1943).

12. María Rosa Lida de Malkiel, *Juan de Mena: Poeta del prerrenacimiento español* (Mexico City, 1950); see also the review by J. E. Gillet, *HR*, XX (1952), 159–66.

13. That this "culture" was like a candle casting its beams in a nonhumanistic environment has been apparent to any thoughtful reader of the sources. It has recently been proved by Nicolas G. Round in "Renaissance Culture and Its Opponents in Fifteenth-century Castile," *MLR*, LVII (1962), 204–15. I agree with his conclusions (p. 211): patrons and scholars of fifteenth-century Castile must have been aware of themselves as an isolated and untypical minority. Mena and his congeners were only pioneers. The concept of the inferiority of learning (compared to the warrior's prowess) persisted as a decisive cultural influence well into the reign of Ferdinand and Isabella.

from another, a glancing allusion from a third, transformed into something authentic" (Gillet, *op. cit.*, p. 159). The essential quality of Mena's *Laberinto de Fortuna* is medieval: he appears curiously indifferent to the objective exactness of the traditional data he used. He was strongly influenced by Dante and, like Dante, by the *Aeneid*. His geographic panorama of the world is definitely connected with the medieval *De imagine mundi* ascribed to St. Anselm. Yet, as a contemporary of Henry the Navigator, he looks out upon the world with avid senses. He systematically introduces mythological allusions, not for their exemplary value, but as ornament and pomp. He knows that in his translation of "Homer" (i.e., of the *Ilias Latina*) he has access to merely a pale reflection of a majestic poem which he, not knowing Greek, could not possess directly. He distinguishes clearly between the genuine Homeric tradition and its medieval deformation (Mrs. Malkiel, *op. cit.*, p. 531), and he comes out in defense of the ancient poet, stressing the power that poetic creation possesses to determine forever attributes and characters, and declaring: "The last hours of Priam were no more lamentable than Homer wished them to be, nor was Hector more lamented, nor Paris more enamored, nor Achilles more renowned . . . , nor Ilium more beautiful, nor the harbors more crowded with warships . . . , nor the temples with sacrifices, than the rich pen of Homer, guided by his wise hand, willed that they should be for all posterity." [14]

From the national standpoint, the hope of monarchial unity (soon to be realized) is an essential aspect of Mena's *Laberinto*: a future single monarch will inspire Spain, under the leadership of Castile, to complete the reconquest of all her territory from the Moors. And, though *Plus Ultra* lies some years in the future, there is a prophetic imperial note: the Spanish king will rule not only over Spain, but over the world (*ibid.*, pp. 542–43).

"What Mena wrote and what Mena was," writes Professor Gillet (*op. cit.*, p. 164), "is probably less important than what he achieved in others. His own time certainly found in him an answer to its needs, and . . . his position . . . as patriarch of Spanish letters was hardly ever challenged." Specific indebtedness is shown, in masterly fashion, by Mrs. Malkiel. His commentator Hernán Nú-

14. Mena's *Prohemio*, cited by Mrs. Malkiel, *op. cit.*, pp. 531–32.

ñez, known as el Comendador Griego (see below), declared him to be "very eminent and outstanding, particularly in his use of metaphor and simile, so that I proclaim him comparable, not to other Spanish poets, but even to the most excellent Latins." And he consents that Mena be called heroic: "We may call Juan de Mena heroic, since he deals in this poem with many illustrious heroes." [15] This is a fundamental preoccupation of the Spanish Renaissance. In classical theory the epic was the noblest genre, and much of the energy of Renaissance poets, in all of Europe, was devoted to the search for the heroic poem — the poem which seeks to declare all, or at least the essential, truth in any age or generation. Juan de Mena did not write such a poem, nor did any of his countrymen, only the Portuguese Camoëns having been fully successful in his *The Lusiads*.[16] But Mena pointed the way, and won the respect of later generations. He was cited as an authority, a source book; he was the Spanish poet *por antonomasia*, par excellence: throughout the Golden Age it was felt sufficient to refer to him as *El Poeta Español*.[17] Lope de Vega admired him, and Tirso de Molina actually put him on the stage, with full honors (Mrs. Malkiel, pp. 376 ff.). His position as a "primitive classic" is thus somewhat parallel — *longo intervallo* — to that of Dante as a "classic" during the Italian Renaissance.[18]

1458

This year marks the death of the Marqués de Santillana, Don Iñigo López de Mendoza, author of the first-known example of Spanish literary criticism and literary history — the famous *Carta Prohemio* prefacing the copy of his works which he sent as a gift to Don Pedro de Portugal. As a literary historian *avant la lettre*, Santillana "was the first to see the art of the troubadours as a literary

15. Cited in O. H. Green, "Juan de Mena in the Sixteenth Century: Additional Data," *HR*, XXI (1953), 138–39.
16. See William J. Entwistle, "The Search for the Heroic Poem," in the University of Pennsylvania Bicentennial Conference volume, *Studies in Civilization* (Philadelphia, 1941), pp. 89–103.
17. Green, "Juan de Mena . . . ," p. 139.
18. See Michele Barba, *Della fortuna di Dante nel secolo XVI* (Pisa, 1890); Bernard Weinberg, *A History of Literary Criticism in the Italian Renaissance* (Chicago, 1961), II, chs. XVI, XVII: "The Quarrel over Dante."

tradition in which different nations cooperated." [19] As a literary theoretician, Santillana follows Boccaccio in his definition of poetry: "And what is poetry . . . except an imagining of useful things, covered or veiled with a most lovely covering, composed, set off, and scanned in accordance with a certain syllable count, weight, and measure?" (cited *ibid.*, p. 249). Here he emphasizes the play of fantasy, with its immediate purpose of creating beauty, the essential requisite of metre, and the didactic end of poetry. His definition was not rendered obsolete during the Renaissance, though there were poets, like Góngora (as well as prose writers like Quevedo), who on occasion disclaimed the didactic purpose of literature.[20] Santillana's enthusiasm for poetry and his equating of literary fame with martial fame are definitely Renaissance characteristics.

In Santillana, as in his friend Juan de Mena, we again encounter a deep concern for learned, as against light and circumstantial, poetry. When Santillana cites Livy or Dante, he is not moved by the medieval desire to authenticate every statement, but rather by the urge to show off — with an innocent vanity that is never offensive — what he has recently learned. No Spanish poet of his own or of earlier times could compete with him in the vast sweep of his interests; [21] none had given himself over so avidly to the Latin classics [22] (in compendiums or translations) or to the great writers of Italy.

This intention to create a body of learned poetry for Spain had as a natural consequence the introduction into Spanish of words adapted from Latin and other languages. Another consequence was the cultivation of a rhetorical style, reminiscent of that of the *Grands Rhétoriqueurs* of contemporary France. Cicero's *De Inventione* and *Rhetorica ad Herennium* were available in Spanish translation, and Santillana's use of rhetorical *elegantiae* shows a clear awareness of form; rhetorical devices are successfully, though not always spontaneously, employed. Mythological invocations appear

19. This was shown by Werner Krauss in "Wege der spanischen Renaissancelyrik," *RF*, XLIX (1935), 119–25 (cited by Rafael Lapesa, *La obra literaria del Marqués de Santillana* [Madrid, 1957], p. 253).

20. On the persistence of the didactic aim, see Weinberg, *op. cit., passim.* On the poet as giver of fame, see Mrs. Malkiel, *La idea de la fama en la Edad Media castellana* (Mexico City–Buenos Aires, 1952), Index, *s. v.* Santillana.

21. See Mario Schiff, *La bibliothèque du Marquis de Santillane* (Paris, 1905).

22. In his *Carta Prohemio* he reserves the adjective "sublime" for those poets who composed in the Greek and Latin languages.

at the beginnings of his longer poems and, internally, in the initial stanzas of the subdivisions. As early as 1436 Santillana had developed a style of his own, brilliant and ostentatious, which surpassed that of his contemporaries. Juan de Mena learned much from him, although Mena, owing to his mastery of Latin, acquired poetic resources that were denied to the Marqués (Lapesa, *op. cit.*, pp. 160 ff.).

Santillana has yet another claim to our attention: inspired by Petrarch, he composed forty-two *Sonetos al itálico modo*, written at intervals during the last twenty years of his life. Some of these are occasional pieces, lamenting the death of a prominent personage or celebrating a royal entry; others have a political intention. One invites the princes of Christendom to restore Byzantium, recently conquered by the Turks. Another gives counsel to the new king, Enrique IV (*ibid.*, pp. 179ff.). We have to do, therefore, not with a poetic whim, but with a consistent and prolonged effort to introduce the sonnet form — a form deliberately chosen and especially difficult. Yet Santillana's *sonetos* do not show a development, an increasing mastery; the last ones, like those at the beginning of the series, are marked by flashes of genuine poetry, but also by deficiencies characteristic of an experimenter.

The occasional sonnets constitute a minority; most of Santillana's forty-two *sonetos*, like the majority of those in Petrarch's *Canzoniere*, are amatory. They do not reveal, as do those of Petrarch, successive stages in the transformation of the poet's emotional life. Few in number, they show only separate phases of the amorous experience: love at first sight, absence, glances, the appearance of gray hairs, the joy of a renewed relationship. All of them seek to express, in vocabularly, tone, and style, the feeling as well as the form of the Italian *dolce stil nuovo* and of Petrarch's *Canzoniere*.[23] "Into these Petrarchan molds," writes Lapesa, "enters all the subject matter of chivalric love" (p. 187). Santillana's Petrarchism is a new, fair, and prestigious form, a *fermosa cobertura*, such as all true poetry required, according to his own definition (p. 189).

None of Santillana's contemporaries and immediate followers was inspired to follow his example. Some sixty years later a few sporadic efforts were made by Spaniards to use the sonnet form, but

23. See our Volume I, Index, *s. v.* Santillana.

the language employed was Italian. It remained for Juan Boscán, and for the infinitely more gifted Garcilaso de la Vega, to naturalize the sonnet in Spain; yet Fernando de Herrera in 1580, in his commentary on Garcilaso, did justice to the forerunner: "The Marqués de Santillana, a great Spanish captain and a brave knight, first made the plunge, with noteworthy boldness, into that unknown sea, and did so with singular success, and returned to his native shores with the spoils of foreign conquest. Testimony of this are some sonnets of his, worthy of veneration because of the nobility of him who wrote them, and because of the light they cast amid the shadows and confusion of that time" (cited in Lapesa, pp. 201–2).

The shadows and confusion of that time . . . Herrera is aware, in 1580, that there has been a sudden development in Spanish literary culture, that his country, between Santillana's day and his own, has seen the beginning of a new cultural span. But we must not get ahead of our story.

1473 [24]

This is the year of the return to Spain of Antonio de Nebrija (or Lebrija, d. 1522), father of Spanish philology, after his years of humanistic study in Italy.[25] Nebrija, neither knight nor cleric but a simple lay scholar, represents the linguistic and philological as well as the scriptural preoccupations of the early Renaissance.[26] There is a striking parallel between Nebrija's conviction in these matters and that of Roger Bacon (d. 1294), who wrote that "no Latin[27] will be able to understand the wisdom of the sacred Scrip-

24. Many months after my section on Nebrija was written I received vol. XLIII (1960) of the *Revista de filología española,* dated "Madrid, 1962" but actually issued in late 1963 or early 1964. It contains a valuable article by Eugenio Asensio, "La lengua compañera del imperio: Historia de una idea de Nebrija en España y Portugal" (pp. 399–413).

25. See Ignacio González Llubera's introduction to his edition of Nebrija's *Gramática de la lengua castellana* (Oxford, 1926); Cipriano Muñoz, Conde de la Viñaza, *Biblioteca histórica de la filología española* (Madrid, 1893); H. Keniston, "Notes on the *De liberis educandis* of Antonio de Lebrija," *Homenaje ofrecido a Menéndez Pidal* (Madrid, 1925), III, 127–41; F. de Onís, "El concepto del Renacimiento aplicado a la literatura española," in his *Ensayos sobre el sentido de la cultura española* (Madrid 1932), pp. 195–223.

26. The initial preoccupations of Renaissance criticism "are linguistic and philological even before they are rhetorical and stylistic." See Weinberg, *op. cit.,* II, 837–74.

27. I. e., no scholar whose only ancient language is Latin. The quotation is from

ture and of philosophy unless he understands the languages from which they were translated." Nebrija was primarily a Latinist, and his concern was with the correcting of the text of the Vulgate; his position was new in that he proposed to apply all the resources of the new philology of the Italian Renaissance to the understanding of the Scriptures. Italy was the mistress of Spain's Christian humanists.[28]

Ingram Bywater points out[29] that an adaptation of Nebrija's *Vocabularium* was found in the library of Henry VIII, and that as late as 1631 there appeared in England *A Brief Introduction to Syntax . . . Collected for the most Part of Nebrissa his Spanish Copie. . . .* The credit for the working out of a theory of ancient Greek pronunciation is due, says Bywater, not to Aldus Manutius or any other Italian, but to the great Spanish humanist Antonius Nebrissensis, the prophet of the new learning among his countrymen, whose labors gave to Spain a place of her own in the intellectual history of the sixteenth century which, though not so distinguished as that of Italy or France, surpassed anything that was possible in Tudor England.

The seventeenth-century bibliographer, Nicolás Antonio, marshals Nebrija's writings under seven headings: grammar, philology, poetics, history, jurisprudence, medicine, and Biblical studies. To ancient geography Nebrija contributed an edition of Pomponius Mela and a dictionary of ancient place names. As editor or commentator he produced a Virgil, a Persius, a Prudentius, a Sedulius, and

The Portable Medieval Reader, eds. J. B. Ross and Mary M. McLaughlin (New York 1953), p. 604; see p. 613 for the similar position of Richard de Bury (d. 1345) and the provision by Clement V at the Council of Vienne (1312) that courses in Hebrew, Greek, Arabic, and Aramaic be offered in the Universities of Paris, Oxford, Bologna, and Salamanca.

28. M. Bataillon, *Erasmo y España* (Mexico City–Buenos Aires, 1950), I, 59. Loofs, in his *Dogmengeschichte*, quoted with approval by Harnack *(History of Dogma* [Boston, 1905], VII, 36, n. 2), enumerates among the conditions and tendencies in Catholicism prior to the Council of Trent (1545–63) the reorganization "in strict medieval sense" of the Spanish Church by the Crown under Ferdinand and Isabella; the zealous fostering by the mystics of Catholic piety; the humanistic efforts for reform; the ennobling of theology through humanism. The only inaccuracy here lies in the words *in strict medieval sense,* applied to the Spanish pre-Reformation. The Spanish theologian-humanists of the fifteenth and sixteenth centuries sought to ennoble theology by applying to the critical study of the Bible the methods and spirit of Renaissance philology.

29. In his brief study, *The Erasmian Pronunciation of Greek and Its Precursors, Jerome Aleander, Aldus Manutius, Antonio of Lebrixa* (London, 1908).

also an edition of the Vulgate Psalms. Interested in Hebrew as well as in Greek and Latin, he had some hand in the editing of the Alcalá or Complutensian Polyglot edition of the Bible, of which we shall have more to say below. His position was essentially that of Erasmus: in all matters of interpretation, the first duty of the interpreter is to go back to the original texts. The true text of the venerated Vulgate might need to be determined, he declared, by consulting the ancient manuscripts. So bold were Nebrija's declarations that his post at Salamanca became untenable; but he moved on to the newly created University of Alcalá, where he remained until his death. As royal historiographer he was commissioned to write the official history of the reign of Ferdinand and Isabella.

In the introduction to his *Spanish-Latin Dictionary*, Nebrija tells how he became convinced that, however great the learning of his preceptors in grammar and logic, *en dezir sabian muy poco* — i.e., they were not masters of the Latin language. "And although I had," he continues, "sufficient ability and training to earn a good living and to obtain honors, I was unwilling to tread the common road, but sought out a path, by God's grace revealed to me alone, namely, to go to the source where I might slake my own thirst and that of my countrymen. . . . So it was that at the age of nineteen I went to Italy,[30] not as others do to obtain a benefice or to bring back formulas of civil or canon law, or to return with merchandise: but to restore to the land they had lost[31] the authors of Latin literature, who for many centuries had been exiled from Spain."

1492

This *annus mirabilis* is a year of many beginnings. In January Granada fell to the besieging forces of Ferdinand and Isabella, and Spain's centuries-old thrust to the south not only met with final success but entered a new phase: Spanish domination extending into North Africa. In August, Columbus set sail from Palos, initiating

30. He obtained a scholarship at the Spanish College of St. Clement, which since the fourteenth century had been attached to the University of Bologna. For the intellectual climate there, see González Llubera's introduction (previously cited, note 25).

31. A number of important Roman authors were born in Spain, among them Seneca, Lucan, and Martial.

the great policy of expansion to the west and balancing the eastward movement which had begun in the Middle Ages with the conquest of the Balearic Islands and had carried the Aragonese and Catalans to victories in Greece.[32] In a less martial field of endeavor, the year saw the birth of the secular theater in Spain, as Juan del Encina put on the first of his eclogues in the palace of the Duke of Alba. It is, finally, the year which gives us the most eloquent expression of Spain's consciousness of her mission as a carrier of civilization — and the arts of peace — to distant lands and populations as yet unknown.

In 1492, almost certainly after Columbus had set sail but assuredly before his return (March 15, 1493), Nebrija published his *Gramática de la lengua castellana*, the first grammar of a Romance language written with all the rigor of the new philology. This book, says González Llubera in the introduction to his modern edition (cited above), "has a very real and symptomatic importance. An intense and cultured patriotism pervades it. The author is conscious that Spain has begun to accomplish great deeds, that the Castilian people are on the threshold of an age of conquest. The eloquent pages with which the book opens belong to the noblest utterances inspired by patriotic feeling; and when we reflect that they immediately precede the discoveries of Columbus, we cannot resist the impression that their tone has something of the prophetic."

In his prologue Nebrija addresses Queen Isabella. "When I reflect, most gracious and illustrious Queen, and view in retrospect the antiquity of all the things of which we have written records, I come to one conclusion: that language was always the companion of Empire, so that together they began, increased, and flourished, and together fell into decline." He then sets forth his classical concept of the cyclical movement of history — not too greatly different from that of the modern Spengler — and traces the linguistic and political history of the Hebrews, the Greeks, and the Romans. The Latin language, as those of his generation inherited it from their fathers, "had little more to do with the Latin of the years of Rome's glory than with Arabic."

32. See Roger B. Merriman, *The Rise of the Spanish Empire in the Old World and the New* (New York, 1918–34). Spain's expansion to the fourth cardinal point — the north—will come later, when Charles I (Charles V of the Empire) incorporates the Low Countries into the possessions of the Spanish crown.

And what of Castilian? It had its inception in the early centuries of the judges and kings of Castile and León; began to show its strength in the time of Alphonso the Learned (d. 1284); spread to Aragon and Navarre; and finally, in the fifteenth century, was car- ried to Italy, "following the princes whom we sent to rule [*imperar*] in those Kingdoms" (Naples, Sicily). "So it has grown, up to the moment of unity, peace, and power that we now enjoy, wherein the pieces that formerly composed Spain have been brought together in a union such that many centuries, and the ravages of time, will not be able to break or disunite it."

Thus, with the infidel crushed and expelled, with Christian unity established, all that remains is to foment the arts of peace, among which language occupies first place as the instrument of the human reason. Heretofore the Castilian language has lain in neglect, with- out learned regulation, and subject to popular forces of change as each generation treated and mistreated it according to whim.[33] In order that whatever shall be written in Castilian in the future may have linguistic permanence and continued validity, the authority of grammar is indispensable. Nebrija would do for Castilian what the grammarians of antiquity did for Greek and Latin. He himself, he continues, has reduced Castilian to rule "in the most opportune time that ever was, since our language is at the height of its develop- ment."

And there is another way, he says, in which his new *Grammar* will serve the public weal: when he offered the presentation copy to Her Majesty in the city of Salamanca, and the Queen asked the nature of its usefulness, "the reverend Bishop of Avila answered in my stead, saying that after your Majesty shall have placed under her yoke barbarous nations with strange tongues, and, having con- quered them will need to impose on them the laws of the conqueror, and therewith our language; then, by means of this my *Castilian Grammar*, they will come to know that language, just as we now depend on my *Latin Grammar* when we need to learn Latin."

We have already read, in Nebrija's own words, his statement of Renaissance individualism, as he sought out a path revealed to him alone, and of the humanist's desire to return to the sources, to make — as Américo Castro has brilliantly expressed it — "a critical

33. He objects to the liberties taken by the authors of the novels of chivalry.

edition of the universe"; we have seen his interest in both profane and sacred antiquity; and we have heard him express his noble concept of an empire devoted to the arts of peace, to the work of civilization. To all this we should add a quotation expressive of his sense of being a reformer, to the greater glory of his nation. He says, in the prologue to his *Latin-Spanish Dictionary*:

I never ceased to try to hit upon some way whereby I could break through the barbarism that is spread so widely throughout Spain. And I remembered the decision of Saints Peter and Paul, the princes of the apostles, in their determination to banish heathenism. For just as those apostles, in order to lay the foundations of the Church, did not lay siege to obscure and unknown towns, but one of them to Athens, and both to Antioch, cities famed for the study of letters, and thereafter to Rome, queen and mistress of the world, so today, in order to banish ignorance from the men of our nation, I began by attacking no meaner center than the University of Salamanca, which, once taken like a fortress captured by storm, I doubted not that all the other towns and cities of Spain would come to offer their surrender.

So noteworthy was his doctrine, he continues, that even his enemies conceded:

I was the first who set up my campaign tent, proposing to teach Latin and daring to raise a standard of new precepts; I banished from Spain the harshness of the old-style grammarians, so that if any proper sort of Latin is possessed by the men of our nation, all of this must be attributed to me.

In the prologue to the 1495 edition of his *Introductiones Latinae*, Nebrija tells of being busily engaged in the study of the antiquities of Spain and declares that, when once this task is finished, he intends to devote himself exclusively to Biblical studies. This statement leads us to our next symbolic year, or rather span of years.

1502–1517

Between these two dates the edition of the great Complutensian Polyglot or Alcalá Bible, was completed. In it Nebrija saw the partial realization of his ideals of Biblical scholarship: the restoration of the sacred texts by means of a return to their philological sources. The great cardinal Cisneros (Francisco Jiménez de Cisneros, d. 1517) brought together a brilliant group of Hellenists, Latinists, and Hebraists (their names will concern us later), obtained for them the best manuscripts that could be found, and spared no expense in materials or printing. The work was begun in 1502; the printing, begun in 1514, was completed in 1517. Volumes I–IV contained the Old Testament in Greek, Latin, Hebrew, and Chaldean; volume V, the Greek and Latin texts of the New Testament; volume VI, a Hebrew-Chaldean vocabularly, an index of names, and a Hebrew grammar. It was the first polyglot Bible to be printed, and it was the high-water mark of early scriptural science. The Alcalá New Testament in Greek preceded by some two years the Greek New Testament of Erasmus.

Nebrija, who for years had been devoting himself to the study of the texts of the Scriptures, accepted (at a late date) the position of Latin editor on Cisneros' board. He declared: "I came to Alcalá to take part in the emendation of the Latin, which is normally corrupt in all the Latin Bibles, by collating it with the Hebrew, the Chaldean, and the Greek." His proposed emendations aroused the opposition of those who defended the Vulgate text as something untouchable, and Nebrija withdrew from the enterprise.[34] Nebrija's activity in this field of textual criticism had preceded the project of Cisneros. He represents, as Marcel Bataillon says, the autonomous effort of the humanists to restore antiquity in its entirety, Christian as well as pagan, and he deserves a place of his own in the history of Christian humanism. In this field of Biblical studies he is not only a predecessor of Spanish Erasmism but a precursor of Erasmus himself. Bataillon sees in him the heir of the boldness of method of Lorenzo Valla in matters of Biblical philology, perhaps also of Valla's critical attitude in regard to the traditions of the Church.[35]

34. He had earlier suffered the indignity of seeing some of his papers sequestered by the Inquisitor General. "The incident," writes Bataillon, "does not assume tragic proportions. In those happy days which precede Luther's excommunication, humanists have the right to laugh if they become convinced that 'official' science has made a *gaffe*. The ecclesiastical authorities do not resent the laughter, at least not when he who laughs is a man of the quality of Cisneros" (*Erasmo y España*, I, 44).

35. Valla had died before Nebrija went to Italy, but the latter lived and studied there in the atmosphere that Valla had created. When, back in Spain, Nebrija found that his old teacher Pedro de Osma was condemned for expressing bold—almost Reformational—ideas concerning confession, Nebrija maintained silence regarding the condemnation, but he did praise Osma publicly in his *Dictionary*, and he ridiculed the theologians responsible for the denunciation (*ibid.*, pp. 30–31).

1508

Ever since becoming primate of Spain, Cardinal Cisneros had devoted large sums from his personal income to the furtherance of learning. His plan to found a university which should be a complete organism for ecclesiastical training [36] strongly based on the humanities, and whose faculty of theology should be open to the novelties of the new scriptural science and the new erudition in the three languages, finally took shape, and he chose Alcalá as the seat of the new university. In 1499 the necessary papal bull was granted; the foundation stone was laid in 1500; instruction began in 1508.

The reason that a new university was felt to be necessary was precisely that in the older University of Salamanca tradition still held sway. Cisneros was determined that, at Alcalá, theology should use as its handmaidens the other sciences and arts — as the statutes of the University (art. XLV) clearly specified. The founding of this university marked not only a triumph of Renaissance humanism, but also a rebirth of Christian antiquity — a fact which differentiates it profoundly from the Collège de France (1530). From the *Distichs* of Cato, beginners in Latin passed to the hymns and prayers of the Church before starting to read Terence; the first half of the next year was devoted to such Christian poets as Sedulius and Juvencus, the pagan Virgil being postponed to make room for them. The Chair of Rhetoric was held by Hernando Alonso de Herrera, one of the first Spanish Erasmians (in the sense that, like Erasmus of Rotterdam, he called for a reform of institutions and of culture); his successor in this chair was none other than Nebrija. In philosophy, Duns Scotus was placed on an equal footing with Thomas Aquinas. And, after centuries of Scholasticism, there was a direct return to the Church Fathers: Jerome, Augustine, Ambrose, Gregory. The Greek Fathers were read in the original; Cisneros established a university press and had published, at times at his own

36. On the shocking ignorance prevalent among the clergy, see the *Estudio Preliminar* of Francisco Márquez (see note 7 above), especially pp. 47–48 and nn. 38, 39; see also the principal source utilized by Márquez, Nicolás López Martínez, *Los judaizantes castellanos y la Inquisición en tiempos de Isabel la Católica* (Burgos, 1954). See also Bataillon, *Erasmo y España*, I, 12–26.

expense, the necessary Greek textbooks.[37] Greek took root in Alcalá because it was the language of the New Testament, of many Church Fathers, and of the great source of Thomist theology, Aristotle. Had Cisneros not died in 1517, there would have been produced at Alcalá a bilingual edition of Aristotle in Greek and Latin. The work had already begun.

The creation of this university thus reminds us rather strikingly of the motivation that prompted the founding of Harvard, somewhat over a century later. Men of immensely different backgrounds and beliefs, in two completely different environments, sought to provide adequate instruction for the spiritual leaders of their respective societies.

In later chapters of the present volume we shall perceive, as Bataillon's great work has enabled us to see with respect to its special field of study, that the problems which led to the wars of religion in sixteenth-century Europe were present also in Spain; that the Spain of Cisneros contained the germ of all that was to develop in the reign of Charles V (d. 1558), all that the efforts of Philip II (d. 1598) would strive to preserve.[38]

1526–1532

In the first volume of *Spain and the Western Tradition* (Chapter IV), we devoted some attention to another *annus mirabilis*, 1526 — the year when a suggestion from the Venetian ambassador to the

37. See Emile Legrand, *Bibliographie hispano-grecque* (vols. XI–XIII in *Bibliographie hispanique*, comp. R. Foulché-Delbosc [New York–Paris, 1905–17]).

38. Even the admirable Cisneros has his "negative side." In 1499 political forces became active which brought the blameless Fray Hernando de Talavera — the man who first raised the cross over the fortress of the Alhambra in 1492 and who served as the first archbishop of Granada — into serious trouble with the Inquisition. When the Court left Granada in 1499, Cisneros remained behind with full powers to deal with the problem of the newly converted Jews. Abandoning the policy of peaceful assimilation initiated by Talavera (and supported by the Queen), Cisneros preferred the swift harsh method of physical compulsion. A revolt followed. Besieged in his residence, Cisneros owed his life to the intervention of Talavera, who promised to restore the status quo, only to be overruled later with ultimately tragic results. When Isabella died in 1504, Talavera was left without a protector and in 1505 was publicly arrested, charged with relapses into the practices of Judaism. Vindicated from the ridiculous charges in May, 1507, he died that same month. See Márquez's (previously cited) *Estudio preliminar* to Talavera's *Católica impugnación* . . . , pp. 13–16; see also p. 48.

court of Spain, Andrea Navagiero, convinced the poet Juan Boscán of the desirability of naturalizing in Spain the poetic forms so brilliantly developed in the Italy of the "three modern classics," Dante, Boccaccio, and Petrarch. As a result of Navagiero's persuasiveness and the efforts it inspired on the part of Boscán and — much more to the purpose — of his supremely talented friend Garcilaso de la Vega, a world of new symbols and of entirely new artistic possibilities was opened to the Spaniards, affecting the development of their literature to the present day. Because this was treated at some length in our earlier volume, it will not be necessary to retrace here the growth in literary beauty and power as the new poetic symbols were taken over, together with the new poetic instrument: the Italian hendecasyllabic line, arranged in new strophe-forms — sonnet, *canzone, terza rima,* eclogue, and others.

Lapesa rightly insists on the decisiveness of the Italian influence.[39] Great as was Garcilaso's debt to Virgil, it was to Petrarch — primarily — and to Sannazaro, Ariosto, Tansillo, and Bernardo Tasso, that the Spanish poet was indebted for the molds into which he cast his personal conception of the world of poetic beauty. Guided by these masters, Garcilaso moves from the gloomy, despairing, and psychologically-abstract imagery of earlier Spanish *cancionero* poetry to the gentle notes of light and color which make possible his new treatment of the physical beauty of his beloved, the hauntingly inaccessible Isabel Freyre — moves so successfully that he was able to surpass in poetic authenticity the entirety of the lyric of the Italian *Cinquecento.* From his Italian models he learned how to write learned poetry, full reminiscences exquisitely re-elaborated and made new, endowed with a delicate sense of plasticity and form. By the time Garcilaso achieved the spiritual peace of his Neapolitan period (from 1532 until his death four years later), he had reached the fullness of his powers. It is to this period in Garcilaso's career that I applied, in my earlier volume, C. S. Lewis' designation of *golden.* We may well permit ourselves to repeat here Lewis' statement of what he means by golden poetry: "In a Golden Age the right thing to do is obvious: 'good is as visible as green.'" The artist has only "to find the most beautiful models, pose them in

39. *La trayectoria poética de Garcilaso* (Madrid, 1948), ch. II: "The Assimilation of the New Art."

the most graceful attitudes, and get to work. . . . Men have at last learned how to write; for a few years nothing more is needed than to play out again and again the strong, simple music of the uncontorted line and to load one's poem with all that is naturally delightful — with flowers and swans, with ladies' hair, hands, lips, breasts, and eyes, with silver and gold, woods and waters, the stars, the moon and the sun." [40] In Garcilaso de la Vega all this is achieved; it is the triumph, in the lyric, of the Spanish Renaissance.

Not all genres reach their plenitude at the same time. The drama, fiction, and the essay reach maturity only in the period "when ingenuous taste has been satisfied," when it becomes necessary "to seek for novelty, to set oneself difficult tasks," even "to make beauty out of violence," (*ibid.*) as do Góngora and Quevedo in the baroque. We shall leave discussion of this for Volume IV. In the meantime, there are two additional dates for us to consider.

1580

In 1580 Fernando de Herrera republished the poems of Garcilaso de la Vega, separating them for the first time from the works of Garcilaso's more pedestrian friend Boscán, and providing them with a learned commentary which marks the full tide of the Renaissance in the field of criticism. Some six years earlier, to be sure, the humanist Francisco Sánchez de las Brozas (el Brocense) had made an edition of Garcilaso "with commentary and emendations," but this edition was completely overshadowed by Herrera's. El Brocense's edition is to be recalled only for the principle underlying its avowed purpose: the demonstration of Garcilaso's excellence in terms of his close kinship with the "classical" poets of Italy and Rome. "I say and affirm," wrote el Brocense, "that I do not regard as a good poet him who fails to imitate the excellent poets of antiquity. And if I am asked why, among so many thousands of poets as exist in our Spain, so few can be accounted worthy of this name, I reply that there is no other reason, except that they are not equipped with the knowledge, languages, and doctrine which

40. *English Literature in the Sixteenth Century Excluding Drama* (Oxford, 1954), pp. 64–65.

would enable them to imitate." [41] Herrera had much to say in the same vein; William C. Atkinson suggests that "had he too been merely a university professor the significance of his commentary might likewise have gone no further. Fortunately he was, instead, a poet" (*ibid.*, pp. 208–9). Atkinson points up the positions taken by Herrera in what amounts to a chapter in the "Quarrel of Ancients and Moderns" [42] — positions that attest the maturity of the Spanish Renaissance in the field of criticism applied to the lyric (a genre almost completely disregarded in Aristotle's *Poetics*). Herrera's positions are (1) that the day for Spain's inferiority complex in the matter of culture and civilization is over; [43] (2) that the complaint, so often repeated throughout the century, against the literary neglect and inadequacy of Castilian is no longer valid; (3) that Spaniards have it within their power to write poetry as immortal as any; (4) that poetry is a heightened mode of expression that may address itself to the initiate with words chosen for their sound, their associations, and their symbolism, and that this poetic language is often beyond the grasp of the common man; (5) that languages have their special character, their genius, and that Spanish is incomparably more "grave," is possessed of a greater spirit of magnificence than all the others now called "vulgar"; (6) and that the poet, if he will learn all that the ancients and the Italians have to teach, may hope to set out from that point to achieve his own conquests. [44]

1585

This year marks the triumph of Castilian prose, as 1580 does that of Castilian as a vehicle for poetic expression. Dr. Francisco López de Villalobos, physician to the Catholic Sovereigns and to Charles

41. William C. Atkinson, "On Aristotle and the Concept of Lyric Poetry in Early Spanish Criticism," *Estudios dedicados a Menéndez Pidal*, VI (Madrid, 1956), p. 201.

42. This famous quarrel was principally between Boileau and Charles Perrault, but the subject of the quarrel is everywhere. See William A. Nitze and E. Preston Dargan, *A History of French Literature* (New York, 1922), Part II (*Modern Times*), Bk. I (*The Transition from Classicism*), ch. I: "The Quarrel of the Ancients and Moderns: Results"; see also the *Petit Larousse illustré, s.v. anciens.*

43. See pp. 208 ff. of Atkinson's article for the supporting quotations.

44. See Oreste Macrí, *Fernando de Herrera* (Madrid, 1959), pp. 69 ff. ("Programa y teoría literaria").

V, felt that his miscellany entitled *Libro de los problemas*, published in 1543, would suffer from the fact that he had written it in Spanish rather than in Latin; and, although many apologies for, and praises of, the Spanish language appeared during the sixteenth century (we shall study them in a later chapter), "it took the voice of Fray Luis de León to make clear once and for all that Castilian was equal to Latin." After the publication of Book III of Fray Luis' *De los nombres de Cristo*, "all understood . . . that the hour of the vernacular had sounded, announcing and promising for it a brilliant career in the future, and proclaiming that henceforth the fruits of philosophical or religious meditation would be available to all readers," whether they knew Latin or did not.[45]

Fray Luis had published Books I and II of *De los nombres de Cristo* in 1583 and had been censured (in spite of the very successful religious works composed in Castilian by Fray Luis de Granada and others) for venturing to compose them in the vernacular. In 1585 he replied to the censure by reprinting the first two books, with a third book added. In the introduction to the latter, Fray Luis accuses his detractors of contempt for their own language, since they refuse to read matter composed in it which — were it not for the circumstance of the linguistic vehicle — they would gladly read and regard as good. These detractors, he says, in their ignorance think that to write in the vernacular is necessarily to express oneself as the common man does, carelessly and without giving thought to the sequence and disposition of concepts and words (*desatadamente y sin orden*). Fray Luis explains that, on the contrary, he gives to every word its proper place in the general orchestration (*concierto*). Effective expression requires judgment and special study. Words have their appropriateness, not only as to meaning but as to sound; the master prose writer actually counts syllables and even letters, weighing and composing for clarity, harmony, and sweetness. Readers of good taste, wise and serious readers, refuse to apply themselves to the perusal of what has been badly or carelessly written. Fray Luis' present book is intended for readers of this kind, and its author has naturally given thought to their requirements.

45. Alain Guy, *La pensée de Fray Luis de León: Contribution à l'étude de la philosophie espagnole au XVIᵉ siècle* (Limoges, 1943), p. 203.

If any should chance to say that this is a novelty, a departure from established ways, Fray Luis willingly admits that it is indeed a new thing to lift ordinary discourse to a higher plane, to give it harmony and rhythm. This is a new path [46] which he has purposely opened, not out of a presumptuous sense of superiority, but rather with the purpose that those having the strength to do so may be encouraged henceforth to treat their native language as the wise and eloquent writers of the past treated theirs, and that by so doing they should make it the equal of the languages which are considered the best — over which Castilian has, in Fray Luis' considered judgment, the advantage of many virtues peculiar to it alone.[47]

SUMMARY AND CONCLUSION

The "symbolic dates" singled out for special attention to represent successive stages of advance, as Spain emerges from the Middle Ages and assumes her place among the cultured nations of Europe, have exemplified various aspects of this cultural coming-of-age: an early awareness of the beauty bequeathed by a more learned past to modern Europeans; the first clearly conscious efforts to give to Castile a literature worthy of mature and learned men, a literature ennobled by its having come to terms not merely with a part of the ancient heritage but with all of it; a conscious turning toward Italy as to a mistress already in possession of many of the things that the Castilians desired for themselves — the keys to the ancient languages and the philological method that would make possible the restoration, in all their purity, of the sources of the Christian culture which Spain, like her sister nations in Renaissance Europe, had inherited from Palestine, Greece, and Rome. Not that the newly enriched culture sought to become a replica of what had gone before; rather, the new culture, now aware of its powers, was entering into possession of ancient treasures which, through neglect and unawareness, had not yet given their modern fruit. Concretely, we have seen how the Christian humanists of Spain set about the ac-

46. Fray Luis seems not to have been satisfied with the efforts of his predecessors in these matters.

47. I have followed the text as given by R. Menéndez Pidal, *Antología de prosistas castellanos* (Madrid, 1920), pp. 160–62.

complishment of these ends by making available for Christian scholars and theologians the complete body of Holy Writ in its ancient languages, for purposes of determining what, exactly, the Holy Ghost had wished to convey to mankind. We have seen also how the same desire for a renewal of the life of the mind and of the spirit led to the creation of a special university which should cultivate the new learning and to the establishment of a university press which should provide the needed books.

Passing from intellectual and religious to literary history, we have seen how a new poetic instrument, and the approach, by means of it, to Italian models, lent an altogether new dimension of expressiveness and beauty to the Spanish lyric; how the awareness of this achievement found its expression in literary criticism and brought the conviction that the ancients were not giants upon whose shoulders mere moderns stood as pygmies, but rather that the moderns, would they but follow the road marked out by their ancient predecessors, could be as sublime as they and aspire to the same literary immortality. Finally, we have gone one step further and seen how the same spirit manifested itself in Castilian prose, as matters of the highest spiritual significance were set forth in a prose style which consciously aimed to be worthy of the supreme dignity of its subject matter.

With this, the Spanish Renaissance may be regarded as launched. Many of its triumphs still lie ahead; Fray Luis de León could have had no inkling of the vast new literary world soon to be created by Lope de Vega and given expression in the national drama. He could not conceivably have foreseen the rich, human triumph of Cervantes, as he created the modern critical novel and opened to writers of fiction a marvelously new scheme of "incarnation," placing authentic human creatures upon the stage of the imagination, there to work out their destinies to the permanent enrichment of mankind.

Nor was it possible, in 1585, to know that after noonday would come sunset and twilight and dark. Nebrija had considered that his country would develop the arts of peace under a firm governmental organization that could not be broken during any time span he could foresee. By no conceivable stretch of the imagination could

Nebrija, before his death in 1522, or even Fray Luis, before committing his spirit into the hands of his Maker in 1591, have known that Quevedo, born in 1585, would one day utter the disconsolate cry:

Life, life, ahoy! Alas, life does not answer! [48]

These complications, these shadings from darkness to light and from light to darkness, we shall investigate in later portions of our study.

48. "¡Ah de la vida! ¡Nadie me responde!" This is the first line of one of his sonnets.

II · *Plus Ultra:* Geographical Expansion

How wonderful beyond words is the conquest
Of the Divine Indies, that great world
Which human sight may dream of, but not see!
Francisco de Aldana (d. 1575)[1]

This is one of the great treasures of the
Christian life: these spiritual Indies, this
patrimony of the sons of God.
Fray Luis de Granada (d. 1588)[2]

THE INDIES AND HUMAN ASPIRATION

The two quotations that follow the chapter heading have been chosen because they show how, almost a century after 1492, the word *Indies* had become a part of the vocabulary — of the thought and feeling — of the Spaniards; how the word was used to designate the wonder of the ineffable or the scarcely expressible. Aldana's "Divine Indies" signifies what for him was the supreme human aspiration: mystical union with the Godhead — a conquest no less awe-inspiring than that of the conquistadors; Granada's "spiritual Indies" are closer to the experience of the ordinary worshipper who "enters into the joy of his Lord." One wonders if any writer using English — in the Old World or in the New — has expressed a similar thought, has seen in the newly discovered lands of America a thing as wonderful as the Land of Canaan, as bright and glorious as the New Jerusalem.[3]

1. "¡O grandes, o riquísimas conquistas/ de las Indias de Dios, de aquel gran mundo/ tan escondido a las mundanas vistas!" (*Obras completas*, ed. M. Moragón Maestre [Madrid, 1953], I, 82).

2. *Guía de pecadores*, Bk. I, ch. 18. On the impact of the discoveries on the Spanish imagination, see Joseph E. Gillet, *Torres Naharro and the Drama of the Renaissance* (Philadelphia, 1961), pp. 164–69. (This work, volume IV of *Propalladia and Other Works of Bartolomé de Torres Naharro*, was edited, transcribed and completed by me; it will hereafter be referred to as Gillet-Green.)

3. Edmundo O'Gorman in *La invención de América* (Mexico City, 1958) points to a phase of *geographical adaptation* to the idea of the newly discovered lands, which was in time followed by a *moral adaptation*. Slowly, the earth came to be thought of as the cosmic dwelling place of the human species, as man appropriated unto himself the entire universe. O'Gorman (see p. 81 and n. 108) dates the change from the publication of Mercator's map in 1538.

In 1552 Francisco López de Gómara wrote, in the dedication to the Emperor Charles V of his *Victorious Spain: First and Second Parts of the General History of the Indies* (published at Saragossa), the following:

> Sire: The greatest event since the creation of the world — if we except the Incarnation and Death of Him Who created it — is the discovery of the Indies, and for that reason they call it the New World. . . . God chose to reveal to mankind the Indies in the days of Your Majesty, and to Your Majesty's vassals, to the end that Your Majesty might convert them to His holy Law. . . . The conquest of the Indies began as soon as the conquest of the Moors was completed, that the Spanish nation might ever continue to war against infidels. This conquest was recognized by the Pope. Your Majesty took a new armorial device, *Plus Ultra*, to symbolize the overlordship of the Indies. Is it therefore right that Your Majesty lend your favor to the conquest and to the conquerors, having at the same time great regard for the welfare of the conquered.[4]

The Indies in History

López de Gómara had had important predecessors in the new field of American history; he was not an eyewitness of the events he recorded; his history met with official disfavor, for unspecified reasons, and was banned, though it was translated into various foreign languages, as the author (he included a "Note to Translators") assumed that it would be. One highly respected predecessor, Gonzalo Fernández de Oviedo, likewise wrote an *Historia general de las Indias* (1535), a portion of which — *Summary of the Natural History of the Indies* — he published separately in 1527 in anticipation of the main work. As the title suggests, he treats in this summary the subject that concerns us here — the new scientific dimension, particularly in biology, which the discoveries had added to the European world view. Oviedo obviously considered this exotic material to be important or, at least, interesting; yet he lacked scientific imagination. His account is descriptive, factual, and dry. Some of his chapters contain but a single sentence: on leopards, on foxes, or on deer. It is not to Oviedo but to López de Gómara — though he wrote twenty-five years later — that we must turn for the sense of wonder and of expanding knowledge that characterizes the Renaissance period as a whole.

4. *BAE*, XXII, 156. López de Gómara was private chaplain to Hernando Cortés after the latter's return, as the Marqués del Valle, from Mexico to Spain.

The world is vast and beautiful. The first words of Gómara's history are these: "The world is so vast and beautiful, and contains so many things each different from the other, that he who contemplates it well and ponders it must be moved to amazement. There can be few men, unless they live on the level of the brutes, who do not sometimes pause to consider its marvels, since the desire to know is a natural human trait." Although Solomon declared that "man judges with difficulty the things of the earth," not on that account (continues Gómara) is man incapable or unworthy to understand the world and its secrets. Since this is true, "let us not waste through negligence our God-given rights and privileges."

All the earth is habitable. In the next chapters Gómara contradicts the philosophers who conceived of a plurality of worlds; declares the earth to be round and not a concave disc; insists, contrary to the belief of Thales, Pythagoras, Aristotle and "almost all the Greek and Roman schools," and even of such moderns as Pico della Mirandola, that the earth is habitable in all its zones, the frigid and the torrid as well as the temperate. "Experience, our sure guide in everything, has become so extended and unceasing in the navigation of the ocean and in the traversing of the land, that we know that all the earth can support population and does indeed support it. Glory to God and honor to the Spaniards, who discovered the Indies, the home of the antipodes, and who, as they discover and conquer them, sail the great Ocean Sea, pass through the torrid zone [5] and go beyond the Arctic circle — scarecrows, all of them, to the Ancients" (*ed. cit.*, p. 159b).

The antipodes exist. St. Augustine, in the ninth book of *The City of God*, denied the existence of the antipodes, probably because (as Gómara conjectures) they are not mentioned in the Bible,

5. Gómara could scarcely have known that the torrid zone had been crossed (*ca.* 1341) by John of Marignolli, who wrote: "we came to the Cyollos Kagon, . . . the Sand Hills thrown up by the wind. Before the days of the Tartars nobody believed that the earth was habitable beyond these. . . . But the Tartars . . . did cross them, and found themselves in what the philosophers call the torrid and impassable zone; and so did I, and that twice. 'Tis of this that David speaketh in the Psalms, 'Posuit desertum,' etc." (*The Portable Medieval Reader*, eds. J. B. Ross and M. M. McLaughlin [New York, 1953], p. 483; see also H. Yule (ed.), *Cathay and the Way Thither* [London, 1914]).

and also because he preferred to avoid inconvenience, as some people say (*a lo que dicen*, p. 159b); for had St. Augustine admitted their existence, he could ill have proved that the antipodes, like all the men of the then-known world, were descendants of Adam and Eve, and consequently he could hardly have made those hypothetical human beings citizens of his heavenly City.[6] And Spain's own St. Isidore of Seville declared in his *Etymologiae* that there was no reason to believe in the existence of such men, inasmuch as the physical character of the earth made this impossible and inasmuch as there was no historical proof but only the imaginings of poets. Yet the contrary view was held by Plutarch, by Macrobius, by "almost all the philosophers," and — first among Christian theologians — by Clement, the disciple of St. Peter.[7] Gómara's next chapter heading reads: "Who and Where the Antipodes Are, and What They Are Like," and the following chapter — under a caption declaring that "The Antipodes Are Accessible, Contrary to the Opinion of the Philosophers" — sets forth, as proof, a simple fact: "All has now been traversed and all is known, for every day our Spaniards go there, as it were, with their eyes shut, so that experience opposes philosophy." Gómara says that he will omit mention of the many ships that make the normal crossing from Spain to the Indies, and will speak of only one, the good ship Victoria, "which circumnavigated the globe, and, touching at the lands of both sets of antipodes, made manifest the ignorance of Antiquity and returned to Spain three years after her departure, as I shall declare at length when I speak of the Strait of Magellan" (p. 160b).

The voyage of the Victoria. Some fifty-eight columns farther on, Gómara tells of that first circumnavigation of the globe. I translate:

They crossed the torrid zone six times, unconsumed by fire (contrary to the opinion of Antiquity). They spent six months in Tidore, where live the antipodes of Guinea, thereby showing that we can communicate with them; and although they lost sight of the North Star, they still shaped their course by it, since the compass needle pointed straight at it, even at forty degrees below the Equator, as accurately as if they were in the Mediterranean. . . . Near the

6. The ancients held that there *were* men whose feet were opposed to theirs, but that communication with them was impossible ("no se podían comunicar con nosotros," p. 159b).

7. As reported by Origen and Jerome.

southern, or Antarctic, pole there appears always a small, whitish cloud and four stars that form a cross, with three others near, resembling our North Star and Ursa Major. These are the signs of the other axis of the heavens, which we call South. Great was the navigation of the fleet of Solomon, but greater was that of these ships of our Emperor and King Charles. Jason's ship Argo, now placed in the heavens as a constellation, sailed but a meager distance in comparison with the Victoria, which should be placed in the shipyard of Seville as a memorial. The goings and comings, the dangers and hardships of Ulysses were as naught compared to those of Juan Sebastián de Elcano; [8] because of this exploit Elcano took the World as his crest, with this legend: *Primus circumdisti me* — You were the first to sail around me — a device most appropriate to the navigation that he completed, for the truth is that he did precisely what the legend says: he circumnavigated the globe (p. 219a).

SIC ET NON [9]

Were one to judge by López de Gómara's enthusiasm, it might be concluded that the Spaniards were as affected by the great news of the discoveries as men in our own time have been by news of an explosion over Hiroshima or a Sputnik orbiting the earth. No such assumption would be justified. While we shall marshal a reasonably impressive number of positive testimonies from sixteenth- and seventeenth-century writers, there are cases — perplexing cases — of inconceivable ignorance or disregard of the new events, as well as of general vagueness with respect to them. Americus Vespucci's revelations were a dead letter in Spain, where men only slowly became convinced that the new lands were not India or a part of it; Spain was enlightened, not by Vespucci, but by the achievements of its own navigators.[10] Indeed, historians have considered it probable that King Charles at first regarded the American continent as an unfortunate barrier lying between his kingdom and the wealth of the Orient. Such a negative attitude could not

8. Elcano took charge and finished the voyage after Magellan's death in the Philippines.

9. This phrase, also used in Volume I (especially Chapter I) and Volume II, expresses the great dichotomy of the life and thought of the Middle Ages and the Renaissance, particularly in Spain where the Church was strong and where the faithful were obliged to steer a careful course between obedience to religious dicta and the often totally opposite tendencies of an acquisitive, expanding society.

10. M. Bataillon, "L'idée de la découverte de l'Amérique chez les Espagnols du XVIᵉ siècle (d'après un livre récent)," *BHi*, LV (1953), 23–55. See also Gillet (ed.), *Propalladia* . . . (Bryn Mawr, Pennsylvania, 1943–51), III, 117, n. 87, and 635, n. 187.

have remained long in his mind, however. From three million *maravedís* of income accruing to the royal coffers from the new lands in 1503 (the year of the founding of the Casa de Contratación at Seville), the figure rose to forty-six million in 1518 (one year after Charles' arrival in Spain) and continued to increase spectacularly. In 1519 the Council of the Indies was created to control the vastly increased business of administration — all of this before the delivery of the fabulous sums derived from the ransom of Atahualpa in Peru (1534).[11]

Public Ignorance and Vagueness

In 1547 Pero Mexía (or Pedro Mejía) published at Seville a book of *Diálogos o coloquios* which proved very popular at home and in other countries. In the *Dialogue of the Sun*, the interlocutor Paulo explains the circumnavigation of the globe by Magellan-Elcano, the problem of the antipodes, and — in a rudimentary manner — the nature of gravitation which pulls all things (including men's feet) toward the center of the earth. In the midst of this explanation another of the speakers, Petronio, exclaims: "Saints preserve us! Is that really so?" Another, Ludouico, interrupts to admit: "I had already heard about that; Antonio even showed it to me the other day on the globe or *mapamundi.*" Not so Petronio, who confesses: "Well, I swear, until now I had not known that that navigation had been as you say." [12] This, though twenty-five long years had elapsed since the event.

The foregoing seems surprising, but what is truly incredible is that the humanist Hernán Núñez, in his commentary on Juan de Mena's *Laberinto de fortuna* (1499), should have adhered to the explanations of the ancient and medieval philosophers regarding the uninhabitability of three of the earth's zones, without correcting their obsolete views by a reference to the first three voyages of Columbus, all of which had penetrated the torrid zone; and that the error of the first edition should have been perpetuated in the edition of 1552, one year before Núñez's death and many years after both the Spaniards and the Portuguese had made the torrid zone a

11. Marcos A. Morínigo, *América en el teatro de Lope de Vega* (Buenos Aires, 1946), pp. 12 ff.
12. Ed. M. L. Mulroney (Iowa City, Iowa, 1930), pp. 97 ff.

highway for their ships. In this edition of 1552 we read: "Mathematicians divide the earth as a whole into five zones or bands, of which the extreme two are uninhabitable because of the great cold, and the middle zone likewise because of the excessive heat." Of the two temperate zones, he says that one is inhabited by the portion of the human race of which knowledge is available; the other, separated from Asia, Africa, and Europe by the torrid zone, is the land of those who are called Antichthones (i.e., antipodes), "of whom we have never had nor shall we have in all eternity any knowledge because the torrid zone, which is uninhabitable by reason of its terrible heat, lies between us and them. . . ." Núñez's source is Macrobius' commentary on Cicero's *Somnium Scipionis*.[13] The printing of such scientific nonsense in 1552 is the more surprising in that this commentary by Núñez is essentially an encyclopedia of humanistic knowledge far exceeding the dimensions required merely to elucidate Mena's text.

Diego Guillén de Avila wrote his *Panegyric in Praise of Queen Isabella* (Valladolid, 1509) without mentioning the discovery in which the Queen had herself had so large a part.[14]

The humanist Hernán Pérez de Oliva (d. 1531?), probably the first translator of a work by Sophocles into a modern language (from a Latin version?), wrote in the *Diálogo de la dignidad del hombre*, which he modeled on Pico della Mirandola's *Oration on the Dignity of Man*, that many parts of the earth are forbidden to us by the cold, others by the heat, still others by the surrounding waters, and others by the unfavorable atmosphere, thus perpetuating the myth of impassable climatic barriers.[15]

Hostility

There was not only indifference, but also hostility to the novelty of the discoveries. Friar Francisco de Osuna, whose treatises on mystical theology and mystical experience contributed so greatly

13. *Todas las obras de Juan de Mena . . .* (Antwerp, 1552), p. 55 (commentary on Mena's *Copla XXXIV*). These questions have been reviewed in Gillet-Green, *op. cit.*, pp. 164. ff. Much of the material there presented was obtained from my own notes and, when it is appropriate, I make use of the same material here.
14. M. Menéndez y Pelayo (ed.), *Antología de poetas líricos castellanos* (new ed.; Santander, 1944–45), III, 103.
15. *BAE*, LXV, 378a.

to the clarifying of St. Teresa's interpretation of her own sense of union with God, in 1530 admonishes the aspirant to that blessed mystical state: "Concern yourself not over the affairs of Rome or Cyprus or Greece; let not your heart be troubled to know the changes occurring to the universe, the condition of kingdoms, the events of the New Isles and of the Mainland [*Tierra Firme*]." [16] This attitude is, on the part of a mystic, reasonable;[17] Thomas à Kempis had given similar advice in *The Imitation of Christ*: "What can you see elsewhere that you cannot see here? . . . What would it be but an unprofitable vision?" [18] Osuna's concern was not with the worldly importance of the newly discovered wealth, or even with the urgency of converting the Indians. Of first importance to him was the inner spiritual development of the souls about him. Mystical religion is by nature individualistic.

European Disinterest

Europe in general was slow to perceive the meaning of the discoveries. As for England: "In the sixteenth century the imagination still turns more readily to ancient Greece and Rome, to Italy, Arcadia, to English history or legend" [19] than to the new lands in the West; French humanists are more interested in the progress of the Turks in Central Europe, and *Voyages to Jerusalem* or *Letters from Constantinople* are the best sellers; [20] the discovery of printing looms larger in the imagination than the Great Discoveries.[21] Jacques Signot's *Description du monde* was printed in 1539, in 1540, and four times again during the sixteenth century without making mention of America.[22] It was not until Montaigne, having

16. *Segundo abecedario espiritual*, cited by Fidèle de Ros in *Un maître de Sainte Thérèse: Le Père François d'Osuna* (Paris, 1936), p. 131.

17. See Chapter I of our Volume II: "The Creation and the Creatures."

18. See Gillet-Green, *op. cit.*, pp. 165–66.

19. C. S. Lewis, *English Literature in the Sixteenth Century Excluding Drama* (Oxford, 1954), p. 16; see also Herschel Baker, *The Wars of Truth: Studies in the Decay of Christian Humanism in the Earlier Seventeenth Century* (Cambridge, Massachusetts, 1947), pp. 236, 253.

20. V. L. Saulnier, *Maurice Scève* (Paris, 1948), I, 21.

21. See Saulnier's edition of Rabelais' *Pantagruel* (Paris, 1946), p. xxxix, n. 1.

22. Rosario Romeo, "Le scoperte americane nella coscienza italiana del Cinquecento," *Rivista storica italiana*, LXV (1953), 222–57, 326–79. See also G. Atkinson, *Les nouvaux horizons de la Renaissance française* (Paris, 1935); B. Penrose, *Travel and Discovery in the Renaissance* (Cambridge, Massachusetts, 1952); R. R. Cawley,

read López de Gómara, wrote *Les cannibales,* that the reality of the New World replaced the fantasies of the exotic societies to which Pantagruel had led his readers.

In Spain, Columbus found it difficult to enlist a crew for his third voyage. In 1518 Bartolomé de las Casas was commissioned to travel about Castile exhorting Spanish farmers to emigrate to America. And, while men-at-arms clearly saw that there were glorious exploits to be achieved and great honor to be won fighting the Turks or the European enemies of the King, Indian fighting in far-off lands seemed at best a matter for second choice. It was only in February of 1534, when Hernando Pizarro brought from Peru the royal share of Atahualpa's ransom, that a voyage to the Spanish Indies became a matter of general illusion and concrete desire.[23]

Positive Values

Before 1550. Not all was indifference or Augustinian hostility — *Nolite foras ire.* It is time now to look for indications of active interest in America, ranging from mere topical allusions to deep patriotic concern such as that of Bernardo de Balbuena (d. 1627), for whom Spain's expansion overseas was the final and total crowning of the national genius.[24]

One of the first to glimpse the significance of the discoveries for stay-at-homes[25] was Fray Ambrosio Montesino, who wrote, perhaps as early as 1493:

> Men sail the seas and find far lands:
> When they come back we wait on shore

Unpathed Waters: Studies in the Influence of the Voyagers on Elizabethan Literature (Princeton, 1940); *idem, Milton and the Literature of Travel* (Princeton, 1951); A. L. Rowse, *The Elizabethans and America* (New York, *ca.* 1959), the last chapter.

23. Francisco Pizarro, of course, had felt the pull of the magnet earlier. See Morínigo, *op. cit.,* pp. 12 ff. The latter's assertion that Lope de Rueda's fifth *paso* in *El deleitoso* is a parody of the exaggerated, glowing reports brought back by returned conquistadors is based merely on a gratuitous identification of Rueda's "Tierra de Jauja" or "Land of Cockayne" (a sort of "Big Rock Candy Mountain") with an actual valley in Peru, that of the Jauja River. Corominas in his *Diccionario crítico etimológico* (Bern, 1954), II, 1042, remarks: "The Peruvian origin is far from being certain."

24. Frank Pierce, "L'allégorie poétique au XVIᵉ siècle" (Part II), *BHi,* LII (1950), 209.

25. What follows might be amplified by a selection of additional texts from Morínigo's work and from the interesting article by H. Capote, "Las Indias en la poesía española del Siglo de Oro," *Estudios americanos,* VI (1953), 5–36.

And ask them what they saw;
And if they tell us of strange things,
We scarce can sleep the whole night through
Longing to know what they learned.[26]

In 1496 Juan del Encina, "father of the Spanish drama," published his *Cancionero*, which contains this heading: "Here begins the *Triumph of Fame*, composed by Juan del Enzina, dedicated and applied to the illustrious and victorious Sovereigns King Ferdinand and Queen Isabella, rulers of the Spains, our natural lords and governors, masters of the islands of our Sea."[27] In 1508 Francisco de Avila makes Death speak as follows:

All powers and principalities
Must drink of my bitter draught;
Mandinga, Antilles, Gelof,
Canaries, Eslavonia. . . .
They know me in Calicut
And other unpleasant regions.[28]

In 1517 Torres Naharro, in the dedication of his *Propalladia* to the Marqués de Pescara, compared his own newly launched book to a caravel sailing into the West[29] in search of "new worlds of strange peoples" and "with the deliberate intent of issuing forth to discover new lands." Torres Naharro may have been thinking of the Portuguese discoverers (writes Professor Gillet) whose progress he outlined in his *Comedia Trophea* (1514); but a reference in his *Romance I* to "Indian Islands in the sea" (cited *ibid.*, p. 117, n. 87) shows that his mind was also following in the wake of Columbus and expressing itself in terms which seem to fit the circum-

26. "Los hombres que navegando / hallan tierras muy remotas, / cuando vuelven, que es ya cuando / los estamos esperando / en el puerto con sus flotas / que nos digan les pedimos / las novedades que vieron; / y si algo nuevo oímos / más velamos que dormimos / por saber lo que supieron" (*Cancionero* [1508]; cited in Gillet-Green, *op. cit.*, p. 166). (Unless otherwise stated, translations in this volume are always mine; they are not always line-for-line.) Father Francisco Alvares, in his *Verdadera información de las tierras del Preste Juan*, noted a similar eagerness for news when he returned to Lisbon and Braga after his mission (with Duarte Galvão) to Abyssinia in 1513; see H. Cidade, "La literatura portuguesa y la expansión ultramarina," *Estudios americanos*, XX (1960), 220–21.
27. Ed. facsimile of Real Academia Española (Madrid, 1928), fol. xlix.
28. "Cualquiera otra señoría / purgo bien con mi jarope, / Mandinga, Antillas, Jelope, / Canarias y Esclavonía. . . . / Tambien entré en Calicú / y en otras brutas regiones" (cited in Gillet-Green, *op. cit.*, p. 166).
29. See Gillet (ed.), *Propalladia . . .*, III, 8.

tances existing just after the first voyage. Here in Torres Naharro's opening paragraph, Professor Gillet suggests, is "something new and personal, which is a conception of the *Propalladia* as a poetic voyage of discovery, starting 'from the sheltered harbors of western Spain,' pointing . . . 'toward the sunset,' sailing by 'the planets in their ethereal space,' with the marvellous help of the mariner's compass and the cunning device of the pilot's chart, to procure for the eyes of stay-at-homes 'new knowledge of strange lands.' "[30]

Torres Naharro's play (or pageant), the *Comedia Trophea*, was performed in 1514 at Rome, under Pope Leo, when the Portuguese Tristão d'Acunha was there as ambassador. It was a part of the elaborate entertainment (and propaganda) for the Portuguese, who sought papal support for their recent conquest of the Moluccas or Spice Islands, which they feared might prove to be in the zone already granted to the Spaniards by Pope Alexander VI. Torres Naharro, a Spanish dramatist residing in Rome whose talents were enlisted for the purpose, says, however, nothing at all of the Moluccas, concerning which he was probably kept in the dark.[31] No matter. The play — though its intent be Portuguese — is composed in Castilian by a native of Castile, who thus becomes the author of the first considerable piece of literature concerned with the expanding horizons of the Renaissance. Rather than a true play, the *Trophea* is a spectacle with comic relief, evoking a stirring reality — one still only partly realized and approached in terms of mythology and the humanistic tradition. "The *Trophea*," writes Professor Gillet, "is not, properly speaking, an imitation of a human action, but an action pure and simple — a magic action, with a double purpose, to confirm an acquired situation and to produce one yet unrealized." "Its confirmatory magic lies not only in the homage of the heathen 'kings,'" but also "in the total analogical effect of the performance. . . . [T]here has been a test, and the community feels reassured: the powers that be are favorable and order reigns in the cosmos. The final burlesque flying-scene . . .

30. Gillet-Green, *op. cit.*, p. 165.
31. Gillet (ed.), *Propalladia* . . . , III, 8. There is no need to detail here how Spanish opposition soon developed, how Magellan, under orders from Charles V, reached the Moluccas in 1521, and how the Spanish claims were finally allowed to lapse, leaving the Portuguese in possession (Gillet-Green, *op. cit.*, p. 495). The islands were lost to the Dutch and recaptured by the Spanish in 1606.

seems like a prophetic glimpse of the future" (Gillet-Green, *op. cit.*, pp. 493, 496–97).

Of special interest for the theme of this chapter is the fact that in the *Comedia Trophea* we have an extremely early occurrence of the "Quarrel between Ancients and Moderns." The prestige of Claudius Ptolemy (second century A.D.) as a geographer was immense in the fifteenth century — the century of the Italian humanists — but his *Geography* was a meager and unsatisfactory guide for use in the period of geographical expansion — a fact quite evident to pilots and sailors, who were in possession of better maps than his. Fama, in the *Comedia Trophea*, treats Ptolemy with scorn. The Portuguese King, she says, has discovered more countries than Ptolemy even mentions. The latter, temporarily released from Hell and jealous of his renown, appears on the stage to protest, accusing Fama of favoritism to kings and prejudice against a man of humble station like himself. There is no reason why Fama should not proclaim the glories of King Manuel, Ptolemy admits, but insists that in so doing she should not deprive Ptolemy of his glory. After all, the King may have discovered lands undescribed by Ptolemy, but Ptolemy has mentioned a few that have not yet been conquered by Portugal!

Perhaps it is to be expected that, in a pageant performed before "all the Church" (except the Pope, who was not present in person), the conquests should have been played up as crusades. The elements of Providence and of human service to God are stressed, as later writers will continue to stress them: this Conquest is sacred! In the *Comedia Trophea* Fama speaks of the King:

> How laudably and with what merit,
> By means of what sacred wars,
> He has won and subdued more lands
> Than Ptolemy ever recorded! [32]

Once again, experience has vanquished armchair philosophy and a modern makes obsolete the work of an ancient.

32. "Con quán honesto deseo, / con quán sacratísimas guerras, / ha ganado muy más tierras / que no escriuió Ptholomeo" (*Propalladia* . . . , II, 94: see also Gillet-Green, *op. cit.*, 142 ff., 489 ff.) Tirso de Molina causes Hernando Pizarro to say: "Henceforth there can be no doubt, / In spite of all the world's envy, / That this is a holy conquest, / Since God aids our enterprise" — "No habrá duda / desde hoy

It was to the same King Manuel that the humanist Juan Luis Vives, "father of modern psychology," dedicated his treatise *De disciplinis* (1531). The Portuguese discoverers, he wrote, "revealed to us the existence of fabulous peoples and nations of marvelous and barbaric life, endowed with the dizzying wealth that we contemplate with such eager eyes. . . . There is no one so ignorant of reality as to think that the peregrinations of the mythical heroes extolled by Fame can in any way be compared with these recent Portuguese voyages." In 1543, in the posthumous treatise *Da veritate fidei Christianae*, Vives declared that "human life in the New World in no way differs from that which was lived everywhere a thousand years ago," thus anticipating the value of the discoveries for anthropological studies.[33] He also sounded the utopian note [34] that will loom so large in certain sectors of Spanish thought in regard to the Indies when he wrote to the Bishop of Lincoln: "Navigators returned from the New World . . . report that there exist certain islands where, if any warlike collision has occurred, the greatest honor is given to the party that first comes forward to ask peace of the enemy." [35]

In 1535 Fray Bernardino de Laredo declared that one and the same sun gives its heat and power to Yucatan or Flanders or the Indies of Prester John. In 1538 he announced that the Pope had granted five hundred days of indulgence to any inhabitant of the lands of New Spain (Mexico) who should say a paternoster in honor of St. Joseph.[36]

contra envidia tanta / que esta conquista es santa, / pues Dios nuestra empresa ayuda" (*NBAE*, IV, 595b).

33. Citations from Gillet-Green, *op. cit.*, pp. 167–68.

34. O'Gorman's study (*op. cit.*, p. 89) shows that at the same time that America was seen as an immense territory which could be legitimately appropriated and exploited — a new and unforeseen province of the earth which destiny held in store for Europe for the purpose of achieving supreme historic ends — America was also considered "new ground" in the Toynbean sense, as a world of liberation and promise, the world of freedom and of the future, a new Europe, in short, which — as it surrendered its treasures to the Old World — gradually came to be thought of as the place which would supplant Europe as the site for establishing utopias considered impossible in the circumstances of the Old World. But this was only part of the picture; America was also seen as a hell on earth whose inhabitants might better go to Hell — their inevitable destination — without European help. See below, the chapter on political expansion.

35. Quoted in Gillet-Green, *op. cit.*, p. 167.

36. Fidèle de Ros, *Le Frère Bernardin de Laredo* (Paris, 1948), pp. 123, 180.

By 1534 the Indies had already entered into the realm of the marvelous; in about that year there spread a story that seventy great ships had arrived at Laredo on the northern coast, with ten thousand Amazons aboard who had come to seek fathers for their children among the brave men of Spain and were offering fifty ducats apiece for every pregnancy — on condition that boys born as a result would remain in Spain but girls would go back to Amazonia.[37]

By 1540 Alejo Venegas regarded the discoveries from east to west as being complete, with only the North and South Poles remaining unknown. Why, he asks, did God delay so long in sending the Gospel to the inhabitants of the new lands? This is God's secret. And he proceeds to introduce the idea of "pre-established guilt" which figured so largely in the debates concerning the justice of the conquest and of making war against Indian non-aggressors. Surely God desires the salvation of all men, says Venegas. Perhaps the Indians were not ready to receive the Gospel — until now, in the fullness of time. We must not forget that God forbade St. Paul and St. Timothy to preach in Asia (Acts 16). The reason had its roots in human free will: the natives of America, like those of Asia in the time of St. Paul, would resist the Gospel, and God foreknew it; were it preached to them in such a state of mind, the guilt of their resistance would be multiplied. But even so, they were not without sin, for they steadfastly resisted the still, small, inner voice; they disregarded the "inspiration and knowledge of the truth which God inwardly had given them." In this, their sin — since they had no evangelizers — was less than that of the contumacious Moors.[38]

37. H. Keniston, *Francisco de los Cobos, Secretary to the Emperor Charles V* (Pittsburgh, *ca.* 1959), pp. 161. When in 1631 Tirso de Molina was commissioned to write a pageant in three parts (three plays, probably given on three successive days) to celebrate the restoration of the title of *Marqués* which had been given to Francisco Pizarro but did not pass to his heirs, the dramatist entitled one of the plays *Amazons in the Indies* and utilized these legendary feministic creatures (as conceived by classical writers) as a means to provide the necessary element of prophecy whereby to foretell, in the uncertain days of the conquest, the future glories of Pizarro and his descendants; see O. H. Green, "Notes on the Pizarro Trilogy of Tirso de Molina," *HR*, IV (1936), 201–25.

38. *De las Differencias de libros que ay en el uniuerso* (Salamanca, 1572; 1st ed. 1540), Bk. I, p. 90 and ch. VII. In the second book of this work, chapter X bears the heading, "How each man has an invisible star which guides him and urges him to seek God, as the visible Star guided the Magi"; and on p. 202 Venegas is more explicit: "What more shall I say, except that this light is so clear that it did not fail

By 1549 the topic of the new discoveries had entered the language of poetry as an expression of hyperbole:

> My love is of greater magnitude,
> So vast it is simply *more*;
> It leaves behind a thousand isles
> *With no Columbus to find them.*[39]

Somewhat earlier — Cortés died in 1547 — are these lines which an anonymous compiler addresses to the Marqués del Valle, offering him his book:

> To him who on land and sea
> Hears songs of undying praise,
> With refrains that forever repeat:
> Cortés is the glory of Spain.[40]

After 1550.[41] With this we come to the mid-century mark. In an

to reveal itself even to the Gentiles. Because of it Cicero [*Tusc. disp.*, V] declared that we have seeds of virtues planted naturally in our souls which — if we would allow them to grow and did not stifle them with sins which we voluntarily commit — would guide us to eternal life." For a more complete discussion of the doctrines of natural light and of pre-established guilt, see Chapter IV of Volume II: "The Nature and Destiny of man." An example of how an uninstructed pagan heeds the still, small voice of the true God is found in these lines spoken by Guacolda in Calderón's *La aurora en Copacabana* (*ca.* 1659), Act I: "I know not what natural light . . . makes it abhorrent to me that, though I have committed no transgression, a celestial [heathen] god thirsts for [my] human blood . . . obliging one worshipper to sacrifice another." See Natalicio González, "Calderón de la Barca y el mundo indígena," *América indígena*, II (1960), 28.

39. "Mi querer es de otro talle, / tan otra cosa que es más, / que mil islas dexó atrás / que no hay Colón que las halle" (*Obras de Juan Fernández de Heredia*, ed. F. Martí Grajales [Valencia, 1913], p. 36; emphasis mine). Much later it would enter the language of criticism. Tamayo Salazar conceives of his friend Pellicer analyzing the works of another poet: "and, like a new Columbus, / You trace in his writings / A course for every rhyme, / A pole-star for each line" — "Y, Colón nuevo, / mostráis en sus escritos, / rumbos a cada rima, / nortes a cada verso." See Dámaso Alonso, *Góngora y el "Polifemo"* (4th ed.; Madrid, 1961), p. 228.

40. "Y de quien en mar y tierra / se canta digna alabança, / cuyos cánticos repiten: / 'Cortés es gloria de España'" (*Poesías barias y recreación de buenos ingenios*, ed. John M. Hill [Bloomington, Indiana, 1923], p. 14.

41. I omit discussion of attempts to celebrate the discoveries in various epics written in Castilian at this time. W. J. Entwistle has written: "To the writers of the Spanish Peninsula it seemed that Ariosto had failed for want of truth. There were achievements in the Americas and the East Indies which, they knew, eclipsed in heroism and strangeness anything 'said in prose or rhyme'; and they averred that the poet need only transcribe plain facts. That was what Alonso de Ercilla attempted in his *Araucana*. . . . Every possible subject and style were exploited in the search for the perfect Heroic Poem. . . . But none of these themes gave the desired Epos, so rare is its attainment! . . . None of these themes, that is, save the national theme of Portugal. Camoes' *Lusiads* is probably the only heroic poem of the age which entirely accom-

anonymous work of Erasmist tendencies entitled *El Crotalón* (*ca.* 1552), one of the speakers reviews his past life: "You must know that once when I was young and eager to see new things, there came to Castile reports that the western parts of those great lands of New Spain [Mexico] had been traversed . . . and in order to satisfy in some measure the insatiable desire which I felt to see new lands and new things, I determined to take ship and venture upon that western navigation. . . . They told us what the natives were like, their customs, dress, and disposition; the diversity of animals, birds, fruits, and all things edible. Everything they told us was so admirable, as were all the things shown to us by those who came from over there, that we could not contain ourselves." [42]

Marcos Morínigo, in his study of America in the plays of Lope de Vega (*op. cit.*), has compiled an anthology of references, culled from sixteenth-century works, which in many ways supplements what is given here. He finds that, both in Lope and in Spanish literature in general, the predominant idea of the Indies, as they were gradually elevated to the rank of *symbol* in the Spanish mind, was one of wealth, riches, and overflowing abundance of worldly things. It is interesting to note again that Fray Luis de Granada, in his *Guía de pecadores* (*Guide for Sinners*, 1556; definitive ed., 1567), applies this symbol to the spiritual life. Confidence and hope in the Divine Mercy, he says, constitute "one of the great treasures of the Christian life: these spiritual Indies, the patrimony of the sons of God" (see the second epigraph of the present chapter). In his later *Introducción del Símbolo de la fe* (1582), Granada makes use of information about medicinal plants and animals in his arguments to establish the teleological nature of the world, created by an all-wise Providence as man's home and footstool: "in new lands there are discovered daily new animals with new abilities and new properties, such as have never been known in the territories we dwell in." [43] Even the poisonous rattlesnake is provided by his Creator with a rattle, the best warning against its sting (*ibid.*, p.

plished its purpose. He proposed to sing the heroic soul of Portugal, and his verses are the intimate pulsations of that soul" ("The Search for the Heroic Poem," in *Studies in Civilization* [Philadelphia, 1941], pp. 95–96).

42. In *Orígenes de la novela*, study and ed. by M. Menéndez y Pelayo (Madrid, 1905–15), II, 231b.

43. *Obras*, ed. Fray Justo Cuervo (Madrid, 1906–8), V, 120; see also p. 97.

130). Fray Luis is not always sufficiently critical: God made the four seasons to the end that in them the four bodily humors (corresponding to the elements earth, water, air, fire) might restore themselves and establish an equilibrium of their dominant and recessive qualities. He does not stop to think that in the tropics the seasons have no rotation (pp. 68–69, 76).

The interest in the new medicinal plants was very great. The Portuguese Nicolás Monardes, who practiced medicine in Seville, published there in 1574 *Two Books, One of Which Treats of the Things Brought from Our Western Indies Which Are Useful in Medicine, and the Other of the Stone Called Bezoar.* In 1590 Father José de Acosta, one of the most scientifically inclined of the ecclesiastical writers, insists again on the idea of teleology: God's eternal will chose to enrich the remote lands of the earth, the lands of least civil population, with the greatest abundance of mines ever known, in order by this means to invite explorers to seek them out and possess them, and, in this effort, to communicate their religion and the worship of the true God to the natives who knew Him not, that Isaiah's prophecy might be fulfilled and the Church extend her borders, not only on the right but on the left, which is how St. Augustine declares that the Gospel must be spread — not only by those who sincerely and with charity preach it, but also by those who with temporal and human methods announce it. Thus the Indian lands most blest with mines and wealth have been the ones wherein the Christian religion has been most successfully implanted, as the Lord took advantage, for His sovereign purposes, of our completely human desires.[44]

Fray Diego de Valdés in his *Rhetórica christiana* (1579) finds in the Indies the visible confirmation of the theory of the social contract — the civilizing of barbarians by the persuasiveness of superior men: "This, which seems a mere figment of the imagination, we have seen accomplished in our time in those remote regions of the New World. . . ." As a consequence, Fray Diego regards the discovery — just as López de Gómara had done earlier — as the most memorable event since the beginning of the world. Nothing

44. *Historia natural y moral de las Indias* (Madrid, 1792), I, 185–86.

has so clearly shown the mercy of God "as the conversion, pacification, and conciliation of New Spain." [45]

In 1588 Pedro Malón de Chaide, in *La conversión de la Magdalena*, makes of Peru a symbol of spiritual distance: "There is no Peru so far removed, no China, no island so secret, no torrid zone so glowing with heat, no Arctic or Antarctic Circle so wintry and frozen, that God's hand cannot reach" the sinner and draw him to the light.[46]

The seventeenth century. It has been said — perhaps with exaggeration — that by the turn of the century "all Spain hung upon the arrival of the galleons from America." [47] From this time on the New World — though infrequently made the theme or even the scene of action of literary works — is present, like a pervading leaven, in the thoughts of Spain's writers (though one is at times surprised by the omission of American themes or allusions in places where one would reasonably expect them).[48]

In 1604 Bernardo de Balbuena, who at his death was Bishop of Puerto Rico, published a poem, entitled *Grandeza mexicana* (*The Greatness of Mexico*), addressed to an illustrious lady, Doña Isabel de Tovar y Guzmán. In a salutation to his patroness he states his purpose in eight lines of *ottava rima* that recall the opening stanza of the *Orlando furioso*:

> Of famous Mexico I sing the site,
> Its origin, and greatness of its buildings;
> Its horses, streets, its courteous manners;
> Its fame in letters, virtue, arts, and crafts;
> Its luxury, its means of entertainment;

45. Quoted in Francisco Terrones del Caño, *Instrucción de predicadores*, ed. Félix G. Olmedo (Madrid, 1946), p. c. See also pp. cviii–cix.

46. Ed. P. Félix García (Madrid, 1947), II, 170.

47. From José de Armas, *Cervantes y el Quijote*, quoted in Jorge Campos, "Presencia de América en la obra de Cervantes," *Revista de Indias*, VIII (1947), 389.

48. In *Don Quijote* (I, 48) the Canon of Toledo tells the Don that he might better forget his romances of chivalry and read histories of heroic men-at-arms: Viriatus, Caesar, Hannibal, Alexander, Fernán González, the Cid, the Gran Capitán, Diego García de Paredes, Garci Pérez de Vargas, Garcilaso de la Vega, Don Manuel de León. There is no mention of any conquistador. See Campos, *op. cit.*, pp. 374–75. In the work of Lope de Vega, only Columbus, Cortés, and García Hurtado de Mendoza — among all the conquistadors — appear as protagonists of *comedias heroicas*. See Morínigo, *op. cit.*, p. 221.

> The eternal spring it evermore enjoys;
> Its noble government, both lay and sacred;
> All this and more in this brief poem is ciphered.[49]

It is a paean of praise, by a Spanish priest who (by calling attention to his erudition and his literary skill) aspires to obtain an appointment in the capital. Its tone is, on the whole, worldly:

> Beauty and noble pride, and gallantry,
> Lineage and discretion, perfect neatness,
> Virtue and loyalty and wealth and rank,
>   All that desire might covet and that art
> Might add to nature's prodigality,
> All this will here be found, all this I see,
> All this here has its center and its sphere.[50]

Everything in Mexico is "eminent" (p. 136); there is a world of armorial shields "broidered and decked, each one, with Spanish fame" (p. 142) — the fame of Spanish deeds that subjugated more worlds than others managed to conceive of (p. 144), deeds which, scarcely believed today, will meet with incredulity in the future (p. 146). In a final apostrophe to the homeland, Balbuena voices a prayer:

> O may the world you govern and control
> E'er render you its praise, my sweet fair land,
> And to you return my body, or its ashes.[51]

Amid the gold-bearing ore brought up from the mines by the dusky Indian to fill the holds of the Spanish fleets, the poet offers his own tribute — his desire to celebrate Spain's greatness *in saecula saeculorum*.

Prior to 1611 Pedro Espinosa uses the symbols of the discoveries figuratively in a poem to St. Ignatius de Loyola:

49. "De la famosa México el asiento, / origen y grandeza de edificios, / caballos, calles, trato, cumplimiento, / letras, virtudes, variedad de oficios, / regalos, ocasiones de contento, / primavera inmortal y sus indicios, / gobierno ilustre, religión, estado, / todo en este discurso está cifrado" (ed. Francisco Monterde, [Mexico City, 1941], p. 3).

50. "Hermosura, altiveces, gallardía, / nobleza, discreción, primor, aseo, / virtud, lealtad, riquezas, hidalguía, / y cuanto la codicia y el deseo / añadir pueden y alcanzar el arte, / aquí se hallará, y aquí lo veo, / y aquí como en su esfera tienen parte" (*ibid.*, p. 77).

51. "El mundo que gobiernas y autorizas / te alabe, patria dulce, y a tus playas / mi humilde cuerpo vuelva, o sus cenizas" (*ibid.*, p. 148).

> With favoring wind, across a balmy sea,
> You sail the ocean of God's victory,
> Toward the Indies of the Blest,
> Beyond the Cape of Good Hope.[52]

The first part of *Don Quijote* was published one year after the *Grandeza mexicana*, in 1605. A quotation such as the following is altogether normal: "the judge could not turn aside from the road he was following, since he had heard that within a month the fleet would leave Seville for New Spain, and it would be most inconvenient for him to miss that sailing" (Part I, ch. 42). Two of Cervantes' plays also give prominence to American themes or actually have America as the setting of part of the action: *La entretenida, El rufián dichoso.* The most insistently recurring idea regarding the Indies, with Cervantes as with Lope de Vega, is that of their all-surpassing wealth. America is present in Cervantes' works, "not as a literary preoccupation, but as an integral part of the real world which he drew upon to create his world of fiction" (Campos, *op. cit.*, p. 403).

In one of his *Exemplary Tales*, "The Jealous Husband from Extremadura," there occurs a famous passage which reveals something of the bitterness with which Cervantes regarded his own failure to obtain a post in the administration of the American colonies as a means of repairing the sad state of his fortune: "Finding himself, therefore, so bereft of worldly goods and lacking in friends, he sought relief by taking a step taken by many who in that city are failures, for the passage to the Indies is the refuge and protection of all the desperate men of Spain, the safe hiding place of those in revolt, the safe-conduct of murderers . . . , the lure of women of easy virtue, the will-o'-the-wisp of many, and the private help of few" (quoted *ibid.*, p. 384). This is not really a condemnation of the lands of the American frontier which, like all frontiers, offered at least the possibility of rehabilitation — as the protagonists of the picaresque novels were often aware, and as Mateo Alemán, the author of the *Guzmán de Alfarache* (1599), himself experienced (*ibid.*, p. 385).

52. "Viento en popa, mar bonanza, / sulcáis el mar de victoria / a las Indias de la Gloria, / Cabo de Buena Esperanza" (*Segunda Parte de Flores de poetas ilustres de España*, comp. J. A. Calderón, ed. F. Rodríguez Marín [Seville, 1896], p. 260).

In Lope de Vega (d. 1635) there are many expressions of ardent patriotism, but relatively few evocations of the glories of the American conquests. On many occasions when the poet marshals by name the lands and kingdoms ruled by the Castilian monarchs he makes no mention of the Indies, though he includes them in other listings, of which this one may be considered typical:

> Unconquered Caesar, Sun, and ruling Monarch
> Of Europe and America;

or

> The world of Antarctica is yours;
> The distant Indian pays you tribute; 53

or again:

> Triumphant Monarchy . . . ,
> Four crowns are yours
> That crown you monarch of the world,
> Victorious in Africa and Europe,
> In Asia and America undefeated . . .54

The frequent omissions of reference to *la gesta de América,* both in Cervantes and in Lope, are not to be interpreted as indications of disdain. What they do indicate is that Spain had other interests, other claims to glory, and that these — victories against the Turks, the defense of Christendom against heresy, the subjugation of Italy, hegemony in Europe — frequently came first to mind. Of the expressions of patriotism gathered by Gino de Solenni in his edition of Lope's *El Brasil restituido,* most evoke the European and Mediterranean theaters of Spain's exploits.

The Negative Side

We shall consider in a following chapter the inhumanity of the conquest: the Indians will appear as objects of Spanish greed, ambition, and injustice. There are, however, other negative aspects that may appropriately be noticed here. According to a persistent

53. "Invictísimo César, Sol, monarca / de América y Europa . . . " ; "El mundo antártico es vuestro, / hasta el indio os viene a ver" (cited in Morínigo, *op. cit.,* pp. 244–45).

54. "Inuicta Monarquía . . . , / quatro coronas tienes, / con que del mundo a coronarte vienes, / tú, en Africa y Europa, / en Asia y en América triunfante." See Lope's *El Brasil restituido, Together with a Study of Patriotism in His Theater,* critical edition by Gino de Solenni (New York, 1929), p. 33.

legend, popularized by ballads, Charles V rejected Cortés and treated him with a certain scorn and cruelty. In Lope de Vega's *La mayor desgracia de Carlos V y hechicerías de Argel*,[55] the Emperor says to Cortés, now Marqués del Valle and an old man:

> All that you say is true, señor Marqués;
> Let Montezuma in his chains be witness,
> And all the forces of Tlascala and Mexico.
> You're an old man, Fernando . . .

Cortés himself, in Act II of this play, exclaims bitterly:

> Oh would to God that I had by my side
> Those loyal Spanish troops, a full half-thousand,
> With whom in those far lands I was respected.[56]

Quevedo in his *Vida de Marco Bruto* cites Cortés among the vassals who, after conquering kingdoms for their sovereigns, are victims of the envy of the Court and of their masters' distrust (cited *ibid.*, p. 233).

The Pizarros in Peru all came to violent ends — one murdered, one beheaded for treason by royal order, one imprisoned in Spain for twenty years, and one (a half-brother) killed in battle. These facts were pointed out by historians, and it is therefore not surprising that the four brothers were not celebrated in song and story — except in the dramatic trilogy in which, long after the events, Tirso de Molina successfully undertook their rehabilitation[57] (as Luis Vélez de Guevara appears to have done also in a play, now lost, entitled *The Glory of the Pizarros* . . .). Mateo Alemán reflected the general hostility to this family when he wrote in his picaresque novel *Guzmán de Alfarache* (1599): "He turns out to be a rebel, like the Pizarros in Peru" (II, ii, 4).[58]

---

55. It is possible that this play might not be Lope's, although S. G. Morley and C. Bruerton (in their *The Chronology of Lope de Vega's Comedias* [New York, 1940]) do not seem to doubt the attribution. See Morínigo's note, *op. cit.*, p. 231. The lines translated read in the original: "Verdades son, marqués, ciertas y llanas; / dígalo Moctezuma en las prisiones, / las fuerzas de Taxcala y mejicanas. / Viejo estáis ya, Fernando" (cited by Morínigo, *op. cit.*, p. 231).

56. "¡Ay, cielo! ¡Quién tuviera / los quinientos soldados a su lado / con que en las Indias fuí tan respetado" (cited *ibid.*, p. 232).

57. The title of Marqués de la Conquista was revived and bestowed on Francisco's descendants in 1631. Tirso used the materials compiled by the family lawyer as a means of winning over the Council of the Indies; see my article, "The Pizarro Trilogy . . . ," previously cited.

58. See Morínigo's section, "Los Pizarros," *op. cit.*, pp. 237–38. Morínigo is evidently

The Indies themselves, unassociated with any Spanish hero or anti-hero, were regarded by some writers as the cause of a certain moral decline in the exploiting country. Bartolomé Leonardo de Argensola (d. 1631), in a poetic epistle to Don Nuño de Mendoza, condemns a

> Song, that with their gold the Indies send
> To weaken and destroy us — like the gold —
> And entertain us with barbaric sound.[59]

FINAL ESTIMATE

In 1606 the Spanish crown retook the Molucca or Spice Islands from the Dutch, who had driven out the Portuguese. This event marks one of the very last acts of imperial expansion by the Spanish. The Conde de Lemos, president of the Council of the Indies, appointed Bartolomé Leonardo de Argensola (d. 1631, as canon of the Metropolitan Church of Zaragoza) to write the history of the campaign. As a result, Argensola published in 1609 his *Conquista de las Islas Malucas*, "one of the most esteemed works in the bibliography of the history of the Philippines." [60] It is natural that the author's viewpoint should be ecclesiastical, but the book — written by official order — must have expressed official attitudes with reasonable accuracy. "People said," writes Argensola, "that the Monarchy, spread far and wide and separated by so many seas and climates, can scarcely be held together, nor is human providence able to bind into a unit . . . provinces which Nature set so wide apart . . . ; that these reasons are not sophistic, but born of experience . . . ; and that the most suitable action would be for the King to increase his strength in Europe." The "people" referred to were the ministers in charge of finances. To this reasonable analysis King Philip replied that all the treasures yet to be discovered in the mines should be applied to the propagation of the Gospel. What would the enemies of the faith conclude if they saw

assuming also that Cervantes introduced the conqueror of Peru in his *Persiles*. The Don Francisco Pizarro in question is almost certainly a descendant.

59. "Canción que de Indias con el oro viene, / como él, a afeminarnos y perdernos, / y con sonido bárbaro entretiene" (*Rimas* [Zaragoza, 1634], p. 595). For a slightly different text, see Blecua's edition (Zaragoza, 1950–51), II, 103.

60. W. E. Retana, *Aparato bibliográfico de la historia general de Filipinas* (Madrid, 1906), I, 58.

that, for mere questions of difficulty, the King of Spain abandoned the Philippines, depriving them of light and of the missionaries that carry it? Why should he allow Gentiles and Mohammedans to invade his territories in the Far East, when in Northern Europe all possible rigor is used to stamp out the Protestant heresy? Argensola's history, the author says, proclaims the King's zeal to maintain inviolate the faithfulness of his subjects in the Indies and to improve the disposition of idolatrous souls to receive the faith. The new history makes clear the King's determination to introduce into all corners of the world "our vigilance," ever at the service of this mystical empire, to the end that it may triumph. The natives of the Spice Islands are exposed to the heresies of the Dutch and the abominations of Islam; the "cause of the Faith" does not permit the abandonment of that Asiatic outpost. Even though in the enterprise of preaching the Gospel there are intermixed at times "the avarice and the excesses of our captains and soldiers," such excesses do not render the cause less just; nor can the Spanish nation listen to "reasons of state." [61]

There is an eloquent passage in another work of Argensola, his *Anales de Aragón* (Zaragoza, 1630). Recounting the history of the reign of Charles V, he gives ample space to the Spanish conquests during that reign. "Who is not silenced by God's preordination?" he asks (p. 580). "Who will ask of His providence why He chose, or tolerated, the long delay in bringing the Light to those regions? We may reverently believe that the Lord of Creation withheld the extension of His truth and the good news of the Redemption, to the end that the sword of our King Charles, placed in the hand of each and every soldier, carried forward by particular favor of Heaven to the unknown and unsuspected confines of the globe, might through fighting free them from oppression and darkness" (see also pp. 2, 76, 160, and *passim*).

Argensola's younger contemporary, Francisco de Quevedo (d. 1645), wrote in his *España defendida*:

As God of Battles, sometimes He protected us — and these occasions were many — with the might of our Patron Santiago [St. James]; at other times with the Cross, which, powerful to overcome death itself, can give life to all those whom it unites, as the standard of God. We were His militia at Las Navas de

61. *Conquista de las Islas Malucas* (Zaragoza, 1891), pp. 84–85, 127–26, 160–61.

Tolosa [1212]. The right hand of God won victories through the Cid [d. 1099], and the same right hand took Gama and Pacheco and Alburquerque as its instruments in the East Indies in order to deprive idols of their peaceful possession. Who other than God, whose hand is fearful above all things, protected Cortés in his happy acts of daring, the reward of which was an entire New World? It was the voice of God — ever obeyed in everything — that enabled Cisneros to prolong the day in the battle of Orán, where a Franciscan's cord girdle was more powerful than all the squadrons of the world.[62]

The Saint with His Feet in the Sea

If we turn back to consider once again the paintings on the sails of King Charles' flagship as he approached Spain's shores at the beginning of his reign in 1517, we find that the symbolic figures were prophetic of reality. Between that date and 1606, the year of the reconquest of the Spice Islands, nearly a century has elapsed, and the world has become a vast expanse of oceanic and continental distances. The Empire has grown top-heavy and the monarchy, weak. Yet the old ideals persist. Across the waters, in Asia now, there still lie tasks for Spanish arms and Spanish missionaries, tasks which Spaniards think of — in the last analysis — as part of an inescapable duty to their religion and their God. The Indies have become the source of unimagined wealth, in the administering of which Spain has grown poor. The discovered lands are thought of as a place of high adventure, the home of exotic plants, birds, and animals, of exploitable Indian labor. They have revolutionized man's conception of the globe he inhabits and have compelled revision of scientific, philosophic, even of religious preconceptions. *How was it that St. Augustine had no knowledge of these things?* [63] References to the Indies, figures of speech born of the great explorations, even personalities such as the conquistador, the humble Indian, and the returned nabob pervade the literature of the time with an insistence that indicates their incorporation into the normal life and thought and imagination of the Spaniards. Things bad as well as good have been encountered — crimes of exploitation and

62. *Obras en prosa*, ed. L. Astrana Marín (Madrid, 1932), p. 259b. On Cisneros' personal presence in the battle of Orán (1509), see Bataillon, *Erasmo y España*, I, 62 ff. In this victory Cisneros perceived a miracle, and he entered the conquered city repeating from Psalm 115: "Not to us, O God, not to us, but to Thy Name give glory."

63. "Querría saber qué fué la causa que no alcançó esto Sant Agustín" (P. Mexía, *Diálogos, ed. cit.*, p. 100).

of disloyalty, attacks of pirates, the insidious sapping of spiritual strength, even vile new diseases (and the drugs that cure them). Taken together, the good vastly overbalances the bad. The suffering of bodies is of no ultimate consequence; what matters is the salvation of souls, the routing of the powers of superstition and of evil, the growth of God's kingdom on earth, achieved by frail and sinful human beings who, because of their heroic faith, are miraculously aided by the Divine hand.[64] Spain has herself been a Christopher. Even in the days of decline (1606), religious considerations win the day against the statistics of the king's treasurers. The cord girdle of another saint — St. Francis — is more powerful than the might of arms (at Orán). Valiant Spain, in the words of Balbuena (*op. cit.*, p. 142), wears the crown of the Old World and of the New, receiving from the one the homage of fear,[65] from the other the tribute of vassalage. For nearly two centuries the vassalage will continue; and when, after a painful parturition, the vassal countries establish themselves as independent states, they will retain, consciously and by an act of will politically expressed,[66] the Christ brought across the waters by the Saint whose name was also the name of Columbus.

64. In Calderón's *La aurora en Copacabana*, the second act relates the conquest of Cuzco in Peru, but the author gives us neither a chronicle of the warfare nor an apologia for the harsh and pitiless Spanish captains. The fighting takes place against a religious background. Man, to Calderón, is "a metaphysical being who acts on the plane of the eternal. Beyond the material acts, disconnected, often senseless, God and the Devil move, weaving with their struggles and contradictions the fabric of history. This supernatural core illumines with flashes of rare beauty the clashes of passions and interests, and makes us perceive our unrecognized destiny." The invaders are shown as essentially powerless against the hosts of the Incas. Calderón makes use of a legend taken from the *Royal Commentaries* of Garcilaso de la Vega, el Inca: Our Lady of Copacabana, attended by angels, descends from Heaven to extinguish the flames of battle and stop the flight of the arrows. The outcries of the besieged are converted into ineffable melodies. See Natalicio González, *op. cit.*, pp. 29–30. The same legend was used by Tirso de Molina in his Pizarro trilogy.

65. As Garrett Mattingly has shown in *The Armada* (Boston, 1959), the English had a sobering fear of the Spaniards even after 1588.

66. John Lloyd Mecham, *Church and State in Latin America* (Chapel Hill, North Carolina, 1932).

III · Cultural Expansion: Castile Transplanted

Only a partisan in the "war of myths"
would dare to claim that the ideals
announced by the Spanish crown were generally
followed in the American territory under
Spanish rule. Nor should anyone claim that
the Spaniards fully accomplished their
purpose: to incorporate the mass of New
World Indians into a Christian and a
European world.

> *Lewis Hanke* [1]

CULTURE FOLLOWS THE FLAG

Italy

Not only is it true, as Antonio de Nebrija explained to Queen
Isabella, that language and empire go ever hand in hand; [2] it is
equally true that the conqueror of a territory imposes his culture
on the vanquished — or succumbs to the greater attractiveness and
power of the culture he has conquered, as happened between
Greece and Rome in ancient times and, in a limited sense, between Spain and Renaissance Italy. As regards Spain and Italy, the
relationship must be stated with great caution. Spain was indeed
"conquered" by the brilliance of Italy's modern adaptations of the
two great ancient cultures to the needs of modern intellectuality
and modern literary enjoyment; but in the matter of literary originality it was Spain that created the powerful new genres and sub-
genres: the tragi-comedy in prose, as exemplified by *La Celestina*;
the purely national drama which — in this matter of national representation — only the English came to match; the picaresque novel;
the pastoral novel (as against the prose-poem interspersed with
verse that was Sannazaro's *Arcadia*); the modern critical novel that

---

1. "The Dawn of Conscience in America: Spanish Experiments and Experiences
with Indians in the New World," *Proceedings of the American Philosophical Society,*
CVII (1963), 91a.

2. See Chapter I of the present volume.

sets forth the gist of human experience (*Don Quijote*); and others of minor interest, such as the epistolary novel. All of these types were imitated in Europe as a whole.

For all the early creative force of *La Celestina*, Spain was at first primarily receptive of Italian influence; in the very first stages she was not yet really able to receive. King Alfonso V of Aragon, who in the fifteenth centry moved the seat of his kingdom to Naples and there rivaled all secular princes in his enthusiasm for antiquity, turning over "stubborn" Aragon to his brother and devoting himself exclusively to his new Italian possessions, restored his castle according to the principles of Vitruvius, kept the classics always within reach, spent great sums to maintain such scholars as Lorenzo Valla, and paid Poggio Bracciolini five hundred pieces of gold for translating Xenophon's *Cyropedia*;[3] yet he did not alter the interests or the taste of the Aragonese courtiers who accompanied him from the ruder Peninsula, though many of these gentlemen established themselves in Italy, founding families whose names have remained illustrious down to modern times.[4] Though Alfonso is reported to have declared that "even more than the trumpet excites the noble warhorse, I am inflamed by the trumpet of imperial fame"[5] — and his fame endures to the present — the poetic output of his Catalan and Aragonese courtiers as preserved in the *Cancionero de Stúñiga* is far less "learned" than the work of contemporary Castilian poets like Mena and Santillana. This is true, even though the poets of Alfonso's entourage "gaily imitated popular Italian poetry and made abundant use of Italianisms in their lyrics."[6] The day of Boscán and of Garcilaso, when under Italian influence Spanish poetry would become "golden," had not yet dawned.

That day would come, however. Though patriots complained of the Spanish yoke (while more realistic observers perceived that Spain's control at least secured the disunited Italian states from

3. J. Burckhardt, *The Civilization of the Renaissance in Italy*, trans. S. G. C. Middlemore (New York, 1958), I, 51, 231.

4. Francisca Vendrell Gallostra, "La corte literaria de Alfonso V de Aragón y tres poetas de la misma," *BRAE*, XIX (1932), 476.

5. Baltasar Gracián, *El héroe. El discreto* (Buenos Aires–Mexico City, 1939), p. 47.

6. Arturo Farinelli, *Italia e Spagna* (Turin, 1929), II, 76; see also J. Terlingen, *Los italianismos en español* (Amsterdam, 1943).

relapsing into barbarism under the Turks),[7] Spain's presence as a cultural force was progressively felt in Italy.[8] Spanish romances of chivalry and sentimental novels were read, and not only by the ignorant: Isabella d'Este in 1514 sought in vain in the bookshops of Milan for a copy of Diego de San Pedro's *Cárcel de amor*, and Bernardo Tasso, father of the great Torcuato, composed his poem *Amadigi*, based on *Amadis of Gaul*.[9] The Spanish cleric Francisco Delicado, fleeing from the sack of Rome in 1527, found that his scandalous *Lozana andaluza*, which he caused to be printed in Castilian at Venice the next year, gave him royalties and a living that his more learned works could not provide. Torres Naharro put on his plays at Rome in Castilian. One of them contains scathing attacks on the corruption of the Roman Curia; their contribution to the theory of comedy antedated anything that the Italians had as yet done.[10] Spanish theologians were respected and famous at Rome, where Juan de Torquemada taught canon law for twenty years. Luigi Tansillo in a well-known poem hailed Charles V as the single shepherd of the universal sheepfold, and even a Neapolitan burgher wrote of him in his *Chronicle*: "Wise and just Emperor!"[11] *Don Quijote* and the *Exemplary Novels* of Cervantes had their vogue, and, at the height of the baroque, Giambattista Marino copied sonnets from Lope de Vega.[12]

In addition to the bibliographies and studies of cultural and

7. The suggestion was first made in 1510 by Fedra Inghirami. See Burckhardt, *op. cit.*, I, 112–13 and n. 1.

8. In the second half of the sixteenth century there were published, at Venice alone, 724 translations from the Spanish and 71 editions of works in the Spanish language, as against 93 and 16, respectively, in the first half of the century. These figures were compiled by E. E. Guzzoni in a dissertation in the Faculty of Foreign Languages and Literatures of the University of Venice; see Franco Meregalli, "Las relaciones literarias entre Italia y España en el Renacimiento," *Thesaurus*, XVII (1962), 620, n. 8.

9. Benedetto Croce, *La Spagna nella vita italiana durante la Rinascenza* (Bari, 1917), p. 64.

10. See J. E. Gillet, *Torres Naharro and the Drama of the Renaissance* (vol. IV of *Propalladia and Other Works of Bartolomé de Torres Naharro*, ed. Gillet), edited, transcribed, and completed by O. H. Green (Philadelphia, 1961), Index, *s.v.* Comedy. Hereafter this volume will be cited as Gillet-Green.

11. Croce, *op. cit.*, pp. 87, 243.

12. See J. G. Fucilla, *Relaciones hispanoitalianas* (Madrid, 1953), p. 49, n. 1, and works by G. Hainsworth and E. Mele cited therein. See also Fucilla, *Studies and Notes (Literary and Historical)* (Naples–Rome, 1953); *idem, Estudios sobre el petrarquismo en España* (Madrid, 1960).

literary influence that have already been cited, there are two specialized bibliographies that point up cogently the extent to which, in Italy, culture followed the flag of Castile. In 1908 E. Zaccaria issued at Carpi the second edition of the first part of his *Bibliografia italo-iberica*, which lists 783 titles of Spanish and Portuguese works printed in Italy.[13] And between 1927 and 1931 E. Toda y Güell published in Catalan at Barcelona his *Bibliografia espanyola d'Italia* which lists, from the origins to the year 1900, Italian printings of original works by Spanish authors, translations of Spanish authors into Italian or Latin, Spanish translations of Italian works, and works of Italian authors that insert Spanish texts. The whole amounts to four large volumes, plus a fifth of indices. The portion of the listed works dating from the Renaissance and baroque periods is impressive and important. For example, Italian editions in Spanish of the works of Fernando de Rojas and Bartolomé de Torres Naharro are fundamental for the bibliographical and textual history of the books in question.

Flanders

Although the force of Spanish cultural expansion made itself felt in France, in England, and in Germany, it was only in Italy and in the Low Countries that European territories were actually governed (however ineffectively) by the Spanish monarchy.[14] Numerous Spanish dramas — written by Spaniards for Spaniards — recall the wars in Flanders of the second half of the seventeenth century; others, called by Gossart *drames militaires*, portray the army that maintained the authority of the king and the valor of the Spanish troops, as well as various individual types, such as the soldier of fortune and the Spanish officer. Naturally, the Flemings have only a secondary role in these plays. Spanish lyric poets of the sixteenth century — few in number — portray such figures as the Duke of Alba, Alessandro Farnese, and Don John of Austria. Juan Rufo, in his epic *La Austriada* (1584), celebrates the exploits of the

13. His second volume would have listed translations.

14. E. Gossart has not given us, in his *Les Espagnols en Flandre: Histoire et poésie* (Brussels, 1914), the equivalent of the studies which we have utilized for Italy, but his book is nevertheless a useful guide.

conqueror of Lepanto, but declares himself unable to follow his
hero to Flanders, unable to do justice to an unjust war (the resistance by the Flemings) that involves such great cares, sufferings,
and struggles on the part of the valiant Spaniards. Literature in
prose is still less interesting, with the exception of the anonymous
semi-picaresque novel *Estebanillo González* (1646). Though there
is truth and realism in the best of these works, they cannot concern
us here: they do not represent the imposition of the Spanish way of
life on a conquered territory, or, to any great extent, the peaceful
penetration of one culture by another.

On the other hand, the testimony of the printing industry, as it
produces countless editions of important Spanish works, is proof
that the influence of Spanish civilization in the Low Countries was
profound and prolonged, and that the enterprising printers and
book dealers of those countries took full advantage of that state of
affairs during the sixteenth and seventeenth centuries.[15] Between
1607 and 1670 thirteen editions of works by Cervantes are listed.

Many editions were issued without date, including Nebrija's
Dictionarium, *La Celestina*, the works of Boscán, the *Propalladia*
of Torres Naharro, various writings of Antonio de Guevara,
Mexía's *Silva de varia lección*, the famous *Cancionero de romances
sin año*. The first dated book (1520) is a dictionary of French,
Spanish, and Flemish. In 1528 we find — very interestingly — a work
that links the occupied Low Countries with the newly conquered
possessions in America: Pierre de Mura's (i.e., Pedro de Gante's)
Christian Doctrine in the Mexican Language. From then on the
printings and reprintings follow each other with surprising regu-
larity: the *Celestina*, Guevara, Mena, Mexía, Boscán (including
his translation of Castiglione's *Cortegiano*), López de Gómara's
history of the Indies, Gonzalo Pérez's translation of *The Odyssey*,
Lazarillo de Tormes (the first picaresque novel), Montemayor's
Diana and his *Cancionero*, Gil Polo's *Diana enamorada*, much of
Fray Luis de Granada, Ercilla's American epic *La Araucana*, and
other first-line works, together with holdovers from an earlier age
such as San Pedro's *Cárcel de amor* and Juan de Flores' *Historia de*

15. See Maurice Sabbe's preface to J. Peeters-Fontainas' *Bibliographie des impressions espagnoles des Pays-Bas* (Louvain–Antwerp, 1933).

Aurelio y Isabella. The seventeenth century sees editions of Huarte's *Examen de ingenios,* Lope de Vega's *Arcadia* and some of the *Partes* of his collected plays, works of St. Teresa of Avila, the picaresque *Guzmán de Alfarache,* and the *Obras* of Quevedo. Anything like a complete enumeration would be tiring. Suffice it to say, in the words of J. Peeters-Fontainas, that the decision of Martin Nuyts, or Nutius (Nucio in Spanish), to print three Spanish *romances* or ballads on the otherwise blank leaves at the end of his edition (1546) of the *Questión de amor y Cárcel de amor* ("in order not to be guilty of selling blank paper") was a "providential inspiration." His customers from the Spanish colony apparently enjoyed the novelty and encouraged him to provide them with more of such reading matter. His *Cancionero de romances,* without date but evidently of 1547 or 1548, assures him immortality in the history of Spanish literature. By this means he saved for posterity a great number of old Spanish ballads gathered from oral tradition or from ephemeral broadsides which are now lost. In 1549 this same Martin Nucio had the pleasure of receiving in his shop some of the important Spanish personages who accompanied Charles V and the future Philip II on their "most happy voyage" to visit Brabant and the Marquisate of Antwerp. By them he was encouraged to multiply his Spanish editions.[16]

Another printer of Antwerp, Christopher Plantin, achieved immortality in a different way. It was his idea to reissue the Alcalá Polyglot Bible "with a marvellous display of typographical resources." Through the good offices of the humanist and Biblical scholar Benito Arias Montano, chaplain to Philip II, the King agreed to support the project, which was to be much more than a simple reproduction of the Alcalá Bible. Known as the Biblia Regia, or Royal Bible, it made use of the totality of Biblical scholarship, Catholic, Protestant, and Jewish — a degree of boldness which might have prevented its publication except for the death of Pius V and the diplomacy of Arias Montano. Thus scriptural science marched forward, without allowing itself to be held back by the

16. J. Peeters-Fontainas, *L'officine espagnole de Martin Nutius à Anvers* (extr. du *Bulletin de la Société des Bibliophiles Anversois "Le Compas d'Or,"* XXXIV [1956]). The reprint has 106 pp.; see p. 17.

restrictive "exigencies of the new orthodoxy" born in Trent.[17] The eight magnificent volumes were printed between 1569 and 1573.

From Europe to America

In Italy the influence of Spanish culture made itself felt naturally by reason of the political importance and power of the occupying nation and without any effort either to suppress or to greatly alter the Italian way of life. If Annibal Guasco suggested to the aspiring Italian lady of the court that her models be the Spanish ladies with which the court of Savoy was filled, since they surpassed all others "in the pleasing gravity and grave pleasantness . . . so natural to this nation,"[18] it was simply because such a suggestion recommended itself — spontaneously — to the writer. In connection with graver matters, it should be remembered that the Roman and Spanish Inquisitions were independent of each other and did not act in unison. In Flanders — Spain's "daughter turned rebellious" — matters were altogether different, and the severest measures were taken in an attempt to reduce the Provinces to political and religious obedience. The failure of the effort is known to all. The world was split asunder, and the imperial might of Spain was powerless to heal the breach. In neither of these areas — the Italian Peninsula or the Low Countries of Central Europe — could Spanish ideals be implanted in their purity and in their fullness, as they were implanted in the virgin New World.

To her possessions in the Western Hemisphere Spain sought to carry the heart and the mind of Castile. The seed implanted there took root and bore its own peculiar fruit. If the harvest was in the long run disappointing, it was because Spain herself had chosen a way of life that was not the way of Europe or the way of the future, so that she ultimately was confronted with a Europe which was not of her making and in which she seemed to have no place. She withdrew behind her borders, clinging to the culture pattern that she held dear. Brilliant though her contributions to Europe have been since then — particularly in the literary and artistic fields —

17. M. Bataillon, *Erasmo y España* (Mexico City–Buenos Aires, 1950), II, 356–58.
18. Ruth Kelso, *Doctrine for the Lady of the Renaissance* (Urbana, Illinois, 1956), p. 225; see also my review, *HR*, XXVI (1958), 71–75.

she has not yet emerged from her retreat. But we must return to our Indies.

SPANISH CULTURE IN THE NEW WORLD

Mexico

It will be impossible for us to review Spain's cultural expansion from Cuba to the Philippines, though the history of printing in the several regions, as set forth in various works by José Toribio Medina, would be most instructive.[19] We shall choose Mexico for special study, principally because the materials are so abundant and so available.

As Marcel Bataillon has pointed out, the Spaniards, faced with the human reality of the New World, took — each one according to his inner condition and his outer circumstances — one of three positions. Some, like López de Gómara, placed themselves within the religious philosophy inherited from the Middle Ages: in their view, the New World was made known at the precise time when the scepter of the Roman Empire passed to the hands of the king of the Goths in Spain; this last incarnation of the Roman Empire would forever be the last, and would endure to the end of time. Others, men of politics who held the evangelization of the Indies to be merely one of the duties devolving upon conquering Spain, were less convinced of the glorious future awaiting the Christianized Indians; they considered the discovery to have been an act of Providence intended to give to Spain — the champion of the faith in Europe — a new source of wealth and power. A third group was composed of the evangelizers: to them — with no thought of empire — the Indians were members to be incorporated into the mystic body of Christ, who had commanded his apostles to preach the

19. Were we attempting to tell the whole story, we should begin with Santo Domingo, where Diego Columbus (son of Christopher) set up his court in the manner of a Renaissance prince. Fourteen years after its founding in 1496, Santo Domingo "had already become a thoroughly Spanish city with convents, schools, and a bishopric." The bishop, a protégé of Leo X, caused the coat of arms of the Medici to be engraved on the cathedral, and the choir loft was decorated in a graceful Florentine pattern. A few years later the poet Lázaro Bejarano "would harbor the subversive humanism of Erasmus, with its ideas of free inquiry, tolerance, and the condemnation of war." See M. Picón Salas, *A Cultural History of Spanish America*, trans. I. A. Leonard (Berkeley–Los Angeles, 1962), pp. 42–46.

Gospel to every living creature; when this should be accomplished, the world could end and history could come to a close.[20]

"The year 1492 might have marked Spain's awakening to a new reality; instead, it marked the coming of a new dream, a new utopia."[21] The culture of the conquest was, as George Foster has pointed out,[22] *sui generis*. By a sort of paradox, the Spaniards, though bent on ennobling cities and setting up kingdoms, were really more self-centered than the English colonists who, though on the surface more self-seeking, were really more socially minded. "The Spaniard, with his hospitals, foundations, cathedrals, colleges, and marquisates, raised a monument to his own self."[23] If some of the conquistadors came seeking gold, and others in search of souls, still others came "in search of order." Their deity was the absolute monarch; their religion, the new religion of the reason of state. Here, in the Indies, the representatives of the crown saw the possibility of escaping "the limitations of internal Spanish politics. . . . Wealth from the Indies would underwrite a state standing above all classes" and this state would "speak with a new voice, with a new will." The New World could be planned, "projected into reality by the royal will and its executioners."[24]

Perhaps nothing is more instructive than an engineer's drawing showing Spanish town planning in Mexico about 1580, reproduced

20. M. Bataillon, "L'idée de la découverte de l'Amérique chez les Espagnols du XVIe siècle (d'après un livre récent)," *BHi*, LV (1953), 48.
21. Eric R. Wolf, *Sons of the Shaking Earth: The People of Mexico and Guatemala —Their Land, History, and Culture* (Chicago, 1962; 1st ed., 1959), p. 159.
22. In "Aspectos antropológicos de la conquista española de América," *Estudios americanos*, VII (1954), 155–71 (cited *ibid.*, p. 280).
23. Salvador de Madariaga (cited *ibid.*, p. 161), in *The Rise of the Spanish Empire* (New York, 1947).
24. Wolf, *op. cit.*, pp. 162–63. This proved to be an unwise policy: "attempting to civilize the Indians by urbanizing them led to many curious experiments and experiences, and in the end was fatal for large numbers of natives. George Kubler has pointed out that 'to urbanize the Indian populations was to dislocate and destroy the patterns of indigenous culture. Such cultural extirpation brought about, in turn, the biological decrease of the Indian race. . . . Each building, and each colonial artifact, was nourished by the destruction of a culture and the decline of a race'" (Hanke, *op. cit.*, p. 84a). See also George Kubler, *Mexican Architecture in the Sixteenth Century* (New Haven, 1948), I, 66–67; Howard Cline, "Civil Congregations of the Indians of New Spain, 1598–1606," *Hispanic American Historical Review*, XXIV (1929), 349–69. Wolf and Kubler's analyses may well be excessively grim: the Indians could indeed have said, "Our cup is broken"; but they were given a new cup. See below, the remarks on Christian baptism as a rite of "essential humanity."

by Eric Wolf in *Sons of the Shaking Earth*. The Indians lived in scattered hamlets. "Let there be a law to force them to live in nucleated towns, each with its own church" and with its own fields within a radius of 560 yards from the church steeple, so that they "can learn to order their lives to the tolling of the bells and the commands of the royal officers." No problem was too insignificant to demand legal solution (p. 164).

In this newly conceived utopia, there were many mansions. Let the gold seeker seek his gold, and let him who desired Indian subjects exercise his rule over them in the spirit of the new order. If another sought to save souls, let him follow the example of the Erasmists with their new interpretation of Catholicism, de-emphasizing ritual and stressing the promptings of the "inner" voice, following the lead of Sir Thomas More (d. 1535) and Juan Luis Vives (d. 1540).

Many of the friars who came early to the New World had taken part in the Erasmist revival of Cardinal Cisneros. The so-called Apostolic Twelve, particularly, had earlier been engaged in the spread of the gospel of "primitive" Christianity in southern Spain. The first archbishop of Mexico was a follower of Erasmus and was familiar with the teachings of More. Vasco de Quiroga, the first bishop of Michoacán, actually founded a replica of More's Utopia in his bishopric. This utopia, like the utopias of gold and of power, was to founder — "impotent in the face of stubborn secular demand" (Wolf, *op. cit.*, p. 166); yet "more surprising than the . . . survivals of pre-Conquest ideas and rituals among the Christianized Indians is the [religious] success of the Catholic utopia in a country of different religions and languages" (*ibid.*, p. 167). The Catholic Church destroyed old idols, "but it also offered the common man a way in which he could cast his traditional attachments into new forms" (p. 171). Pedro de Gante (whose book of *Christian Doctrine in the Mexican Language* has already been mentioned in this chapter), an exemplary Franciscan and a relative of the Emperor, baptized Indians in Mexico City by the thousands (p. 173). "To the Indian, the rite of baptism . . . proved an assertion of his essential humanity," of which "no colonist or royal official could rob him."

His new religion was "at once his opium, his consolation, and his hope for ultimate justice." [25]

In due time we shall have to study, as Wolf does in *Sons of the Shaking Earth*, the retreat from utopia. For the present, we must observe how the Spaniards transferred, with considerable success,[26] the mind and heart of Castile to the new land.

The Spaniards did not regard the Mexican land as "merely the scene of passing military adventure but rather as a place in which to settle and take root," a place wherein the Indians, too, should "cooperate in the formation of a new society" (Picón Salas, *op. cit.*, p. 49). The practical steps taken to achieve these ends, such as the importation of agricultural plants and beasts of burden from the Old World, cannot be specified here: they belong to the history of colonization, not of intellectual expansion. Nor shall we speak, in this chapter, of the evangelizing activities of the friars. Rather, we shall examine the conditions which made it possible for Francisco Cervantes de Salazar (d. 1575), a friend, perhaps a pupil, of Juan Luis Vives, to compose dialogues in Latin as a means of familiarizing his Mexican students "with a graceful style of Latin conversation on topics and events of the day," following the model provided by Erasmus (*ibid.*, p. 50). By 1554 the Spanish schools and colleges were beginning to accept Indian and half-caste pupils, moved by the Greek dream of a "microcosm, a synthesis . . . of two opposite worlds" (pp. 51–52).

It will be remembered that Nebrija, half a century earlier, had conceived of the Spanish monarchy placing beneath its yoke "barbarous nations of strange tongues," and of these nations as needing his *Castilian Grammar* as a means of acquiring the language of the new ruling power, "just as we now depend on my *Introductiones Latinae* for our learning of Latin" (see Chapter I). Remarkably

25. *Ibid.*, p. 175. See also Silvio Zavala, *La "Utopía" de Tomás Moro en la Nueva España y otros estudios* (Mexico City, 1937).

26. In 1581 the Portuguese skeptic philosopher Francisco Sánchez wrote in his *Quod nihil scitur*: "In Italy, in France, in Spain, such a thing as a doctor [of philosophy] was not even conceivable [i.e., in the time of ancient Egypt and Greece]. . . . Now, the Muses dwell among us and Christ is with us. And in the Indies, what ignorance reigned until today! Now, however, they are little by little becoming more religious, more keen, more learned than we ourselves" (Spanish trans., *Que nada se sabe* [Madrid, n.d.], p. 162).

enough, the prediction proved true. Not only did the Indians learn Spanish; they also learned Latin, and so well that on October 20, 1541, Jerónimo López, advisor to the Viceroy of Mexico, wrote to the Emperor in Spain that the Indians had not only learned to read and write, to play instruments and become musicians, but that they were learning Latin grammar so efficiently that "there are lads . . . who are talking as elegant Latin as Tullius." [27] We may readily believe that Marcus Tullius would have been shocked by the sound, perhaps by the structure, of this "Aztec" Latin; but it is a fact that Nebrija's *Latin Grammar* was from the first a best seller in the colonial book trade. Perhaps more copies of it were sent to the New World than of any other book.

The ability to read, acquired so readily by these Indian pupils, was cause for concern to the authorities and produced fruitless efforts at legislation intended to exclude from the new lands all "frivolous" literature. As early as 1506 King Ferdinand decreed, "for the good government of the Indies," that "there should not be permitted the sale of books dealing with profane, frivolous, and immoral matters so that the Indians may not take to reading them" (*ibid.*, p. 80).

It is noteworthy that it is Indian innocence, and the Indian "utopia," that the monarch sought to protect. Apparently there was no hope of preventing the Spaniards (Christians, as they are called in the early reports) from indulging in frivolous and worldly reading; the decrees against light literature are repeated too often for us to believe that they were ever effectively enforced. When we begin to have documentary records of books actually transported to the New World under the control of the Spanish House of Trade (*Casa de Contratación*), we perceive that the prohibitions were a dead letter, as far as the exportation of polite literature was concerned.

On April 4, 1531, the Queen of Spain commanded the authorities of the House of Trade to stop the circulation in the New World of "books of fiction in the vernacular which are unrelated to religion . . . , since this is bad practice for the Indians" (*ibid.*, p.

27. Irving A. Leonard, *Books of the Brave: Being an Account of Books and Men in the Spanish Conquest and Settlement of the Sixteenth-century New World* (Cambridge, Massachusetts, 1949), pp. 86–87.

81). Five years later a decree makes it even clearer that the main purpose of the prohibitions was to protect the innocence of the natives: Spaniards are directed not to "have these books in their houses" nor to permit the Indians to read them, "as we are informed that some of the natives of that country are already beginning to be adept in Latin." The Indians, it was argued, would be unable to distinguish between books true and false, between the Acts of the Apostles and the adventures of Amadis of Gaul (pp. 81–82).

In the year 1500 a German printer and bookdealer, Jacob Cromberger, went to Seville and helped to make that city the most important publishing center in Spain during much of the sixteenth century. By some means unknown to us, he managed, in 1525, to obtain from the emperor the monopoly of the book trade with Mexico. About 1539 a son of Cromberger, with an Italian partner, contracted to set up the first printing press in Mexico City and almost immediately issued the first book printed in America, *The Spiritual Ladder to Heaven* by St. John Climacus. Some three years later would-be competitors made a formal petition requesting that the special privileges of the Cromberger family be abolished in exchange for their own pledge to set up printing presses in Mexico and to charge only a reasonable profit. There is no record that this effort was successful, but the document gives testimony of the importance of the book trade, even at this early date, in the Mexican dependency (pp. 96–97). The inventory of the stock left by the younger Cromberger at his death in 1540 shows that, even during the period for which no ships' manifests are available, thousands of volumes had been sent to the former Aztec capital. Of *Amadís de Gaula* there were on hand 446 copies; of *The Mirror of Knighthood*, 1,017; of *Robert the Devil*, 557 (p. 98).

Two additional documents should be cited for the period before we have ships' manifests with their lists of titles transported; both are of the year 1576. One of them covers the purchase of some 341 books, plus maps, woodcuts, and drawings. The amount of secular literature, and indeed of classical literature as against the earlier soldiers' fare which consisted of tales of chivalry, is surprising; the purchase list includes works by Virgil, Lucan, Martial, Seneca, Ovid, and the Eight Parts of Erasmus of Rotterdam (p. 203). The second document is an order for books, not only from Spanish presses but also from those of Lyons, Paris, Rome, and Antwerp. The Mexican dealer ordered 35 copies of Sallust; 18 of Caesar's *Commentaries* in Latin; 12 of Josephus' *Jewish Antiquities*; 26 of Cicero's *De Officiis*; 2 three-volume sets of Cicero's *Orations*; 67 Virgils; 25 copies of Martial's *Epigrams*; 9 of Ovid's *Metamorphoses*; 9 of Seneca's *Tragedies*; and 2 of Apuleius' *Golden Ass*. Spain was best represented in his order by *La Celestina*, the greatest masterpiece of Spanish literature before *Don Quijote*; by the anonymous *Lazarillo de Tormes*, the first novel of roguery; and by the *Diana* of Jorge de Montemayor, known to all students of the Renaissance pastoral.[28]

By the year 1600 the ships' manifests with their book lists specifying the exact nature of this part of the cargo are available in considerable richness. We shall concentrate our attention on a single shipment — that carried by the ship *La Trinidad* from Luis de Padilla in Seville to Martín Ibarra at San Juan de Ulúa — consisting of a number of cases of books to be sold at the latter's discretion for cash or for credit.[29] The list contains some 700 titles and provides a remarkable index of the cultural development of the colony, less than a century after its pacification.

These books cover an amazing range of fields: bibliography, encyclopedic works, history, biography; medicine, law, mathematics, natural science, geography, archaeology; theology and ecclesiastical literature; education; philology and lexicography; numismatics; music; political science; military science; black arts, ephemerides, and miscellaneous (joke books, books on games, accounts of festivals, cipher writing, etc.).

In spite of the garbling occasioned by the custom of taking down the titles as a clerk dictated them, nearly all of the books were identified, after which it was possible to classify them according to the various fields of knowledge. They fell into two broad cate-

28. *Ibid.*, pp. 205 ff. Professor Leonard, our authority in these matters, also has chapters entitled "Best Sellers of the Lima Book Trade, 1583" and "One Man's Library, Manila, 1583"; but we will not change our focus from Mexico.

29. What follows forms part of chapter XVI of *Books of the Brave*; it was originally published in *HR*, IX (1941), 1–40, with the title, "On the Mexican Booktrade in 1600: A Chapter in Cultural History," by Otis H. Green and Irving A. Leonard; see p. 1, n. 1.

gories: the philosophical and natural sciences, and the humanities, with numerous subdivisions.

Of the 155 titles classified as theological and ecclesiastical works, the greater part should have no mention here: they are compendiums and manuals with which the local priesthood might well have been satisfied. But apparently there were select spirits among the priests and friars, persons who would buy from an ordinary merchant Bibles with the text in Greek or Hebrew (there are 6 of these), as well as commentaries and concordances in surprising number.

In philosophy one distinguishes, first of all, the clearly medieval note, as exemplified by Ramón Lull's *Ars Magna*. Then come 3 texts of Plato, 1 each of Plotinus, Iamblicus, Philo Judaeus, and Maximus Tyrius, 1 commentary on Porphyry, 2 Ficinos, 2 Pico della Mirandolas, 1 León Hebreo, and 2 Bembos. That there was considerable interest in the Jewish Kabbala is shown by the inclusion of Pico's *Conclusiones cabalisticae et theologicae*. There are 4 titles in the Senecan and Stoic tradition, among them 2 works of Justus Lipsius. Some 16 works represent the Aristotelian tradition of the Renaissance, in both its conservative and its advanced forms.

Among the representatives of the eclectics we find Niphus, Cardano's *De Sapientia*, Gómez Pereira's *Antoniana Margarita* (which anticipates some aspects of Descartes), Bernardino Telesio's *De rerum natura* (which sought to free natural science from Aristotle by basing it on observation), and — last of all — the greatest, Nicholas Copernicus' *De revolutionibus orbium caelestium*.

Of all the sciences, the first to emerge in the Renaissance was botany, because of its connection with the healing arts. Our list proceeds from the ancient botanists to the modern commentators (Andrés Laguna) and the sixteenth-century herbalists (Mattioli, Fuchs); the latter, together with Brunfels, mark an epoch in the history of botanical iconography. Special interest in the flora of the Indies is shown by the presence of treatises by Fragoso and Acosta.

The works of the physicians of antiquity were still in demand, as they were in Europe, along with their sixteenth-century continuators, such as Trincavellius. Their opponents are also represented in our Mexican list by Manardo and Fernel. Pre-Vesalian anatomy is represented by Massa. Paré, the founder of French surgery, is present, as is another first-class physician of the sixteenth century, Conrad Gessner, together with Fracastoro, who holds first place among Renaissance students of epidemics. No less distinguished among those on our list are Brasavola and Caspar Wolff, author of the first collection of gynecological treatises ever published.

Renaissance astronomy is represented by Peuerbach, corrector of Ptolemy; by his pupil Regiomontanus, author of the first complete treatise on geometry published in the West; and by Rheinerus Gemma, whose reputation as an astronomer caused him to be consulted by Charles V. The composition of the list attests considerable interest in comets, and in such mathematical exercises as the squaring of the circle.

Also present are works of other scientists, distinguished even in the strictly modern sense: Benedetti, who seconded Galileo's researches on falling bodies; Ciruelo, who reformed the theory as astronomical refraction; Guidubaldo del Monte, the friend and protector of Galileo; and Erasmus Reinhold, who offered the first application of the theories of Copernicus.

Geology is represented by Albertus Magnus; by Besson; by Fracastoro, who held with Leonardo da Vinci that fossils had been living organisms; and by Georgius Agricola, the principal geologist of the sixteenth century. There are various works on applied science (mining, agriculture, architecture), on the astrolabe, on clocks, on measurements.

Turning to the humanities, we begin with bibliography. There is but one entry: Muzio Pansa, *On the Vatican Library. In Which an Account Is Given of This Library; And Also of the Famous and Celebrated Libraries Throughout the World; And of All Men Illustrious in Letters, with Certain Discourses on Books.* It went to Mexico in 1600 in good company: Middendorp's *Academiae celebres in universo terrarum.*

Next we note the encyclopaedic works. Though medieval in tone, they were nonetheless the best that the age afforded: Vincent de Beauvais, whose work was not superseded until the eighteenth century; and Bartholomaeus Anglicus, whose *De proprietatibus rerum* was still well known to Elizabethan writers.

In geography (considered as an adjunct of history and of belles-lettres) there is one contemporary: Peter Apian, in the revised edition by Gemma Frisius. The historians of Greece and Rome are present, as well as the modern writers on the history of Spain, France, Italy, Austria, Hungary, Albania, Turkey, and China. There are numerous biographical works, and others on political science, on Egyptian and Roman archaeology, and on ancient coins.

In philology we find a dictionary in six languages, 8 Hebrew grammars, 3 copies of Clenardus' Greek grammar, the Greek grammar of Budé, 2 Latin-Greek dictionaries, an Arabic grammar by Pedro de Alcalá, and the Syriac grammar of Caninius. There are collections of Roman inscriptions, and some half dozen books on general classical erudition. Of considerable interest is an Italian glossary of all the words used by Dante, Petrarch, and Boccaccio. There are 2 Latin-French grammars, a French grammar, and a grammar of the Inca language of Peru.

There was general interest in the principles of rhetoric and stylistics, and in the various literatures, which are represented on the list as follows: Greek (29 titles); Latin (32 titles); Neo-Latin (Petrarch, Poliziano, Enea Silvio Piccolomini, Pontano, Erasmus); Italian (from Dante to Torcuato Tasso); and Spanish (27 titles).

The arts are not forgotten: the listing includes Daza and Narváez on lute music; and Francesco Colonna's *Dream of Poliphilo*, published by the Aldine Press in 1499; the latter is an allegorical novel of love in which the plot is but a pretext for a hymn of adoration — more fervent than any other in the fifteenth century — to the beauty and art of antiquity. *Poliphilo's Dream* went across the Atlantic in the year 1600, bringing to the land of the Aztec pyramids its vision of the grandeur of ancient Greece and Rome.

This list, with its nearly 700 titles, and numerous other such lists, analyzed by Irving Leonard in *Books of the Brave*, show that it is impossible to think of the period of the Spanish colonial regime — as it has so constantly been thought of by serious scholars — as three centuries of theocracy, obscurantism, and barbarism. Some dozen titles in the list were on the Inquisition's Index; yet the shipper had no hesitancy about sending them to his agent in Mexico, not for clandestine distribution, nor for use by some scholar or scholars who had been granted ecclesiastical permission to read forbidden books, but for public sale to any who might wish to buy — for cash or for credit as the agent might think best.[30]

A year much greater than 1600 for the history of Hispanic culture is the year 1605. For that year we have, as Professor Leonard has shown (*Books of the Brave* and earlier studies), a spate of ship's manifests whose reports vary from the relatively insignificant notation of "three books of *Don Quijote de la Mancha*" sent on the galleon Nuestra Señora del Rosario, to the listing of 262 copies of that book carried on the good ship Espíritu Santo for delivery to one Clemente de Valdés of Mexico City. Another substantial book shipment of the same year included 100 copies of Cervantes' novel for delivery at Cartagena. Indeed, when all the shipments of copies of the 1605 edition of *Don Quijote* to the Indies are totaled up, they appear to have equalled nearly the entire first edition. In the year 1607 representations of the two main characters of the great novel, Don Quijote and Sancho Panza, appeared in a public festival in Peru.

On September 28, 1605, Alonso de Dassa — a mere passenger — declared to the interrogating authorities at Vera Cruz that "for his own entertainment he was bringing the First Part of Mateo Alemán's picaresque novel *Guzmán de Alfarache*, *Don Quijote de la Mancha*, and the romance *Flores y Blancaflor*; for his prayers, a book of devotion by Fray Luis de Granada, a copy of St. John Chrysostom, and a *Book of Hours of Our Lady*" (*Books of the Brave*, p. 271). Other statements of the same sort could be cited.

Let us look back one year. In 1604, another Spanish writer of genius, Lope de Vega — called by Cervantes the "Prodigy of Nature" — declared that his dramatic works were read by admirers not only in Spain, Italy, and France, but also in the Indies. This was true. An unidentified Peruvian [31] lady, known only by the pastoral

30. It is interesting to compare this laxity with the rigorous control exercised by the Canadian authorities. La Hontan reported that the priests "prohibit and burn all books but books of devotion." And the saintly recluse Mlle. Jeanne le Ber declared that to teach poor girls to read was to waste their time unless they wished to become nuns. "Nor was she far from wrong," observes Francis Parkman, "for in Canada there was very little to read except formulas of devotion and lives of saints. The dangerous innovation of the printing press had not invaded the colony"; see his *The Old Régime in Canada* (Boston, 1893), pp. 349, 359. For England, see C. R. Gillett, *Burned Books: Neglected Chapters in British History and Literature* (New York, 1932).

31. For the sake of clear presentation and conservation of space, we have directed our attention primarily to Mexico, but the Peruvian picture is essentially the same,

name Amarilis, "versed in the fine intricacies of Renaissance poetry," [32] addressed to Lope an epistle, full of admiration, in elegant
stanza form. So complete are the records that we can trace the rise
and decline of Lope's popularity in the colonial book lists (and in
the colonial theaters) very nearly as accurately as it is possible to do
with regard to Spain itself.

The University of Mexico [33]

John Tate Lanning (*op. cit.*) entitles his first chapter "The
Transplantation of the Scholastic University." This chapter heading is expressive of the idea which I seek to emphasize in the present
portion of this volume: that Castile extended to her new possessions her mind and heart, or — to state it perhaps more accurately —
that she added to herself a great new American dimension. In
periods both of expansion and of contraction, Spanish America is
revealed, not as a mere satelite, but as a daughter of the metropolis.

The encouragement which Pope Martin V (d. 1431) gave to the
University of Salamanca (he was antagonistic to Paris) had made
the school of theology in that Spanish city "little less than the
oracle of Catholic Europe." [34] As Spain became the leading empire
of the world, Salamanca's influence increased. It was natural that
the American colonies should petition for similar institutions.
Shortly after the discovery, the newly founded (1508) University
of Alcalá rose to its pinnacle of glory.

though the development comes somewhat later: only in 1578 did the University of
San Marcos at Lima reach a point of development comparable with that of the University of Mexico in 1553 (John Tate Lanning, *Academic Culture in the Spanish Colonies*
[London–New York–Toronto, 1949], p. 21). The cultural picture in the great centers
of population such as Lima was reflected also in far-off places. Books, including books
of entertainment, found their way to the frontiers. Not only did a large portion of the
first edition of *Don Quijote* make its way by muleback to the great mining center of
El Cuzco; even in so remote an outpost as our own city of Santa Fe there were readers
in the seventeenth century of Spanish ballads, of *Orlando Furioso*, of *Don Quijote*,
of the picaresque novel *Marcos de Obregón*, and of the collected comedies of Lope
de Vega and his school of dramatists.

32. Pedro Henríquez Ureña, *Literary Currents in Hispanic America* (Cambridge,
Massachusetts, 1945), p. 75.

33. See Francisco Cervantes de Salazar, *México en 1554: Tres Diálogos traducidos
por J. García Icazbalceta* (Mexico City, 1937); Gabriel Méndez Plancarte (ed.),
Humanismo mexicano del siglo XVI (Mexico City, 1946), especially the good introduction.

34. *Ibid.*, p. 11. Page numbers in parentheses in the following paragraphs refer to
Lanning's study.

Though it is possible that no university began to function in Santo Domingo until after 1558, it was twenty years earlier that the Dominicans obtained from the pope a bull which raised their college in that city to the rank of a *studium generale* (p. 12). In 1551 Charles V and the Queen Mother authorized the universities of Lima and Mexico City, giving them statutes the same as those of the University of Salamanca. It was the Mexican university that became the first active major university in the New World: courses began in 1553, antedating Lima by some twenty-three years.

The Mexican viceroy, Antonio de Mendoza, "eager to Hispanize the natives and to bring the educational amenities to the viceroyalty," contributed some cattle ranches to the new institution by way of endowment, having urged, as early as 1545, the founding of a university "of all the sciences," open to both natives and *criollos* (American-born Spaniards). It was not he, however, but Viceroy Luis de Velasco who opened the University of Mexico, which had been given all the franchises and privileges of the academies of Spain (p. 17).

From the beginning, the force of the Counter Reformation was felt.[35] The new institution gave pre-eminence to the chair of Scholastic theology. Some of its occupants held the highest degrees from Spanish universities and some had studied under such eminent masters as Domingo de Soto. Their task was "to impugn, to destroy, to vanquish, and to extirpate that which does not conform to the faith" (p. 18).

The Universities in Other Colonies

During the colonial period some twenty-one universities were founded in Spanish America in addition to the pioneer institutions at Mexico City and Lima (p. 23). The reason for this diversification was, quite naturally, distance. The Jesuits, arriving in Peru in 1569, shortly thereafter opened a college in Cuzco and another in La Paz, followed by a Jesuit house in Potosí in 1577. Members of this order came in force to Upper Peru: the University of Chuquisaca (Sucre), though founded late (1624), caused that city to

---

35. "The Counter Reformation reached American intellectual life in two fundamental respects — it imposed the system of orthodoxy devised by the Council of Trent and gave to the New World the Jesuit Society" (*ibid.*, pp. 21–22).

become "the Athens of South America" to Peruvians and Argentines, and "the Oxford of South America" to a traveling Englishman, General Miller (p. 23); it was governed by the Jesuit order until the expulsion (1767). The Dominicans (already mentioned in connection with Santo Domingo) continued to be active, competing fiercely with the Jesuits. They conferred degrees in New Granada (Colombia), Chile, and the Philippines and, after prolonged opposition, established a Thomistic university at Bogotá (1655).

Of the twenty-three universities recorded by Lanning, ten are classified by him as major ones. All of the latter were "royal and pontifical"; three were modeled on Salamanca, one on Alcalá, others on Mexico, Lima, and Santo Domingo. Of the minor universities, most were Jesuit; four were Dominican; one, Augustinian; one, Franciscan. "In reality they were the very warp and woof of the church," according to Lanning (p. 33), and "the very solid rock upon which colonial culture, in all its formal aspects, rested in closest parallel to that of Europe."

The Last Stand of the Schoolmen

In these universities, Scholastic philosophy — the Aristotelian-Thomistic world view — made its last stand.[36] This world view was not to prevail, and the legend of intellectual stagnation in the Spanish-American universities "is founded upon considerable truth." "The cloister of Salamanca may not have been unrepresentative," Lanning observes, when in 1771 it rejected modern philosophers and physicists because of the difficulty of reconciling their teachings with revealed truths (p. 63). But the picture has two sides. For all the emphasis on rote memory and on the general philosophical principle of authority, innovation crept in. The Cartesian system of methodical doubt "came to be accepted, everywhere in America, between 1736 and 1800" (p. 74). Newton was "an accepted institution a half-century after the publication of his *Principia Mathematica*." It was at the universities of Chuquisaca, of Caracas, and of San Carlos de Lima — where the most retrogressive principles of the Schoolmen had been vanquished — that the

36. See Lanning, ch. III: "The Last Stand of the Schoolmen."

revolutionary leaders of Spanish America were trained (p. 86).[37]
But such considerations take us far beyond the period covered in
this book and belong, rather, to a study of Latin America and the
Enlightenment.[38]

End Products: Renaissance and Baroque

In his first printed work, the pastoral novel *La Galatea* (1585),
Cervantes chose to insert as a poetic interlude the one hundred
and eleven octaves which comprise the *Song of Calliope*: generous
praise meted out to the poets and prose writers of the Hispanic
world. In stanza 66 the Muse casts her eye on "the Antarctic region" and announces her intention of mentioning, as representative men, one "sovereign genius" from Peru and one from Mexico.
In the following discussion we shall consider Cervantes' Mexican —
along with two other persons from Mexico and one from the territory that is now Colombia — as typical of the fruitfulness, in literature, of Spain's transplantation of her world view and her value
system to the New World.

The Mexican "genius" singled out by Cervantes for praise in
the *Canto de Calíope* is Francisco de Terrazas (d. 1600?), whose
flowing verses have given to his native land — according to Cervantes' Muse — a new Hippocrene, a new fountain of poetic inspiration.[39] The modern recovery of Terrazas' fragmentary poetic
production made clear the early existence in New Spain of a
literary culture as closely related to Peninsular literature as the
viceroyal policies were to the policies elaborated in the royal councils of Madrid.[40]

37. Impressed by this fact, Lanning ventures to suggest that "a scholastic discipline
—which we laymen sometimes loosely call methods—ultimately combined with the
liberal experimental approach in a non-scholastic society, is an ideal formula for col-
legiate education" (p. 87).

38. See A. P. Whitaker (ed.), *Latin America and the Enlightenment* (2d ed.; Ithaca,
New York, 1961). In the eighteenth century "authors and editions of textbooks were
changed without corresponding alterations in the university statutes: when a controversy in the eighteenth century led the professors of medicine to mention their
authorities, it appeared that they were teaching the circulation of the blood, and extant textbooks show that they were using the medical treatises of the latest and most
eminent Dutch, French, Italian, British, and Spanish authors (Lanning, *The University in the Kingdom of Guatemala* [Ithaca, New York, 1955], p. 121).

39. *Obras completas*, ed. A. Valbuena Prat (Madrid, 1956), p. 750.

40. Jorge Campos, "Letras de América: La protesta del petrarquista Francisco de
Terrazas," *Insula*, núm. 185 (April, 1962), p. 11. See also J. García Icazbalceta, *Fran-

One of Terrazas' sonnets, often reprinted in anthologies, has been called "the richest jewel of Mexican Petrarchism." The poet aspired, however, to greater honors and began an epic — the noblest of genres — entitled *The New World and Its Conquest*, of which fragments have been preserved. At times merely a rhymed chronicle full of names and facts and figures, its most poetic part relates an Indian idyll, a love story rudely interrupted by the slave-seeking Spaniards. The beloved is seized; the lover, Huitzel, unable to free her, yields himself to capture. Escape provides a happy ending to the romantic episode. We have here not so much a foreshadowing of nineteenth-century attitudes as a sixteenth-century expression of the ideas of the Apostle to the Indians, Father Las Casas: [41] the poet condemns the early settlers for the system of enforced Indian labor. Aware of the Sepúlveda-Las Casas debate, Terrazas refrains from taking sides philosophically (as he says); he states that the practice itself was forbidden, observing at the same time that the prohibition came too late. The pre-Columbian existence of the natives is idealized.

And in another respect Terrazas speaks for his generation: he, the unrewarded son of the Mexican conquest (though in earlier stanzas he praises Cortés as hero), as he thinks of himself and his companions finds that their hopes have been deceived and that unhappy Mexico is

> Falling from age to age in greater sadness,
> In deeper misery, poverty, and hunger.[42]

These lines are written from the point of view of a special class: that of the hidalgos who are sons of conquistadors. Cortés promised his followers a kingdom, a promise never redeemed; mer-

---

cisco de Terrazas y otros poetas del siglo XVI (Madrid, 1962). Icazbalceta's work first appeared in 1883.

41. "The 'Natural Man' is, of course, an ambivalent image. He may be conceived as ideally innocent. From that conception descend Montaigne's essay on cannibals, Gonzalo's commonwealth in *The Tempest*, the good 'Salvage' in *The Faerie Queen* (VI. iv, v, vi), Pope's 'reign of God,' and the primeval classless society of the Marxists. It is one of the great myths. On the other hand, he might be conceived as brutal, subhuman: thence Caliban, the bad 'Salvages' of *The Faerie Queen* (VI. viii), the state of nature as pictured in Hobbes, and the 'Cave Man' of popular modern imagination. That is another great myth" (C. S. Lewis, *English Literature in the Sixteenth Century Excluding Drama* [Oxford, 1954], p. 17).

42. "de tiempo en tiempo siempre en más tristeza, / en más miserias, hambres y pobreza" (cited by Campos, *op. cit.*).

chants, farmers, and picaros have taken over. What Terrazas failed to understand, says Jorge Campos, was that a new society was forming willy-nilly — a society which, for all the desire to create a utopia, was to be both un-utopian and something less than fully Spanish: it was to embrace the good and the bad of the experiment in transoceanic living. Terrazas, the refined Petrarquist who moved among the gentlemen and ladies of Mexico's high society, hated human slavery — even though the enslaved persons were of another race — nor could he bear the thought that the creators of all these possibilities did not enjoy the comforts and the privileges of their fathers.[43] In this poet we perceive an unusual amalgam of Renaissance refinement and post-Renaissance decline.

Because he is next in chronological order, we bring in at this point our example from Colombia, Juan Rodríguez Freyle (d. 1640?), who wrote a "scandalous chronicle," full of choice anecdotes of love and quasi-picaresque adventures, of the life of his country and of his own life, entitled *The Conquest and Discovery of the New Kingdom of Granada* (popularly known as *El Carnero*). The author was interested, says Alessandro Martinengo, in revealing himself as a man of culture and in displaying his Scholastic and medieval learning, which had taught him to set every event against the complex background of traditional ethical and religious ideas, portraying the modest occurrences of provincial life in a colonial capital in the light of universal history, or, more precisely, relating these humble events to the story of salvation which began with the creation and the fall and will end with the end of time.[44]

The literary — and rhetorical — character of many of Rodríguez Freyle's "debates" and satires is shown by Martinengo. Rodríguez Freyle cites *exempla* of the ten Sibyls and quotes *La Celestina* on the nature of women; he elaborates on Horace's rustic beatitudes in the *Beatus ille*, yet laments the disillusions and miseries of peasant life (which he claims to have experienced). The sources of his erudite excursus are few: the Bible, especially Ecclesiastes; Saint Augustine (the *Confessions* only); Virgil; compendiums of classical

43. Terrazas' father had been *mayordomo* to Cortés.

44. "La cultura letteraria di Juan Rodríguez Freyle: Saggio sulle fonti di una cronaca bogotana del Seicento," in the *Annali* (of the Istituto Universitario Orientale), *Sezione Romanza*, IV, i (Naples, 1962), 59. Martinengo questions the much-repeated picaresque filiation of the *Carnero*; he finds no direct influence (see p. 79).

lore; and perhaps (though chronology makes this as difficult as it is enticing to suppose) Quevedo. This is indeed small intellectual baggage for one selected as a "representative man" of Spanish colonial culture. He is here chosen for that role, not because he shows the heights to which Spanish colonial education and environment could enable one to mount, but because he adheres so faithfully to the Spanish tradition: the Bible, the Church Fathers, Scholasticism.

Our third "end product" is a Mexican nun. "The most lively, charming, and resonant voice of the baroque period in Spanish America was that of Sor Juana Inés de la Cruz,"[45] a contemporary of Calderón (d. 1695). She has been pictured by Pedro Salinas as a spirit born too soon: she could have been happy, clad in blue jeans, hair flying in the wind, on a bicycle at Bryn Mawr or Mt. Holyoke.[46] Certain it is that her passion for intellectual understanding and achievement was incompatible with the possibilities open to a woman in seventeenth-century Mexico. She has left her own record of unhappiness:

As soon as I heard [that in Mexico City there were a University and schools in which the sciences were studied] I began to beseech my mother with urgent and persistent entreaties to allow me to change my manner of dress [disguise herself as a man] and go to Mexico City in order to study and to attend the University while living in the home of some relatives. She did not permit me to do so — and quite rightly — but I satisfied my desire by reading many different kinds of books belonging to my grandfather, without letting punishments or reprimands stop me.[47]

In time she came to advocate the establishing of a system of education for women, imparted by women.[48] Her personal wish was to live alone, to be responsible to no one, to have no occupation that would interfere with her freedom to study, to hear no nun-made noises in the quiet of her seclusion. This could not be, and "all the impertinences" of her remarkable temperament yielded and bent themselves to the yoke. Not interested in marriage, her only choice

45. Enrique Anderson Imbert, *Historia de la literatura hispanoamericana* (Mexico City, 1954), p. 64.
46. "En busca de Juana de Asbaje," *Memoria del Segundo Congreso Internacional de Catedráticos de Literatura Iberoamericana* (Berkeley–Los Angeles, 1941), p. 191.
47. Carlos González Peña, *History of Mexican Literature*, trans. G. B. Nance and F. J. Dunstan (Dallas, Texas, 1943), p. 107.
48. This and what follows is taken from Anderson Imbert, *op. cit.*, pp. 65 ff.

was to enter a religious order. This she did, taking with her not only her own person, as she records, but also her greatest enemy, that intellectual bent which — for some reason — Heaven had given her. The impulse, instead of being deadened by the new environment, "exploded like gunpowder." She continued to read and study, with no other teacher than her books. Because of this she suffered persecution and endured hatred. A saintly and foolish abbess commanded her to desist; she obeyed during three months — the length of her superior's administration. As for not studying, this was simply impossible; when denied books she studied "in all the things that God created," in the book of the universe.

Her theology was orthodox, beyond a doubt, but her activities could only be a cause of conflict. The final asceticism of her years of renunciation may have been, as Anderson Imbert suggests, less religious in character than it has been thought to be.

She explained and defended her position in verse and in prose: in verse in her *Primero sueño*, in prose in a *Letter to Sor Filotea de la Cruz* (1691). Anderson Imbert calls the latter one of the most admirable autobiographical essays in the Spanish language, expressed in a prose which is delicate, flexible, and sharp. It was a case of intelligence defending itself against impertinence, prejudice, lack of comprehension, stupidity: an intelligence fully aware of the strength of its own position, yet forced by circumstances into a posture of humility. The defense is remarkably effective. Why does she write verses and plays? A heresy against art, she says, is punished not by the Inquisition but only by the laughter of the discreet. She is much too aware of her limitations to dare to write on sacred subjects. What she reaffirms is her inability to desist from her life's vocation. In the *Primero sueño*, composed in the baroque style of Góngora's *Soledades*, she tells of the upward flight of her spirit toward knowledge. At night, in dreams, the spirit can mount in a single flight to a vision of all creation — only to return, humbly, to struggle toward conceptual understanding, step by step.

Part of Sor Juana's tragedy may be explained by the recent discovery that she was born out of wedlock. But Professor Leonard has shown, convincingly it seems, that her essential trouble lay deeper: "She yearned for a newer, freer era of widening horizons, of a differing approach to truth which she did not realize was beginning. But the religious institution, of which she was a part and which was so concerned for her salvation, was wholly identified with the old ways of thinking that did not attract her. Rather, her attachment to the unorthodox kind of thinking became a compulsion against which she struggled constantly, fearful of its implications for her eternal security in its radical departure from ecclesiastical authoritarianism." [49]

Sor Juana's Mexican world, unable to understand the fundamental needs of her forward-looking spirit, demanded of her the sacrifice of her truest self. Yet it did not fail her altogether: her grandfather's library afforded her the books in which her young mind found the nourishment it needed, and the society in which she lived — colonial though it was — enabled her to assemble a personal library of some four thousand volumes, which she sacrificed, alas! in the final years of asceticism. Could she have been happy even in England or in New England in that half-century extending from 1648 to 1695?

The final "end product" to be noted — though his life extended nine years beyond our period — is the Mexican Carlos de Sigüenza y Góngora (d. 1700). More savant than man of letters, he wrote on astronomy, astrology, ethnography, mathematics, history, and, to a smaller and much less significant extent, on literary subjects, sometimes in verse. "His radical disposition is apparent in a bluntly expressed disrespect for authority in learning, in his belief in methodical doubt, in his conviction of the necessity of demonstration, and in his reliance on mathematics as a means of measuring natural phenomena." He assembled "the best collection of treatises and instruments then to be found in the New World," and these he willed to the Jesuits (the order from which, to his unending unhappiness, he had been expelled for a breach of discipline) "in gratitude to, and as an adequate compensation for, the good training and good instruction I received from the reverend fathers during the few years that I lived with them." It is a curious paradox, observes Professor Leonard, that just as Sor Juana's secret sorrow

49. *Baroque Times in Old Mexico* (Ann Arbor, Michigan, 1959), p. 185; see also *idem*, "The *Encontradas correspondencias* of Sor Juana Inés: An Interpretation," *HR*, XXIII (1955), 33–47.

"was the impossibility of escaping into a world of wider horizons, Sigüenza's private grief was the impossibility of returning to the strict rule of a religious community." [50] In his will Sigüenza y Góngora directed that his cadaver should be turned over to the medical authorities for autopsy and scientific study.

POSTSCRIPT AND CONCLUSION

In this chapter our concern has been to show the extension of the Castilian way of life and the Castilian spirit into new territories, "following the princes whom we sent to rule in those kingdoms," as Nebrija expressed it in 1492 to Queen Isabella. The evidence of this extension has been impressive, both in the European and in the American theaters of expansion. Yet it would be wrong to assume that the influence was, in any theater, unilateral. We may apply to the conquistadors the lines from Stephen Vincent Benét's *Western Star*:

> And those who came were resolved to be Englishmen,
> Gone to the World's End, but English every one,
> And they ate the white corn kernels, parched in the sun,
> And they knew it not, but they'd not be English again.

A Mexican writer, Agustín Yáñez, in a monograph entitled *The Social Content of Hispanic American Literature*, finds as the dominant note in this literature what he calls *mestizaje*: the blending of European and American elements to form something organically new. Spanish-American literature is not Spanish literature; as a Spanish writer has put it, the old instrument, which was the Castilian language, acquired in America a new timbre, overtones not heard before.

Speaking of early literary works produced on American soil by Spaniards, Yáñez says: "Though these works have a genuine Spanish ring, they cannot be incorporated into the literature of the Peninsula. . . . There has been injected into them a new spirit: even the language is interspersed with words and turns of phrase born in the antipodes. They are conditioned by forms of thought and feeling inconceivable in Spain. . . . A pre-existing language

50. *Baroque Times* . . . , pp. 203, 208.

has come into contact with a new reality, which . . . inevitably must become the basis of a new racial, sociological, and cultural creation." [51] Even the Indians who learned to write in Castilian produced works which no pre-Columbian Indian could have conceived: the *Mexican Chronicle* of Tezozomoc; the *Relation of the Conquest of Peru*, by Titu Cussi Yupanqui, baptized as Diego de Castro; the *New Chronicle and Good Government* of Huamán Poma de Ayala. Other accounts and documents, written in native languages but with the Castilian alphabet, are likewise conditioned by the presence of the Spaniards and have meaning only in relation to the Spanish frame of reference — whether the native writer accepted or repudiated the white man's way.

It is thus possible — as a Spanish writer has done — to view all the Hispanic lands as forming a single vast republic whose president is Miguel de Cervantes — a republic whose citizens, though their homes be separated by thousands of miles, feel immediately at home with each other upon meeting. Whether these bonds of a common culture, forged in the Renaissance and post-Renaissance, can withstand the destructive forces of our own day is a problem for the future.

51. *El contenido social de la literatura iberoamericana (Jornadas, 14)*, (El Colegio de México, Mexico City, n. d.), pp. 21 ff. Henríquez Ureña, *op. cit.*, p. 214, n. 17, gives a list of Indian and half-caste writers and artists during the colonial period.

IV · Political Expansion: The Idea of Empire[1]

My name, illustrious friend,
is Gerardo; the noble and
famous city of Madrid, most
worthy seat and dwelling of
our Catholic Sovereigns, is
my beloved home, common and
universal mother of diverse
peoples and remote nations.

Gonzalo de Céspedes y Meneses [2]

Ranke correctly maintains
that as we pass from the
Empire of the Turks to the
Empire of Charles V, we pass
from a regime of slaves to a
regime of free men.

Juan Antonio Maravall [3]

That union was a pact, a
personal alliance. The
parts of that monarchy were
heterogeneous. . . . A keen
sense of independence, nourished
by the frequent meetings
of the Cortes, had a place
deep in the heart of those
indomitable peoples.

Juan Beneyto Pérez [4]

1. See Felix Gilbert, "Political Thought of the Renaissance and Reformation: A Report of Recent Scholarship," *Huntington Library Quarterly*, IV (1941), 433–68.

2. *Poema trágico del Español Gerardo y desengaño del amor lascivo*, 1615 (*BAE*, XVIII, 124a).

3. *Carlos V y el pensamiento político del Renacimiento* (Madrid, 1960), p. 43. See also J. M. Gallegos Rocafull, *El hombre y el mundo de los teólogos españoles de los siglos de oro* (Mexico City, 1946), p. 28: "To the supposed dominion of the emperor over all the world [Francisco de Vitoria] opposes natural law which makes all men free. No one can deprive them of that liberty which Nature gave them: positive law can regulate it, but never annul it. The Emperor Charles V governs those peoples by reason of legitimate titles which he possesses; but he has no right over other peoples, nor can he, therefore, use force to bring them under his dominion. . . . Peace and concord among men must be established, but not imposed from the outside by legal compulsion; they must spring from within in answer to an imperative of the conscience"; see also p. 38.

4. "Los medios de cultura y la centralización bajo Felipe II," *Ciudad de Dios*, CL (1927), p. 250. The reference is to the spiritual union achieved by Ferdinand and

In the year 1568 the Emperor Charles V was a memory. For thirteen years his son, Philip II, had held the reins of government. The great palace-monastery at El Escorial — symbol of Philip's personality and of his government — had been under construction for five years. It was a time of optimism. Though the victory of Lepanto was three years in the future, the humanist Juan de Mal Lara, in the dedication to Philip of his huge work *Filosofía vulgar*, speaks of the "prosperous reign" and the "admirable prudence" of King Philip, so great that war cannot disturb the "repose and blessedness" in which the entire Kingdom lives amid "general happiness," nor can the fact of this *pax hispanica* embolden potential enemies to forget the awe wherewith they are wont to regard His Majesty — ever in a state of preparedness, armed "with all those things which sustain the power of a happy state." This, all of it, by the grace of God, is in recompense for Philip's vigilance as defender of Catholicism.[5]

Mal Lara also expresses two additional ideas: first, that the fruits of thought, conceived in the minds of learned men, are the best fruits of the country, those most worthy to be offered to one's sovereign; second, that the Spanish Empire is vast. "What can one offer to so magnanimous a Prince, to so Catholic a King, to so genuine a Father of his Country, so appropriately as letters, and the creations of the mind? Each one will offer what he has and what he knows, for therein lies the greatness of so vast an Empire."

It will be well to go back and observe the growth of this idea of empire. It found expression even before Antonio de Nebrija prophesied in (1492, as we have seen) the extension of the Castilian language to lands of "barbarous nations with strange tongues," as the star of empire moved southward into Africa, eastward to

Isabella, and to the various peoples that composed the Spanish monarchy in the Peninsula. The unifying process was slow (pp. 256–57); Philip II cannot be accused of exacerbating the process of centralization (p. 262). On the lack of homogeneity between Castilians, Aragonese, Catalans, etc., see p. 242. Unification really began under the Conde-Duque de Olivares (d. 1643) and culminated under Philip V (of the House of Bourbon; d. 1746); see p. 242, n. 4.

5. Ed. A. Vilanova (Madrid, 1958–59), I, 55. In another place we shall have to give attention to this work. It is a remarkable example of the Renaissance belief in the wisdom of the folk—a notion which owed much to Erasmus and his *Adagia*. Mal Lara collected popular proverbs and made them the basis of a treatise showing that the wisdom they express is the same as that found in the classics and in the literature of the learned.

Italy, westward across the Atlantic, and — in 1517 — northward to the Netherlands. The concept is still present several generations later when Baltasar Gracián (d. 1658) speaks of the two "universal languages, the Latin and the Spanish, which today are the keys of the world." [6]

Prior to 1492, probably in 1490, Gonzalo de Santa María had published his translation of the *Lives of the Fathers* attributed to St. Jerome, prefacing it with a prologue, inspired by the *Elegantiae* of Lorenzo Valla (d. 1457), in which, somewhat earlier than Nebrija, Santa María makes statements similar to those of the father of Spanish philology. We read in this prologue: "And since the royal empire [7] which we have today is Castilian, and the most excellent King and Queen have chosen as the site and seat of their kingdoms the Kingdom of Castile, I decided to render the present work into Castilian; because language normally follows empire, to a greater extent than anything else." [8]

The novelty of Santa María's attitude in the year 1490 lies in its essentially Renaissance concept of the dignity of letters, rather than in its acceptance of the proposition that the kings of Castile-

6. *El Héroe. El Discreto* (Buenos Aires–Mexico City, 1939), p. 165.

7. The term "royal" is naturally associated (but see note 9) with the term empire, for, in the new centralized dynastic states of the Renaissance, "the king was the state." Not until the time of the French revolution did "the survival of the Christian and Stoic traditions, the regard for the universally human, the faith in reason, one and the same everywhere, and in common sense" become sufficiently weakened to allow nationalism to develop its true tendencies and "to disrupt the society of man" (Hans Kohn, *Nationalism* [Princeton–New York–Toronto, 1955], pp. 14–15). The idea of a Spanish empire arose in the Middle Ages: "Vicentius . . . glorifies Spain and the Spanish and believes that the Spanish are superior to the French and the Germans, and by their virtues merit the empire they have won and are expanding. This empire, however, is not the old, theoretically universal, Holy Roman Empire . . . [but] the Empire of Spain, of the Iberian Peninsula. . . . The true Spanish Empire was only by accident joined to the Holy Roman Empire in the person of Charles V" (Gaines Post, "*Blessed Lady Spain*–Vicentius Hispanus and Spanish Nationalism in the Thirteenth Century," *Speculum*, XXIX [1954], 208). For material concerning the medieval expectation of a new Golden Age (preceded by a triumph over misbelievers and a new harmony among Christians) and the general tendency of medieval chroniclers to see even in the most unlikely monarchs the Last Emperor, a messianic *rex iustus*, or a new David, see Norman Cohn, *In Search of the Millennium* (Fairlawn, New Jersey, 1957), pp. 20, 58.

8. Cited by Eugenio Ascensio, "Juan de Valdés contra Delicado: Fondo de una polémica," in *Studia Philologica: Homenaje ofrecido a Dámaso Alonso* (Madrid, 1960–61), I, 106; see also *idem*, "La lengua compañera del imperio: Historia de una idea de Nebrija en España y Portugal," *RFE*, XLIII (1960), 399–413.

Aragon properly rule, or should rule, over many kingdoms.[9] In Spain it had long been traditional to consider the king's primordial duty to be that of warring against the infidel — which implied seizing the enemy's lands and (ideally) extending Spain's victories to include a reconquered Jerusalem. Throughout the Middle Ages there was thought of a possible conquest of North Africa; and when Ferdinand the Catholic (d. 1516) became the principal king of Christendom (as Machiavelli believed), he assumed as his first objective the struggle against the Mohammedans throughout the Mediterranean. The idea of "holy war" meant, for every Spanish king, the duty of defending and propagating the faith — which was also the chief means of acquiring new territory, power, and fame. Ferdinand, as Gracián (d. 1658) declared, "joined Heaven and earth" by combining the two objectives, the religious and the political — to his own immense profit. It was in 1509 that Cisneros, by his attack on the Moroccan city of Oran, launched what might be called Ferdinand's African policy.[10]

SPAIN AND THE HOLY ROMAN EMPIRE

The problem of Spanish imperial power and responsibility became greatly complicated when Charles V was elected Roman Emperor in 1519. This state of affairs lasted only until the time of Charles' abdication in 1556. Yet "the Western realm, which by Charles V and his conquistadors in the Indies had been enlarged to dimensions widely surpassing those of any rival power in Europe, was, by common consent, also endowed with a name which suggested a comparison with the Imperium Romanum and its predecessors in antiquity. It was called 'the Spanish Monarchy' " — a term symbolic, not simply of a kingdom, but of a state towering above all others (Koebner, *op. cit.*, pp. 55–56). The words signified nearly "universal monarchy." When the heritage of this "Spanish Mon-

9. In exact language, the word *empire* was by international consent reserved for the countries over which the Roman Emperor, together with the German Diet, presided, and also for the Turkish Empire (which had defeated the empire of the Greeks). See Richard Koebner, *Empire* (Cambridge, 1961), pp. 55–56.

10. R. Menéndez Pidal, "Los Reyes Católicos," in *Mis páginas preferidas: Estudios lingüisticos e históricos* (Madrid, 1957), 209–31. I am deeply indebted to this study and to another by the same author and included in the same collection of reprints: "La idea imperial de Carlos V," pp. 232–53.

archy" passed to Charles' successors, the Imperium Romanum fell into decline.

Pax Christiana

There were other complications for Charles. Ferdinand had passed on to his grandson the determination to defend the Church (principally from the French); to strive for a general *Pax Christiana* in Europe; and to win victories from the Mohammendans of Africa and Asia Minor. These points were summarized by Pedro de Quintana, Ferdinand's secretary of state, upon that king's death in 1516: "The end and purpose of His Majesty was always the achieving of a general peace among Christians, and war against the infidel; these two ends were as dear to him as the salvation of his soul." [11] This policy was reaffirmed by Charles in a speech delivered at Madrid in 1528, redacted by Fray Antonio de Guevara, preacher to His Majesty and royal historiographer, in words frequently identical to passages in Guevara's *Dial of Princes*.[12] In his speech Charles protests that he does not wish to acquire the states of other rulers (this, with his eye on the French, he calls tyrannical ambition), but only to conserve what he has inherited and to unify Christian Europe: he wishes, in other words, to transmit to Europe the sense of Christian crusade which had been the life and breath of Spain for centuries. As for the mastery of the whole world, he could not aspire to it. His theological advisers, all of them, agreed with Francisco de Vitoria: [13] neither by natural law nor by divine law nor by human law was the emperor master of the world. An irenic ideal of Christian pacifism thus became Charles' unswerving policy, though some members of his entourage, like Mercurino di Gattinara,[14] urged him to pluck the "fruit" offered by his election as head of the Imperium Romanum.

11. Cited by Menéndez Pidal, "Los Reyes Católicos," p. 219.

12. Menéndez Pidal, "Fray Antonio de Guevara y la idea imperial de Carlos V," in *España y su Historia* (Madrid, 1957), II, 108–13.

13. Vitoria was the first to elaborate an exposition of the *jus gentium* (law of nations) at the same time that he laid down the fundamental lines of what, in his opinion, the Spanish Empire was and should be (Gallegos Rocafull, *op. cit.*, pp. 142, 145). He was influenced by Erasmus' *Enchiridion Militis Christiani* and *Querela Pacis* (P. Mesnard, "Erasme et l'Espagne," *Revue de la Méditerranée*, III [1946], 75).

14. "Gattinara brought to the King's entourage a wholly new point of view. Humanist and man of learning, he was imbued with the idea of world empire and for a dozen years he preached his doctrine to Charles and guided his steps, as far as he could, to

A Time of Troubles

Instead of peace, Charles experienced a time of troubles. In 1525 he characteristically refused to permit public celebration of the victory at Pavia since it had been obtained at the cost of Christian blood. When in that same year Francis I of France arrived at Madrid as his prisoner, Charles sided against Gattinara, rejecting any thought of conquest and aggrandizement, choosing instead a policy of clemency and reconciliation. In 1526, the year before the sack of Rome, he addressed to the Pope the bitterest possible recriminations because of that pontiff's devious policies which militated against the Emperor's irenic dream. Then, in 1527, came the assault on the Eternal City — lamented by Charles, but in the last analysis approved by him and stoutly defended by his secretary for Latin letters, Alfonso de Valdés, in two brilliant literary dialogues to be studied below.[15] In 1530 Charles received the imperial crown from the hands of the pope. "To many Italians and Spaniards [he] was the champion of a united world that could combat the Turk and bring concord to a Europe divided by religious strife." It was not to be. Though Charles, "by strange coincidences and native ability, had plausible claims to universal recognition . . . he was frustrated at every turn by a complexity of problems, which finally overwhelmed him."[16] He abdicated in 1556 and withdrew to a monastery in Extremadura, where he died in 1558.

Charles' dream became impossible: first, because the Mohammedan lands could not be conquered; second, because the schism created by Protestantism would not be healed. Yet,

the Empire, which had come to him in such diminished state, he converted into a vigorous reality; he ceased to be merely the honorary chief of the German Princes. For the Spanish branch [of the Empire] he retained the Spanish Peninsula, Flanders, Naples, and Sicily. His brother . . . , the favorite grandson of Ferdinand the Catholic and a disciple of Cisneros, reigned in Hungary

the realization of his bold dream" (H. Keniston, *Francisco de los Cobos, Secretary to the Emperor Charles V* [Pittsburgh, *ca.* 1959], p. 50. The words "as far as he could" imply Charles' fundamental rejection of the idea of empire as the Romans and Gattinara conceived it.

15. The sack of Rome, it was held, was a just punishment visited by Heaven upon the Holy See.

16. Milton A. Buchanan, "Annotations, III: Hernando de Acuña's Sonnet Addressed to Charles V," *HR*, XV (1947), 446.

and Bohemia. Spanish armies fought the infidel from Vienna to Algiers. The Church was given new strength by the Spanish Society of Jesus, by the Spanish theologians at the Council of Trent (1545–1563), and by the new Scholastic philosophy [of Suárez, Soto, Cano]. Diplomacy was invaded by Spanish ministers and Spanish practices, and the Spanish language came to be used everywhere, especially after Charles employed it in a parliament with the pope in 1536 in the Vatican.[17]

A New King: Compromise Rejected

With the abdication of Charles in 1556, the headship of the Imperium Romanum passed to non-Spanish hands. Henceforth the imperial title would be merely honorary, lacking universal value. Charles was the last Roman Emperor crowned by a pope. Yet, in spite of frustrations and failures, the idea of unifying Christendom, so stoutly defended by Charles as a heritage from his grandfather Ferdinand the Catholic, continued to be the basis of Spain's foreign policy, pervading life and literature in the Peninsula. To that policy Spain sacrificed her progress, becoming as it were a fossil state in a Europe that was marching already toward the Enlightenment and the industrial revolution. It is typical of the nation's choice of path that when Philip II assumed power in 1556, the theologians whom he consulted concluded that, in view of the evils which would befall the Church as a result of the imminent rebellion in Flanders, the king might — without hurt to his conscience — grant to the cities of Flanders the freedom of worship they demanded; yet Philip, more unyielding than they, made his own decision, swearing that he would never permit religious disruption, that he was unwilling to rule over heretics. The result was, of course, the loss to Spain of her possessions in the Low Countries.[18]

17. Menéndez Pidal, "La idea imperial de Carlos V," pp. 249–50. The bibliography on this subject is large. An older work is R. B. Merriman, *The Rise of the Spanish Empire in the Old World and in the New* (4 vols. New York, 1918–34). See, *inter alia multa*, J. Beneyto Pérez, *Espíritu y estado en el siglo XVI* (Madrid, 1952), and Maravall, *op. cit.*

18. Menéndez Pidal, "Las dos Españas," in his (previously cited) *Mis páginas preferidas* . . . , p. 291. On this general subject see Louis B. Wright, *Religion and Empire: The Alliance between Piety and Commerce in English Expansion, 1558–1625* (Chapel Hill, North Carolina, 1943); J. L. Meacham, *Church and State in Latin America* (Chapel Hill, North Carolina, 1934).

EXPANSION IN AMERICA

Again, we must go backward in time, to consider the American aspect of Spain's political expansion. Charles was "the last Emperor to have seen the Earthly City and the City of God united, the last universal Emperor." He was the European politician who most sincerely believed in a United States of Europe — a Europe united politically, as it had always been united culturally by its common Christian heritage, a Europe symbolized by Augustus, Trajan, Charlemagne, Frederick II, and Boniface VIII.[19] He, alone among the emperors, ruled directly over the most widespread and distant territories as the first emperor of both Europe and America. He sought to Hispanize America, to bring it into the ecumenical sheepfold [20] of a unified Christendom. And to guide him in this purpose he had — along with such official advisors as Mota, Valdés, Guevara, and Vitoria — his unofficial American advisor, Hernando Cortés. Cortés, more than any other of the conquistators, was concerned with humanizing the cruelty of the conquest of the New World, and with evaluating and lifting up the conquered lands. In 1522 he wrote to Charles: "Your Majesty can call yourself the first Emperor of all the land, with a title no less distinguished and no less meritorious than that of Emperor of Germany, which Your Majesty already possesses." Cortés voiced the desire that the emperor should devote to the New World all the interest due to a true empire, in matters of religion, government, historical records, respect and concern for the ethnography and the treasures of Mexico. Charles sought, as his grandparents had sought before him, to give to the new American empire a foundation of justice based on law.[21] Out of

19. Menéndez Pidal, "La idea imperial de Carlos V," p. 251. It must be remembered that this union was to be achieved, not by invasion and conquest of lands held legitimately by independent princes, but by a federation of Christian states. Only the Mohammedan states and rebellious territories (like Flanders) were legitimate objects of military conquest. Concerning the legitimacy of conquest in America, see below; and see our Volume II, Chapter IV.

20. For discussion of the popular concept of the "universal sheepfold," see below, the section "The Reign of Charles V."

21. See Volume II, Chapter IV. Among the authorities listed there, see especially Lewis Hanke, *The Spanish Struggle for Justice in the Conquest of America* (Philadelphia, 1949); see also the unsigned review of this book in the (London) *Times Literary Supplement* (May 25, 1951): "Probably never before or since has a mighty emperor in the full tide of his power ordered his conquests to cease until it could be decided whether they were just."

that concern, out of the disputes between Sepúlveda[22] and Las Casas,[23] grew the "admirable laws of the Indies" (1542) which, whatever their lack of success in practice,[24] do honor to Spain as a colonizing nation.[25]

Ideal Justice vs. Accomplished Facts

The colonial ethics of the Siglo de Oro, based on Scholastic theological and political thought, became a theory that was perfectly thought out and methodical and that derived from two great sources: natural law (*lex naturalis*) and Christian revelation.[26] Though Dante, Bartolo da Sassoferrato, Enea Silvio Piccolomini, and others had argued for the universal monarchy of the emperor, in the Spain of the Siglo de Oro the idea of the sovereignty of all states — that is to say, the nationalist idea — had become so strong that not a single theologian, and few jurists, defended the Dante-Piccolomini thesis.[27] Though Charles V seemed about to attain to

22. Teodoro Andrés Marcos, *Los imperialismos de J. G. de Sepúlveda en su "Democrates alter"* (Madrid, 1948). On Sepúlveda's "détestable politique de violence" see Alain Guy, *La pensée de Luis de León* (Limoges, 1943), p. 339.

23. Bartolomé Leonardo de Argensola, in his *Anales de la Corona de Aragón* (Zaragoza, 1630, pp. 147–48) is admirably impartial in regard to Las Casas: "when he exposed the acts of violence committed by captains, judges, discoverers and patroons [*encomenderos*] none of [his] opponents [the text reads *pocos amigos* but should read *poco amigos*] contradicted his facts, though they might excuse or discount them. Usually, not being able to deny the iniquities . . . , nor make any accusation against him personally, they went to extremes in their condemnation of the vehemence with which he exaggerated violence and injustice. They said that he was indiscreet and without modesty in his procedure, excessive in his zeal, insufferable in his manner, ruining his case by his altogether unfortunate methods."

24. Though there developed — in spite of all theories — an abyss between conquerors and conquered, it is yet a fact that the government of Mexico City actually suggested that there be always six Indians on its Council (O. H. Green, "The Concept of Man in the Spanish Renaissance," *The Rice Institute Pamphlet*, XLVI [1960], 52). In 1545 Cardinal Pacheco pointed out to the emperor the desirability and the justice of bringing as delegates to the Council of Trent "some prelates from the Indies" inasmuch as "this is the first general council to be held since those lands were won" (F. Cereceda, *Diego Laínez en la Europa religiosa de su tiempo, 1512–1565* [Madrid, 1945–46], I, 223).

25. Menéndez Pidal, "La idea imperial de Carlos V," pp. 252–53. "A few Puritan clergymen . . . asserted that the Indians were children of the devil who might profitably be wiped out and their lands appropriated. But the prevailing belief was that missionaries must carry the Gospel to the savages" (Louis B. Wright, *Religion and Empire*, p. 86). And note also the quotation from the *Times Literary Supplement* (see above, note 21).

26. Joseph Höffner, *La ética colonial del siglo de oro: Cristianismo y dignidad humana*, trans. F. de Asís Caballero (Madrid, 1957), pp. 509–10; other page references in the present paragraph refer to this work.

27. "In the *De Monarchia* (II, 1, 2), Dante confesses that in former days he believed,

universal sovereignty, not even Sepúlveda made bold to bolster his concept of colonial dominion with the old imperial argument, preferring to rely on religious and theocratic considerations (pp. 367–68), as well as on the anthropological proposition of the natural inferiority of certain peoples (see pp. 90–91, 223, 380). Though Spain considered herself an *orbis Christianus* on a reduced scale, her ideals took a course differing from the imperial one (p. 103): in accordance with traditional theological thought, political power was granted by God to princes and to kings, as well as to the emperor, through the mediation of the Church (p. 10). Even though this mediation might be absent, as it clearly was in America, the conclusion — necessarily frustrating to Charles and to his successors — was that the political states of the heathen were as legitimate as those of the Christians (pp. 341–42) since every state was based on natural law and, being "natural," was ordained by God; [28] that, in short, in the New World there existed true sovereign states and that "in no case could the emperor occupy the provinces of the 'barbarians,' deposing rulers, setting up new ones, and collecting taxes" (p. 371). St. Augustine had declared in the heading of chapter XIII of Book V of *The City of God* (London, 1620): "the ancient Romans obtained the increase of their kingdoms at the true God's hands, being that [i.e., although] they never worshipped him." [29] We are thus again faced — as so often in the course of our

with Saint Augustine, that the Romans obtained the government of the world only by violence, by right of arms. He abandoned this view when it dawned on him that the Romans by conquering the world simply fulfilled the supreme mission imposed upon them by God himself. . . . Dante's Rome Idea outgrew the Augustinian-Orosian pattern of world history and developed an almost religious embracement of the ideas of Virgil. . . . To Dante, the world appeared at its best when the pagan Augustus and the Lord simultaneously treaded [sic] the ground of this earth." Thus "Augustine tried to demolish the myth of universal and eternal Rome; Orosius attempted to Christianize it. . . . Dante's universalism extended to pagan as well as Christian times" (Ernst H. Kantorowicz, reviewing Charles Till Davis, *Dante and the Idea of Rome* [Oxford, 1957] in *Speculum*, XXXIV [1959], 104–5).

28. On the *Lex Naturalis* as (in the last analysis) the will of God, see Höffner, *op. cit.*, p. 338; the *jus gentium*, on the other hand, is human (pp. 390, 393).

29. All of this Book V is pertinent to our problem. See François de Dainville, *Les Jésuites et l'éducation de la société française* (Paris, 1940), p. 225. There were three principles governing human action: natural law, Mosaic law, and faith. As for the first: Nature (or natural knowledge) illumined the Gentiles with a great light, enabling them to live well, as St. Paul showed clearly in his Epistle to the Romans. In Mosaic law, God provided a still brighter light. The law of Grace (faith) provides the ultimate, supernatural light.

study — with a *Sic* and a *Non*.[30] The conquest was an accomplished
fact; the conquered must be governed, and by Spaniards. The New
Laws of the Indies of 1542 were, perhaps, the only possible compromise.

With respect to Spain's sense of her mission, the following text
is of interest. It is taken from Part II (1574) of the *Pontifical
History* of Gonzalo de Illescas, one of the first histories of the
popes to have been written in a vernacular language. In it we are
given a confrontation of Cortés and of Luther which is eloquently
indicative of the state of Spanish opinion during the rule of Philip
II. Illescas gives an account of Luther's humble birth, born of "vile
persons of low station." In that same year of 1485,[31] he says, there
was born in Medellín, in Extremadura, that noble and famous man
Hernando Cortés, Marqués del Valle. The one was born in Saxony,
to upset the world as a test and a trial of God's elect, to place beneath the banner of the Devil many faithful and Catholic Christians who before his coming had lived in peace in the Christian
religion. Cortés, on the other hand, "was born in Spain, to lead into
the Church an infinite multitude of barbarous peoples who for so
many years had lived under the dominion of Satan, sunk in vice
and blind in their idolatry. . . . Just as these two men were born
at the same time, so in the same year each entered upon his task:
Luther, to corrupt the Gospel among those who had already received it; Cortés, to proclaim and promulgate the Gospel, with all
purity and sincerity, to nations that had ever been ignorant thereof, never having heard preached the word of Christ." [32]

The Orbis Christianus

In popular thought (as opposed to the reasoning of the theologians), the old idea of an *Orbis Christianus*, successor to the

30. Michael Seidlmayer, in *Currents of Mediaeval Thought with Special Reference
to Germany*, trans. D. Barker (Oxford, 1960), p. 97, discusses the "revolution" in
political thought brought about by Scholasticism and concludes: "Its effects can be
seen most clearly and simply in the change in the theory of dominion. Here it led to
the recognition of the legitimacy of the individual national states because they were
the result of natural laws and forces, and this was regarded as sufficient justification
for them. There was no longer implicit acceptance of a universal and sacred empire."
   31. Actually, Luther was born in 1483.
   32. Winston A. Reynolds, "Gonzalo de Illescas and the Cortés-Luther Confrontation," *Hisp.*, XLV (1962), 402.

Imperium Romanum, persisted: "people's minds change more slowly than their environment. So, throughout Europe, right up to the year 1500 and beyond, most people went on thinking in terms of the hierarchically ordained great society, and passing judgment on its parts in terms of how proper they were for that society's overriding final ends. As long as they did so their attitude towards the state was bound to be . . . different from that of modern times. . . ."[33]

LITERATURE AND THE EXPANSION OF CASTILE

In literature, and in peripherally literary texts, we find the two attitudes — for and against universal dominion — eloquently expressed, with respect both to Spain and to the Indies.

Early Texts

Though "the belief in the unity of Western Christendom had at various times in the course of the Crusades been seriously shaken, and Frederick II [d. 1250] had probably outgrown it,"[34] it remained as an ideal from St. Augustine to Bossuet (d. 1704).[35] To the thirteenth-century historian and archbishop of Toledo, Rodrigo Jiménez de Rada, the crusade against the infidel was a task not for Castile or Aragon separately, but for the united Spanish people.[36] Although from the reign of Alfonso the Learned (d. 1284) to that of Juan II of Castile (d. 1454) there was more internal civil

33. Garrett Mattingly, "Changing Attitudes toward the State during the Renaissance," in William H. Werkmeister (ed.), *Facets of the Renaissance* (Los Angeles, 1959), p. 26. See also Silvio Zavala, *La filosofía política en la conquista de América* (Mexico City, ca. 1949). Alois Dempf's *Christliche Staatsphilosophie in Spanien* (Salzburg, 1937) "serves mainly to show how fruitful an investigation in this field might be" (Gilbert, *op. cit.*, p. 466); J. H. Parry's *The Spanish Theory of Empire in the Sixteenth Century* "is concerned with the importance of the colonial possessions for the development of absolutism in theory and practice" (*ibid.*); see also my brief note on Parry, *HR*, VIII (1940), 370.

34. J. Burckhardt, *The Civilization of the Renaissance in Italy*, trans. S. G. C. Middlemore (New York, 1958), I, 110.

35. This was true of France and Germany no less than of Spain. In the Peninsula, more than elsewhere, it was an *idée-force*, an impelling idea; but it was not an obsession. See M. Bataillon's review of Juan Sánchez Montes, *Franceses, protestantes, turcos: Los españoles ante la política internacional de Carlos V* (Madrid, 1951) in *BHi*, LIV (1952), 208.

36. Gifford Davis, "The Development of a National Theme in Medieval Castilian Literature," *HR*, III (1935), 149–61; see also p. 152.

strife in Spain than active war in the cause of the faith, the age-old hope of union found expression both in action and in verse. Even the weak Enrique III won victories against the Moors, and sent his fleet to Tetuán in Africa and two embassies to Tamerlane. On the occasion of Enrique's death (1406), Fray Diego de Valencia de León called for Castilian unity in a poem preserved in the *Cancionero de Baena* (1445): "If only this people were brought into concord, and were to advance together unified in heart, I know of no corner of the world that they would not conquer, including Granada." [37] To Enrique's successor, Juan II, Alfonso Alvarez de Villasandino addressed (1409?) a poem of similar tone: the Mohammedan nations, descended from Hagar, will be conquered and destroyed, and the survivors will be converted or put to death. Ecclesiastical reform will go hand in hand with the war against the infidel: the great schism of Western Christendom (1378–1417) will be healed, and Alexander V — considered by Spain to be an antipope — will be ejected from St. Peter's throne:

El pueblo agareno de mala natura	Hagar's evil descendants will be
será conquistado e todo estroydo.	conquered and destroyed. In this
En aqueste tienpo será obedecido	time there will be but one Vicar
vn solo vicario segunt la Escriptura,	of Christ, as the Gospel proclaims,
será desatada la çisma e orrura	and the horrible schism that
porque era el mundo dañado e perdido.	ruined the world will be ended.

The identity of the usurping pope and the date of the poem are established, I believe, by the next lines:

El frayle profeso será requerydo	The friar will be forced to leave
que dexe las çeldas de que es capellán,	the cell of which he is chaplain;
montañas e puertos del flumen Jordán	to surrender the mountains and
que con tiranía gran tienpo a tenido.	harbors of the River Jordan
	which he has long had under
	tyrannous control.

Of all the popes of this period only one, Alexander V (1409–1410), was both a friar — he was a Franciscan — and was denied the obedience of Spain.[38]

37. "Ca sy esta gente fuese concordada / e fuesen juntados en vn coraçón, / non sé en el mundo vn solo rrencón/ que non conquistassen, con toda Granada" (cited by Américo Castro, *Aspectos del vivir hispánico* [Santiago, Chile, 1949], p. 22).

38. See the *Catholic Encyclopedia, s. v.* Alexander V. The poem is no. 756 in the *Cancionero castellano del siglo XV*, ed. R. Foulché Delbosc. Erasmo Buceta in an

There is nothing strange or unusual in this poem of Villasandino. It restates the age-old ideal of victory over the Mohammedan
enemy and of cessation of discord among Christians. Indeed, in
this same reign of Juan II (d. 1454) we even have an out-and-out
declaration against the idea of empire-as-conquest by Alfonso de la
Torre in his *Visión delectable* (ca. 1440): the allegorical figure of
Justice, exiled from earth by a wicked mankind, declares that if
she had retained her earthly residence Alexander the Great would
not have made his campaigns at the expense of distant lands; nor
would Hannibal have destroyed the Spanish towns of Murviedro
and Sigüenza; nor would the Romans have subjugated — unjustly —
the nations brought under their sway; nor Scipio have won battles
in Spain; nor Caesar and Pompey have engaged in internecine
strife. There simply would have been no evil — private or universal — in the world. For if men were just, they would follow the
Golden Rule.[39]

Juan de Mena

Such is the background against which we must understand the
position of Juan de Mena. He was "one of the first who had a vision
of a Spain that should be united, whole, glorious, . . . as the sixteenth century actually integrated her again." [40] In his *Laberinto de
Fortuna*, with its Dantesque circles for the blessed and for the
damned in various categories of human conduct, he reserves first
place in the fifth Order (Mars) for the heroes of the Spanish reconquest, at the same time that he gives first place among the damned
to *los belicosos en causas yndinas* — "makers of war in causes un-

article on this poem entitled "Ensayo de interpretación de la poesía . . . número 199
del *Cancionero de Baena*," *RFE*, XV (1928), 354–374, would consider our poem as
written in 1420, on the basis of his political interpretation of the veiled allusions.
Without seeking to account for the politics (might not events of 1409–10 be equally
applicable?), I hold to my choice of dates because Buceta's application of the "schism
verses" to Benedict XIII is impossible; Benedict was never a friar.

39. *BAE*, XXXVI, 390a.

40. Menéndez y Pelayo, *Antología de poetas líricos castellanos* (new ed.; Santander,
1944), II, 174. For the background in greater detail, see the section entitled "Idea
Nacional" in María Rosa Lida de Malkiel's *Juan de Mena: Poeta del Prerrenacimiento
español* (Mexico City, 1950), pp. 537 ff., especially the lines from Gonzalo Martínez de
Medina addressed to the King (cited p. 541): "Placing his seat in Jerusalem, / Crowning his head with the Emperor's crown" — *En Jerusalem su sylla poniendo, / rreçi-
biendo corona de alto Emperador.*

just." In stanza 230 he calls upon Juan II to unite the Spanish kingdoms,

O príncipe bueno, o novel Agusto,	O new Augustus, good Prince
o lunbre de España, o rey mucho justo,	of Castile, King of Hispania,
pues rey de la tierra vos fizo El del Cielo.	mighty in justice, since the King of Heaven made you king of earth.

And in stanza 255 he addresses all men in authority:

por ende, vosotros, essos que mandades,	Therefore, O rulers of men, dis-
la yra, la yra bolued en los moros.	charge your anger and fury on the Moors.

The Marqués de Santillana

In his *Comedieta de Ponça*, written before the poet could have learned that Alfonso V of Aragon had successfully renewed his campaigns in Italy, Santillana announces, or causes Fortune to announce, campaigns never undertaken: the conquest of the Holy Land, of Babylon, India, and Egypt. This poem transcends the limitations of local kingdoms: the poet, a nobleman of Castile, laments the misfortune of the kings of Aragon and of Navarre at the same time that he magnifies their prophesied triumphs. The *Comedieta*, no less than Mena's *Laberinto*, advocates a providencialist goal: Christian and political unity, final victory over the infidel.[41]

Juan de Lucena

In a treatise entitled *Libro de vida beata* (1463), translated and adapted from a Latin work of similar title by Bartolomeo Fazio, Lucena exclaimed: "What do you mean when you say 'his?' And what, when you say 'another's?' One law, one faith, one religion, one homeland, one sheepfold and one shepherd [see John 10:16] for all: He is most 'mine' who partakes most of this spirit." [42] The Biblical note here sounded will be repeated again and again during the next two centuries.

41. Rafael Lapesa, *Los decires narrativos del Marqués de Santillana* (Madrid, 1954), pp. 48, 58–60.
42. Cited by Margherita Morreale, "El tratado de Juan de Lucena sobre la felicidad," *NRFH*, IX (1955), 8.

The Reign of Ferdinand and Isabella

Gómez Manrique (d. 1490?), in a poem called *Instruction for Princes*, included four lines which look forward, as it were, to the moderation of the imperial policy by Charles V (*Cancionero castellano . . .* , II, 119):

A las conquistas injustas
no vos quiero prouocar;
mas, señor, para cobrar
las cosas que vos son justas.

Not to unjust conquests would I incite you, sire; But rather to the recovery of what is justly yours.

At some time prior to his death in 1492 Pedro de Cartagena, in *coplas* (*ibid.*, p. 521) addressed to the Queen, gives special significance to each of the letters of her name.

que la *I* denota imperio,
la *S* señorear
toda la tierra y la mar . . .

For the *I* denotes *imperium*, and *S* signifies your rule over all lands and seas . . .

The four remaining letters of the name do not concern us here, but after using the six letters in Isabel, he then adds the *R* of *Regina*:

Dios querrá, sin que se yerre,
que rematés vos la *R*
en el nombre de G*R*anada: . . .
no estarés contenta bien
hasta que en Jerusalem
pinten las armas reales.

God will assuredly grant that the *R* shall win for you not only the *R* of G*R*anada; nor will Your Majesty rest till she sees her royal crest on the walls of Jerusalem.

Power on land and sea; Jerusalem conquered. . . . In 1496 Juan del Encina, the father of the Spanish secular drama, voiced the additional note of peace among Christians, writing in the dedication of his *Cancionero*: "May your Majesties be pleased to receive this small present from your servitor, with those triumphant hands and the serene countenance that sheds light on all the Spanish Monarchy, moderates and governs the Western Region, and invites to the friendship of peace not only the princes of the Christian religion, but even a great part of the barbarous nations of the West." [43] There is here no hint, it will be observed, of bringing

43. Ed. facsimile (Madrid, 1928), fol. xxxi *verso*. The poet recognizes the pope's famous dividing line established in the Treaty of Tordesillas (1494) whereby lands to the east of that line were assigned to the Portuguese, with Spain retaining the lands to the west.

legitimate Christian princes under the imperial rule of Spain. On the following folio of this same *Cancionero*, Encina dedicates to Prince John, son of the Catholic Monarchs, his translation and adaptation of Virgil's *Eclogues*, declaring that the Prince (whose untimely death changed the course of the "Monarquía Española") will extend the bounds and limits, not only of knowledge, but also those "del imperio."

In his *Triumph of Fame*, in the same volume (fol. li), Encina sounds two notes not heard before — somber notes of persecution, characteristic of that age in all countries [44] — as the poet visualizes thieves and traitors suffering adequate penalties, and in addition:

al vn cabo estavan ereges quemados y al otro la fe muy mucho ensalçada; por un cabo entrava la santa cruzada, por otro salían judíos malvados.	At one side I beheld the burning of heretics, at the other the exaltation of the holy Faith; at one side the Crusade with its flying banners, at the other, the accursed Jews marching off to exile.

In 1504 Isabella passed to her reward, leaving to her people a mandate for military and political action in Africa. After her, Cisneros, as archbishop of Toledo, gave new impulse to the idea of the crusade. Islam must be annihilated, Christianity restored to the purity of its primitive origins, Jerusalem reconquered.[45]

The Spanish campaigns in Italy against the invading French, with the famous victories of Cerignola, the Garigliano, and Gaeta, were celebrated in Latin verse by Giambattista Cantalicio.[46] To the hero of that war, the "Great Captain" Gonzalo Fernández de Córdoba (d. 1515), Juan de Narváez dedicated in 1506 his poem *Las valencianas lamentaciones*, in which a more aggressive sense of

44. Religious tolerance came only as a result of stalemate in the religious struggles of the sixteenth and seventeenth centuries. The dream of peace and good will on earth was to be realized by force if, and whenever, necessary. This attitude will be discussed below.

45. M. Bataillon, *Erasmo y España* (Mexico City–Buenos Aires, 1950), I, 61.

46. B. Croce, *La Spagna nella vita italiana durante la Rinascenza* (Bari, 1917), pp. 125, 199; see also Menéndez y Pelayo, *op. cit.*, III, 144–45. Earlier, in 1495, when the French successes in Italy were cause for official worry in Spain, Ferdinand commissioned Francisco de Madrid to write a dramatic *Eclogue*, a propaganda piece, probably performed before the Spanish court, to present a public explanation of the emperor's position. See the edition (with introduction) by J. E. Gillet in *HR*, XI (1943), 275–303. Its appeal is for peace, in line with the Spanish irenic ideal (pp. 278–79).

empire is discernible: "The Spaniards hold sway over the lands they have conquered, sail 'unnavigable' seas, take by storm 'impregnable' fortresses, obey no overlord except God who gives them the victory. If they do not command the whole world, it is not because they lack the power to do so" — this last point being, of course, determined by Charles' limited ambition to retain what was already his (see above).[47]

In 1509 Cisneros launched his campaign against Oran in Africa. On August 22 the French Christian humanist Charles de Bovelles wrote in glowing terms celebrating the victory. The road to Jerusalem, he said, will be opened: *Erit sepulchrum eius gloriosum* — Christ's sepulcher will be rendered glorious. On March 10, 1510, Bovelles writes again, communicating electrifying news: the king of the Persians has accepted baptism. May God bring back the times sung by Virgil: *Iam redit et virgo* — a Virgin returns. May one faith and one Prince reign throughout the world (Bataillon, *op. cit.*, I, 65 ff.).

In 1513 Bartolomé de Torres Naharro composed his *Psalm* on the glorious victory of the Spaniards over the Venetians (allied with the French), with its highly significant line, *que somos reyes del suelo* — "we are the lords of the earth." This is still not "empire" in the sense of the empires of antiquity. The poem ends:

Alçemos a Dios las manos,	Let us lift our hands to God to
suplicando sin siniestros	beg for peace among Christians,
que ponga paz en christianos:	free from unnatural struggles:
cuando no, vençan los nuestros.	until then, may the king's arms win.[48]

In 1516 the same poet wrote his *Romance I*, a lament on the death of Ferdinand the Catholic in which he enumerates the King's victories — Granada, Naples, Navarre (usurped by the French), and the *islas Indias por el mar* — the Indies, still thought of as islands, not a continent. The Christian note is sounded as Torres Naharro

47. "No sólo nos son tractables / las tierras que conquistamos, / mas los mares navegamos / que fueron innavegables. / Pugnamos quasi impugnables, / a ninguno obedecemos, / salvo a Dios, por quien tenemos / las victorias memorables. / E aún si carescemos / del mundo todo mandar, / la causa quiero callar, / pues mostramos que podemos" (Menéndez y Pelayo, *op. cit.*, III, 110).

48. *Propalladia and Other Works of Bartolomé de Torres Naharro*, ed. J. E. Gillet (Bryn Mawr, Pennsylvania, 1943–51), I, 234–35, 241.

visualizes the King's entry into heaven to join the Great Captain, who preceded him by a year *(ibid.,* pp. 218, 222):

Con el cathólico nombre	With the Catholic name he bore
su biuir ha conformado.	his life was ever consistent. . . .
. . . .	Such a King and such a Captain
Tal rey y tal capitán	never entered heaven before.
nunca en el cielo han entrado.	

Alonso Hernández in his *Historia Parthenopea* (1516) reviewed the reign just ended *sub specie voluntatis Dei,* as a manifestation of God's will: *Y aquestas son cosas del alto tejidas* — "And these are things ordained from on high" (Menéndez y Pelayo, *op. cit.,* III, 121).

The Reign of Charles V

In spite of Charles' protestations that he sought only what territories were his by legal right, there crept into the consciousness of the Spaniards during his reign a broader concept, born, perhaps, of the influence of his minister, Mercurino di Gattinara. Gattinara, inspired by Dante's *De Monarchia,* hoped to establish a universal Christian empire and — as Keniston noted — guided Charles toward the realization of this ideal "as far as he could" (see above). I shall first quote a poem of 1532, composed by Pedro Barrantes Maldonado in praise of his Spanish compatriots, a poem which, as he set off to the war in Germany against the Turk, he posted on walls in all the places through which he passed. It begins:

Españoles, españoles,	Spaniards, Spaniards, bear in mind
¡cuánto debéis al Señor;	the greatness of your debt to God:
que todos os han temor!	all the world stands in your fear.

The *caballero* who recites it declares:

Desde Alcántara hasta Hungría	From Alcántara to Hungary I
vuestro nombre puesto he	have posted your name in every
en cada *logis* que veía	lodging-house I saw, with a device
y una letra que decía:	to all declaring: *Far from home,*
Cuanto más lejos más fe.	*yet ever true.* This sign I set up
Púselo en España, Francia,	in Spain, in France — Aquitaine,
Aquitania y Normandía,	Normandy, Brittany and Picardy.
La Bretaña y Picardía,	I posted it in Burgundy, in Flan-
Borgoña, Flandes, Brabancia;	ders and Brabant too; I left

en los Alpes le dejé,	it behind in the Alps, in Swabia
en Suevia y la Franconía,	and Franconia, while I in Ger-
y en Alemania quedé,	many remained, with a device to
una letra que decía:	all declaring: *Far from home, yet*
Cuanto más lejos más fe.	*ever true.*[49]

The author of these lines, untouched by the irenic spirit of European conciliation entertained by the Emperor and his theological
counselors, writes these words *en loor de los españoles* — extolling
the men of Spain. These Spaniards are feared everywhere, and this
in itself is a Divine blessing: *¡Cuánto debéis al Señor!* — "How great
your debt to God!" Pedro Barrantes Maldonado, like Alonso Hernández at the ending of the preceding reign, finds that "these
things are ordained from on high." Barrantes is "drunk with sight
of power" and he writes in the spirit of Dante, of Gattinara, of Juan
Ginés de Sepúlveda.

Fiet unum ovile.[50] At some time after 1530, probably after the
victory over the Protestants at Mühlberg (1547), Hernando de
Acuña (d. 1580?) penned what is perhaps the most famous of all
the expressions of the Gattinara dream. It is addressed to the King:

> The time draws near, or seems at length fulfilled —
> The age of glory promised us by Heaven —
> When on this earth one shepherd of one flock
> Shall rule in singleness our destinies.
>
> Your Majesty's true zeal, your victories,
> Mark the beginning of the happy age
> And to the expectant world at length foretell
> One King, one Empire, and a single sword.
>
> The earth in part now knows, in part awaits
> The extension of this happy monarchy,
> Won by your arms in wars forever just;
>
> For he who bears Christ's standard shall receive
> From the Almighty Hand, not that alone,
> But, by His grace, dominion universal.[51]

49. Gallardo, *Ensayo*, II, col. 38, no. 1314.
50. "There shall be one sheepfold."
51. Ya se acerca, Señor, o es ya llegada / la edad gloriosa en que promete el Cielo /
una grey y un pastor solo en el suelo, / por suerte a vuestros tiempos reservada; / ya
tan alto principio en tal jornada / os muestra el fin de vuestro santo celo, / y anuncia
al mundo para más consuelo / un monarca, un imperio y una espada; / ya el orbe
de la tierra siente en parte, / y espera en todo vuestra monarquía, / conquistada por
vos en justa guerra; / que a quien ha dado Cristo su estandarte, / dará el segundo

These ideas were widespread. In the 1532 edition of his *Orlando Furioso* Ariosto had declared that God had designated Charles to be the possessor of the diadem of Augustus, of Trajan, of Marcus Aurelius, and of Severus, and to possess all the earth: under this emperor there shall be but one sheepfold, one shepherd. Antonio Minturno in his *Rime et prose* (1559) repeats the prophecy: "un ovile ed un pastore." [52]

The idea of their king as "good shepherd" had not always appeared so obvious to Charles' Spanish subjects. Indeed, he began his reign with the country in a state of general tension which broke out into open warfare. When he confronted the *Cortes* of Valladolid in 1517 [53] he did not receive unanimous support, being recognized only as joint ruler with his mother (Queen Juana la Loca), and that only after a solemn promise to maintain Castilian privileges and to exclude foreigners from office. Four years later, with the battle of Villalar and the executions that followed the royal victory, Charles' personal authority became firmly established — so firmly that Juan Rodríguez de Pisa, deputy of Granada to the *Cortes* of Valladolid in 1523 and a man of very considerable political independence, could declare that Spain's present moment was worthy to be sung by Virgil himself: "The Golden Age so long awaited is now with us, and we have the great happiness of being ruled over and governed by a Prince who is glorious, most just, most prudent, God-fearing, and — a miracle in one so young — a perfect epitome of virtues. . . . The Prince who governs us is the most excellent in all the world . . . , deserving of other empires and other dominions — if there be any such — greater than those he possesses." [54]

más dichoso día / en que vencido el mar, venza la tierra" (in *Spanish Poetry of the Golden Age*, ed. M. A. Buchanan [Toronto, 1942], p. 46).

52. See Buchanan, "Annotations . . . ," pp. 466–67. Luigi Tansillo (d. 1568), in a *Canzone a Carlo V*, repeated the phrase "un pastor solamente ed un ovile" (cited by Croce, *op. cit.*, p. 243).

53. This royal visit to Valladolid was celebrated by the performance of a *Royal Eclogue* by the Bachiller de la Pradilla. The play voices the fervent desire that Charles succeed to the throne, and contains a prophecy of his future greatness. J. P. W. Crawford says of it: "it is chiefly interesting as an attempt to glorify the future emperor by a biased presentation of facts" (*Spanish Drama before Lope de Vega* [Philadelphia, 1937], p. 59).

54. Cited by Juan Sánchez Montes, "Actitudes del español en la época de Carlos V," *Estudios americanos*, III (1951), 194–95.

With the victory over the French at Pavia (1525), events began to move faster, as a minority of Spain's elite — among whom some of the King's most powerful advisers were most active — became more convinced that Charles would impose religious peace (Bataillon, *op. cit.*, I, 262). After the sack of Rome (1527) and the victories over the Turks at Mohacz and Buda, the faith of this minority was raised to feverish pitch: political and religious forces worked together to form a complex dream of Spanish hegemony, Christian unity, and general reform (*ibid.*, pp. 262–63).

Literature as propaganda. Since the time of Ferdinand the Catholic, literary works, especially dramatic performances, had been used as vehicles of publicity and royal propaganda.[55] The battle of Pavia (1525) was celebrated by a play — which perhaps was actually performed — by Andrés Ortiz, in which all Nature and, with her, certain shepherds rejoice at the good turn in the fortunes of *el grande Pastor, Señor de la España* — "the great shepherd, Lord of all Spain." The King of France is presented as suffering retribution for having interfered (by invading Navarre) with Spain's plans to defeat the Moors in the time of Ferdinand. Even Rhodes would not have been lost to the Turks if Francis I had been loyal to the Christian cause. Now, after the victory at Pavia, it is certain that Charles will exercise hegemony (*pujar*) over all kings and will conquer the Holy Land.[56]

When the Treaty of Cambrai in 1529 ended the rivalry of Spain and France in Italy, another play was written to celebrate the event, a *Farsa* by Hernán López de Yanguas, stressing again the note of peace, exactly as Charles himself was to stress it in 1536 when, speaking in Spanish before Pope Paul III, he sharply denounced France as the disturber of the tranquility of Christendom, challenged Francis I to single combat, and concluded with the almost ritualistic formula: *I want peace, I want peace, I want peace.*[57]

France was not the only source of trouble; there was also the Holy See. Before the peace of Cambrai there occurred the sack of

55. See above, note 46, on the *Egloga* of Francisco de Madrid.

56. J. E. Gillet (ed.), "A Spanish Play on the Battle of Pavia (1525)," *PMLA*, XLV (1930), 521, 523, 526.

57. J. E. Gillet in the introduction to his edition of Madrid's *Egloga* (previously cited, note 46), p. 279.

Rome, a dazzling victory over the pope, as terrible to contemporaries as the fall of France was to us in 1940, yet also a source of
hope: at last the Emperor had the power and the opportunity to
restore the Church (Bataillon, *loc. cit.*).

It is impossible here to give an account — as Bataillon has done
so admirably — of these incredible events. Suffice it to say that
Charles chose to deny responsibility for the alarming turn they had
taken,[58] and to offer in advance his own submission to the decisions
of a general council of the Church. Charles' message to all Christian princes was redacted by his Latin secretary, Alfonso de Valdés,
and it is to Valdés' two literary dialogues that we now turn. In them
the sack of Rome is represented as the judgment of an offended and
angry God. In them, also, we have the boldest expression of Spanish
Erasmianism in its religious, moral, and political aspects. To present the possibility that good may redound from the disaster, Valdés
wrote a satirical colloquy, more harsh than any of Erasmus,[59] entitled *Dialogue on the Recent Happenings in Rome*, following it
a year later with a continuation, the *Dialogue of Mercury and
Charon*.[60]

Valdés opens with a declaration of the innocence of the Emperor
and, as his second point, of the justice of the Eternal City's punishment. The one who broke the peace, he claims, was Clement,
though the doctrine of Christ condemns overwhelmingly the monstrous scandal of a warring pope. The religious aspects of the
dialogues, the argument between the interlocutors over what constitutes the inner essence of Christianity, must be left for our discussion of Erasmus in Spain. Here our concern is with the imperial
policy voiced by the emperor's secretary. That policy becomes clear
in the second of the two dialogues: if, as is hoped, Charles now
succeeds in reforming the Church, he will not only perform a great
service to God; he will obtain for himself in this world the greatest
fame ever achieved by a ruling prince, and it will be said, from
now till the end of the world, that Christ founded the Church and
the Emperor Charles reformed it.[61] The reform, as Valdés con-

58. The blame was cast upon evil-intentioned advisors of Pope Clement VII.
59. I follow closely Bataillon, *op. cit.*, I, 430 ff.
60. *Diálogo de las cosas ocurridas en Roma* and *Diálogo de Mercurio y Carón*, ed.
J. F. Montesinos (Madrid; 1928, 1929).
61. Juan Luis Vives expressed the same thought in almost identical language

ceives it, is to be carried out in the spirit of the Evangelical Christianity of Erasmus. The religion of Christ will at last be made worthy of its founder. In the *Dialogue of Mercury and Charon* the events of Rome are in the background and the new enemies are France and England. Valdés presents his sovereign as a king whose soul is exceptionally suited to its great function, "one of the loftiest incarnations of human nobility" (Bataillon, *op. cit.*, I, 454). The political principle defended is that of Erasmus' *Training of a Christian Prince*: the king reigns only to serve his people. This principle, incarnated in Charles, is set over against the arbitrary tyranny of his royal enemies, Francis I and Henry VIII. The whole dialogue is an affirmation of an ideal, that of a return to Christian responsibility—in all the purity of the words and the intention of the Galilean. Valdés favors a patriarchal monarchy, yet without shade or shadow of absolutism: royalty illumined by Grace.[62]

In 1528 Fray Gonzalo de Arredondo y Arévalo published at Burgos and dedicated to Charles V an *Exhortation to Attack the Turks and Defeat Them and Annihilate the Mohammedan Sect as Well as All Other Infidels, and to Win the Holy Land in Blessed Triumph*. This forms part of a collective volume entitled *Mighty Fortress of the Faith*.[63] On August 3, 1529, Juan Luis Vives wrote to Erasmus: "Spain is the Empress and directress of all things. . . . You must have heard that the Emperor set sail from Barcelona with a mighty fleet . . . : in addition to the Court and the flower of Spanish nobility, as many as ten thousand marines, hand-picked from all Spain."[64] In 1532, the year of the withdrawal of the Turks from before Vienna (also the year of the comet), Juan Maldonado, newly appointed professor of humanities at Burgos, in a Latin dialogue entitled *Somnium* (modeled on Cicero's *Somnium Scipionis*), tells of being caught up, in a dream, into interplanetary space. Among his visions is one of recently Christianized America, where the good savages are so eager to test their orthodoxy in the

(Bataillon, *op. cit.*, I, 445). See M. Puigdollers, *La filosofía española de Luis Vives* (Barcelona, 1940), p. 20.

62. See our Volume II, Index, *s.v.* Grace, divine.

63. See José Simón Díaz, *Bibliografía de la literatura hispánica* (Madrid, 1961), VI, 71, no. 720.

64. *Obras completas*, trans. L. Riber (Madrid, 1947–48), II, 1715–16.

new faith that they ask the interplanetary traveler serious questions concerning Christian rites. The friar replies that he is unable to satisfy their curiosity without access to his books. The Spaniards, he says, are settled on the coast; soon they will come to dispel the last shreds of ignorance. In the meantime, the Indians should pray that their utopia be preserved in all its purity (Bataillon, *op. cit.*, II, 251–52).

In 1535–1536, as we learn from the private correspondence of Juan de Valdés (the semi-Protestant and self-exiled brother of Charles' Latin secretary Alfonso), it seems that Spain wished to make possible, even at the expense of her own welfare, a general European enterprise not unlike the unification of Spain by Castile during the two preceding reigns. There existed the keenest desire that Europe, having finally resolved to live in peaceful coexistence, should confront the Mohammedans in battle and speed the reform of Catholicism — discipline, uses, organization, and worship — thus restoring to Christianity the meaning and sense of purpose it had lost or was in danger of losing. If necessary, it was felt, this should be imposed by the superior force of Spain and the Empire.[65]

In 1540 Pero Mexía wrote, in his much translated miscellany *Silva de varia lección*, the following:

> Thus Christianity is sustained and protected by his [Charles'] solicitude and care, as he spends his income and his patrimony in its defense, subduing in person kingdoms and cities acquired by the Turk . . . with great personal effort and great danger to his life; it is sustained no less by his holy purpose and his diligence in continuing along the same path, until he shall have restored the Imperium Romanum and the Faith of Christ to the estate and power that they had in antiquity. And surely we must believe that if the emperors who ruled in the time of Mohammed had been of this mettle, the empire would not have suffered the fate it did; and if God gives life to the emperor we now have, those errors of former times will in large part be corrected.[66]

Alejo Venegas expressed the same confidence in 1540 in his *Differencias de libros que ay en el vniuerso*:[67] "though the Devil wander loose throughout the world, he shall not prevail against the unity of the Holy Catholic church." In 1547, two years after

65. *Cartas inéditas de Juan de Valdés*, ed. J. F. Montesinos (Madrid, 1931), Introduction, p. cxi.

66. Ed. La Sociedad de Bibliófilos Españoles (Madrid, 1933–34), I, 87.

67. Ed. Salamanca (1572), fol. 413v.

the convocation of the Council of Trent, an anonymous Spanish humanist wrote in a *Dialogue between Charon and the Soul of Pedro Luis Farnese*: "The Emperor has taken the matter so to heart and has carried it so far, that [God's will] cannot fail to be done." [68]

In 1548 Prince Philip, the heir apparent soon to be crowned Philip II of Spain (1556), made a state visit to his future possessions "in lower Germany." Passing through Milan on the way, he was greeted by a triumphal arch, with this inscription in Latin: "Fortunate descendant of the Caesars, the Christian Religion rejoices to receive you, because you are the son of your father — greatest of all the Caesars — and because you will extend the boundaries of the Christian empire to the farthest lands of the earth." [69] Here again it will be observed that the expansion hoped for is religious — the Christian empire shall fill all the world. There is no thought of extending the secular Empire by subjugating Christian princes.

The Emperor's withdrawal. In accordance with his Erasmian ideals, Alfonso de Valdés had presented Charles in 1528 as the "good shepherd" of his people. In 1556, when Charles in his weariness and frustration — not a single one of his victories had been definitive — laid down the burden of empire and passed on to his son the responsibilities of the Spanish monarchy, he was eulogized, in a sermon by Fray Cipriano de Huerga, as "the good shepherd who gives his life for his sheep." At times the humanists — those more influenced by imperial Rome than by Erasmus and his Christian pacifism — had placed great hope in the Emperor's sword. The abdication came less than ten years after his great military victory over the Protestants, at Mühlberg (1547). Now, at the end of his reign, Charles is pictured as consumed by care, by the ravages of age, by the bitterness of the gall he had had to drink. His greatest sorrow is his failure to pacify Germany as a "good shepherd," his inability to cure the rebellious land of its illness. Neither sword, nor fire, nor the word of God has been of any avail. Philip, already king of England and now head of the Spanish monarchy, must

68. *BAE*, XXXVI, 7.
69. J. C. Calvete de Estrella, *El felicísimo viaje de . . . Don Felipe . . . a sus tierras de la Baja Alemania*, ed. La Sociedad de Bibliófilos Españoles (Madrid, 1930), I, 62.

continue to imitate the "good shepherd" [70] — his father, Charles I of Spain.

The Reign of Philip II

During this reign there was a brief period — between the victory over the Turks at Lepanto (1571) and the defeat of the Armada (1588) — when Spaniards could believe that their dream of universal pacification under Spanish hegemony would become a reality.[71] Yet in this reign also strong voices were raised against the imperial idea. Fray Cipriano de Huerga, in his sermon on Charles' retirement from the government in 1556, spoke of him — without protest — as having sought to achieve the healing of Christian society by means of fire and sword, as well as the word of God. Others protested. Francisco de Vitoria (d. 1546), whose *Relectiones Theologicae* were printed in 1557, opposed the modern imperial views of diplomats like Diego Hurtado de Mendoza (d. 1575), who had insisted that Milan must be held as a power lever and key to Italy, or like Sepúlveda (d. 1573), who based his concept of empire on military and political supremacy and cultural superiority (Maravall, *op. cit.*, pp. 310, 330). Vitoria has been called the destroyer of medieval Christianity. This is an exaggeration, to be sure, but it is a fact that Vitoria "founded a new universalism that did away with the limitations of Medieval civilization" (*ibid.*, p. 262). Vitoria and his followers, dedicated intellectually to a new system including a plurality of states, "disassembled, piece by piece, the old structure of the Medieval Empire" (p. 248).

Vitoria was unwilling to rely on the sword. War in itself, he contended, cannot establish the truth of the faith. Therefore, infidels defeated in war will not believe; they will merely feign belief. To be a party to such a fiction is a monstrous sacrilege (Gallegos Rocafull, *op. cit.*, p. 35). Vitoria taught categorically that it is not permissible for a Christian prince to make war in order to enlarge his territories, to win glory, or to obtain any other advantage

70. M. Bataillon, "Charles-Quint bon pasteur, selon Fray Cipriano de Huerga," *BHi*, L (1948), 398 ff., especially 402–3. See also M. Morreale, "Carlos V Rex Bonus, Felix Imperator," *Estudios y documentos: Cuadernos de historia moderna*, núm. 3 (1954), pp. 7–20.

71. Pedro Laín Entralgo, *La antropología en la obra de Fray Luis de Granada* (Madrid, 1946), p. 366.

(*ibid.*, p. 37). A just war is always and exclusively an instrument of justice; the victorious prince is to consider himself a judge between the attacking state and the victim-state, since, as Vitoria believes, the just cause must prevail (p. 39).[72] Thus the idea of empire is given a new and restricted interpretation. In effect, it amounts to the submission of individual and sovereign peoples to a single norm of justice. The Spanish *imperium*, therefore, does not annihilate the right of the Indians to enjoy self-government; let them retain their laws and usages within the superior judicial order.[73]

Leaving the professional theorists, let us listen to the opinions of a humanist, dramatist, and man of letters, in the year 1568. Juan de Mal Lara in his *Filosofía vulgar* declares that for forty years certain Spaniards in the New World have been heading for hell, since their purpose is to acquire gold and silver.[74] He here refers (without naming them) to the Pizarros in Peru, rebellious tyrants in the Indies, sons of honorable fathers, who yet went there "in search of evil for themselves, though unthinking persons consider it a good" (*ibid.*).

Américo Castro has seen in Fray Luis de León, whose *De los nombres de Cristo* appeared first in 1583, "an absolute anti-imperialist."[75] The assertion may be excessive, for there are two lines in Fray Luis' poem on the death of Prince Carlos, son of Philip II, which voice the grief, not only of Spain and Flanders, of Germany and Italy, but of

> That fair and rich New World
> Compared to which all empires are as naught.[76]

Fray Luis does not, therefore, condemn the Spanish-Portuguese adventure in the Indies as Fray Juan de Pineda will condemn it a few years later (see below). What Fray Luis does condemn is the

72. Loopholes were necessary, and Vitoria provides one: where there is no hope of reducing the enemy to peace, the conqueror may, even after surrender, exterminate the enemy combatants (*ibid.*, p. 40).

73. This "superior judicial order" is an abstract concept — as abstract as "Roman law" became when once the Roman Caesars had disappeared (*ibid.*, pp. 135–36).

74. Ed. A. Vilanova (Barcelona, 1958–59), III, 85.

75. "Erasmo en tiempo de Cervantes," *RFE*, XVIII (1931), 354, n. 2.

76. From the poem beginning *Quien viere el suntuoso*: "y de aquel mundo nuevo y rico, / con quien cualquier imperio es corto y chico."

use of the sword to obtain merely the fruits of war: "You hope to obtain land—an ephemeral good —, though God's word promises you Heaven. . . . You hope to be lords of others; all God promises is that you may be masters of yourselves. . . . To conquer other peoples — well do we know what that means: the value of weapons is daily apparent to us; there is nothing that the flesh understands so well, so eagerly desires, as wealth and dominion." [77]

We have mentioned Fray Juan de Pineda, whose *Agricultura Christiana* has been cited so often in other volumes of the present work, and again we quote his opinion. Man was born to labor, says Fray Juan, and this labor should be in the service of his Lord and Master, who is God — just as the ox labors in the service of the man who owns him. Yet men slave instead in the service of covetous avarice, penetrating diverse kingdoms and swallowing up diverse seas. "If you doubt it," he continues, "look at what happens to the Spaniards as they penetrate the Orient and the Occident, enduring dangers and hardships such that no sane man could consider them as having anything to do with sanity. The adventurers would appear to be as irrational as Ovid's frightened cow, as told in the fable of Io." [78]

Sic et Non — Fray Luis and Fray Juan condemn selfish or worldly conquest in works whose subject matter is not political theory but the Christian life. But Fray Luis, for all his harsh words against self-seekers at the expense of others, viewed the New World — object of conquest though it had been — in a light which is certainly not one of condemnation: *y de aquel mundo nuevo y rico, / con quien cualquier imperio es corto y chico.* His view, had he expounded it fully, must surely have been similar to that of the Jesuit José de Acosta in 1590: "And to Spain has come this great treasure of the Indies, in accordance with the desire of Providence that certain kingdoms serve others . . . if these use wisely the goods which they have." [79] Acosta writes at a time when the possessions (and the crowns) of Spain and of Portugal are united

---

77. Quoted by Castro, *loc. cit.* See also the remarks of Ricardo del Arco on Fray Luis in *La idea de imperio en la política y la literatura españolas* (Madrid, 1944), pp. 344–45.

78. Ed. Salamanca (1589), I, fol. 160v.

79. *Historia natural y moral de las Indias* (Madrid, 1792), I 192–93.

(since 1580), and he writes with awe and wonder. The Jesuits in their annual letters report (he tells us) that great new provinces are being discovered between Peru and Brazil. Time will determine whether or not this is so; for, knowing the diligence and daring of the discoverers to date, one may well believe that the process will go on, "in order that the Holy Gospel may be preached throughout the universe of men, since the two discovering powers have been joined together, coming full circle. The two crowns have united their discoveries, and it is a marvelous and sobering thought that sailing east the Portuguese came to China and Japan, while the Spaniards, traveling west, reached the Philippines, next door to China" (*ibid.*, pp. 170–71).

This joining of the possessions of the two crowns Acosta regards as a "special favor of Heaven," to the end that they should encircle the globe with their power. God has done this for the benefit of the dwellers in those territories, far removed from the seat of the Church, which is Rome, and from the head of the Church, who is the pope, since only by obedience to the faith can their souls be saved. And God has done it also to strengthen the faith and the Church in Europe, where heretics combat both. Since God, who gives and takes away dominion, has so ordained it, all should pray for the success of the Catholic king, who in this cause expends what he receives from the Indies, and needs much more (pp. 202–3).

And what of the poets? Being poets, they were more prone to be swept up to heights of enthusiasm by the thought of Virgil's famous line — *parcere subjectis et debellare superbos*, an expression of the ideal of secular empire which strangely has almost exact literal support in a sentence from St. Paul (I Peter 5:5): "God resisteth the proud and giveth grace to the humble." Fernando de Herrera, in his exhaustive commentary on the poems of Garcilaso de la Vega (1580), devotes brilliant pages to an expression of patriotism, to exalting Spanish achievements: the fifteenth-century reduction of all Spain to the religion of Christ; the taking of the measure of France and the reduction of her haughtiness; the penetrating of distant regions and unknown seas; the exploits of the Great Captain in the time of Ferdinand; the conquest of Mexico by Cortés in the reign of Charles; and the domination of the powerful heathen peoples of the West in an action that pushes into the shade the achievement of the ancients.[80]

Herrera's *Ode on the Victory of Lepanto* (1571) has been called "perhaps the greatest political poem in the Spanish language." [81] "The Song of Moses over the drowned Egyptian chariots, the Lament for Tyre, and a couple of Psalms were gathered by Herrera to make a statement of Spanish theocratic nationhood" (*ibid.*) — but hardly of the sense of empire. To Herrera, the victory is not man's but God's, though achieved by the faith and the strong hand of a Christian prince.[82] On the other hand, in a sonnet of Herrera to Philip II, urging him to avenge the defeat of the Portuguese at Alcazarquivir (1578), the idea of empire — Christian empire — is present:

> Who against you, and who against your Spain
> Would dare to give defiance and risk the fate
> Of being crushed beneath your conquering feet? [83]

In an ode to the Marqués de Tarifa (*Si alguna vez mi pena*), Herrera exults in

> The everlasting glory
> Of the unconquered Spaniards;[84]

and in a retrospective sonnet to Charles V he winds the martial trumpet:

> There now remains no spot in all the earth
> But is a trophy of your conquering power,
> And Mars lays down his laurels at your feet.[85]

Alonso de Ercilla (d. 1594), though in his epic *La Araucana* he is ready to admit the harm done by Spanish greed (the end of Canto I), is thrilled by the power of his nation to strike down the proud. Praising Charles' abdication (after treading with victorious feet Arctic and Antarctic regions, the Emperor triumphed over

---

80. The text is given by Adolphe Coster, *Fernando de Herrera (El Divino), 1534–1597* (Paris, 1908), p. 256, n. 2.

81. William J. Entwistle, *Cervantes* (Oxford, 1940), p. 21.

82. *Poesías*, ed. V. García de Diego (Madrid, 1914), pp. 44–45.

83. "¿Quién contra vos, quién contra el reino Esperio, / bastará alçar la frente, qu'al instante / no se derribe a vuestros pies rendido?" (*ibid.*, p. 198).

84. "La siempre insine gloria / d'aquellos Españoles no domados" (p. 109).

85. "Que ya en la tierra i mar no queda parte / que no sea trofeo de tu gloria, / ni le resta más onra al fiero Marte" (pp. 167–68).

Fortune and turned his thoughts toward heaven), the poet extolls (Canto XVII) the exploits of Philip—of him who, at Saint Quentin,

> Struck down with one swift stroke the arrogance,
> The presumption and the pride of hostile France,

and who, at Lepanto,

> Upset the overweaning pride of Turkey,
> Reducing to mere matchwood all her fleet.[86]

Amid all this exultation, the Evangelical note of one sheepfold and one shepherd is not forgotten. In 1584 Juan Rufo, in his *Austriada* (Canto XXIV), remembers the emotional appeal of a hope still cherished against all hope:

> The time shall come when in the whole world's vastness
> One shepherd shall hold sway, one monarchy.[87]

Another author of a heroic poem, Cristóbal de Virués (d. 1609), in his *Monserrate* (Canto XX) sings of

> A single shepherd in a single fold.[88]

About the year 1590, as we pass inevitably from the Renaissance to the post-Renaissance period—during which the frustrations become definitive as the victories had never been—a certain Licenciate Lorenzo de Valenzuela, in an ode to the patron saint of Seville, nevertheless imagines Seville's river, the Guadalquivir (or Betis in poetic language), as receiving—not giving—tribute from the ocean and as imposing its laws on the latter. The thousand sails coming out of the West are filled, not with air but with treasure, which converts the river's sand into mountains of silver. All this is true, yet it is because of a higher reason—the blood of her martyr—that Seville has always been

> Shield of the Faith, Honor of Spain, envy of the World.[89]

86. "para bajar de la enemiga Francia / la presunción, orgullo y arrogancia"; "la soberbia otomana derrocada, / su marítima fuerza destruída" (quoted by Del Arco, *op. cit.*, p. 284).

87. "Tiempo vendrá en que el mundo dé aposento / a un pastor solo y a una monarquía" (quoted *ibid.*, p. 223).

88. "Solo un pastor en un aprisco solo" (quoted *ibid.*).

89. "En ti siempre ha tenido / la fe escudo, honra España, imbidia el mundo" (*Cancionero de la Academia de los Nocturnos de Valencia*, ed. F. Martí Grajales [Valencia, 1905–12], II, 162).

EPILOGUE

Here we end our account of Spain's political expansion at the floodtide of the Renaissance, in the reign of Philip II. Having begun it with a soldier's boast of his far-flung campaigns: *Far from home, but ever true*,[90] we end it with a similar outpouring of cherished memories by another old campaigner (also cited above, note 86), Alonso de Ercilla:

> Many the lands I trod, many the nations:
> Over the frigid wastes of northern climes,
> South to the bitter cold of the Antarctic,
> Conquering your enemies in the Antipodes.
> Climates I changed, beheld new constellations;
> My frail ship sailed unnavegable gulfs,
> Extending as it went, my Sire, your glory
> To where the austral ice stands barrier.
> Not in America only; on sea and land
> Your standards led me on to Italy,
> Augsburg and Flanders, and from there to England
> (When that far kingdom sought you as its king).
> Then to Peru I passed, where swords rebellious
> Were raised in your disservice. . . . To the Araucan
> Wilds I passed next, and ever as before
> I left behind me enemies subdued,
> Only to seek new conquests, lands unheard of,
> Out on the world's far rim, in wars unending. . . .[91]

In a later volume we shall record not only the retreat from utopia, as already promised, but, in a broader sense, the decline toward the sunset of the dream — and the reality — of Spanish grandeur.

90. Pedro Barrantes Maldonado; see above, pp. 100–101.

91. "¡Cuántas tierras corrí, cuántas naciones / hacia el helado Norte atravesando, / y en las bajas antárticas regiones / el antípoda ignoto conquistando! / ¡Climas pasé, mudé constelaciones, / golfos innavegables navegando, / extendiendo, Señor, vuestra corona/ hasta casi la austral frígida zona! / ¿Qué jornadas también por mar y tierra / habéis hecho que deje de seguiros, / a Italia, Augusta, a Flandes, a Inglaterra / cuando el reino por rey vino a pediros? / De allí el furioso estruendo de la guerra / al Perú me llevó por más serviros, / do con suelto furor tantas espadas / estaban contra vos desenvainadas. / Y el rebelde indiano castigado / y el reino a la obediencia reducido, / pasé al remoto Arauco, que, alterado, / había del cuello el yugo sacudido; / y con prolija guerra sojuzgado, / y al odioso dominio sometido, / seguí luego adelante las conquistas / de las últimas tierras nunca vistas" (cited by Manuel de Montolíu, *El alma de España y sus reflejos en la literatura del siglo de oro* [Barcelona, n. d.], p. 48).

V · *Ut Sapientior Fiat:* Intellectual Expansion

The waters came to the surface first in Italy.
From that spring, and directly from Antiquity,
we Spaniards drank deep.
                    Dámaso Alonso [1]

In the preceding chapter we saw how Juan de Mal Lara, in the
dedication to Philip II of his *Filosofía vulgar,* declared that the
fruits of thought conceived in the minds of learned men are a
country's best fruits, the fruits most worthy of being offered to
one's king. Twenty-eight years later, Alonso López Pinciano causes
an interlocutor to say in his *Filosofía antigua poética:* "Study letters, and learn to appreciate them; thereafter — provided you have
bread and water — you will scorn all the treasure in the world compared with the pleasure they will give you." [2] This exaltation of
the intellectual life, the recognition of it as the supreme achievement of the individual and of the nation, was a product of the
Spanish Renaissance, a period best defined, perhaps, as the transition from a time of intellectual and aesthetic deficiency and imma-
turity to one of confident possession, in overflowing abundance, of
the goods of the mind and of the spirit. When the Renaissance is
over, when the period of transition has ripened its rich fruit, Francisco de Quevedo (d. 1645) will write this sonnet on the joy of
study:

> Withdrawn from the world's clamor, in the peace
> Of this rusticity, amid my books,
> I live in converse with the long departed
> And with my eyes I listen to the dead.
>   Not always understood, but ever open,
> They lead me onward, or restrain my impulse;
> And in their silent counterpoint they sing
> Mysterious notes of life's swift-moving dream.

1. *De los siglos oscuros al de oro* (Madrid, 1958), p. 197.
2. "Estudiad letras y sabed gustar dellas, y, en teniendo pan y agua, no estimareys
en un ardite todo el thesoro del mundo en comparación con el gusto que recibireys'
(ed. A. Carballo Picazo [Madrid, 1953], I, 136).

> The master spirits who preceded us
> The printing press has freed, dear friend José,
> From the dire ravages of vengeful Time.
> Each hour, once past, is gone for evermore;
> But if one has with happy study enriched me,
> My whitest counting-stone records its passing.[3]

How it became possible, in Spain, to write such glowing testimonies to the intellectual wealth of the culture in which their authors were immersed, is the theme of the present chapter.

The generally unsatisfactory state of culture in fifteenth-century Castile — in spite of the symbols of change noted in Chapter I — has been documented in a study by Nicholas G. Round.[4] In 1417 Don Enrique de Villena urged gentlemen not to scorn the sciences; their reputation as men of valor will not suffer, he says, though many hold the contrary opinion and the more liberal-minded (*modernos*) consider it sufficient for a knight to know how to read and write (cited *ibid.*, p. 207). The same condition is again reflected in 1445, in the prologue to an anonymous translation of St. Basil's homily *De legendis antiquorum libris.* The insecure position of learning at the court of Juan II and its decadence in the court of Enrique IV are implied by Juan de Lucena in his *De vita beata* (1463). At about the same time Fernán Pérez de Guzmán lamented the fact that "in Castile there always was, and there still exists, a lack of interest in antiquities" (cited *ibid.*, p. 209).

Though Round's conclusion that "Classical learning at the court of Juan II was subordinate to theological studies" (p. 214) may be accepted and extended to all of the Spanish Renaissance and post-Renaissance, the widespread apathy and hostility toward learning which we have noted in the two preceding reigns was to be largely

3. "Retirado en la paz de estos desiertos, / con pocos, pero doctos libros juntos, / vivo en conversación con los difuntos / y escucho con mis ojos a los muertos. / Si no siempre entendidos, siempre abiertos, / o enmiendan o secundan mis asuntos; / y en músicos callados contrapuntos / al sueño de la vida hablan despiertos. / Las grandes almas que la muerte ausenta / de injurias de los años vengadora / libra, ¡oh gran Joseph!, docta la imprenta. / En fuga irrevocable huye la hora; / pero aquella el mejor cálculo cuenta, / que en la lección y estudios nos mejora" (*Obras en verso*, ed. L. Astrana Marín [Madrid, 1932], pp. 424–25).

4. "Renaissance Culture and Its Opponents in Fifteenth-century Castile," *MLR*, LVII (1962), 204–15.

corrected in the Spain of Ferdinand and Isabella and their successors. The date of Nebrija's return from Italy in 1473 has already served (see Chapter I) as one of our "symbols of change"; it is now necessary to look more deeply into the effects produced by Nebrija's renewal of Latin studies and his innovations in philological method.

SPANISH LOGICIANS IN FRANCE

Before proceeding, we may well pause to consider the position of Spanish savants in the intellectual world of Europe, particularly in France, before and after 1473. Adolfo Bonilla y San Martín, in his studies of Fernando de Córdoba and of Juan Luis Vives,[5] has brought together evidence showing that, at the end of the fifteenth century and the turn of the sixteenth, the field of logic — with its Scholastic syllogisms so detested by Vives and by Rabelais — was largely dominated by Spanish teachers, both in the University of Paris and elsewhere, citing by way of proof the writings of Juan de Celaya, at one time rector of the University of Paris (published 1500–1516, mostly at Paris); the *Argutiae* (Paris, 1506) of Agustín Pérez de Oliva, who taught in the same university; the *Tractatus* (Paris, 1507) of Luis Coronel, professor in the Collège de Montaigu; and numerous treatises of identical or similar character published in France as late as 1528 — not to speak of books published by Spanish logicians in Spain. All these authors, says Bonilla, were medieval dialecticians who sought absolute knowledge resting on absolute proofs.

Fernando de Córdoba and His Triumphs

No less absolute and no less medieval in his attitudes was Fernando de Córdoba, who belonged to an earlier generation (d. 1486?). Stephen Paschal, on the basis of a history in manuscript written by an eyewitness, gave this description of him:

In the year 1445 there came to the Collège de Navarre a certain youth of twenty summers who was past master of all good arts, as the most skilled

5. *Fernando de Córdoba, 1425?–1486? y los orígenes del Renacimiento filosófico en España* (Madrid, 1911) and *Luis Vives y la filosofía del Renacimiento* (Madrid, 1903).

masters of the university testified with one accord. He sang beautifully to the lute: he surpassed all in numbers, voice, modes, and symphony. He was a painter and laid colours on images best of all. In military matters he was most expert . . . none dared to fight with him. . . . He was master in arts, in medicine, in both laws, in theology. With us in the school of Navarre he engaged in disputation, although we numbered more than fifty of the most perfect masters. . . . So shrewdly and cumulatively did he reply to all the questions . . . that he surpassed the belief, if not of those present, certainly of those absent. Latin, Greek, Hebrew, Arabic, and many more tongues he spoke in a most polished manner. . . . Nay more, if any man should live to be a hundred and pass days and sleepless nights without food and drink, he would never acquire the knowledge which that lad's mind embraced. . . . He argued four doctors of the church out of countenance; no one seemed comparable to him in wisdom. . . .[6]

In his study of Córdoba, Bonilla gives a rapid survey of the contents of late-medieval Spanish libraries in order to show that cultivators of learning were not rare at that time in the Peninsula. Yet the education which the boy wonder had received in Spain was purely medieval,[7] as may be inferred from the eulogy just quoted.

Fernando de Córdoba reached Paris in 1445, sent by the King of Spain. On his way there he held disputations in all the *gymnasia* of Italy and France.[8] At Paris he continued to produce general stupefaction. According to one contemporary report, it was difficult to believe that Aristotle knew more. Back in Italy, Córdoba delivered a public discourse — at a banquet offered to him at Genoa — "On the Location of the Stars, and On the Soul." He became a friend of Cardinal Bessarion, owing to whose influence he was named subdeacon to the pope. When he died, Cardinal Da Costa caused a Latin epitaph to be placed in the Church of San Giacomo degli Spagnuoli at Rome.

Some fourteen works of his are extant, of which the most important is entitled: *Method for Investigating and Discovering All*

6. Trans. L. Thorndike in *University Records and Life in the Middle Ages*, quoted in *The Portable Medieval Reader*, eds. J. B. Ross and M. M. McLaughlin (New York, 1953), pp. 596–97.

7. Nebrija received the same sort of training prior to his journey to Italy; and so did Vives, even after he took up residence at the University of Paris.

8. Lorenzo Valla, in a letter of 1444, mentions him with considerable praise — especially for his prodigious memory — and some dispraise for his Latin style; and Poggio Bracciolini remarks that Córdoba defended Valla when the latter was accused of impiety by the Inquisition at Naples (cited by Bonilla).

That Can Be Learned from Nature, unedited until published by Bonilla.[9] It is a thoroughly medieval book, based principally on the logic of Aristotle and on the *Ars Magna* of Raymond Lully (Raimundo [or Ramón] Lull).

THE NEW SPIRIT

Antonio de Nebrija

The picture which emerges from this review of Spanish philosophy before Nebrija is that of a country where impressive learning was by no means unknown, but where forward-looking spirits did not find a congenial home. Nebrija has left an eloquent expression of the personal dissatisfaction which led him to seek the fountainhead of true intellectual discipline in Rome (Chapter I, above). To pass from the Spain of Fernando de Córdoba's *De Artificio . . . omnis natura scibilis* to the post-1473 Spain symbolized by Nebrija's declaration of the principles governing his philological and Biblical researches is to pass from an essentially alien and outmoded milieu into one that we recognize as modern. The difference between Nebrija's drive for genuine knowledge and Fernando de Córdoba's amazing achievements is the difference between the medieval absorption of authorities and the Renaissance urge to restore by critical methods the purity and the authenticity of a religious doctrine and a secular culture that together had become vitiated by centuries of separation from their original sources. Keniston, summarizing Nebrija's activity as an educator,[10] stresses his importance as a bridge between the old and the new types of learning (p. 141): "[He] had drunk at the same fountain as had his predecessors in the field of education in Italy; . . . the methods which he himself followed and which he inculcated in others were based on the classic tradition. Implicit in these facts is the corollary that the young men — and the young women too — of the reign of Ferdinand and Isabella were trained in those liberal studies and

9. As an Appendix (pp. ii–lxxx) of the study upon which I have been drawing for this material.

10. "Notes on the *De liberis educandis* of Antonio de Lebrija" (i.e., Nebrija), *Homenaje ofrecido a Menéndez Pidal* (Madrid, 1925), III, 127–41.

with the humanizing purpose which marks the beginning of modern education."

We are thus at a critical period in Spanish cultural history. Within Nebrija's lifetime (d. 1522) Spaniards passed from the unsatisfactory intellectual environment of the late Middle Ages to the state of learning which, though unable to satisfy Vives (who refused to return to Spain) or Erasmus (who refused to go there), justified Spanish pride of achievement as it justifies our own admiration for Nebrija and his fellow intellectual pioneers.

Marineo Sículo and Pedro Mártir

In 1484 and 1487 respectively two Italian humanists emigrated to Spain, identifying themselves with the intellectual life of the nation. The first was Lucio Marineo Sículo,[11] who went to Salamanca from Sicily at the instigation of the Admiral of Castile, Don Fadrique Enríquez, statesman and patron of letters.[12] At the university Marineo alternated with Nebrija as professor of humanistic studies until 1496, when he passed to the service of Ferdinand and Isabella, joining the staff of the palatine school as a colleague of Pedro Mártir. There is no document to show the terms of this appointment, but the nature of his duties is made clear in an early letter to the Queen: "After it pleased Your Majesty . . . that those who serve you in divine ceremonies and in other ways, and all the youthful nobles who follow your court, should be taught by me the liberal arts and the Latin tongue . . ." (Lynn, op. cit., p. 113).

Marineo's *Familiar Letters* and his *Praise of Spain*, both composed in Latin, are valuable sources for the history of Spanish humanism. The latter constitutes a veritable *Who's Who* of illustrious Spaniards and furnishes data regarding the University of Salamanca not obtainable from any other source.[13] Marineo was

11. See Caro Lynn, *A College Professor of the Renaissance: Lucio Marineo Sículo among the Spanish Humanists* (Chicago, 1937). See also my review, *HR*, VI (1938), 176–78; the chapter entitled "School Days" in Hayward Keniston's *Garcilaso de la Vega: A Critical Study of His Life and Works* (New York, 1922); and the first chapter of A. F. G. Bell, *Luis de León* (Oxford, 1925).

12. M. Menéndez y Pelayo (ed.), *Antología de poetas líricos castellanos* (Madrid, 1890–1916), XII, 251. On Don Fadrique's interest in the religious movements of the time, see Bataillon, *Erasmo y España* (Mexico City–Buenos Aires, 1950), I, 214–15.

13. See Bataillon, *op. cit.*, I, 22, n. 32. Marineo's writings are listed by Lynn, *op. cit.*, pp. 268–69.

happy in his adopted country, finding there " a new Elysium." [14] "Castile," he was able to write with pride, "follows me with honor and with love; almost all the Castilian princes drew their love of letters from my store." [15]

In 1487 the Conde de Tendilla,[16] returning from his embassy in Rome, brought with him Pietro Martire d'Anghiera (known in Spain as Pedro Mártir de Anglería) who, like Marineo, was to have an honorable career in the service of the Catholic Sovereigns and a marked influence on the development of humanistic studies in Spain. In the entourage either of Tendilla or of King Ferdinand, he witnessed the last campaigns against the Moors prior to the fall of Granada in 1492. Taking holy orders, he became apostlic prothonotary. As a member of the Council for the Indies, he dealt personally with the great navigators — Columbus, Magellan, Vasco da Gama — and from their lips obtained data which he utilized in his valuable writings on the history of the New World. Finally, Charles V appointed him Prior of the Cathedral of Granada, where he died in 1526.

Though he made no connection with the University of Salamanca, Pedro Mártir did create general excitement in the university city when he went there to lecture at the invitation of the Chancellor, Gutiérrez de Toledo. Caught on the way by storms that mired the horses, he finally walked into Salamanca to be welcomed at a thronged reception on the autumnal equinox, 1488. His lecture was delayed by unseasonal snows, and with the delay the expectation grew. In a humorous letter to Tendilla he tells of that amazing

14. A. Farinelli, *Italia e Spagna* (Turin, 1929), I, 405, n. 4.

15. Lynn, *op. cit.*, p. 111. Alfonso Segura wrote: "When Lucio was summoned to the court, the king directly gave him the charge of instructing his attendants and the members of his household; and the queen put him to the task of improving the Latin of the palatine priests; and in the time left over from these duties he used to read either prose or poetry to the young nobles" (cited *ibid.*, p. 113).

16. William Hickling Prescott said of Tendilla (in *A History of the Reign of Ferdinand and Isabella* [Philadelphia, 1860], II, 196–97): "He was the brightest ornament of his illustrious house. His family, rendered yet more illustrious by its merits than by its birth, is worthy of specification, as affording altogether the most remarkable combination of literary talent in the enlightened court of Castile" (cited by Hermann Schumacher, *Petrus Martyr, der Geschichtsschreiber des Weltmeers* [New York–Leipzig–London, 1879], p. 103). He was a grandson of the famous Marqués de Santillana; his son, Diego Hurtado de Mendoza, was (to use Schumacher's phrase) "the Sallust of the war against the Moriscos," and his daughters were celebrated in the literary world.

lecture on Juvenal's second Satire: the throng was so great that he had to be carried to his desk and lectern; sandals and berets were lost in the press; a beadle lost his crimson cloak and sought to collect damages from the speaker. The lecture lasted some three hours. When it was over, Mártir "was carried home like a victor from Olympia." [17] In spite of its playful exaggeration, this letter "is a document of the greatest significance, for it reveals that already learning was held in respect and was sought for with eagerness." [18]

In 1492 — with Granada taken — Pedro Mártir was given by Isabella the post of director of the palace school for the young nobles of the court, among whom, assuredly, were the future poets Juan Boscán and Garcilaso de la Vega. On July 1 of that year he wrote to Cardinal Ascagno Sforza, contrasting his pupils with those of Socrates and Plato in ancient times. His own pupils (alas!) "think that learning will interfere with soldiering in which they center their ambitions. . . . Only a soothsayer could foretell the harvest." The result was better than he imagined. In September he wrote to the Bishop of Braga: "they are turning little by little to the love of letters. They are beginning to admit that letters are not a hindrance . . . but even an actual help. I try to persuade them that no one becomes a distinguished man either in peace or in war by any other path" (Lynn, *op. cit.*, p. 110). In these words we have the myth of the Renaissance stated in all its purity: the study of letters, ancient letters, constitutes the ideal life-preparation for the man of distinction, whether the scene of his endeavors be *mar, Iglesia, o Casa Real* — the seven seas, the Church, or the courts of kings.[19] The "lack of interest in antiquities" that Fernán Pérez de Guzmán had complained of two generations earlier by this time no longer exists. The Spanish sixteenth century will produce soldier-poets, some of them of the very highest order, all of them steeped in the poetic lore of the classical world and guided in their self-expression by a classical sense of form.

17. Lynn, *op. cit.*, p. 95. See also Schumacher, *op. cit.*, pp. 20–21.
18. Keniston, *Garcilaso de la Vega*, p. 23.
19. His *Opus epistolarum* is a sort of diary of the important events of his time. Among his historical works may be mentioned *De orbe novo Decades octo* and *De insulis nuper repertis et incolarum moribus*; see Schumacher, *op. cit.*, pp. 96–97.

GREEK STUDIES [20]

Fernández de Heredia

"The cosmopolitan Aragonese Hospitaller, Juan Fernández de Heredia (d. 1396), who closed a long and active military and diplomatic career as Master of the Knights of St. John of Rhodes, was responsible for the first mediaeval translations from the Greek into a Western tongue of Plutarch's *Lives*, and of other Greek texts until then unknown in the West."[21] Coluccio Salutati said of Heredia's library at Avignon that it contained any book one might require. From it he sent to the Aragonese court a series of manuscripts which profoundly influenced the development of Catalan humanism (*ibid.*). It is unlikely that Heredia ever acquired more than a smattering of the Greek language. It was the Dominican Nicholas, titular bishop of Drenopolis, who made Heredia's Aragonese translation of Plutarch from contemporary Greek. Dimitri Calodiqui, the translator of Plutarch from classical to demotic Greek, was also employed by Heredia to acquire, preserve, and copy various manuscripts, one of which may have been the Plutarch. From about 1382 onward, Heredia produced translations of Greek histories, having brought with him to Avignon "a philosopher from Greece who translates for you books from Greek into our language" (cited *ibid.*, p. 404). Shortly after 1395 several Italian versions of Heredia's manuscripts were circulating in France. On his death he left "three large volumes of the histories of Greece" (*ibid.*, p. 405). This work, important as it is, "was not the fruit of a precocious humanism but the achievement of an intelligent bibliophile with a thoroughly medieval passion for every aspect of universal history" (p. 407).

Arias Barbosa

In a Latin dialogue entitled *De poetis nostrorum temporum* (1548), the Italian humanist Lilio Gregorio Giraldi recalled the

20. Consult Emile Legrand, *Bibliographie hispano-grecque* in *Bibliographie Hispanique* (The Hispanic Society of America: New York, 1915-17), *Première Partie, 1477-1560* (vol. I of 3 vols.).

21. Anthony Luttrell, "Greek Histories Translated and Compiled for Juan Fernández de Heredia, Master of Rhodes, 1377-1396," *Speculum*, XXXV (1960), 401.

names of various Portuguese and Spanish poets, many forgotten today; among them he includes the Portuguese Arias Barbosa (d. 1540), who had been a pupil of Angelo Poliziano (d. 1494) and later taught at Salamanca.[22] Barbosa appears to have completed his studies and returned to Spain about the year 1490 to introduce the study of Greek at Salamanca under strictly secular auspices (Bataillon, *op. cit.*, I, 22–23, especially n. 32).

To him, by general consent, went the credit for establishing Greek studies in Spain: also by general consent, he was granted eminence in both Greek and Latin. He published very little: a work entitled *Epometria*, another called *De prosodia* (in which he departed not infrequently from the precepts of his master Poliziano), and a collection of Latin epigrams, *Epigrammatum seu operum poeticorum libellus*. Extending his interest — as did so many other humanists in the Peninsula — to Christian antiquity, he issued a long commentary on the Portuguese-Latin Christian poet Arator; this was a work of his old age. Nicolás Antonio, in his *Bibliotheca Hispana Nova*, lists various eulogies of Barbosa, including that of Giraldi. Barbosa did not, however, make a place for himself in the history of general Greek scholarship, as Nebrija did with his anticipation of Erasmus in the matter of determining how ancient Greek was pronounced.

Hernán Núñez

A much greater philologist than Barbosa was his pupil Hernán Núñez (d. 1553), known sometimes as El Pinciano — he had been born at Valladolid, ancient Pincia — and very frequently as El Comendador Griego, since he was a knight commander of the Order of Santiago and a great Hellenist. Like Nebrija, under whom he studied also, Núñez completed his education at the Spanish College in Bologna. He knew Hebrew and also Arabic, which he had learned at Granada when in the entourage of the Conde de Tendilla. Living in the Alhambra at Granada, he made an intensive study of the works of St. Jerome, whose ascetic life he endeavored to imitate. He was described as chaste, a celibate, and a merry raconteur. He worked on the Greek text of the Alcalá Polyglot Bible. In 1519 he succeeded Demetrios Doucas — a native of Crete

22. Benedetto Croce, *Ricerche ispano-italiane* (Naples, 1898), p. 19.

—in the chair of Greek at Alcalá. Seriously involved in the civil strife attendant upon the accession of Charles V to the Spanish throne, he was forced to flee Alcalá in 1522 and take refuge in Salamanca. There, on Nebrija's death in that same year, he succeeded to the chair of Greek, becoming the teacher of such outstanding humanists as Francisco de Vergara (d. 1533), León de Castro (d. 1585), Juan de Mal Lara (d. 1571), and Francisco Sánchez de las Brozas (d. 1600). Núñez was the most eminent humanist of his time.[23]

At the University of Bologna he studied with an obscure Greek from the Peloponnesus and with the Italian Philippo Beroaldo, whose method appears to have influenced Núñez in the choice of his own method. Beroaldo's commentary on *The Ass of Gold* of Apuleius is typical. After defining the meaning of a word or phrase, a syntactical turn or a stylistic peculiarity, the editor may propose an emendation of the text, citing all manner of Greek and Latin authorities both pagan and Christian, and — most characteristically — enlivening his work with lengthy digressions, some of them bearing on contemporary events or personal experiences. He describes the farm of his friend Roscio, tells of his recent marriage, recalls the invasion of Italy by the French, allows himself to praise the talents of a relative. These tendencies appear later in Núñez's own commentary on Juan de Mena.

Invited by the Conde de Tendilla, Núñez returned to Spain as preceptor to the Count's children at Granada, where he remained many years. It was in that city in 1499 that he dedicated to the Count his elaborate edition of Mena's *Laberinto*. Núñez was the first to undertake the elucidation and amplification of Mena's great work.[24] In doing so he imitated, in many respects, the garrulous type of commentary that as a student he had admired in Beroaldo's

23. See Antonio Vilanova's *Prólogo* to his edition of Mal Lara's *Filosofía vulgar* (Barcelona, 1958–59), I, 17–18; see also Bataillon *op. cit.*, I, 17–23, and Index.

24. Mena was to become the most edited, most commented, and most revered Spanish poet of the fifteenth century. The greatest humanists took him under their protection, finding delight in his frequent imitations of classical poets and in his erudition — remarkable for his time — in matters historical, mythological, ethical, and political. Since the *Laberinto* was the chief repository of what was then known, its encyclopedic character invited commentators to display their own learning as they explained the poet's language, not infrequently obscure, and his innumerable recondite allusions.

Apuleius: many observations and disquisitions were included merely because he saw fit to include them.[25] In 1509 Núñez published a Castilian translation of the *History of Bohemia* by Enea Silvio Piccolomini (later Pope Pius II) and dedicated this also to the Conde de Tendilla.

Núñez became associated with the philological work of the Alcalá Bible only at a late date, when the volumes were already being printed; but it seems reasonable to suppose, as Bataillon does (*op. cit.*, p. 29), that he had for years been examining the text of the Bible with a philologist's eye. We have already noted how at Granada he sought to imitate the ascetic life of St. Jerome. Furthermore, in his edition of Mena he tells of a long walk with his revered master Nebrija, during which they talked of Christian, not classical, antiquity. It seems possible that even in those early days he was studying St. Jerome with the thought of making a critical edition of the Vulgate.

His editions of Greek texts with interlinear translation in Latin — Moschus, 1519, and St. Basil, 1521 — can be easily overestimated. Legrand (*op. cit.*) gives their description: they are textbooks, as Núñez himself clearly states in the dedication to Nebrija of his *Moschus*. Núñez's original contribution to philology lay, rather, in his application of Greek philology to the elucidation and emendation of Latin texts. He corrected Seneca in the same manner. In his edition of Pliny's *Natural History* he emended the text on the basis of his own corrected *Pomponius Mela*. Justus Lipsius praised his *Seneca* and Commelin reproduced his *Pliny* in the edition which he issued in 1593. Modern editors of Mela still cite the text and the commentary of El Comendador Griego.[26]

Núñez's collection of *Refranes* (Spanish proverbs), a work of his old age, became a classic of early Spanish paroemiology. Edited after the master's death by his pupil León de Castro (1555), it testifies to the Renaissance interest in the wisdom of the folk. We lack a statement by Núñez of his philosophical attitude toward popular

25. This work, like his later collecting of popular adages, was secondary in the interest of Núñez. Aware of the popular character of his commentary, he eliminated in the second edition all Latin quotations. The work is really a manual of ancient mythology and geography, along with other arts and disciplines which the commentator considered of value for the unlearned.

26. J. E. Sandys, *A History of Classical Scholarship* (Cambridge, 1903–8), II, 159.

adages. His editor attributed to him an aim similar to that actually carried out by Mal Lara: "to declare these adages and to place beside them the expression of the same thought, from Greek and Roman authors." [27]

In a funeral dirge (*Epicedio*) composed on the occasion of Núñez's death, Valerio Francisco Romero described — in the style of Dante and Juan de Mena — a vision of the great man, surrounded by the Muses and the eminent personalities of antiquity, on the Mount of Fame:

> His undying glory will endure forever,
> Age after age and world without end.[28]

GREEK STUDIES AFTER NÚÑEZ

Aubrey Bell declares that during the first half of the sixteenth century Spain produced ten Greek scholars for every one produced in England (*op. cit.*, p. 24). This statement I am unable to verify; it may well be an exaggeration. We do know, however, that Cranmer appointed Francisco de Enzinas professor of Greek at Cambridge.[29] Whereas the first book in Greek printed at Rome bears the date 1515, the Alcalá Greek New Testament was issued in 1514, preceding by two years the edition in Greek by Erasmus. The Colegio Trilingue for the teaching of Latin, Greek, and Hebrew at Alcalá was established two years prior to the founding of the Collège de France. Not all was glory, however; the dark side of the Spanish Renaissance — it was dark in other countries too [30] — mani-

27. From León de Castro's introductory epistle, cited by Mal Lara, *Filosofía vulgar*, ed. cit., I, 96–97.

28. "Será sempiterna su verace gloria / y siempre en los siglos será duradero." The almost medieval form and tone of this poem are surprising in 1553, nearly a score of years after Garcilaso's death. The poem is included in the Madrid (1803–4) edition of Núñez's *Refranes o proverbios*. . . .

29. On Melanchthon's advice Enzinas made an excellent translation of the New Testament from the Greek. He died at Strasbourg in 1552. See David Rubio, *Classical Scholarship in Spain* (Washington, D.C., 1934), p. 59.

30. In France: On the night of October 17–18, 1534, placards were posted against the mass, the pope, and the cardinals in various French cities. The repression was atrocious. That evening six heretics were burned. At Paris more than twenty Lutherans went to the stake, after having had their tongues pierced or their hands cut off; some two hundred more were banished after confiscation of their property. In England: John Foxe pleaded vainly to save the Anabaptists from the stake in 1575 and the Jesuits from the gallows in 1581. In Switzerland: The Spanish humanist-

fested itself in the tragic case of the heretic humanist Juan del Castillo, hunted by the Spanish Inquisition in Italy, located at last at Bologna (where he earned his living teaching Greek), arrested easily because of the emperor's presence in that city in 1533, and eventually sent to the stake.[31]

The Belgian Nicolas Clenardus, whose main purpose in going to Spain was to learn Arabic, and who taught Greek for a brief time at Salamanca but principally taught in Portugal, published at Louvain in 1530 an excellent Greek grammar which was used well into the eighteenth century. This book was surpassed by Francisco de Vergara's *De omnibus Graecae linguae Grammaticae partibus* (Alcalá, 1537), a work fully appreciated by Scaliger, who commented that "the best parts had been borrowed by Canini."[32] The physician Andrés Laguna made a translation (1566) of Dioscorides' *Materia medica*, with notes that occupy twice the space of the text. Both Vergara[33] and Laguna were Christian humanists, deeply involved in the Erasmian movement in Spain.

Juan Ginés de Sepúlveda

Greek studies took root at the University of Alcalá, says Bataillon, only because Greek was the language of the New Testament, of many of the Church Fathers, and of Aristotle. Catholicism had need of the Greek language as a necessary instrument for the newly conceived ideal of going back to the metaphysical sources of its faith and of deciphering the ancient texts of divine revelation. These beginnings of Hellenism in the university city must not be thought of as an easy flourishing, but rather as that sweet, hard fruit that San Juan de la Cruz spoke of as the product of a cold, dry land (Bataillon, *op. cit.*, I, 25).

The ideal of reaching backward from corrupt to pure texts of

anatomist-theologian Miguel Servet was burned at Geneva by Calvin. See J. Plattard, *François Rabelais* (Paris, 1932), p. 197; C. S. Lewis, *English Literature in the Sixteenth Century Excluding Drama* (Oxford, 1954), p. 300; Roland H. Bainton, *Hunted Heretic* (Boston, 1960), pp. 202 ff. See also the section entitled "Social Control," Chapter XII below.

31. Bataillon, *op. cit.*, II, 62; see also pp. 220–21, and Index, *s.v.* Castillo, Juan del.

32. Sandys, *loc. cit.*; A. Roersch, *Clénard peint par lui-même* (Brussels, 1942), p. 7.

33. Vergara published also a collection of Epistles in Greek at Alcalá in 1524. See P. U. González de la Calle, "Francisco de Vergara y la pronunciación de la z griega," *Boletín del Instituto Caro y Cuervo*, IV (1948), 249 ff.

the Bible became a reality in the Alcalá Polyglot. There was no similar edition of the Greek fathers, merely sporadic efforts: St. John Climacus was printed in Spain in 1504; Dionysius the Areopagite in 1541; Gregory Nazianzenus in 1549; Cyril of Alexandria in 1576; St. Ambrose in 1585. Cardinal Cisneros did intend, however, to produce a modern edition of all of Aristotle; had he lived a few years longer, he and the scholars of his scriptorium would have produced, as a companion to the Alcalá Bible, a Graeco-Latin Aristotle. The Greek text would have been accompanied by a species of "vulgate," i.e., one of the Latin paraphrases then current, and by a new literal Latin translation. The latter, entrusted to Juan de Vergara, brother of Francisco (see above), had been begun in 1514, and the *Physics*, the *De Anima*, and the *Metaphysics* were finished by the time of the Cardinal's death in 1517 (*ibid.*, pp. 25–26 and n. 40). The enterprise remained at a standstill, and then was finally completed, at Rome, under the sponsorship of the Prince of Carpi, the young Ercole Gonzaga, and the pope. One of the chief workers in the completion of the enterprise — undertaken and then abandoned by the men of Alcalá — was Juan Ginés de Sepúlveda (*ibid.*, p. 476 and n. 14), whose interest in Aristotle first manifested itself (when he was a student at Bologna) in his writing of a now lost book of *Errata Petri Alcyonii in interpretatione Aristotelis*; he continued in the same vein with a translation of the *Parva naturalia* (Bologna, 1522), of the *De generatione et interitu* (Rome, 1523), of the *De mundo* in that same year, and of Alexander of Aphrodisias' commentary on the *Metaphysics* (Rome, 1527). Sepúlveda sided with the anti-Erasmian party, defended Scholastic philosophy and dialectics, and anticipated, in his own attitudes, the dogmatic restoration achieved at the Council of Trent (*ibid.*, p. 477).

Limiting ourselves to a consideration of the effectiveness of Sepúlveda's philological work,[34] we may trace his influence as a

34. Aubrey Bell, in his monograph *Juan Ginés de Supúlveda* (Oxford, 1925), after reporting (p. 21) that in his will (1571) Sepúlveda bequeathed his Greek books and manuscripts to the cathedral of Cordova (not to the king's library at El Escorial), sums up (p. 22): "His long life had been a crowded one. He had seen all the horrors of the sack of Rome, had been in danger of starving at Naples, had conversed intimately with Pope Clement VII and the Emperor Charles V, had met Alfonso de Valdés at Piacenza, dined with Cardinal Pole at Toledo . . . , had known a host of Italian and Spanish scholars and men of letters . . . , had discussed Aristotle at Madrid with Alejo Venegas and Honorato Juan; had taken part in many literary and philo-

Hellenist into the nineteenth century. The translation of Aristotle's *Politics* which he published at Paris in 1548 was the best that had appeared up to that time; it was still regarded as the best when Griphanius prepared his *Commentarii* on the *Politics* in 1608; it is reported as the best, on Griphanius' authority, by Fabricius in the *Bibliotheca Graeca* (1705–7); it came as a revelation to Johann Gottlieb Schneider when he was preparing his own edition in 1809; and it is the earliest Renaissance text used in establishing the critical edition of Franz Susemihl (1879).[35]

Gonzalo Pérez

Gonzalo Pérez began life as a soldier and as a scrivener in the office of Alfonso de Valdés, the imperial secretary. When Valdés died in 1532, Pérez — by dint of effort and ability — rose gradually to become secretary of state in the government of Charles V. Taking holy orders, he was appointed archdeacon of Sepúlveda in Old Castile. His desire to become a cardinal was never satisfied.

During his moments of relaxation — one wonders how there could have been such moments in a life so filled with travel and with official and unofficial activity — he busied himself making a translation into Spanish blank verse of Homer's *Odyssey*. The first thirteen books were printed at Salamanca and at Antwerp, in two nearly simultaneous editions, in 1550. The completed twenty-four books appeared first at Antwerp in 1556.

Pérez was something of a Maecenas, favoring poets, humanists, historians, printers. Bernardo Tasso immortalized him in a stanza of his epic poem, the *Amadigi* or the adventures of Amadis of Gaul. When Pérez died in 1566, Philip II acquired his Greek books and manuscripts for the royal library at El Escorial.

Although Angel González Palencia has published or summarized hundreds of documents having to do with Gonzalo Pérez, little is known of his education except that he studied at Salamanca. There is no record of his having taken a degree at that institution.

sophical and religious discussions in the palace of Carpi and the gardens of the Vatican: he had deciphered Latin inscriptions in the garden of Angelo Colocci, and he had corresponded with Erasmus and many other famous men of the day."

35. See the note of R. D. Hicks in his revision of Susemihl's text, *The "Politics" of Aristotle* (London, 1894), p. 7; O. H. Green, "A Note on Spanish Humanism: Sepúlveda and his Translation of Aristotle's *Politics,*" *HR*, VIII (1940), 340.

Five editions of the *Vlyxea de Homero* were printed in the six-teenth century and one in the eighteenth (1767). The translation is faithful, but rough and careless in its versification. This defect, in the opinion of Menéndez y Pelayo, gives to Pérez's unrhymed hendecasyllables a certain air of patriarchal rusticity which is not out of keeping with the character of Homer's poem.[36]

ARCHAEOLOGICAL STUDIES

The study of ancient archaeology is best represented by Antonio Agustín (d. 1586), who taught law at Padua. He was in constant communication with the most eminent scholars of his generation. His masterpiece, writes Sandys (*op. cit.*, II, 160–61), was his book of dialogues on coins and other antiquities, posthumously published in 1587 and translated into Latin by Scaliger in 1617. "He breathes the spirit of the Italian humanists when he writes with rapture to his Roman friend Orsini, telling him of the discovery of the Excerpts on Legations from the Encyclopaedia of Constantius Porphyrogenitus: 'Somewhere in Spain a Greek manuscript has been found containing the fairest fragments of the ancient historians. I have a large part of them in my hands . . . , while the rest are being promptly copied. If they were pearls or rubies or diamonds, they could not be more precious. I have also in my hands some beautiful fragments of Dionysius of Halicarnassus, fragments as lucid as crystal and well-nigh as bright as the stars.' "

LATIN STUDIES

Juan Luis Vives

Of all Spanish humanists, whether Hellenists or Latinists, the one who had greatest impact on the intellectual life of Europe was Juan Luis Vives (d. 1540). Vives' towering stature makes it possible to limit our account of him to a suggestion, rather than an exposition, of his greatness. In Monroe's *Encyclopaedia of Education* we read that Vives, Erasmus, and Budaeus (Guillaume Budé) made up

36. *Orígenes de la novela*, II (Santander, 1943), 164. See also A. González Palencia, *Gonzalo Pérez, Secretario de Felipe Segundo* (Madrid, 1946), and Julio Palli Bonet, *Homero en España* (Barcelona, 1953).

the "Triumvirate of Letters" of his time: "Of these the most systematic and thorough-going was Vives. In 1519 Vives, in his *In pseudo dialecticos*, broke finally with the Old Scholasticism and the Parisian Schools by his fierce protests against medieval disputational dialectic, and in place of it, his advocacy of the New Renaissance materials of knowledge and inductive methods of inquiry. As an advocate of the inductive method of observation, Vives ranks as a pioneer of Bacon." While this is unquestionably true, it must not be thought that Vives rejected outright the Scholastic philosophy: Part III of his *De anima* is based on St. Thomas Aquinas; he was a friend of Erasmus and Sir Thomas More and a tutor to Catherine of Aragon; in his own generation he was acclaimed "the second Quintilian." He was, according to William Harrison Woodword, "the first humanist to submit to systematic analysis the Aristotelian psychology and to regard the results of his study in their bearing upon instruction; . . . he stands forth conspicuously amongst the scholars and teachers of his century." [37] The *Enciclopedia Italiana* states that his is the earliest pedagogical system marking the transition from the age of humanism to the modern age. The *Encyclopedia Britannica* points out that Vives preceded Bacon in his emphasis on induction as a method of intellectual discovery, and preceded both Descartes and Bacon in his attention to psychological theory. He may even be regarded as a predecessor of John Dewey: his central idea was that knowledge is of value only when it is put to use. Because of Vives' importance as a Christian humanist, we shall return to his contribution to the Spanish Renaissance in another connection.

Hernán Pérez de Oliva [38]

Hernán Pérez de Oliva (d. 1531) composed a geographical work, *Imagen del mundo*, which has been lost but which was utilized by

37. *Studies in Education During the Age of the Renaissance* (Cambridge, 1906), beginning of the chapter on Vives. B. G. Monsegú's *Filosofía del humanismo de Juan Luis Vives* (Madrid, 1961) is a complete study that sets Vives in the Renaissance world and details his solutions of the problems of the period.

38. For reasons of space and of proportion it is necessary to limit our consideration of early Latin studies to Vives and Pérez de Oliva (a much less important but immensely interesting figure). For a brief but more comprehensive survey of Spanish Renaissance humanism, see my article, "A Critical Survey of Scholarship in the Field of Spanish Renaissance Literature, 1914–1944," *Studies in Philology*, XLIV (1947), 228–64, especially 238–44.

his nephew Ambrosio de Morales in his own *Antiquities of Spain*. Pérez de Oliva studied at Salamanca and Alcalá, at Paris, and at Rome, where an uncle of his was in the service of the pope. On the death of his uncle, Oliva was offered his post, but the young man preferred a life of study and returned to Paris, where he taught for three years. In 1524 he went back to Spain, and two years later he began teaching at Salamanca. In 1527 he took part in the famous scrutiny of the works of Erasmus at Valladolid. As rector of the University of Salamanca he was extremely active, at the expense of his teaching duties. Fortunately, Charles V named him to serve as tutor to Prince Philip, born in 1527; but he died at the early age of thirty-seven, only four years after his appointment.

In addition to cosmography — surely the subject of the lost *Imagen del mundo* — Oliva had other scientific interests: among his lost works are one on magnetism, one on light, and another on the "Operation of the Intellect." He actually foresaw, in his study *De Magnete*, the possibility of communication by means of the telephone, according to Morales.

One of Oliva's chief concerns, long before Joachim Du Bellay (1549), was the "ennoblement" of the Spanish language. He himself confesses that only after he had made his adaptations in Castilian of dramatic works of Plautus, Sophocles, and Euripides did he dare undertake to express in his native language the philosophical concepts of his *Dialogue on the Dignity of Man*. Earlier than that, in 1515, he had made a curiously conceived test of the two languages. In that year Juan Martínez Silíceo, Oliva's preceptor, published at Paris a work on arithmetic with a prologue written by Oliva in Latin, but with words which had — every one of them — cognates in Castilian. In the title itself — in strange Latin, but Latin nonetheless — Oliva goes so far as to assert the superiority of Castilian. The prologue is a philological tour de force; here is one sample, which is both Latin and Spanish: "Claramente cognosco, praestantissima Fama, quantos philosophos exaltas, quantos difuntos vivificas." Even his dramatic adaptation of Plautus' *Amphitryon* bears the title *Sample of the Castilian Language in the Birth of Hercules, or Comedy of Amphitryon*. In the dedication to his nephew Augustín de Oliva, the author states that "a very important quality of the discreet and intelligent man is to know his native language well." This adapted play, in spite of its meta-physical reasonings and moral subtleties, has its own *vis comica*, its own sprightliness of dialogue, its own Spanish realism.

To Oliva belongs the honor of having been the first to translate Sophocles into a modern language (probably through the inter-mediary of a Latin version). He made an adaptation of *Electra* (1528); he also adapted Euripides' *Hecuba* (which remained un-edited until 1586, when Morales printed his uncle's *Obras*). Oliva's purpose was not to make an accurate rendering but to show that lofty ideas could be expressed in Castilian. Both of the plays are excellently written, well able to stand comparison with the best works of the time. Neither in England nor in Germany were trans-lations made of these Greek dramatists in the sixteenth century. In France the first translation of Sophocles was in 1537; of Euripides, in 1550. In Italy, the first version of Sophocles bears the date 1533. The only European effort in this line preceding Oliva's in date was G. B. Gelli's Italian translation of *Hecuba*, about 1519.

The models for Oliva's *Dialogue on the Dignity of Man* are Pico della Mirandola's *Oration on the Dignity of Man* and the dialogues of Cicero. In it we have the first attempt by a Spanish humanist to express lofty philosophical concepts in his native language. Herein, rather than in the concepts themselves, lies Oliva's originality. The *Diálogo* is a debate between pessimism and confidence in the good-ness of the universe. To the ideas of Aristotle, those of Christian ethics are added. The thought content will be examined in our own discussion of optimism and pessimism in the Spanish Renais-sance and baroque.[39]

Women Scholars [40]

In an earlier study I made the observation that Spanish human-ism was democratic, that it extended to women, and in one famous

39. See W. C. Atkinson, "Hernán Pérez de Oliva: A Biographical and Critical Study," *RHi*, LXXI (1927), 309–484; Pedro Henríquez Ureña, "El humanista Hernán Pérez de Oliva," *Cuba contemporánea*, VI (1914), 19–55; J. P. W. Crawford, *Spanish Drama before Lope de Vega* (Philadelphia, 1937), pp. 125, 160–61; and A. E. Swaen, "Sidelights on *Amphitryon*," *Studia Neophilologica*, XIX (1946), 93–118.

40. See my reviews of P. W. Bomli, *La femme dans l'Espagne du siècle d'or* (The Hague, 1950), in *HR*, XX (1952), 255–57; and of Ruth Kelso, *Doctrine for the Lady of the Renaissance* (Urbana, Illinois, 1956), in *HR*, XXVI (1958), 71–75. On the subject of women scholars, see also F. de Llanos y Torriglia, *Una consejera de Estado: Doña*

case to a Negro slave.[41] From among the various women "Latinists"[42] whose careers it would be interesting to discuss I have chosen two: Luisa Sigea, because she left published works of merit, and Luisa (Lucía) de Medrano, because we have a thoroughly documented exposition of all that is known about her.

Luisa Sigea (d. 1560?) was taught by her erudite father and entered the service of the Infanta María of Portugal, sister of Charles V. Later, she and her husband became attached to the emperor's court at Valladolid. Her fame was immense: she knew Latin and Greek, Hebrew and Chaldean, and was well read in history, philosophy, and poetry. Her best work, the Latin poem entitled *Cintra* (Paris, 1566), has been translated into Spanish verse by Menéndez y Pelayo. The countryside near Cintra in Portugal is described in elegant bucolic style, with a feeling for nature which is genuine but not profound. Luisa also described rustic life in her Latin *Dialogue between Two Maidens on Courtly and Private Life,* displaying an erudition which amazed the Archdeacon of Alcor, translator of Erasmus' *Enchiridion.*[43]

Lucio Marineo Sículo wrote of Lucía de Medrano:[44] "In Salamanca [prior to 1514] I met Lucía Medrano, a most eloquent maiden. I heard her not only speak as an orator, but also read and expound publicly Latin books in the University of Salamanca." Indeed, there is to be found in Marineo's *Opus epistolarum* a letter addressed to her (*ibid.,* p. 331). Her actual performance of a teaching assignment in the university is corroborated by the testimony of

Beatriz Galindo, "La Latina" (Madrid, 1920); and two articles by S. G. Morley, "Juliana Morell: Problems" and "Juliana Morell: Postcript," *HR,* IX (1941), 137–50 and 399–402.

41. "A Critical Survey . . . " (cited above, note 38), p. 239. Spain was the only Catholic country in which the *Colloquia* of Erasmus were made freely available to the public at large (Bataillon, *op. cit.,* I, 360); see the title page of the Spanish translation, where the translator's popularizing purpose is set forth, and A. Castro, "Juan de Mal Lara y su *Filosofía vulgar," Homenaje ofrecido a Menéndez Pidal* (Madrid, 1925), III, 563.

42. The designation "La Latina" was during a certain period commonly applied to all women versed in Latin; see Thérèse Oettel, "Una catedrática en el siglo de Isabel la Católica: Luisa (Lucía) Medrano," *Boletín de la Academia de la Historia,* CVII (1935), 312.

43. Several of her Latin letters were published in 1901 by Adolfo Bonilla y San Martín in his *Clarorum Hispaniensium epistolae ineditae* (*RHi,* VIII, 183–308).

44. She is generally called "Lucía," perhaps because of Marineo's mistake, although her name was Luisa; see Oettel, *op. cit.,* upon which I have drawn for the following discussion.

Pedro de Torres, rector of the university in 1513, who wrote in his manuscript *Cronicón*: "A. D. 1508, 16th day November at the third hour. The Medrano girl lectured from the chair of canon law." From a study of the university's program, it would appear that her lecture was on the dramatist Terence. It is possible that in 1508–9 she was substituting for Nebrija, who in the course of that academic year was absent from his classes during a period of four months. She has left no works, either printed or in manuscript.

Juan Latino [45]

The slave-child Juan, brought as an infant — *ab ipso lacte*, to use his own words — from a land which in his writings he calls Ethiopia but which his modern biographer A. Marín Ocete has shown must have been Guinea, by a turn of good fortune and by his own talent and industry acquired in his new country freedom and a new name: Juan Latino. Tradition has it that he became professor of humanities in the University of Granada. This is doubtful, since Marín Ocete has found no trace of this in the university's records. Nicolás Antonio in his *Bibliotheca Hispana Nova* is probably correct when he states that the Negro held the chair of Latin grammar and speech in the Cathedral School of Granada: "sanctae ecclesiae Granatae cathedram grammaticae et Latini sermonis moderandam quam per viginti annos feliciter moderatus est."

Juan Latino was born around 1516; the date of his death is unknown. He was brought to Spain as a slave of the Duque de Sessa, grandson of the Great Captain, conqueror of the Kingdom of Naples, and was assigned as page to the son of this grandee. Attending the University of Granada with his master, he learned the same lessons as the young nobleman, attracting the attention of the professors with his translations of Horace. He is said even to have translated from the Greek some poems of Menander. Sessa gave him his freedom, and he soon won distinction and honor, marrying a white woman "not lacking in nobility," according to Nicolás Antonio, and winning acceptance in aristocratic circles on a footing of equality: he was a friend of Don John of Austria, victor over the Turks at Lepanto. He published at Granada in 1573 his book of Latin epi-

45. See A. Marín Ocete, *El Negro Juan Latino* (Granada, 1925).

grams, *Epigrammatum liber*, a collection overshadowed by his *Austriadis libri duo*, a poem in hexameters on the exploits of Don John, in which pagan mythology is mingled, in true Renaissance style, with Christian imagery. His fame extended throughout Spain. In 1605 Cervantes mentions him in the first of the burlesque poems that preface *Don Quijote*. The sorceress Urganda la Desconocida speaks:

> Pues al cielo no le plu-
> que saliese tan ladi-
> como el negro Juan Lati-
> hablar latines rehu-,

"since Heaven did not choose to make me as clever as Juan Latino, I refuse to speak in Latin." At some time prior to 1633, Diego Ximénez de Enciso composed a play entitled *Juan Latino* in which details of the humanist's life are romanticized. Facts of his biography are also utilized in Lope de Vega's *El negro del mejor amo*.[46] There are two references to him in the *Hispaniae Bibliotheca, seu de Academiis ac Bibliothecis . . .* (Frankfurt, 1608) of the Belgian scholar Andreas Schott (Schottus).

EARLY HEBREW STUDIES

The most conspicuous achievements of Hebrew scholarship in Spain came during the baroque period, when "the greatest luminaries of their age" in this field of learning were Spanish, according to William J. Entwistle.[47] Here we are concerned with beginnings only. The study of Hebrew was introduced at Alcalá in 1512. In 1526 Alonso de Zamora published his Hebrew grammar. Born of a family of *conversos*, Zamora knew Hebrew as his native tongue. At Alcalá in these early years there was no divorce between the old and the new theology; languages were the key to the Scriptures and the true introduction to the Erasmian *Philoso-*

46. See the review by U. González de la Calle of Marín Ocete, *op. cit.*, in *RFE*, XIV (1927), 278–79; my review of V. B. Spratlin, *Juan Latino, Slave and Humanist* (New York, 1938), in *HR*, VII (1939), 359–60; R. Schevill, "The Comedias of Diego Ximénez de Enciso," *PMLA*, XVIII (1903), 194–210; E. Juliá Martínez's edition of Ximénez de Enciso's *El Encubierto y Juan Latino* (Madrid, 1951).

47. In his review (*MLR*, XXVI [1931], 489) of A. F. G. Bell, "Notes on the Spanish Renaissance," *RHi*, LXXX (1930), 319–652.

phia Christi.[48] Only later would a Hebraist, by the mere fact that he was one, be the natural object of suspicion.[49]

DESINANT DOCTISSIMIS HISPANIS MALEDICERE

"In view of the foregoing exposition, let the railers cease to speak ill of our most learned Spaniards. In respect to the antiquity of the arts among us, to the abundance of erudite men in our midst, to mental power, or to their application to the interests of mind or soul, the men of our nation have as ancient a record as any, nor have any surpassed us in quality, since the days of the Greeks and Romans." These words were written, probably in 1553 (the date of their publication) by Alfonso García de Matamoros as a summing up of the evidence presented in his *Pro adserenda hispanorum eruditione* — an apology in defense of Spanish culture — published at Alcalá.[50] The purpose of the writer was clearly set forth by Rodrigo Caro (d. 1647), who had family ties with him: "He defended Spain as a whole against the calumny of certain foreigners who, envious of her glorious and fear-inspiring name, were willing enough to praise the warlike exploits of her invincible arms, yet condemned her writers as if they were Scythians or African Garamantes. Against this most unjust charge Alfonso García de Matamoros set himself valiantly . . ." (*ed. cit.*, p. 151).

The charge of anti-intellectuality, made by some native Spaniards [51] as well as by many foreigners, had been voiced in a particularly offensive way by the geographer Sebastian Münster, inspiring, in 1542, a riposte in a Latin epistle *Pro defensione Hispaniae* by Damião de Góis, in which this Portuguese humanist wrote to Jacob

48. M. Bataillon, in the introduction to his edition of Juan de Valdés, *Diálogo de doctrina cristiana* (Coimbra, 1925), p. 58.

49. See Miguel de la Pinta Llorente, *Proceso criminal contra el hebraísta salmantino Martín Martínez de Cantalapiedra* (Madrid–Barcelona, 1946).

50. *Pro adserenda hispanorum eruditione*, ed. and trans. José López de Toro (Madrid, 1943). This *Apología*, as the title reads in the Spanish translation (see *ed. cit.*, p. 231), was reproduced by Andreas Schott in his *Hispania illustrata* (Frankfurt, 1608), II, 801–23.

51. Among them Gonzalo Pérez (see above) in the prologue to his translation of the *Odyssey*: "the Spaniards are more inclined to war than to study." See also B. Croce, *La Spagna nella vita italiana durante la Rinascenza* (Bari, 1917), ch. VI, especially p. 102. Examples could be multiplied.

Fugger: "Spain gives birth to hard-campaigning soldiers, to most expert strategists, to orators of the greatest eloquence; Spain is the mother of the loftiest poets, of judges, of princes. . . ."[52] This lyrical rejection of the resented charge is, of course, a predecessor of Matamoros' work, but lacks its methodical approach and its fullness of statement.

Matamoros goes back to remotest antiquity, tracing through the ages the facts and legends (which he lacks the critical sense to distinguish carefully) touching upon intellectual achievement by Spaniards. He does not disdain to include the illustrious Moors: Rasis, Avicenna, Averroës. He pays tribute both to the great and to the provincial universities, to "the incredible fame and glory of the *Academia Complutensis*" (Alcalá). Though he attacks the Spanish dialecticians of the fifteenth and early sixteenth century (see above), he praises the baroque Scholastics (Soto, Cano), and overpraises El Tostado (Alfonso de Madrigal, d. 1470?): "had he lived in another century, Spain would not need to envy St. Augustine or St. Jerome." The University of Salamanca is the mother of Licurguses and Solons, and of learned monks whom the emperor has recently sent to the Council of Trent, he says (*ed. cit.*, p. 211). There, at Salamanca, Hernán Núñez holds a chair, "a man without superior in the world, either in knowledge of ancient literature or of the Greek and Latin languages" (*ibid.*).

Similar praise is bestowed on the others, though important names are forgotten. There is little interest in writers who used the vernacular. There is no mention of Spain's greatest scholarly achievement to date, the Alcalá Bible; but the Christian note of the Spanish Renaissance is sounded with a clarion blast: "in short, the most erudite, the most brilliant, the most divine among Spanish savants of our time are the theologians. . . ."[53]

The subject of *España defendida* — of the "defense" of Spain in matters intellectual — will receive full treatment in Chapter IX. In the year 1553 the battle seems, at least to Matamoros, to have been won.

52. Cited in *Pro adserenda . . .* , *ed. cit.*, p. 77.
53. This is true, he says, in spite of the fact that the race of logic-choppers is not extinct in Spain; but, now that theology has been "restored," there is no fear that it will again be vitiated by *theologastri* (pp. 231–32).

SUMMARY

In the present chapter, as in those that have preceded it, we have witnessed a transition from a state of affairs which Spaniards regarded as unsatisfactory to a situation which gave cause, if not for complete satisfaction — since not all shared Matamoros' complacency — at least for self-congratulation. Though the ancient intellectual glories of Spain — Seneca, Lucan, Martial, Quintilian, not to speak of the fictional ones — had always been available to apologists and were utilized from time to time in the early and late Middle Ages, Matamoros' comprehensive and modern *Apologia* could not possibly have been written before the university reforms instituted by Nebrija and Cisneros and continued, with fruitful results, by their collaborators and successors. Spain had experienced an expansion of intellectual energies to match her expansion in the fields of exploration, colonial enterprise, and imperial power.

VI · *Ac Inde Melior:* Religious Expansion

It would be well to say a few words
about the anticlericalism of the
Renaissance, which is the same as
saying, of the Middle Ages. For,
here again, one can almost go so
far as to say that the sixteenth
century did not have a single
malicious thought that the twelfth,
the thirteenth, or the fifteenth
did not have before it.

Lucien Febvre [1]

RELIGIOUS ABUSES AND DESIRE FOR REFORM

"The desire to correct the abuses was general and of long standing in the Church of God. Ever since the Council of Vienne in 1311 the ritualistic phrase had been heard: 'Reform of the Head and of the members'; it resounded again and was repeated in the Council of Pisa (1409), and again in the Council of Constance (1414), and yet again in the Council of Basel (1431), and, more powerfully than ever in the Fifth Lateran Council during the reign of Pope Julius II" (convoked in 1512).[2] John Busch, writing of monastic reform in the monastery of St. Martin in Ludinkerka, in fifteenth-century Friesland, gives a general complaint and a case history which could be duplicated a hundred-fold: "None of them was chaste, all were proprietors, and they had nuns with them in the monastery who sometimes brought forth children. I knew an abbot there, a learned man, whose father had been called a convert, and his mother a nun.

1. Lucien Febvre, *Autour de l'Heptaméron* (Paris, 1944), p. 264.
2. F. Cereceda, *Diego Laínez en la Europa religiosa de su tiempo, 1512–1565* (Madrid, 1945–46), I, 184. The documentation could be endless. Gerard Groote (d. 1384), founder of the Brotherhood of the Common Life, declared that "this schism cannot be healed without some terrible blow to the Church, which has long been in a position of decrepitude, ready to fall to pieces, and now the head itself is in a sad condition" (cited in Albert Hyma, *The Christian Renaissance* [New York–London, 1924], p. 28). See also Odo of Rigaud's report on "The Habits of Priests in Normandy" (thirteenth century) in *The Portable Medieval Reader*, eds. J. B. Ross and M. M. McLaughlin (New York, 1953), pp. 78 ff.; see also pp. 75–77.

He afterwards resigned his abbacy and entered into a monastery of our chapter near Haarlem, and having there become a monk, he ended his days well." [3] St. Catherine of Siena (d. 1380) called the corrupt clergy of her day "stinking flowers of the garden of Holy Church." [4]

The protest against abuses goes back much farther than the Council of Vienne, and in the vast literature of protest Spain has a place of some honor because of a Latin satire of very high quality which until recently was largely overlooked by the historians of medieval Latin letters. It is the *Garcineida* of García de Toledo; its complaint is against simony, particularly at the Roman Curia, and against attitudes and activities (and sloth) unworthy of an institution whose founder was Christ. It fustigates Urban II and his court and especially Bernard de Sédirac, first archbishop of the newly reconquered Toledo (1086). The date of composition appears to have been about 1099. In his satire (and parody) García de Toledo includes all western Europe. His work shows impressive classical learning, the use made of Ovid, Horace, and Terence giving evidence of direct and attentive reading. He points up the conflict between Spanish ecclesiastical interest and the policies of the French Order of Cluny, with its tendency to erase local and national differences. His ingenious parody and *vis comica* place him far outside the circle of the frivolous satirists whose works make up so much of medieval Latinity.[5]

Unsatisfactory Condition of the Church in Spain

Censure of the clergy in Spain has the same character as elsewhere. There are bitter protests in the anonymous fourteenth-century *Libro de los gatos*,[6] though these may be discounted since the book is a translation of the *Narrationes* or *Fabulae* of the English monk Odo de Cheriton. Of purely native stock, on the other

3. *The Portable Medieval Reader*, pp. 67–68.
4. Cited by G. Volpi in *Il Trecento* (Milan, n.d.), p. 341. It should be remembered that to the Catholic soul the unworthiness of persons never compromised the sacred character of the institution. See J. Huizinga, *The Waning of the Middle Ages: A Study of the Forms of Life, Thought and Art in France and the Netherlands in the XIVth and XVth Centuries* (London, 1924), p. 48.
5. See María Rosa Lida de Malkiel, "La *Garcineida* de García de Toledo," *NRFH*, VII (1953), 246–58.
6. Ed. John E. Keller (Madrid, 1958); see pp. 48, 70, 78.

hand, is the didactic novel *Blanquerna* of the Catalan Raimundo
Lull (d. 1315). The story he tells of Anastasia and her daughter
Cana reveals disinclination among the worldly to regard nuns as
in any way sacred. The mother, angered because during her absence
her daughter has taken the veil, calls her relatives together and
explains to them the cause of her anger. Sharing her fury and directing it against the convent, the relatives present themselves outside its walls, determined to obtain possession of the girl by force,
to kill the nuns and burn their dwelling. The nuns are so frightened that Cana has to call them sharply to their duty. Haranguing
the crowd, she throws the keys of the building from a window: the
trust of the besieged, she says, is in God; women have no need to
defend themselves; the nuns will die rather than give up Cana. The
attackers, impressed by this act of boldness and faith, repent and
ask for prayers. Anastasia, too old to enter the order, lives thereafter "under the direction" of the nuns.[7]

Another episode of very similar character is told in the same
work. A bishop sends a canon to excommunicate a certain prince
because of his acts of violence against the Church. The accused
resents this greatly, and orders the canon to be stripped, tied,
flogged, and put to death. The canon, as he endures his mistreat-
ment, continues to pray for his enemies and to thank God for the
opportunity to perform his own necessary penance in this way.
The prince is touched, suspends the torture, and asks the reason
for the remarkable change in the character of the clergy in this
diocese: there obviously has been a rebirth of virtue among them.
The canon tells the story of Bishop Blanquerna and his reforming
zeal — so effective that the eight canons of his government sym-
bolize in their manner of life the eight Beatitudes of the Gospel.
The prince declares that such a bishop and such a body of canons
henceforth must be obeyed. He makes amends, is relieved of excommunication, and commends himself to the good graces of both
the bishop and the cathedral chapter (pp. 371–72).

Alfonso Martínez de Toledo (d. 1470), in his moralizing and
realistic *Arçipreste de Talavera* (or *El Corbacho*), warns clerics of
ruination if they give themselves over to worldly love (Part I, ch.
XI); and in another chapter (Part II, ch. X), on woman's propen-

7. Ed. L. Riber (Madrid, 1944), pp. 121–28.

sity to falsehood, offers "one more example: another woman had a friar hidden behind the bed. . . ."

No social or doctrinal importance can be given to such friars "behind the bed." They appear frequently as comic types in the literature of the Middle Ages and the Renaissance, and long after it might be supposed that the Council of Trent (1563) had banished them forever.[8] In Cervantes' dramatic interlude *La Guarda cuidadosa*, the Soldier speaks to Cristina: "You abandon and scorn this fair flower, this flower garden of military honor, and cast in your lot with an assistant sexton — contemptible as a manure heap — when you could easily have a sexton full-fledged, and even a canon."[9] In another dramatic interlude, *The Old and Jealous Husband*, Cervantes presents in sprightly conversation the mismatched beauty Cristina and Hortigosa, the older woman who promises to remedy Cristina's yearning for male companionship. Cristina says: "Look, Señora Hortigosa, I want him attentive and good-looking, well-groomed, free and easy, a bit bold, and, above all, young." After some minutes of discussion she repeats her request: "Señora Hortigosa, be so kind as to bring me a youthful friar, small of stature like myself, with whom I can have some satisfaction." "I'll bring him pretty as a picture," is the reply. "I don't want a picture," protests Cristina, "but a live man — alive and small, like a little pearl" (*ed. cit.*, p. 597b). The volume containing these interludes was published in 1615 with the usual ecclesiastical "Approbation," written by a distinguished author of religious dramas, Master José de Valdivielso.

In 1640 the Inquisition finally decided to subject Fernando de Rojas' *Celestina* (1499?) to expurgation, and it deleted some fifty lines. The expurgator was concerned with matters of doctrine, not with the unfavorable depiction of the customs of certain members of the clergy. One is amazed at what was allowed to pass untouched. Celestina, recalling the days when she had a house full of young girls — "cattle most difficult to guard" — speaks of her clients as including "gentlemen old and young, abbots of all ranks, a bishop, all the way down to sextons" and continues: "there was even one individual who, on seeing me enter as he was saying mass, was

8. See Vittorio Cian's history of satire in Italy, *La Satira* (Milan, n.d.).
9. *Obras completas*, ed. A. Valbuena Prat (Madrid, 1956), pp. 565a.

thrown into such confusion that he couldn't do or say a single thing properly." Sempronio remarks: "I am dumbfounded by the tales you tell of such religious folk and such blessed tonsures." [10] The Index that permitted all of this to stand was issued in 1640. [11]

Not that there was no perceptible effect in 1640 of the decrees of the Council of Trent concerning literature. The situation is complex. The Erasmian *pues vestir no haze al monge* — the mere wearing of a habit does not make a proper monk [12] — may (or may not) give way, in any given literary work, to the opposite attitude. Juan de Mal Lara, in an early section of his *Filosofía vulgar*, explains "The Quality of the Proverbs which are Discussed." He refers to Philip II's ban (inspired by the decrees of Trent) against licentious sayings and songs, and indicates his compliance: he has removed from his glossary, he says, all proverbs invented by the "licentious masses," all those "not approved by all or not common in the language of decent people"; he has disregarded, furthermore, all those that express hostility to monks and nuns, since these can give rise to scandal and seem more characteristic of the excessive "liberties" of Germany than of Spain, being, in addition, "dangerous in these times — so favorable to the derisive scorn of the accursed heretics." Américo Castro, in his study of Mal Lara, pointed out that this Spanish folklorist showed a defensive attitude in regard to anything that might affect ecclesiastical doctrine as affirmed at Trent. [13] Mal Lara's modern editor, quoting Castro's observation, points out that "in spite of the energy with which the Spanish humanist condemns Lutheran heresy and anticlerical satire, he

10. M. Seidlmayer (*Currents of Mediaeval Thought with Special Reference to Germany*, trans. D. Barker [Oxford, 1960], p. 130) remarks that "there was . . . complete freedom in sexual matters. Even smaller towns had their brothels, whose inmates enjoyed a place in local society . . . and had their own pews in church." He refers to P. Browe, *Beiträge zur Sexualethik des Mittelalters* (Breslau, 1932).

11. O. H. Green, "The *Celestina* and the Inquisition," *HR*, XV (1947), 211–16; a fuller discussion of literary censorship will be given in a later chapter. See also Menéndez y Pelayo, *Antología de poetas líricos castellanos* (new ed.; Santander, 1944–45), III, 363: "Nothing that we read on the subject of friars, priests, and hermits in . . . all the authors of our primitive comedies, farces, and eclogues has any novelty or significance at all." An author who today would be regarded as "an out-and-out enemy of the ecclesiastical estate was not so regarded then."

12. See *Cuatro obras del Bachiller Hernán López de Yanguas, Siglo XVI*, ed. facsimile (Cieza, 1960), penultimate folio.

13. "Juan de Mal Lara y su *Filosofía vulgar*," in *Homenaje ofrecido a Menéndez Pidal* (Madrid, 1925), III, 563–92.

nevertheless retained in his collection a considerable number of adages of definitely anticlerical flavor."[14]

Another case is that of Alonso López Pinciano, who in his *Filosofía antigua poética* (1596) causes Fadrique to say to his fellow interlocutors: "In my opinion all religious are very good, and very chaste, and worthy of much esteem; I, at least, confess that when I see one covered with his order's habit, though he be an ignorant lay brother, I regard him with great respect because of the excellencies which I contemplate beneath that robe." To this he adds: "One who thought otherwise would be guilty of mortal sin."[15] Twenty years earlier, in 1576, a Portuguese censor reported of a certain book that, though it contained "nothing against our holy religion," he had struck out a line that "touched upon members of religious orders, which in these days is dangerous."[16] Yet the life of monks and nuns continued to be denigrated, even by so upright and severe a "censor" of public morals — *Leonardo, recto juez, Catón severo* — as Bartolomé Leonardo de Argensola (d. 1631), who in his *Sátira del incógnito* rhetorically "refrains" from inquiring into a certain delicate problem of ecclesiastical morals:

> Nor would I ask with what justification
> Report would have it that the Antichrist
> Was ill-begotten in an evil hour
> By a mounting friar and a mounted nun.[17]

And Quevedo's railing at friars would fill a small anthology, though he respected the Jesuits.

But let us go back to the fifteenth century. The poet Hernán Mexía cannot bear to contemplate a situation wherein abbots send invitations to the weddings of their sons.[18] Fray Iñigo de Mendoza declares that if the sea were ink and every fish a scrivener, it would

14. Antonio Vilanova (ed.), *Filosofía Vulgar* (Barcelona, 1958–59), I, 83, especially n. 2.

15. Ed. A. Carballo Picazo (Madrid, 1953), III, 66.

16. Cited by I. S. Révah in *La censure inquisitoriale portugaise au XVIᵉ siècle* (Lisbon, 1960), p. 64; see also p. 65.

17. "Ni ssi con justo título achacaron / a fray Montante y soror Ensillada, / que al Antichristo ser comunicaron" (*Rimas*, ed. J. M. Blecua [Zaragoza 1950–51], II, 479).

18. *Cancionero castellano del siglo XV*, ed. R. Foulché-Delbosc (Madrid, 1912–15), I, 274.

be impossible to list all the followers of Sensuality, from all three estates: bishops and cardinals; dukes, kings, and emperors; and tillers of the soil and artisans (*ibid.*, p. 83). An anonymous *Mirror for Clerics* of this century has a chapter (XVIII) titled "On the Priest and his Concubine." [19]

The hostility encountered by Cisneros in the carrying out of his reforms points up the contrast between the desires of the mass of the clergy and the aspirations of a small, select number. The secular clergy, in particular, had in large measure turned its back on its sacred mission. It is for this reason that a society whose concern for personal salvation was stronger than ever regarded friars like Cisneros as the true representatives of ideal Christianity.[20] The ranks of these reformers became progressively stronger, and their activity more popular (*ibid.*, p. 6). But the way of the reformer was then — as always — difficult (p. 10). In 1508 Fray Francisco de Avila printed at Salamanca a poetic work entitled *On Life and Death*, in which there is a section "Against Bad Prelates" — those men in authority who "take away the milk and wool without caring for the sheep," using the proceeds to provide splendid weddings for their daughters; men who extend the boundaries of their estates and build worldly palaces, while the poor, ground down in their misery, die in the poorhouse. Let all such evil men, says the poet, be assured that they will not escape the eternal punishment reserved for those who lay up treasure on earth (Gallardo, *Ensayo*, I, col. 343).

Typical of the reformers of the generation after Cisneros (d. 1517) is the Erasmist [21] Juan Maldonado, whose ideas are set forth in his *Pastor bonus* of 1529 (printed 1549). In it the author draws a detailed picture of the corruption of ecclesiastic customs and outlines a program of regeneration (cited by Bataillon, *op. cit.*, I, 383). Bishops, he says, are given over to wealth, luxury, and pleasure — an example being Don Juan Fonseca, whom Maldonado

---

19. Bartolmé José Gallardo, *Ensayo de una biblioteca española de libros raros y curiosos* (Madrid, 1863–89), I, col. 737. Hereafter this work will be cited simply as *Ensayo*.

20. M. Bataillon, *Erasmo y España* (Mexico City–Buenos Aires, 1950), I, 5.

21. "We can never emphasize sufficiently the extent to which the Counter Reformation in Spain was molded by the discussions that centered about the thought of Erasmus" (Bataillon, *op. cit.*, I, 382).

knew at Burgos, a great lord as corrupt as any other until his change of heart and his redemption of former abuses by means of the good deeds of his later years. The daily life of such great ecclesiastical lords is given in full and unedifying detail (*ibid.*, p. 384). Maldonado stresses the ignorance of the ordinary priest, and his conduct — aided and abetted by the fine-collecting discipline of the bishop (p. 388). It is obvious that much remained to be done, twelve years after the death of the great Franciscan reformer.[22]

In 1535 Ignatius de Loyola had returned from Paris and was living in Azpeitia, preaching and doing good, as he tells in his autobiography, and correcting such vices as he could. In many cases, a young girl, he says, following the custom of the Basque country, went with uncovered head until her marriage; or until she had become the concubine of some priest, to whom she remained faithful and whose concubine she declared herself to be by covering her head and saying that she had done so "because of such and such a person," — being known thereafter by that connection.[23]

By 1537 — the date of the preliminaries of Alejo Venegas' *Agonía del tránsito de la muerte* — matters had improved somewhat, at least in some cities, for Venegas was able to exclaim:

How much more meritorious is the person who lives a saintly life in Wittenberg . . . among the vipers spawned by the serpent Hydra, than the man who is a Catholic in the city of Toledo, where the sanctity of the Church automatically invites him to live in a saintly manner! Over and above the excellence and the great number of the clergy and the multitude of monasteries of all the religious orders — for though Toledo is in the center of Spain it lacks an establishment of only one order, the Carthusian, a lack compensated for by the Friars Minor and (formerly) by the Knights Templar of Jerusalem in the Castle of San Servando —, over and above so many examples of the religious life, there are confraternities of the devout in this city, so numerous that one would think that all such organizations in all of Spain had gathered for a convention in Toledo. For all of these reasons, the man who, in spite of the example of such strict observance of the Christian life, wanders from the broad highway of the Church deserves a much greater penalty than the sinner who, living in Wittenberg, follows the lead of the evil masses in that city.[24]

22. On luxury-loving bishops, see Fidèle de Ros, *Un maître de Sainte Thérèse, le Père François d'Osuna* (Paris, 1936), p. 133; see also A Castro, "Lo hispánico y el erasmismo," *RFH*, II (1940), 23.

23. *Obras completas*, ed. Ignacio Iparaguirre (Madrid, 1952), p. 95.

24. *NBAE*, XVI, 241a.

Serious Concern in Literature

Lazarillo de Tormes. The anonymous *Lazarillo de Tormes* —
first in the famous series of Spanish picaresque novels — has long
been dated around the year 1554, the year of the first editions, but
recent scholarship makes it appear likely that it was composed
about 1525, when Erasmian agitation was approaching its first
great crisis (1527).[25] Bataillon insists that Erasmianism "was always something very different from a simple movement of protest
against the 'abuses' of an unworthy clergy and of ignorant monks:
it was a positive movement, striving for spiritual renovation, an
effort of intellectual culture dominated by an ideal of piety" (*op.
cit.*, I, 395–96). Applying this test (Bataillon's criterion for true Erasmism) to the *Lazarillo*, Asensio (*op. cit.*) has demonstrated its author's intention to criticize religious practices: of the nine masters
whom Lázaro serves, five are — in one way or another — men of the
Church. Asensio's demonstration becomes even more impressive
when it is remembered that two of Lázaro's other masters are tran-
sitional figures of practically no importance (the bailiff and the
painter of tamborines). Furthermore, Lázaro's service with the
blind man — a lay figure — is charged with religious significance:
in this episode there is constantly a question of the validity of
charity, of prayer, and of good or bad examples; of the exploitation
of the simple faith of the poor; of the turning of a trustful boy
into a lying schemer. The other lay figure of importance, the
squire, in his blind attachment to aristocratic values and in his
lack of moral responsibility, evokes the censure not only of the
serving-boy with his limited mentality but also — directly — of the
author: "Oh Lord, how many like him must be scattered through
the world; men who suffer, for the unfortunate thing they call
honor, pangs and miseries that they would not endure for Thee!"

All the personages of the book are without a productive trade;
not one is willing to earn his bread with the labor of his hands. We
are thus given a picture of social parasitism, with members of the

25. On the matter of the date, see Manuel J. Asensio, "La intención religiosa del
Lazarillo de Tormes y Juan de Valdés," *HR*, XXVII (1959), 78 ff. Asensio's findings
are almost completely acceptable to me, and I rely on them heavily in the treatment
that follows. Whereas Bataillon (*op. cit.*, II, 211–12) denies the Erasmianism of the
anonymous author, it seems to me that Asensio, reviewing the question, has the
better part of the argument.

clergy in the forefront; the Erasmists declared, on the other hand, that the true Christian should earn his sustenance by working.

In all of this there is what Asensio calls a "mental chastity, a cleanness" altogether absent in medieval satires against the clergy. The author portrays an ambient — poverty, hunger — in which men who shirk their Christian responsibility and set bad examples sow the seeds of religious disillusionment in the mind of a child, converting him to the tricks of deceit, parasitism, and materialism, and leading him finally to consent to his wife's prostitution — a progressive spiritual and moral deformation.

The child-youth Lazarillo is a believer: the name of God is ever on his lips — a God who gives succor to the afflicted and glory to those who deserve it. This God is his ally, ready to answer his prayers even when these prayers and desires are not what they should be. Some of the prayers produce a comic effect; yet beneath them lies something more serious. Their satire is directed against persons more knowing and responsible than Lazarillo who nevertheless allow themselves to make a similar travesty of prayer. Even the geographical names, and the one historical personage mentioned in the book, point up the author's religious intention. The villages of Maqueda, Torrijos, and Almorox are not far from the seat of the Duque de Escalona, who in 1523 brought to his palace a lay preacher, Pedro Ruiz de Alcaraz, to preach the doctrine of the semi-mystical Iluminados (see below) to his household.[26] This Illuminist movement has been related by Bataillon to the similar efforts of various European reforming groups whose members were characterized by their lack of confidence in acts of exterior worship. The author of the *Lazarillo* appears to share the aggressiveness of the group gathered about the Duque de Escalona, especially in his mocking of public manifestations of religious rapture and ecstasy, such as the extremists of the time were wont to indulge in even within the Illuminist movement itself. The ignorant Lazarillo — surprisingly — is able to use correctly, in his description of the pretended rapture of his master the Seller of Indulgences, the

26. The Duke's household included Juan de Valdés, a Renaissance Spaniard whose activity as a religious reformer came to be felt in Spain, Italy, Switzerland, France, Poland, the Low Countries, and England. Domingo Ricart, *Juan de Valdés y el pensamiento religioso europeo en los siglos XVI y XVII* (Mexico City, 1958); see also my review, *HR*, XXVIII (1960), 401–2.

language of mystical experience: "transported into the divine essence." Lazarillo parodies unwittingly, in his non-edifying activities, many things which the Inquisition was unwilling that the faithful should take lightly or condemn — things clearly specified in that tribunal's sentence pronounced against Escalona's lay preacher, Pedro Ruiz de Alcaraz. In short: it seems difficult not to perceive in *Lazarillo de Tormes* "palpitations of the religious disquietude and perturbation which had its center, around 1525, in Escalona and Toledo."[27] That religious disquietude is characterized by a typically Renaissance desire for authenticity — in the character of the religious experience itself, in its outward manifestations, and in social organizations or groupings: "where two or three are gathered together" (Matt. 18:20).

Viaje de Turquía. The author of the *Viaje de Turquía (ca.* 1555), now identified with reasonable certainty as the physician Andrés Laguna, translator and commentator on Dioscorides' *Materia Medica*, was an Erasmist, not an *iluminado* (or *dejado* or *alumbrado*).[28] The *Viaje* was published for the first time at the beginning of the twentieth century. It is, according to Bataillon, the best literary work produced by a Spanish Erasmian humanist. Its author was obviously a Hellenist, a man instructed by life as well as by libraries, a man endowed with an exceptional sense of humor, a master of dialogue, a Spaniard who was at the same time a "good European," a man free in his judgment of the world of nature and of human affairs. Not an autobiography, the *Viaje de Turquía* is a novel in dialogue, after the manner of Erasmus, which incorporates many personal recollections of its physician-author.

It is extremely Spanish in character; three of its interlocutors are personages taken from Spanish folklore. Cervantes wrote a play about one of them: Pedro de Urdemalas. Another, Juan de Votadiós, is a hypocritical cleric who exploits the credulity of

27. Asensio, *op. cit.*, pp. 90–92. We are not concerned here with accepting or rejecting Asensio's hypothesis that Valdés may have written the *Lazarillo*. I agree with Asensio: if the author is ever identified and proves not to be Valdés, he will at least resemble him greatly (p. 102).

28. See Battaillon, *op. cit.*, II, *Indice analítico, s.vv. dejamiento, iluminismo*. In the discussion in this section I follow closely Bataillon's commentary, pp. 279 ff. See also *idem*, "Sur l'humanisme du Docteur Laguna: Deux petits livres latins de 1543," *RPh*, XVII (1963), 207–34.

simple folk as he tells of the Holy Land, which he has never seen, and collects money to found hospitals. The third, Mátalascallando, is a cynical companion of Juan, jolly and frank, who makes fun of Juan's hypocrisy.

As Juan and Mátalascallando chatter on the outskirts of Valladolid, watching the pilgrims come and go on the way to Santiago de Compostela, they are accosted by a strange-appearing pilgrim speaking in a language — Greek — unknown to them. A discussion follows in which Juan is unable to make good — by displaying a knowledge of Greek — his claim to have traveled in the Levant. In spite of this the stranger shifts to Spanish and embraces the others, former fellow-students of his at Alcalá; he is none other than Pedro de Urdemalas, returned from captivity in the land of the Turks. His monk's habit has been his disguise, and he has bound himself by an oath not to change it until he can hang it as an offering at Santiago de Compostela. The encounter is worthy of Rabelais. Pedro's odyssey is told in the first part of the *Viaje*; the second part expounds the life, religion, government, and military discipline of the Turks and describes their capital city.

In his captivity, Pedro feigns medical knowledge and practices that profession with eminent success. Indeed, only a physician could have written the book. Certain pages make it clear that the author is an authority on *materia medica*. It happens, strangely, that Pedro has in his knapsack a diploma in medicine from Bologna. That Pedro is Doctor Laguna in person may be accepted as a reasonably certain hypothesis.[29]

The book is severe in its attitude toward the papacy, impartial in its interpretation of Turkish culture (*ibid.*, p. 146). It is severe also in its judgment of Spain (*Erasmo y España*, II, 295). When Pedro discusses the ritual of the Greek Orthodox church, he makes it clear, in Erasmian fashion, that ceremonies are a variable thing, of minor importance. Pedro's God, like the God of Erasmus, is the God of the Gospels and of St. Paul. The Erasmian ideas expressed

29. In 1956 Bataillon took up the problem again in answer to William L. Markrich (*The "Viaje de Turquía": A Study of Its Sources, Authorship and Historical Background* [unpub. dissert., U. of Calif.; Berkeley, 1955]) and César E. Dubler (*D. Andrés Laguna y su época* [Barcelona, 1955]), who had questioned his Pedro-Laguna identification. See his "Andrés Laguna, auteur du *Viaje de Turquía*, à la lumière de recherches récentes," *BHi*, LVIII (1956), 121–81; for the decisive argument, see especially pp. 146–49.

in the *Viaje* are exactly those of the historical Dr. Laguna who, at Metz and at Cologne, exerted to the utmost his moral authority in an effort to effect a reconciliation between Catholicism and Protestantism (*ibid.*, p. 296). His critical rationalism joins hands with the new *Philosophia Christi* to oppose the metaphysical spirit of the traditional theologians (p. 298), bound hand and foot in their slavery to Aristotle (p. 299). "We witness here," says Bataillon, "a conflict of two disciplines, one of which is governed by authority, the other by reason and experience" (*ibid.*).

Pedro de Urdemalas believes in a philosophy which is not disputatious, whose master is Jesus Christ, and which can be imbibed at the pure spring of its origin by any sane spirit possessing humanistic knowledge and techniques of inquiry. It is, in short, the religion of the Gospels and of the Church Fathers. Laguna is a layman of the Renaissance type, able to give lessons in theology to professional theologians (p. 300).

Confessors, he charges, cater to a wealthy clientele. The clergy exploit shamelessly the credulity and the sense of charity of the public. He renews the theme (so dear to Alfonso de Valdés) of bogus relics of the saints. He is a Catholic and a sincere one; but he is willing to grant to the opposing party a considerable amount of reasonableness. He calls into question the merit of hypocritical paternosters and sees in a simple ejaculatory prayer a means of opening the gates of heaven (p. 303). The *Viaje* opens with a quotation from Homer and ends with a quotation from St. Paul — a discreet token of homage, as Bataillon suggests, to the master of the fiction of adventure and to the master of inspired faith. This book is the finest example of that literature, at once entertaining, edifying, and profitable for the spirit, which was produced by the Spanish followers of Erasmus. Bataillon supposes that its remaining unprinted was in accordance with the author's intention: that it was written for the delight of the author and his intimate friends. It is a work of the greatest historical significance. Written in those years when Spain was beginning to enclose herself within her frontiers,[30] it constitutes the *Odyssey* of Spanish Erasmianism; it is, in fact, the Erasmists' farewell to Europe and return to Spain (p. 304).

30. The first Spanish Index of forbidden books bears the date 1559.

RELIGIOUS REFORM: DIRECTED AND SPONTANEOUS

Of the six reform movements produced as reactions to the unsatisfactory state of religion in the early sixteenth century, three were repressed or suppressed and three were successful. Included among the successful were two efforts at directed reform: a program of education and renewed emphasis on scholarship for the clergy and, later in the century, the conscious return to ecclesiastical tradition. Orthodox mysticism, a spontaneous reaction to religious abuses, also flourished vigorously before yielding eventually to the pressures for a return to tradition. The heterodox reformers and the heterodox mystics were fully repressed. The Erasmist movement too was suppressed, but its pervasive doctrine (*Philosophia Christi*) continued to be influential in many ways not officially recognized.

Clerical Reform

Cardinal Cisneros' noteworthy reform of the clergy through education and scholarship achieved its end in large measure. However, some of the energies developed at Alcalá came to fruition elsewhere. It was at Rome, as we have seen, that Sepúlveda and his sponsors and collaborators brought out the Greek-Latin Aristotle that had first been conceived by the men of Alcalá. Similarly, the Antwerp or Royal Polyglot Bible — to be studied later — was brought out, under Spanish auspices and in a country still nominally part of the Spanish monarchy, but not on Spanish soil. Yet the reform of the clergy took time.

Prior to 1540, Francisco de Osuna wrote in his *Fifth Spiritual Alphabet* (cited by Ros, *op. cit.*, p. 662):

You must know that there are two types of bishops: one type is instituted by God our Lord. . . . There is another type of bishop who possesses the ring and the staff and great authority in order to eat and adorn himself with the patrimony of the Crucified. These are symbolized by the "bishops" which are made of pig meat and served at table in Castile; they bring together scraps and bones of the pig, and if possible add spices and eggs, throwing in all sorts of odds and ends, and they pour it into a pot and invite a lot of guests. . . . With this in mind, you will find in the Church of Christ many more bishops of the second than of the first type, because the wicked always outnumber the good.

In or near 1557 Luis Hurtado de Toledo completed the dramatic work begun by Micael de Carvajal entitled *Death's Parliament* (*Cortes de la Muerte*). Death addresses the poor man:

> Who are they who most afflict you,
> You, the poor, for you have seen it;
> Who are they who do not teach you?

and the poor man replies:

> Who are they? The ones who govern
> The holy Church of Jesus Christ
>
> . . . .
>
> It is they who will not hear us,
> It is they whose ears receive not
> Our tearful cries of misery.[31]

In another place Satan charges that there is no woman whom the clerics do not corrupt, especially orphaned maidens; and another enemy of the soul, the Flesh, seeks to defend herself from the righteous indignation of a priest, alleging that

> I have ever been the friend of
> Pious hermits for I give them
> Pleasure with my company;
> They, indeed, are never weary
> Of my witty entertainment.[32]

Such texts as these prove two things, according to Ros: that in Spain Catholic moralists were as ready as Luther to denounce in energetic terms the disorders of the clergy; and that the Inquisition, permitting the circulation of their denunciations, gave proof of broadmindedness. Under Philip II, he continues, administrative disorders disappear. The new king filled vacant bishoprics only with men who were eminent because of their learning and their virtue (*op. cit.*, pp. 134–35).

31. "¿Quién son los que más afligen / esos pobres, pues lo has visto, / y los que no los corrigen?" — "¿Quién son? Aquellos que rigen / la Iglesia de Jesu Cristo / . . . / qu'ellos cierran los oídos / a nuestros continuos lloros / y a miserias y gemidos (*BAE*, XXXV, 14c).

32. "Pues yo amiga suelo ser / de ermitaños religiosos, / y aun suelen tomar placer / conmigo y no aborrescer / mis dichos lindos, graciosos" (p. 8a).

The Philosophia Christi

The history of Spanish Erasmianism is an inspiring story. Seldom has a lost cause been so nobly defended, and seldom has a suppressed doctrine lived on with more effectiveness in spite of the suppression.

Bataillon's researches prove beyond doubt that the intellectual complications of sixteenth-century Europe were present in Spain, but were there simplified by the *Philosophia Christi* which had appeared in Spain as a natural growth [33] and which in the course of its development was given new impetus by Erasmus (*Erasmo y España,* II, 429):

> Between the publication of the Polyglot Bible at Alcalá and the printing of *Don Quijote,* the Christian humanism of Erasmus had, beyond the Pyrenees, a singularly productive career. The history of Spanish Erasmianism illustrates the meaning of Erasmus in the spiritual revolution of his time. With him, humanism sets itself the task of restoring the Christian message in its authentic purity, and of achieving a consensus of the best human thought centered about a *Philosophy of Christ* in which modern man might find joy and peace. To accomplish this end, all that is necessary is for man — through the mediation of Christ — to participate in the Divine, thus entering into the kingdom of love and of liberty. . . . In spite of all the differences between Erasmus and a Savonarola or a Luther, he is closer to them — because of his philosophy — than he is to the "paganizing" humanists.

During a number of years this doctrine of spiritual renewal through a process of stripping off the accretions of ages met with the favor and the support of the highest authorities: the Emperor, his secretary Alfonso de Valdés, and the Inquisitor General Manrique. What is remarkable is that, in spite of such favor in high places, the opposition was strong enough to make it seem prudent to Alfonso's brother, Juan de Valdés, to absent himself permanently from Spain and take residence in Italy — for no other offense than having published a catechism exhibiting Erasmian tendencies, the *Diálogo de doctrina Cristiana* (1525). Only two years later, the general theological scrutiny of Erasmus' works in the city of Valla-

33. The ennobling of theology through humanism, already noted (Chapter I, note 28) as one of the tendencies in Catholicism prior to the Council of Trent, was the outstanding characteristic of Cisneros' reform program — which was well under way before the influence of Erasmus as a theologian became general.

dolid was adjourned — the city being threatened by pestilence — without having reached a conclusion but in such a manner as to leave fear in the hearts of the Erasmists.

The situation was grave because two different interpretations of Christianity were contending for supremacy: ceremonies opposed to inner prayer and devotion; individual responsibility of the Christian to his God opposed to institutional, organizational control of religion. Fundamentally, any doctrine that tended to make each man his own priest — and therein lay the danger of certain mystical tendencies — was a threat to the institutionalized Church. An example of the Church's attitude toward such doctrine is found in its treatment of Fray Luis de Granada's *Book on Prayer* and his *Guide for Sinners*, which were condemned by the Inquisition (in 1559) until corrected. A collation of the original and the revised versions shows that what Luis de Granada did to obtain approval was to play down mental prayer — direct communion of the soul with the Deity — and play up ritual. Very typical of the changes made to placate the censors are the long glosses introduced into the *Book on Prayer* for the purpose of re-establishing in their dignity "the sacred ceremonies and external good works"; the new insistence on the degree of respect due to the doctors and preachers of the Church, as well as on the necessity of practicing active virtues; and the placing of fasting and alms-giving on an equal footing with mental prayer.[34] Luis de Granada had not been unorthodox in the earlier versions; in the judgment of the censors he had merely failed to emphasize sufficiently certain Catholic teachings.

Little by little, Erasmus the theologian became a banned author — though his *Adagia*[35] continued to be cited even after the condemnation of his religious writings had become, for practical purposes, complete. As early as 1580 it seemed to certain writers prudent to refer to Erasmus, not by name, but anonymously, as *quidam* (*ibid.*).

Two conceptions of the Christian life thus came to grips — not culture against its opposite but two different subcultures opposing

34. Bataillon, *Erasmo y España*, II, 373.
35. O. H. Green, "Additional Data on Erasmus in Spain," *MLQ*, X (1949), 47–48; see also Bataillon's observations on this article, *Erasmo y España*, II, 339, n. 30.

each other. Fray Luis de Carvajal, a disciple of Josse Clichtowe, appeared in 1528 as the leader of the party opposed to Erasmus: "As for us, we have faith in the ceremonies and in the other good works which we accomplish for the glory of Christ" (cited *ibid.*, I, 376). This attitude of the traditionalists eventually became official and was imposed progressively by the authority of a state which — having become fully authoritarian,[36] with orthodoxy as its party line — changed its earlier attitude of support to one of hosility. Erasmus and his supporters, though they were victorious in 1527 (the date of the "scrutiny" of Erasmus' works at Valladolid), and though for a few years (1527–32) they had the support — and supported the policy — of the Emperor and the Grand Inquisitor, suffered persecution from 1557 onward and, with the publication of Cardinal Quiroga's *Index Expurgatorius* (1583–84), were forced back "into the shadows." In Spain, therefore, the party with Protestant leanings — the party of reason and loyal protest, the party of renewal rather than rebellion — lost out in the protracted struggle; yet the good that it accomplished lived on. The great reformers, the apologists, and the inquisitors of the Counter Reformation properly so called (i.e., after Trent, 1563) absorbed and incorporated into their own work of reform much of the spiritual energy of the early Spanish Erasmists.[37]

36. The Erasmians were as eager to impose their ideas by discipline from above as were those who came to be their victorious adversaries. The published correspondence of Juan de Valdés proves this amply. That authoritarianism was congenial to the Spanish mind may be gathered from this quotation from the *Agricultura christiana* of Fray Juan de Pineda (Salamanca [1589], fol. 16): "All republics [i.e., commonwealths] that developed into flourishing states were governed by common laws even in matters that might appear now as inconsequential, for neither eating nor dressing nor taking a wife was left to the choice of the individual: a thing we observe in Rome and in Sparta especially, and therefore those two states achieved great worth and power. . . . Portugal has insisted very properly on sumptuary legislation in dress, and this has been very necessary for them, since their land is so unproductive, and their people are so proud, that they would ruin themselves with fancy clothes and costly inventions, as occurred when they were given freedom to dress as they pleased for the disastrous expedition of King Sebastian."

37. The sequence of events from the time when the Erasmists were approved in powerful quarters until the time of their ultimate repression has been traced in masterly fashion by Bataillon in three chapters of *Erasmo y España* (vol. I, ch. VIII, and vol. II, chs. IX and XIII). In the same work (vol. II, chs. XI, XII, and XIV), he has traced the Erasmian influences in devotional literature, in secular literature, and in the two great works of the "twilight" of that influence: Luis de León's *De los nombres de Cristo* (1585–95) and Cervantes' *Don Quijote* (1605–15).

The Heterodox Reformers [38]

The debate between the supporters and the opponents of Erasmus was much more than a dispute between theologians. For the most sensitively Christian souls, it was a question of saving a new and powerful sense of Divine Grace, a sense of grace which had been developed only at the cost of reducing confidence in human acts of worship and devotion — indeed, in all human acts. The "Protestants" — and there were those who might be called Protestants in Spain — were the ones who went furthest in this withdrawal of confidence from the human, the ones who insisted that man must be justified by faith alone.

As we view these events a posteriori, it is easy to assume that Trent was a complete and sweeping victory for the traditional orthodox party. Such a view is simplistic. At Augsburg in 1548 (three years after the convocation of the Council) a declaration on Grace was issued — the joint effort of the Saxon Erasmist Julius Pflug and the Spanish theologians Fray Pedro de Soto and Pedro Maluenda — which would have been able to satisfy even the refugee reformer Juan de Valdés (p. 85).[39] In the same year of 1548 some of the sermons of Savonarola (martyred fifty years earlier), translated into Latin by a Spanish Dominican, became popular at the imperial court (p. 87, n. 21). Erasmus was still respected by Spanish theologians (pp. 90 ff.): his *Coloquios* had been forbidden only in 1537; in 1551 the prohibition was made more inclusive but by no means complete (p. 88), the Spanish Inquisition appearing more liberal in these matters than the Sorbonne (p. 89). The struggle, for the most part, was not so much between orthodoxy and clearly defined heresy as between two special kinds of orthodoxy, the one

38. The parenthetical page references in the following discussion are to *Erasmo y España*, II, ch. X: "The Spanish Reformation during the Period of the Early Meetings of the Council of Trent" (i.e., after 1545).

39. It was only some twenty years later that Spain became the champion of Tridentine orthodoxy in its definitive formulation (see below). In order to understand the seesawlike history of these developments, it is necessary to consider, alongside the position of the traditionalist Diego Laínez, second General of the Society of Jesus (d. 1565), evidence of a Spanish position which was opposed to his. It should be remembered that in this interim of approximately two decades between the opening of the Council of Trent and Spain's settling into a strongly orthodox position the nation's official attitude was so liberal that in 1556 Pope Paul IV called Charles V a heretic and brandished over him and his heir the threat of excommunication.

liberal and lenient, the other suspicious and exacting (p. 91). The increasing suspiciousness appears clearly in the second and the third editions of Fray Alonso de Castro's *Adversus omnes haereses*: in the first (1534), Erasmus is spoken of as *vir vere pius* — a man truly devout; in the second (1539), this defense is suppressed; in the third (1543), the author, perhaps under pressure, feels constrained to speak of him as *vir utinamn tam pius quam doctus* — a man whose piety unfortunately does not match his learning (pp. 91–92). Even so, Castro remains essentially broad-minded (p. 92).

The fact was that if the theological restoration required the reprobation of Erasmus' boldness, it required no less a correction of the degeneration against which Erasmus had fought (p. 93). In 1548 the Bishop of Guadix published a work *On the Divine, Apostolic, and Ecclesiastical Traditions*, which is the most original predecessor of the Scholastic restoration of Melchor Cano, Domingo de Soto, and Francisco Suárez (*ibid.*). In this book the author declared that "there exists a multitude of pious men, learned, experienced, ceaselessly given to prayer, who energetically reprove the abuses of the Church and the evil life of many of its ministers, who desire that true doctrine reign in the Church, together with purity and simplicity of life, and who are . . . far removed from the teachings of the Lutherans" (cited p. 95).

Over against these faithful protesters we must place the heterodox reformers, some of whom — Juan de Valdés, with his Neapolitan disciples, Francisco de Enzinas who taught Greek at Cambridge — emigrated to other countries. Others remained in Spain and in 1558 suffered persecution for their alleged Lutheranism. These have been regarded as Spanish Protestants (pp. 103 ff.). The chief charge against them was their insistence on the doctrine of justification by faith. The most prominent among these men had once been leaders in the party whose triumph Charles V, *defensor fidei*, strove to bring about. Their religious ideas had their origin in Spain in the *iluminismo* of the Spanish Erasmists (p. 105). They show pietistic tendencies opposed to the intellectualist theology of Melchor Cano, that is to say, of the triumphant party (p. 107). One of them, Dr. Agustín Cazalla, perished at the stake. By 1554 the situation had become alarming to the authorities (p. 133): Fray Felipe de Meneses reported in that year that the news of religious revolt in France and Italy had aroused in Spain "an unbounded appetite for liberty" (cited p. 134).

Thus there appeared in Seville and other parts of Spain a doctrine which could be called "Protestant," derived from Erasmian *iluminismo* (see below) but without destructive implications for Catholic dogma. Beside it there developed, in the reformed monasteries and in the young Society of Jesus, a spiritual movement which, though resolutely Catholic, sought renovation through a renewed sense of grace. These two groups had much in common — though just how much it appears impossible to determine in the present state of our knowledge (p. 137).

The Heterodox Mystics

Insofar as this reform was accompanied by mystical tendencies, it was considered almost as dangerous as the Lutheran movements of protest. The reason is simple: mysticism tends to dispense with the ceremonies. In order to understand the relation of the Spanish mystics to the problem dealt with in this chapter, it will be necessary to be aware at all times that prior to, and partly contemporaneous with, the orthodox mysticism of the great Carmelites — St. Teresa, St. John of the Cross — there existed a heterodox mysticism which carried with it unquestionably dangerous possibilities.

Henry C. Lea, in a discussion of the Mystics and the Illuminati,[40] expounds the methods prescribed by the mystical theologians of the Middle Ages whereby the soul could rise above itself, reach the Divine Essence, and become divinely illumined. It was not only the orthodox, Lea points out (p. 214), who ventured into these perilous paths of human ecstasy; there were many who were far from orthodox: the Amaurians and their followers, and the Brethren of the Free Spirit, commonly known in Germany as Beghards and Beguines.[41] They invented the term *Illuminism* to describe the condition of a man so illumined by the Divine Spirit that he was no longer subject to external laws. The perfect adept could commit no

---

40. *Chapters from the Religious History of Spain Connected with the Inquisition* (Philadelphia, 1890).

41. See Norman Cohn, *The Pursuit of the Millenium* (Fairlawn, New Jersey, 1957), Index. *s. v.* Beghards, Beguines, Brethren (or Adepts) of the Free Spirit; Ernest W. McDowell, *The Beguines and Beghards in Medieval Culture, with Special Emphasis on the Belgian Scene* (New Brunswick, New Jersey, 1954).

sin; whatever he did was righteous. Such a doctrine had of necessity to be intolerable to the Church, and was condemned at the Council of Vienne in 1312.

During the Middle Ages, according to Lea (*op. cit.*, p. 215), Spain was "singularly free from mystic aberrations." However, one begins to find references to these unorthodoxies in fifteenth-century Spanish sources. There is a passage on the Beguines in the *Spill* of the Catalan Jacme Roig (d. 1478);[42] and in Rojas' *Celestina* (1499?) Pármeno says to the procuress Celestina: "I would prefer that you not entice me by a promise of sensual delight like those who, lacking all rational foundation for their position, formed sects enveloped in sweet poison for the purpose of capturing the wills of the weak and throwing the dust of sweet passion into the eyes of reason."[43]

Some thirteen years later (1512), there appeared a mysterious *iluminado* called Fray Melchor, who is denounced in preserved documents. He was born in a family of converted Jews, merchants of the city of Burgos. His divine "call" was as irresistible as that of St. Francis. His "prophecies" bring to mind those of Charles de Bovelles in France: the Church was to be transformed within twelve years; the Roman Empire was to be destroyed; the kings of all Europe must die and their kingdoms disappear; the Church would return to its ancient seat in Jerusalem, and the divine leader of that return would be Melchor himself.[44] The movement Melchor represented was to make its presence felt for nearly fifty years (p. 73).

Time will pass before anyone in authority speaks of an Illuminist "peril," but in that same year (1512) a document refers to a certain Franciscan as "illumined by the darkness of Satan" (p. 79). About the same time a woman known as The Bigot of Piedrahita became famous for her trances. A "Mother Martha" of Toledo was re-

42. Joseph-S. Pons, "Le *Spill* de Jaume Roig," *BHi*, LIV (1952), 6. Huizinga (*op. cit.*, p. 179) tells of the nobleman who confessed "that the sin of lust did not prevent him from loving God; on the contrary, it inflamed him to seek for and taste more eagerly the sweetness of divine love." See also J. M. Pou, *Visionarios, beguinos y fraticellos catalanes (siglos XIII–XIV)* (Vich, Catalonia, 1930).

43. Ed. J. Cejador (Madrid, 1913), I, 108.

44. Bataillon, *Erasmo y España*, I, 75. Again I follow Bataillon closely, and parenthetical page numbers continue to be from this work throughout this and the following two sections.

garded by Cisneros as being favored with supernatural gifts — naturally, perhaps, because Cisneros considered himself the instrument of a miraculous renewal of Christianity. Indeed, the "Messianic" hopes of these Spaniards centered about Cisneros, and some of them thought of him as a future pope (p. 82). In this heated atmosphere — an atmosphere which the Inquisition was already endeavoring to restore to normality (p. 194) — the influence of Erasmus first made itself felt in Spain (p. 83).

The danger from the Illuminists was less than it appeared to their contemporaries, who could not judge the movement in its relationship to Erasmianism. The tendencies of Spanish Illuminism are clearly analogous to those of the religious revolution in all of Europe. It was, quite simply, an inner Christianity of the heart, a keen awareness of the need, and of the efficacy, of grace (pp. 194–95). The type of mysticism encouraged by Cisneros is best represented by Fray Francisco de Osuna, the thoroughly respectable Franciscan whose works have been so often cited in the course of the present study. He preached *recogimiento,* a withdrawal into the inner sanctuary of the self whereby the soul, totally shut off from the world, sought God in its own bosom. His boldness consisted in declaring, in terms that cannot be surprising to readers of Volume II of *Spain and the Western Tradition,* that the contemplation of the humanity of Christ — wounded head, hands, feet, side — is not a means of joining oneself directly to God. Union must be achieved by rising above the creatures, by purifying the passions and desires. (p. 196).

There is no trace of disregard for Christian tradition, no trace of quietism in Cisneros' system. The *Iluminados* preached, on the other hand, a worship of *abandono* which was more subject to the dangers of sin and heresy. The adepts of this *abandono* aimed at a quietistic union with God, thinking of nothing. The act of delivering oneself to God so organized the personality, they claimed, that one "could not sin either mortally or venially." A certain female adept was said to have become so perfect that "continence was no longer necessary to her." This doctrine was related to Luther's view of the human will as slave. There thus developed, in these restless circles, a "cloudy admixture of sensuality and mysticism" (p. 201).

Yet the accusations of the Inquisition against the Spanish adepts were not accusations of departing from common morality or of holding secret orgies; it was the doctrine that was feared.

The *Iluminados* did, of course, oppose all religious formalism. Why should it be that one prayed in church more efficaciously than elsewhere? (p. 203). Why pray orally? There is really only one prayer: *Thy will be done.* Of what use were saints when one has the Scriptures? Protestant as these teachings may seem, it is not easy, at this stage, to separate the orthodox from the heterodox. The edict of 1525 denouncing the *Iluminados* associated their propaganda with certain of the propositions of Lutheranism (*ibid.*). Yet what we perceive today is simply a religion of freedom with respect to the ceremonies, and of confidence in a God who gives peace and joy. Suffering is regarded as the result of an insufficient harmony with God (p. 205). Both branches of the movement — the preachers of *recogimiento* and of *abandono* — resolutely turned away from that harsh and lachrymose devotion which evokes the sufferings of the Lord and weeps. The *Abandonados* rejoiced no less on Holy Thursday than on Resurrection Sunday. Osuna, the apostle of *recogimiento*, declared that his exercises were not for men "naturally melancholy" (p. 206).

Both Spanish Illuminism and the general European religious revolution had their roots in the *Devotio Moderna* of the Brethren of the Common Life of medieval Holland. From about 1523 Spanish *Iluminismo* was decidedly influenced by Erasmianism. The year 1525 marks the beginning of the persecution of some members of the movement. This was the same year that three boatloads of books by Luther were impounded in a port of the Spanish kingdom of Granada (p. 221). The edict against *Iluminados* or *Abandonados* was issued on September 23 of the same year. By way of defense, the condemned sought to bolster their position by associating their teaching with that of the prestigious Erasmus, none of whose books was as yet condemned by the theologians, though some of them were perfect manuals of "inner" Christianity. From 1527 to 1532 there occurred a veritable "invasion" of Spanish translations of works by Erasmus (p. 325).

But the master himself came to be an object of censorship and persecution. The attack on the *Iluminados* was renewed in 1529–31.

Two men, one a priest, were condemned to the flames (II, 13). María Cazalla was arrested in 1532 (II, 53 ff.) and in October of 1534 was subjected to torture. Her sad case illustrates the hostility which came to be felt for a quietistic Illuminism that had evolved in the direction of a rationalized pietism under the new Erasmian influence (II, 57). In 1558 every doctrine suspected of even a shadow of Illuminism became the object of persecution (II, 206). Had the Inquisition acted less vigorously, the Illuminist groups might have evolved into genuinely Protestant groups comparable to those in France (II, 320).

The Orthodox Mystics

Because of the exigencies of our exposition, Francisco de Osuna (d. 1540?) and his *recogimiento* have been mentioned among the heterodox mystics, though he was not one of them; Cisneros himself, blameless as his life and teachings were, could not be separated from the complicated interplay of orthodoxy-heterodoxy in the early years of Spain's uncertain vacillation between innovation and tradition, between *Sic et Non*. The truly orthodox branch of Spanish Catholic mysticism asserted itself powerfully only later, at a time when the Illuminists were facing their final ruin.

By 1555 the great monastic orders, "rich in saints," as a contemporary called them, had consolidated their position so completely that they could not be the object of the easy censure: *Monachatus non est pietas* — "the wearing of the habit is meaningless." They had produced, in impressive number, men like Pedro de Alcántara (later canonized) whose ascetic life was of a purity beyond question. Fray Luis de Granada speaks of multitudes of the poor who hungered and thirsted after righteousness, some of whom "sought out the austerest and most rigorous monasteries, desiring not fatness but hunger; not wealth but poverty; not bodily ease but a cross and mortification of the flesh" (II, 201). Thousands of men and women had heeded the call to practice the inner life.

Saint Teresa of Avila was of this number. Having experienced the state of ecstasy before she had stifled her self-love, she suffered when her Jesuit confessors endeavored to guide her along the path of a more traditional intellectualized type of prayer which visualized the humanity of Christ and lingered in contemplation of the creatures when her soul longed to rise above them. Another of the select group was Fray Juan de la Cruz (not the Saint), who argued against the Erasmian position: even the "perfect" were not exempt from the ceremonies, which would endure, he declared, until the Judgment Day. Avoidance of all thought of the Crucified Christ would be disastrous for the sacraments instituted by our Lord (II, 203 ff.). Thus, it was recognized that the *Philosophia Christi*, as taught by Erasmus and as expressed in many of his books, contained a real and present danger for traditional Catholic dogma, in spite of the saintly life of many of its practitioners. Luis de Granada's *Book of Meditation and Prayer* (1554) closes one epoch and opens another in the history of Spanish spirituality. This book aroused debates which would be cut — like a Gordian knot — by the Inquisition. Henceforth Spanish mysticism, though its greatest triumphs lay ahead, would need to be ever on its guard against the charge of disguised Illuminism, even of masked Lutheranism. I cannot follow Bataillon in his pessimism over this development. "The spiritual life of Spain is going to be destroyed," he writes. "The golden age of the book is near its end" (II, 207). Whatever the persecutions were — and we shall list some of them in a moment — the fruit of this age of repression is, in the work of the greatest Spanish mystics, nothing short of marvelous. The *Philosophia Christi*, revitalized by a Platonic meditation on the universe and man, speaks a thrilling language in Luis de León's *De los nombres de Cristo*. This work is one of the enduring treasures of Spanish spirituality:

When one recalls that the "scarecrow of Illuminism" lifted its flapping arms at every crossroads of Spanish spiritual life, that Estella's Latin *Commentary* on St. Luke was censured, that the reform of the Carmelite Order was rudely attacked, that St. John of the Cross was accused of Illuminism, that the Jesuit Baltasar Alvarez, twenty years after having confirmed Saint Teresa in the way of inner prayer, saw his own type of prayer condemned by his superiors, one can measure more accurately the importance of this manual of Christianity of the spirit, composed in spite of everything as an enduring and outstanding treasure of religious literature in the Castilian language (II, 390).[45]

True though it be, on the one hand, that Luis de León's book "could scarcely bring about . . . the revolutionary effects once

45. There may well be some impropriety in implying that Luis de León was a mystic in the same way that St. Teresa was. There is no evidence in his writings that he experienced union.

produced by Erasmus' *Enchiridion*" and, on the other, that the book was fully intelligible only to those who could read between the lines, the Inquisitor Quiroga judged León's theological position to be sound. The book had four editions in thirteen years. All was not lost. The strength of the Spanish Counter Reformation was due, in part, "to its ability to assimilate and conserve the spirit of the early days of the complex spiritual revolution of sixteenth-century Spain" (II, 391) — that spirit which Erasmus had preached before the coming of Luther. *De los nombres de Cristo* is far from being the only great religious book produced after the condemnation of Erasmus. It was to have illustrious company, as we shall see in the appropriate place.

Ignatius de Loyola and the Return to Tradition

We had a significant reminder of the strength of ecclesiastical tradition at the very opening of our period: it will be remembered that Nebrija withdrew from participation in the work of the Alcalá Polyglot Bible because Cardinal Cisneros would not allow him a free hand in his task of revising the text of St. Jerome's Vulgate translation of the Bible. The "sacredness" of the long-established, of the long-revered, will be a constant force throughout the Spanish sixteenth century; it will be a drag and a threat to the makers of the Royal Bible of Antwerp in the century's second half; it will cause Hebrew scholars to be the object of suspicion and persecution merely because they manipulate Jewish texts; it will cause the designation "lover of newness" to be almost prima-facie evidence that the man so called — be he ever so great a scholar — is an enemy of the public weal. This love for the static will, in the end, be the cause of Spain's decline, of her retirement into a cocoon of insulation and defeat. It is fitting that we study it here, both as a positive and as a negative force.

It will be remembered also that the opposition to the Erasmist reformers came not from ignorant, blind, and bigoted monks of medieval mind; it came from monks, to be sure, but from monks who were learned and devout, men of good will — men unconvinced, however, of the advisability or the possibility of renouncing any considerable portion of the Church's traditions: to do so, they declared, was to endanger the Church itself, even to lose the meaning of sacraments instituted by Christ.

The fact that the Society of Jesus became after 1560 a great force in the struggle against Protestantism does not mean that St. Ignatius was primarily an anti-Luther. The Reformation began before Luther and continued after him (II, xiv).

In a section of *Erasmo y España* bearing the heading "From Illuminism to Erasmianism," Bataillon points out an important fact: around the year 1525 Ignatius de Loyola appeared in the role of an *Iluminado,* an actor in the spiritual revolution whose leader was to an ever increasing extent Erasmus of Rotterdam (I, 247). Ignatius, as a student at Alcalá, witnessed the first great sweep of popularity of the Erasmian *Enchiridion.* The future saint's own confessor urged him to make of that book his personal manual. For the future organizer of the Jesuit Order, with its military inspiration and organization, the title — *Manual of a Christian Soldier* — of Erasmus' work could have been significant. Historians of the Jesuit Order are not clear in this connection; some say that Ignatius preferred not to use a book by an author who was the object of public discussion; others, that he read it and found it unsuited to his needs. What we do know is that, with some fellow students, he became an apostle of a Christianity more ethical than dogmatic. He and they were examined (1526–29) and found free of Illuminist contamination; but they were forbidden to teach before having studied three years in the university. Ignatius was protected by the Archbishop of Toledo, Maecenas of Erasmists. When he passed to Salamanca, the subprior of the Dominican monastery there warned him of the dangers of his position and of his actions "in this time when so many errors are propounded by Erasmus and many others who have deceived the world." When Ignatius came to found his order, he gave it a secular character, its members being uncloistered and without obligation to sing in choir (I, 249).

We have already seen, following Bataillon, that between 1535 and 1555 there was a period during which the dividing line between the orthodox and the heterodox movements was imprecise. If the conservative school, with its respect for the sacraments and ceremonies, and the radical school, committed to the doctrine of justification by faith rather than by works, had really been in conflict, one would scarcely be able to explain the indecisive position of the new Jesuit Order in the trials of Constantino and Carranza in 1558 (I, 138). When, in 1555, instructions were given to the Jesuit colleges to scrutinize their books, the works of Erasmus and of Vives were not burned but were ordered set aside until the General (Loyola died in 1556) should make a decision regarding them (II, 140). It would thus be an error, as we study the early years of the new Order, to establish too decisive a contrast between Erasmian meditation and that advocated by Loyola.[46] Only in 1549 does Ignatius add to his *Exercitia Spiritualia* new rules on orthodoxy in which adhesion to the institutions, loosened by Erasmus, is insisted upon.

When the Index of 1559 was making objections to the type of inner devotion urged by Luis de Granada, the Society of Jesus found it possible to make the necessary adjustments. Laínez, the second General of the Order, avoided the most obvious dangers. The works of the northern mystics were abandoned in favor of Ignatius' own *Exercitia* (with their 1548 rules on orthodoxy); prudence was required in all matters (e. g., questions of predestination, justification by faith, grace) that could weaken the incentive to good works. Far from deprecating a worship which dwells on the creatures, especially the humanity of Christ, the *Exercitia* made of such contemplation the first step in the soul's approach to God. Far from favoring a limitation or diminution of the importance of the physical, organized Church, the Jesuits set out to strengthen and re-establish the authority of the ecclesiastical power that had its center in the Eternal City.

Cano, Soto, Suárez — and Trent. Out of all the intertwining doctrines of the early sixteenth century, out of all the conflicting tendencies, there emerged a Spain committed to the Thomistic-Aristotelian world view and to the Catholicism of the Scholastics. Spanish theologians — Cano, Soto, Suárez — undertook the great task of bringing Scholastic philosophy up to date, a task they performed so successfully that their writings have in our own time become the object of a renewed interest, as they were an important object of interest to Spinoza and to Leibnitz. This Scholastic restoration,

---

46. See the dedication to Ignatius and to his Society in the Cologne (1555) edition of the works of the mystic Henry Herph, made by the Carthusians in that city (cited *ibid.*, p. 188, n. 5).

sometimes called the Scholasticism of the baroque, is studied in Chapter X of the present volume.

Back of this work of consolidation — even at the Council of Trent itself — there was the ever-present interplay of a doctrinal *Sic* and *Non*. Some twenty years after the first meeting in 1545, Spain will emerge as the champion of "Tridentine orthodoxy," and will take pride in the part Spaniards played in the formulation of that orthodoxy:

> Laínez's part in the debates on justification by faith will be played up with great satisfaction, while arguments on the other side will be glossed over. Nevertheless . . . the records show how other Spaniards, at Trent, were the despair of Gian Battista Scotti because of the extreme freedom of their speech. . . . Dr. Arnedo did not hesitate to say, in a bookstore in Bologna, that "in all St. Augustine there was no mention of purgatory nor could a trace of it be found." In this episode we have a distant echo of a spiritual world now submerged (II, 86).

The first meetings of the Council were held in an atmosphere of tension between Spain and Rome, a conflict reminiscent of the passionate days of 1526–27. Documents of the earlier conflict were brought out and published; indeed, a new satiric dialogue was produced. Later, in 1556, the Pope called Charles V a heretic (see above, note 40).

In the course of eighteen years passions were gradually stilled. In 1563 the decrees of Trent were issued, to exert their force down to the present day. After ninety years (1473–1563) of stormy evolution, the Spanish position was at last crystallized — but not without cost. Henceforth Spain was to be what she had not always been — a nation with a single purpose, intent upon making that purpose prevail in troubled times, times when new European powers were rising to confront and challenge her. Yet neither the decrees of Trent nor the *Exercitia* of Loyola represented the totality of Spanish thought and feeling. "The will to orthodoxy did not stifle the criticism of lifeless ceremonies, the censure of logic-chopping bereft of Christian spirit." The best forgers of the Spanish Counter Reformation — Luis de Granada, Luis de León, and others to be studied later — were "spirits incapable of being contented merely with the *Rules* of St. Ignatius; they were men firmly committed to all the exterior acts of worship, to be sure, but men who did not fear to denounce any suppression of inward devotion by outward ritual; men, in short, who had a profound relationship with Erasmus but differed from him by reason of their resolute adherence to the dogmas and the rites of Catholicism" (II, 409).

UNITY ACHIEVED

When these men came into their own — often not without suffering persecution, as both Luises did — Spain had passed from an unsatisfactory and unsatisfying state of religion within her borders to a condition of disciplined conformity for which the nation as a whole had been willing to pay the necessary price and to make the necessary sacrifices — including its loss of illustrious sons to exile or to execution.

The spiritual unification of Spain is nowhere more clearly observable than in the national theater as created (about 1588) by Lope de Vega — "the entrancing pageant of a vanished age, a society vivid, picturesque, noble, blazoning its belief in God, the King, the Point of Honor, as imperious realities governing the conduct of an entire nation." [47] The two great poles of that theater, as Arnold Reichenberger has so convincingly shown, are: in the secular sphere, honor; and in contrast to the secular, the faith.[48] As early as 1589 Pedro Simón Abril wrote that eloquence, in Spain, was restricted to the pulpit, since government did not depend on swaying the multitudes and lawsuits were decided on the basis of written briefs. Two generations later the "modern" school of pulpit orators contended that, now that religious assent was universal, the preacher should avoid the exposition of ideas, there being no longer anything to prove, and should use his originality to invent conceits and devices to move the will of his listeners, to incite them to follow after virtue.[49]

An expression of this majority assent is Dr. Tomás Cerdán de Tellada's praise of the Inquisition in his work entitled *True Government of this Monarchy* (Valencia, 1581). It is that institution,

47. James Fitzmaurice-Kelly, *Lope de Vega and the Spanish Drama* (Glasgow–London, 1902), pp. 62–63.
48. "The Uniqueness of the *Comedia*," *HR*, XXVII (1959), 308.
49. See my article, "*Se acicalaron los auditorios*: An Aspect of the Spanish Literary Baroque," *HR*, XXVII (1959), 417, 421.

Cerdán says, that keeps Spain safe from the disasters of Germany, France, and Flanders. Owing to the king's zeal, "our religion and its precepts are well preserved; and this, in my opinion, is the principal cause of the peace, tranquility, and calm of this our Spain."[50] It was an institution, however, that could strike with numbing terror men innocent of heretical intent, and its power — political, even academic, as well as religious — was more sinister than Cerdán's statement would imply. Yet one fact remains: there were no wars of religion in Spain.[51]

It was this new society, bound together at last in a spiritual unity born of struggle and yet separated by political cleavages which led in 1640 to the separation of Portugal from the Spanish crown and the bitter War of Catalonia, that produced, strangely enough, the great masterpieces of that period of maturity in which Spain most successfully expressed and realized herself.

50. Fol. 68v; cited by J. Zarco, "Ideales y normas de gobierno de Felipe II," *La Ciudad de Dios*, CXLIX (1927), 286.

51. See Fray Hernando de Talavera, *Católica impugnación* . . . , ed. F. Martín Hernández, with a highly important *Estudio Preliminar* by Francisco Márquez (Barcelona, 1961); see also A. A. Sicroff, *Les controverses des statuts de "pureté de sang" en Espagne du XVᵉ au XVIIᵉ siècle* (Paris, 1960).

PART II

Christian Renaissance

VII · Reply to the Devil's Advocate

If a medieval tradition held sculpture
in suspicion, a Renaissance dogma held
sculpture the major art, since God had
practiced it to form man.
> *Robert J. Clements* [1]

The renewed interest of fifteenth-century
Florence in the Early Christian Fathers . . .
made the patristic similes current once
again, and, automatically, these revived
ideas found visual expression in such
sculptures as Donatello's *Davids*. . . . Thus
the enthusiastic study of the nude by
Renaissance artists . . . becomes very much
clearer as an historical phenomenon.
> *Ruth Wedgewood Kennedy* [2]

Pulchritudo est splendor divini vultus.
> *Marsilio Ficino* [3]

It will be well to begin our detailed inquiry into the Christian
character of the Renaissance in Spain [4] with an examination of the

1. *Michelangelo's Theory of Art* (New York, 1961), p. 301.
2. In a review of *De Artibus Opuscula XL: Studies in Honor of Erwin Panofsky,* ed.
Millard Meiss, *Renaissance News,* XV (1962), 12.
3. Cited by Clements, *op. cit.,* p. 5.
4. This is a subject which obviously has been touched upon in nearly every chapter
of the present work, beginning with Volume I. In the remaining six chapters of this
volume something different is proposed, namely: to present evidence that Spain, by
a determined choice, devoted her spiritual and material strength to the defense of
an ideal which we find exemplified, for England, in the Christian humanism of Milton
(d. 1674) in contradistinction to the scientific-materialistic ideals of Bacon (d. 1626)
and of Hobbes (d. 1679). This we shall endeavor to accomplish by presenting, first,
a chapter whose argument is negative: Spain was not enticed by the possibilities
which other countries were realizing as they developed a much more secular culture.
This will be followed by a presentation of Spain's positive preference for the religious
orientation of public and private life. The next chapter, on the "quarrel between
ancients and moderns" (and Spain's self-defense against the charge of being unable
to receive or develop what the new centuries had to offer), shows those areas of modern
endeavor in which Spain had the advantage, as well as those other fields — science,
philosophy, classical scholarship — in which Spain was an absorber and a user, not a
creator, of things new. The chapter on philosophy is of similar import (yet not
without surprises). The chapter on optimism and pessimism has to do with the

"received idea" that the period is to be understood as an un-Christian age opposed, if not openly and declaredly at least covertly and unconsciously, to Christian values. Over against this simplistic view we may set that of Paul Oskar Kristeller: "Since the religious convictions of Christianity were either retained or transformed, but never fully challenged, it seems more appropriate to call the Renaissance a fundamentally Christian age. . . . The medieval traditions of religious thought and literature continued without interruption until and after the Reformation. Italy was no exception to this rule." [5]

Gilbert Highet makes very specific the charge of paganism in one department of Renaissance literature — the pastoral: "The same applies to all these pastoral books: the Christian religion, its creed and its church, are never mentioned . . . only Greek deities appear . . . powerful spirits, who are sincerely worshipped and can protect their votaries. . . . This was not merely a fad, or a wish for dramatic propriety. It was a genuine rejection of the austere and otherworldly Christian ideals, and an assertion of the power of this world and human passions, as personified in those Greek figures who were called immortal because the spirits they hypostatized lived on forever in the heart of man." [6]

To write thus is simply to fail to understand the symbolic world of the pastoral and to ignore well-known facts. Sannazaro wrote not only the *Arcadia* in Italian prose, but also two works in Latin verse: the *Piscatory Eclogues,* in which he sought to rival Virgil's *Bucolics* and in which the Christian religion, its creed, and its church, very appropriately are not part of the subject matter; and the *De partu Virginis,* whose theme is the bringing of the Christ Child into the world by the Virgin Mary. Jorge de Montemayor, author of the first true pastoral novel (as opposed to Sannazaro's prose-poem with interspersed passages in verse), composed also a *First* and a *Second Spiritual "Cancionero."* He was one of the first

thorny problem of the transition from Renaissance to baroque (a subject to be fully treated in our Volume IV). The chapter on literature and society records the strains that developed as the concept (almost universal) of the literary art as ancillary to mental health and eternal salvation came into conflict with an opposing idea: that literature possesses an autonomy of its own.

5. *The Classics and Renaissance Thought* (Cambridge, Massachusetts, 1955), p. 73.

6. *The Classical Tradition: Greek and Roman Influences on Western Literature* (New York–London, 1949), p. 169.

in Spain to perceive the majestic poetry of the Psalms, the first to try to give it popular expression — by means of the Castilian hendecasyllable; in his religious verse he shows the influence of Erasmian piety, as well as that of the martyred Savonarola.[7] In Cervantes' pastoral novel *La Galatea* (1585), the antiphonal song honoring the deceased Meliso unquestionably places the newly ascended soul in the Christian Empyrean.[8] I have counted eight passages in Cervantes' works which reveal how deeply he was affected by the great words from St. Augustine's *Confessions*: "Thou has made us for Thyself, and our hearts are restless till they rest in Thee." To Cervantes, God was everywhere: "not a leaf in the forest, not a worm in the ground, not a bird in the air stirs without God's will."[9] The real core of the tradition concerning Renaissance paganism is, as Kristeller indicates, "something quite different: it is the steady and irresistible growth of non-religious intellectual interests which were not so much opposed to the content of religious doctrine, as rather competing with it for individual and public attention" (*op. cit.*, p. 72).

Reviewing Kristeller's lectures on *The Classics and Renaissance Thought*, I pointed out that whereas Kristeller, perhaps more than any other scholar, has shown us that the charge of paganism cannot be sustained, his argument that the Renaissance was a fundamentally Christian age could have been more impressively made. The tragedy of the sixteenth century — what Ronsard called "the wretchedness of this time" — was war, "cold" and "hot," not between Christianity and paganism but between opposing camps within the body of Christian believers.[10] "Luther attacked not the ribald Aretino or the trifling Boccaccio but rather the great restorer of primitive Christianity, Erasmus of Rotterdam. And Calvin came to grips not with the scoffing Luigi Pulci, but with the passionate herald of a new day of the Lord, Michael Servetus [Miguel

---

7. M. Bataillon, *Erasmo y España* (Mexico City–Buenos Aires, 1950), II, 208–9.

8. *Obras completas*, ed. A. Valbuena Prat (Madrid, 1956), pp. 743–44.

9. A. F. G. Bell, *Cervantes* (Norman, Oklahoma, 1947), p. 158.

10. See *RPh*, X (1957), 282–83. Since writing that review I have found the following in Hans Kohn's *Nationalism: Its Meaning and History* (Princeton, 1955), p. 13: "The European peoples of the sixteenth and seventeenth centuries did not fight for national values but for dogmatic truth. People were expelled or punished not for ethnic or linguistic differences but for religious heresy or apostasy."

Servet]."[11] Humanism, says Kristeller, "was in its core neither religious nor irreligious, but a literary and scholarly orientation that could be and often was pursued without reference to religious topics, by fervent or nominal members of Christian churches" (*op. cit.*, pp. 74–75). Christian humanism, in its specific sense, he limits to those scholars with a classical and rhetorical training who explicitly discussed religious problems, and he discusses the ennoblement of theology through philology that we have studied in an earlier chapter. There is still more to be said about it, however. Christian humanism had as its main tenet the Christianized Socratic doctrine that all knowledge produces virtue — Christian virtue. Its philosophical and theological position rested on the acceptance of the natural world and on belief in the importance of the rational faculties of man — a position not very different from that of the Thomists on the problem of nature and grace;[12] its difference therefrom lay in its fuller acceptance of the total corpus[13] of classical literature: learning could not corrupt, it could only purify. A new educational program was not only necessary; it was all that was necessary.[14]

"The alleged cases of openly pagan or atheistic convictions are rare and dubious," writes Kristeller.[15] We find, of course, that in the fifteenth century the dying Captain Bétissac said to his comrades: "Beaux seigneurs, . . . I believe and say . . . that there is no such thing as a soul,"[16] but such isolated instances are extremely difficult to duplicate, much less to multiply.[17] Serious skepticism "is

11. Roland H. Bainton, "The Thirst for God in the Renaissance," *Renaissance News*, V (1952), 10.

12. See in our Volume II, Chapter V: "Reason," and Chapter III: "Three Aspects of Nature."

13. "The Renaissance represents the historical moment when European thought was ready to come to terms with the whole of its ancient heritage, not merely with some part of it" (James Hutton, "The Classics in Sixteenth-century France," *The Classical Weekly*, XLIII [1950], 131).

14. See Myron P. Gilmore, *The World of Humanism* (New York, 1952), pp. 204–7.

15. *Op. cit.*, p. 86. The question of atheism was touched on briefly in Volume II.

16. J. Huizinga, *The Waning of the Middle Ages: A Study of the Forms of Life, Thought and Art in France and the Netherlands in the XIVth and XVth Centuries* (London, 1924), p. 148. In the sixteenth century, the "pure" humanists whom Erasmus suspected of being "more pagan than pagan letters" and who, he charged, found the Gospel "inconvenient" — they showed no interest in his return to the more primitive Christianity of the Gospels — nevertheless "proclaimed their orthodoxy" (Bataillon, *op. cit.*, I, 178).

17. María Rosa Lida de Malkiel cites the words *No creo en Dios* — "I do not believe

scarcely discoverable prior to the very end of the sixteenth century, in Bruno, Campanella, and Vanini, and they expiated their temerity at the stake [or in the torture chamber] after the manner of the High Middle Ages." [18] Kristeller, after reading the philosophical sources commonly regarded as anti-Christian, found that "never is the existence of God called into question and especially discussed in that body of writing." [19]

Bainton concludes, in a statement which we may make our own: "If the Renaissance be defined as a *movement* to be set over against the Reformation, that movement was marked by an exaggeration of the Hellenic elements in the Christian synthesis, with an ever-present tendency to open the door, not to irreligion but to universal religion, and, in some quarters, a secularistic tendency which relegated religion to the periphery of life. If, on the other hand, the Renaissance is a *period* which includes the Reformation [and I, with Kristeller, so regard it], then one may say that, although the unity of the Church was shattered, the Christian consciousness of Europe was restored." [20] The time was not ripe for agnosticism. Even in the seventeenth century, most scientists were "men of piety who believed they were advancing the Kingdom of Heaven by their earthly labors." [21] The real theological difficulties were not to take shape until after the Renaissance, when men would have to deal with new concepts that would shatter the outer walls of the medi-

in God" — used as an oath by Juan de Osorio, a young officer who accompanied the conquistador Don Pedro de Mendoza on his campaigns in the River Plate territory, and by Luis de Miranda, the first poet in the same region. See her *La originalidad artística de La Celestina* (Buenos Aires, 1962), p. 697, n. 2. Burckhardt reports the case of Alfonso, Duke of Calabria, who "openly avowed his contempt for religion and its usages" (*The Civilization of the Renaissance in Italy*, trans. S. G. C. Middlemore [New York, 1958], I, 52 and n.). The Middle Ages offer similar case histories: see M. Seidlmayer, *Currents of Mediaeval Thought with Special Reference to Germany*, trans. D. Barker (Oxford, 1960), p. 99, for the thirteenth and fourteenth centuries. See also below, Chapter X, the section entitled "Skepticism."

18. R. H. Bainton, "Man, God, and the Church in the Age of the Renaissance," in *The Renaissance: A Symposium* (Metropolitan Museum of Art, New York, 1952), p. 59.

19. "El mito del ateísmo renacentista y la tradición francesa del libre pensamiento," *Notas y estudios de filosofía*, IV, núm. 13 (1953), p. 5. Kristeller has made a brilliant summary of the findings of recent scholarship in his article, "Studies on Renaissance Humanism During the Last Twenty Years," *Studies in the Renaissance*, IX (1962), 7–30, with selective bibliography; see especially p. 18 ff.

20. "Man, God, and the Church . . . ," pp. 57, 62; italics mine.

21. Don Cameron Allen, *The Legend of Noah: Renaissance Rationalism in Art, Science, and Letters* (Urbana, Illinois, 1949), p. 49.

eval universe and disperse the stars throughout infinite space, showing them to be suns possibly having inhabited planets revolving about them.[22] Even with these dismaying realities to be faced, "it would be difficult to find a first-rate scientist [of the seventeenth century] who was an agnostic" (Allen, *op. cit.*, p. 30).

"ATHEISM" IN SPAIN

"Although paganism held attractions which the poets dulcetly expressed, there were no practising pagans in Tudor England."[23] "The word atheist was used against the seventeenth-century scientist, and undoubtedly there were some scientists worthy of that epithet; but it is difficult to investigate this charge, for though there were many books written against atheism, there were none in its favor" (Allen, *op. cit.*, p. 25; see also p. 59). It should be remembered that the age was intolerant — everywhere; that "it was no less criminal to believe in Christianity in a manner different from orthodoxy than to abandon religious belief altogether."[24] Even in the case of Giordano Bruno (d. 1600), "it is hard to decide whether he was a heretical Christian or an outright unbeliever. . . . It all depends on how we define religion" (*ibid.*).

Assuming that — as the Spanish proverb has it — "if the river is noisy, there is water in the channel," it is reasonable to ask what were the doctrines against which the epithet *atheist* was launched? While leaving room for all sorts of shades and gradations, we may say that the enemies of the orthodox protesters very probably professed or seemed to profess either the hedonism of Epicurus' continuators[25] or the disbelief in personal immortality which

22. Arthur O. Lovejoy, *The Great Chain of Being* (Cambridge, Massachusetts, 1948), pp. 117–18; see also Index, *s.v.* Infinity.

23. Harry Levin, "English Literature of the Renaissance," in Tinsley Helton (ed.), *The Renaissance: A Reconsideration of the Theories and Interpretations of the Age* (Madison, 1961), p. 130. See also pp. 135–36: "Mr. Bush's Alexander Lectures of 1939, *The Renaissance and English Humanism*, had a healthy sobering effect upon the temptation to paganize the Renaissance."

24. P. O. Kristeller, "Changing View of the Intellectual History of the Renaissance since Jacob Burckhardt," in Helton (ed.), *op. cit.*, p. 44.

25. On Epicurus himself, see Allen, "The Rehabilitation of Epicurus and His Theory of Pleasure in the Early Renaissance," *SP*, XLI (1944), 1 ff. The fifteenth-century Juan de Lucena took pains not to appear to be an Epicurean (see M. Morreale, "El tratado de Juan de Lucena sobre la felicidad," *NFRH*, IX [1955], 1, n. 3); on "la devise facile" of "vivre, boire, et jouir" in sixteenth-century France, see L. Febvre,

characterized the Latin Averroists. So widespread was the acceptance of the latter teaching that the Lateran Council of 1512 found
it necessary for the first time to establish the immortality of the
soul as a dogma of the Church.[26]

References to unbelief in literary and in other works must be
interpreted with care. The following four lines, from *The Twelve
Triumphs of the Twelve Apostles* by the fifteenth-century Juan de
Padilla might be taken — except for the heading that introduces
them — for a social document:

En fin, que me trujo mi triste pecado	In short, my accursed sin
a un vil oficio de baratería:	brought me to engage in vile
allí renegaba, y allí descreía,	tricks of deception; I blasphemed,
allí sotilmente hincaba mi dado.[27]	I gave up my belief, as I slyly
	rolled my dice.

The heading makes it clear, however, that the speech is that of a
hypothetical and imaginary renegade: "These words are supposed
to be pronounced by a sinner in Hell."

Much more concrete is the warning of Gómez Manrique (15 c.),
in a poem *On the Training of Princes*, against being enticed by the
conviction (held by certain wicked men) that in the matter of life
and death there is no difference between men and animals — a
conviction which leads to bestial acts requiring social discipline.
Such beliefs cause wars and famine; because of them cities are destroyed and converted into swamps.[28] On the the other hand,
Hernando de Ludueña writes a *Doctrine of Gentility* which, though

Le problème de l'incroyance au XVIᵉ siècle (Paris, 1947). In the seventeenth century,
Quevedo and the Jesuit J. E. Nieremberg rehabilitated Epicurus (see Quevedo's
Obras en verso, ed. L. Astrana Marín [Madrid, 1932], pp. 718ab, 793b).

26. Ernst Cassirer *et al.* (eds.), *The Renaissance Philosophy of Man* (Chicago, 1948),
p. 17; see also p. 140.

27. *Cancionero castellano del siglo XV*, ed. R. Foulché-Delbosc (Madrid, 1912–15),
I, 311. The word *renegaba* is ambiguous: it may be translated as "blasphemed" or,
more seriously, as "gave up my Christian religion to adopt the Mohammedan." The
heading reads: "Presupone cómo fabla un pecador que penaba." In any case, the
sinner is an imaginary figure.

28. "Mas guardaos de presumir / lo que tienen los maluados, / que non ay en el
biuir / sino naçer e morir / como saluajes venados," etc. (*Cancionero castellano . . . ,*
II, 115–16). Rafael Lapesa comments on this passage of Manrique's poem: "Gómez
Manrique does not state the source of the religious agnosticism for which he demands
punishment; but in any event he provides evidence that in fifteenth-century Castile
there existed adepts of a naturistic materialism." See his review of Mrs. Malkiel, *op.
cit.*, in *RPh*, XVII (1936), 61; see also I. S. Révah, "Les marranes," *Revue des études
juives*, 3d ser., I (CXVIII) (1959–60), 58.

it reports disbelief to be embraced by many "nowadays," seems to be directed against some sort of fashionable frivolity of high society: it is the romantic lover (*galán*) who is warned to avoid such wickedness in his own person and to condemn it in others. Anyone finding satisfaction in such attitudes must surely be basely born. A man's reputation for "gentility" does not suffer from an outward profession of Christianity, but rather is the gainer; for virtue is an essential factor in courtly success, and he who is not virtuous is a fool. The keeping of these precepts is as essential to the courtier "as her mirror is to the lady." [29]

Yet more was involved — or had been involved, and would again be — than a certain fashionable affectation to which ladies and gentlemen of high society were inclined. In the early fourteenth century Ramón Lull (d. 1315), following — in his own original fashion — the example of St. Thomas' *Summa contra gentiles*, attacked Averroism as the greatest peril threatening men's minds in his generation. With his usual confidence in his own powers, Lull — while complaining of the general indifference of his contemporaries in religious matters — believes firmly that his arguments and his writings are the new weapon, providentially made available, by means of which the pestilential philosophy of materialism is to be exterminated.[30] Two generations later, in 1399, the Catalan humanist Bernat Metge takes up the question of the death or immortality of the soul in his allegorical work *The Dream*. The author relates in the first person how, being unjustly imprisoned, he had an unusual dream in which three personages appeared before him, one of whom was the recently deceased King Juan I. The dreamer rejects the idea that he is talking with the spirit of the King, since he personally believes that the soul dies with the body. There follows a discussion on the immortality of the soul according to the testimonies of the ancient philosophers, of the Old Testament, of the New Testament, of the Fathers, and of the Mohammedans. The King also corrects Metge's belief in the identity of the souls of men and animals. In the end Metge's doubts re-

29. "Mirad bien, yo os lo consejo, / porque es muy gran aparejo, / e sabéis quánto pro tiene, / que al gentil hombre conuiene / como a la dama ell' espejo" (*Cancionero castellano* . . . , II, 724).

30. Mauricio de Iriarte, *Genio y figura del iluminado Maestro B. Ramón Lull* (Madrid, 1945), pp. 52–53.

garding the destiny of the soul are resolved.[31] Earlier, perhaps as early as 1388, Metge had prepared a sort of preliminary study of these problems in a work entitled *Apología* "in which will be . . . defended various impugnations against the truth, and our doubts will be satisfied by Divine grace" (p. 76 of the prologue).

The chief seedbed of these Averroistic ideas in the Spanish Peninsula was, from the fourteenth century on, the "displaced" (i.e., newly converted) Jews known as *Marranos*. The studies of Isaac Baer[32] have shown that during the Middle Ages rationalistic, skeptical, and Epicurean tendencies spread among the highly placed Jews — financiers and physicians — of the Peninsula. Averroist philosophy especially managed to avoid, by means of allegorical symbolism, dogmas which it found uncongenial, substituting for them its own deistic interpretations. When in 1532 the Portuguese João de Barros composed his *Ropica pnefma* or *Spiritual Merchandise* for the religious edification of the recent converts from Judaism, he sought to combat not only their secret relapses into the practices of their former religion, but also their propensity to deny the immortality of the soul.[33] These tendencies persisted even into the seventeenth century: in 1659 Spinoza, living at Amsterdam in intimate contact with Dr. Juan de Prado, came under his influence. Prado preached the mortality of the human soul, a thesis which Spinoza was to replace by his own theory of non-personal immortality (*ibid.*, p. 15).

There were, therefore, atheists (or deists) in Spain during the Middle Ages, in Portugal in the early sixteenth century, and in Marrano circles in Holland in the seventeenth. With regard to sixteenth-century Castile, on the other hand, it will be well to note Bataillon's insistence (*op. cit.*, I, xvi) that Erasmianism was a rationalistic piety (with all the risks that this involved for orthodoxy) but not a movement looking forward to eighteenth-century-style "free thought." How could Erasmus have thought otherwise?, Bataillon asks; the most profound historian of the sixteenth century, he says, has shown the anachronism of giving to the word *atheism* a modern

31. *Obras de Bernat de Metge*, ed. Martín de Riquer (Barcelona, 1959), pp. 76, 130 ff. of the prologue (with page references to the text of *Lo Somni*).

32. *Die Juden im christlichen Spanien* (Berlin, 1929–36).

33. I. S. Révah, *Qu'est-ce que les Marranes?* (Conférence faite le 8 Juillet 1958 aux Journées Pédagogiques de l'Alliance Israélite Universelle), p. 6.

content,[34] and has characterized that century as marked by its will to believe. As an illustration of the loose and uncertain use of the word *ateo* in Castilian, we have a very enlightening text of the early seventeenth century, by the Carmelite Friar Jerónimo Gracián (d. 1614). Three years before his death, in 1611, Fray Jerónimo published at Brussels a work entitled *Ten Lamentations on the Wretched State of the Atheists of Our Time*. The title brings one up with a start: were atheists that numerous at the end of Gracián's lifetime, even in the Low Countries? But the Friar's definition makes all clear: "Atheist, godless. The word godless could be applied to all those who are in mortal sin, for they lack His grace. . . . Likewise all heretics — whose knowledge is far removed from the true God, from His law and His faith — could be called atheists. Speaking more properly, we here apply the name atheist to heretical sinners who have reached such depths of misery that they deny there is a God, or speak ill of His Divine Essence, or live beyond the pale of law or reason." That Fray Jerónimo, in spite of the title of his work (i.e., "the atheists of our time"), was not limiting his analysis to the contemporary scene, or the word *atheist* to its normal meaning, is proved by the title of his Fifth Lamentation: "Concerning spiritual atheists, namely the Pythonesses, the Essenes and Sadducees, Messaliani, Beghards and Béguines, *Alumbrados* and *Abandonados*; as well as the modern Perfectists [Familists] in our own day, and certain Catholics of evil spirit who are the cause of many errors." Speaking of "the atheism which now reins in Germany," he mentions the Anabaptists, and other "persons who have been deceived by this atheism"[35] — persons he has actually encountered in his travels.

When once it has been shown that the word atheist could be applied to passionate believers in the Lord merely because their beliefs and actions met with social and ecclesiastical disapproval, it becomes apparent that any charge of impiety or unbelief made

34. I suspect that the historian to whom Bataillon refers is Lucien Febvre. See Henri Beer, preface to Febvre, *op. cit.*, p. xi: "Le mot athée n'avait pas alors le sens précis que nous lui assignons: 'il s'employait dans le sens qu'on voulait bien lui donner', et 'c'était l'injure suprême que les polémistes de tendances très diverses s'envoyaient les uns aux autres.'"

35. Domingo Ricart, *Juan de Valdés y el pensamiento religioso europeo en los siglos XVI y XVII* (Mexico City, 1958), pp. 69-70 and n. 46. I have not seen Gracián's book.

on the basis of the use of that word can have no historical value. We are therefore prepared to discount the word as used by Quevedo in his *La Constancia y Paciencia del Santo Job* (1641), a work which was given the following approbation by Fray Francisco Polanco: "I have seen this book, whose subject is the defense of Divine Providence against atheism. . . . "[36] In his *Providence of God, Suffered by Those Who Deny It and Enjoyed by Those Who Confess It* (1641–42) Quevedo continues the same line of argument. The word *atheist*, he says, means *godless* in Greek, and has been "usurped" by the vernacular languages (*ibid.*, p. 1028a). He is clearly arguing against the "few" ancient philosophers who absolutely deny God's existence (Diagoras, Protagoras, disciples of Democritus and Theodorus, Bion, Lucian) and against those who, denying Providence, do not confess God's existence (Epicurus, Lucretius, Democritus, Heraclitus). Among moderns he cites (*ibid.*, p. 1029a) Torcuato Tasso who, in his dialogue *The Messenger*, forestalled condemnation by saying in the dedication: "Let me argue as a philosopher though I believe as a Christian." [37] In this most learned disputation Quevedo cites all manner of authorities, leaning heavily on Jesuit writers of his own time. But in Castile where, as one witness has already testified for us (see above), "there remains nothing to be proved," whom is he addressing? The question must remain rhetorical.[38]

Similarly, the allegorical figure named Atheism in Calderón's eucharistic drama (*auto sacramental*) entitled *La divina Filotea* [39]

36. *Obras en prosa*, ed. L. Astrana Marín (Madrid, 1932), p. 978a.

37. *Il Messaggero* is one of Tasso's more famous dialogues; in it a "familiar" spirit explains to the author the hierarchy of beings from the Deity down to man. Quevedo accuses Tasso of following an erroneous opinion of Tertullian who, "badly persuaded by a verse of Lucretius," held that the soul "has a sort of body." Tertullian was a Stoic materialist, one of the few major Christian theologians to hold to the materialistic doctrine that only the body is real (J. H. Randall, Jr., *The Role of Knowledge in Western Religion* [Boston, 1958], p. 39).

38. Francisco Cascales in his *Cartas filológicas* (1634) equates the word *ateismo* with anything execrable. Inveighing against the new poetic style of Góngora and his school, Cascales sums up: "In short, this is a gross humor which has risen from the body to the head of the author of this atheism—and to the heads of his followers. Like any bodily humor, it is bound to evaporate and gradually resolve itself into nothingness" (cited by W. C. Atkinson, "On Aristotle and the Concept of Lyric Poetry in Early Spanish Criticism," *Estudios dedicados a Menéndez Pidal*, VI [Madrid, 1956], 189).

39. In *Autos sacramentales desde su origen hasta fines del siglo XVII*, ed. Eduardo González Pedroso (*BAE*, LVIII), pp. 531 ff.

quite obviously represents the deniers of immortality of the school of Epicurus and Epicurus' continuators, the hedonists: Atheism (the personage) follows after World (another allegorical speaker) because World is necessary to him,

> And since my god is my belly,
> Let us eat and drink today,
> For tomorrow we shall die —
> And on with the dance! [40]

Atheism is disgusted for having allowed himself to be persuaded to come to a place where so little thought is given to living, "since beyond this life there's nothing" — "siendo así que no hay más vida" (p. 539b). Later he addresses Faith:

> Though this life's the end of all,
> I flee from your fury.[41]

Surely Calderón did not expect that there would be atheists in the audience, or that his hearers had had any direct contacts with modern Epicureans. Was atheism, then, unreal in Golden Age Spain? Yes and no. Heretics were, of course, common enough to produce *autos de fe*, but heretics are not atheists. Avowed atheists, to all intents and purposes, were non-existent in Castile during the Golden Age. But the moralists of the day knew that individual cases of troubled unbelief were a perfectly concrete reality.[42]

One of these concrete cases remains anonymous. Fray Luis de Granada tells in the prologue of his *Guía de pecadores* of having heard from the lips of a member of the General Council of the

---

40. "Y mi dios mi vientre siendo, / comamos hoy y bebamos, / que mañana moriremos,/ y dure lo que durare" (p. 536b).

41. "Aunque no hay más que vivir, / huyendo iré tu furor" (p. 540a).

42. We can only conclude that Father José de Acosta is complaining merely of insufficient piety (not of atheism) when, at the beginning of his *Historia natural y moral de las Indias* (Madrid, 1792, I, 3-4), he exonerates certain Doctors of the Church of their obvious ignorance of cosmological matters (their concern was the Creator, not the creatures) but condemns "the savants and vain philosophers of this century who, knowing and perceiving the essence and the order of these creatures, the course and movement of the heavens, did not, in their blindness [*los desventurados*] recognize and know the Creator and Maker of all this; persons who, completely concerned with these creatures—Divine works of such great loveliness—did not lift up their thoughts to discover the Supreme Author, as the Book of Wisdom bids us do (*Sap.* 13); or who, knowing the Creator and Lord of all, did not serve Him and glorify Him as they should, blinded as they were by their own inventions and discoveries." I can read into these words only the charge that the scientific authors in question treated holy matters in a purely secular fashion.

Inquisition in Portugal the story of a man "who came to beg mercy of the Holy Office of his own free will, not having been accused. He confessed that because of his habit of reading many books, he had lost his faith so completely that he privately believed that human existence was merely a matter of birth and death; but that later, either incidentally or because Providence so ordered, he began to read books of good doctrine; and giving himself over to this type of reading, he emerged from the darkness of his doubt, and asked for pardon, and received it." The books which led this honest soul astray were, apparently, works of Epicurean philosophy or treatises with Averroist tendencies; they denied the immortality of the soul.

Another reader of books, medical books by Arabic authors (he mentions Avenzoar, the teacher of Averroës), was the physician Juan López de Illescas, a man whose paternal ancestry, perhaps significantly, was not free from the "taint" of Jewish blood. That this man was an atheist is certainly not supported by the recorded evidence. What he admitted over and over, and what caused him distress to the point of impairing his health and causing him to fear insanity, was a persistent "temptation" to reject the inner will to believe and to listen to the still small voice that whispered: "There is no God." In 1539 he fulfilled the penance imposed upon him by the Inquisition and removed from the town of Yepes to the town of Tembleque, accepting a post as local physician in the latter place.[43]

How frequent such individual cases may have been it is impossible to know, even approximately, until all the papers of the Inquisition have been studied. What the present state of our knowledge does show conclusively is that Doctor López de Illescas, with his "evil temptation" to believe that there was no God, must have felt terribly isolated in the Spain of his time.[44]

43. See Angela Selke de Sánchez, "¿Un ateo español en el siglo XVI? Las tentaciones del doctor Juán López de Illescas," *Archivum*, VII (1957), 25–47. A study by the same author of a similar case, "El caso del Bachiller Antonio de Medrano, iluminado epicúreo del siglo XVI" (*BHi*, LVIII (1956), 393–420), has nothing to do with atheism, or even with intellectual Epicureanism, but rather with a perverted "thirst for God" in a person of strong sensual impulses and neurotic tendencies. The index to Menéndez y Pelayo's eight-volume *Historia de los heterodoxos españoles* lists no Spanish case of atheism.

44. This observation is made by Manuel Durán, *La ambigüedad en el Quijote* (Xalapa, Mexico, 1960), p. 26, n. 11. Durán errs, however, in seeing in Spain "an almost absolute predominance of orthodoxy or of slight heretical deviations, in some

We conclude this section with a *quod erat demonstrandum*: Renaissance Spain had its heretics; it probably had, as Portugal did as late as 1532, social groups (mainly Jewish) attracted to certain philosophical doctrines that denied personal immortality; it had also — though these cannot be numbered — some isolated individuals who, at given stages in their lives, denied or were tempted to doubt the existence of God. But the nation as a whole was overwhelmingly a nation of believers, passionately seeking personal salvation through belief in a personal God.

LITERARY "PAGANISM"

The interpenetration during the Renaissance of pagan and classical forms of literary expression and of other forms that were Christian — Biblical or patristic — has been shown to us in a new light by recent scholarship. The first Christian to transfer the ethical implications of the Greek and Roman athletic contests into Christian similes was none other than St. Paul: "a crown of glory that fadeth not away" (I Peter 5:4) recalls the laurel wreath granted to the athletic prizeman (see also I Cor. 9:25; II Tim. 4:8). This transfer of symbols [45] was continued by John Chrysostom, as Colin Eisler has demonstrated,[46] and patristic similes of this and similar types became the object of enthusiastic study by Renaissance artists. Thus the interest in the human nude, long held to be a mark of "paganism" in the visual art of the Renaissance, is seen to have been on the contrary an enrichment — like that of St. Paul — of the means of interpretation and persuasion at the disposal of the Christian sculptor or painter. There were, of course, frivolous artists in the Renaissance, as there were also frivolous writers. The coming

cases, like that of the Erasmists and that of the *Alumbrados*" (*loc. cit.*). Unity was achieved, as was shown in our chapter on religious expansion, at very considerable human cost.

45. "At least by the third century A.D. Christian doctrine had assimilated from the extraordinarily influential philosophy of Stoicism the notion of an equalitarian State of Nature which was irrevocably lost. And although it was hardly possible to talk of social and economic organization of the Garden of Eden, orthodox exegesis nevertheless managed to use the Graeco-Roman myth to illustrate the dogma of the fall" (Norman Cohn, *The Pursuit of the Millenium* [Fairlawn, New Jersey, 1957], p. 201).

46. In the first of the studies in honor of Panofsky (see the reference, note 2, above).

to terms with the totality of the pagan heritage produced artistic and literary products of both the frivolously pagan and the Christianized pagan type. The point to be made here is that the presence of the frivolously pagan does not constitute evidence that the sculptors and their patrons, or the users of the literary similes and their readers, were in any sense "pagan."

The final chapter of our Volume I — "Truancy and Recantation" — provides impressive evidence of this truth: no matter how jolly or inspiring the company of the wayward pagan Muses may have been, the time almost always came when the poet turned away from the dazzling colors of his soul's outward walls — "so costly gay" in the words of Shakespeare — and took thought for the salvation of the soul within. Even the merriest medieval laughter (see Chapter II of Volume I) gives way on occasion to the muted voice of religious meditation as the Archpriest of Hita asks that God not forget him, or as the boisterous sixteenth-century Cristóbal de Castillejo remembers that his name is Christopher, that is to say, Bearer of Christ. The palinode — the recantation, the regret over time lost and youth squandered in a life both too brief and too demanding for all but the heroically virtuous — all the palinodes, in their insistent chorus of unanimity, proclaim that the gaiety was only gaiety. They bear testimony, in a manner no less valid than do the wars of religion, that Europe did not cease to be Christian in the Renaissance.

But what of the Muses? Were they accepted as easily as St. Paul accepted the imagery of the Olympic games, as easily as the Stoic myth of an original equalitarian state of nature was incorporated into the dogma of the fall? While many writers were as able as Paul of Tarsus to make adaptations of this sort, and to do so with a clear conscience, the issue at times presented itself to others as a choice between the licit and the illicit. To what extent was it possible to "despoil the Egyptians" in order to adorn God's Temple? To what extent were images and concepts, originally pagan and known to have been such, usable — indeed seemingly indispensable — in the poetry and prose of our Siglo de Oro? In what cases were they not properly adaptable? Under what circumstances was the "fragrance of the vessel" felt to be foreign and unsuitable?

"The poets feign"

The Middle Ages were not ages of literary theory or criticism: "the direction of theoretical thinking in these ages was elsewhere. . . . In short it was an age of . . . theologically oriented and theocratic society." [47] Throughout our period Spain continues this theological thinking — a medieval thinking grown mature under the pressure of Renaissance aspirations, achievements, and failures — in a society theocratically oriented though by no means a theocracy. Boccaccio insisted that the pagan poets were good theologians. [48] Villani asserted that Dante had reconciled the fictions of the poets with moral and natural philosophy and with Christian literature, and had shown that the ancient poets were divinely inspired to prophesy Christian mysteries, thus making poetry pleasing not only to the learned, but also to the common and uneducated. In our own time Antonio Belloni, in his history of epic and mythological poetry in Italy, [49] writes that it was the religious writers themselves who, when they treated sacred subjects, felt the need to avail themselves of the imagery of the pagan gods. And Ernst Walser, [50] attacking what was to him the error of earlier students of the Renaissance (namely, the belief that the Christian piety of the humanists had been shaken by the revival of enthusiasm for antiquity), sets forth as the one fundamentally new and differentiating element in Renaissance humanism its newly acquired artistic conception of the formal beauties of antique art and letters. The "paganism" of the Renaissance, he maintains, was a purely external, fashionable, formal element. The elaborate care "with which the Scholastics . . . had reconciled classical philosophy with Catholic doctrine had its influence in the fact that the humanists, for the most part, simply

47. W. K. Wimsatt, Jr., and Cleanth Brooks, *Literary Criticism: A Short History* (New York, 1957), p. 154. These statements are on the whole true, and have their bearing on our present problem; but one should not forget that E. de Bruyne's *Estudios de estética medieval*, so often cited in Volume I of the present study (in translation by Fr. A. Suárez [Madrid, 1958-59]), is a solid three-volume work.

48. C. G. Osgood, *Boccaccio on Poetry* (Princeton, 1930), pp. 121 ff.; see also my article, "*Fingen los poetas*: Notes on the Spanish Attitude toward Pagan Mythology" (in *Estudios dedicados a Menéndez Pidal*, I [Madrid, 1950], 275–88), in which I discuss this question in detail and give complete documentation.

49. *Il poema epico e mitologico* (Milan, n.d.), p. 328.

50. In his *Studien zur Weltanschauung der Renaissance* (Basel, 1920), cited by Cassirer *et al.* (eds.), *op. cit.*, p. 149.

took it for granted that there was no conflict between Catholicism and the classics: that the latter were pagan in form but Christian in content; that the Greek mythology and pantheon might legitimately be employed for expressing thoughts about Christian holy persons and saints." The words "for the most part" in the statement just quoted allow for the *Sic et Non* which is the leitmotif of *Spain and the Western Tradition*. It will be well, from the start, to document this *Sic et Non* as we find it in Renaissance Spain.

Cristóbal de Villalón (d. 1581?) in *El Scholástico*, inspired more or less directly by Castilgione's *Courtier*, combines a glorification of classical literature with a violent (and exceptional) diatribe against pagan poets and philosophers, since "their work . . . is not seasoned with the salt of Christ." This does not keep him from censuring severely those parents who do not educate their children in humanistic studies, "as if the exercise and the work of good letters could dull the lance of the knight of Christ and servant of God." [51] More normally, the works of the classical poets and philosophers were regarded as propaedeutic to Christian teaching. In the fifteenth century Juan de Mena addresses God as Jupiter with perfect naturalness [52] (*El Laberinto de Fortuna*, stanza I); Pedro de Santa Fe writes a poem in praise of the Virgin, addressing her with a succession of classical names — Diana, Cybele, Minerva, Juno — just as Alcuin (d. 804) had referred to God the Father as Jove the Thunderer. [53]

The "mixture of Golgotha and Olympus" — the phrase belongs to Mrs. Malkiel (*loc. cit.*) — continues in the seventeenth century with Quevedo, whose *canto épico*, *To the Risen Christ*, contains a scene (derived from the epic hell of Tasso's *Jerusalem Freed*, IV) wherein Alecto, Tisiphone, Megaera, and Rhadamanthus, and Discord with her vicious sisters, are given a place and part in a Virgilian setting noteworthy for its blending of classical literary

51. Cited by Margherita Morreale, *Castiglione y Boscán: El ideal cortesano en el Renacimiento español* (Madrid, 1959), I, 196.

52. So do Santillana (*Cancionero castellano* . . . , I, 461); Juan de Andújar (*Cancionero de Stúñiga*, eds. the Marqués de la Fuensanta del Valle and Sancho Rayón [Madrid, 1872], p. 194); Gerónimo de Artés (*Cancionero general*, ed. La Sociedad de Bibliófilos Españoles [Madrid, 1882], no. 937).

53. Mrs. Malkiel, *Juan de Mena: Poeta del prerrenacimiento español* (Mexico City, 1950), p. 162, n. 2.

tradition and Christian metaphysics.[54] Even in far-off colonial America, a near-contemporary of Quevedo, Hernando Domínguez Camargo (d. 1659), began his *Poema Heroico de San Ignacio de Loyola* with an appeal to Euterpe, the Muse of music. May the poet be granted both the quill and the sonorous voice of the swan: so mighty a warrior is the founder of the Society of Jesus — *vizcaíno Marte*, the "Biscayan Mars" — that any song addressed to him should have the ring of steel.[55] At the end of stanza VIII, "an ostentatious series of paradoxical antitheses is resolved in the miracle of the Faith — a synthesis of Plato and the Old Testament, of Horace and the love-poetry of the Renaissance, of Góngora and the mysticism of St. John of the Cross" (*ibid.*, p. 109).

Rhadamanthus sitting in judgment in the Christian hell, the war god of Olympus identified with a Christian saint: how can these things be? The answer will become clear as we proceed historically from Mena to Calderón. But first let us examine an explanation offered in 1617 in a treatise on the art of preaching, by Dr. Francisco Terrones Aguilar del Caño, preacher to Philip III. In the fourth chapter of this *Arte o instrucción* [56] he treats of the composition and the matter of the sermon. A consideration which gives rise to controversy among very devout and spiritual preachers has to do, he says, with the bringing in of "things human." Men without humanistic training, those who have studied "only Aristotle and St. Thomas," reject "human studies" most violently. Others are so steeped in humanism that the greater part of the sermon is taken up with classical allusions. The second "opinion" is "abominable" — it is a very worldly thing to clutter the pulpit with chaff (*burlas*) and to prefer paste jewelry to diamonds. For this reason the saints and "serious authors" have argued against the humanistically oriented sermon. And yet these same saintly Doctors in their writings give evidence that they themselves studied and learned and made use of classical subjects, and they even advise and praise the practice. Among many authorities, Terrones cites

54. Frank Pierce, "The *Canto Épico* of the Seventeenth and Eighteenth Centuries," *HR*, XV (1957), 8.

55. See Eleanor Webster Bulatkin, "La Introducción al *Poema Heroico* de Hernando Domínguez Camargo," *Thesaurus*, XVII (1962), 51–109.

56. Don Francisco Terrones del Caño, *Instrucción de predicadores*, ed. Félix G. Olmedo (Madrid, 1946), pp. 80–89.

St. Cyprian on the despoiling of the Egyptians. Origen said that the substantial wheat of scripture should be adorned by the preacher with lilies and flowers from belles-lettres. The list of authorities seems endless, among them some very modern Spanish and Portuguese theologians and moralists. Terrones then speaks for himself: in books "of humanities" and even of "vanities" many useful arguments are found for the confirmation of our faith and the improvement of our culture; even St. Paul on three occasions repeats verses from the poets. Terrones' conclusion is that a middle ground should be chosen between the two extremes which he first listed: the classics should be studied, especially in one's youth, and from them one should take what they have to offer, avoiding doctrinal error and all licentiousness (*errores y ruines costumbres*). We should abhor not their eloquence (*elegancia*), but only their errors.

If this humanistic material is "true" — i.e., natural, moral, and intellectual philosophy or political history — four, six, or even eight points may be incorporated into a sermon, with a special place for Seneca, who never says anything in excess and surpasses all others in compelling pithiness. If, on the other hand, the material is "feigned" — emblems, fables — only the most sparing use should be made of it. Not more than two emblems should be allowed per sermon. A fable from time to time is a pearl; but let it not be a fable about Venus. If she be mentioned, let the preacher show his disdain by the words he uses to introduce her. In short: the use of classical material must always have — very clearly — an instrumental value.

The end which Dr. Terrones had in view in writing these instructions was strictly homiletic. Other eminent divines were far more literary in their practice.[57] Fray Hortensio Félix Paravicino (d. 1633) in his sermons — he also wrote *obras humanas* — sought to do what Góngora did in verse: to give the freest possible play to the imagination in the creation of a learned and breath-taking imagery intended to produce "surprise and delight, amazement and enjoyment."[58] And ascetic writers like Malón de Chaide in his *Conversion of Mary Magdalene* did not hesitate to use classical allusions

---

57. O. H. Green, "*Se acicalaron los auditorios*: An Aspect of the Spanish Literary Baroque," *HR*, XXVII (1959), 413–22.
58. "sorpresa y deleite, maravilla y entretenimiento" (*ibid.*, p. 418).

even in an exhortation addressed to Christ himself. Pleading Mary Magdalene's case, Malón de Chaide addresses Him whose feet she was to wash: "And you, Redeemer of Life, will you not speak to her? Beware lest this sad woman be converted into a fountain, like another Byblis or Arethusa; those tears of hers are not tears of water, but of fire." [59] Both Byblis and Arethusa were Ovidian heroines, objects of a pagan metamorphosis.

It is time to retrace our steps somewhat in order to document from the fifteenth century onward this attitude toward the "feignings of the poets" that made it possible for a writer on a sacred subject to call to the attention of the Founder of Christianity the sad, sentimental fate of the Ovidian Arethusa and Byblis.

In seeking an explanation of this phenomenon we must go beyond the fact that the poetry of the ancients was too closely intertwined with contemporary culture to be ignored; we must find a cause closer to the wellsprings of human nature. This has been suggested by C. S. Lewis:

No religion, so long as it is believed, can have that kind of beauty which we find in the gods of Titian, of Botticelli, or our own romantic poets. [And he continues:] For poetry to spread its wings fully, there must be, besides the believed religion, a marvellous *that knows itself as myth.* For this to come about, the old marvellous, which was once taken as fact, must be stored up somewhere, not wholly dead, but in a winter sleep, waiting its time. . . . The decline of the gods, from deity to hypostasis and from hypostasis to decoration, was not, for them nor for us, a history of sheer loss. For decoration may let romance in. The poet is free to invent, beyond the limits of the possible, regions of strangeness and beauty for their own sake.[60]

Strangeness and beauty for their own sake — here again we must make a restriction. Strangeness and beauty were, in the literature of our period, ancillary to the aim of spiritual or moral profit. "How else can we define poetry," wrote the Marqués de Santillana, "than as a feigning of useful things, covered over and veiled by a most lovely covering, composed, set off, and scanned in accordance with a certain number, weight, and measure?" [61] Throughout the

59. Ed. P. Félix García (Madrid, 1947), II, 212–13.

60. *The Allegory of Love: A Study in Medieval Tradition* (Oxford, 1936), pp. 83, 75 (italics mine).

61. Quoted by Rafael Lapesa, *La obra literaria del Marqués de Santillana* (Madrid, 1957), p. 249.

Renaissance, whether in Italy or in Spain, there will be very few theorists indeed who will accept beauty and strangeness merely for their own sake.[62] Yet beauty and strangeness are part and parcel of Renaissance literature, and in Spain classical mythology and the pagan Parnassus were a part — an increasingly essential part — of the "most beautiful covering" that was to serve as the "veil" of deeper truth.[63]

Jean Seznec's *La survivance des dieux antiques* (London, 1940) is from beginning to end a record of the adaptations whereby the "feignings" of the pagan poets were converted into allegories and symbols suitable for use by Christian writers. The adaptation was not, however, perfect: it produced a certain *gêne*, a certain uneasiness, even bad conscience. Tertullian sought (ineffectually) to eliminate the pagan names of the days of the week. Certain writers on astronomy sought to transform Cepheus into Adam and Cassiopeia into Eve. The Priscillianists replaced the signs of the Zodiac by the twelve apostles. Later, Pope Pius V chased the "idols" from the Vatican, and Sixtus Quintus ordered that the fountain of Acqua Felice be adorned by a statue of Moses, not of Neptune. While these efforts are but ripples on a mighty current, they correspond to an essential reality: "many sincere believers who were at the same time fervent men of letters, naïvely associated their worldly erudition and their faith; for them allegory was a flowery path that enabled one to pass from the one realm to the other. But — we must recognize it — allegory is very often a mere imposture: it served to reconcile the unreconcilable . . . it was a dangerous rationalization." [64]

62. B. Weinberg, *A History of Literary Criticism in the Italian Renaissance* (Chicago, 1961), *passim*.

63. It is difficult not to imply more than one should. Not for a moment can one hold the idea that all literature in Renaissance Spain actually "veiled a deeper truth." But the demands of that deeper truth were nearly always felt, and concessions were made to them. In the novels of chivalry, in the picaresque novels, in the drama, there was usually an overt recognition of these demands—pauses in the narration or the action, not unlike our modern pauses for "commercials," in which the author looked to his doctrinal defenses. The lyric was the freest genre; yet we have cited in our Volume I (Chapter VII) a rich harvest of palinodes, whose significance has already been referred to in the present chapter. At the very least, frivolous or merely merry literature claimed the instrumental value of serving to "relax the bow," to give rest to heads and spirits bowed down with responsibility or merely weary from daily tasks. These questions will be treated below in the chapter "Literature and Society."

64. Seznec, *op. cit.*, pp. 240–41; see also my *"Fingen los poetas,"* p. 277.

"The religious significance of the Muses during the decline of paganism," writes E. R. Curtius, "is in all likelihood the fundamental reason for their express rejection by early Christian poetry. This rejection then becomes a poetic topos itself, the history of which can be traced from the fourth to the seventeenth century. It is an index of the rise and fall of dogmatic rigorism. It is frequently connected with an attempt to find a Christian substitute for the antique Muses." [65] Yet, "from the first, the rejection of the Muses by Christian poets is scarcely anything but a badge of conventionally correct ecclesiastical thought. The more vehemently it is expressed, the less does it carry conviction. . . . But even the outworn topos of rejection of the Muses can become alive in the mouth of a true poet. It found its finest expression in Jorge Manrique . . . " (ibid., p. 240).

We cannot accept fully Curtius' reduction of this matter to a topos, a mere conventionality.[66] The Muses were acceptable or unacceptable, depending on two factors, one of them constant, one variable. The constant factor had to do with whether the poet was treating a sacred or a secular theme; the variable factor was none other than the poet's own rigorism or liberal attitude. We shall begin by giving our attention to the dissenting rigorists.

Both Jorge Manrique (d. 1478) and Gómez Manrique (d. 1490?) reject the "pagan" — or rather the pseudo-pagan — invocation. I shall quote from Jorge, the more outspoken of the two:

Dexo las ynuocaçiones	I will have none of the invocations
de los famosos poetas	used by great poets and orators: I
y oradores;	reject their "feignings," for their
no curo de sus ficciones,	sweetness conceals a hidden poison.
que traen yeruas secretas	To Him alone I entrust myself, Him
sus sabores;	only do I invoke, whose deity the
A Aquel sólo me encomiendo,	world knew not, though he came
aquel sólo inuoco yo	unto the world.
de verdad,	
que en este mundo biuiendo,	

65. *European Literature and the Latin Middle Ages,* trans. W. R. Trask (New York, 1953), p. 235. See also p. 236: "Patristic allegoresis makes the Muses harmless through euhemeristic explanations and reinterprets them as concepts in musical theory. . . . "
66. The reason for our reservations will become apparent below as we cite a text from Encina.
67. *Cancionero castellano* . . . , II, 229. Curtius quotes these lines, and his translator inserts Longfellow's translation (pp. 240–41). The poetic translation does not

el mundo no conosció
    su deydad.[67]

Don Pedro de Portugal (d. 1466), using the same figure of speech
— poison — is equally outspoken. Juan de Mena, who in the first
stanza of the *Laberinto* speaks of God as Jupiter, in his *Stanzas on
the Capital Sins* turns away, not only from the amorous follies of
his youth, but also from concern with the sensuous delights of
poetic "fables." Addressing his Christian Muse — *Canta tú, Christiana Musa* — he dismisses the "sirens" (*serenas*)

Que en la mi edad pasada	Who in years past poured through
tal dulzura emponzoñada	my veins such poisoned sweetness.
derramastes por mis venas.	

Then, "using a comparison of St. Basil the Great in his famous sermon on the profit which can be obtained by reading the books
of the gentiles," he adds: "Having thus thrown away all that is
superfluous and harmful in pagan poetry, I shall continue in the
company [of the poets] as a true Catholic, reducing their output in
such a way that the part which I take unto myself will be of more
value than the whole." [68]

This is essentially the position of Juan de Padilla, the Carthusian
(d. 1522?), who in his *Retable of the Life of Christ* makes it clear
that in his case, as in that of Mena, the turning away from the
delights of secular poetry is analogous to the turning away from
the delights of courtly love.[69] But there is one added circumstance
— the poet is now writing on a sacred theme:

> Let them be gone, the cursed Muses,
> To the Stygian realm of Pluto;
> In any such noble song as ours
> Our Christian doctrine can give them no place;
> For here we write on a subject celestial.[70]

make it clear that Manrique rejects not the poets, but their habit of invoking the
Muses.

68. "De la esclava poesía / lo superfluo así tirado, / lo dañoso desechado, / seguiré
su compañía, / a la católica vía / reduciéndola por modo / que valga más que su
todo / la parte que fago mía" (see my *"Fingen los poetas,"* pp. 279–80, for this and the
following three quotations; I draw upon this article also for much of the discussion
following).

69. "We portrayed [their falsities] in our youth; now, in the presence of Supreme
Virtue, I recognize that they are the death of the soul" — "Pintamos en tiempo de la
juuentud, / agora mirando la suma virtud, / conozco que matan a los corazones."

70. "Huyan, por ende, las musas dañadas / a las Estigias do reina Plutón, / en

He proceeds, however, to correct the impression of a general and total condemnation of "vain poetry":

> Secular poems, with their attendant dangers,
> I leave to one side, taking only the good,
> Like the man who winnows his grain from the chaff
> Or casts out the pith in the making of cider.
> Such a decision has saintly approval,
> And holy decretals by no means reject it,
> Intending thereby that nations and kings
> Should have due regard for secular learning.[71]

The prose writers are no less explicit. The stern moralist Juan Luis Vives recommends that the reader of the ancient writers "proceed as over a terrain known to be poisonous, that is, with the antidote close at hand." Pedro Mexía, in the prologue to his translation of Isocrates, remarks: "And also, since Isocrates in some passages speaks as a gentile, I have taken care to translate him in Christian terms." To Fray Luis de Granada, in the moment of temporary pessimism in which he composed his *Book of Prayer and Meditation* (1554), "the study of the pagan authors would be, at the most, a sort of inevitable calamity." Granting that these studies are necessary, he yet warns: "we should nonetheless regard them as a great plague of our life, since they still take from us so much of our time"; and he insists, "inasmuch as man's miserable condition has imposed this necessity upon us, we should assign to it a suitable time." Later, in 1556 and in 1582, Fray Luis becomes much more reasonable in these matters (*ibid.*, p. 281).

The most curious protest of all has already been quoted in the present study, in the final chapter of Volume I ("Truancy and Recantation," pp. 294–95). Composed at a time when the educational program of the Jesuits had long since resolutely integrated pagan letters into Christian education, and when Fray Juan de Pineda had proclaimed tolerance toward the "feigning of the poets," we have from the pen of a certain Licenciate Agustín Calderón a *Psalm* (*ca.* 1611) in which he confesses as the worst of his

nuestro divino muy alto sermón / las tienen los santos por muy reprobadas. / Aquí celebramos las cosas sagradas."

71. "Los vanos poemas, que pueden dañar, / dexemos aparte, tomando lo sano; / como quien quita la paja del grano, / y más de la cidra su mal amargar. / Esta sentencia, por muy aprobada, / tienen los santos decretos y leyes; / porque no tengan los pueblos y reyes / la ciencia terrena por menos preciada."

sins his former ascription of deity to "the idols of the gentiles" and his having invoked Apollo and the Muses — "with a devout if heretical soul." This palinode voices the extreme attitude of that minority in Spain that saw evil in the *Diana* of Montemayor and rewrote, in pious *contrafacta*, not only the romances of chivalry, but also the works of authors whose writings were essentially pure, like Boscán and Garcilaso. This minority felt with Fray Luis de Granada in his *Book of Prayer and Meditation* that the greatest preoccupation of man should be to "learn how to die well." The great majority, like Granada in his *Introduction to the Creed* (1582), had no such scruples ("*Fingen los poetas*," pp. 281–82). It is time to turn our attention to this majority.

Earlier in the present section we noticed a fifteenth-century poem by Santa Fe in which the Virgin Mary is addressed as Minerva, Juno, Pallas — but always with a Christian adjective: "sanctified Minerva, Juno our advocate, Pallas illuminated." At the very end of the following century we have this statement in a sermon of Fray Alonso de Santa Cruz: "Men have never had success in their efforts to fight against God or to place themselves on an equal footing with Heaven. Consider the fall of the rebellious angels, the punishment imposed on the giants, the end of Pharaoh and his army." The giants, it will be remembered, were fabled sons of Earth and Tartarus who stormed the heavens but were smitten by Jupiter and buried under Mount Aetna. They are mentioned as an illustration — in a sermon — side by side with Lucifer and his host ("*Fingen los poetas*," p. 283).

To both poet and preacher, in the fifteenth, sixteenth, and seventeenth centuries, the *merveilleux païen* — the pagan marvelous — was but a "feigning," a figment of the literary imagination: "the poets feign. . . . " The phrase is repeated endlessly. Furthermore, what the poets feigned "does not fail to have concealed mysteries in some of its parts, for though it was a figment, the poets set forth beneath those fables, and in those poems, a great part of the truth — great and admirable secrets and mysteries." [72] A similar explanation is given by Hernán Pérez de Oliva in his *Dialogue on the Dignity of Man*. The heroes of Greece and Rome were real men, he tells us, but their identities have been lost in the course of the centuries

72. From the anonymous *El Crotalón*; see *ibid*, p. 283.

and "when we use their names we evoke not the actual heroes, but others, feigned and created by the poets in their fables." [73]

We now come to our most enlightening text. Juan del Encina (d. 1529) in his *Arte de la poesía castellana* employs the words *figment, fiction, feigned* to explain the common use by the poets of the pseudo-pagan invocation, e.g.: "Oh lucid Jupiter" (Santillana); "Oh supreme Jove" (Gerónimo de Artés); "Mighty Jupiter" (Juan de Andújar); and numerous others. Encina, speaking of "the divinity of poetry," explains that the ancients considered poetry divine because they ascribed its origin to their gods and to the Muses:

This we infer from the invocations of the ancient poets, from whom the practice has passed on to us, not because we believe as they did, assigning divinity to those gods by invoking them (which would be an intolerable error and heresy); but because we wish to imitate their elegance and their poetic practice [*gala y orden poética*]: that is, when we propose to narrate or tell some grave and arduous fiction, we feel the need to make an invocation; so that, the work itself being fiction, it is quite appropriate that its invocation be no less fictitious and unreal. But when we undertake to write some work of lofty or devout theme, or one touching on the substance of our Faith, we invoke Him who is Truth itself, or His precious Mother, or some saint or saints, asking that they be intercessors and mediators for us to the end that we may obtain grace. [74]

In 1585 there was published at Madrid a work by Juan Pérez de Moya entitled *Secret Philosophy, Wherein under the Veil of Fabulous Histories May Be Found Much Useful Doctrine for All Studies, with the Origin of the Idols or Gods of the Pagans.* His title makes his attitude clear: he sees in mythology a "hidden philosophy." His fifth book is devoted to a study of fables which inspire men to be virtuous, and his seventh and last treats of those fables that were invented "to inspire the fear of God" ("*Fingen los poetas,*" p. 286).

Four years later there appeared at Valladolid a translation by Pedro Sánchez de Viana of Ovid's *Metamorphoses*, "with Commentary and Explication of the Fables, Reducing Them to Moral and

73. *BAE*, LXV, 289b.
74. In Menéndez y Pelayo, *Antología de poetas líricos castellanos* (Madrid, 1890–1916), V, 32–33. Curtius (*op. cit.*, p. 237) found this distinction between ordinary poems and poems of devotion to be characteristic of Carolingian humanism. Alcuin granted the Muses a place in secular poetry but banned them from spiritual poetry.

Natural Philosophy, Astrology [i.e., Astronomy], and History." Here there is complete accord between the classic myths and Christian belief. This is shown particularly in Book I (Annotation xxvi), where Sánchez de Viana treats of the end of the world, of the new heaven and of the new earth (*ibid.*).

The year 1589 also saw the publication at Salamanca of Fray Juan de Pineda's *Agricultura Christiana*, in which "the author sought to include the most varied, profitable, curious, and pleasant and best proved doctrine that he could find" — a book long familiar to the readers of *Spain and the Western Tradition*. On folio 20 we read that Homer among the Greeks, and Ovid among the Latins, were regarded as most learned men, not as liars. And one should remember that "to feign is not to lie," since Christ himself feigned on the road to Emmaus; "and the poets feigned . . . [their] tales to veil and cover many truths, both physical and moral [as the Scriptures do also], in order to cause the unlearned to esteem things which, if told in common and ordinary language, they would scorn; therefore all peoples have used symbols and mystic ceremonies in their worship, for the purpose of lifting the masses up to God by means of rites which they do not understand" (cited *ibid.*, p. 287).

In 1620 there was issued at Salamanca the *Theater of the Pagan Gods* by Fray Baltasar de Vitoria, with an *Aprobación* by Lope de Vega. There is nothing in this history of mythology, Lope certifies, which is injurious to the faith or to morals. On the contrary, the material is important for the understanding of many books. For the ancients developed their philosophy under the veil of fables, under the beautiful adornments of poetry, to guard from the too-ready perception of the vulgar eye the most secret verities (*ibid.*).[75]

Philosophy under the veil of fables — Lope de Vega's phrase restates the position taken by Juan del Encina, more than a century earlier, in regard to ancient mythology. The seventeenth century is at one with the fifteenth. To this extent Olympus did indeed "live merrily and peacefully with the Christian Paradise," as Arturo

---

75. Seznec, *op. cit.*, pp. 285–86, says that it was not until the eighteenth century that mythology became purely decorative. See p. 287, n. 2, of my *"Fingen los poetas"* for a discussion of Luzán's (d. 1754) censure of Camoëns for having introduced Jupiter, Venus, Bacchus, etc., into a poem "written to be read by Christians"; see also the very learned article of Edward Glaser, "Manuel de Faria e Sousa and the Mythology of *Os Lusíadas*," *Miscelánea de Estudos a Joaquim de Carvalho*, No. 6 (Figueira da Foz, 1961), 614–27.

Farinelli asserted (cited *ibid.*, p. 277). But we must not disregard the dissenting voices, unknown to Farinelli, ranging from that of the sixteenth-century Juan de Mena to that of Agustín Calderón in the early seventeenth century. Such dissent is generally uttered toward the end of a writer's life and is analogous to the palinodes which we have studied in Volume I. This dissent represents what Curtius calls moral and dogmatic rigorism (*ibid.*, p. 278, n. 3). The rigor was born of personal attitudes on the part of the writer: Fray Luis de Granada felt the need for it in 1554, before the promulgation of the decrees of Trent, only to soften his attitude in later years, when those decrees were known to all. The two Calderóns, Agustín and Pedro, represent the two poles: we have already quoted from the former, a rigorist, who preceded the latter in time; for the latter, mythology was again a veil hiding the greatest truths — indeed, a preparation for the law of Grace (*ibid.*, p. 285). Of far greater significance than the minority voices of protest is the fact that the majority felt as Encina did: "since the work itself is fiction, it is proper for its invocation to be a figment also." Encina's distinction between the types of poems that allow the pseudo-pagan invocation or exclude it is fundamental. It is almost certain that a thorough study of the invocations in Golden Age poems would show that Encina's rule was adhered to. Jorge Manrique set the tone and the style when he rejected the pagan invocation in his pious meditation on the death of his father — the most famous poem in Spanish literature.

La Celestina

In an earlier volume (Volume II, Chapter III) we examined and disproved the charge of paganism based on the treatment of Nature in *La Celestina*: the beginning speech, in which the lover "sees the greatness of God" in His having assigned to Nature power to endow the beloved with such dazzling beauty, is entirely within the framework of orthodox theology, for Nature is indeed the handmaiden of God, the continuator of His work of creation. Similarly, the charge of a radical and universal pessimism in this work, based on the statement (taken from Heraclitus) that "all things come to pass through the compulsion of strife," has been weighed and found wanting (Volume II, Chapter II): the "compulsion of strife" is

resolved in universal harmony. Fernando de Rojas was not expressing a life philosophy in his prologue; he was merely anticipating
the strife of "bards and reviewers" which he felt would certainly
be stirred up by his venturing—with no more preparation than a
legal degree—into the dangerous realm of authorship. Neither
La Celestina's elevation of Nature to the rank of God's vicegerent,
nor the prologue's reference to the universal strife of the elements
(fire against water, etc.), ever met with any official stricture.

The same leniency resulted in no exception being taken to the
scandalously frank portrayal of the sexual mores of members of
the clergy when *La Celestina* was finally expurgated.[76] The Spanish
Inquisition did not alter the text of *La Celestina* for more than one
hundred and forty years, and then it ordered the deletion of only
some fifty lines which, in one way or another, but not always obviously (as we see things today), touched on matters of doctrine.
This late action took place in 1640. In 1667 Luis Ulloa y Pereira
published his *Defense of Works of Fiction and of the Proper Poems
and Plays Which Custom has Caused Us to Accept.* His remarks
on *La Celestina* are pertinent to our problem here:

> If certain hyperboles are placed on the lips of the lovers, this is never done
> with approval, or to arouse admiration, so as to make the lovers appear
> idolatrous, even in their greatest excesses. Calisto in his amorous frenzy (and
> reproved by his servant Sempronio) says: "What's that to me?" And when he
> is reprehended by the question, "Aren't you a Christian?" he replies: "I am
> a Melibean." And he continues to utter unbridled excesses which very prop-
> erly were ordered expunged in the latest expurgatory Index, since it was
> considered unwise to allow ignorant folk to make speculations regarding what
> had for so many years been allowed to pass—this out of a general awareness
> of the morality and the ethical teaching which lay back of those words. . . .
> And the rest of the book was permitted to stand, though there are slips and
> mistakes in the remainder, in view of the book's intention to show the disas-
> trous end which awaits all those who indulge in illicit love affairs.

As I have shown in a separate study,[77] the expurgator's treatment
of the entire book is remarkably tolerant. The book's moral mes-

---

76. "Bezüglich der Obscönitäten war die portugiesische Censur strenger als die
Spanische. . . . In Spanien wurde die [erste] Celestina erst 1793 verboten." The In-
quisitors allowed it to circulate "mit einigen Streichungen (und die verordnet erst
Sot [omayor in 1640])"; see Franz Heinrich Reusch, *Der Index der verbotenen Bücher:
Ein Beitrag zur Kirchen- und Literaturgeschichte* (Bonn, 1883–85), I, 594. The Lisbon
Index of 1581 forbade the *Celestina* and its sequel by Feliciano de Silva.
77. "The *Celestina* and the Inquisition," *HR*, XV (1947), 211–16.

sage, recognized early by the pious Luis Vives (*ibid.*, p. 216), has been admirably expounded and demonstrated by Marcel Bataillon: "If Rojas did not exert himself unduly to demonstrate the exemplary character of *La Celestina*, it is because the matter was obvious to him and to his contemporaries." "He was fully aware that he had written a work which was at one and the same time scabrous and serious." [78]

Both Celestina and Calisto call for confession as they die, and Melibea says of her lover: "The Fates severed his thread, they cut off his life without confession." *The Fates . . . confession*: this juxtaposition of the pagan and the Christian was permitted to stand in 1640, as it had been through the preceding years. Melibea, in the *turbación* [79] — the derangement — of her last hours, appeals to God before her suicide, expecting in spite of it to be joined with Calisto in heaven. Some critics, scandalized, have taken comfort in the thought that the author was a converted Jew. The Inquisition's expurgator made no objection.[80]

Suicide [81]

The matter of Melibea's suicide, of all suicides in Spanish literature, raises a problem. May an author cause his heroine to sacrifice herself as Dido did on the pyre at Carthage? Certainly we have a case in *La Celestina*, but here the answer to the problem is easy: these lovers come to a disastrous end because the author has willed that

78. *"La Célestine" selon Fernando de Rojas* (Paris, 1961), pp. 213, 219. Mrs. Malkiel combats Bataillon's thesis in her *La originalidad artística . . .* ; see the *Índice de nombres y de obras, s. v.* Bataillon, Marcel. I review all the evidence in my article "The Artistic Originality of *La Celestina*," *HR*, XXXIII (1965), 15–31, especially 26; see also p. 30: "The moral theme, insisted on by Bataillon and minimized by María Rosa is *there*—but less importantly than Bataillon believes. Similarly, the artistic perfection insisted on by 'our' María Rosa is *there* — though not in the exact measure she claims."

79. This *turbación* (upon which we remarked also in Volume I) is a sort of madness, and it greatly reduces a lover's responsibility: see the *Tractado que fizo . . . el Tostado por el cual se prueba por la Santa Escritura cómo al ome es necessario amar e que el que verdaderamente ama es necessario que se turbe*, ed. A. Paz y Melia in *Opúsculos literarios de los siglos XIV a XVI* (Madrid, 1892). See also my *Courtly Love in Quevedo* (Boulder, Colorado, 1952), pp. 41–42.

80. See my article, "Did the 'World' 'Create' Pleberio?" written in answer to Stephen Gilman's "Fernando de Rojas as Author," *RF*, LXXVI (1964), 255–90; my article will appear in the same journal in 1965.

81. The question of suicide in literature and the attitudes towards it was touched upon in various places in Volume I, especially pp. 271–72.

by their personal disaster they shall show the inevitable wages of sin.

Not too many years later, in Boscán's *Fábula de Leandro y Hero*, the heroine is made to cast herself down from her seaside tower, to fall upon the body of her lifeless lover and join him in death. But Hero is Grecian, not a Christian young woman.

The *Egloga de Plácida y Vitoriano* of Juan del Encina (d. 1529) was placed on the Index of 1559. In it Plácida, after tears and laments, stabs herself. Vitoriano, seeing the body, would have taken his own life, but is restrained by a friend who tells him that by so doing he would lose his soul. There follows a parody of the Office of the Dead, reminiscent of the parodies of Juan Ruiz (see Volume I, Chapter II). Another character, Sulpicio, preparing to die without confession, commends his soul to Venus, but the goddess stays his hand, assuring him that Plácida is not really dead and offering to restore her to her lover. The girl is finally brought back to life by the goddess, and the play ends with singing and dancing.[82]

The Inquisition was right in banning this play in the year 1559 — for times had become, as other witnesses have already told us, "dangerous." But with our knowledge of the nature of burlesque and parody of things sacred we shall not too quickly conclude that the play was written with any "pagan" intent. It was written, obviously, as entertainment. Furthermore: the suicide is not genuine and the "resurrection" is accomplished, by the intervention of mythical deities, in an atmosphere of unreality. "Side by side with the believed religion," we may repeat with Lewis (see above, note 60), "there is need for a marvellous that knows itself as myth." Bruce Wardropper has said that the secularization in Encina's play of the miracle of resurrection "is so startling that it has the impact of a parody, if not actually a blasphemy." [83] This we readily grant. But neither the author nor his audience were overstepping the limits of what was permitted by the conventional "medieval taste for humorous blasphemy." [84]

Keeping in mind these three examples with their three heroines — Melibea, Hero, Plácida — we shall analyze the problem of suicide in Spanish Renaissance literature in the light of what was theo-

---

82. See J. P. W. Crawford, *Spanish Drama before Lope de Vega* (Philadelphia, 1937), pp. 26–27.

83. "Metamorphosis in the Theater of Juan del Encina," *SP*, LIX (1962), 41–51.

84. The phrase, frequently quoted in Volume I, was coined by Lewis.

retically and officially acceptable on the one hand, and, on the other hand, what the authors actually did with characters and situations.

In Chrétien de Troyes' verse romance *The Knight of the Cart* (*ca.* 1170), Lancelot in a moment of despair places a noose about his neck and, commending the outcome to God, slips out of the saddle. Fortunately for Lancelot — and for the ultimate morality of the story — his guards save his life.[85] Some four centuries later, in Torcuato Tasso's *Jerusalem Delivered* (XII, stanza 83), Tancred, having slain Clorinda unaware of her identity, tears open his wounds in order to destroy himself. He swoons as he does so, else he would surely have died. Reproved by Peter the Hermit, he is terrified at the thought of the eternal damnation he has so narrowly escaped (86–89). Between these two dates, and for many years after the second one, we find in Spanish literature numerous episodes in which the problem of suicide — contemplated, threatened, attempted, accomplished — presents itself to the author as a usable theme, though beset with difficulties. It will be well first to consider the matter from the standpoint of doctrine.

The condemnation of suicide by the Church is easy to understand. The suicide abandons the post in life assigned him by his Maker. This rebellion against, or defiance of, the Almighty was considered the greatest sin of all; some writers condemned Judas Iscariot more for his self-destruction than for his betrayal of his Master (of which, had he lived, he could have repented). St. Augustine taught (*Of the City of God*, I, 25) that no man should kill himself out of fear of temporal miseries. In chapter 22 of the same book he condemns the Roman Cato of Utica for taking his life in order to avoid falling into the hands of Caesar. Vives, in his commentary on this passage in Augustine, does not discuss the issue but does refer to Cato as "this worthy man."[86] The anonymous glossator who expounded the "added stanzas" of Juan de Mena's *Laberinto* says of Cato: "Seneca called this man the living image of virtue, the

85. Hermann J. Weigand, *Three Chapters on Courtly Love in Arthurian France and Germany* (Chapel Hill, North Carolina, 1956), p. 12.

86. St. Augustine, *Of the City of God*, ed. J. L. Vives (London, 1620), p. 32; Cato was, of course, not a Christian.

original *sapiens*" (philosophically wise man).[87] Mena himself absolves Cato of his act of suicide as Dante had done.[88] This he could do by placing Cato within his own culture, in his own time and place — that is to say, by considering him as an ancient Roman.

The examples cited thus far give inklings of various ways in which the problem will be faced, evaded, or solved in Spanish literary works. The problem is merely evaded when suicide is threatened, as it constantly is, in works whose theme is courtly love. If the threat does not lead to action, the only sin committed is a sinful thought, and repentance can come at any moment; it can, indeed, be many times repeated.

Suicide in the fifteenth-century lyric. Pierre Le Gentil, in his study of the Spanish and Portuguese lyric at the end of the Middle Ages, finds suicide rare in the French *roman courtois*, or courtly romance, as well as in the French lyric. He remarks: "Unrequited love can kill; no weapon is needed; it suffices to give oneself over to despair." [89] Suicide is equally rare, by LeGentil's calculation, in the Spanish poetry of our period (*op. cit.*, p. 150, nn. 163, 164). Yet it is not so rare but that a full treatment of the theme in Spanish Renaissance literature would require a monograph.

The problem is complex. Mrs. Malkiel wrote in 1942: "But if the art of the Spanish Renaissance admitted, in *La Celestina* [1499?] and in the *Cárcel de Amor* [1490], the use of suicide as a poetic solution, the art of the Counter Reformation did not tolerate it," and as proof she adduced "the humorously frustrated suicides de-

---

87. Mena, *Obras* (Antwerp, 1552), p. 585.

88. Menéndez y Pelayo (ed.) in *Antología de poetas líricos castellanos* (new ed.; Santander, 1944–45), II, 176.

89. *La poésie lyrique espagnole et portugaise à la fin du moyen âge*, I (Rennes, 1949), 268 and n. 80; see also p. 279. On this subject, see the section on death in my *Quevedo*, pp. 62 ff. In Juan de Padilla's *Twelve Triumphs of the Twelve Apostles* a suicide in hell (*yo triste maldito*) expounds the theological aspects of self-destruction, exonerating some persons who, like Samson, appear to have killed themselves with Divine approval and others, such as certain Roman heroes, who thought that thereby they were rendering service to "their gods," but condemning others who, like himself, had no proper excuse: Saul, who killed himself to escape from the Philistines, and others who committed the act "with little prudence," "without reverence," or "with slight power of resistance." See *Cancionero castellano* . . . , I, 366. On the Divine approval of certain suicides, see Pedro Ciruelo, *Reprovación de supersticiones* (Salamanca, 1539), fol. 30v. (marked by error xl).

picted by Lope de Vega in his songs and ballads." [90] It is evident, however, that even in the early Renaissance the toleration was not altogether easy and that the fifteenth century often looked upon such a solution as unacceptable.

The contemplation of suicide was, of course, common enough, as we know. Suicide could also be threatened by the despairing lover, as by Juan de Mena in a *Carta* to his *belle dame sans merci*:

Esta braua disciplina	If the suffering meted out by your
que con manos atan crudas	cruel hands is not mitigated, you
vos me days, si no se afina,	will soon see me driven to despair
me vereys vos muy ayna	like Judas Iscariot.
desesperar como Iudas.[91]	

A similar text, later in date (before 1549), has to do with a theoretical, a contemplated suicide that is not quite threatened. If the jealousy which the lady provokes were aroused by a rival suitor, the remedy would be easy enough:

Matalle, y con él a vos,	To kill him, and you also, and
y a mí con ellos matarme,	myself with the two of you; thus I
siquier por no atormentarme	at least would escape the torment
de mirar qué hazeys los dos.[92]	of seeing what you do together.

Santillana — already quoted in the brief discussion of suicide in Volume I — allows himself to envy Cato Uticensis, but he recognizes that Cato's choice of the means of escape from an intolerable life is denied to Christians:

¡ O quánd bien murió Catón,	How nobly Cato met his death,
si permitiesse	if only our religion permitted
nuestra ley e consintiesse	and allowed such a solution!
tal razón! [93]	

Gómez Manrique (d. 1490?) expresses an identical escapist mood and an identical rejection of it (*ibid.*, II, 127):

Vida tan desesperada	A life so full of despair as the life
como yo biuo syn vos	I endure because of you should

90. "Dido y su defensa en la literatura española," *RFH*, IV (1942), 239; see also 209–52 and 313–82.

91. Judas, stricken by remorse for having betrayed his Lord, went out and hanged himself. *Desesperar*, in the Spanish of our period, frequently means to commit suicide. The text is in Mena's *Obras* (*ed. cit.*), p. 809.

92. *Obras de D. Juan Fernández de Heredia*, ed. F. Martí Grajales (Valencia, 1913), p. 25.

93. *Cancionero castellano* . . . , I, 445.

no deue ser deseada,
mas con mis manos tirada,
sy lo permitiese Dios.

be the object of no man's desire, but rather thrown away by my own hand, if God permitted such an act.

This poet is perfectly clear in regard to the consequences involved: those who die as suicides (*desesperados*) put an end to their fame, to their person, and to their life, remaining submerged forever in the fires of hell (*ibid.*, p. 20):

poniendo fin a sus famas,
a sus personas y vidas,
cuyas almas son perdidas
y por siempre submergidas
en las infernales flamas.

Suicide in early fiction. Barbara Matulka has reported that "suicide constituted a stock theme of the sentimental novel in Spain," [94] citing four cases in addition to the one — the best known today — in Diego de San Pedro's *Cárcel de amor* (1492).[95] Miss Matulka makes no attempt to determine how the theme was conceived and treated.

The *Cárcel de amor* (1492) was eventually put on the Index, probably — in the opinion of Menéndez y Pelayo — because of the "nonsense" contained in its defense of women rather than because of the suicide of its hero Leriano.[96] This hero, however, was most certainly guilty of the sin of despair: it was published throughout the court and the kingdom that Leriano was allowing himself to die of hunger. Another sentimental hero, Aliso in *El triunfo de las donas* by Juan Rodríguez del Padrón, the most celebrated novelist of the reign of Juan II (d. 1450?), kills himself because he is the object of disdain. In the same author's *Siervo libre de amor*, Ardanlier, like Pyramus, falls on his sword in despair over the death of Liessa; the embalmed bodies of the two lovers were preserved in "two rich tombs" against the fateful day when the roars of the four beasts should be heard after their long sleep and the "very purified" souls

94. In *The Novels of Juan de Flores and Their European Diffusion* (New York, 1931), p. 158. The novels were composed about 1495; translated into Italian in 1521, into French in 1520, into English in 1556; one of them was used in a bilingual text for the instruction of persons wishing to learn Spanish.
95. Miss Matulka cites also the suicide of Melibea, although the *Celestina* is not a sentimental novel.
96. *Antología de poetas* . . . , new ed., III, 171.

of the lovers should enter into eternal blessedness.[97] Here again we have truancy, and also the medieval taste for blasphemy and for parody of things sacred, in a work (strangely enough) in no way humorous.

In Juan de Flores' *Grisel y Mirabella* (1495?), Grisel leaps into the flames surrounding the stake where Mirabella is shortly to be placed to die. Mirabella seeks to follow him but is restrained, one victim being considered sufficient. Succumbing to her despair, the maiden leaps from a window and is devoured by the captive lions below.

In Juan de Segura's *Quexa y aviso contra Amor* (first printed, 1548) Lucindaro, deep in despair because of the death of his beloved, allows himself to starve to death after having swallowed the ashes of her body.

In all of the foregoing cases there is, along with the suicide itself, an attendant element of apparent approval of the "worthy" act of tragic self-destruction on the part of noble and sensitive lovers. There exists also another series of works of fiction in which suicide appears but is punished or condemned — many long years before the Counter Reformation could have been dreamed of.

In Martorell's *Tirante el Blanco* (1490) the widow Reposada "kills herself out of fear of Tirante." It is to be noted, however, that she is a wicked character and appears not to be responsible for her act: "she was driven to distraction by her great love for the hero." [98] This perturbation is, at the very least, a factor that greatly extenuates her guilt.

Juan de Flores wrote not only *Grisel y Mirabella* but also *Grimalte y Gradissa* (printed 1495?), "a curious treatment on a single plane of life and literature, ending with a view of Hell." Grimalte, rejected by Gradissa, joins the Pánfilo of Boccaccio's *Fiammetta* and witnesses the horrible vision which torments Pánfilo three times each week: Fiammetta appears surrounded by devils who, after tormenting her because she died a suicide, carry her off in a cart through a storm-wracked forest.[99]

97. Ed. A. Paz y Melia (Madrid, 1884), pp. 64, 70.
98. This love "de todo la hacía salir de seso" (*Libros de caballerías españoles*, ed. F. Buendía [Madrid, 1954], p. 1655b; see also pp. 1479a, 1481a).
99. Mrs. Malkiel, *La visión de trasmundo en las literaturas hispánicas* (an Appendix in Howard R. Patch, *El otro mundo en la literatura medieval* [Mexico City, 1956]),

In the "primitive" redaction of *Amadís de Gaula* — the version reworked by Rodríguez de Montalvo in 1508 and known to us only through a few scattered fragments and through scholarly reconstruction — Oriana committed suicide by jumping out a window, an act which our early sixteenth-century author reinterprets allegorically and thus eliminates.[100] The *Amadís* of 1508 reports various suicides, but never with approval. In chapter XIII of Book I, Dardán, smitten with remorse, plunges his sword into his own body. We are told by the author that for the most part the witnesses rejoiced, for this knight, though valiant, was haughty and arrogant, esteeming more the valor of his heart than the judgments of the Lord. Amadís' squire Gandalín, in despair through no fault of his own, would have cast himself into the sea "had he not remembered that by so doing he would lose his soul." He seeks his master and begs him to cut off his head; otherwise, he says, he will kill himself. Amadís replies: "How did you come to lose your mind, or what misfortune is this?" (II, lxi). In the next chapter we witness the self-destruction of Matalesa, the "terrible damsel" (*desemejada*), only to be reminded on the same page of the helplessness of the human being when, given over to the dictates of free will, he finds himself without the grace of God. When Amadís himself is thrown into despair and retires to the mountains of the Peña Pobre, the author takes care to keep him from overstepping the ultimate limit of desperation. Convinced that he can only "die in this mountain," Amadís yet asks a pious hermit to direct him for the good of his soul. He is commanded to eat: "You are subject to my command and I bid you eat; otherwise your soul would be in great danger should you die in this condition." The hero, who has fasted for three days, obeys (II, xlviii).

In four lines of verse in the anonymous *Questión de amor* (1512), a despairing lover voices the old lament:

Acostado	Lying restless on this bed, I would
sobre un lecho, tan cansado	gladly end my life if I but feared
que quisiera	not the penalty that is reserved

pp. 427–28. (This book is a Spanish trans. of Patch's *The Other World According to Descriptions in Medieval Literature* [Cambridge, Massachusetts, 1950]).

100. Mrs. Malkiel, "El desenlace del *Amadís* primitivo," *RPh*, VI (1953), pp. 284–85, 289.

matarme si no temiera   for the suicide.
el morir desesperado.[101]

In 1534 Feliciano de Silva (whose prose was parodied by Cervantes in *Don Quijote*) published his *Segunda Comedia de Celestina*. In Rojas' work the bawd Celestina had been murdered by her accomplices in evil doing. Silva resurrects her, actually bringing her back from the nether regions — a somewhat ticklish business. Poncia, as well as other characters in the new book, is curious and asks: "Mother, do tell me, did you see Melibea in the other world?" "Young lady," says the old hag, "that's not the first time they have asked me that question. Such secrets, my child, can not be discussed. I can only remind you that Melibea was her own murderer." [102]

Juan de Segura's *Processo de cartas de amores* (1548) is Europe's first epistolary novel. In it flirtation, replete with coquetry, soon turns serious, becoming all but tragic. The lady, separated from her lover by her relatives, yet manages for a time to communicate with him by means of an exchange of letters. In letter XXXVI she confesses: "if I had not had a reply from you, my lord and master, I should have given surcease to my burning heart in such wise that my soul would have been forever in torment and my fame [as a martyr of love] would have spread throughout the world." [103]

Suicide in Renaissance drama, lyric, and fiction. In Encina's dramatic *Eclogue of Three Shepherds* (1509) [104] we are dealing with a close adaptation of an Italian original: the second eclogue of Antonio Tebaldeo. The author follows the Italian poet in de-

101. *Orígenes de la novela*, study and ed. by M. Menéndez y Pelayo (Madrid, 1905–15), II, 66a.

102. Ed. J. A. Balenchana (Madrid, 1874), p. 224. Melibea, it will be remembered, threw herself down from her tower because her lover had accidentally met a similar death as he hastily left her apartment.

103. Ed. and trans. by Edwin B. Place (Evanston, Illinois, 1950), p. 144 (I have departed slightly from Place's translation). The lover himself contemplates, but does not consummate, his own suicide because of his lack of courage. In the same letter (XLI) in which he announces his intention to take his life, he asks (with a confusion and *turbación* that recall Melibea's words before her fatal plunge) that masses be said to the Holy Ghost, to Mary Magdalene, and to the Magian Kings. For other condemnations of suicide prior to the promulgation of the decrees of Trent, see Pérez de Oliva, *Diálogo de la dignidad del hombre, ed. cit.*, p. 395b; Pero Mexía, *Silva de varia lección*, ed. La Sociedad de Bibliófilos Españoles (Madrid, 1933–34), I, 352.

104. See above, early in this section on suicide, the analysis of the problem in another play of Encina.

scribing the suicide (by stabbing) of Fileno, but he adds a comic character, Zambardo. To a considerable extent, at least in one version of the play (see below), the comic element offsets the suicide. What is certain is that a safeguard — the word *loco*, "madman" — is made use of. Fileno, bent on self-destruction, tells his well-meaning friend, Cardonio, "I want no advice," and receives the rebuke: "A madman's reply." "Sane or mad, that is what I say," exclaims Fileno. Over against all this, there can be no question that we are dealing with a literary presentation of tragic love.

A powerful argument that a spirit of burlesque was present in the author's mind, and was intended to be conveyed to the audience, is provided by certain lines found only in a separate edition of this play (not in the 1509 edition of Encina's *Cancionero*) — lines which suggest the type of blasphemous parody that we encountered in Juan Ruiz's burlesque funeral sermon and his apotheosis of his old bawd Trotaconventos (see Volume I, Chapter II). The comic character Zambardo objects to Cardonio's suggestion that the two surviving friends prepare a funeral for the suicide. "Do not pray for him, for he is a saint and we should regard him as such. Let us go without restraint to the Pope in Rome that he may canonize him." [105]

The element of parody or burlesque is present in our next play, the *Farsa o cuasi comedia del soldado* (also of 1509), by Encina's imitator, Lucas Fernández. Love among shepherds is again the subject. The play begins with a burlesque of the preparations for suicide in Encina's play (mentioned above) *Egloga de tres pastores*. The shepherd Pravos takes leave of his flocks and of all things dear to him. The soldier enters and learns that Pravos is in love — the same "disease" which in the Encina play caused the stabbing of Fileno and occasioned no end of trouble to other shepherds. Fernández mentions in the course of his *Farsa* five of his predecessor's plays, along with one of his own, and, according to Crawford (*op.*

---

105. "No rueguen por él, Cardonio, que es sancto / . . . . / Pues vamos llamar los dos sin carcoma / al muy santo crego que lo canonice: / aquel que en vulgar romance se dice / allá entre groseros el Papa de Roma" (see A. Valbuena Prat, *Literatura dramática española* [Barcelona–Buenos Aires, 1930], pp. 31–32). Perhaps the omission of these verses from the 1509 edition of Encina's *Cancionero* may be taken as additional proof that not even the early Renaissance tolerated easily or readily what was to be condemned much later (1563) by the decrees of Trent. (Note the use of the word *loco* in the 1509 text.)

cit., p. 69), does not take Fileno's death "with all of the seriousness which its author might have expected." Crawford appears not to have remembered the burlesque tone of the lines which we have quoted from the *suelta* imprint of Encina's eclogue.

The anonymous *Farça a manera de tragedia* (1537) deals with a guilty love, inasmuch as the beloved, Liria, is married. The lover Torcato receives a letter, apparently signed by Liria but actually a forgery, in which he is told of the discovery of their secret and of the cooling of her love for him. Torcato writes a letter in his own blood and stabs himself, and Liria commits suicide on discovering her lover's body. This play is strongly influenced by Encina's two plays of suicide and shows, according to Crawford, "considerable progress in typing up the emotions which lead to the inevitable catastrophe" (*op. cit.*, p. 100).

There is no case of a genuine suicide in the plays of Bartolomé de Torres Naharro (d. 1520?). Gillet, discussing death and resurrection as one of the primitive themes in Torres Naharro's theater, remarks: "There is something peculiar in the frequent occurence in Torres Naharro's plays of the idea of death in a form which seems to reveal an essential connection with the primitive theme of Death and Resurrection." In the *Comedia Calamita* "the process is presented in full as a comic interlude. It might be summed up as: death is feigned to test a wife's faithfulness, and it might well have been current folklore in Torres Naharro's time. . . . Essentially it is a form of the old Death and Resurrection theme." The other cases are suicides, "yet only apparently so." [106]

Alonso de la Vega's *Tragedia llamada Seraphina* (1566) ends with the suicide of the two protagonists, Seraphina and Athanasio. Menéndez y Pelayo, the play's modern editor, found it "a fantastic muddle, a mixture of themes mythological and pastoral," suggestive of the lightness of a Spanish dramatic interlude (*entremés*). There is the nonsense of the Simpleton; there are wild men right out of the Middle Ages; [107] there are also two well-known characters

106. J. E. Gillet, *Torres Naharro and the Drama of the Renaissance*, ed., transcribed, and completed by O. H. Green (Philadelphia, 1961), pp. 46–47; see also the Index, *s.v.* Suicide. (This work is volume IV of *Propalladia and Other Works of Bartolomé de Torres Naharro*, ed. J. E. Gillet; it will be cited as Gillet-Green.)

107. See Richard Bernheimer, *Wild Men in the Middle Ages* (Cambridge, Massachusetts, 1952).

from classical antiquity, Paris and Narcissus; and finally, there is — as one of the *dramatis personae* — Cupid himself, the god of love. The scene is Italy.[108]

In the later drama of the Golden Age, suicide may be threatened as readily as in the lyric, or as in any other genre. In *Los balcones de Madrid* of Tirso de Molina (d. 1648), Elisa decides either to marry her lover or to die.

> Ever firm and ever faithful
> I shall resist their rigors;
> And if they prevent me I'll find
> The perfect remedy in death.[109]

Suicide may even be attempted, as in Lope de Vega's youthful play *Belardo el furioso*, where the heroine attempts to kill herself by swallowing a ring.[110] As we have noted above, such rash desires or heedless (and unsuccessful) attempts can always be readily atoned for. For the rest (so far as I know), suicide is unacceptable in the later drama, unless those who take their lives are noble pagans. The mass suicide of the defending Numantians in Cervantes' *La Numancia* is characterized as "praiseworthy."[111] In *El dueño de las estrellas* by Juan Ruiz de Alarcón (d. 1639), Licurgus chooses suicide as the only means of preserving his honor: "I myself shall give to my life / An honored end and endless fame." [112] Cervantes, in his play *El rufián dichoso*, declares that Judas Iscariot was more blameworthy for having killed himself than for having betrayed his Lord — a conviction which is repeated in another of his plays, *La Gran Sultana*, in which he insists that to kill oneself is cowardice.[113]

In the lyric the attitude is very similar. Suicide may be threatened by any despairing lover; it may even be attempted, if a friend, or

108. See Menéndez y Pelayo's introduction to his edition in *Gesellschaft für Romanische Literatur* (Dresden, 1905), pp. xxiii–xxiv. Suicide is contemplated, or threatened, or all but consummated in the anonymous *Egloga pastoril* (1519?); in the *Comedia Grassandora* of Uceda de Sepúlveda (1539); in the *Farsa de la hechicera* of Diego Sánchez de Badajoz (1552); and in the anonymous *Farsa llamada Rosiela* (1558). See Crawford, *op. cit.*, Index.

109. "Siempre firme, siempre verde / sus rigores me verán; / y si en perseguirme dan, / morir es total remedio" (*BAE*, V, 556); cf. p. 561: "O morir o ser tu esposa."

110. See J. M. Blecua's ed. of Lope's *La Dorotea* (Madrid, 1955), p. 35, n. 11.

111. Aubrey Bell, *Cervantes*, (Norman, Oklahoma, 1947), p. 48, n. 20, Cf. Mexía, *Silva de varia lección, ed. cit.*, I, 352.

112. Cited in A. García Valdecasas, *El hidalgo y el honor* (Madrid, 1948), p. 196.

113. Bell has listed the passages, *op. cit.*, p. 48, n. 20.

some natural agency such as the wind, prevents the consummation of the act. The fact is that the ancient example of Pyramus and Thisbe exerted a strong attraction, which was seconded by the whole tradition of *Liebestod* in the literature of courtly love. Fray Juan de Pineda wrote in his *Agricultura christiana*, with reference precisely to Pyramus and Thisbe: "Such deaths always inspire pity." "What they ought to inspire," says another interlocutor, "is a warning and a horrible example . . . wherein the most pitiable aspect is the loss of the lovers' souls, which went down to hell, where their fate was worse than that of the Crab killed by Hercules and placed by Juno in the heavens as a constellation." [114]

A generation ago, critics tended to regard Garcilaso de la Vega as a neo-Stoic who, by reason of his man-centered philosophy, recognized any person's right to choose the moment of his death. In 1948 Rafael Lapesa wrote of a character in one of Garcilaso's eclogues:

Finally that shepherd, who marches "with long stride and unswerving heart" toward suicide, shouts, with a rebellion as pronounced as that of Garcilaso himself in Sonnet IV, and with the same reminiscence from Petrarch:

> Can I not die? Can't I make my departure
> From here, from there, from whencesoe'er I please,
> A disembodied soul, or man in the flesh? [115]

What others have not pointed out, insofar as I am aware, is that: (1) no suicide is consummated in any of Garcilaso's poems; (2) similar truancies, too numerous to be documented here, occur in all the various genres; (3) the tradition of such outbursts is independent of Stoic philosophical trends, being a concomitant of courtly love; and (4) Garcilaso himself, in this same *Egloga II*, makes it clear that the shepherd who marches so resolutely toward suicide is a deranged person, in need of what today would be psychiatric care. He is turned over to a learned and wise friar for treatment. The word *loco*, "mad," is applied to him numerous

114. Ed. Salamanca (1589), I, fol. 204.
115. "¿No puedo yo morir? ¿No puedo irme / por aquí, por allí, por do quisiere, / desnudo espíritu o carne y hueso firme?" (*Egloga II*, vv. 880 ff). See Lapesa, *La trayectoria poética de Garcilaso* (Madrid, 1948), p. 110, and Margot Arce Blanco, *Garcilaso de la Vega: Contribución al estudio de la lírica española del siglo XVI* (Madrid, 1930), p. 67.

times (vv. 951, 1003, 1027, 1876), and his friend Salicio, in the remonstrations which he addresses to him, remarks:

> As long as you're alive, it well may be
> That in some way I can get through to you
> And blend my tears with yours;
> It's best to have some one with you at your gallows
> To give advice and share your misery.[116]

Garcilaso may indeed have been only a nominal Christian, but the body of the poetry he has left suggests that he was more than that: with the deepest poetic emotion he places the soul of his own lost Elisa in the Christian Empyrean.[117]

Gutierre de Cetina (d. 1557?), one of Garcilaso's continuators in the new Italian style of lyric poetry, appears to have been the victim of an attempted assassination inspired by jealousy, though the nature of his stabbing is shrouded in mystery. In true courtly fashion he expressed envy of the death of a lackey crushed by a carriage which carried Lucía Harielo: "O to be crushed by so beautiful a weight!" In Sonnet CCXXVII (also quoted in volume I, p. 272) he re-echoes the wish — expressed by Santillana and by so many poets of the fifteenth century — to put an end to *Liebessehnsucht* by an act of self-annihilation:

> If our religion but permitted it,
> As did that of the ancients, whose concern
> Was merely to die well, how gladly would I
> End all I suffer, following their example.[118]

Gabriel López Maldonado, a friend of Cervantes, published his *Cancionero* in 1586 at Madrid. One of the poems expresses an inclination to suicide, a desire a thousand times experienced and always thwarted because the object of the poet's affections and the cause of his despair is unwilling that he should take his life. What

116. "que mientras estás vivo, ser podría / que por alguna vía te avisase, / y contigo llorase; que no es malo / tener al pie del palo quien se duela / del mal, y sin cautela te aconseje" (vv. 360 ff.)

117. See Volume II, Chapter IV, and my article, "The Abode of the Blest in Garcilaso's *Egloga Primera*," *RPh*, VI (1953), 272–78, especially the concluding paragraph.

118. "Si nuestra religión lo permitiera, / como aquella gentil, que solamante / de un hermoso morir tuvo cuidado, / yo sé por menos mal lo que hiciera" (*Obras*, ed. J. Hazañas y la Rúa (Seville, 1895), I, 198. See R. Lapesa, "Gutierre de Cetina: Disquisiciones biográficas," *Estudios hispánicos: Homenaje a Archer M. Huntington* (Wellesley, Massachusetts, 1952), 321 ff.

greater cruelty can there be, he asks, than this: she who kills her lover with sadness demands of him cheerful long-suffering (fol. 18).

Fernando de Herrera, who flourished at the same time, addresses his Luz:

> Only permit, since I must absent be,
> That I pour out my grief in these wild places
> Ere I with this keen sword my throat shall sever,
> Bequeathing to the fire my lifeless body.[119]

In Francisco de la Torre's *Egloga VI*,[120] Florelo laments the cruelty of "the more than divine Galatea" and addresses to her an apostrophe: since she wills that her lover shall die *desesperado*, let her at least have sufficient mercy to show her face to him who loves her as his God (p. 151, line 30). This places us, of course, in a medieval setting: this is the courtly "religion of love" (see Volume I, Chapter III). The hyperboles of this "religion" are continued throughout the soliloquy. The distraught lover invokes the gods of the crystalline waters and of the serene sky, of the night and of the sea. Perhaps with good reason he also addresses Hecate, in ancient times appealed to for aid against attacks of insanity; but the help that Florelo most desires is assurance that his act of self-sacrifice is pleasing to Galatea. The gods respond: we are told that Florelo would have cast himself downward into the sea if he had not heard a choir of goddesses of the white-capped waves singing and calming the waters. The remainder of the eclogue is spoken by Leucothea, the daughter of Cadmus received among the sea gods. Her song tells the story of Iphis who hanged himself at the door of the relentless Anaxarete, the rich and beautiful maiden of Cyprus whom Venus in anger converted into a block of stone. The song ends with an appeal to Florelo to remember that good and evil fortune are equal parts of life, and that halcyon weather follows storm.

There is a thwarted suicide in one of Lope de Vega's lyric poems[121] (no less than in his *Dorotea*) and a threatened suicide in a sonnet of Francisco de Figueroa (d. 1620).[122]

119. *Rimas inéditas*, ed. J. M. Blecua (Madrid, 1948), p. 164: "Solo permite, ya que estoy ausente, / quexarme de mi mal a este desierto, / primero que a la espada entregue el cuello / y el cuerpo al fuego que me tiene muerto."
120. See his *Poesías*, ed. A. Zamora Vicente (Madrid, 1944), pp. 149 ff.
121. *Poesías líricas*, ed. J. F. Montesinos (Madrid, 1941), II, 17.
122. *Obras*, ed. facsimile by A. M. Huntington (New York, 1903), p. 2.

This theme offered no difficulty to the censors. La Torre's poems were issued with the customary statement that they contained nothing at variance with the Catholic Faith or "our modest customs," signed by the well-known theologian and sacred dramatist José de Valdivielso. The verses of Francisco de Figueroa were printed at Lisbon in 1626 with this statement by Friar Tomás de Santo Domingo: "It is my opinion that they ought to be printed many times, to the end that all interested persons may enjoy such good poetry as this poetry is."

An elaborately frustrated attempt at suicide is described in *Desengaño de amor en rimas* (1623) by the Gongorine poet Pedro Soto de Rojas. In his *Egloga IV* he presents dramatically the despair of Fenixardo, who after a long lament endeavors to cast himself down from a great height. At that moment "the fury of an angry wind" causes him to fall backward, not forward; and there the dawn finds him, bathed in tears and still unconscious. He is discovered by his friend, who reproves him gently. From time to time the poor man shakes his head gloomily as he recovers, not daring to meet his friend's gaze, "since guilt deprives a brave man of his courage." Other shepherds gather to receive him and kindly lead him to his hut, where he may recover from his wounds, both spiritual and physical.[123]

In Gaspar Gil Polo's pastoral novel, the *Diana enamorada* (1564), there is a thwarted suicide: "I wished to pierce my wretched bosom with a sword, and I would have done so had not those sailors restrained me by word and deed." [124]

In 1565 Antonio de Villegas published in his *Inventario* a quasi-pastoral tale entitled *Absence and Solitude of Love*. It is in the willful and wayward tradition of medieval courtly love. The speaker, a despairing lover, sets out upon "the path of solitude and perdition," saying: "Oh sadness, absence, and solitude (three enemies of my soul and body), vent your rage upon me; for if you would go to the final lengths, you have here brought me to a place where I may punish myself and take vengeance upon you; here I have a fountain in which to drown myself, a tree from which to hang my-

123. *Obras*, ed. A. Gallego Morell (Madrid, 1950), pp. 201–9.
124. Menéndez y Pelayo, *Orígenes de la novela, ed. cit.*, II, 349b. The decrees of Trent were published in 1563. It seems impossible that the passage could have been influenced by them as early as 1564.

self, and a tomb in which I may be enclosed." He neither dies nor kills himself, however, but falls into a trance, during which various "cases" of unhappy lovers are solved before his eyes. After this he revives and finds himself again at his point of departure. The author is of course aware that thoughts of suicide are dangerous: the speaker's mental state and outward circumstances are "enemies" of his soul and body.[125]

In 1586, twenty-three years after the promulgation of the decrees of Trent, Bartolomé López de Enciso published at Madrid a didactic novel, *Desengaño de celos*, on the irrational nature of jealousy — a work which is not accessible to me but which is analyzed at some length by Avalle-Arce. In it, says Professor Avalle-Arce, the author passes repeatedly from a consideration of jealousy to "the most universal problems of ethics" (*op. cit.*, p. 159). These discussions are so strongly tinged with Stoic — that is to say, rational — philosophy that Professor Avalle-Arce has seen in this Stoicism a reason explaining the author's "treating resolutely a theme which was forbidden at the time he was writing. When one of his shepherdesses has to choose, on the one hand, between forcing her will and her reason, and producing her own death as the only alternative, she kills herself with fortitude" (*ibid.*). I regret not having the text of this work. I suspect that the prohibition of Trent is in one way or another taken into consideration by the author. Almost certainly — and the word almost makes it clear that I am offering a mere hypothesis — the prohibition of Trent will be found, on close reading, to have been respected. Since the tale is conceived and constructed on the basis of a rational conception of proper human conduct, I assume that the author, by some means, shows the unfortunate shepherdess to have been driven to distraction, so that emotion and agitation obfuscate the light of reason. The word *loco*, so insistently repeated in Garcilaso's *Egloga II* and in other texts we have examined, is probably inserted here, perhaps with such nouns as *locura*, *turbación*, *desvario*. In any case, suicide cannot be said to "disappear as a literary theme in Spain during the second half of the sixteenth century," as Professor Avalle-Arce states, though it is true

125. See J. B. Avalle-Arce, *La novela pastoril española* (Madrid, 1959), pp. 34–37; M. Bataillon, "¿Melancolía renacentista o melancolía judía?," in *Estudios hispánicos: Homenaje a Archer M. Huntington*, p. 46.

that "a suicide in 1586 must be attributed to . . . ideas totally unacceptable to the new reformers in control at the moment" (p. 160).

In the following year (1587) an actually accomplished suicide is depicted in the allegorical novel *Viaje y naufragios del macedonio* by Juan Bautista de Loyola (Salamanca, 1587). In an interpolated episode in verse, the author gives his own interpretation of the Ninth Story of the Fourth Day of Boccaccio's *Decameron*. A jealous husband has overheard his wife engaged in amorous conversation with his trusted servant. Killing the servant, the husband sets the dead man's heart as a viand before the offending wife, telling her that it is the heart of a deer. When he asks her, "Did you enjoy eating Arpago, your lover?" she rushes to her quarters and hangs herself.[126] Here again, I do not have access to the Spanish text. This is a clear case of truancy. The fact that the scene is laid in Italy, in an atmosphere far away and long ago, may have had some part in determining the acceptability of the episode. It would be well to scrutinize the text, either for some reference to a temporary onset of madness (if the wife is a sympathetic character), or for indications that she is an evil person naturally consigned to damnation.

Cervantes condemns suicide as an infamous and cowardly "remedy" for human sufferings. He does so in *La Galatea* (1585), in his *Exemplary Novels* (1614), and in the *Persiles* (1616).[127] Yet he himself uses the theme in various ways. In *La Galatea* Artidoro leaves a note affixed to a tree, proclaiming that a trail of blood drops will lead to where he is and asking that — though his love is scorned — a final sad farewell be not denied to his body.[128] The suicide is not consummated. Another character, Rosaura, would have stabbed herself to death had she not been prevented by friends (*ibid.*, p. 685). Still another, Galercio, to whom the adjective *desesperado* is more than once applied, struggles violently to keep his head under water as two shepherdesses, with the help of friends, prevent his suicide (p. 761).

In *Don Quijote* (1605), the case of Grisóstomo has been much discussed. There can be no doubt that he actually did kill himself.

126. See John D. Williams, "Notes on the Legend of the Eaten Heart in Spain," *HR*, XXVI (1958), 94.
127. Bell, *op. cit.*, p. 48, n. 20.
128. *Obras*, A. Valbuena Prat (Madrid, 1956), pp. 637–38.

He is denied burial in sacred ground and is buried "out in the fields, like a Moor" by his shepherd friends, as they lament his pitiable case. His death is attributed to *porfía, impaciencia, arrojado deseo* — intractability, unwillingness to suffer, intemperate desire: irrational elements, all of them. These three attributes given him, and his burial in the fields where his flocks had wandered, are Cervantes' only condemnation of Grisóstomo.[129] The shepherds themselves treat Grisóstomo's case with something of the respect, even reverence, that we noted in the fifteenth century in Rodríguez del Padrón's *Siervo libre de amor*.

In 1602 Mateo Alemán, author of the extremely successful picaresque novel *Guzmán de Alfarache* (1599), had a bitter experience which some years later Cervantes would share with him: an impostor, "Mateo Luján de Sayavedra," brought out a spurious "second part" to the famous tale of Guzmán. Alemán's reaction differed from that of Cervantes in 1614. Very cleverly, he incorporated Sayavedra into the *dramatis personae* of his own *Segunda Parte*, making him commit suicide. But there is a point that must be taken into account: before leaping from the storm-tossed galley into the raging sea, Sayavedra goes completely mad — *loco*.[130]

In the spurious second part of *Don Quijote* by "Alonso Fernández de Avellaneda" (1614) we have the tale of *The Despairing Rich Man* with its double suicide and murder. The guest of a rich Fleming deceives the latter's wife and succeeds in obtaining her favors, only to be killed by his host. The dishonored wife, on realizing that she has lain with a man who was not her husband, takes her own life, whereupon the husband, in desperation, kills both his daughter and himself. All are consigned to hell.

In the *Poema trágico del español Gerardo y desangaño del amor lascivo* (1615–17) of Gonzalo de Céspedes y Meneses, suicide is con-

---

129. See Bell, *op. cit.*, p. 48, n. 20; and *Don Quijote*, I, 12 ff. It does not make sense to assume, as an eminent critic has done, that the fact that Grisóstomo's death was self-inflicted is brought out "semi-clandestinely" by revealing it in the verses of chapter XIV—verses which the ordinary reader supposedly "habitually skipped." The character of the act is very strongly suggested by the use of the words *desesperado, desesperarse, canción desesperada, versos desesperados*, the latter occuring in the heading of the chapter that contains the "song of despair." See Américo Castro, "Los prólogos al *Quijote*," *RFH*, III (1941), 337.

130. See E. Moreno Báez, *Lección y sentido del Guzmán de Alfarache* (Madrid, 1948), pp. 47–48, and the review by Ch. V. Aubrun in *BHi*, LI (1949), 195, 197.

templated, threatened,[131] and actually attempted: Gerardo comes upon Clori, "who in that very moment, with diabolical and desperate daring, had just thrown herself down from a large holm oak and was hanging suspended by a strong noose and unyielding knot." She is cut down, whereupon she opens her eyes and "with frail voice prayed to all-pitying God for mercy" (175b–76a).

Thus, in the various literary genres from the fifteenth (even the fourteenth) century onward, Spanish writers are both attracted and repelled by suicide. At no time is it admitted "easily" — that is to say, without traces of bad conscience — as a literary theme. In the serious works which are exceptions to this statement, there may be admiration for the Stoic serenity and fortitude of ancient heroes [132] such as Cato Uticensis, or gentle pity for lovers like Pyramus and Thisbe — a pity akin to that so strongly felt by the theologian Dante as he contemplated the eternal punishment of Paolo and Francesca. If either of these emotional resources is used in a work of literature, it is normal to set the scene in antiquity or, if not in the world of the ancients, at least in a setting that has about it something of the long ago and far away, or something of essential unreality — the world of the allegorical or the pastoral tale. There is no clear-cut cleavage between the pre- and the post-Tridentine periods except, perhaps, in the drama:[133] the national theater created by Lope will be found to show — I suspect — remarkably few cases of the use of the theme. In the novels of chivalry — of which I have read so few! — the self-destroying characters will be found, I am sure, to be persons whose consignment to hell is natural in view of their general inhumanity. In the sentimental novel, the rare personages who take their own lives are normally driven by the overwhelming force of that *turbación* which (once one has given himself over to his passion) weakens both the reason and the will.

In short, the literature dealing with suicide is not "pagan" literature. The temptation to admire the pagans in this respect is gen-

131. *BAE*, XVIII, 125b–26a; see also 135b–36a, 149b.
132. Quevedo admires the suicide of Portia, the wife of Brutus: "Oh wise, and at that time pious, scorn of personal health!" (*Obras en prosa, ed. cit.*, p. 607a.)
133. In which the dangerous theme does indeed seem to be rather more avoided than disallowed in the seventeenth century (witness our quotation from Tirso de Molina, and Lope's *Belardo el furioso*).

erally resisted. Only some very few works — the *Cárcel de amor* and the *Siervo libre de amor*, both prior to the full tide of the Renaissance, and the 1547 imitation of Rojas' *Celestina*, the *Tragedia Policiana* [134] — present suicide without condemnation or extenuation; in such cases the truancy is like any of the other truancies discussed in the final chapter of Volume I ("Truancy and Recantation"). [135]

"Paganism" of the Flesh

After what has been written in the two preceding volumes of this study it will not be necessary to dwell for long on this aspect of Renaissance literature. Just as the sainted Sir Thomas More composed Latin epigrams that were sometimes salacious (for example, the one about a rapist), so Spanish churchmen of great religious respectability and purity of life allowed themselves to write things which today appear unseemly. I have studied this at some length in other places, [136] and in general I refer the reader to those studies. Though Renaissance literature is cleaner in Spain than in other countries, it can also be scabrous. Poems of the *Venus and Adonis* type were indeed written, but their Spanish authors were not "pagan" any more than King David was pagan when he looked with sinful eyes upon Bathsheba. Such poems are symbolic structures, created by Christians in and for a Christian society — a society whose Hebrew-Graeco-Roman-medieval synthesis, though far from perfect, was strangely enough workable, as I have shown in the initial chapter of Volume I. The expression of sensuality is a matter of style and genre. Things acceptable in laugh-provoking tri-

134. Before Policiana plunges her dead lover's sword into her bosom, she entrusts her soul to God, at the same time expressing the hope that her body may join in death "him whom it [the body] was unable to enjoy in life." Her father's lament over her makes no reference to the manner of her death, and is quite secular except for the five Latin words which end the story: "All things pass away except the love for God." See *Origenes de la novela, ed. cit.,* III, 57, 59.

135. See the discussion of suicide in Book IV of Sidney's *Arcadia.* On the Italian regard for the Christian attitude toward suicide in tragedy, see G. Guarini, *Compendio della poesia tragicomica* (Bari, 1914), 234–42. See also Mario Monaco, "Racine and the Problem of Suicide," *PMLA,* LXX (1955), 441 ff.

136. "On Francisco de Aldana: Observations on Dr. Rivers' Study of 'El Divino Capitán,' " *HR,* XXVI (1958), 117–36; *Quevedo,* pp. 13 ff., 69–82; my review of A. Mas, *La caricature de la femme, du mariage et de l'amour dans l'oeuvre de Quevedo* (Paris, 1957), in *HR,* XXVIII (1960), 72–76.

fles — *obras de burlas* — may be objectionable in a lyric poem, just
as things regarded as seemly in the *Book of Good Love* of the Archpriest of Hita, in an introit to a play by Torres Naharro, or in one
of the *Dramatic Interludes* of Cervantes (not to mention the later
novelas cortesanas of Juan Pérez de Montalbán or María de Zayas y
Sotomayor) may seem indelicate (or may simply never appear) in
a Lopean *comedia. Tirant lo Blanc* and *Amadís de Gaula* express
delight in physical passion in a way that one seeks for in vain in the
Diana of Montemayor — though one finds it in festive poets like
Baltasar del Alcázar and Gregorio Silvestre. Lope's "action in
prose," *La Dorotea,* still heated by the embers of his youthful passion for Elena Osorio, is cast in a far different key from Cervantes'
chaste *Persiles.*

Toward the end of the sixteenth century there appears in the
lyric a greater freedom in these matters, and Francisco de Medrano
(d. 1615?) could write "with contours of flesh, with effervescing
desire" (the words are Dámaso Alonso's):

> When she — oh lovely sight — bends down her neck
> To the ardor of my kisses, and, besought,
> Denies with easy anger what she wishes
> (More than her lover could) to have taken from her
> With a loving show of force . . .[137]

And there is the Quevedo of the Sonnets: *¡Ay, Floralba! soñé que te
. . .¿dirélo?* ("I dreamed, Floralba . . . oh, I cannot tell it!") — or
the Quevedo of the poem beginning:

> Those two white columns fair,

with its suggestion of the orgasm (couched in words that recall
Hemingway's "the earth moved!" in *For Whom the Bell Tolls*):

> The great mountains trembled,
> The whole earth shuddered,
> As all things returned
> To their primeval essence.[138]

137. "Cuando ella tuerce — ¡oh, cómo hermosa! — el cuello / a mis ardientes besos, y
rogada, / con saña fácil niega / lo que ella, más que el mismo que la ruega / dar
quisiera robada . . . " (cited by Alonso in *Vida y obra de Medrano* [Madrid, 1948–58],
I, 107).

138. "Temblaron los montes / y estremecióse la tierra, / convirtiéndose las formas /
en su primera materia" (*Obras en verso, ed. cit.,* p. 256b).

All of this proves one thing: there occurred in Spain a forward-moving change in taste that made it more seemly than before to express sensuality in lyric verse. All of the creations of the poet as maker — be they seemly or unseemly — constituted the poetic expression of that unquestionably Christian nation that was Spain. Not infrequently they produced bad conscience. Then the poets, growing older — or old! — turned their gaze toward heaven, regretting not only the works written, but

> The good works that in my unbridled youth
> I offered not to God as my hand scattered
> A seed more sterile than sterility.[139]

SUMMARY AND CONCLUSION

The conclusions which follow from our necessarily lengthy analysis of Spain's position in the important matter of the supposed paganism of Renaissance thought and literature are for the most part obvious, each in its own section. There was some talk of atheism, but atheists can scarcely be identified. Assumptions by earlier critics that a literary or philosophic reference to the creative power of Nature, to the cruelty of the world (not of the universe), or to the Stoic integrity of certain historical or fictional personages could be taken as evidence that the faith of the Age of Faith had weakened have been shown to be without foundation. *Natura naturans* is at all times God's vicegerent; cosmic strife is ever resolved into cosmic harmony; when Stoic attitudes [140] lead "resolutely" to suicide, the necessary religious safeguards are found to be present — or else the literary personage is an evil creature, sent by his own willfulness to hell. "Paganism of the flesh" is simply sin, recognized as a truancy in literature as it was in life — in the life, for example, of that passionate yet repentant sinner whose name was Lope de Vega.

The "devil's advocate" has thus not proved his case. At no time did Spain, or any appreciable part of her population — of the population, that is, whose life is known to us through the written

139. "Triste de tantas [obras] que tan vanamente / en la sin freno edad pude negalle [a Dios], / sembrando esterilísima simiente" (Francisco de Aldana [d. 1578], *Obras completas*, ed. M. Moragón Maestre [Madrid, 1953], II, 39).

140. On the early assimiliation of Stoic ethics into the Christian ethical system, see below, Chapter X.

word [141] — cease to be naturally and obviously Christian. The Renaissance, which Kristeller and others have shown to be, in Europe as a whole, "fundamentally a Christian age," was in Spain a Christian Renaissance.

141. I am writing cultural history, not history. That there were, among the "converted" Jews, an appreciable number of persons who denied the soul's immortality (following the teaching of Epicurus) has been shown by the researches of Baer, Révah, and others. Another unassimilated minority was that of the Moriscos (Mohammedans who remained in Spain after the expulsion under Ferdinand and Isabella). They revolted in 1568 but were subdued by military action. Finally, in 1609–10 the entire body of the king's subjects of Moorish descent was expelled, but with a noteworthy exception: all Moriscos who were priests, monks, or nuns were allowed to remain. The Moriscos — agriculturalists and artisans — "no longer possessed an Averroës or an Ibn Hazm, and their writings . . . have no special value" (Américo Castro, *La realidad histórica de España* [Mexico City, 1954], p. 99). The dramatist Guillén de Castro took a commanding part in the expulsion of 1610; see Luis de Mármol Carvajal, *Historia de la rebelión y castigo de los moriscos del reino de Granada* (Málaga, 1600?); Jaime Bleda, *Crónica de los moros de España* (Valencia, 1618); Henry C. Lea, *The Moriscos of Spain* (Philadelphia, 1901), especially ch. X; O. H. Green, "New Documents for the Biography of Guillén de Castro y Bellvís," *RHi*, LXXXI (1933), especially pp. 12 ff.

VIII · Religious and Ethical Orientation

> The Spaniards were the first among all nations
> to profess letters, and they are the most ancient
> theologians and canonists (except the Apostles);
> they are the first legislators of the world.
>
> > *Fray Benito de Peñalosa y Mondragón* (1629) [1]

> Finally, the most learned, illustrious, and godlike
> group of men that Spain can point to at this time
> consists of the theologians, if we make exception
> of a few insignificant and old-fashioned ones
> trained at the Sorbonne at a time when true elo-
> quence was exiled from that institution. . . .
>
> > *Alfonso Garcia de Matamoros* (1553) [2]

> Among all the other sciences . . . theology has by far
> the greatest dignity and excellence, and there is
> no other to which the true Christian should devote
> more time; so that, if it were possible for us, we
> should let no day pass without taking into our
> hands some book of Holy Scripture, because you
> will generally see that a man's character is
> shaped by the science in which he most takes
> delight. . . .
>
> > *Hernán Núñez, el Comendador Griego* (1499) [3]

Although theology "was the most engrossing subject of Renaissance thought" throughout Europe (politics being the second), although in countries other than Spain Hebrew was considered the greatest of languages because it was "nearest the original magic of God's voice," [4] there is none the less something peculiarly Spanish in the

1. *Libro de las cinco excelencias del español*, cited by Albert A. Sicroff, *Les controverses des statuts de "pureté de sang" en Espagne du XVᵉ au XVIIᵉ siècle* (Paris, 1960), p. 292. I cite these three texts in reverse chronological order to show their independence of any "mandate" by the authorities of the Counter Reformation.

2. *Pro adserenda hispanorum eruditione*, ed. and trans. José López de Toro (Madrid, 1943), pp. 231–32.

3. Commentary on *Copla* CXII of Juan de Mena's *Laberinto de Fortuna* (ed. Antwerp, 1552), p. 231.

4. Hardin Craig, *The Enchanted Glass: The Elizabethan Mind in Literature* (New York, 1950), pp. 47, 170. See also Dean P. Lockwood and Roland H. Bainton, "Classical

preference, among all intellectual activities, for the theological. The religious, cultural, spiritual, and social revolution that we call the Renaissance seems infinitely varied in its general European manifestations, yet greatly restricted in its manifestations in Spain. From Italy to Scotland,

it assumes the most diverse aspects, from the return to paganism advocated by a Marsuppini and a Plethon to the renewal of the "myth" of Prometheus; from the exaltation of man as an authentic microcosm by Giannozzo Manetti and others, to the Neoplatonism of Marsilio Ficino; from the syncretism of Pico della Mirandola to the inner, illumined religiosity of Erasmus; from the philological criticism of sacred texts inaugurated by Valla, to the literal exegesis of men like Socino; from the "Epicureanism" of Valla to the cult of glory and individualism in life, politics, and art, as shown by Burckhardt; from the abandonment of Scholastic intellectualism to the bold experimentalism of Telesio and Bacon, and, later, of Galileo, all of whom tended to undermine the "authority" of medieval gnosiology; from the cosmic organicism of León Hebreo to the panpsychism of Bruno; from the exaltation of the demiurgic power of art compared to the creative action of God, to the cult of "harmony" of men like Ariosto and Leonardo; from the rebirth of the ethics of the Roman state to the free-thinking pragmatism of Niccolò Machiavelli.[5]

Of all the movements here enumerated, there are scarcely more than six or seven that had important repercussions in Spain, and this is not due to the supposed fact that Spain was "shut off from the light," nor because there existed in Spain "no calm, no possibility to bring about a general conversion of religious values into other values of secular character." [6] Even when Spain was fully "open" to the light, when even the Inquisitor General and the emperor's secretary for Latin letters were Erasmists, Spain gave no evidence of wishing to convert religious values into secular values. It was not

and Biblical Scholarship in the Age of the Renaissance and Reformation," *Church History*, X (1941), 16: "The Age of the Renaissance and Reformation gave, if possible, an even greater stimulus to Biblical than to classical studies, because the Bible as a document of antiquity and a textbook of religion enlisted the interest alike of the humanist and of the reformer."

5. Edmondo Cione, *Juan de Valdés, la sua vita e il suo pensiero religioso* (Bari, 1938), pp. 77–78.

6. The first phrase quoted is William Hickling Prescott's (I consider it unnecessary to cite chapter and verse). The second quotation was written by Américo Castro in 1929, and corresponds generally to the "received idea" of an effective suppression of thought by the Inquisition; see his "Gracián y España," in *Santa Teresa y otros ensayos* (Santander, 1929), p. 260. Castro now seeks the explanation along very different lines.

a question of conversion, but simply of the direction Spanish religiosity should take.

Another critic, Karl Vossler, has asked: "Why did not Spain produce a Rabelais, a Voltaire, a Beaumarchais, a Heine, that is to say, a critic?" Vossler regards the reason as historical, and states that it must be sought in "the lack or the weakness of ideas opposed to Catholicism and absolutism: the heretical and revolutionary ideologies had spent their energy as they were absorbed into the work of the great reformers, apologists, and Inquisitors."[7] Castro, in *España en su historia* (1948) and its subsequent re-elaborations, would explain everything by the interplay — opposition and adaptation — of three cultures: Christian, Moorish, Jewish.

The first argument, based on the idea of suppression, commits what Lucien Febvre has called the ultimate historical sin, the sin against chronology. As we have seen, Spanish humanists began by devoting their main energies to Biblical exegesis; they did not turn to that activity when other aspects of philological inquiry were closed to them (they never were). The second argument, that the innovating ideologies lost their force as they were absorbed into the work of the giants of Spain's Counter Reformation, leaves unexplained why the Spaniards were impelled to be reformers, and not revolutionaries, in religious and intellectual matters. The third argument, that based on the interplay of cultures, rests on insufficient evidence or on spurious evidence — on examples that do not carry conviction or that can be matched by contrary examples. I simply decline to enter those lists. Acculturation was surely a factor, but there is no single key to the mystery. We are simply faced with a certain value system, a certain "culture pattern" — the Spanish. The rise, decline, and fall of value systems seems to be governed by forces as arbitrary as those that select, from out the countless possible sounds of which the human vocal apparatus is capable, certain ones — few in number — to serve as carriers of conceptual meanings and to constitute a language. It is a matter of choice, of social choice. I can see no ultimate cause for the direction taken other than the leadership of strong individuals who impose their ideals on their social group. One great service rendered by Américo Castro's recent

7. *Introducción a la literatura española del siglo de oro* (Madrid, 1934), pp. 116–17.

books and monographs is his demonstration of the fact of the Spanish preference for religious values. The device which the Marqués de Santillana (d. 1458) carried into battle, or into a tourney, was *Dios y Vos*, "God and you." The *Vos*, he explained, was the Virgin Mary.

Lest I myself be accused of having "an inspired method of selecting examples," it will be well to present further proof of this Spanish preference for religious, and — when once the struggle over Erasmianism is terminated — for orthodox Catholic values.[8]

It should first of all be made clear that, though a call to the inner life of the spirit was heard and heeded by thousands of men and women in the Spain of the first half of the sixteenth century — a call present in the pages of Savonarola, Erasmus, Francisco de Osuna (*fl.* 1527), Bernardino de Laredo (*fl.* 1535), and numerous others; though a veritable "throng" of Spaniards was seeking the means of acquiring the joy and the peace of inner prayer,[9] we have to do with something more than a religious revival. The religious revival was a real phenomenon — no one, after Bataillon's researches, can doubt that. As an example we may take Fray Alonso de Madrid, author of one of the first devotional works of an ascetic character written in a modern European language, the *Arte para servir a Dios*, of 1521 (definitive form, 1526). Fray Alonso, obviously influenced in his writing by the new trend toward classical imitation; diametrically opposed to Luther in his insistence on free will; deeply imbued with the doctrines of traditional philosophy and theology; a man of noble birth, a humanist and a director of souls, gave to Europe, and particularly to the Franciscan Order, an effective and personally conceived summary of traditionalist doctrine: the Gospels, the Fathers, Thomas Aquinas, Cajetan, Diony-

8. It is not easy to find reasons why England chose to follow the lead of Hobbes and Bacon, rather than that of Milton, Donne, or Butler. For Milton the search for impractical knowledge was reprehensible: in *Paradise Lost*, Raphael pauses in his discussion of the solar system to state that it does not much matter whether Ptolemy or Copernicus is correct. Butler's conclusion was very much like Donne's — man spends too much time numbering the hairs in the lion's mane. Yet by the third quarter of the seventeenth century the hairs were counted and man was trying to add up the atoms in the universe. See Don Cameron Allen, *The Legend of Noah: Renaissance Rationalism in Art, Science, and Letters* (Urbana, 1949), p. 38; E. L. Marilla, "Milton on 'Vain Wisdom' and 'False Philosophie,'" *Studia Neophilologica*, XXV (1953), 4.

9. Marcel Bataillon, *Erasmo y España* (Mexico City–Buenos Aires, 1950), II, 201.

sius the Areopagite, Gregory of Nyssa, Gregory the Great. The bibliographical history of this work, which went through some twenty editions at regular intervals and was translated into French, Italian, and Flemish (five editions), proves that a great effort at sanctification was indeed being made, on the widest imaginable basis, by souls who had remained faithful to the Church.[10] But there was more than this: there was a desire to know, to understand — a desire which, though it went hand in hand with the desire to know and to enjoy God, involved secular learning and invited the worshipper to study the ancient philosophers. In 1499 Hernán Núñez, the knight commander and professor of Greek, in his comment on *Copla* XIX of Mena's *Laberinto* remarked:

> This is the reason for what we read, namely, that many wise men abandoned their properties in order the more expeditiously to give themselves over to study, for example: Anaxagoras, Democritus, Crates, Zotus. This was understood by Lactantius Firmianus, when he said in the prologue to his *Divine Institutions* these words: "These men were worthy to know the truth, which they thirsted after so eagerly that they placed it ahead of all other things; for as we know, some philosophers left their possessions and withdrew from the delights of this life, in order thus naked and unimpeded to follow after virtue — herself one, unique, and unclothed" (*ed. cit.*, p. 38).

This recognition of the values and the need of secular learning and philosophy is brought out clearly by Pedro Ciruelo in his *Reprouación de las supersticiones y hechicerías* in 1539. Ciruelo was "an illustrious mathematician and philosopher, author of the first course of exact sciences to be drawn up in Spain, and a luminary of the Universities of Paris and Alcalá." [11] Referring to Aristotle's assertion that all men naturally desire to learn, he warns that this natural inclination must be controlled in accordance with the law of reason and the law of God, as expressed in the Bible by "the wise man": Do not go about searching the secrets of things that are too high for your intellect, and do not be curious to know all things; it is sufficient that you know the things that God commands you to know.[12]

10. Pierre Guillaume, "Un précurseur de la Réforme Catholique, Alonso de Madrid: *L'Arte para servir a Dios,*" *Revue d'histoire ecclésiastique*, XXV (1929), 260–74.

11. M. Menéndez y Pelayo, *Historia de los heterodoxos españoles* (Madrid, 1947–48), IV, 365; see also J. M. Llorente y Pérez, *Biografía y análisis de las obras de matemática pura de Pedro Sánchez Ciruelo* (Madrid, 1921).

12. The references given by Ciruelo are "Eccli. iii." and "Prouer. 25"; see Eccles.

"There are other things," Ciruelo continues, "which although they can be known by natural reason, require effort and a certain passage of time, and the making of experiments and the hearing of lectures by masters; and for acquiring this knowledge there are true sciences, founded and written by learned men, setting forth effects as the result of causes; and in this way men have come to know the virtues and the properties of stars, stones, herbs, fishes, birds, and other animals of the earth." Then follows the application of all this. Merely curious and lightweight minds do not distinguish between the knowable and the unknowable; and furthermore they are likely to take to magic as a short-cut to avoid the long road of true science (*ed. cit.*, fols. xxii–xxiii).

Ciruelo here speaks of organized study in institutions which appear to be universities. It will be well to omit, for the time being, the testimony of other Spaniards of the 1530's and to consider, in 1553, the ideal of García de Matamoros: religious piety, he says, will erect temples; enthusiasm for letters will construct "academies." In a section of his *Apology* for Spanish erudition, Matamoros praises the Conde de Ureña, Don Juan Téllez Girón (whose parents were the patrons of Francisco de Osuna, to be discussed soon). According to Matamoros, in this Spanish grandee there had been revived the piety to erect new churches and the "literary fervor" to construct academies so famous that not only from the provinces of Andalusia but even from America "innumerable" men of talent came in search of the "good letters" available at the University of Osuna.[13]

In another portion of this work Matamoros praises Don Francisco de Borja (d. 1572, later canonized), a grandee of wealth and power, the father of children, beloved by all his household and esteemed by strangers, who had turned his back upon his inherited position to join the Society of Jesus. This man is so evident a model of virtue and love "that I do not dare to risk injuring his greatness with the clumsiness of my pen; but who will prevent me from celebrating his noble and glorious enterprises in behalf of good studies, and the arts? He founded in Gandía . . . a famous college and

3:22 and Prov. 25:3. Compare Eccles. 7:23–24: "All this I have proved by wisdom; I said, I will be wise; but it was far from me. That which is far off, who can find it out?"

13. *Pro adserenda* . . . , *ed. cit.*, p. 37.

provided generous endowments to pay the salaries of the professors and contributed to the support of the religious of the Society of Jesus" (*ibid.*, p. 205).

Furthermore, Borja "wrote a pious book on Self Knowledge, worthy . . . of being at all times in our hands. Therefore, if Pliny commands young men to learn by heart the *De Officiis* of Cicero, and the Greeks, by means of the interpretation of Hesiod, gave to their children the rudiments of eloquence and the first standards of conduct, why should we not have ever in our hands a Commentary whence flow — full of grace — religious sanctity and piety?" (*ibid.*).

Would not a fully consummated "marriage" of science and piety, such as this passage hopefully suggests, have been of great benefit to Spain and to the Europe of which she formed a part? Perhaps, in 1553, one could think of the marriage as on the point of becoming a reality. Indeed, if we move forward eight years, we find that a Spanish Augustinian, Fray Diego de Zúñiga, actually adopts the astronomical system of Copernicus, so that it becomes the object of official study at the University of Salamanca in 1561.[14] But alas! to arrive at this year we have skipped too easily over the year 1559 wherein — one hundred and ninety-five years after the founding of the Spanish College at the University of Bologna — the King of Spain forbade Spanish scholars to study at any foreign university, with the exception of Naples and Coimbra. Indeed, one should not overstress the fact that Copernicus became a part of the Salamanca curriculum in 1561. Though the new astronomy was adopted by Fray Diego de Zúñiga, it was attacked by the Jesuit Father Pineda. And the Dominican Mancio de Corpus Christi (one of the teachers of the great Fray Luis de León) came to the conclusion that the Catholic Faith was bound up with the Aristolelian concept of the universe, since this was the world system adopted by St. Thomas. Unfortunately, Mancio prevailed and Ptolemy returned to Spanish classrooms, where he remained almost until the nineteenth century. In these same classrooms Scholasticism became gradually impoverished, for lack of independence and genuine research in philosophy,

14. A. F. G. Bell, *Luis de León*, Sp. trans. by Celso García (Barcelona, [1928]), p. 67.

and for lack of research and criticism in theological studies. It is therefore not strange that in 1610 there was only one candidate for the professorship of Hebrew, Master Gonzalo Correas, and that, in the Spain which had conceived and carried through to successful execution the great projects of the Alcalá and the Antwerp Polyglot Bibles, Professor Correas could not find Hebrew characters to print his *Gramática hebrea*.[15] We shall discover a similar unfortunate decline when we investigate philosophical studies in Spain.

Not all was antiscience.[16] Not that Spain ever produced a Leonardo, a Copernicus, a Vesalius, a Galileo; but she did produce humbler conceivers of scientific ideas whose work was appreciated, printed, and read by contemporary Europe. Juan Huarte de San Juan (a witness soon to be cited on the other side of the ledger) wrote Europe's first book on educational psychology and vocational guidance, the *Examen de ingenios para las ciencias*, translated into English by R. Carew in 1594. Speaking of the book's reception in Elizabethan England, Hardin Craig says: "Let nobody think that Huarte is anything less than learned, practical, wise, and ingenious, or look down with scorn upon this early scheme for vocational guidance. The book went through many editions, must have been read by many parents and schoolmasters, and have enjoyed great influence during the seventeenth century (*op. cit.*, p. 121)." Mauricio de Iriarte, S. J., lists twenty-four editions in French before the death of Calderón in 1681, and during the same years there were eight editions in Italian, five in English, three in Latin, and one in Dutch, as well as two editions in German in the eighteenth century.[17] In this same field of education, we have not only the immense achievement of Vives — carried on, to be sure, outside of Spain — but also the pioneering work of Pedro de Ponce and Juan

15. P. M. Vélez, *Observaciones al libro de Aubrey F. G. Bell sobre Fray Luis de León* (El Escorial, 1931), pp. 17–18.

16. It is inaccurate to say, as Américo Castro has said in his otherwise brilliant essay, "Incarnation in *Don Quixote*," that "the Hispanic world to which Cervantes belonged never dreamed of changing the structure of reality by the adoption of new ideas; the scientific nature of things remained that bequeathed by inert tradition, modified here and there only under pressure from imported scientific knowledge" (in *Cervantes Across the Centuries*, ed. Angel Flores and M. J. Benardete [New York, 1947], p. 143).

17. *El Doctor Huarte de San Juan y su "Examen de ingenios"* (Madrid, 1948), pp. 85–86.

Pablo Bonet, whose method for teaching deaf mutes was the first known in Europe.[18]

In other fields, also, Spanish scientific work was esteemed — in certain areas necessarily and inevitably. Pedro de Medina's *Art of Navigation* was translated into French in 1554 and reprinted in that language four times within our period. It had numerous editions in Italian, English, and German. A similar book by Martín Cortés had two separate translations into English. Bourne declared in 1577 that "no other book in the English language explains, with a method so brief and simple, so many, and such rare secrets." Europe, therefore, learned navigation from the Spanish (*ibid.*, p. 546).

Ortega's arithmetic was printed at Lyon, Rome, Messina, Cambrai. He preceded Harwitz in studying the theory of irrational quadratics. Martín Cortés studied the causes of magnetic variations before Norman or Gilbert, and Alonso de Santa Cruz preceded Halley by over a century in drawing a map of such variations. Santa Cruz, Cortés, and Enciso preceded Mercator and Wright in the attempt to draw spherical maps. Jerónimo Muñoz corrected the great Tartaglia. Europe learned modern botany and pharmacopeia largely from Spanish-Portuguese sources: Monardes, De Orta, Hernández, Acosta. Fray Domingo de Soto preceded Galileo by fifty years in formulating a law of accelerated motion; and in the modern age the list of the discoverers of new metals is headed by Spaniards (*ibid.*, p. 546–47).

To point out these small scientific triumphs is not to repeat the error of Menéndez y Pelayo in endeavoring to prove that Spain's claim to attention in these fields is a claim to greatness in them: one speaks today of "the great Tartaglia," not of the great Jerónimo Muñoz; and the fact remains that Spain, owing to choices dictated by her own value system, remained in a very real sense caught on a sandbar while other European ships of state moved on to greatness. In the Age of the Enlightenment she produced only one genius — Goya.

Perhaps the cause may be perceived in the frame of mind which we are now prepared to document, and of which the first example chosen reads as follows:

18. Claudio Sánchez Albornoz, *España: Un enigma histórico* (Buenos Aires, 1956), II, 547.

To arrive at this truth, for which there is one first cause on which all other causes are dependent, it was not necessary to engage in abstruse studies; because, as the perceptive poet [Ovid] says, "it was for this reason that God gave to man an elevated face, so that he is able to look up to heaven and consider the movement of the stars"; and if from the contemplation of this movement it were not possible for men to arrive at the knowledge of God, the Apostle would not have said (Rom. 1.): "The invisible things of God from the creation of the world are clearly seen." [19]

The text just cited is from a book first published in 1540. Before entering upon our chronological exposition of similar declarations, it seems helpful to cite a text from the year 1599. In that year Lupercio Leonardo de Argensola, as historiographer to Philip II for the kingdoms of Aragon, began to compose a *General History of Hispania Tarraconensis*, a work the author died without completing. In a letter dated April 29, 1599, Argensola outlined his plan to his friend Dr. Bartolomé Llorente. He will write, he says, the early history of the territory known as the Crown of Aragon prior to the year 1118, with which the great Jerónimo Zurita had begun his *Anales de Aragón*. He will not concern himself with the age of myth: first, because the main source — Giovanni Annio da Viterbo and his invented book of "antiquities" — is held in general disrepute; and second, "because, even if these sources were fully authentic, I do not consider it a matter of great importance to record the barbarous ancient times of those people who did not know the true God." He will therefore, he says, leave those centuries "as rude and formless matter" and begin his new history with the most happy times of Augustus, in which God sent his Son and the foundations of the Church were laid." [20] Argensola was a layman.

Thus the natural curiosity of the human being, Aristotle's "natural desire to know," is restricted — with a surprising exclusiveness — to inquiries which have a meaning that bears directly on Spain's chosen system of values. This same Argensola, when commissioned to prepare a compendium of Aragonese history to be printed on the margins of the official map of Aragon, explained his disinclination

19. Alejo Venegas, *De las diferencias de libros que ay en el uniuerso* (Salamanca, 1572), fol. 51.

20. O. H. Green, *The Life and Works of Lupercio Leonardo de Argensola* (Philadelphia, 1927), pp. 127–28.

to dwell on things having to do more especially with geography — topography, resources, climate — and his decision to record "those most important things, which are the actions of men. . . . The most worthy of inclusion appeared to me to be the saints, the kings, the captains, in short: *los hombres*." Aragon, he explains, was (according to revered traditions) the first province of Spain to receive the Catholic religion, having heard it from the lips of the Apostle St. James himself, who made more converts in that province than in all the rest of the Peninsula (*ibid.*, p. 155).

These texts are a clear statement of the Spanish preference for "the sciences of paper" — theology, law, history — as against the sciences of the laboratory — even geography. Ancient history itself is held to be of slight importance in comparison with the history of Christianity.

But let us return to our chronological review of these attitudes. Francisco de Osuna, the mystic who in many respects opened the way for Teresa of Avila and who flourished about the year 1527, wrote of "the new science of these days" that the Church might very well say of it, in the words of the mother of Tobias: "Would that we had not sent our son away for such coin; our poverty was sufficient unto us." [21] He continues his attack: there exists the danger that there will no longer be a single faith and a single baptism; that every arrogant scholar will scatter through the world the ideas born in his own head; and since these are expressed in elegant Latin, with a heading in Greek, and are spiced with Hebrew quotations, they can easily appeal to the human appetite, ever fond of novelties, so that each man will read in his own manner. A curse upon the intelligence of the arrogant men of these days, for they have taken Christ from us and split the Church in schisms; they have taken from us profound knowledge, and all we have left is: 'so reads the Greek'; 'so it appears in the Hebrew' " (*loc. cit.*).

In 1530, in the convocation address at the opening of the Tri-Lingual College at Alcalá, Lope Alonso de Herrera expressed disdain for the arrogant science of the doctors, exalting the inner science of things divine (Bataillon, *op. cit.*, I, 400–401).

In 1533 Rodrigo Manrique, son of the Inquisitor General, wrote

21. Fidèle de Ros, *Un maître de Sainte Thérèse, le Père François d'Osuna* (Paris, 1937), pp. 661–62.

from Paris to Vives complaining that in Spain "no one henceforth can possess a certain degree of culture without being accused of heresy, errors, Jewish tendencies." The trouble is not altogether Spanish, however; the young man reports that at Alcalá some would like to wipe out the study of Greek altogether — "a thing which many, furthermore, would like to do here in Paris" (ibid., II, 75–76).

Venegas, in 1537, expressed the wish that Plato might fall from the hands of the Italians, in spite of the defense of Plato by Cardinal Bessarion.[22] Unlike López de Gómara, whose eloquent words in favor of experience (the corrector of books) we quoted in another chapter of this volume, Venegas insists on "how much more excellent it is to believe than to prove and to experiment; . . . how much better it is for the Christian to believe firmly that which, in the name of God, the Church commands him to believe, than to seek out with his own judgment reasons whereby he may believe . . . for [according to Matt. 12] 'an evil and adulterous generation demandeth a sign'" (ibid., Appendix). In matters not affecting "one faith and one baptism," however, Venegas could show a true scientific spirit. In his Diferencias de libros, Book II, chapter 16, he explains: "I have written all this to the end that — inasmuch as in Spain we have the summa of cosmography — many persons might make copies of these figures according to the originals of their author [Alonso de Santa Cruz], so that a man's science may not perish with the man, especially a man who, together with these instruments, intermingles the history and the chorography of the places which he describes, throughout the world" (ed. cit., fol. 84r.).

In an early work concerned with "the quarrel of ancients and moderns," Cristóbal de Villalón's Ingeniosa comparación entre lo antiguo y lo presente (1539), the author is abundantly optimistic. He would gladly tell of the learned men of all nations: many living today in Italy and France, whose doctrine is more advanced than that of the ancients; certain ones in Germany who, in spite of the general plague of heresy, are "Catholics of great value." Scholars are not wanting in Flanders and in England and in Holland. And if we were to proceed to Spain, time would run out on us, for Spain is no less flourishing in these matters than other nations, but rather

22. Agonía del tránsito de la muerte, NBAE, XVI, 245.

more so. And he specifies the admirable number of jurists and canonists and their great learning; the sincerity of the theologians; the special curiosity and industry of the physicians; the subtlety and inventiveness of the philosophers; the elegance and eloquence of the rhetoricians and of those well trained in humane letters, consummate masters in the Latin, Greek, and Hebrew tongues. Finally, he could easily dwell on the prudence, skill, and learning of the men who govern the country.[23]

Juan Luis Vives, the father of modern psychology, died in 1540. For him the only things of real importance in life were the avoidance of vice and the cultivation of virtue.[24] Eternal life is to know God the Father and his Son Jesus Christ. The path to this knowing is self-knowledge (*ibid.*, p. 108). Other sources of knowledge are Divine revelation and the world of the creatures (p. 60). "All human learning," he wrote, "when compared with our Christian religion, is as mud and blindness and folly. All that we read in the works of the gentiles — gravely, prudently, even piously and religiously spoken — all that which we praise in them and exalt to heaven (good God!) — how incomparably more simple and easy and open, how direct and brief do we have it set forth in our Christian religion, the knowledge whereof is true wisdom. . . . " (p. 64). Only God's doctrine can bring light to our understanding (p. 44).

For all his influence on humanist culture, for all his insistence on the need for reforms in the transmission of knowledge — and these have given him a permanent place in the history of education — Vives' attitude is not that of the man of science. He holds (with St. Paul) that we should not seek to know more than is needful for us; we should avoid uncertain or heretical opinions of philosophers; we should never take in our hands books which, because of their licentiousness, are not conducive to virtue. But, with these exceptions, all the rest is most profitable to know and to learn. Humane letters may be studied in order that — among other things — we may the better defend our faith when others question it. They may also spur us to live more virtuously, as we consider the purity of many pagan lives given over to virtue without the aid of Christian-

23. Ed. Manuel Serrano y Sanz for La Sociedad de Bibliófilos Españoles, vol. XXXIII (Madrid, 1898), pp. 163–64.
24. *Introducción a la sabiduría* (Madrid, 1944), p. 28.

ity. Over and above all this, humane letters enable us to judge the things of the world — an ability at times, and to some people, quite needful (pp. 43 ff.). Thus learning is esteemed for its instrumental value; there is no encouragement of inquiry for its own sake. St. Paul is the guide, not Aristotle.

In 1554 Fray Luis de Granada published his *Book on Prayer and Meditation*. In it, following the lead of St. Augustine, St. Bernard, and Thomas à Kempis, Fray Luis proclaims that the knowledge of oneself is superior to the knowledge of the stars and of the earth.[25] For him biological life, political life, and supernatural life are but three parallel planes whereon the Creator and the creation come together — a position which no one, perhaps, in Golden Age Spain would have contested.[26] In a later work, *Introducción del símbolo de la fe* (1582), he declares that no one should entertain doubts regarding the marvels of nature, "since both the efficient cause (which is God) and the final cause (which is the manifestation of His glory) make these works the more credible in proportion as they are the more amazing and the consequent testimony of God's glory is the greater."[27]

A letter from the humanist Pedro Juan Núñez to the historian Jerónimo Zurita, dated February 17, 1556, reveals how scholarship had become more difficult and more discouraging as Spain sought — in ways not altogether unlike those of our own troubled times — to defend her chosen way of life. He has been greatly encouraged, writes Núñez to Zurita, by the latter's approval of his researches; without this encouragement he would despair, having no one with whom to consult and determine matters of accuracy or interpretation — "not because there is a lack of learned persons in this city, but because they follow different paths; and the worst of it all is that they would prefer that no one should engage in these studies

25. Robert Ricard, "Notes et matériaux pour l'étude du 'socratisme chrétien' chez Sainte Thérèse et les spirituels espagnols" (Part I), *BHi*, XLIX (1947), 33. This is the position of Pascal in his *Pensées*.

26. Pedro Laín Entralgo, *La antropología en la obra de Fray Luis de Granada* (Madrid, 1946), p. 226.

27. "no debe nadie tener por increíbles las cosas que acerca desto se dijeren, pues así la causa eficiente (que es Dios) como la final (que es la manifestación de su gloria) hacen todas estas obras tanto más creíbles, cuanto son más admirables, y mayor testimonio dan de la gloria del Criador" (*Obras*, ed. Fray Justo Cuervo [Madrid, 1906–8], V, 109).

of humane letters because of the supposed danger which lies in them — danger that the humanist, just as he corrects a passage in Cicero, might make bold to correct a verse of the Bible, or might criticize the Doctors of the Church as readily as he disapproves of the commentators on Aristotle." [28]

The sermons of the Augustinian friar Tomás García (later St. Thomas of Villanueva, d. 1555) were collected and printed at Alcalá in 1572. Fray Tomás repeats the doctrine of St. Augustine: "should you be ignorant of logic, of philosophy, and of all the liberal and mechanical arts, of law and of medicine, you could still be saved; but if you do not know yourself, you will not obtain salvation" (cited by Ricard, *op. cit.*, p. 182).

In his *Examen de ingenios para las ciencias* (1575), Dr. Huarte de San Juan, following Aristotle and his own theories regarding the effects of geography and climate on the human intellect, arrives at the conclusion that the outstanding trait of Spaniards is the intellect, as against the memory and the imagination; and power of intellect, in his view, is the distinguishing trait of the "theological" mind. He distinguishes three types of theologians: those who compile mosaics of theological truths from other authors; those who specialize in homiletics; and those whom he calls Scholastics — the real thinkers and exegetes of Scripture.

To the mere compiler Huarte assigns a low rating. The specialist in preaching resembles the compiler in some ways, for he too is a butterfly seeking his honey where he may find it; his work is decorative rather than firmly intellectual. The Germans, Huarte, says, excel in erudition and technical studies: "these possess a great memory for languages, and combine it with a good imagination, so that they invent watches, or a device to lift water from the Tagus to the city of Toledo, or create machinery and works of ingenuity — things denied to the Spaniard because of his lack of imagination. But when it comes to dialectics, philosophy, Scholastic theology, medicine, and law, the Spanish man of intellect can say more wonderful things in his barbarous terms than any foreigner, and this beyond all comparison, because if one were to deprive foreigners

28. Adolfo Bonilla y San Martín, *Luis Vives y la filosofía del Renacimiento* (Madrid, 1903), cited by F. Cereceda, *Diego Laínez en la Europa religiosa de su tiempo, 1512–1565* (Madrid, 1945–46), I, 29.

of the elegance and brilliance with which they write, they could not say a single thing that is original or well-conceived" (cited by Iriarte, *op. cit.*, p. 270 and n. 26).

Thus Dr. Huarte admits as true one of the charges launched against Renaissance Spaniards by the scholars of other nations — particularly the Italians — that their Latin is barbarous and that they do not excel in "erudition." We shall hear more of this in the following chapter. Huarte's position is not anti-intellectualist, for the very subject of his book is the intellect and its wise direction; but it is anti-humanist and pro-theology. To Dr. Huarte, theology and its related professions are the object of a very special interest. He assigns to the expositor of Holy Writ the supreme category among intellectuals and declares that this endeavor requires the very highest degree of mental power. His modern biographer (*ibid.*, p. 212) believes that he must at some time in his career have devoted himself to theological studies "with some degree of specialization." Perhaps so; but it should be remembered that we began this chapter with three quotations, separated by well over a century, which stress the pre-eminence of Spanish theological scholars. We shall soon quote still another of similar import, and one no less eloquent.

In an earlier chapter we cited Father José de Acosta's essentially scientific interpretation of the biological phenomena encountered in the New World. Yet in his *Historia natural y moral de las Indias* (1591) he too stresses the supremacy of theological contemplation over the acquisition of scientific knowledge: "He who does not pass beyond a mere understanding of their properties and usefulness may well be curious in acquiring knowledge or greedy in its attainment; to him, in the end, the creatures will be, as the Wise Man says, a noose and a net unto his feet (*Sap.* 4. 11). To the end, then, that the Creator may be glorified in his creatures, I intend in this book to set forth some of the many things worthy of note in the Indies — metals, plants, and animals. . . . "[29]

In a work entitled *Spain Defended*, Quevedo (d. 1645) stresses, just as did Huarte de San Juan in *Examen de ingenios*, the eminence of his countrymen in the "substantial" disciplines: "In the

29. Ed. Madrid (1792), I, 183.

solid sciences, such as philosophy, theology, canon and civil law, medicine, and Scriptural exegesis, all nations are inferior to us, though they scorn us as barbarians because we do not expend our efforts on grammar and humanistic studies; which things the Spaniards are not ignorant of, but show little regard for, as things inferior." [30]

Inferior? Quevedo was immensely proud of his ability to translate from, and to study in, the ancient languages. Yet in his *Politics of God and Government of Our Lord Jesus Christ* he insists on the scant utility of bringing together "authorities" from Aristotle and other philosophers who, in the darkness of paganism, picked up some crumbs of truth, whereas the King Christ Jesus in the Gospel reveals to all monarchs the truth, the life, and the way that constitute the essence and method of royal justice (*ibid.*, 313b). In another work, *Militant Virtue*, he remarks: "I shall perhaps cite certain things that were said by the authors of pagan antiquity, not to teach the Christian, but to shame the bad Christian by forcing him to read, in the works of the gentiles who lived without the true light of faith, thoughts more noble than in the writings of authors born at a time when Light illumines, and Faith reigns in, the world" (p. 951b).

In view of what has here been presented, one may well ask: In what light did the Spaniards themselves regard their literary and intellectual progress, from the insufficiently sophisticated fifteenth century to the thoroughly adult seventeenth? What was the nature of their achievement?

The most obvious answer is that they entered upon this path of progress with the perception — a dim one in most cases — that St. Augustine and the Church Fathers had renounced more of the ancient pagan heritage than was necessary; that they could do better — much better, indeed — by giving more heed to the world, which was now to take its place beside the cloister. They felt it necessary to enter into fuller possession of the legacies of a wiser past, to guide their lives more directly by the wisdom of the *antiguos sabidores* — the ancient knowers. [31]

30. *Obras en prosa*, ed. L. Astrana Marín (Madrid, 1932), 300a.
31. This was set forth in the fifteenth century by Alonso de Cartagena. See Juan

What happened was that a new secular faith came to supplement the old and still-revered religious faith — a new belief that widely disseminated secular knowledge was a power that could set men free and lift them to nobler heights. Vives said that he would give heed to those who defended their reading of novels of chivalry if he could but see them, at the same time, reading Cicero and Seneca, St. Jerome and Holy Scripture, and mending their conduct with the help of these twin sources of wisdom, pagan and Christian.[32]

One of the conversations that constitute Luis Alfonso de Carvallo's (or Carballo's) *Cisne de Apolo* (1602) turns on the origin of Egyptian hieroglyphics and of Renaissance emblems. One interlocutor has quoted authorities to show that figural representation had its beginnings among the Hebrews. Zoylo (representing the man-in-the-street) finds it difficult to believe that the Egyptians could have imitated Hebrew and Chaldean figures. "The reason is," says Lectura (Study personified) "that the Hebrews and Egyptians dwelt together for long periods, and in the intercourse which learned men inevitably establish with each other, they engaged in reciprocal imitation in all matters that did not conflict with their religions." This, Lectura insists, is "a thing perfectly licit, and practiced today." [33]

This eclecticism, "practiced today," sought to enrich the traditional Christian culture, not to replace it; beneath the figments of the imagination of heathen poets there lay hidden heavenly truths: *Sub poetico figmento semper res diuinae latent (ibid.,* p. 99). This Spanish eclecticism often has a special, personal flavor not matched in other countries of Europe. Juan de Mal Lara, the collector of proverbs which in his view constituted a most respectable "popular philosophy," sought to instruct his countrymen in virtue by tapping this traditional source of wisdom, at the same time amplifying and enhancing it in every possible way. When treating of the theme "Honor thy father and thy mother," he brings in, not only the Decalogue and supplementary Biblical quotations, but in addition "all the authorities among the gentiles," covering many pages with

Marichal, *La voluntad de estilo (Teoría e historia del ensayismo hispánico)* (Barcelona, 1957), pp. 32–33.

32. Cited by Henry Thomas, *Spanish and Portuguese Romances of Chivalry* (Cambridge, 1920), p. 163.

33. Ed. Alberto Porqueras Mayo (Madrid, 1958), I, 108.

citations from Greek and Latin authors. He brings in his own teachers (for these are, in a sense, second fathers), singling out by name
Pedro Ciruelo, Pedro Hernández, León de Castro, and several
others; and at length he mentions his own father in the flesh —
Diego de Mal Lara, who was the first to influence him to devote
his life to the study of letters and whom, "after my mother," he
feels most bound to revere. Many pages later he mentions his
brother, Fernando de Mal Lara, who, though far away in the Indies,
has never forgotten his parents and continues to honor them in
word and deed.[34]

This folksy bringing together of father, brother, teachers, the
ancient sages, and Holy Writ — all to the end that their combined
testimony and example may lead men along the path of virtue — is
a manifestation of typically Spanish integralism: life is seen steadily
and seen whole, and the little is frequently not separated from the
great. So powerful is the Spanish sense of the oneness of truth that
it can express itself with perfect ease, not only in the serious works
of which we have cited so many, but also in burlesque. The following lines were addressed by the highly respected Dr. Villalobos to
the Constable of Castile:

> Galen and Hippocrates
> Were gentiles, who can doubt it?
> Yet with their blooming recipes
> Millions we've killed, no doubt about it.
> Avicenna was a Moor,
> And Jews, Aben Ruy and Moses,
> Yet no physician on that score
> Their books of physic ever closes.[35]

The same spirit manifests itself with equal freedom in parody.
We have, for example, a parody written by a man whose Christian
devotion is attested in numerous writings but who, in this sonnet
addressed to an unspecified lady, chose to make jocose use of the

34. *Filosofía vulgar*, ed. A. Vilanova (Barcelona, 1948–49), III, 10–54; see especially pp. 28, 54.

35. *Cancionero de Sebastián Horozco*, ed. La Sociedad de Bibliófilos Andaluces
(Seville, 1876), p. 91: "Galieno e Hipocrás / gentiles fueron por cierto, / mas con
ellos hemos muerto / un millón de hombres y más. / Avicena moro es; / Aben-Ruy,
Rabí Moysés / judíos son de natura, / mas por eso su escritura / no es reprobada
después."

Augustinian principle of the "figural" or "prefiguring" interpretation of literature:

> Not only Helen for her beauty bright
> Is known throughout the world, nor is Paris the only
> Lover who knew good fortune; nor was Troy
> The only city to be razed by war.
> If Helen in her beauty was perfection,
> 'Twas of your beauty but a first faint inkling;
> Nor could she perfect be, since her fair face
> Was of your loveliness but the forerunner.
> And Paris, too, prefigures my presumption
> In loving you, my boldness and my daring
> In choosing you as the lady of my thoughts.
> And Troy? Ah, Troy, alas! prefigures
> The life of one who in fire is e'er consumed
> And, burning, would burn on forevermore.[36]

There thus came a time, in the course of Spain's cultural maturing, when there was a vision of glorious achievement which seemed to lie ahead: a new age of Pericles — or of Augustus, for the Spanish ideal was Roman, not Greek — could be experienced, men hoped and believed, on Spanish soil. This vision of splendor and glory was attractive and all-pervading, touching and enlivening all aspects of the national culture. (We shall see it at work in chapters concerning "Spain defended," optimism and pessimism, literary theory, and others.) The vision came to be clouded by adverse factors which we shall analyze when we deal with the Spanish baroque: the retreat from utopia was inevitable. What is important for the understanding of our present chapter is that at no time was there any thought that the bright vision was to be realized at the cost of self-surrender, that the nation's past culture was really inferior, that its God and its saints were false. No Spaniard during our period is known to have held — with Hobbes — that all reality was reducible to the concept of bodies in motion, or — with the

---

36. "No fué la linda Helena celebrada / por su sola beldad y hermosura, / no fué de solo Páris la ventura, / ni Troya sola fué desventurada. / Si Helena fué perfecta y acabada, / señal fué que de ti nos dió Natura, / que no fué perfición, mas fué figura / do tu sola beldad fué figurada. / También Páris figura el pensamiento, / que en tu valor osó ser empleado / con su sobrado amor y atrevimiento. / ¿ Pues qué Troya será, sino el cuitado / que está contino ardiendo, y tan contento, / que no querría acabar de ser quemado?" (*El Cancionero del poeta George de Montemayor*, ed. La Sociedad de Bibliófilos Españoles [Madrid, 1932], p. 52).

later Gibbon — that Christianity's taking over of the Roman Empire had been a deplorable historical accident. The superiority of Christian virtue over ancient virtue is expressly stated by the Jesuit Alonso Rodríguez (d. 1616):

> The Redeemer of the world very truly says that we must learn this virtue from Him; because Plato did not point it up, nor Socrates, nor Aristotle. When they discussed other virtues, such as fortitude, temperance, justice, the pagan philosophers were so far from being humble that in the very works they wrote, and because of their personal virtues, they sought to be esteemed and to leave behind them the memory of their fame. . . . They did not achieve real disregard of self, which is the essence of Christian humility; not even by name did they know this virtue of humility; this is our own, our special virtue, defined and set before us by Christ.[37]

Any Spaniard of our period could have said with Rodríguez: "Lest it seem that we are overstressing the spiritual side, it will be well for us to set forth a few reasons and considerations of a purely human character, for these are more natural and more suited to the weakness of our humanity; to the end that, convinced not only by way of the spirit, which is the way of perfection, but also by natural reason, we may be led to scorn the honor and the esteem of the world and to follow the path of humility" (ibid., pp. 63–64).

We conclude with a quotation from Jorge de Montemayor's Diana (mistakenly declared, as we have seen, by Gilbert Highet to be — along with the other Renaissance pastoral books — a rejection of the other-worldly ethic of Christianity): "Therefore, seeing that his son had reached an age at which it was proper to devote his energies to some virtuous exercise, he determined to send him to the University of Salamanca with the intention that he should apply himself to that study which raises men to a degree and to a rank that is more than human; and this he did." [38] The study in question, with its elevating power, was the then Queen of Sciences, theology.

And a final word. The Spanish national theater, created out of pre-existing and disparate elements as a new and original genre by the poetic genius of Lope de Vega (d. 1635), was conceived and constructed around two main pivots or poles: [39] in worldly matters,

37. Ejercicio de perfección y virtudes cristianas (Madrid, n. d.), pp. 9–12.
38. In Orígenes de la novela, ed. M. Menéndez y Pelayo (Madrid, 1905–15), II, 288b.
39. Arnold G. Reichenberger, "The Uniqueness of the Comedia," HR, XXVII (1959), 303–16.

honor; in spiritual matters, the Catholic faith. And Lope de Vega, himself remarkable as a sinner, was chiefly responsible for the canonization of St. Isidro, the farmer of Madrid who was made the patron saint of that city. The canonization was prepared, solicited, and finally brought to fruition through the influence on public and ecclesiastical opinion of an epic poem and three dramatic works by Lope himself, and two poetic contests which he organized. Such was the power of poetry and of Christian devotion in the Spain of 1599, 1617, 1620, and 1622 (Vossler, *op. cit.*, p. 61).

IX · Spanish Belles-lettres: From Inferiority to Equality[1]

It appears quite evident that poets writing
in the Italian language have existed much
longer than in our own; we may take as
examples Dante and Petrarch, and other noteworthy poets who preceded them and followed
them from whom our own poets took over a
great body of outstanding poetic material.

Juan del Encina (1496)[2]

We do not have books, or songbooks, on
half the subjects that we should. . . . We
have, until now, been very deficient in all
sorts of books for lack of authors . . . ,
though in Arabic, German, and other tongues . . .
there are a hundred thousand on any subject —
a fact not too noticeable . . . until we
Spaniards left our kingdoms to go to the
war of Naples; but now we should cultivate
and adorn our language as the Romans
exalted theirs.

Cristóbal de Castillejo (d. 1550)[3]

I have lived in a time when the Spanish
Monarchy was so abundantly filled with
gallant spirits in arms and in letters
that I do not believe Rome possessed any greater;
and I venture to say that that nation did not have
as many, or of such stature.

Vicente Espinel (1618)[4]

Three attitudes towards Spanish culture are expressed in the three
passages chosen as epigraphs to this chapter. In the first, Spain is

1. See Hans Baron, "The *Querelle* of the Ancients and the Moderns as a Problem
for Renaissance Scholarship," *JHI*, XX (1959), 3–22.

2. From his *Cancionero*, cited by W. C. Atkinson, "Mediaeval and Renaissance: A
Footnote to Spanish Literary History," *BSS*, XXV (1948), 213.

3. *Obras*, ed. J. Domínguez Bordona (Madrid, 1926–28), IV, 207–8.

4. *Vida del escudero Marcos de Obregón*, ed. S. Gili Gaya (Madrid, 1922–23), I,
Prólogo al lector.

readily conceded to be, in the field of letters, a lesser nation,[5] in relation both to antiquity and to contemporary Italy. In the second, the same admission is made, but with the optimistic qualification that Spaniards have only to bestir themselves, and the fault will be easily remedied. In the final passage, all signs of inferiority have disappeared. These three texts, and the historical problem they indicate, offer a considerable challenge to analysts of national feelings of inferiority and superiority.

Concerning the first attitude — that of general inferiority — it must first be noted that the unfavorable comparison may be (and often is) made with a vanished culture — with Greece or Rome, of which the Spaniards felt themselves to be the diminished heirs; or it may be made with a contemporary culture such as the Italian, whose superiority many Spanish authors readily admitted. It may also be made, either with antiquity or with contemporary Europe, but with a softening of the unflattering implications — as is the case in our second quotation and in a large number of other texts that I shall present: the inferiority is there, to be sure, but it can be, and should be, overcome. If writers are few, talent is everywhere; what is needed is for these talented persons to give greater attention to enhancing the nation's fame by providing the books which shall make Spain as eminent intellectually as she has become in the fields of war, exploration, and government.

Thus the problem of the inferiority (whether or not inherent) of modern man when compared with the Greeks and the Romans is constantly entangled with a quite different problem: the inferiority (actual, accidental, or non-existent) of modern Spain in relation to contemporaries (Italy, France). We have to do with a triple manifestation, of which one aspect is a supposed inferiority according to nature (the ancients were giants) or inferiority through calumny (contemporary nations are unfair); another is a similarly supposed inferiority through non-realization (the Spaniards have not realized their own potential); and the third is the opposite of

5. Cf. the complaint of Konrad Celtis in 1502 that Italians call all Germans barbarous drunkards, and his admission that this is often sadly true: "It is our infamy and shame to have received the empire and to neglect the arts by which it was produced and grew" (cited by Eugene F. Rice, Jr., *The Renaissance Idea of Wisdom* [Cambridge, Massachusetts, 1958], p. 97).

all inferiority (the Spaniards are the equals or the superiors of any other people).

The sense of inferiority in comparison with ages past was not unique to Spain. It had philosophical roots. The ancients were closer, it was held, to Nature; the moderns, being further removed from Nature and from divinity than were the ancients, could not really equal their predecessors.[6] This thought was in line, it seems to me, with two interpretations of the universe — or at least with one. I make the reservation because, for my first supposition, I have no authority to rely on. But I seem to see at work here the Platonic doctrines of the *fall of the soul into matter*, and of *reminiscence*: the further we are removed in time from our divine source, the weaker the ties of attachment must of necessity become. (Heaven bends above us in our infancy, but its light dims as we grow old.) The second interpretation of the universe that I find involved here is a perfectly clear one; it is the *theory of universal decay*, built on the classical myth of successively degenerate ages: the Golden Age, the Age of Silver, the Iron Age. For example, Edmund Spenser (d. 1599) chose to treat mutability in terms of elementary, seasonal, and planetary inconstancy, and seems almost in spite of himself to sympathize with a personified Mutability's claims of universal sovereignty:

> Since within this great wide universe
> Nothing doth firm and permanent appeare.[7]

This decay theory was basic in the Renaissance concept of imitation: "since the first writers were the best, subsequent literature has represented a steady decline, and man's safest strategy is to imitate the mighty dead." Even in the eighteenth century, Dr. Johnson (d. 1794) declared that "early writers are in possession of nature, their followers of art."

The decay theory seems to have found great favor with British Protestant preachers and moralists. Sheltoo à Geveren, in his *Of the Ende of this Worlde and the Second Commyng of Christ* (1577),

---

6. Robert J. Clements, *Michelangelo's Theory of Art* (New York, 1961), p. 402.

7. Cited by Herschel Baker, *The Wars of Truth: Studies in the Decay of Christian Humanism in the Earlier Seventeenth Century* (Cambridge, Massachusetts, 1952), p. 69; the quotations following are from the same page, n. 90.

finds "the ayre oftentymes corrupt . . . , now with too much cold, now with extreme heat," and the fruitfulness of the fields "not such as it hath been aforetyme." Another argument set forth in the same work is that "all good Arts and learning . . . almost in euery place come to decay."[8] And John Dove, in *A Sermon . . . Intreating the Second Comming of Christ* (1594), proclaims that "Nature beginneth generally to intermitte her wonted course" as the elements lose their qualities and the "naturall vigor which they had before," and the stars and planets "wax dimme and olde" (cited *ibid.*, p. 51).

By no means all thinkers and writers accepted this gloomy philosophy. The idea of progress was too strong, too well supported by facts, to permit the uninhibited flourishing of a philosophy of decay. Milton (d. 1674) in his *Areopagitica* considered his countrymen's acuteness to invent, their "subtile and sinewy discourse," as not "beneath the reach of any point the highest that humanity can soar to."[9] Sir Thomas Browne (d. 1682) held that "man still has the faculties for attaining truth." The evidence was visible to all: the compass, gunpowder, printing — cited by Cardan, Bodin, Bacon, Campanella, Louis Le Roy, and many others — seemed to offer clear proof that at least in certain respects the modern age had improved upon the past, and that man might hope for further gains (Baker, *op. cit.*, p. 81).

In Spain, as we have seen in various parts of the present work,[10] the idea of progress was strong. I have not encountered in my reading a single Spanish text that accepts the pessimistic view, although references to its existence and to the general respect in which it was held are easily found. In 1529 Cristóbal de Villalón wrote the dedication to his *Ingenious Comparison between Ancient Times and the Present*, a dialogue in which the defender of the pessimistic thesis dwells on the idea that Nature is growing old and as a consequence is losing her powers, while the champion of the present seeks in the ancient myths evidence of successive victories obtained by the human mind over man's primitive bestiality. Passing over

8. Cited by Ernest L. Tuveson, *Millenium and Utopia: A Study in the Background of the Idea of Progress* (Berkeley–Los Angeles, 1949), p. 45.

9. Cited by Carlton J. H. Hayes, *Nationalism: A Religion* (New York, 1960), p. 40.

10. For example, in Volume II, the chapter, "The Nature and Destiny of Man"; in the present volume, the initial chapter on geographical expansion.

(for reasons of political prudence) the restoration of theology by the methods of the humanists, Villalón prefers to dwell upon the flourishing state of the arts. His observations on Spanish painters and sculptors, musicians and iron workers, even on Spanish typography, are of genuine interest today. Cristóbal de Andino, he says for example, has created the most beautiful iron gratings to be found anywhere in the world. He sums up: "In short, if we but examine carefully every science and art, we shall find the world so well provided that I believe that future generations will venerate us no less than we venerate those who were outstanding in antiquity."[11]

We have another rejection of the idea of decay in 1573, in the first volume of the *Medendi Canonum* of Francisco Villarino. "The way to great theories was not open exclusively to the ancients, nor did the flower of all learning dry up. Nature has not become exhausted, as certain people believe, because of the productivity of past centuries. . . . Nature is the same as she has always been, nor is she . . . less able to produce illustrious geniuses. Many things remain to be done in the field of science; many have been discovered in our time; . . . coming generations will be amazed that we were ignorant of things so obvious. . . . Anyone, if he wishes, can add something new. . . . "[12]

Nearly a century later Baltasar Gracián (d. 1658) composed his *El Criticón*. In Crisi V he causes a character to remark: "Every day the various fields of study make progress, and forms of expression become more subtle. . . . " "How can you say that," the speaker is asked, "when all agree that everything has reached its summit and is at the peak of its power and is, indeed, so far advanced — whether we speak of nature or of art — that nothing can be improved?" "Whoever says that is altogether mistaken," is the reply, "when we see that all things invented by the ancients are mere child's play with respect to what is thought today; and that this will be even more true tomorrow. . . . All that is written in all the arts and

11. *Ingeniosa comparación entre lo antiguo y lo presente*, ed. M. Serrano y Sanz (Madrid, 1898), p. 168. My discussion follows that of Bataillon, *Erasmo y España* (Mexico City–Buenos Aires, 1950), II, 265.

12. Cited by Antonio La Granda, "Huarte de San Juan y Francisco Villarino," *Estudios de historia social de España* of the Instituto Balmes de Sociología (Madrid, 1940), I, pp. 660–61.

sciences is a mere drop of water in the great ocean of knowledge. . . . Not only have things not reached their apex, but they are not half as high as they can go." [13]

There is in Spain obviously no connection — in this matter of a pessimistic or an optimistic view of cosmic and human progress — with the progressive disillusionment traceable in the seventeenth-century — and generally considered a "baroque" phenomenon. Spaniards at all times seem to have rejected the idea of the universe as an unwound clock running down. Thus, very early (1493), Gonzalo García de Santa María states in his *El Catón en latín e en romance* that if the production of books is inadequate, the reason is a practical one: lack of patronage. Honors and rewards maintain the arts and sciences. Nor is there any reason "why we could not have today another Aristotle or Demosthenes or Cicero. For already in their time the diminution of the ages and the change in human life [*el discurso del vivir*] had occurred. Not one of those men lived to be ninety years old. No one can allege that the life span was then greater; the forces of Nature are not diminished to the extent that today we could not produce a man as excellent as they, now as easily as then." [14]

The modern Spaniard thus stands vindicated. He is not inherently or cosmically inferior to the ancients: he, like his fellow-Europeans, may aspire to exceed their achievements. There is no particular virtue in having lived milleniums ago, says Vicente Espinel in the same *Prólogo* (1618) that gave us the third epigraph for this chapter: "Neither are the ancients better for the mere fact that they are ancient, nor the moderns less estimable and less useful by reason of their modernity."

REACTIONS TO INFERIORITY FEELINGS

By some the accusation of cultural backwardness is admitted without qualification. By most it is admitted but explained away,

13. Ed. M. Romera-Navarro (Philadelphia, 1938–40), III, 155–56. See also B. L. O. Richter, "The Thought of Louis Le Roy According to His Early Pamphlets," *Studies in the Renaissance*, VIII (1961), 173–96, especially 192; G. Atkinson, the chapter "L'idée du progrès" in his *Les Nouveaux horizons de la Renaissance française* (Paris, 1935).

14. See B. J. Gallardo, *Ensayo de una biblioteca española de libros raros y curiosos* (Madrid, 1863–89), III, col. 31. This work will hereafter be cited as *Ensayo*.

though others — as our epigraph from Espinel makes evident — were able, with rare optimism, to regard the inadequacy as overcome, and even to claim superiority for their nation. What today causes surprise is the vitality of the idea that *elegantiae* were really not for the Spaniards. As Huarte de San Juan made bold to state in a text reproduced in our preceding chapter, a Spanish theologian could say more wonderful things in his "barbarous" Latin than all the proud stylists of Italy. To Huarte, the poor Latinity of his country-men was quite acceptable.

As early as the fifteenth century, Alonso de Cartagena (d. 1456) had endeavored to justify the absence of humanistic activity in Spain on the basis of lack of leisure: *Hispanos quod regiâ curâ sint occupati, calamo vacare non posse* — Spanish courtiers, weighed down with the affairs of the monarchy, had no time to trim their pens with nicety. This called forth the scorn of Leonardo Bruni, who pointed out that the Italians with their nicely trimmed quills yet managed the world affairs of the Vatican.[15] Many Spaniards felt obliged to admit that such scorn was justified. Somewhat after the middle of the next century (1553), Valerio Francisco Romero composed a *Dirge on the Death of Master Hernán Núñez*, in which he wrote, in the heavy stanza form of *arte mayor* so characteristic of the fifteenth century:

> I know not what sleep or what dullness of senses
> Keeps men of our nation so sorely oppressed
> That they care not a whit for such noble endeavors
> Nor give their attention to things that abide.[16]

It will be well to document this conviction of deficiency with some degree of thoroughness.

Humility before 1550

Our first witness is Alonso Hernández de Sevilla, who in his *Historia partenopea* (1516) interrupts his eulogy of El Gran Capitán (Gonzalo Fernández de Córdoba) to voice his dismay:

15. *Epistolae* (Basel, 1535), p. 309; cited by Robert B. Tate, "Italian Humanism and Spanish Historiography in the Fifteenth Century," *Bulletin of the John Rylands Library*, XXXIV (1951), 139, n. 1.

16. "Que no sé qué sueño, o qué torpedad / tiene los nuestros tan fuerte apresados / que nunca las mientes en tales cuidados / ponen, ni en cosas de eternidad." See Núñez's *Refranes o proverbios* (Madrid, 1803-4), IV, 7.

In only one thing are Spanish men negligent,
And why they should be so I never will know;
They seat not their sons at the table of learning
So that in humane letters they ever are indigent.[17]

Vives in 1524 is equally convinced of Spain's ignorance (though he perceives a change and has hopes for the future). He writes to Erasmus: "Our Spaniards also are interested in your works. . . . I hope that, if they become accustomed to this sort of reading, and to books of the same kind, they will lose their rough edges and cast off certain barbarous conceptions of life, conceptions with which these keen but ignorant spirits are imbued, and which they pass on to each other from hand to hand" (Bataillon, *op. cit.*, I, 182). In 1534 Garcilaso de la Vega wrote in the dedication which precedes Boscán's translation of Castiglione's *Courtier*: "I know not what misfortune has ever been ours, that scarely anyone has written in our language anything but things we could very well do without." There are, in other words, no Spanish classics, no proper literary models for the aspiring writer.

In 1535 Miguel Servet (Servetus), the father of comparative geography, declared that the Spanish land is arid and that, although the inhabitants are well endowed to pursue the study of the sciences, "they study little and badly, and when they are half trained they think themselves great authorities"; they care little for letters and print few books, importing French ones; they have many barbarous customs inherited from the Moors.[18] Juan de Valdés, perhaps in the same year, protested in his *Diálogo de la lengua* that Spain had no writers comparable to Boccaccio and Petrarch, and that the Spanish language must be considered more "vulgar" than the Italian because "it has never had anyone who wrote works in it with sufficient care and nicety" that these works might serve as authorities in matters of style.[19]

17. "En solo una cosa no han advertencia / y desto me spanto, no quieren hazer: / no ponen sus hijos doctrina aprender   / y han en las letras muy gran negligencia" (cited by José López de Toro in his ed. of Alfonso García de Matamoros, *Pro adserenda hispanorum eruditione* [Madrid, 1943], p. 249, n. 1).

18. Cited by M. Menéndez y Pelayo, *Historia de los heterodoxos españoles* (Madrid, 1947–48), III, 355.

19. Ed. J. F. Montesinos (Madrid, 1928), p. 8. Valdés is a "modern," however, in his perception of the literary, and even stylistic, values of earlier Spanish literature. He esteems the *Celestina*: in his opinion there is no book written in Castilian in which

Our much cited Alejo Venegas, in *Agonía del tránsito de la muerte* (1537), complained: "The fourth vice [peculiar to Spain] is that the Spanish people neither know nor desire to know; for which reason they do not seek mentors to give them good counsel, but tell anyone who out of charity wishes to offer advice . . . to mind his own business and not meddle in other people's." [20] About 1539 Cristóbal de Villalón, in *El Scholástico*, after expressing the conviction that in the universities of Castile there were more stipends and rewards than learning, sounded the call for writers who would exalt the Spanish language and bestow upon it "that elegance and ornamentation that the Greeks and other peoples bestow upon theirs." [21] The results, he said, would be no less satisfying than in Greece. Yet in his *Ingeniosa comparación* (*ed. cit.*, pp. 142–43) he is pessimistic: there is in Spain no real desire to learn.

The *Discurso sobre la lengua castellana* (1546) by Ambrosio de Morales is called "the most substantial, the best reasoned, and the most brilliant" apology of the Castilian vernacular written in that century.[22] Yet, though it is an eloquent statement of the position of the moderns, made with full knowledge of Italian movements to vindicate the vernacular, it still sounds the familiar note: Spain, culturally, is an underdeveloped country. "Who could point to many Spanish books in the confidence that, if they were read and imitated, perfection would be achieved, or at least that there would be an outstanding and generally recognized improvement in the use of our language? . . . I am well aware that certain books could be pointed out which, in recent years, are read with general applause by the uneducated, who regard them as very elegant. But I address myself to learned men of good judgment, who recognize the lack I have indicated and who agree with me in my complaint." Seeking for the cause of this deficiency in a nation which has always

(when once its stylistic faults are corrected) "the language is more natural, more proper, or more elegant." He regards with favor, "many of the ballads which are in the *Cancionero General*" and praises Jorge Manrique highly. See Franco Meregalli, "Las relaciones literarias entre Italia y España en el Renacimiento," *Thesaurus*, XVII (1962), 622.

20. *NBAE*, XVI, 174b. This failure is not here referred specifically to book-learning.

21. Cited by José F. Pastor, *Las apologías de la lengua castellana en el siglo de oro* (Madrid, 1929), pp. 29–30.

22. M. Romera-Navarro, "La defensa de la lengua española en el siglo XVI," *BHi*, XXXI (1929), 219.

produced men of good minds, many of them actually employed in literary endeavors and trained in the art of effective expression, he finds it in a general disinterest in ennobling the mother tongue: "when mere love stories and vain romances were the only things written in Castilian, who would venture to express in it better and more substantial matters?" And he compares the language to an earthen vessel which has been employed for "vile uses," so that no one would pour into it anything noble and precious.[23]

In 1550 Gonzalo Pérez, the translator of Homer's *Odyssey*, could not shake the old sense of dissatisfaction: "We do not have as good books as other nations . . . because of our laziness and our disregard for the public good, and because we are more inclined to war than to study." [24]

Early Exhortations

We are dealing here with what amounts to an endlessly repeated *défense et illustration* of the Castilian language — a call to cultivate literary excellence and to exalt the fame of the nation. Juan de Mena (d. 1456) is the first poet to claim, for poets using the Castilian language, the prerogative of the poets of old — that of bestowing fame on heroes: the deeds of the Cid, he proclaims, were not inferior to those of the heroes of antiquity, but the fame of these modern deeds lies hidden in oblivion *por falta de autores* — for lack of a Homer to sing them.[25]

The same proclamation is made in prose by Diego Enríquez del Castillo (d. 1504) in his *Crónica de Enrique IV*: the immortality of the man of action lies in the hands of the man of letters: Spanish heroes are as glorious as any that ever fought, but most Spaniards have been more familiar with the habit of war than with the style of speech. The author has chosen (he says) "to awaken the great deeds of the deceased . . . and proclaim the achievements of those now living, that their names and their fame may be sounded abroad

23. Germán Bleiberg (comp.), *Antología de elogios de la lengua española* (Madrid, 1951), p. 57.
24. Cited by Margherita Morreale, *Castiglione y Boscán: El ideal cortesano en el Renacimiento español* (Madrid, 1959), I, 40, n. 3.
25. Cited by María Rosa Lida de Malkiel, *La idea de la fama en la Edad Media castellana* (Mexico City, 1952), p. 285.

as a stimulus to the good, a shame and reproach to cowards" (cited *ibid.*, pp. 257–58).

Amadis de Gaula was reworked and printed for the first time in 1508. The revisor, Rodríguez de Montalvo, repeats the old refrain: the deeds of the nation, greater than those of the ancients, have lacked authors to extol them (cited *ibid.*, pp. 263–64). In his *History of Ferdinand and Isabella*, Andrés Bernáldez (d. 1513) points up a crying need: if poets and historians have established the fame of Hector and Achilles, "how much more should the deeds and virtuous achievements of the noble knights of Spain be made known, their persons and their temperaments described?" (cited *ibid.*, pp. 258–59).

For the year 1546 we may point to the more positive side of the position of Ambrosio de Morales in the brilliant *Discurso* already noted. Spain may have — most certainly has — a deficiency of model authors. But (he insists) Pedro Mexía has written with great purity of style; Florián de Ocampo in his histories has shown a skill in expression that "prudently adorns the language." In earlier times, Hernando del Pulgar's *Letters* showed a familiar style of great elegance, and in his *Histories* much of the charm of Latin was transferred to his mother tongue. Boscán's *Cortesano* is not inferior to Castiglione's *Courtier*; and Morales here goes so far — his boldness is excessive — as to equate Boscán's verse with its Italian models. Garcilaso competes with the Italians in bringing to the vernacular the best that Virgil and Horace have to offer. In philosophy there is Alejo Venegas. And Fray Luis de Granada treats of divine and celestial matters with purity, gravity, and force (*ed. cit.*, pp. 57–62).

Yet the note of inferiority is still present in Morales' thought: the language must be studied. And to those who accuse him of favoring affectation in style he replies: "I do not ask you to employ cosmetics to adorn the Castilian language, but merely to wash its face. Do not paint its cheeks, merely remove the grime. Do not dress it in brocade or embroidery, but do not deny it a dress of dignity and decorum" (Romera-Navarro, *op. cit.*, p. 220).

Cristóbal de Castillejo (d. 1550), in the prologue to his translation into Castilian of Cicero's treatises *On Friendship* and *On Old Age* for an unidentified Maecenas, makes a bold and optimistic bid for patronage to raise the state of Spanish letters: "If Your Lordship

will favor the good poets and other writers of his nation, as Maecenas did in his own country in the time of Augustus, we shall have
no lack of Martials, of Virgils, or of Petrarchs" (*Obras, ed. cit.,* IV,
207).

Early Claims of Equality or Superiority

Hernán Núñez, El Comendador Griego, wrote in his *Commentary* (1499) on the *Laberinto* of Juan de Mena a declaration of
Mena's ability to stand comparison with the best poets of ancient
Rome: "Though he is eminent and singular in all other things, it
is principally in his similes that he is so apt that I declare him comparable not only to other Castilian poets . . . but even to the most
excellent Latins." [26] Two years later Fernando de Rojas, in the
verse prologue to the 1501 edition of *La Celestina*, made a remarkable eulogy of the unknown author (whether real or imaginary we
cannot be sure) [27] to whom he ascribed the first division or "act" of
the work which he was publishing. It is an amazing statement, even
for the first year of the golden *Cinquecento*:

> I never have seen in the tongue of the Romans
> In all my born days, nor has anyone else,
> A work so noble in style, so exalted —
> In Tuscan, in Greek, or our eloquent Spanish.
> There's no sentence or maxim from which there distills not
> Wisdom that makes its author eternal. . . .[28]

We pass to the year 1520. "Whenever Spain, eager for spiritual
renovation, opens its doors to some foreign influence," writes Marcel Bataillon, "that unconquerable land delegates one of its sons
to say No! to the invader." [29] No sooner had Erasmus' New Testament in Greek arrived in Spain than Diego López de Zúñiga

26. Ed. Antwerp (1552), commentary on *Copla* CLXII, p. 373.
27. The late Mrs. Malkiel, in *La originalidad artística de La Celestina* (Buenos
Aires, 1962), has argued very cogently that the unknown author was not Rojas himself.
The probability that she is right is great.
28. "Jamás yo no vide en lengua romana, / después que me acuerdo, ni nadie la
vido, / obra de estilo tan alto e sobido / en tusca, ni griega, ni en castellana. / No trae
sentencia, de donde no mana / loable a su auctor y eterna, memoria" (ed. J. Cejador
[Madrid, 1913], I, 13).
29. In this paragraph I am utilizing *Erasmo y España*, I, 107 ff. See also Pedro
Sainz Rodríguez, *Las polémicas sobre la cultura española* (Madrid, 1919); Dolores
Franco, *La preocupación de España en su literatura* (Madrid, 1944). (The latter
work begins with Cervantes.)

launched his counterattack. His assault against Erasmus was of course unfair, yet its exaggerated claims are not without interest for our purpose: it contains a defense of "Spanish science," and no little scorn on the part of a Latin for the "barbarous" sons of the North. The Spanish race, because of its Roman origins, Zúñiga asserts, is superior. Erasmus forgets (in his slighting remarks about the Spanish pronunciation of Latin) that Spain gave emperors to Rome and masters to Latin literature. Until recently, one must admit, the struggle against the Moors deflected the national energies away from literary pursuits; but universities are burgeoning everywhere; Nebrija's Latin grammar and dictionary are praised throughout the world; and Greek authors, from Homer to Thucidides, are now better known in Spain than were formerly the most trivial works of Latin literature. And finally there is the Alcalá Polyglot Bible with its irrefutable proof of Spanish competence in the field of philology.

In 1542 the Portuguese Damião de Góis wrote to Jacob Fugger an *Epistola pro defensione Hispaniae*. The title suggests a sense of insecurity, and indeed the author's purpose is to combat the "calumnies" of the geographer Sebastian Münster's *Cosmographia*. De Góis says of Spain: "She produces hard-fighting soldiers, expert captains and generals, eloquent orators, lofty poets; she is the mother of judges and of princes." [30] Seeking to relieve Spain of the charge of producing few books, he stresses Spanish originality: "If at present the Spaniards do not smear with ink as much paper as others do . . . they are not to be esteemed less than those who cultivate their own praise by committing thefts of books. The Spaniards bring forth few things, but what they bring forth is their own" (cited by Bataillon, *op. cit.*, II, 247, n. 57).

Francisco Cervantes de Salazar sums the matter up in his *Obras* of 1546: Spain, more than other provinces, had long been "bárbara"; but in his own time "wherever you go you will find learned men." [31]

30. Cited by López de Toro (ed.), in García Matamoros, *Pro adserenda* . . . , p. 77.
31. Cited by A. F. G. Bell, "Notes on the Spanish Renaissance," *RHi*, LXXX (1930), 335.

Insecurity after 1550

Worry about the charge of cultural backwardness goes on, with endless fluctuations, to the middle of the seventeenth century and beyond. When the river roars, surely there is water in it. As proof, we point out the need, felt and expressed by the Spanish theologians at the Council of Trent (ended 1563), to improve Spanish Latinity in order to render it an attractive vehicle for Spanish erudition and theological authority. Melchor Cano conceded that, at least until Francisco de Vitoria (d. 1546) came to Salamanca, it was not normal for the professors there to give emphasis to style, and that "los escolásticos" (the Spanish Baroque theologians) were careless in this regard.[32]

In the anonymous *El Crotalón* (*ca.* 1553) there is an account of a "witty colloquium" in four languages: Italian, Spanish, French, and Portuguese. In it the entertainer offers to prove that the Italians appear learned and indeed are; that the Spaniards appear learned but are not; whereas the French appear crazy without being so, and the Portuguese appear crazy and are so indeed."[33] There is horseplay here, but these attitudes toward the four national cultures obviously existed. Another set of international comparisons — between Italians, Spaniards, Frenchmen, Germans — was provided by Juan Arce de Otálora in his manuscript *Coloquios* of 1550. He concludes that the Italians excell in literature, the Spaniards in navigation, the French in charm and courtesy, and the Germans in the mechanical arts.[34]

In 1555 Dr. Andrés Laguna, in the prologue to his edition and translation of Dioscorides' *Materia medica* published at Antwerp in that year, complains that the Spanish tongue, "through our carelessness or because of the baleful influence of some constellation," has always been the least cultivated of all (cited by Morreale, *op. cit.*, I, 40, n. 5).

32. F. Cereceda, *Diego Laínez en la Europa religiosa de su tiempo* (Madrid, 1945–46), I, 403–5.

33. M. Menéndez y Pelayo (ed.), *Orígenes de la novela* (Madrid, 1905–15), II, 226b–27a.

34. See the unpublished dissertation of Patricia O'Connor, *Juan Arce de Otálora, Coloquios de Palatino y Pinciano, an Erasmian Dialogue of the Sixteenth Century: A Critical Analysis of the Unpublished Manuscript* (University of Texas, 1952), p. 173.

About 1557 the same Dr. Laguna completed his fictional *Viaje de Turquía*. Although his complaint against Spain in this book has to do rather with well-ordered living [35] than with learning per se, his damaging testimony must be taken into consideration: it is the old charge that Spain was essentially uncivilized, and it comes from a patriotic and enlightened Spaniard. In the dialogue, Mátalascallando observes: "In short, we here live like beasts, and foreign nations exceed us in all skills." He demands to know what there is in Spain (great as she is) that can compare to the Italian mail service. Juan then asks: "Is Spain, then, in such a wretched state?" "Yes indeed, with respect to Italy," is the answer. And Juan concludes: "Now I declare that Mátalascallando is right; they might as well harness us all with packsaddles; we do not know how to organize anything in a decent manner." [36]

We have already seen that in 1575 Huarte de San Juan stressed the intellectual superiority of the Spaniards in spite of their bad Latin. The badness of the latter he is always quick to admit: "by his good Latin we recognize that the author is a foreigner; by a barbarous and rough style, we gather that he is a Spaniard." [37] In 1586 Pedro Simón Abril, in the dedication of his *Greek Grammar*, gave voice to the hope that "we Spaniards may lose that bad name that we have among other nations, namely that we do not enjoy ancient letters because of a lack of knowledge and use of the languages in question" (*ibid.*, p. 45, n. 3).

In 1578 Jerónimo de Lomas Cantoral published his *Obras* at Madrid with a prologue to the reader in which he says: "we should greatly esteem the small remnants that have been left to us in the few Greek and Latin books that were spared by the fury of time and the barbarians; our greatest regret should be that, although in all the other arts and disciplines the recovery has been complete (and so felicitous that in many things our age surpasses past ages) . . . the Spanish nation . . . has singled out Poetry as the object of its scorn, so that it lacks an art which delighted the ancients." [38]

In 1587 Alfonso Sánchez de la Ballesta, in his Castilian-Latin

---

35. For example, the Italian system of locating houses and buildings in the cities by means of painted signs (a horse, a lion, etc.).

36. *NBAE*, II, 91a.

37. Cited by M. Morreale, *Pedro Simón Abril* (Madrid, 1949), p. 52, n. 6.

38. Gallardo, *Ensayo*, III, cols. 401–3.

dictionary published at Salamanca, said frankly: "The lack of the Latin language among Spaniards is so noticeable to other nations that any effort to correct or remedy it should be well received." [39]

The years pass but the complaint continues. In 1609 Quevedo, in large part moved by the estimate of Spain and the Spaniards published in the *Atlas Minor* (1607) of the Flemish cartographer Gerardus Mercator, issued his treatise, *España defendida*. He quotes Mercator as having said: "The Spaniards, though quick of mind, do not learn easily; among them half-learned men call themselves learned; they are fond of the illfounded reasonings of the sophists; and in the schools they speak Spanish more readily than Latin, mixing with it not a few Arabic words. They rarely publish their works, and foreigners are still less willing to publish them for them, because of the bad style." [40]

In 1611 Sebastián de Covarrubias issued his *Tesoro de la lengua castellana o española*. Discussing the word *cuervo* ("crow"), he reports that the Egyptians in their hieroglyphics compared flatterers to crows. "It is a shameful thing," writes our lexicographer, "that, though this is so well known, we do not learn our lesson, with the result that virtue and letters are no longer shown favor, and only jesters and similar men get on with princes; a five-stringed guitar in the hands of a fool gives better fruit than all the seven liberal arts in the mind and understanding of a sane man." After much discussion and a quotation from Martial, Covarrubias goes on to state that such frivolous entertainers have brought poetry into disrepute, "so that men who could ennoble the Spanish language by imitating the Greek and Latin poets do not dare to publish their works, lest they be considered foolish men of little consequence, like those to whom our people have become accustomed." [41]

With this we come to Cervantes and the second part of *Don Quijote* (1615). In his discussion (ch. XVI) of the books that make up his private library, Don Diego de Miranda — "a discreet gentle-

39. *Dictionario de vocablos castellanos, aplicados a la propriedad latina*, cited in J. E. Gillet, *Torres Naharro and the Drama of the Renaissance*, ed., transcribed, and completed by O. H. Green (Philadelphia, 1961), p. 574. (This work, vol. IV of *Propalladia and Other Works of Bartolomé de Torres Naharro* [ed. J. E. Gillet], will hereafter be cited as Gillet-Green).

40. *Obras en prosa*, ed. L. Astrana Marín [Madrid, 1932], pp. 283b–84a. Quevedo's indignant ripostes will be recorded in the appropriate section below.

41. Ed. Martín de Riquer (Barcelona, 1943), p. 385a.

man of La Mancha" — reports that some of the works are in Spanish, some in Latin; that romances of chivalry never cross the threshold; that he reads more frequently works of pure entertainment than works of devotion, provided the former be such that they "give delight by their skillful use of language, and cause admiration and wonder by the cleverness of the authors' invention, although of this last kind there are very few in Spain."

One must not identify too readily the speech of a created character with the thought of his creator; but Cervantes is probably complaining that Spain has no *Orlando furioso*, and only one *Don Quijote*. In a speech that in more general terms is really a defense of the moderns, the Manchegan knight takes up the subject of literature as he discusses with Don Diego the future of the latter's poet son. To this also we shall return in the appropriate place. But first we must hear those who continue to insist, in the latter part of the Siglo de Oro, that though new heights are attainable by Spaniards, they have not yet been attained. Thus we again encounter the plus-minus sign, the *Sic et Non*.

New Clarion Calls

Fernando de Herrera, in the famous *Anotaciones* which he published in his edition of the poetry of Garcilaso de la Vega (1580), makes a spirited defense of the Castilian language, "its chasteness and culture, its admirable greatness and spirit," whereby it exceeds all other vernaculars. That the Italians have been more perfect and complete poets than have the Spaniards, no one can deny (Herrera continues), the reason being that the Italians have given attention to these matters and applied their minds to them, with striking results. The Spanish, on the other hand, ever involved in wars to restore their kingdom to the Christian religion, have lacked the quiet and calm necessary for the studious life, with the consequence that they have very little knowledge of the poetic art and are scarcely able to light up the darkness of so many years. But now that "good letters" have entered into Spain and the people have shaken off the yoke of ignorance, even though poetry is not so honored here as in Italy, a few men cultivate the art with such skill and felicity that they can justly arouse the fear and the envy of the inventors of poetry ("los mismos autores de ella"). Spain, at last, is coming into her own; present achievements are great. But Spain has only now cast off her ancient fetters; she is still behind Italy.[42]

Herrera's edition of the *Obras de Garcilaso de la Vega con Anotaciones* was preceded by a prologue by Francisco de Medina in which the pluses and minuses of the Spanish situation with regard to the liberal arts are reviewed in great detail. One impediment was, of course, military: the liberal arts could not flourish in a country that for so long had been partially occupied by a barbarian enemy. Another was ignorance and lack of a concerted effort to develop those arts whereby the light and the discourse of the understanding are made manifest. A third was lack of princely patronage. Various lesser impediments are enumerated and given due weight. But now that Garcilaso (and Herrera after him) has shown the power and force of *un excelente ingenio de España* — "a first-class Spanish mind" — "it is no longer impossible for our language to approach the heights reached by the Greek and the Latin tongues — if we Spaniards do our part" (*no la desamparásemos*). In his own time, Medina contends, there have been excellent poets; so excellent, indeed, that they can be compared with the ancients. Medina's is a much more reasoned estimate than the premature ones of Juan de Mena, Fernando de Rojas, and others who in the fifteenth century had embraced the cause of the moderns. Yet two swallows do not make a summer: the days of true glory — a glory which is "not impossible" — lie ahead (pp. 95 ff.).

Pedro Malón de Chaide's *Conversión de la Magdalena* was issued in 1588. In it the author expresses his encouragement over the success of Fray Luis de León in *De los nombres de Cristo*, a book showing all "the adornment which those who are zealous for the good name of the Spanish language could desire." His most persistent thought is that Spain can catch up: "I expect from the diligence and care of those who are zealous for the honor of Spain . . . that, with God's aid, we shall soon see all manner of curious and grave things written in our vernacular language; we shall see the Spanish

---

42. I have followed the excerpts given in Bleiberg (comp.), *op. cit.*, p. 89. Following paraphrases and quotations from Medina, Malón de Chaide, and Aldrete also are from Bleiberg's anthology, with page references given in parentheses following the material used.

tongue raised to the height of its perfection, so that it will have nothing to envy in comparison with any of the languages of the world. . . . We shall take back from other nations the glory that they have won over us in this respect, just as we have done in the realm of arms. And until that happy time arrives (it is now near) we must have patience with our detractors" (p. 84).

We move on to the year 1600, which sees the publication of Bernardo de Aldrete's *Origin of the Castilian Language Which Today Is Used in Spain* (Rome, 1600). Aldrete's praise of the Castilian tongue will be examined in our next section. In the present section it is appropriate to point to his use of the conditional tense to speak of a possible future: "If, as the Romans honored their language by never losing an opportunity to polish it and extend it, the Castilians would give the necessary effort to elaborating their own and to adorning it, not with affectation but with nicety of expression and with careful usage . . . , it would not be inferior to the others which the world esteems and praises, and in certain things would surpass them." Some writers have already begun to lift it to the height of perfection; should this effort continue, "I doubt not that it would equal the Latin language and in certain respects leave it behind" (p. 129).

El curial del Parnaso of Matías de los Reyes (1623) tells of a "public audience" held by Apollo at which Horace appears in anger before the god and reports a dispute that had arisen between the Latin and the Spanish poets. In one respect only are the Latins allowed to retain the palm, but the department in question — heroic verse — is decisive, since in Renaissance theory the epic shared with tragedy the distinction of being the highest form of human expression. In lyric verse, Spaniards and Latins are declared to be equal. In satire — the lowest form of all — Quevedo is so much Juvenal's superior that the very mention of Spanish satirists causes the Roman to shiver.[43]

In 1627 there appeared at Seville an anonymous *Panegýrico por la poesía*, in which the old inferiority complex is once again (at this late date!) in evidence. The author, after showing that poetry had

<hr/>

43. See Ruth Lee Kennedy, "The Madrid of 1617–25: Certain Aspects of Social, Moral, and Educational Reform," *Estudios Hispánicos: Homenaje a Archer M. Huntington* (Wellesley, Massachusetts, 1952), pp. 279–80.

been cultivated in Spain in ancient times, remarks: "From this, one can see how capable our language is of surpassing in this art certain nations that regard us as barbarians; and barbarians we are, because of our neglect in artfully polishing our language as if it were a mine of finest gold, as has been done in so many other places." Indeed, when he reads certain old Spanish verses, composed within the limits of the deficient knowledge of the poetic art which was then available, they seem to him rich, uncut and unpolished diamonds, capable of satisfying him in a way that the most cultured output of other languages cannot do.[44] Thus, more than a decade after the publication of Góngora's *Soledades*, Spain could still be held to be "negligent" in matters poetic when compared with other countries.

And the end is not yet reached. Gracián in his *Agudeza y arte de ingenio* (1649) explains that, in this very special kind of "rhetoric," he has taken his examples from any language in which he found them: "for if Latin praises the great Florus, Italian boasts of the admirable Tasso, Spanish of the cultivated Góngora, and Portuguese of the tender Camoëns . . . , so I, preferring Spanish, do so because Spaniards have the most wit, as the French have the most learning, the Italians the most eloquence, and the Greeks the most invention" (cited by Curtius, *op. cit.*, pp. 298–99). So, though we are almost at the end of the Golden Age (there is no great Spanish prose writer after Gracián), we still find a foreign nation — this time France — regarded as having the most learning. There is, however, another side to the complex picture, and in the following section we shall examine essentially unadulterated expressions of Spanish superiority.

Hispania victrix

In 1574 Melchor de Santa Cruz de Dueñas published at Toledo his *Floresta española* to fill what he regarded as an unfortunate gap: "amid the multitude of books . . . which the fertility of the good minds of our nation" has produced, there exists (he says) no collection of noteworthy sayings and *sententiae* by famous Spaniards. Since the men of this nation have shown no less keenness and acu-

---

44. Cited by E. R. Curtius, *European Literature and the Latin Middle Ages*, trans. Willard R. Trask (New York, 1953), p. 557.

men, no less weight and gravity, than did the great personages of the ancient world in the treasured nuggets they bequeathed to us, and have in part excelled their predecessors (as the compiler promises to show), it has seemed wise to him to assume the task of making a fitting compilation.[45] In the very same year the humanist Francisco Sánchez de las Brozas published his edition of the poems of Garcilaso de la Vega "with commentary and emendations," guided by the avowed purpose of showing Garcilaso's excellence in terms of his close kinship with the "classical" poets of Rome and Italy.[46] In this enterprise Sánchez de las Brozas was to be followed six years later by the incomparably greater critic, Fernando de Herrera.

Herrera's edition of Garcilaso (1580) makes the following points: (1) Spain's inferiority in the matter of culture and civilization belongs to the past: "Garcilaso is not inferior to Virgil, but greater." Mentioning various specific poems, Herrera expresses the doubt that their equals could be found in the body of modern Italian poetry. (2) The complaint — so fully documented in our present chapter — of the neglect and inadequacy of Castilian is no longer valid: "there is nothing a man can think that cannot be adequately declared in our language." (3) Spaniards have it within their power to write poetry as immortal as any, even to soar to heights still unscaled. Respect for the ancients can be overdone: "they were men like ourselves; . . . they could make mistakes, and they made them." Francisco de Medina, our previously cited writer of the prologue for Herrera's Garcilaso, expresses the same attitude of triumph: "in our time there have been excellent poets, so excellent that they can be compared with the ancients" (Bleiberg [comp.], op. cit., p. 100).

In his first published work, the pastoral La Galatea (1585), Cervantes declares Spain to be fertile in genius and rich in poets, so that "our age is more fortunate than that of the Greeks and Romans." Great is the number, he says, "of the divine geniuses which today live in this our Spain." [47]

45. Gallardo, Ensayo, IV, col. 484.
46. See W. C. Atkinson, "On Aristotle and the Concept of Lyric Poetry in Early Spanish Criticism," Estudios dedicados a Menéndez Pidal, VI (Madrid, 1956), 201. I follow this article in what I say below about Herrera.
47. Cited by Aubrey F. G. Bell, Cervantes (Norman, Oklahoma, 1947), p. 13 and n. 11. See also William J. Entwistle, Cervantes (Oxford, 1940), pp. 55–56; "Calliope's

Two years later, in 1587, Miguel Sabuco de Nantes issued a work entitled *A New Philosophy of the Nature of Man* which, though written by himself, he chose to attribute to his daughter, Doña Oliva Sabuco de Nantes. In this work the following dialogue occurs:

Antonio — Garcilaso de la Vega depicted this happiness very successfully in his Eclogue.

Veronio — You cite Garcilaso when you could cite, instead, Aristotle, Seneca, Plato, and Cicero?

Antonio — The antiquity of an author is a matter of small concern when a thing is well said, as Garcilaso expressed it, saying. . . .[48]

Quevedo wrote a whole treatise, *España defendida* (1609), in an effort to combat unfavorable public opinion at home and abroad in the matter of Spain's cultural importance.[49] He insists passionately: "few are the nations that in abundance and renown and elegance of authors have equaled us, either in the vernacular or in [Latin]." [50] Quevedo makes no mention of Cervantes' recent and amazing success, the *Don Quijote* of 1605, or of Lope de Vega's new drama (a genre in which Quevedo himself on occasion tried his skill). "But tell me," he asks, "leaving aside things of great moment, what have you in any language, be it Greek, Hebrew, Latin, or all your modern tongues . . . which will stand comparison with that exemplary tragedy, *La Celestina*, or with *Lazarillo de Tormes*?" (*ibid.*, p. 294b).[51]

Song [inserted in *La Galatea*] was one more document *de adserenda Hispanorum eruditione*" (Entwistle, p. 60).

48. Cited by Florencio M. Torner, *Doña Oliva Sabuco de Nantes, siglo XVI* (Madrid, 1935), pp. 150–51.

49. He is not always temperate in his defense, as when he asks: "What have you [foreigners] comparable to the divine [Cristóbal de] Castillejo?" (*Obras en prosa, ed. cit.*, p. 294b). See Raimundo Lida, "La *España defendida* y la síntesis pagano-cristiana," in his *Letras hispánicas* (Mexico City–Buenos Aires, 1958), pp. 142–48.

50. I believe my interpretation is correct, although the language is not altogether clear. Here is Quevedo's Spanish text: "son pocos los que en copia y fama y elegancia de autores en el propio idioma y en el extranjero nos han igualado" (*ed. cit.*, p. 284a). "The foreign tongue" appears to mean Latin.

51. It is interesting to observe that Quevedo perceived a tragic force in *La Celestina*. This is still a moot question, but is, it seems to me, resolved in the negative by Marcel Bataillon in *"La Célestine" selon Fernando de Rojas* (Paris, 1961). Bataillon shows with a convincing marshaling of texts that the love which causes the death of the two protagonists is "ce misérable amour" — a love completely lacking in moral dignity and hence non-tragic. And yet Quevedo, like numerous modern critics since the romantic period, sees elements of tragedy in the sweet-sad tale of disastrous young love. I have written in Volume II of the present study against a tragic interpretation

From Quevedo's *España defendida* we pass to Covarrubias' dictionary, the *Tesoro de la lengua castellana*. Defining the word *cerca*, Covarrubias cites a popular song, and two lines from Garcilaso's *Third Eclogue*, adding by way of self-justification: "One may with no less authority and gravity cite the divine Garcilaso — to prove a point concerning the Spanish language — than Virgil and Homer in matters pertaining to Latin and Greek; and I would say the same of any old ballad or song that lives among the people; and so, when it is desirable to cite them to support a point of view regarding the language, I do not disdain to do so (*ed. cit.*, p. 408a).

The whole of the "learned" and consciously hermetic output of Luis de Góngora was written "deliberately for immortality, written to the resolve that it should have as much significance for the twenty-seventh or any other century as for the seventeenth . . . a resolve . . . indubitably postulated and . . . studiously executed" (W. C. Atkinson, *op. cit.*, p. 213). This resolve is most evident in Góngora's *Soledades* and *Polifemo* (both of the year 1613). There is in his work a clear intention to imitate (as the Renaissance understood *imitatio*) [52] the great masters of Italy, Rome, and Greece; but the intention goes far beyond that. It is what Dámaso Alonso calls "una intención superadora," an intent to surpass. "Góngora purifies and refines, he polishes, intensifies and perfects . . . ; he increases the possibilities of allusion, he forces images and metaphors until they crackle. . . . He has something new and different to express . . . a beauty of the summit, absolute." [53]

In 1615, in the dedication of Part II of *Don Quijote* and again in the *Voyage to Parnassus*, Cervantes makes clear his awareness of having given to the world literary works embodying an absolute novelty which would give him enduring fame. In the dedication he playfully writes to his patron, the Conde de Lemos, that among those who have expressed most eagerness to see the new *Quijote*

of Rojas' prologue. As for the work itself, the only tragedy I perceive is this: it is part of the *lacrimae rerum* that a love of such passionate surrender, the source of so much earthly bliss, should be rooted so obviously in unworthiness; that a statue so fair should have feet, not of clay, but of mud. See my review of Mrs. Malkiel's *La originalidad artística* . . . in *HR*, XXIII (1965), 15–31.

52. See Antonio Vilanova, *Las fuentes y los temas del "Polifemo" de Góngora* (Madrid, 1957), especially I, pp. 249, 266, 396.

53. *Góngora y el "Polifemo"* (Madrid, 1961), I, 212–13.

(1615) is "the Emperor of China," who recently sent him by special messenger a letter begging him to send the novel to China — where it would be adopted as the textbook in a college specially established to teach the Castilian language — and offering to Cervantes the presidency of the new institution. In the *Voyage to Parnassus* (ch. IV), Cervantes' ringing self-vindication — and complaint against a society that favors others who have done far less — is such that it should have impressed the conscience of the somewhat nonchalant god Apollo. His *Exemplary Novels*, Cervantes asserts, have "opened a road" that makes possible the writing, in Castilian, of fiction which can satisfy the mind and excite Aristotelian wonder (*admiratio*); his "beautiful" *Galatea* will not fall into oblivion; as for his greatest achievement,

> I am the author who in inventive powers
> Leaves behind many rivals. . . .[54]

Cervantes did not live to see the publication of his serious romance, the *Trabajos de Persiles y Segismunda*, but he was able to write its dedication and prologue a few days before his death. In the prologue he tells of riding with two friends from Esquivias (where his wife had her family estate) to Madrid, and being overtaken by a student who, on learning the identity of the great author, threw himself down from his mount so hastily that his cushion and portmanteau fell to the ground and rushed to grasp Cervantes' left hand (the one injured by a musket ball at Lepanto), saying: "Yes, yes! This is he of the powerful wounded hand, the giver of joy, in short, the darling and the delight of the Muses!" This posthumous novel carries only two prefatory poems, both of them epitaphs. One of these, a sonnet by Luis Francisco Calderón, I must translate:

> Traveler, this unpretentious marble slab,
> This urn, more humble than a funeral pyre,
> Contains the sacred ashes of a mind
> That dares defy oblivion and time.
>   The grains of sand that Tagus rolls to sea
> Are not more numerous than the widespread nations

---

54. "Yo soy aquel que en la invención excede / a muchos. . . ." It is this quality of inventiveness that was Cervantes' greatest pride, and it is, essentially, this quality that makes Don Quijote himself a dreamer of dreams and a seer of visions. See my article, "El *ingenioso* hidalgo," HR, XXV (1957), 175–93.

That marvel at his eloquence, which gives
To Spain the laurels that are justly hers.
   His books with many graces are adorned,
With sweet expression and with charming style,
Moral decorum and devout invention.
   His fame Spain's writers spread throughout the world,
And, as they lay to rest his frail remains,
They offer tribute of unceasing tears.[55]

On the subject of the "quarrel of the ancients and the moderns" Cervantes made himself quite clear: "the great Homer did not write in Latin, because he was a Greek; nor did Virgil write in Greek, for he was a Roman. In short, all the great poets of antiquity wrote in the language that they learned at their mothers' knee . . . and it would be proper for this custom to extend to all nations, so that the German poet should not be denied esteem if he writes in his language, nor the Castilian or even the Basque who composes his work in his native tongue." [56]

Lope de Vega, when in 1609 he recited before the Academy of Madrid his famous verse dissertation "On the New Art of Writing Comedies Nowadays," assumed (probably with gleeful irony expressed by gesture and facial expression) an apologetic attitude with respect to the precepts of the ancients (unities of time and place, separation of the comic and the tragic, decorum, etc.). Later, in 1632 especially, he gave evidence of the pride with which he regarded his own powerful contribution to the art of the drama.

Before citing Lope himself, we shall hear, in their chronological order, two defenders of Lope's creation — the "new comedy" of Castile. The first is Vicente Espinel, whose semi-picaresque story of *Marcos de Obregón* gave one of the epigraphs to this chapter. In *Descanso* XIX of that work Espinel asks: "Who could be so inhuman as to accuse one of flattery were he to tell Lope de Vega that there never existed in all antiquity a genius who excelled him in his

---

55. "En este, ¡oh caminante!, mármol breve, / urna funesta, si no excelsa pira, / cenizas de un ingenio santas mira, / que olvido y tiempo a despreciar se atreve. / No tantas en su orilla arenas mueve / glorioso el Tajo, cuantas hoy admira / lenguas la suya, por quien grata aspira / a el lauro España que a su nombre debe. / Lucientes de sus libros gracias fueron, / con dulce suspensión su estilo grave, / religiosa invención, moral decoro. / A cuyo ingenio los de España dieron / la sólida opinión que el mundo sabe, / y al cuerpo, ofrenda de perpetuo lloro."

56. *Obras completas*, ed. A. Valbuena Prat (Madrid, 1956), pp. 1325–26a.

own chosen department [*por el camino que ha seguido*]?" The second is Tirso de Molina. In a miscellany of tales and plays entitled *Cigarrales de Toledo,* composed about 1620 and published in 1624, Tirso places on the lips of one of the gentlemen who have just witnessed a private performance of his comedy, *El vergonzoso en Palacio,* the most spirited of all the defenses of the new Lopean *comedia* against those who show little esteem for it because of its disregard of the classical "rules." The defender interrupts a carping critic to say:

I cannot agree with you, because the comedy just now performed respects the dramatic laws now in use; and — if you ask me — the plays now enacted in this our Spain, when compared with those of antiquity, have obvious advantages over them, however much they may sin against the regulations of the genre's first inventors.

Referring to the time-limit of twenty-four hours, the defender continues:

What greater objection can we lay to the charge [of the ancients] than that in so brief a time, a discreet gentleman should fall in love with a sensible lady and should serve her and court her so energetically that, without even a whole day having elapsed, he should become master of her emotions to the extent that, having begun to woo her in the morning, he should marry her that night? . . . How can a lover be judged to be faithful and constant unless there pass some days, months, and even years wherein he may give proof of his constancy?

Tirso then proceeds to compare the compression of time and place achieved by the theatrical illusion to the similar compressions of a history book (time) and a painting (space), after which he attacks the problem of the ancients and moderns:

And if you argue that we who engage in this type of writing are obliged to observe the precepts of the first inventors of comedy . . . I reply that, although we owe them veneration . . . we must — at the same time that we leave intact the substance of their creation — improve it in its details.

Nature, he continues, cannot change: the pear tree must ever give pears; yet climate and soil produce variations even here. What wonder, then, that comedy should alter its laws and mingle the tragic with the comic, producing a pleasant cross between the two genres, introducing into one and the same play the noble characters of tragedy and the merry and ridiculous ones of comedy? And what of the argument from authority? We arrive at the same conclusion: If Aeschylus and Euripides, Seneca and Terence, by the mere excellence of their dramatic production, established the laws so hotly defended by their modern adherents, "the excellence of our Spanish Vega so clearly surpasses them in both departments [*entrambas materias*] . . . that the force of his superiority is sufficient to abrogate their statutes." Nay, more: When Lope, in various places in his works, says that he departs from ancient precept merely to please the crowd, "he does this out of modesty . . . but we must revere him as the reformer of the new *comedia*":

Since he has brought the *comedia* to the perfection and the clever excellence [*sutileza*] that it now displays, he is sufficient to found a school by reason of his authority, so that we, who take pride in being his disciples, have every right to rejoice at having such a master, and to defend at every moment his doctrine against those who out of prejudice [*pasión*] would impugn it.[57]

Turning again to the lyric, we find a similar sense of having surpassed the ancients in the prologue to the *Cancionero antequerano* compiled in the years 1627 and 1628 by Ignacio de Toledo y Godoy: "In the general flowering which we have witnessed in our time, universal applause has been accorded to our poets, all the more so since in their excellent works they have used, as a lavish display of adornment and perfection, entirely new modes of expression which were unknown in the ancient world."[58]

In 1631 Juan de Robles published at Seville *El culto sevillano*, in which Fray Luis de Granada is declared to be "the Christian Cicero" and Juan de Mariana "the Spanish Sallust." Other Spanish

---

57. Cited by M. Menéndez y Pelayo, *Historia de las ideas estéticas en España* (Santander, 1946–47), II, 312–13. See also M. Romera-Navarro, "Lope y su autoridad frente a los antiguos" in his *La preceptiva dramática de Lope de Vega y otros ensayos sobre el Fénix* (Madrid, 1935), pp. 11–59; E. C. Riley, "The Dramatic Theories of Don Jusepe González de Salas," *HR*, XIX (1951), 183–203, especially 199; O. H. Green, "On the Attitude Toward the *Vulgo* in the Spanish *Siglo de Oro*," *Studies in the Renaissance*, IV (1957), 190–99, especially 197 ff. Tirso in 1635 proclaims Spanish superiority over Italy's Tassos, Ariostos and Petrarchs. See his *La patrona de las Musas*, ed. R. Froldi (Milan, 1959), p. 63.

58. The language of this statement is so conceptistic that it seems best to give the original: "Universal ha sido el aplauso que en lo florido de nuestros tiempos se le ha dado a los escritos de los poetas y tanto mayor cuanto lo excelente de la obra, en cuya ostentación y pulimento han usado en el decir modos tan peregrinos que no alcanzó la antigüedad (ed. Dámaso Alonso and Rafael Ferreres [Madrid, 1950])."

writers are cited to prove that "our language is in the state of development that the Latin language enjoyed in the time of Cicero" (Bleiberg [comp.], *op. cit.*, p. 148).

In 1632 Lope de Vega added his own voice to that of his admirers. In the *Egloga a Claudio* he wrote the following bold but true words:

> Though I have departed from the rigidity of Terence, and though I am far from questioning the credit due to the three or four great geniuses who have guarded the infancy of the drama, yet to me the art of the *comedia* owes its beginnings. To whom, Claudio, do we owe so many pictures of love and jealousy, so many stirring passages of eloquence, so copious a supply of all the figures within the power of rhetoric to invent? The mass of today's production is mere imitation of what art created yesterday. I it was who first struck the path and made it practicable, so that all now use it easily. I it was who set the example now followed and copied everywhere.[59]

In 1651, in his *Genio de la historia*, Fray Jerónimo de San José finds that at length the Spanish have almost brought their eloquence to the same degree of perfection as their valor, joining arms and letters and surpassing all the nations of the world: "And this so greatly, that this our Spain, once considered crude and barbarous in the use of language, today exceeds the most flourishing culture of the Greeks and Latins" (Bleiberg [comp.], *op. cit.*, p. 171).

In his *Agudeza y arte de ingenio* (1648), Gracián traces the tradition of personal literary expression from Seneca and Martial (both born in Spain) down to his own day: "This taste for individuality was bequeathed as an inheritance to this fertile century, in which Spanish genius has flourished as each man expressed his thought with freedom and originality [*a lo libre*]." [60]

"With freedom and originality" — even the Aristotelian critics of the seventeenth century were forced to concede that in these two respects Spain had won her cultural independence. There existed "a higher preceptor than Aristotle" — Nature. And in the Spanish public itself, in the unruly audiences of the theaters, there was yet another preceptist through whom Nature worked.[61] The Italian Renaissance was over, French neoclassicism was not yet born. Italy

---

59. Cited by James Fitzmaurice-Kelly in *Chapters on Spanish Literature* (London, 1908), p. 176.
60. Cited by Juan Marichal, *La voluntad de estilo* (Barcelona, 1957), p. 174.
61. Riley, *op. cit.*, pp. 197–99.

and France could reconcile their literary practice and their aesthetic theories more easily than Spain, whose literature the classical theories "did not readily and obviously fit" (*ibid.*, p. 201). Criticism was consequently forced, *de facto*, to recognize Spain's creation of essentially new genres. For the Aristotelian preceptists "there existed two possible courses in their embarrassing situation": they could openly deplore departures from the "rules" or they could expound Aristotle's *Poetics* as "poetic philosophy," as an exposition of ancient, not modern, literary practice. Both these courses were followed. Just as the Greeks achieved eminence by taking Nature (not Aristotle) as their preceptor, so modern Spaniards, it was said, could — indeed must — do the same (*ibid.*, p. 197). It was evident that they had done and were doing exactly that. The success of Lope's dramas, of *La Celestina*, of *Don Quijote*, of Góngora's hermetic poetry, of Quevedo's *Sueños*, could not be denied. Though Lope de Vega sought in *La Dorotea* (1632) to employ all the "colors of rhetoric" which the Greeks had bequeathed to the modern age and actually ended the acts of his "action in prose" with choruses, the result of his *Literarisierung des Lebens* — of his using personal experience as the raw stuff of literature — was something new and Spanish. Like his dramas, this autobiographical novel in dialogue sounds — though with new and highly sophisticated resonances — notes that had long vibrated only in Spain. Indeed the Spanish Renaissance was over also. Gracián and Calderón would continue to revere and "imitate" the ancients and would turn for inspiration to Italy; but the spirit of the new and confident age — the Spanish seventeenth century — is summed up in the phrase which we have quoted from Gracián: *a lo libre*, "with freedom and originality."

CONCLUSION

The "quarrel of the ancients and the moderns" of Desmarets de Saint-Sorlin, Boileau, and Perrault (1687–1700) appears — after our survey in this chapter — as a curiously revived anachronism. The Italians had achieved awareness of their cultural independence a century and a half earlier. The Spaniards, years before the death of Perrault (1703), had overcome all doubts concerning the expressiveness of their language and the originality of their literature. But the evolution of that Spanish awareness is a complex one. The expressions of a sense of inferiority and the exhortations to Spaniards to do better are intermingled with a self-praise which is at times aggressive, at times based on reasoned analysis, with the result that in the classifications of our chronologically marshalled texts there is inevitable overlapping. The meaning of our exposition is, however, clear: Spain did overcome — impressively — her early sense of inadequateness as she compared her own achievements with those of a past generally held to have been wiser and with those of the modern Italians, whose obvious brilliance was difficult to match. The problem would reappear in Spain in aggravated form in the neoclassic Age of the Enlightenment (when Voltaire called Dante "cet homme sauvage"), but at the height of the Golden Age the old doubt had vanished: in the world of belles-lettres the Spaniards recognized no overlordship, either ancient or modern.

X · Philosophy

As a propositional system we
cannot say that there is a Spanish
philosophy. But as a mode of
human being . . . we can say, not only
that the expression "Spanish
Philosophy" has a sense, but even
that Spanish philosophy is one of
the philosophical systems of thought
in which the condition of being a
function of our existence is fully,
and wonderfully, realized. . . . A
people which . . . prefers *to be* reality
rather than to become an operator of
reality is, of course, most suited
to become the color bearer of
philosophy as a mode of human being
and the most unrepentant enemy of
any philosophy as a *mere* system of
propositions.

José Ferrater Mora [1]

To satisfy your insistence, I shall
introduce a few philosophical
persuasions and reasons that do not
conflict with our holy Catholic faith.

Pero Díaz de Toledo [2]

I, however, shall follow the great
St. Peter Chrysologus in denying
confidence to the philosophers, and
I shall obey St. Thomas by not
writing except what I find in the
Saints of the Church, remembering
what St. Augustine said in his
Confessions, that in the works of
Plato he had never been able to learn
charity or humility.

Francisco de Quevedo [3]

1. "Is There a Spanish Philosophy?" *HR*, XIX (1951), 9. See also Jacques Chevalier, "Y a-t-il une philosophie espagnole?", *Estudios eruditos in memoriam de Adolfo Bonilla y San Martín* (Madrid, 1927), I, 4.

2. "Diálogo e razonamiento en la muerte del Marqués de Santillana," ed. Antonio Paz y Melia in *Opúsculos literarios de los siglos XIV a XVI* (Madrid, 1892), p. 253.

3. *La virtud militante*, in *Obras en verso*, ed. L. Astrana Marín (Madrid, 1932), p.

"The philosopher's crown," wrote the Italian Arturo Farinelli in 1923, "has been ardently desired by few men in Spain, though there are not lacking spirits inclined toward solid and persevering meditation, capable of rising up to the high regions where pure ideas have their domain and where the deep, unplumbed mysteries of life exist in apparent interconnection." [4] The Spanish philosopher Xavier Zubiri, ten years later, expressed the wish "that Spain, the land of light and of melancholy, will some day rise up to metaphysical concepts." [5] Yet "the fact is . . . that Europe, *during two centuries*, learned metaphysics in the writings of Suárez, though they did not learn the metaphysics *of* Suárez." [6] We have seen in an earlier chapter how, at the beginning of the sixteenth century, Spaniards seemed to dominate the teaching of old-fashioned logic at the University of Paris, publishing their textbooks in that city and in other cities outside of Spain. Three or four generations

952a. Lest Quevedo be judged too harshly for thus preferring "the Saints of the Church," I would point out that Sir Thomas More, author of the "rationalistic" *Utopia*, weighed "the comfort of Scripture against that of pagan philosophers" and concluded that the seventh chapter of Ecclesiastes "containeth more fruitful advice and counsel to the forming and framing of man's manners in virtue and the avoiding of sin, than many whole and great volumes of the best of old philosophers or any other that ever wrote in secular literature" (cited by Herschel Baker, *The Dignity of Man: Studies in the Persistence of an Idea* [Cambridge, Massachusetts, 1947], p. 264). The humanists were normally bookish and "anything but philosophical. Just as most of them preferred piety to dogma, they preferred ethics to metaphysics and epistemology" (*ibid.*, p. 272).

4. "Consideraciones sobre los caracteres fundamentales de la literatura española," *Archivum Romanicum*, VII (1923), 266. Américo Castro has gone so far as to print this sentence: "If the relations of man to the cosmos were *never* posed or rethought by the Spaniards, the situation of man with respect to himself was perceived and revealed as a luminous reality which could be investigated in works of literature" (emphasis mine). I quote the Spanish text: "Si las relaciones del hombre con el cosmos nunca fueron planteadas o repensadas por los españoles, la situación del hombre respecto de sí mismo fue vista y destacada como realidad luminosa y manejable literariamente" (*De la edad conflictiva* [Madrid, 1961], p. 204). This is the thesis of Castro's writings from 1948, the date of publication of *España en su historia*, onward.

5. Cited by Castro, "El enfoque histórico y la no hispanidad de los visigodos," *NRFH*, III (1949), 226. See W. J. Entwistle in his review of A. F. G. Bell's "Notes on the Spanish Renaissance" (*RHi*, LXXX [1930], 319–652): "Spanish thinkers are all eclectic. Like Fox Morcillo they reconcile Plato and Aristotle, or like Suárez they build up a new Scholasticism. . . . Above all they do not, and apparently cannot, abstract thought from life. Man, the whole man, is their preoccupation" (*MLR*, XXVI [1931], 489.

6. Julián Marías, *La escolástica en su mundo y en el nuestro* (Pontevedra, 1951), p. 89.

later, Spanish theologians held positions on the faculties of "nearly all" the universities of Europe: Francisco de Toledo, Suárez, De Lugo, Esparza, and Silvestre Mauro at Rome; and Maldonado at Paris, "to mention only a few." [7] Francisco Suárez, whose *Disputationes metaphysicae* were published in 1597, was a contemporary of Cervantes. Authoritative critics of the present day consider him worthy to rank with St. Thomas and Duns Scotus.[8] Shortly after his *Disputationes* were published, and in the very years when Bacon, Kepler, Grotius, Harvey, Galileo, and Descartes were laying the foundations of strictly modern philosophy (1609–44), Suárez's great work penetrated the philosophic thought of the young philosophers of Europe. And not only that of Suárez. In the early seventeenth century Jesuit teachers and philosophers, schooled in the metaphysics of the Jesuit Suárez, spread over Europe: Ingolstadt, Vienna, Würzburg, Mainz, Trier, Prague, Cologne, and Freiburg im Breisgau.[9] As Julián Marías has pointed out, Suárez's vogue was natural, even necessary. Aristotle's *Metaphysics* is not a complete treatise on the subject; for St. Thomas metaphysics was merely ancillary to theology; only in Suárez does metaphysics appear as a discipline which, though dependent on Aristotle, is not Aristotelian — a discipline that separates metaphysics from theology in a manner essentially "modern" (though Suárez intended his metaphysics to be propaedeutic to "the queen of sciences"). In sum: seventeenth-century philosophy needed what Suárez offered.

It is unquestionably true that "modern" thinkers used Suárez and esteemed the work of his followers: editions multiplied as the universities of Europe read and commented on his work right down to the eighteenth century. This came about because Suárez provided the metaphysical base — disciplined and systematic — which

7. See Peter Tischleder, *Ursprung und Träger der Staatsgewalt* (München-Gladbach, 1923), cited by Joseph Höffner, *La ética colonial española del siglo de oro: Cristianismo y dignidad humana*, trans. F. de Asís Caballero (Madrid, 1957), p. 341; see n. 41.

8. See Marías, *op. cit.*, and J. Ferrater Mora, "Suárez y la filosofía moderna," *Notas y estudios de filosofía*, II (1951), 269–94.

9. *Ibid.*, p. 281. The influence of Scholasticism on Descartes has been studied by Gilson, Koyré, and Hertling; its influence on Spinoza, by Freudenthal; on Locke, by Küppers; on Gassendi, by Pendzig; on Leibnitz, by scholars ranging from Von Nostiz-Rieneck to Paul Schrecker. Most of these scholars paid too much attention to "classical" Scholasticism, too little to the new Scholasticism of the baroque — to Spanish Scholasticism. The balance has been redressed by Ferrater Mora and Marías (see note 8).

was essential to the burgeoning philosophy that was to lead to Newton, to Darwin, and eventually to William James and Einstein.

The Spanish and Portuguese metaphysicians did not hold the keys to the future. They would fall into oblivion because their metaphysics, however useful to the "new" philosophers, was primarily religious — Christian: its ultimate task was conceived of as the understanding of the Divine. In the coming years, the new philosophy would be progressively divorced from religion, though its leaders proclaimed something other than that; its success, and the failure of Spanish baroque Scholasticism, arose from the fact that it analyzed and interpreted, ever more insistently, that portion of reality which could be measured and weighed, abandoning the rest as "notional." To so great an extent was this true that in the nineteenth century metaphysics was to become an all-but-forgotten discipline, relegated to the corners of the academic world, even eliminated as a study without meaning in the day of *philosophie positive* and *religion positive*.

Spain clung tenaciously to her Dominican-Jesuit tradition, as we have seen earlier in the chapter on Spain's intellectual expansion in the New World. Later in the present chapter we shall revert to this problem, that is to say, to the "collective choice" that wedded Spanish thought to its cherished concept of the universe as forever determined and organized by the will of the Almighty — an unchanging universe, as against a universe newly conceived as an evolving and expanding organism. At no time shall we be able to present clear-cut causes determining this particular choice: history is what happens to happen.

SCOTISM, THOMISM, NOMINALISM, HUMANISM

Spain, as we have seen, never lacked "spirits inclined to meditation," nor were these ever ignorant of what abstract thinkers had done and were doing elsewhere. As the sixteenth century began, Cardinal Cisneros (d. 1517) sought to restore, at his newly created University of Alcalá, the dignity and the prestige of theology and philosophy.[10] A Franciscan, he conceived the project of introducing

10. M. Bataillon, *Erasmo y España* (Mexico City–Buenos Aires, 1950), I, 15, n. 12.

into the recently founded institution the philosophy of Duns Scotus — perhaps stimulated by the example of the Dominicans, who at Valladolid "had lit a bonfire of Thomism" (*ibid.*, p. 12). Thus Scotus, the great Franciscan philosopher, came to enjoy at Alcalá a position of equality with St. Thomas (*ibid.*, p. 19). At about the same time, the young Dominican Francisco de Vitoria (d. 1546) was imbibing at the Sorbonne the atmosphere of the French nominalist revival (*ibid.*, pp. 12–13). Soon he would return to Spain to initiate a general philosophical reawakening.

At Toledo, meanwhile, another attempt was made to establish the teaching of Scotus. Salamanca became alarmed when Cisneros introduced the "novelty" of nominalism at Alcalá, and by way of reaction decreed the establishment of three nominalist chairs of its own: one each for theology, philosophy, and logic (*ibid.*, p. 20). Hernando Alonso de Herrera's *Brief Dispute . . . against Aristotle and His Followers* (1517) was one of the first assaults made by the new humanism on the medieval "corruption" of the liberal arts (*ibid.*, p. 18) and was a predecessor of the work of the great Vives.

SYNCRETISM

Having established the fact that Spaniards were not philosophically ignorant, we may anticipate a statement that might well have its place in the conclusion of this chapter but can be more useful here as an indication of the line of thought we are to follow: philosophically, that is to say as users of philosophy, the Spanish did not differ greatly from the English at this time. Theodore Spencer points out "the remarkable unanimity with which all serious thinkers, at least on the popular level, express themselves about man's nature and his place in the world." [11] These thinkers "combined elements of Aristotelianism, Platonism, Neo-Platonism, Stoicism, and Christianity" so that they "were almost indistinguishably woven into a pattern which was generally agreed upon and which, in its main outlines, was the same as that of the Middle Ages" (*ibid.*).

11. *Shakespeare and the Nature of Man* (New York–Cambridge, Massachusetts, 1945), first page.

There were, of course, new ideas, such as those discovered through reading Plato in the original, but these "were treated either as additions to the accepted picture or as fresh ways of interpreting the one universal truth about which there was no question" (ibid.). Dispute was about details. No one, in England, doubted the importance of reason in the process of knowledge, or the existence of the kingship; all knew that "there was an eternal law, a general order — in the universe, in the ranks of created things,[12] in the institution of government — and it was the business of thoughtful men to discover and describe it so that through knowledge of it they could fulfill the end for which God had made them."[13]

It is necessary to insist on this spirit of syncretism in Christian philosophical and theological thought. Richard P. Jungkuntz, in an article entitled "Christian Approval of Epicureanism,"[14] explains the baffling existence, in Patristic literature, of expressions of approval of all three divisions of Epicurus' system (canonic, physics, ethics) on the ground that this eclecticism was in harmony with the Fathers' tolerant definition of philosophy itself. He cites (p. 279) Clement of Alexandria, who wrote: "By philosophy I do not mean the Stoic nor the Platonic, or the Epicurean and Aristotelian, but everything that has been well said by each of the schools and that teaches righteousness along with science marked by reverence; this eclectic whole I call philosophy." Clement's definition corresponds quite closely to the one which, according to Theodore Spencer, prevailed in Elizabethan England. It was equally applicable in Golden Age Spain.

Epicurus was, of course, a much maligned philosopher. Though Cicero condemned him at all times, Filelfo (d. 1481) showed how he could be interpreted "cristianamente."[15] In 1463 Juan de Lucena adopted the Ciceronian stand, causing Juan de Mena (appear-

12. The reference is, of course, to the Great Chain of Being; see Volume II, Chapter I, for a discussion of this concept.

13. Ibid. Spain differed from England in that Spain remained faithful to this settled state of belief, whereas England pioneered changes. Quevedo, a contemporary of Hobbes, lived in a philosophical world which was — apparently — infinitely removed from Hobbes' reduction of everything to matter and energy, to "bodies in motion."

14. Church History, XXXI (1962), 279–93.

15. Luigi Tonelli, L'amore nella poesia e nel pensiero del Rinascimento (Florence, 1933), pp. 253–54.

ing as one of the interlocutors in Lucena's *Libro de vida beata*) to say that he prefers not to make a defense of the pleasures of the senses "lest you call me a disciple of Epicurus, whose opinions and school I always abhorred." [16] On the other hand, Alejo Venegas defended Epicurus from the slandering *vulgaje*, or common mass of men, who assumed "that he spoke of bodily pleasure and not of the pleasure of virtue, as Epicurus himself meant." [17] In the sixteenth and seventeenth centuries respectively, Francisco Sánchez de las Brozas and Francisco de Quevedo defended Epicurus stoutly against the charges of hedonism and disbelief in the immortality of the soul. Quevedo dismissed the latter charge, using as his criterion the signs of the disbeliever given in the *Book of Wisdom*, and explained the former one away: "this opinion of Epicurus came to be greatly abominated because it was poorly understood by his followers and was interpreted in a bodily sense, defaming its inventor." [18]

In exactly the same spirit of syncretism, Fray Luis de Granada, apparently with no sense of strain, "Christianized the Greek physician Galen." [19] Of the Arabic physician Avicenna, Fray Luis said, as any thinker could have said anywhere in Europe, "a great philosopher, though a Moor" (cited *ibid.*, p. 234).

God's truth being one, expressions of it could be taken from any source at all. Many things had indeed been "well said" by Greeks and Romans and Moslems. Bataillon writes of the fifteenth-century Alonso de Cartagena (and of his contemporaries and successors as well) a paragraph that applies to Spanish thought during the whole Renaissance: "Whether it be a question of Aristotle, of Seneca, of Boethius or of Petrarch, their philosophy is considered as a preparation for the imitation of Christ. Boethius is regarded as a saint and martyr. It is supposed that Seneca was in correspondence with St. Paul. Cicero is one of the ancient eloquent orators who, though they did not possess the true light of faith, had a shining spark of natural

16. Ed. Paz y Melia, in *Opúsculos literarios . . .* , p. 151.

17. *Agonía del tránsito de la muerte* (Appendix), in *NBAE*, XVI, 298a.

18. *Obras en prosa*, ed. L. Astrana Marín (Madrid, 1932), pp. 753a and 762a. Covarrubias in his *Tesoro de la lengua castellana (s.v. Epicuro)* rejects the idea of hedonism but accepts that of atheism.

19. Pedro Laín Entralgo, *La antropología en la obra de Fray Luis de Granada* (Madrid, 1946), p. 225.

reason that enabled them to say many things which, 'brought together and subordinated to the faith,' can serve as a means of making the reading of the Scriptures more profitable to the Christian" (*op. cit.*, I, pp. 59–60).

AUGUSTINIANISM

Though the philosophical bases of Christianity were laid in the Gospel according to St. John (in the beginning was the Word, i.e., the Greek *Logos*), it was St. Augustine who provided the new culture with the firm philosophical foundation which was held to be valid for nearly a thousand years and which, though having to compete with later and differently oriented systems, did not lose its validity in the Renaissance. "Augustine, the most philosophical of the fathers, poured most scorn upon philosophy" (Baker, *op. cit.*, p. 138). He railed against the discords of the various pagan schools: philosophers, with God's help, he contended, may approach the truth, but only to fall back into error; only Christians "rest easy in the certainty that they have attained it" (*ibid.*). In truth, this rest was at best uneasy, as the history we are recording makes clear.[20] Spanish shifts away from, and back toward, the Augustinian view of man and his relationship to God have been traced in the chapter "Free Will" in our Volume II. It was, of course, an overwhelming belief in the rightness of the Augustinian "anthropology" that separated Protestants from Catholics in the sixteenth century: Luther pitted Augustinianism against Thomism.[21] Even Descartes, in his principal writings, "gives priority to a rather crude and ill-digested Augustinianism," only "to set to work with enthusiasm to provide a radically mathematical interpretation of the physical universe."[22]

20. Pomponazzi's *De immortalitate animae* (1516) was publicly burned at Venice, while at Rome Nifo refuted it by order of the Pope. Pomponazzi replied in his *Defensorium*. Cardinal Contarini took part in the controversy, demonstrating the soul's immortality in an interview with Pomponazzi at Padua. According to legend, Pomponazzi committed suicide "to see who was right." See Angel Losada, *Juan Ginés de Sepúlveda* (Madrid, 1944), p. 38, n. 13.

21. Roland H. Bainton, *The Reformation of the Sixteenth Century* (Boston, 1952), p. 36.

22. J. V. Langmead Casserley, *The Christian in Philosophy* (New York, 1951), pp. 98–99.

In the last analysis, however, the difference between Augustinianism and Thomism was one of emphasis rather than of definition. Thomas also posited that in the end everything depends upon God; though he insisted that man is able to contribute to his salvation. Seizing upon this point, Luther was rigorously logical: if all depends upon God, nothing is left over for man (Bainton, *loc. cit.*). In the contest that followed, Spain generally preferred the more optimistic view of Thomism: man has freedom of action; his efforts to achieve salvation can be efficacious. However, in spite of this preference, *The Confessions, The City of God,* and *De Doctrina Christiana* were at all times important influences on Spanish thought. We have more than once had occasion to cite Vives' edition with commentary of the *De Civitate Dei*, which received the honor of translation into English nearly a century after Vives' death (London, 1620).

In addition to the fact that Augustinianism was too strongly rooted in human experience to be completely supplanted, even by the more optimistic (and more scientific) doctrine of St. Thomas, there existed two powerful reasons for Augustine's popularity in the Renaissance: he was the epitome of classical and Christian antiquity (*ibid.*, p. 23); his philosophy was "one of the major roots or antecedents of Renaissance Platonism." [23] Kristeller has shown how the humanists, when attacked by theologians, liked to quote the Fathers both as examples and supporters of their own intellectual ideal, and, actually, as precursors of their own essentially *literary* movement of reform: the attitude of Petrarch toward Augustine determined that of most other humanists (*op. cit.*, pp. 347–48). From the *philosophical* point of view, the influence of Augustine "attained its full significance only when Renaissance Platonism reached its culminating point in Marsilio Ficino." The fact that there were two aspects of Augustine — the Christian classicist, the Christian Platonist — had been forgotten (or de-emphasized) during the later Middle Ages; but because of them the two leading intellectual currents of the early Renaissance — humanism and Plato-

23. Paul Oskar Kristeller, "Augustine and the Early Renaissance," *Review of Religion* (May, 1944), pp. 352–53. This article was first published in *International Science,* I (1941), 7–14.

nism — "were kept within the boundaries of the Christian tradition" (*ibid.*, pp. 353, 357–58).

In the chapters "Fortune and Fate" and "Free Will" in our Volume II, we saw that the fifteenth-century Fray Martín de Córdoba, in his *Compendio de la Fortuna*, presented philosophical and theological solutions of those vexing problems based firmly on the doctrine of St. Augustine. This is a mere beginning: to go on to catalogue the Augustinian reminiscences in Siglo de Oro literature would involve the writing of another book.[24] I shall here simply point out Augustinian traits in three authors who, at first blush, might seem unlikely to show them.

The first is a conquistador, Gonzalo Jiménez de Quesada (d. 1579?), who in 1539 led an expedition into what is now Colombia. A wielder of both sword and pen, he has been likened to Don Quijote in his "wild oscillation between reality and imagination."[25] He identified himself with his fellow Spaniards as the destined instruments of God, charged with the task of establishing the "City of God" on this planet — of late so vastly expanded by Spanish exploration and conquest. And he identified Spain's detractors with the denizens of the utterly opposed "City of Satan." Jiménez de Quesada was obsessed by Paolo Giovio's *Historiarum sui temporis libri XLV* (1550–52), which, according to his own Quixotic view, voiced an anti-Spanish attitude representative of that very Adversary who sought to thwart and to make impossible Spain's divine mission on earth. He actually wrote, in his American isolation, a work which he entitled *Antijovio* to oppose the onslaughts (often imagined) of the Italian historian. Still more fundamental than this opposing of the two "Cities" is another aspect of Augustinianism present in Jiménez de Quesada's book: the doctrine concerning God as an Absolute Power, including the idea of the predestination of the

24. One isolated example: Lope de Vega's *Carlos Quinto en Francia* is dedicated to the chapel master in the Royal Monastery of El Escorial. Lope says that he considers music a gift of God and quotes Augustine to that effect. St. Augustine did not, as did Plato, exclude poets from the Republic, but held them to be identical to, or allied with, musicians: "los admite por músicos." See Arnold G. Reichenberger's critical edition of this autograph play (Philadelphia, 1962), pp. 59–60.

25. Enrique Anderson Imbert, *Historia de la literatura hispanoamericana* (Mexico City–Buenos Aires, 1954), p. 28. See also F. A. Kirkpatrick, *The Spanish Conquistadores* (London, 1934), pp. 310 ff.

elect and of the damned. For example, in referring to a body of Spanish soldiers killed by the Turks in their reconquest of Castelnuovo — soldiers identified by Giovio as having earlier been involved in a rebellion in Lombardy and characterized by him as thieves — Jiménez de Quesada observes: "Even if all or most of these soldiers were the same men who revolted in Lombardy, it may well be that one of the thieves crucified with the Redeemer of the world had committed greater thefts than had these Spaniards; yet the Redeemer kept him for God himself, in the state of blessedness that all men know; and so now, in this case reported by Giovio, I believe that God had reserved for Himself many thieves." The Augustinianism of this conquistador–knight-errant, of this erudite chronicler who used ink as readily as he spilled blood, *ad majorem gloriam Hispaniae,* has been convincingly shown by Victor Frankl.[26]

The view that Cervantes' ethic was a naturalistic ethic, a this-worldly morality based on strictly human considerations, is untenable today. Convinced as he was of the physiological basis (the four bodily humors and their admixture) of human personality traits, indeed of many human actions, Cervantes was no less firmly convinced of an over-arching, higher harmony which was in its essence Augustinian-Platonic. As Don Quijote, lying on his death bed, suddenly awakens from the sleep which had, by renewing the moisture of his brain, restored the knight-errant to sanity and to his former identity as Alonso Quijano the Good, he utters a great shout, saying: "Praised be God Almighty, who has granted me such blessedness! His mercies are without limit, nor are they diminished by the sins of men."[27] There is in this death scene an aura of eternity which invites us to think that the dying man is keeping to himself more thoughts than he expresses. There is, however, nothing approaching mysticism in what he next proceeds to say and do. He renounces his devotion to the romances of chivalry; makes his will as any Christian should; thinks of the fame as a good man (no

26. See his article, "Augustinismo y nominalismo en la filosofía de la historia según Gonzalo Jiménez de Quesada," *Estudios americanos,* XVI (1958) 1–32, especially pp. 12–13.

27. This is an expression of the doctrine of Divine Grace, freely given provided the penitent will receive it; see Volume II, Index, *s.v.* Grace.

longer as a "famous knight") that he wishes to leave behind him; and in secret makes his confession to the Curate.

Is there something more than this? Perhaps. Throughout all his works, Cervantes gives evidence of having been impressed by the eloquent words of St. Augustine — perhaps the most perfect expression ever made of what the Christian life really is — from the first chapter of his *Confessions*: "Thou hast made us for Thyself, and our hearts are restless till they rest in thee." I have found eight references to it. Here is one from his early pastoral, *La Galatea* (1585): "But our Maker and Creator, seeing that it is the very nature of our souls to be ever in a state of perpetual movement and desire, since they cannot rest except in God, as in their proper center. . . ." [28] And here is another from his posthumous *Persiles* (1616): "Since our souls are in continual movement, and cannot stop nor rest except in their true center, which is God, for whom they were created . . ." (*ibid.*, p. 1627a). Indeed, there is in the *Persiles* a near-death scene which closely parallels the death scene in *Don Quijote*. Auristela, having been changed into a loathsome creature and brought to death's door by an act of witchcraft, at length begins her return to health, and "giving thanks to Heaven for the mercies and the joys which she has just received [29] . . . one day she calls Periandro and . . . says to him . . .: 'I could wish that this happiness might go on forever, and last as long as my life. Our souls . . . are ever in continual movement, and cannot rest except in God, as in their center. In this life our desires are infinite, each linked to the other so as to form a chain that sometimes reaches Heaven'" (p. 1706b). If Cervantes, from his first printed work until his last, could not forget these haunting phrases from the *Confessions*, it must be that they had meaning for him. We may believe that the mercies received by Alonso Quijano the Good on his deathbed resembled, in Cervantes' mind, the mercy and joy, the happiness which Auristela experienced in death's antechamber; that is to say, that from this side of the Great Divide those who are near death can perceive the Truth, the Universal Absolute. In the light that radiates from that Eternal Reality, all things human — including

28. *Obras completas*, ed. A. Valbuena Prat (Madrid, 1956), p. 701b.
29. The reference is again to an awareness of having received the gift of Divine Grace.

the plots of Cervantes' novels — cease in their movement as they find their Center.[30]

Quevedo, much more than Cervantes, is widely considered to be a man "of the earth, earthy." Constantino Láscaris Comneno offers an exposition of Quevedo's thought as a function of the two principal influences apparent in his writings: that of Seneca and that of Augustine.[31] Quevedo's sense of cosmic discord impels him to use the introspective method and is (according to Láscaris) reflected in his idea of man, which is centered about the conception of *cuidado*, of *Angst*, or disquietude. Here Quevedo's solution is based on Seneca, a Seneca interpreted, however, by St. Peter Chrysologus. When finally Quevedo comes to grips with the problem of faith, he investigates three themes: God, the soul, Providence. Here his argument is developed in harmony with the Augustinian spirit (*ibid.*, p. 462). Because I am unable to offer a resumé of this long study, I shall limit myself to the description of Láscaris' treatment of one of these themes: the nature of God (p. 484–85). Quevedo follows the "negative way" of the Saint: the nature of God is inscrutable. For God, time is an eternal present; God's today is all eternity. Quevedo repeats the eloquent Augustinian phrases: The earth is not God, nor are the beings that inhabit it — men and animals, the fishes of the sea, the fowls that fly through the air. The sun and the stars and the moon are not God, nor are the Angels, the Virtues, the Powers and Principalities, the Archangels and Thrones. What, then, is God? The only answer: that which is not. These are the words of St. Augustine in his commentary on Psalm LXXV (Vulgate numeration). Beyond this, Quevedo's thought cannot go. One can only think, he says, that "God is His own host and His own lodging"; but "even to speak the truth about God is an act of excessive daring," as Saint Augustine himself had declared it to be — a declaration which Quevedo makes his own and accepts as his guide to wisdom.[32]

Where, in all this, does philosophy end and theology have its

30. See my article, "Realidad, voluntad y gracia en Cervantes," in *Ibérida: Revista de filología*, III (1961), 113–128, especially 125–26. This issue is an *Homenagem a Marcel Bataillon*.

31. In "Senequismo y agustinismo en Quevedo," *Rev. de filosofía*, IX (1950), 461–85.

32. The principal works of Quevedo cited by Láscaris are *The Cradle and the Grave, The World Seen from Inside, Providence of God and Government of Christ, Discourse of All Devils, Virtue Militant, Epictetus Translated,* and *Marcus Brutus.*

beginning? I am not sure that professionals in the two fields could draw the line.[33] The lay historian of Spanish intellectual culture certainly cannot. My aim has not been to write — *absit omen!* — an essay in the history of philosophy. It has been, rather, to show a part of the philosophico-theological substructure of the literature of our period.

ARISTOTELIANISM

The philosophy of Aristotle and its derivatives — Latin Averroism, Scholasticism (Christian, Arabic, and Jewish),[34] and (later) Renaissance Neo-Aristotelianism — constitute by far the most powerful of the currents we are to study. Aristotelian philosophy gave to the Church — from the thirteenth century onward — the metaphysical basis for its faith, which it was to reaffirm at Trent and to which in many fundamental respects it adheres to the present day. This philosophic system survived the attacks of the Renaissance anti-Aristotelians; it was not thrown into the shade by the new popularity of Plato after Ficino; and it persisted, "steady as a church," through the Renaissance and into the Post-Renaissance without visible break. In some ways the tradition of Aristotelianism "even increased rather than declined." Aristotle's influence at the Renaissance "was clearly linked with a tradition that originated in the later Middle Ages." [35]

33. "For this type of Christian thought no hard and fast distinction between reason and revelation, between theology (based on faith and authority) and philosophy (based on pure reason), is possible. According to Aquinas, and most of the Neo-Scholastics who follow him to this day, philosophy can take us, so to speak, part of the way . . ." (Casserley, *op. cit.*, p. 69).

34. "But when we reach this point an objection naturally comes to mind: Scholasticism is not a unity, there are three scholasticisms: the Christian, the Arabic, and the Jewish. How can one assume the general prevalance of Christianity, when large numbers of scholastics were formed by Judaism or Islam? The answer is easy. Not even religiously is it possible to isolate Judaism, Christianity, and Mohammedanism. With respect to the first two, the relationship is obvious; as for the third, it can only be understood as a Judaeo-Christian heresy. Furthermore, the three religions live together historically in the Middle Ages, and the gravitational center is, of course, Christianity. Secondly, the three religions coincide *philosophically* in their essentials: theism, monotheism, creation, the place of man; they have common postulates and antecedents — the Greek tradition which nourishes impartially Christians, Arabs, and Jews; above all, in their period of closest contact, their common postulate is Aristotelianism" (see Marías, *op. cit.*, pp. 24–25).

35. Paul Oskar Kristeller, *The Classics and Renaissance Thought* (Cambridge,

The Arabs acquired at an early date an almost complete corpus of Aristotle's systematic writings. Inasmuch as they inherited Aristotle from the Neoplatonic tradition of late antiquity, their Aristotelianism was affected by Neoplatonic interpretations and accretions. Thus altered, Aristotle attained among the Arabs an authority that he never possessed in Greek antiquity.[36]

This Arabic Aristotelianism exercised a powerful influence upon the Jewish thought of the later Middle Ages. Maimonides became the leading representative of Aristotelianism and strongly affected the philosophy of the Christian West (*ibid.*, p. 29).

During the period of philosophical activity that extended from 1050 to 1250, numerous translations from the Arabic and from the Greek made available in Latin new materials which stimulated and tended to transform Western thought. These materials constituted a nearly complete corpus of Aristotle, to which were added the works of his Arabic commentators, especially Avicenna and Averroës. By 1250 Aristotle and Averroës became the basis of philosophical instruction in the universities (*ibid.*, p. 31).

The fact that Jews and Moslems had been the transmitters of this material intensified the revolutionary character of the renovation. The greatest and most influential of these transmitters, Averroës, the Arabic physician and philosopher (d. 1198), was at the same time the least sympathetic toward any form of theistic religion, whether Moslem or Christian. The result of all of this was a crisis in Christianity.

For the Aristotelian thinker, all human thought is rooted in the physical perception of the external world and what cannot be given in such perception, or deduced from it, cannot be known at all. Thus many thirteenth-century Christians were faced with a sort of

Massachusetts, 1955), pp. 24–25. See also *idem*, "Humanism and Scholasticism in the Italian Renaissance," *Byzantion*, XVII (1944–45), 346–74, especially 369; and *idem*, "Changing Views of the Intellectual History of the Renaissance since Jacob Burckhardt," in *The Renaissance: A Reconsideration of the Theories and Interpretations of the Age*, ed. Tinsley Helton (Madison, 1961), pp. 39–42. In this collection of essays Kristeller says (p. 42): "Quite differently from Spanish Aristotelianism of the sixteenth century, which was closely linked and identified with scholastic theology, Italian Aristotelianism before and during the Renaissance was markedly untheological, closely linked with medicine, and centered upon the subjects of logic and natural philosophy or physics."

36. Kristeller, *The Classics . . .*, p. 28.

Darwinism *avant la lettre*: philosophy seemed incompatible with faith. A way out of the difficulty was sought by the invention of the doctrine of the "double truth": what was true in the sphere of reason need not be true in the sphere of faith. St. Bonaventure (d. 1274), however, went so far as to deny that Aristotle could provide Christians with an adequate philosophy of religion (Casserley, *op. cit.*, pp. 72–73).

The discovery and the acceptance or rejection of these new and compelling possibilities produced what amounted to a thirteenth-century "discovery of the world and man." The Church now desperately needed a genuinely Christian philosopher who sincerely shared the dominant Aristotelianism of the thirteenth century, a man who should show his contemporaries "that it was possible to be a progressive thirteenth-century intellectual and a Christian at the same time. This synthesis was the achievement of St. Thomas Aquinas" (*ibid.*, p. 74).

The Double Truth

Postponing for the moment our discussion of Thomistic Aristoteliansim, let us examine the earlier compromise, that of the "double truth," according to which a proposition may be philosophically true though theologically false. Belief and rational knowledge were first divorced in the twelfth century by Averroës, who regarded the two as hostile opposites.[37] A second divorce occurred when William of Ockham (d. 1349) treated rational and theological truth as two separate spheres that simply had nothing to do with each other — a variant of the "double truth" theory which "brought a strong doubt and uncertainty into the foundations of learning, morals, and religion."[38] The Renaissance Aristotelians, while they resorted to the position that faith may be at variance with reason, and though they made a significant effort to defend and strengthen the neat separation between the realm of natural reason and the realm of faith (i.e., between philosophy and theology) "never [held] the

37. It is doubtful whether Averroës himself held the "two-truths theory," but it was taught by the Latin Averroists, who gained great influence in spite of the Thomistic reconciliation.

38. Michael Seidlmayer, *Currents of Mediaeval Thought with Special Reference to Germany*, trans. D. Barker (Oxford, 1960), p. 146.

crude view that there is a double truth, as some unsympathetic historians have claimed."[39] This bifurcation of truth, though it made inevitable incessant attacks on the "notional" and syllogistic method of the Scholastics, was not necessarily hypocritical or scandalous. Ockham and Calvin argued — and who will say they were wrong? — that the inscrutable ways of God lie beyond the scope of man's reason. This being so, reason must turn to the investigation of the things that it can understand, leaving aside the rest.[40] Consequently, the iconoclasts of the seventeenth century in both theology and science came to believe that a theology and a natural philosophy both deriving from a common set of "notional" assumptions "could yield no proper knowledge either of religion or nature" (*ibid.*, p. 305). Yet it was possible for Joseph Glanville (in his *Plus Ultra*, 1668) to offer a facile answer: render unto faith the things that belong to faith, but be sure not to confuse them with the empirical data of the new philosophy (*ibid.*, p. 88). Indeed, the problem is still present in Kant: "you can have one world in which science is true, and another in which religion is true. This, extremely crudely put, is the principle of Kant's solution."[41]

As for Renaissance Spain, the reconciliation of reason and faith was normal and not excessively difficult: Francisco Suárez maintained the possibility of holding one and the same truth by both science and faith.[42] Spanish theologian-philosophers held that the

39. Kristeller, "Changing Views . . . , p. 43. See also Etienne Gilson, "La doctrine de la double vérité" in *Etudes de philosophie médiévale* (Strasbourg, 1921); Ernst Cassirer *et al.* (eds.), *The Renaissance Philosophy of Man* (Chicago, 1948), pp. 12, 272, 275. It is interesting to note that even in Andreas Capellanus' *Art of Courtly Love* and *Rejection of Love* we have, respectively, an exposition of the two parts of the proposition that what is true according to nature and reason can be false according to grace and divine authority; so that "there emerges in his work the doctrine of the so-called 'double truth'" (A. J. Denomy, *The Heresy of Courtly Love* [New York, 1947], p. 45; see also pp. 46–47, 48–52).

40. Herschel Baker, *The Wars of Truth: Studies in the Decay of Christian Humanism in the Earlier Seventeenth Century* (Cambridge, Massachusetts, 1952), p. 167.

41. W. T. Stace, *Religion and the Modern Mind* (Philadelphia, 1952), pp. 191–92.

42. *Catholic Encyclopaedia*, s. v. Suárez (XIV, 319b). Raimundo Sabunde, in his *Theologia Naturalis*, does not seek, as Raimundo Lull had done, to convert the Moors by rational argument. He addresses himself, rather, to incredulous men in general, "especially to the radical nominalists who then maintained the dangerous theory of the double truth. . . . It is on their own ground and with their own weapons that Sabunde strives to demonstrate by natural and necessary reasons the truth of the dogmas of the Church, in that profoundly troubled century in which three main

means given by God to man for solving the difficulties of his life is his reason; when this vacillates or fails, faith (which does not annul reason but rather elevates and fortifies it) enables man to know divine truth.[43] Miguel Sabuco de Nantes differentiated absolutely between discursive reasoning and scientific knowledge on the one hand, and religion on the other. In each of these departments different laws are valid, he claimed, and they can coexist without mutually destroying each other.[44] The Jesuit Antonio del Río in 1593 urged that young men in the Jesuit schools should not "usurp" the phrases: *unum fidei, alterum rationi* (we hold one thing according to faith, another according to reason), "for faith never is at variance with the truth, but if one thing is true its opposite must be false." [45] Quevedo takes Torcuato Tasso to task for having used the old "double-talk"—"Let me argue as a philosopher, believing as a Christian"—in the dedication to *Il Messagero*. He might have done better, says Quevedo, had he reasoned as a Christian philosopher.[46] Gracián, it has been suggested by Karl Vossler, inclined toward the Averroist position: two types of concepts march side by side, a temporal series and a different series which is eternal; unity will be achieved only in the life to come. On earth there reigns an insuperable ambiguity.[47] I believe that in Vossler's observation there is considerable truth: Gracián, usually, is concerned with the ambiguities of existence on earth, *de tejas abajo*, from the roof downward. That there exists, on the other hand, an ultimate harmony of all opposites in the universe as a whole — Time plus Eternity — he never doubts. Even the writers whom we shall study soon in the section headed "Skepticism" would have agreed with him.

rivals disputed the headship of the Empire and three prelates the throne of St. Peter, while the scandalous corruption of ethical standards was denounced by Wycliffe and John Huss . . . " (Alain Guy, *Les philosophes espagnols d'hier et d'aujourd 'hui*, I [Toulouse, 1956], 41).

43. José M. Gallegos Rocafull, *El hombre y el mundo de los teólogos españoles de los siglos de oro* (Mexico City, 1946), p. 20.

44. Florencio M. Torner, *Doña Oliva Sabuco de Nantes* (Madrid, 1935), pp. 31–32.

45. François de Dainville, *Les jésuites et l'éducation de la société française* (Paris, 1940), p. 238.

46. *Obras en prosa*, ed. cit., p. 1029a.

47. *La soledad en la poesía española*, trans. José Miguel Sacristán (Madrid, 1941), p. 285.

The Two Tendencies in Aristotelianism

Just as we saw that both St. Augustine and St. Thomas, greatly as they differ, agree in reserving for God alone the solution of the drama of human salvation — and of human philosophical understanding —, so Aristotle and Plato, for all their opposition, have much in common. Aristotle is much less permeated by religious feeling than Plato; "nevertheless he too maintains a teleological view of the world. . . . Belief in cosmic purpose was not the invention of Christianity" (Stace, *op. cit.*, p. 30). Like the Italian Renaissance Platonists, the Italian Renaissance Aristotelians "began discussing God, freedom, and immortality in relation to the individual soul; but, unlike them, they arrived through Aristotle at naturalistic conclusions." [48] This version of Aristotle "without benefit of clergy" is known as Latin Averroism. Though it was condemned in 1270 and 1277 and refuted by the "commanding modernism" of St. Thomas, it took refuge in the Italian medical schools. [49] This current of naturalistic thought leads from Aristotle to Pomponazzi to Zabarella and, finally, to Spinoza (*ibid.*, p. 9). Aristotle "with benefit of clergy" led to the Spanish baroque Scholasticism of the sixteenth century, which gave way to the emerging philosophy based on natural science (i.e., measurement) only in the eighteenth century, and then very reluctantly.

Anti-Aristotelianism

Siger of Brabant (condemned in 1270 and 1277) held that "faith is true, but Aristotle is more interesting," taking an irrationalist position. The fifteenth-century Italian Aristotelians maintained a more decidedly Christian Averroism (*ibid.*, p. 10). Even so, there was opposition to excessive reverence for Aristotle. The first important Spanish anti-Aristotelian was Hernando Alonso de Herrera (d. 1527). In his *Disputation against Aristotle and His Followers* he treats of a secondary aspect of Aristotelian doctrine, with general success but with some deficiencies in his presentation. He is devoted to Aristotle, he says, but not his slave. He expounds the short-

48. J. H. Randall, Jr., the "Introduction" to Pomponazzi in Cassirer *et. al.* (eds.), *op. cit.*, p. 260.
49. Kristeller and Randall, "General Introduction," *ibid.*, pp. 9–10.

comings of the Schoolmen and the dialecticians, especially those at the University of Paris. His critical attitude is noteworthy, not so much for its content as for its having introduced into Spain, before Peter Ramus had been heard from and somewhat earlier than Vives, the movement of philosophic independence from the excessive authority of Aristotle. The book had influence in Spain; other Spanish books issued to achieve the end sought by Herrera were, in the words of Marcial Solana, "innumerable." [50] Herrera's treatise was, according to Bataillon (*op. cit.*, I, p. 18), an entering wedge which would help topple the decaying structure of "pseudo-dialectics." In the view of Bonilla y San Martín, Herrera followed the Pythagorean current as this was represented in the fifteenth century by Nicholas of Cusa. [51]

As an expression of the Spanish anti-Aristotelian attitude I shall quote from a work of critical fiction, the *Viaje de Turquía* by Dr. Andrés Laguna (d. 1560), who perhaps would not have thought of himself as a philosopher at all:

Mátalascallando. — Why is it that I have heard that physicians are better philosophers than theologians are? *Pedro.* — Because the theologians are always tied to Aristotle [and quote him] as if they were saying "The Gospel says it" and can't conceive of going against Aristotle whom they follow without looking where they are going, as if he hadn't uttered no end of lies; but the physicians are eclectic in their search for truth. When Plato says a thing better, they refute Aristotle; when the reverse is true, they say freely that Plato did not know what he was talking about. But just you try to tell a theologian that Aristotle in a certain passage does not know what he is saying; he will pick up stones to throw at you, and if you ask him why what he says is true, he will reply with more naïveté than wisdom, that it is true because Aristotle said it was. So you can judge for yourself what philosophical competence they have! [52]

Finally, it is interesting to note that the Apostle to the Indians, Fray Bartolomé de las Casas (d. 1566), though his Dominican habit would cause us to expect in him a greater respect for the philosopher to whom Scholasticism owed its greatest debt, rejected not only

50. *Historia de la filosofía española: Época del Renacimiento (siglo XVI)* (Madrid, 1941), I, 32.
51. "Un aristotélico del Renacimiento: Hernando Alonso de Herrera," *RHi*, L (1920), 93.
52. *NBAE*, II, 86b.

Aristotle's doctrine of "natural slavery" [53] — he could not have been the Apostle to the Indians had he not done so — but actually went so far as to say that such ideas "proceed from Aristotle, a heathen who is burning in hell." [54] This view is exceptional.

Aristoteles victor

"The common notion that Scholasticism as an old philosophy was superseded by the new philosophy of humanism is . . . disproved by plain facts." [55] This assertion, made with reference to Italy, holds true for Spain (*ibid.*, p. 7).[56] It was Aristotle interpreted "with benefit of clergy" that became the foundation stone of the baroque Scholasticism of Francisco Suárez and his school at the time of the Counter Reformation, just as earlier it was this same Aristotle whose importance as the chief source of Christian metaphysics was a principal factor in the decision to establish a chair of Greek studies at the newly founded University of Alcalá (1508). In general, as the sixteenth century advanced, "Spanish thought gravitated much more toward the doctrine of the Stagirite [Aristotle] than toward the teaching of the founder of the Academy [Plato]. Nevertheless, pure Aristotelians . . . are few . . . in the Golden Age. At a time characterized by the total revision of knowledge it was natural that even the most accepted of doctrines should be critically examined in many of its points" (Torner, *op. cit.*, p. 61). The successful implanting of renewed Aristotelian studies at Salamanca was the work of the Dominican Francisco de Vitoria (d. 1546). The victory of Aristotelianism in Spain as a whole was due to the impulse given it by the Jesuits, with Suárez at their head.[57]

We may take as indicative of this Aristotelian (and Thomistic)

53. See Chapter IV of our Volume II: "The Nature and Destiny of Man."

54. Gallegos Rocafull, *op. cit.*, p. 139. On a Spanish thinker who "not only seeks to destroy the authority of Aristotle but to oppose the wide influence of Petrus Ramus in Spain," see D. W. Bleznick, "Las *Institutiones Rhetoricae* de Fadrique Furió," *NRFH*, XIII (1959), p. 355. Furió Ceriol died in 1592.

55. Kristeller, "Humanism and Scholasticism . . . ," p. 368.

56. In France the Christian humanist Lefèvre d'Etaples was the master of Aristotelian studies as these were renewed at the Renaissance. See Lucien Febvre, *Autour de l'Heptaméron* (Paris, 1944), p. 82.

57. F. Cereceda, *Diego Laínez en la Europa religiosa de su tiempo, 1512–1565* (Madrid, 1945–46), I, 419–20.

triumph the program of studies at Alcalá in 1553–1559, when Juan Huarte de San Juan was studying there. The courses in philosophy consisted of the reading and interpretation of Aristotle. The first year was given over to the *Súmulas* (compendia of the principles of logic), in a text which might be either by Petrus Hispanus, by Francisco de Villalpando, or by Domingo de Soto. In the second year, Aristotle's own works on dialectic and logic were read; in the third year, the *Physics*; in the fourth, the *Metaphysics*. At times the *Ethics* was added. The program as a whole was rounded out by work in arts, mathematics, astronomy, and related subjects.[58] Whether the students with a special bent for philosophy became, as independent scholars, genuine Peripatetics like Sepúlveda; Platonists like Fox Morcillo; independents like Francisco Vallés or Arias Montano; baroque Scholastics like Suárez; Dominican Scholastics like Cano, Soto, Báñez; Jesuits like Molina and (again) Suárez; Franciscans like Alonso de Castro and Luis de Carvajal; or, finally, eclectic Scholastics like Diego Tapia de Aldana, it was from Aristotle that they received their first awareness of the philosophic substratum of Christian thought and their first introduction to philosophic method. We return to Huarte as an example: "His philosophy moves, much more than he himself realizes, within the boundaries of Aristotelian conceptions. Since Aristotelianism was the philosophy currently taught in Spain — the philosophy he had heard at the University — and was likewise the philosophy of the books which he found readily to hand, he regards it as something natural and taken for granted; yet not without criticism and reflection, since we find him discussing many of the points of that philosophy and defending other points against Galen" (*ibid.*, p. 226).

SKEPTICISM [59]

If one should ask why Spaniards were users rather than creators of philosophy, he would find the answer, perhaps, in the typically

58. Mauricio de Iriarte, S. J., *El Doctor Huarte de San Juan y su "Examen de ingenios"* (Madrid, 1948), p. 29.

59. In Chapter V of Volume II (pp. 185 ff.) we gave a less technical account of skepticism in our review of the Spanish attitude toward reason. Here the point of view is that of philosophy as a branch of learning.

Spanish lack of confidence in the merely human, which manifests itself, as we have seen, in the general preference for religious solutions (see above, Chapter VII). This distrust of the Goddess Reason is expressed countless times, in countless works, during Spain's age of greatest intellectual activity. Though Etienne Gilson has observed that the combination of skepticism and fideism is "classical and characteristic of all ages," [60] its presence appears — with unusual strength and persistence — in the writings of Spaniards many of whom are not genuine philosophers but rather Christian humanists, moralists, or ascetics.[61] We shall begin by quoting a moralist, Fray Juan de Pineda. In his *Agricultura christiana*, the interlocutor Pámphilo remarks to the Maestro (Philaletes) that "authorities seem to disagree." The Master admits that this is so, and urges his pupil to see in this circumstance "how fragile are the minds of men, since even in visible and tangible things they cannot achieve unanimity, not to speak of things known only by conjecture, for which reason Socrates abandoned the effort and took up the moral philosophy of the virtues, inasmuch as these can be understood by those who truly seek to live by them." This is most necessary, Philaletes insists, and is sufficient for our salvation; yet men, forgetful of this truth, wear themselves out studying "curious" sciences. And he quotes St. Augustine's contention that, God being wisdom, he who loves God will be a true philosopher.[62] In a very real sense, we have here the reason why one searches in vain, in the Spanish Renaissance, for more than "predecessors" of Descartes and Bacon. Many writers, even though classed as "philosophers," are content to set forth what they regard as moral truths without presenting rational proofs.

60. *La philosophie au moyen âge* (Paris, 1947), p. 655.
61. "The skeptics of the Renaissance went as far as it was possible to go in this strategy of discontent. They were skeptics, but until a genuine alternative to Scholastic rationalism was forthcoming their skepticism could have only one outcome: the symbolic suicide of fideism." Only in the seventeenth century was this skepticism vigorously developed (see Baker, *The Wars of Truth* . . . , pp. 146, 154). See also Helton (ed.), *The Renaissance* . . . , p. 102; Eugene F. Rice, Jr., *The Renaissance Idea of Wisdom* (Cambridge, Massachusetts, 1958), pp. 20–21, 37, 183–84; Margaret L. Wiley, *The Subtle Knot: Creative Scepticism in Seventeenth-century England* (Cambridge, Massachusetts, 1952), pp. 39 ff., 42, 46, 51–52, 59, 214–15; Charles A. Nauert, "Agrippa in Renaissance Italy: The Esoteric Tradition," *Studies in the Renaissance*, VI (1959), 207.
62. Salamanca (1589), II, fol. 45.

The one Spanish writer who holds a place of esteem in the history of European skepticism is the physician Francisco Sánchez, long regarded as a Portuguese, but now known to have been born in Tuy, in the Spanish province of Galicia. His portrait hangs in the auditorium of the University of Toulouse.[63] The skepticism of his *Quod nihil scitur (Nothing Can Be Known)*, printed in 1581, "is a true panoply of the scepticism of the last years of the sixteenth century." In his development of systematic doubt he is a predecessor of Descartes, of Locke, and of Kant. This physician, astronomer, philosopher, and mathematician "offers the quintessence of all the negative aspects of Renaissance criticism."

The distinctive note of his philosophy is that it is less expressive of true skepticism than of agnosticism — "in a positivistic and neo-kantian direction." His doctrine, much more than that of Vives, is an *ars nesciendi*, an art of not knowing. He is, however, a believer, a Catholic. The knowledge of hidden things, he says, was reserved by God for Himself. We must not seek to invade the province of Divinity; it is our duty, rather, humbly to receive our knowledge of "what is hidden" from individuals to whom God chose or chooses to reveal it — from men like St. Paul or the prophets. This negative book was intended to be merely propaedeutic: in various passages it announces the author's intention to found "a certain and easy science," based not on notional imaginings, but on solid, rigorous rational methods.[64]

The rationalist and Christian humanist Juan Luis Vives (d. 1540) at times sounds very much like a skeptic, but it is the skepticism of St. Bernard: *ama nescire*; [65] it owes much to the skepticism of another Christian humanist, Erasmus of Rotterdam, who wrote: "all sublunary matters are enveloped in such a cloud of obscurity

63. Solana, *op. cit.*, I, 378. For the following assessment of Sánchez, I select from Solana, pp. 389–405.

64. This positive contribution would have been based on experience and judgment. It would have limits, however: Sánchez's philosophy does not go beyond probabilism; it does not establish a criterion of truth even for the world of the senses. See José Ferrater Mora, *Diccionario de filosofía* (Buenos Aires, 1951), *s. v.* Sánchez (Francisco), where ample bibliography is given. Sánchez's skepticism was principally directed against the Aristotelian *corpus* and the methods of the late Aristotelians. See Michele F. Sciacca, "La Opera philosophica de Francisco Sanches" in *Miscelánea de Estudos a Joaquim de Carvalho* (Figueira da Foz, 1959), No. 2, pp. 174–75.

65. Maurice Hélin, *A History of Medieval Latin Literature*, trans. J. C. Snow (New York, 1949), p. 122.

that the shortsightedness of human understanding cannot peer through and arrive at any comprehensive knowledge of them. . . . All things being no more than probable, nothing can be known as certain." [66] Vives echoes these thoughts in his *Introduction to Wisdom* (as we saw in our chapter on "Reason" in Volume II). Solana asks: "In the light of [the] doctrines set forth by Vives in the sixteenth century, what reader familiar with the contents of the *Critique of Pure Reason* published by Kant in 1781 does not perceive the stages in the critique of human knowledge . . . by the philosopher of Koenigsberg?" (*op. cit.*, I, 203).

Although Spain produced no Vanini, no Charron or Des Périers or La Mothe le Vayer, no Jean Bodin (author of the *Heptaplomeres*), the attitude of critical skepticism expressed by Pineda and by Vives is quite common in the Spanish sixteenth century; yet it is always accompanied by fideism. Thus Huarte de San Juan in his *Examen de ingenios para las ciencias* (1575), a book so bold that the author had to revise it to meet the demands of the Inquisition, "presents a deluge of doubts and of skepticism" which leaves intact only the truth of divine revelation: along with his ancient authorities Huarte sought the support at all times of the Bible (*ibid.*, pp. 307, 316). As for the theologians, he finds them "uncertain in matters which are not articles of faith because after they have reasoned very well, they can find no infallible proof or evident fact that can indicate which reasons are best, so that each theologian forms opinions as best he can." In matters defined by the Church, no error is possible, since God — aware of the ease with which men deceive themselves — did not consent that matters of such high import should be left to human determination; rather, "where two or three are gathered together in His name, He assumes the presidency, approving what is properly said, rejecting errors, and revealing what cannot be arrived at by human efforts" (*ibid.*, p. 307). Huarte is thus not a materialist (for all his concessions to the power of matter over mind), or even a sensualist or positivist: he openly affirms that the human soul is spiritual and immortal (*ibid.*, p. 311).

Francisco Vallés was born in 1524 in Old Castile. His principal philosophical work, *De sacra philosophia*, printed in 1587, was

66. *In Praise of Folly* (London, 1876), pp. 94–95.

written with the intention of showing that all doctrine — even natural philosophy — is contained in Holy Writ; it was written, furthermore, not that the author might obtain praise, but *ad majorem gloriam Dei*. Nevertheless, the book was expurgated by the Spanish Inquisition and reappeared with corrections and omissions in 1613. Even so, the Roman Inquisition in 1618 demanded further corrections; these apparently were not made, and the book was still on the Roman Index in 1900.[67] In this book there are notes of skepticism and of probabilism, held in check by sincere religious faith. Vallés wrote: "Men, no matter how much they sweat in the study of philosophy, must sometimes inevitably seek reasons and causes of those things which take place under the light of the sun; but it is also inevitable that, in the investigation of these matters — as long as they are enshrouded in the darkness of their human senses — they be more or less deceived (*allucinentur*), and in regard to things which appear most probable, they inevitably, unless they are false to themselves, enter into doubt" (cited *ibid.*, p. 340).

Pedro de Valencia (d. 1620) has been regarded (by Menéndez y Pelayo and by others) as a skeptic and as a predecessor of Kant; but inasmuch as he claims to perceive the absurdity of other thinkers' irrational opinions, he is a believer in rationality and not a skeptic. One of the first (and best) historians of philosophy, he was above all a critic — in philosophy, in archaeology, in ethics and in politics, in literature, in everything (*ibid.*, pp. 375–76).

Quevedo (d. 1645) approved highly of the *Quod nihil scitur* of Francisco Sánchez:

It is perfectly clear that nothing is known, that all men are ignorant; and not even this is certain. . . . If we knew it, that at least would be knowing something. So says the learned Francisco Sánchez. . . .[68]

He falls back into fideism (*ibid.*, p. 1031):

If one sees better persuaded by reason than by looking with the eyes, how much more advantageous is it to believe in God through an act of faith in Him, than to hold to all that is visible without faith.

Quevedo shows the typically Spanish disdain for science (p. 913):

67. Solana, *op. cit.*, II, 297, 306–7.
68. *Obras en prosa*, ed. cit., p. 166.

One who observes you wearing yourself out with syllogisms . . . and undisciplined logic . . . and natural philosophy (they call it natural, though it is fantastic, conceived in a dream) . . . could only pity you. The greatest, the most baseless, and the most dangerous hypocrisy is the hypocrisy of knowledge. . . . Men seem to have formed a compact to believe each other. If you wish to confound them, just try to believe what those . . . men tell you, and you will see that nothing is known. . . .

This does not mean that Quevedo disdains to read philosophy, even modern philosophy. He is not the first man to call the philosophers ignorant; it was from their own works that he learned to do so (p. 914):

If you listen to Aristophanes, Socrates was a fool. They called Plato divine, yet Aristotle condemned his doctrine, as Plato did Aristotle's, and, in our own times, Petrus Ramus and Bernardino Telesio. Plato and Aristotle called Homer the father of wisdom, yet Scaliger and many others call him a doddering and drunken old man. These, in turn, are called worse things still.

It is thus clear that from Spain there came during the Renaissance serious questionings of man's ability to uncover the mysteries of being, to penetrate the truth. Philosophical skepticism led, however, to an affirmation of belief: the truth of divine revelation was not called into question. *Philosophia* was *sacra philosophia*. The ultimate source of knowledge remained the Bible. The skeptic, the probabilist, was always a fideist.[69]

PANTHEISM

Spanish Renaissance pantheism had medieval roots. The Hispano-Jewish thinker Ibn Gabirol, also called Avicebron (d. 1037), with his Neoplatonic philosophy of the universality of matter, influenced especially medieval philosophers of the Franciscan tradition. He has been called "the Spanish Spinoza of the eleventh century."[70] Menéndez y Pelayo wrote (*ibid.*, p. 349) that he seemed to find some pantheistic notes in the writings of the prodigious Fernando de Córdoba, studied in Chapter V of the present volume. The same critic says in another connection that

69. See Arturo Farinelli, *La vita è un sogno* (Turin, 1916), I, 114–15.

70. M. Menéndez y Pelayo, *Historia de los heterodoxos españoles* (Santander, 1946–48), II, 165.

in all the heterodox thinkers of Spain "it is easy to discover the pantheistic germ." [71]

The Spanish Neoplatonist and anti-Trinitarian Miguel Servet (d. 1553) expressed in the most precise terms a pantheistic mysticism derived from the Alexandrian School (Plotinus, Proclus). No one since Scotus Erigena or, more accurately, since Amalric de Chartres and David de Dinant (according to Menéndez y Pelayo) had defended a Christian pantheism in such a consistent and out-and-out exposition as he did. From this point of view, Servet stands as an isolated figure in the history of Spanish Renaissance thought (*ibid.*, III, 384). Rejected by his countrymen and pursued by the Inquisition, he sought refuge in Geneva only to be sent to the stake by Calvin.

Servet's teaching was clear: "I hold it as a general maxim that all things are part and portion of God, that all nature is His substantial spirit"—and he included in the category "all nature," even the Devil.[72] "Christ fills all things," he insisted. "They have a carnal sense who separate Christ from us by placing Him at the right hand of the father." [73] "The more Christ renews our spirit by the fire of his spirit, the more He insinuates himself into our body. . . . Our inward man is God. . . ." Calvin accused Servet of proclaiming that "all creatures are of the proper essence of God and so all things are full of gods. . . . I have no doubt that this bench or anything you point to is God's substance. . . . Even if you are a blind demon you are sustained nevertheless by God."

PLATONISM [74]

C. S. Lewis, in his account of English literature in the sixteenth century, reminds us that Scaliger, Sidney, and Bacon "inherited, in

71. *Ibid.*, I, 59. See also Ferrater Mora, *Diccionario* . . . (*s. v. panteísmo*): "when God is identified with a metaphysical absolute, there is always a tendency toward a depersonalization which is the first step in the direction of an identification of God with nature; of the Absolute . . . with that which emanates . . . from the Absolute."

72. Cited by Francisco Vega Díaz, "Miguel Servet entre la condenación y la gloria," *Clavileño*, VI (1955), 18.

73. This and the following quotations are taken from Roland H. Bainton, *Hunted Heretic: The Life and Death of Michael Servetus, 1511–1553* (Boston, 1960), pp. 136–39, 186.

74. Sergio Rábade Romeo in an article entitled "¿Neoplatonismos medievales?" in *Estudios filosóficos*, VIII (1959), 407–17, contends that the concept of "Neoplatonism"

a Christianized form, the Platonic dualism. Nature was not the whole. Above earth was heaven: behind the phenomenal, the metaphysical. To that higher region the human soul belonged." Therefore the artist who, in his "feigned history," improved on Nature and painted what might be or ought to be was not indulging in escapism: "he was reascending from a world which he had a right to call 'foolish' and asserting his divine origin."[75] It is with this Christianized Platonism that we have to deal here. Its influence is omnipresent in the Spanish Renaissance and baroque.[76] This was natural. St. Augustine had said that the doctrine of the Platonic Ideas was so fruitfully productive that without understanding it no one could become wise. And St. Thomas, the Aristotelian, had cited this sentence of St. Augustine and given it his approval.[77]

In the course of the present study, beginning with the first chapter of Volume I, we have had so many occasions to refer to the Christian derivatives of Plato's teaching that a full treatment here would be repetitious. For our purposes in the present context it will suffice to point up the vitality of the Platonic philosophical-artistic current in the Spanish Renaissance with facts and quotations that seem to have particular significance.

If both Platonism and Aristotelianism were Christianized philosophies — that is, if both were necessary substrata of Christian theology — they must be harmonized. The effort to explain away their points of contradiction went on throughout the Golden Age. For example, there was the *De causis obscuritatis Aristoteleae* of Pedro Núñez, published in 1554 (Solana, *op. cit.*, II, 201). In the same year Sebastián Fox Morcillo issued his *De natura philoso-*

embraces ideas so diverse that they cannot properly be included under this designation, and he distinguishes five philosophical currents (for their enumeration see our Volume I, Chapter I, note 7). These complexities do not diminish in the Renaissance: the distinction between the various kinds of Platonism "depends upon emphasis and terminology rather than upon content. The avenues by which the Greek philosophical tradition passed from ancient to modern times are so numerous, twisted, and complex that only the appearance of precision is gained by labelling these as 'medieval' and those as 'Renaissance'" (William Nelson reviewing Robert Ellrodt's *Neoplatonism in the Poetry of Spenser* [Geneva, 1960] in *Renaissance News*, XIV [1961], 277).

75. *English Literature in the Sixteenth Century Excluding Drama* (Oxford, 1954), pp. 320–21.

76. See the chapter "Renaissance Platonism" by Paul Oskar Kristeller in William H. Werkmeister (ed.), *Facets of the Renaissance* (Los Angeles, 1959), pp. 89–107.

77. A. D. Sertillanges, *Les grandes thèses de la philosophie thomiste* (Paris, 1928), p. 39.

phiae, seu de Platonis et Aristotelis consensione, which Boivin le Cadet, writing in 1817, considered "perhaps the best and most solid treatment ever written on this subject." [78] The contradictions of the two philosophies with Christianity itself were originally very real, but in the sixteenth century men no longer shared St. Bernard's misgivings in this regard; [79] the conflict of the one ancient philosophy with the other, however, not only concerned professional thinkers but also intruded itself into works of literature. León Hebreo in his *Dialoghi d'amore* addressed himself to the problem in this snatch of dialogue: [80]

Sophia — Many of the wisest philosophers deny the existence of the Platonic Ideas, namely Aristotle and his followers the Peripatetics.

Philótimo — . . . What we just said about the Ideas is not denied by Aristotle, nor can he deny it, although he does not use the term Ideas.

What does seem to be a conflict, Hebreo states, is only a matter of terminology.

Plato, in one way or another, was regarded as having had knowledge — or inklings — of the Divine Law which was the Christian patrimony. Here is a text from the fifteenth century: "Plato . . . had knowledge of the law of God, according to St. Augustine." [81] Huarte de San Juan states in 1575: "Plato took from Holy Writ the best *sententiae* that we find in his works; it is because of these that he came to be called 'divine.' " [82] Here is another text, written by Don Bernardino de Rebolledo in 1652: "Not only is this the

78. *Querelle des philosophes du quinzième siècle*, II, 557 ff. (cited by Solana, *op. cit.*, I, 626).

79. St. Bernard had written: "When Abelard sweats blood to make a Christian of Plato he merely proves himself a pagan" (from *Selections from Medieval Philosophers*, ed. Richard McKeon [New York, 1929-30], I, 207; cited by Baker, *The Dignity of Man* . . . , p. 194). Compare this attitude with that of the Renaissance: "Neoplatonic mysticism is not remote from the Christian tradition by which it had been long since appropriated. . . . In the [Italian] Renaissance writers the Christian note is muted though never definitely denied, and the door is thereby opened to pass from Christianity not to irreligion but to universal religion" (Roland H. Bainton, "The Thirst for God in the Renaissance," *Renaissance News*, V [1952], 10).

80. Castilian translation, *Diálogos de amor*, by Garcilaso de la Vega (The Inca), *NBAE*, XXI, 432ab. The differences are set forth on pp. 432-33a.

81. Pero Díaz de Toledo, *Diálogo e razonamiento en la muerte del Marqués de Santillana*, in Paz y Melia (ed.), *Opúsculos literarios* . . . , p. 270. For Augustine's discussion of Plato, see *City of God*, Book VIII. On Hispanic Platonism in the fifteenth century, see R. Ricard, "L'Infant D. Pedro de Portugal et *O livro da virtuosa bemfeitoria*," *Bulletin des études portugaises*, XVII (1953), 50 ff.

82. *Examen de ingenios para las ciencias*, ed. R. Sanz (Madrid, 1930), I, 117.

doctrine of the Church; the Academy [Plato] appears to have taken it from the Bible, only to give it back to . . . St. Dionysius [the Areopagite], since Plato places it on the lips of the learned Diotima, who says: 'All lower beauties are, as it were, stepping stones whereby Love may mount upward little by little until it is enabled to enjoy the Supreme Beauty, which constitutes supreme felicity.' " [83] Quevedo on the other hand, in *La virtud militante*, quotes St. Augustine as having said that "never in the books of the Platonic school had he been able to learn aught of charity and humility." [84] Yet there was no disinclination to cite Plato or the Neoplatonists in works of Catholic devotion. Alonso de Orozco issued his *Victoria de la muerte* in 1583. In it he represents the philosopher Eusonius as having replied to the question *What man achieves a good death?* by saying: "He who firmly believes that the day he is presently living in is his last and who ordains his affairs in accord with this consideration." "The words," remarks Orozco, "would seem to have been said by a faithful Christian, not a pagan without faith." And he continues: "Plato also affirmed that true philosophy is the constant awareness of death. His disciple Aristotle said: 'to leave this life is a good thing.' This he repeated with frequency to the end that his followers might remember their mortality." [85]

In 1589 Fray Juan de Pineda, discussing love in his *Agricultura christiana (ed. cit.,* II, fol. 125), explains that no man loves without giving himself to the beloved, and that no one gives himself without giving also what he possesses. "This was well expressed by Marsilio [Ficino]," he continues, "when he declared that he gave himself only in exchange for himself, meaning that he loved only those who in turn loved him." The selfsame thought is used as an illustration in a sermon on St. John the Evangelist preached in the year 1603 by Fray Hernando de Santiago. After quoting various saints to the effect that nothing is so inborn in human nature as to love him who loves us, and that love can be won only by an outflowing of love from him who desires affection, he remarks: "the cause of this was expressed with great eloquence by Marsilio Ficino in his commentary on the *Symposium* of Plato; he says that love is so free and

83. *Ocios* (ed. Madrid, 1778), I, 657.
84. *Obras en prosa, ed. cit.,* p. 952a.
85. Ed. Biblioteca Renacimiento (Madrid, 1921), p. 48.

esteems itself so highly, that it cannot and will not be bought or sold except at the price of itself." [86]

Alain Guy (*op. cit.*, vol. I: *Epoques et auteurs*) selects eight thinkers as representative of the Golden Age, among them Fray Luis de León. It is questionable whether Fray Luis can properly be called a philosopher, but he was a thinker deeply indebted to the Platonic tradition. Bataillon says of him (*op. cit.*, II, 383, 390):

> When we begin to leaf through *On the Names of Christ*, we find ourselves in the presence of a work of rarer quality. Its perfection, its complexity, its profundity announce a literary and religious genius in every way exceptional. May not Fray Luis owe to the Jewish strain in his inheritance certain secret affinities with the spirit of the prophets and the Psalmist? Perhaps. He shows a no less keen sensitivity to the lessons of harmony taught by Plato. One recalls inevitably the Platonic *Dialogues* as one reads these conversations, so far removed from the *Colloquia* of Erasmus.
>
> . . . .
>
> Fray Luis insists less than does Erasmus on peace between men; he stresses inward peace of spirit, and the great cosmic peace which is communicated to the soul by the serenity of the night. Enriched, renewed by a Platonic meditation on man and the universe, the Erasmian *philosophia Christi* of the first decades of the sixteenth century speaks in *De los nombres de Cristo* a magnificent language.

The claim that the post-Tridentine period in Spain was hostile to Plato is without foundation. Garcilaso de la Vega, the Inca, tells in the dedication to Maximilian of Austria of his translation of Hebreo's *Dialoghi d'amore* (1589) that he was encouraged and even commanded to carry the work through to completion by four distinguished theologians, one of whom, Fray Hernando de Zárate, has erroneously been put forward as an example of a supposed "ascetic hatred" hostile to Platonic immanence. In 1631 the Jesuit Juan Eusebio Nieremberg published at Lyons a work with a typically baroque title, which I translate: *On the Art of the Will, Six Books: In Which the Substance of Platonic, Stoic, and Christian Doctrine Is Digested, All the Juice of the Best Philosophy Having Been Squeezed from Plato, Seneca, Epictetus, Dio Chrysostom, Plotinus, Iamblicus, and Others, Whose More Subtle Meanings Have Been Organized in Artful Manner; Some Things Have Been Corrected, Very Many Things Have Been Added with Novelty and*

86. In *Sermonario clásico*, comp. Miguel Herrero García (Madrid, 1942), p. 39.

Cleverness. In 1641 the same author brought out his *Treatise on The Beauty of God, Telling Why He Should Be Loved Because of the Infinite Perfections of the Holy Being.* This is not properly speaking a work of philosophy, but rather a work of ascetic and practical doctrine, written with the intention of elevating the emotions, "stealing from the saintly doctors their *sententiae,* from the Scholastic philosophers their reasoning, and from the mystics their words." Plato and the Platonists are cited on every hand.[87]

The swan song of the Platonic school in Spain was a *Discourse on Beauty and Love* published at Copenhagen in 1652 by Don Bernardino de Rebolledo, the Conde de Rebolledo. Don Bernardino quotes "los platónicos" as saying "beauty is a ray of Divinity spread and diffused through all material things." He asserts "the existence of a Supreme Beauty, without adornment or defect, eternal, immutable, all act, all virtue, all perfection, which in infinite unity embraces all the excellences and all the pleasure-giving forces that in material things are revealed by only an occasional trait. . . . From the fecundity of this Beauty are derived all the beings of Nature and by its goodness they are attracted, since it is their beginning and their end."[88]

STOICISM

In summarizing Chapter V ("Reason") of Volume II, I pointed out that, of the two types of law provided by God for the government of each Christian — the law of the commandments and the law of grace and love —, the first, the law of rational commandments addressed to the intellect, came to be enriched by the teachings of the ancient sages,[89] to the end that virtue might be made meta-

87. See M. Menéndez y Pelayo, *Historia de las ideas estéticas en España* (Santander, 1946–47), II, 112; see also pp. 102–11.

88. Cited *ibid.,* pp. 56, 59. Further proof of the fruitfulness of the Platonic tradition in Spain may be accumulated by examining one by one the 1,242 items listed in *Filosofía española y portuguesa de 1500 a 1650,* issued by the Biblioteca Nacional for the centenary of Francisco Suárez in 1948 and published at Madrid by the Ministerio de Educación Nacional, Dirección General de Propaganda. See also Joan Estelrich, "Coup d'oeil sur le platonisme en Espagne" (Resumé), Association Guillaume Budé, *Congrès de Tours et Poitiers* (Paris, 1954), pp. 382–83.

89. "Deeply versed in the Hebrew Scriptures, Jerome was saturated with Cicero and Virgil. Cicero had much to do with giving direction to Augustine, and Virgil

physically understandable and ethically attractive to the intellectually inclined. An honored place among those ancient sages was at all times accorded to Seneca, to his predecessors, and to his successors. "It is certain," writes Wenley, "that the Stoic *mens conscia recti* [the mind aware of what constitutes rectitude] became part and parcel of popular Christian teaching" (*ibid.*, p. 123). And not only of popular teaching; Justus Lipsius, who with Isaac Casaubon and Joseph Scaliger formed the "literary triumvirate" of the later sixteenth century,[90] interpreted natural law as God's will, and thought of the Stoic "wise man" in terms of what it meant to be a good Christian man.[91] So pronounced and so persistent was the syncretic tendency that, at the very end of the centuries we are surveying, in most of the plays of Racine (d. 1699) no rigorous separation of Greek, Stoic, and Christian elements is possible.[92]

It was because Stoicism stressed moral philosophy and linked it with profound speculative problems (man's relation to the physical universe, his obligation to the "inner law" of conscience, his ties with his neighbors) that "no limit can be set to its leaven within the undivided Church. The results may have been good, they may have been bad . . . [but] they are there" (Wenley, *op. cit.*, pp. 112, 128). The philosophy of the Stoa, with its perennial appeal to all for whom "knowledge has ripened into meditation and has prompted high desire," vivified the dignity of the man who, sure of the approval of his own conscience, could personally govern the glorious realm of his private self or — by the same sign — "could account himself peculiarly worth the special aid vouchsafed by infinite Grace" (*ibid.*, p. 110). St. Jerome spoke of *Seneca noster* — "our Seneca."

Yet, as always, there was a *Sic* and a *Non* and a need to reconcile them. Christianity had of necessity to reject the Stoic pantheistic

pervades *The City of God*" (R. M. Wenley, *Stoicism and Its Influence* [Boston, 1924], p. 127).

90. See Charles Nisard, *Le triumvirat littéraire au XVIᵉ siècle: Juste Lipse, Joseph Scaliger et Isaac Casaubon* (Paris, n.d.).

91. Jason Lewis Saunder, *Justus Lipsius: The Philosophy of Renaissance Stoicism* (New York, 1955), p. 85. See also the review by Charles Trinkaus in *Renaissance News*, X (1957), p. 34: Lipsius was interested in the possible theology that might be derived from Stoic metaphysics.

92. Mario Monaco, "Racine and the Problem of Suicide," *PMLA*, LXX (1955), p. 444.

identification of nature with the deity; its spiritualist materialism; its denial of reality to the incorporeal; its sense of inexorable fate. The concept of moral progress in the world as a whole was fundamental to the Church Fathers; yet its possibility was denied by Marcus Aurelius (d. 180 A.D.). As against Stoic pessimism, the Christian, defying experience, declared that with God all things are possible.[93] Lactantius, who flourished in the last half of the fourth and the beginning of the fifth century, opposed the severity and the inhumanity of Stoic doctrine: passions should be channelized, not extirpated; fear is holy when it is the fear of God.[94] Augustine (d. 430), insisting as he did on the role of the will, was forced to reject Stoic apathy, as Lactantius had already done. In Augustine's view, suppression of the passions would be a denial of life; he urged that the will, stirred up by appetite, be directed toward worthy objects (*ibid.*, p. 72, n. 47). And then there was the problem of interpreting human history. Augustine could not accept the Stoic theory of repeated cycles; for him history moved in a straight line: nothing so clearly exploded the theory of cycles as the eternal life of the saints.[95] Most fundamental of all was the opposition of Stoic error and the Christian sense of guilt through sin; of the gospel of humility, love, and pity and the Stoic gospel of pride (Alston, *op. cit.*, p. 9).

It will not surprise us, therefore, when — in spite of the impressive favor with which Stoic teaching was adapted to Christianity by Spanish thinkers — we find in the year 1650 a title like this: *Seneca Impugned by Seneca in Political and Moral Questions*, published at Madrid by Alonso Núñez de Castro.[96] For such a book there was ample precedent. The atypical humanist Lorenzo Valla (d. 1457), emphasizing the irreconcilability of reason and faith, "broke decisively with the endeavors of both high Scholasticism and Humanist thought to create a synthesis of paganism and Christianity" and condemned the Stoics in his *De voluptate ac bono*.[97] But what we

93. Leonard Alston, *Stoic and Christian in the Second Century* (London, 1906), pp. 42–43.

94. Baker, *The Dignity of Man* . . . , p. 136.

95. William A. Christian, "Augustine on the Creation of the World," *Harvard Theological Review*, XLVI (1953), 11–12.

96. There was an anti-Stoic movement in France in the latter part of the seventeenth century. See Monaco, *op. cit.*, p. 444.

97. Charles Trinkaus in Cassirer *et al.* (eds.), *op. cit.*, pp. 147–48.

most need to remember is that, in spite of occasional opposition, the favor accorded to Stoic doctrine in Spain was great, in the Middle Ages, in the Renaissance, and in the Post-Renaissance. "The view that there was any hostility between medieval thinkers and the pagan classics (Christianly interpreted, of course) is a figment of some modern imaginations." [98] In like manner it is erroneous to assume, as various critics have done, that the expression of Stoic philosophical attitudes in Spanish Renaissance works shows hostility to Christianity, or even a bold spirit of innovation.

Manuel de Montolíu begins the fourth chapter of his book, *The Soul of Spain and its Reflection in the Literature of the Golden Age*,[99] with a dramatic account of the return of Fray Luis de León to his professor's chair at Salamanca on December 30, 1576, free at last after five long years as a prisoner of the Inquisition; and of the beginning moments, and the beginning words, of his first lecture on that historic day: *Dicebamus hesterna die* — "as we were saying yesterday." This noble restraint, says Montolíu (p. 359), is expressive of the entire Stoic sense of life which at all times characterized the Spanish soul. The idea has been much repeated, both before and after Montolíu's evocation. One scholar finds "an atavistic Senecan tradition" expressed in the fifteenth-century Juan de Lucena's free translation of the *De vitae felicitate* of Bartolomeo Fazio (*ca.* 1445).[100] Another believes that the proverbial assertion of individuality and personal worth, *Soy quien soy* — "I am who I am" —, is not only an extension to the human sphere of the Biblical "I am what I am," but also that it is "a typical manifestation of that Spanish national trait [the Will], derived from Christian Stoicism." [101] Américo Castro is much closer to reality when he insists: "man is not a demigod, master of himself; . . . absolute stoicism is an unreal abstraction. . . . The vaunted inner calm of Stoicism does not make it possible to express the totality of human existence,

98. *Ibid.*; see also Gerald G. Walsh, *Medieval Humanism* (New York, 1942), p. 28. On Seneca, see St. Augustine, *The City of God*, Book VII, chs. 10, 11.

99. *El alma de España y sus reflejos en la literatura del siglo de de oro* (Barcelona, n.d.).

100. Margherita Morreale, "El tratado de Juan de Lucena sobre la felicidad," *NRFH*, IX (1955), 1, n. 3; see also pp. 2, 20.

101. Leo Spitzer, "Soy quien soy," *NRFH*, I (1947), 113–27; see especially p. 127.

and . . . it is surprising that many have centered the most salient traits of the Spanish character in Senecan philosophy. . . . " [102] Quite obviously, Castro's use of the adjective *absolute* detracts from the strength of his statement; yet the statement is valid: we may not accurately speak of "the Stoic sense of life in the Spanish soul," as Montolíu does in a marginal note. What we may say is that much of the Stoic ethic appealed strongly to the men of Christian Spain in the centuries under review.

Going through the ample indices of Solana's *Historia de la filosofía española*, one learns, perhaps to his surprise, that Seneca is given relatively very few mentions; the same holds true for Epictetus, though Cicero fares considerably better. All of these names are thrown into the shade by the name of Aristotle — no Stoic. Seneca and Cicero are used by the philosophers and the near-philosophers very much as they are used by men of letters: as sources of insight and of authority, along with Pliny or the Church Fathers. Vives, in his *De tradendis disciplinis*, classifies writers according to the field or department in which their works are most effective, including among books conducive to good morals: Cicero's *De finibus* and *Quaestiones tusculanae*; Seneca's *De beneficiis*, *De clementia*, *De consolatione*, *De vita beata*; the *De consolatione philosophiae* of Boethius; and the *De utraque philosophia* of Petrarch. A similar departmentalization is offered by Sebastián Fox Morcillo (d. 1560?) in his *De philosophici studii ratione*: Seneca is mentioned as an authority on questions of natural philosophy, along with Aelian, Theophrastus, Dioscorides, Pliny, Georgius Agricola, and Edward Wolton (I, 81, 577).

Yet the importance of Stoic doctrine in the thinking of Spanish writers of all sorts is beyond question. Menéndez y Pelayo's *Bibliografía hispano-latina clásica* devotes seventy-nine pages to the influence of Boethius. [103] The history of that influence is yet to be written; its impact may be sensed by anyone who examines *Hispano-Classical Translations Printed between 1482 and 1699: A Study of*

102. "Incarnation in *Don Quixote*," in *Cervantes Across the Centuries*, eds. A. Flores and M. J. Benardete (New York, 1947), p. 147.

103. Ed. E. Sánchez Reyes (Santander, 1950–53), I, 274–353. On the influence of Boethius in Renaissance England, see E. M. W. Tillyard, *The Elizabethan World Picture* (London, 1948), p. 51.

the Prologues and a Critical Bibliography by Theodore S. Beardsley, Jr.[104]

Limiting herself to Seneca and to one hundred and fifty Spanish writers of ascetic or mystical tendencies in the sixteenth and seventeenth centuries, María Josefa González-Haba confirms her initial statement that "the presence of Seneca is strongly felt in all Spanish literature" by extending it to the principal *espirituales* of the Golden Age: the influence of Seneca, while not exclusive or universal, is "extensive," even "very great." There are authors that can properly be called disciples of Seneca; others that cite him and are influenced by him; still others that show incidental influence. Finally, there are some who show no influence at all. These are few. The great majority endeavor to explain Seneca's thought and to use it to strengthen Christian doctrine.[105]

In the fourteenth century the Prince of Castile Don Juan Manuel wrote in his *Treatise on the Assumption of the Virgin*: "Certain it is that many men, both philosophers and learned men in general, who never knew or never accepted the Catholic faith, said very many and very true things which illuminate the holy faith of the Church."[106] In the following century this eclecticism caused the moralists of Spain during the waning Middle Ages and the budding Renaissance to accept Senecan doctrine as one of their principal sources of illumination.[107] So numerous and widespread is the influence that the only possible procedure here is to offer samples.

About the year 1436, Alfonso de la Torre described an allegorical gathering in the "house" of Reason: "and in the midst of the house was yet another company of very respectable men of great authority, and all through the house wandered other damsels, angelic and beautiful beyond compare, and the two sisters, Reason and Truth, seated themselves above, and the whole blessed gather-

104. University of Pennsylvania doctoral dissertation, 1961; available in typescript or in microfilm.

105. "Seneca en la espiritualidad española de los siglos XVI y XVII," *Rev. de filosofía*, XI (1952), 287, 302.

106. *Libro infinido y Tractado de la Asunción*, ed. J. M. Blecua (Granada, 1952), p. 94.

107. This body of doctrine "dominates without rival" at this time, according to Menéndez y Pelayo, *La Ciencia española*, ed. E. Sánchez Reyes (Santander, 1953–54), I, 213.

ing round about them, except Socrates and Seneca, who sat at their feet. . . . "[108] That these two wise men, one Greek and one Roman, are singled out by name, and are seated not in a vague "round about" but at the feet of Reason and Truth, seems clearly to be a mark of special reverence for their pre-Christian wisdom.

Somewhat later, near 1450, Fray Martín de Córdoba wrote in his *Compendio de la Fortuna*: [109]

And therefore Seneca says to Lucilius . . . : "money will not make you like unto God, for in God there is nothing of the sort; nor will fine raiment . . . for God is naked; nor fame . . . , for He is known to few; nor a horde of servants carrying your bed as you travel over the countryside, for it is God who carries and sustains the world; nor can beauty, health, and strength make you blessed, for all things grow old and wither." Therefore, says Seneca, let us seek that which can make us blessed: . . . an upright, a kind, and a virtuous heart, because if we have this we are similar to God.[110]

As we pass into the sixteenth century, we find that Vives, discussing the proper reading matter for the Christian woman, sets up as a requirement — before one gives herself (or himself) over to the perusal of novels of chivalry — that the admirer of those secular books have read first "Cicero and Seneca, or St. Jerome or Holy Scripture," and have mended his or her life according to their teaching.[111]

Seneca and "Senecan firmness" [112] are to be found on every hand in the poetic works of the generation of Garcilaso de la Vega — a Christianized Stoicism, as we have seen (with particular reference to Garcilaso) in Chapter IV of our Volume I ("Courtly Love and Platonic Vision").

Then comes the generation of the "two Luises," Fray Luis de León and Fray Luis de Granada. The former, as is well known, "with his resolutely austere spirit made his own the severe morality

108. *Visión delectable*, BAE, XXXVI, 377a.
109. Ed. P. Fernando Rubio Alvarez (El Escorial-Madrid, 1958), pp. 49–50.
110. The same ideas and ideals are shared by the poets: Juan de Mena, the Marqués de Santillana, and many others. The Stoic element in Santillana's poem *Bías contra Fortuna* was discussed in the final chapter ("Fortune and Fate") of our Volume II. For Mena, see Rafael Lapesa's "El elemento moral en *El Laberinto* de Mena: Su influencia en la disposición de la obra," *HR*, XXVII (1959), 257–66.
111. Cited by Henry Thomas, *Spanish and Portuguese Romances of Chivalry* (Cambridge, 1920), p. 163.
112. See R. Lapesa, *La trayectoria poética de Garcilaso* (Madrid, 1948), p. 165.

of the Stoa." [113] The other Luis, Fray Luis de Granada, requires treatment at greater length.

In his interpretation of the Christian creed, *Introducción del Símbolo de la fe* (1582), Luis de Granada wrote: "This was understood by that illustrious moral philosopher Seneca, who said in a word much of what our Religion teaches. For, speaking about God, Seneca says that He treats us as we treat Him, indicating thereby that those who reverence and honor God as veritable Lord and Father, are treated by Him as faithful servants and sons. What more could the philosopher have said had he been a Christian? How great and how universal is the doctrine contained in these brief words!" [114]

At an earlier date (1554), when Fray Luis was writing under the influence of Savonarola,[115] he had actually expressed a repugnance toward "gentile philosophers and humanistic studies," accepting them as a necessary evil in a world now devoted to them.[116] It seems appropriate to repeat here what I wrote in my review of Laín Entralgo's study of Fray Luis' concept of man. Among Luis de Granada's principal sources are: the Church Fathers; the *Hexameron* of St. Basil and its adaptation in Latin by St. Ambrose; Galen; Avicenna ("a great philosopher, though a Moor"); and the *History of the Composition of the Human Body* by Juan de Valverde — a follower and adaptor of the findings of the founder of modern anatomy, Andreas Vesalius, whose *De fabrica humani corporis* (1543) was one of the first products of the "new" science. This eclecticism is thoroughly characteristic of Fray Luis' generation in Spain. As was to be expected, Fray Luis professes the Christian idea of man — but in a complex manner. His early work, the *Book on Prayer and Meditation* (1554), is tinged with anthropological pessimism: man has been reduced to wretchedness by the fall. The work of his old age, the *Introduction to the Creed* (1582–85), is radiant with anthropological optimism: man is the crowning glory of the universe, created in God's image. Other works stand between these two ex-

---

113. Alain Guy, *La pensée de Fray Luis de León* (Limoges, 1943), pp. 439–40. See also T. E. May, "Fray Luis de León and Boethius," *MLR*, IX (1954), 183–92; Manuel de Montolíu, "Un tema estoico en la lírica de Fray Luis de León," *Estudios dedicados a Menéndez Pidal*, IV (Madrid, 1953), 461–67.

114. *Obras*, ed. Fray Justo Cuervo (Madrid, 1906–8), V, 281–82.

115. M. Bataillon, "De Savonarole à Louis de Grenade," *RLC*, XVI (1936), 23–39.

116. Laín Entralgo, *op. cit.*, pp. 336–37; see also pp. 21, 22, 68, 96.

tremes. It is obvious that Fray Luis cannot be quoted in support of a supposed progression from Renaissance light to baroque darkness. Indeed, the definitive edition of his *Sinners' Guide* is much more optimistic than the edition condemned by the Inquisition (because of its stressing of inward religion as opposed to exterior ceremonies). Nor is it possible to attribute his increasing optimism to a progressively mystical attitude toward the world as God's temple. He is most mystical in the years 1554–1556.[117] On the first page of the *Símbolo de la fe*, Luis de Granada wrote, referring to Seneca: "And since in this exercise [the contemplation of things divine] the philosophers are in agreement with the Christians, it seems to me proper to insert here an account of the manner in which this great philosopher conducted himself in this regard. To do so will serve to throw into confusion many Christians . . . who never have had an inkling of what this pagan philosopher practiced always." Other passages no less eloquent are quoted by Laín Entralgo (*op. cit.*, pp. 337 ff.).

The need to conserve space compels us to move onward. The year 1588 is the date of Malón de Chaide's *Conversión de la Magdalena*. In it the author takes up again (after the manner of Vives) the question as to whether one should read romances of chivalry. His contention, of course, is that one should not — though the defenders of those books "will persuade you that *Don Florisel* is the *Book of the Maccabees*; *Don Belianís*, the *Morals of St. Gregory*; *Amadís*, the *Offices* of St. Ambrose; and *Lisuarte*, Seneca's *Book of Clemency*" (cited by Thomas, *op. cit.*, p. 175).

We pass on to the years of Justus Lipsius and Francisco de Quevedo. Speaking of England in the same years (George Chapman's *Revenge of Bussy d'Ambois* was printed in 1610), Theodore Spencer says (*op. cit.*, pp. 206–7) that "religion, science, Stoicism or frivolity . . . each in its different way, seemed to take the burden of despair from men's minds." This was the time when Guillaume du Vair, along with Chapman and with Lipsius, was "haunted by the desire to harmonize ancient Stoicism . . . with modern Christian morality."[118]

---

117. See *HR*, XVI (1948), 180; Fray Justo Cuervo, "Fray Luis de Granada y la Inquisición," *Homenaje a Menéndez y Pelayo* (Madrid, 1899), I, pp. 733 ff.; Bataillon, *Erasmo y España*, II, 193, 373.

118. Frank L. Schoell, *Etudes sur l'humanisme continental en Angleterre à la fin*

Though Quevedo imitates Seneca both in his style and in the conduct of his personal life, the years 1630–1635 mark a particularly acute "crisis of Senequism." He associates Epictetus with Seneca and struggles to conciliate Stoicism with Christian faith, following the example of Lipsius and endeavoring to establish a link between Epictetus and the Old Testament, particularly the Book of Job. Yet in none of this activity is there any servile imitation. Quevedo, though he needs a bulwark against the assaults of Fortune, is far removed from the *otium* recommended for the Stoic "wise man" (*sapiens*). And he recognizes, as he could not fail to do, that Seneca is not fully assimilable to Christianity.[119]

Quevedo insists that the chief end of man in this life is the exercise of virtue (*ibid.*, p. 914b). Unable to do without him (as the Church also was), he maintains that Seneca — though keen of mind and admirably learned, though he condenses into small compass "oceans of knowledge," though his style flashes like lightning — offers nothing that cannot be obtained more advantageously in the works of St. Peter Chrysologus (pp. 930–31; see also p. 313b). Quevedo is even hostile to the science of the *Quaestiones naturales*: "It is said of experimental science (and rightly) that it punishes the keenest intelligences" (p. 782a).

He cites the deficiencies of Stoic doctrine: the lack of pity, the suppression of the passions (whereas Christ experienced them), the extolling of suicide (*ibid.*, pp. 747, 749a). He falls back on fideism:

de la Renaissance (Paris, 1926), p. 105. The Jesuits had already made the adjustment: "If the Jesuits were so enthused by 'good old Epictetus,' . . . by Seneca and by Plutarch, whom they assigned as readings or explained to their pupils in class . . . , it was because the sayings and actions of these Stoics are both a powerful affirmation of reason and of the freedom of the will in opposition to Protestant fideism, and are also sources of energy. Their agreement with Christianity — since reason is the sum total of Stoicism and the basis of Christianity — made of them an ideal interpreter which raised the level of ancient wisdom to the heights of truth and girded the will for the greatest possible effort, *Ad majorem Dei gloriam*" (Dainville, *op. cit.*, I, 245). The Jesuit Pedro de Rivadeneyra, in his *Tratado de la tribulación* (1589), wrote that in all his works Seneca "shows himself grave and severe, and in those which treat of human misery and of the strength of spirit necessary to endure it, is marvelous and divine. . . ." Seneca will be cited, the Spanish author says, to reveal to those who possess — as Seneca did not — the light of grace, how much can be accomplished by the exercise of so excellent and so necessary a virtue as Christian patience" ([Madrid, n.d.], pp. 144–45).

119. Pierre Delacroix, "Quevedo et Sénèque," *BHi*, LVI (1954), 305–7. See also J. M. Chacón y Calvo, "Quevedo y la tradición senequista," *Realidad*, III (1948), 318–42. On the belief that Epictetus had contact with the early Christians, see Quevedo's *Obras en prosa, ed. cit.*, p. 991.

though reason is more to be trusted than the fallible senses, much greater is the superiority of faith over reason (p. 1031b). In short, as Ernest Mérimée said of Quevedo: "He remains a faithful disciple of the Scholastics." [120]

In spite of all objections, there is no escape from Stoicism. Quevedo announces his list of "great books": "Never fail to have at hand the Books of Wisdom by Solomon, the *Doctrine* of Epictetus, the *Warning (Conminatorio)* of Phocylides, Theognis, the writings of Seneca, and read with special diligence the books of Job. . . . You will be a student, a good student, if the reading of St. Paul is your main occupation, and the study of the Saints, your task." [121] Phocilides, according to Quevedo, "expressed in precepts . . . all the commandments of the Divine Law . . . rules for Christian conduct . . . though he lived so many years before Christ" (*ibid.*, p. 667a). Quevedo's greatest praise of Montaigne is that the reader of the famous *Essais*, though he read not Plutarch or Seneca, will nonetheless be reading Seneca and Plutarch (p. 757a). Indeed, the Jesuit Juan Eusebio Nieremberg, as he gave his *imprimatur* to *The Cradle and the Grave* (printed 1635), expressed satisfaction over Quevedo's having set forth in that work "the most brilliant Stoic sentiments in the light of the Christian faith." "One could think," Father Nieremberg continues, "that Epictetus has become a Spaniard; that Chrysippus has acquired clarity; that Zeno has become kind; Antipater, merciful; Cleanthes, vivid; and Seneca, Christian." [122]

Gracián (d. 1658), with his constant concern for the enigmas *de tejas abajo*, makes use of Seneca as a source of worldly wisdom. In the foreword to the reader of *El Criticón* he announces that he will

120. *Essai sur la vie et les oeuvres de Francisco de Quevedo* (Paris, 1886), p. 264.

121. *The Cradle and the Grave*, in *Obras en prosa, ed. cit.*, p. 915b.

122. *Ibid.*, p. 898. In his "Approbation" of Quevedo's *Epictetus Translated* (1634), Father Nieremberg wrote: "The Stoics deserve the sacred origin which is here given them. . . . No human being was the Author of the Stoic doctrine in those aspects of it which touch on virtue [de la doctrina estoica, cuanto a la estima de la virtud, no fué hombre Autor]" (*Obras en verso*, ed. L. Astrana Marín [Madrid, 1932], p. 718). See Raimundo Lida, "Cartas de Quevedo," *Cuadernos americanos*, XII (1935), 193–210, especially 196, 203; *idem*, "Quevedo y la *Introducción a la vida devota*," *NRFH*, VII (1953), 656; *idem*, "La *España defendida* de Quevedo y la síntesis paganocristiana," *Imago mundi*, II (1955), 3.

"imitate" — in the best tradition of Renaissance *imitatio* — "the allegories of Homer, the tales of Aesop, the doctrinal *sententiae* of Seneca . . . , the judgments of Boccalini, the satire of [John] Barclay." In the twelfth Crisi (chapter) of Part II he introduces a heading, "Competition of the Sciences," and tells how each one of the various sciences and arts sought for itself the title of queen, of sun of the understanding, of empress of letters. Having made obeisance to Theology as occupying a holy place altogether removed from such competitive designs, the others (and here Gracián actually uses the phrase *de tejas abajo*) are surrounded by their special followings, persons especially gifted with imaginative power gathering about Natural Philosophy, for example, while those of great power of judgment joined the train of Ethics. Among all these, two men stood out: Plato, "eternalizing our thought of divinity, and Seneca, [with his] moral maxims." [123] In Part I, Crisi XIII, there is a conversation between the contemporary Duque de Villahermosa and a lapidary who has in his possession the "philosophers' stone" (a piece of jet). The lapidary says that the stone teaches the greatest wisdom, which is how to live. "In what manner?" asks the Duke. "By not giving a fig for all the world," is the reply; "by not being a fool: that is, this stone teaches how to live like a king, a thing men have not yet learned how to do." This is none other than the Stoic doctrine of *nil admirari*. The Stoic, with his *ataraxia*, is unmoved, though the heavens fall.

This grimmer aspect of Seneca is evident in the title of a work published at Murcia in 1652: *Men against Fortune: Political Schools of Seneca Wherein is Taught How to Resist Misfortune and Be Comforted Amid the Miseries of This Time.* But the other Seneca — not merely the impassive *sapiens* surrounded by political ruin, but the philosopher and moralist who points back to Job — is not forgotten. Somewhat earlier Jerónimo de la Cruz published a work entitled *Evangelical Job, Stoicism Explained: Ethical, Civil, and Political Doctrine* (Zaragoza, 1638).

There were also those who found Stoicism unattractive and who dissented from the acceptance of a Christianized Seneca. The idea

123. Ed. Miguel Romera-Navarro (Philadelphia, 1938–40), II, 342.

that Seneca had been influenced by the Biblical Job was criticized by Juan de Jáuregui in *El Retraído* (Barcelona, 1635).[124] Juan Pablo Mártir Rizo, in his *Norte de príncipes* (Madrid, 1626), showed little enthusiasm for Stoic apathy; as did Diego de Saavedra Fajardo, who in his *República literaria* (1612, 1640) objected to the Stoic conception of fate.[125] Claudio Clemente even classed Seneca, along with Machiavelli, Jean Bodin, and others, among the hated masters of the doctrine of "Reason of State."[126] In 1650 Antonio Núñez de Castro brought out at Madrid his *Seneca Impugned by Seneca in Political and Moral Questions*, in which he aimed to show: that all the apparent truths in Seneca are not necessarily true; and that the Bible is the safest and best source of political wisdom. He remarks in his prologue: "If any Stoic philosopher of these days should take offense and wish to come out in defense of Seneca, I will not oppose him [*le dexaré libre el campo*]."

SPANISH BAROQUE SCHOLASTICISM

The Thomistic philosophy so characteristic of Spanish thought in the sixteenth century was, as we have seen, slow in making headway. The early equality of Thomism and Scotism at Alcalá meant that, opposing the rationalistic positions of the Thomists, there were teachers who maintained the superiority of will over intellect and held that the union of Christianity with Aristotelianism was unsuccessful. At Salamanca, teaching had scarcely been altered by the great European debates over the doctrine of William of Ockham, though nominalism was briefly taught there: Salamanca remained generally faithful to fundamental Scholasticism, to St. Thomas and to Peter Lombard.[127]

124. A century earlier Stoic teaching had colored the attitudes of at least one heretical group in Seville: they developed an asceticism more akin to Epictetus than to the Gospel (Bataillon, *Erasmo y España*, II, 137). This is, so far as I am aware, an isolated example of the tendency, so strong in Italy, to develop a naturalistic ethics based on Stoicism. See Cassirer *et al.* (eds.), *op. cit.*, p. 12.

125. Juan A. Maravall, *La philosophie politique espagnole au XVIIᵉ siècle dans ses rapports avec l'esprit de la Contre-Réforme* (Paris, 1955), p. 58, n. 3.

126. *El machiavelismo degollado por la christiana sabiduría de España y Austria* (Alcalá, 1637, cited *ibid.*; see also *ibid.*, p. 20).

127. Bataillon asks: "What part of nominalism was introduced into Spain at this time? Was it the spirit, or only the dead shell? . . . What was gained when one

There existed, therefore, in the early sixteenth century and in the two leading universities of Spain, a more or less peaceful competition between Thomism, Scotism, and nominalism, but with no powerful thinker to lead the way in any one of the three directions. This situation was corrected in 1526 when the Dominican Francisco de Vitoria assumed the first chair of theology at Salamanca. He made the *Summa Theologiae* of St. Thomas the basis of instruction and put an end to what Vives had termed "pseudo-dialectics." Vitoria died twenty years later, in 1546. He is regarded as the father of international law. His successor, Melchor Cano, whom some would rank next to St. Thomas, at his death in 1560 left in manuscript his *De locis theologicis*, which made his name imperishable. In this work he sought to establish scientifically the foundations of theology. Among his ten *loci* (sources of theology) he included the value of reason as manifested in science. Cano was in turn succeeded by Domingo de Soto, one of the teachers of Suárez (see below). Soto's *De justitia et jure*, a landmark in the philosophy of law, was widely imitated by the philosophers and theologians of his time.

Whereas Luther regarded reason as the enemy of faith, Vitoria, Cano, and Soto upheld the opposite view. Thomism, which up to that time had followed an indecisive course in Spain, became there the dominant philosophy. In a famous series of lectures at Alcalá, Soto "ruined nominalism" (Cereceda, *op. cit.*, I, 55–56).

We thus stand at a threshold. At a time when in the rest of Europe certain thinkers turned their backs on the past — attacking Aristotle with the harshness of a Petrus Ramus or an Hermolao Barbaro, when others sought satisfaction in the natural theosophy of Cardano or of Paracelsus, or in the Averroism of Niphus and Vanini, and still others — like the Romanized Spaniard Juan Ginés de Sepúlveda — defended the Aristotelian school with all their might, in Spain a sort of collective decision was made: the Spaniards silently but firmly cast their vote for the superiority of reason. Spain, soon to

replaced Peter Lombard by *Questions* on Peter Lombard? . . . Nevertheless, it is not impossible that Durand's thought retained enough life to influence the most interesting speculative efforts of the Spanish sixteenth century, that Gómez Pereira received its imprint at Salamanca, as Vives received it at the University of Paris" (*Erasmo y España*, I, 21). See also V. Beltrán de Heredia, "Accidental y efímera aparición del nominalismo en Salamanca," *Ciencia tomista*, LX (1942), 62–101.

become a nation of mystics, turned away from the more mystical and Franciscan tendencies of Scotism; and she also — by rejecting nominalism — chose the path of Milton in opposition to the path of Bacon; she followed the path of Francisco Suárez rather than the path of Hobbes and Locke. Her philosophical efforts would bear fruit in the work of Leibnitz and in the German universities of the Enlightenment; whereas in the nineteenth century the works of her philosophers would become largely a dead letter and would remain so until revived by the renewed interest, almost in our own day, in Spanish baroque Scholasticism. Meanwhile, the industrial revolution, and the philosophic transition from the world view of Aristotle to that of Newton, would be accomplished by other **nations**.

"Already in the Middle Ages the . . . method of Scholasticism had sought to reconcile not only Plato and Aristotle, but Ptolemy and Pythagoras, Epicurus and the other philosophers, Cicero and Boethius, the *Timaeus* and Genesis." [128] In the sixteenth century the task of reconciliation had to be undertaken anew: the Church had been split asunder, a New World had been discovered, Copernicus had challenged Ptolemy. It seems wrong to call Francisco de Vitoria the father of baroque Scholasticism,[129] inasmuch as his latest philosophical work was published in 1539. This leadership belongs, rather, to his successors, though they acquired it as a result of his reform. Much more of a theologian than a philosopher, Vitoria extended the limits of theology to include everything from the attributes of the Deity to the ultimate ramifications of public and private law and converted Spain into "a nation of theologians." His influence, says Menéndez y Pelayo,[130] is everywhere, and through him and his pupils, Spain became "the mother of the most illustrious Scholastic thinkers since St. Thomas." What does that claim really mean?

Kristeller says of the work of Renaissance thinkers in general —

128. Alois Dempf, *La concepción del mundo en la Edad Media* (Madrid, 1958), p. 118.

129. Guy, *Les philosophes espagnols* . . . , I, 51.

130. Cited by Marcial Solana in *Los grandes escolásticos españoles de los siglos XVI y XVII: Sus doctrinas filosóficas y su significación en la historia de la filosofía* (Madrid, n.d.), pp. 26, title page.

and we may apply the statement to our Spanish baroque Scholastics — that it seems "to lack permanent significance because it was superseded when modern science and modern philosophy received a new and more solid foundation in the seventeenth century through Galileo and Kepler, Bacon and Descartes." [131] Referring to nineteenth-century and twentieth-century Neo-Scholasticism and discussing the relation of Scholasticism to modern philosophy, José Ferrater Mora cites two extremes: the position, on the one hand, of those who held that Scholastic philosophy represents a pause — a blank — between ancient and modern thought; and, on the other, the contention of those who asserted that it is modern philosophy that lacks value and significance. These extreme positions, he hastens to add, were quickly abandoned in favor of a great mutual comprehension. Not only have many nineteenth-century Neo-Scholastics found in modern philosophy elements which to them are indispensable; many thinkers of the opposing camps have, in their turn, rediscovered Scholastic values. Especially in the study of the history of philosophy has this been true: various investigators have accentuated the important role played by classical Scholasticism in the origin and development of modern philosophy and have seen in it a bridge between two periods of thought — the ancient and the modern — which, in the eighteenth and nineteenth centuries, were thought of as being completely separate.[132]

Under the heading *Escolástica*, Ferrater Mora refers (*ibid.*, p. 280) to the subject of our present section, that is, to the so-called baroque Scholasticism of Spain, active from 1550 to 1630. This designation separates the Spanish movement from the nineteenth-century Neo-Scholasticism just discussed. The Spanish movement had its influence on Leibnitz and on Spinoza, on the protestant Aristotelians of Central Europe, and very especially on university teaching in Holland, Germany, and Bohemia, especially from the time that Philip Melanchthon decided to make Protestantism "philosophical." The influence of the Jesuit Suárez's *Disputations*

---

131. "Renaissance Platonism," p. 88.
132. *Diccionario* . . . , p. 655. See the long list of names, arranged by countries, on p. 656. Most familiar to the layman, perhaps, will be Cardinal Mercier and the School of Louvain in Belgium, Thomas Harper (d. 1893), and John Rickaby (d. 1927) in England.

is patent. Rigorously speaking it was the Jesuits who, though relying on an earlier movement, were the prime movers in most of these developments. Five generations of Spanish thinkers can be articulated into this "baroque Scholasticism": the first representative is Vitoria (d. 1546); the last, perhaps, Francisco Oviedo (d. 1651).

Before discussing Suárez, it will be well to pause to examine the position, in this matter of philosophy, of the founder of the Society of Jesus, Ignatius de Loyola, whose *Spiritual Exercises* were printed in 1548. St. Ignatius sets forth as his eleventh Rule that it is necessary:

> To praise positive and Scholastic philosophy; because, as it is more characteristic of the positive doctors [St. Jerome, St. Augustine, St. Gregory, etc.] to move the emotions to serve God with all love; so it is more characteristic of the Scholastics [St. Thomas, St. Bonaventure, Peter Lombard, etc.] to define or declare for our time the things necessary for eternal salvation and for impugning all errors and fallacies. Because the Scholastic doctors, being more modern, not only take advantage of the true interpretation [*inteligencia*] of Scripture or of the works of the positive and sainted doctors of the Church, but also being themselves illumined by divine grace [*virtud divina*], avail themselves of the Councils, the canons, and the constitutions of Mother Church.[133]

We thus have, as it were, two "founding fathers" of the philosophical renewal in Spain, neither of whom is, in the strict sense of the word, a philosopher who adduces rational proofs of rational propositions. St. Ignatius, like Vitoria, was to influence the movement of renewal principally through the work of his "sons." Loyola is remembered as a reformer and organizer; Vitoria, as the abolisher of the still prevalent "pseudo-dialecticism" and the originator of the new concepts of international law soon to be taken up and developed by Hugo Grotius (d. 1645).

Francisco Suárez, 1548–1617

So much has already been said about the most distinguished of the Spanish thinkers of the Renaissance and post-Renaissance that it will be sufficient here to give a brief account of his *modus operandi*, that is to say, of the structure of his philosophy, and to touch

133. *Obras completas*, ed. Ignacio Iparraguirre (Madrid, 1952), p. 237.

on his relationship (only recently pointed out) to the philosophers of the present day. Suárez's first task was one of simplification: he gave an account of four centuries of Scholastic tradition. In the general mass of opinion, he sought to define "the true meaning" and to do so "in the light of things" (en vista de las cosas).[134] It is a question of a new confrontation with reality, insofar as reality is accessible to human reason. For him the sources of knowledge are three: sacred and human authority, and reason, "each in its proper rank." He relies on a vast erudition, in which there is only one lacuna — for the subsequent history of philosophy, the most important of all — physical and mathematical science and speculation. Among all his authorities, Aristotle and St. Thomas have special eminence. But Suárez does not "swear in their words." When they appear to be in error, Suárez seeks to discover what, in each case, Aristotle or St. Thomas *meant to say*. This he determines by a collation of the difficult passage with the entire output of the author. Marías reduces to six the main aspects of Suárez's method: (1) the methodical separation of philosophy from theology and revelation; (2) the assumption of metaphysics as the essential base of philosophy; (3) the recognition of philosophy as propaedeutic to theology; (4) the acceptance of the relationship of philosophy and theology; (5) the insistence on philosophy as mediator (*mediatez de la filosofía*) — that philosophy is a moving from present to past and past to present — in order to search out the "true meaning" of Aristotelian-Scholastic doctrine; and (6) a certain "simultaneousness" in the use of the philosophic past, i.e., an interpretative historization of philosophy.

So much for method. Ferrater Mora, in his essay "Suárez and Modern Philosophy" (see above, note 7), finds Suárez's modernity not only in details that he gave to Leibnitz (*puissance obédientielle; potentia obendentialis activa*, etc.; see p. 288), but also in his treatment of essence and existence (pp. 290–91): created beings exist by virtue of an intrinsic principle, not by reason of an external quality; essence is a possibility susceptible of converting itself into being. This reappears in Leibnitz. "It is as if essence had a certain claim to existence, as if *essentia per se tenderit ad existentiam*" (p. 293).

134. I am following Marías, *La escolástica* . . . , pp. 84 ff.

This insight can be much more clearly understood "if we place it under the light of Suárez's rational distinction" (pp. 293–94). The same problem of essence-existence, with a new method and a new terminology, stands at the center of contemporary philosophy: "Both Suárez and Leibnitz seem to us to abandon their historic position and to advance straight toward the forefront of our epoch" (p. 294). Spanish baroque Scholasticism, therefore, is something more than an interesting antique, something other than an object of dissection for historians and scholars. It presents, on the contrary, a "living and palpitating reality" (*ibid.*).[135]

SCIENCE AND RELIGION

The reconciliation of scientific fact and religious faith had been undertaken by Melchor Cano in his *De locis theologicis* (1563), a work which is theological in character rather than philosophic. In the course of our survey of Spanish philosophical writing we have seen a general conservativeness and, opposed to it at times, a surprising boldness in demanding that experience correct authority. In summary it may be said that Spaniards did not tend to embrace the naturalistic philosophy of the Latin Averroists, or to follow their continuators in carefully leaving to one side the "notional" in order to concentrate on those aspects of reality that the human intellect can confidently analyze — *count, measure, weigh* — and by these means interpret. For practically all our Spanish thinkers, the supreme source of authority — considered as the greatest of the books existing in the universe and as constituting the source from which human knowledge is derived — was the Bible. But the Scriptures did not explain everything; nor did the Church Fathers or the Church Councils. Experience insisted that men heed her voice, and men did. Let us examine how they heeded her, taking as example a single author, whose works fall outside the field of phi-

135. The bibliography on baroque Scholasticism is large and can be consulted in philosophical bibliographies. By way of a sample, I mention two studies: K. Eschweiler, "Die Philosophie der spanischen Spätscholastik auf den Universitäten des siebzehnten Jahrhunderts" and *idem*, "Rodrigo de Arriaga, S. J.: ein Beitrag zur Geschichte der Barockscholastik," both in H. Finke (ed.), *Gesammelte Aufätze zur Kulturgeschichte Spaniens*, in the series *Spanische Forschungen der Görresgesellschaft* (Münster i. W.), I (1928), 251–325, and III (1931), 253–85.

losophy properly so-called but nonetheless have great significance because they impinge on cosmology and related subjects.

In his *Historia natural y moral de las Indias* (1590) the Jesuit José de Acosta reports that he felt chilly while crossing the Equator. "Here I confess that I laughed, and made sport of the *Meteorologica* of Aristotle and his philosophy, as I saw that, in the place and at the time that, according to Aristotle's rules, everything should be burning and on fire, I and my companions were cold. Indeed, there is not in all the world a more temperate and pleasant region than the equatorial one, but there is a great diversity in it and it is not constantly the same." [136] Several pages farther on, Acosta remarks: "If one were to write at length of these natural problems, and to do so with the degree of speculation that such notable phenomena require, I doubt not that one could produce a work equal to those of Pliny, Theophrastus, and Aristotle" (*ibid.*, p. 107).

Acosta shows noteworthy independence of mind: "Since all that has just been said appears to be true, certain, and clear — yet is not — only false inferences can be derived from it; inasmuch as the so-called middle or torrid zone of the earth is really inhabited by men, and we ourselves have dwelt in it for a long time, and to live there is very comfortable and pleasant. If that is so, and if as all are aware it is impossible to derive true conclusions from false premises, now that we find the conclusion to be in error — as we do — we must turn back by the same steps and examine closely the premises which were able to deceive us" (*ibid.*, p. 83). The heading of chapter VI, Book II, reads: "Wherein it Is Shown That in the Torrid Zone There Is Great Abundance of Water and Pasturage, Though Aristotle Denies This" (*ibid.*).

Acosta's estimate of the wisdom of the ancients is inevitably diminished: "Therefore we must infer that many things remained outside the ken of the ancients, and that no small part of the world is still hidden from us today" (*ibid.*, p. 47). This, he says, should be a stimulus to present-day thinkers: "In this torrid zone we find so many admirable properties that they rightly stir up and enliven our minds to inquire after their causes, guiding ourselves not so much by the doctrine of the ancients as by true reason and sure

136. Ed. Madrid (1792), I, 92.

experience" (*ibid.*, p. 76). Acosta's respect for Aristotle neverthe-less remains great, and he hesitates to contradict him: "I confess that this objection and this argument arouse such doubt in me that I am almost inclined to join those who reject the idea of compatible and incompatible qualities that Aristotle attributes to the elements . . . [but] I cannot bring myself to oppose Aristotle except in things that are very certain" (*ibid.*, pp. 99–100).

As it could not fail to do, this attitude of doubt extends also to the less-than-omniscient Fathers of the Church. These men, Acosta says, were concerned with knowing, serving, and preaching Christ. This was their main business, and in it they displayed great excel-lence. If in some points of philosophy or natural science they held opinions contrary to "good philosophy," we should not be sur-prised, nor should we marvel that "in the study and knowledge of the creatures they were not always completely accurate" (*ibid.*, p. 3).

A Word on the Inquisition

Acosta was evidently a man gifted with genuine scientific curi-osity. Are we to assume that this curiosity was held in restraint because of a fear of inquisitorial thought-control? In his case, almost certainly not. In our chapter on geographical expansion we saw that Acosta did not hesitate, on occasion, to take a stand completely opposed to what St. Augustine had taught. Certainly in his *Historia* he does not need to approach such thorny problems as those faced by Huarte in the first edition of his *Examen de ingenios*. Huarte's theories on the faculties of the soul were such — as Diego Alvarez said to him — that if they were allowed to stand it would be neces-sary to revise all the Scholastic treatises on the soul, as well as all current teaching in psychology, and even the catechism.[137] What we may assume in regard to Acosta and his task of adjusting long ac-cepted cosmological, biological, and anthropological ideas to re-cently discovered facts is that it was not official pressure, nor the Jesuit habit he wore, but the habitual thought pattern of his time and of his nation that dictated his statements of respect for Aristotle and the Church Fathers. In an age when "no man claimed for

137. See Rodrigo Sanz, the prologue to his (already-cited) edition of Huarte, I, xix–xx. The first edition (1575) of the *Examen de ingenios* had had warm ecclesiasti-cal approval; it was reissued in revised form in 1578 and 1581 with approving licenses.

himself or allowed another the right of believing as he chose" [138] anywhere in Europe, thought-control did exist in Spain as it existed elsewhere.[139] In Spain as in England, "on both sides [of the ecclesiastical revolutions and counter-revolutions of the century] there were heroic martyrs, cruel persecutors, prudent time-servers. If literary texts reflect little of this, their silence can be explained by the well-grounded fears of authors and their printers" (Lewis, *op. cit.*, p. 38). It would be possible to draw, for Spain, an imposing picture of official leniency, and to balance this with a sobering account of the "immanent inquisition" which not only might, but sometimes suddenly did introduce into a writer's life a period of terror (usually relieved by absolution). Yet this much can be asserted with assurance: the Spain of the sixteenth century was not created by the Inquisition; it developed, used, and abused the Inquisition as a means of strengthening, and later of defending, its cherished way of life.[140]

CONCLUSION

It is apparent that Spain did not produce a Hobbes or a Locke, a Descartes, a Spinoza, or a Leibnitz, much less a Newton. Yet she was not without important thinkers. Her most valuable contributions to European thought were, probably, her innovations in the philosophy of law (especially international law) and her modernization, for the sixteenth and seventeenth centuries, of the body of traditional metaphysical thought — a modernization which the philosophers of other countries adapted to the needs of their own philosophical systems and eventually relegated to oblivion as meta-

138. Lewis, *op. cit.*, p. 39; see also pp. 40–42.

139. Suárez's *Defensio fidei* was publicly burned as dangerous to the state — but not in Spain. The burning occurred in England and in France. See Ludwig Pfandl, *Geschichte der spanischen Nationalliteratur in ihrer Blütezeit* (Freiburg im Breisgau, 1929), p. 12, n. 1.

140. Jack Gibbs, reviewing Miguel de la Pinta Llorente's *La Inquisición española y los problemas de la cultura y la tolerancia* (Madrid, 1953), states that the author "shows from selected cases that the Inquisition was not responsible for suppressing scientific research or cultural activities, but that it gained the reputation for so doing as the result of foreign attacks in the eighteenth and nineteenth centuries" (see Modern Humanities Research Association, *The Year's Work in Modern Language Studies* [Cambridge, 1955], p. 180). I am not prepared, without further study, to follow Mr. Gibbs in accepting the validity of Pinta Llorente's conclusions.

physics itself was progressively pushed into the background. It is apparent, also, that Spain was not interested in following the lead of those few of her sons who actually were, in one way or another, predecessors of Bacon and Descartes, that is to say, of her own "critical philosophers": Vives, Gómez Pereira, Vallés, Francisco Sánchez.[141] Her interests, determined by the value system of the culture pattern that she made her own, tended strongly to keep her faithful to Thomistic Aristotelianism, though she renewed that ecclesiastical tradition in her own original way. After 1650 her spirit of inquiry wore itself out. In her universities on both sides of the Atlantic we witness what John Tate Lanning has called "The Last Stand of the Schoolmen." [142]

To trace the movement of Spain's partial re-entry into the stream of European thought in the eighteenth, nineteenth, and twentieth centuries falls outside the province of the present work. What falls within its province is a consideration of the state of philosophy as this is revealed by the titles listed in a ship's manifest of the year 1600 — titles of a shipment of some seven hundred books intended for the "trade" in Mexico. In this list "the old and the new, progress and retrogression, science and superstition and charlatanism appear in strange juxtaposition, proving that sixteenth-century Mexico was but an intellectual outpost of Europe."[143] The main currents of sixteenth-century thought are faithfully reflected in this commercial document. We have already examined in some detail (see Chapter III) the content of this list, but it seems appropriate here to touch upon it once more in view of its significance for our present discussion.

The list first sounds the traditional medieval note: Boethius, the *Ars Magna* of Lull, the interest in logic attested by the inclusion of Fonseca and the *Dialectica* of Titelman. (But it must be remembered that Boethius and Lull are not altogether "medieval": Boethius was at times utilized in Christian thinking, and Giordano

141. Eloy Bullón y Fernández, *Los precursores españoles de Bacon y Descartes* (Salamanca, 1905).

142. *Academic Culture in the Spanish Colonies* (London–New York–Toronto, 1940), pp. 61 ff.

143. Otis H. Green and Irving A. Leonard, "On the Mexican Booktrade in 1600: A Chapter in Cultural History," *HR*, IX (1941), 3.

Bruno (d. 1600) — in a very real sense the first Romantic — was a passionate reader of Lull.)

The Renaissance interest in Neoplatonism is represented by a fairly numerous group of texts: three of Plato, two of Iamblichus, one each of Plotinus, Philo Judaeus, Maximus Tyrius, and the commentary of Montañés on Porphyry, as well as two texts each of Ficino, Pico, and Bembo, and one of León Hebreo.

Closely connected with this current is that of the Jewish Kabbala and, by way of a natural extension, that of the theurgic and extravagant philosophies and superstitions of the sixteenth century. There are twenty-two titles in this category, including Iamblichus' *De mysteriis Aegyptiorum* and Pico's *Conclusiones philosophicae, cabalisticae et theologicae.*

The Stoic current of thought is strong in sixteenth-century Mexico, no less than in Renaissance Europe. Our ship's manifest lists Seneca's *De vita beata*, the *De Constantia* of Lipsius, Cicero's *Consolatio* with Lipsius' essay on it, and Marcellino's *Il Diamerone, ove . . . si mostra la morte non esser quel male che'l senso si persuade.*

There are four Aristotelian texts and thirteen others that represent the Thomistic and Scholastic tradition, and copies also of such Renaissance Aristotelians as Vicomercatus, with his commentary on Aristotle's *De naturali auscultatione*, and J. C. Scaliger, with his reply to Cardano's *De subtilitate.*

Most important of all, if we are to judge by our own standards, are the great eclectics who in one way or another prepared the way for modern philosophy. Pomponazzi is represented only negatively by the work of his opponent Niphus, *De anima*; but we have Cardano's *De subtilitate* as well as Scaliger's attack on it, already mentioned. Cardano, who sought to explain all things naturally, went to Mexico in company with Sextus Empiricus (*Opera omnia*), the late-Greek skeptic who so influenced Montaigne that he placed on his study walls nine maxims from this author; in company with the Spanish nominalist Gómez Pereira, whose *Antoniana Margarita* anticipated certain aspects of the teaching of Descartes; with Bernardino Telesio, who in his *De rerum natura* sought to reform natural science by freeing it from Aristotle and the ancients and by basing it on observation; and with Nicholas Copernicus, the publication of whose *De revolutionibus orbium caelestium* may be regarded as having ushered in the modern age.

It seems fitting to end this chapter — concerned as it is with the ceaseless questing of the human spirit — with an apologetic note, though this is a thing I have heretofore consistently endeavored to avoid in my long survey of the multiple manifestations of the Castilian mind in literature. It seems appropriate to insist here that the "immanent Inquisition" which I have mentioned in the present chapter was not so repressive as has long been thought: a fair number of the books in the list of 1600 were "forbidden books," yet they were freely shipped from Seville and freely received for sale in Mexico. The liberalizing tendencies of the sixteenth century were not so effectively crushed in Spain as has frequently been asserted: Erasmus' *Opus epistolarum* — those witty and humane letters, many of which were so bitter against monks and "Scholastics" — went to New Spain in 1600 in two copies, together with two other works of Erasmus (literary rather than doctrinal ones, to be sure). Spain was not "shut off from the light." We have no right to condemn, with the clichés that in spite of our best scholarship have cat-like tenacity of life, the Spanish colonial regime in America as "three centuries of theocracy, obscurantism, and barbarism." [144]

144. Arturo Torres-Rioseco, *La novela en la América Hispana* (Berkeley, California, 1939), p. 159. Irving A. Leonard has done more than any other person to combat this aspect of the "black legend." See his *Books of the Brave: Being an Account of Books and Men in the Spanish Conquest and Settlement of the Sixteenth-century New World* (Cambridge, Massachusetts, 1949), and numerous other studies by him. For points of comparison, one might well turn to Francis Parkman's *The Old Régime in Canada* ([Boston, 1893], p. 349, 359) and to Charles R. Gillett, *Burned Books: Neglected Chapters in British History and Literature* (New York, 1932).

XI · Optimism—Pessimism

The ultimately moral character of the
universe . . . has been . . . in the West, a
universal belief. . . . The opposite
conception . . . of a blind universe . . .
perfectly indifferent to good or evil —
though it appears . . . in the ancient
world, as in Lucretius — is characteristic only of the Western world during
the last three centuries, and is the
product of the seventeenth-century
scientific revolution.

> *W. T. Stace* [1]

Every one must have two pockets, so
that he can reach into the one or the
other according to his needs. In his
right pocket are to be the words: "For
my sake was the world created," and in
his left: "I am earth and ashes."

> *Rabbi Bunam of Pzhysha* [2]

Behind every system of sixteenth-century
thought, however learnedly it is argued,
lurks cruelty and Ogpu.

> *C. S. Lewis* [3]

Since the second term of our chapter heading — pessimism — refers
to a world view which, strictly speaking, cannot exist (except spo-
radically) in a truly Christian society, we require at the outset a
careful distinction of terms. I shall be dealing with two types of

---

1. *Religion and the Modern Mind* (Philadelphia, 1952), p. 49. "In the Elizabethan age . . . modern science was only a fledgling, and its effect upon poetry was scarcely perceptible. Shakespeare's world-picture was essentially pre-scientific, and Spenser's traditional complaint against the ravages of time in the two powerful *Cantos of Mutability* owed less to science than it did to received medieval thought. In the seventeenth century, however, science became a force too powerful for the poets to ignore" (Samuel I. Mints, review of Douglas Bush, *Science and English Poetry: A Historical Sketch, 1590–1950* [Oxford, 1950], in *JHI*, XII [1951], 155).

2. Cited by Victor Gollancz, *Man and God* (Boston, 1951), p. 8.

3. *English Literature in the Sixteenth Century Excluding Drama* (Oxford, 1954), pp. 200–1.

optimism and/or pessimism: *circumstantial* and *radical*, or — stated more technically — optimism or pessimism *quoad vitam* and *quoad ens*. The first concerns itself with the human condition in the ups and downs of the here and now; the second deals with *being* in the most general and philosophic sense of the word, i. e., with the least possible determination or qualification.

Before proceeding to stricter definitions, I shall quote some Spanish texts illustrative of the two types of optimism-pessimism.[4] Representative of the first — elation or depression over the here-and-now — are these lines from a work published in 1595 by Fray Juan de los Angeles:

> It is true that the world is in its last stages and come to decrepitude, because even in the matter of virtue we find in it a hundred thousand new and crazy ideas, and as for sins, newly invented abominations are without number . . . no theologian can solve the difficulties they present. Therefore, I am persuaded that the saints of undying fame, the generals and captains of Christianity and those of the Round Table have gone never to return, and that the people who nowadays make their way to heaven are infantrymen, insignificant folk of no account, incapable of suffering even a slight vexation for the sake of their God.[5]

This is circumstantial pessimism: the times are out of joint. Radical optimism — concerned with limitless being — is illustrated by this text of 1618: every man must

> know how to force his way through the difficulties of the world, to oppose his bosom to the perils of time and fortune, in order to maintain — with honor and good name — a gift so precious as that of life, which was granted to us by the Divine Majesty to the end that we should render Him thanks and admire this marvelous order of skies and elements, the unerring and inviolable courses of the stars, the generation and production of things, that thereby we may attain to a full knowledge of their universal Maker.[6]

Radical optimism appears also in this sentence by Quevedo (d. 1645):

4. I shall be deliberately exposing the reader to what may appear to be an anomalous succession of dates. This seesaw effect is intended to demonstrate that the attitudes in question are independent of any supposed transition from "Renaissance" to "baroque." Note that my first examples of radical optimism are dated 1618 and *ca.* 1645.

5. *Diálogos de la conquista del espiritual y secreto reino de Dios*, NBAE, XX, 79.

6. Vicente Espinel, *Vida del escudero Marcos de Obregón*, ed. S. Gili Gaya (Madrid, 1922–23), I, initial paragraph. Curiously, this devout text is from a semi-autobiographical, semi-picaresque work of fiction.

To say that God exists is to repeat what all the creation has said from the beginning: rational creatures, with words; the irrational ones, by their every action; the elements, by their religious obedience; the whole structure of the universe, by the providentially ordered consonance of its fruitful harmony.[7]

We may now formulate some stricter definitions. Circumstantial optimism (*quoad vitam*) is based on a general satisfaction with the present and on bright hopes for the near future. A perfect example is the analysis by Antonio de Nebrija of the happy state of Spain in 1492 and his prophecy that, now that the wars are over and the nation is united, a new historic cycle and a new flourishing of the arts of peace are to be expected (see Chapter I above); another example is provided by a letter from Juan Luis Vives (d. 1540) to Erard de Lamarck, congratulating him on his appointment as Bishop of Valencia: "You, for your part . . . , will contribute to that Golden Age of which we dream, to those anticipated happy centuries which I, as in a vision [*soñando*], announce to the world." [8] Radical optimism (*quoad ens*) is independent of time and circumstance: "one is optimistic when one holds that the world is a moral order in which, in spite of all appearances to the contrary, goodness must prevail and justice be done" (Stace, *op. cit.*, p. 179). In this sense, even the bitterest critics of Spanish life and ideals are in reality optimists: Mateo Alemán, Quevedo, Gracián — by their words we shall get to know them.

Circumstantial pessimism (*quoad vitam*) includes a wide range of attitudes: though it believes the world to be very evil, it does not rest in that belief. The ills lamented are curable: by suitable education, by a renewed moral sense, by an awakened religiosity. This circumstantial pessimism has, nonetheless, its own theodicy: our sufferings are blessings in disguise inasmuch as they force us to recognize our weakness as fallen human creatures utterly dependent on Divine Grace and enable us — strengthened by that heavenly gift — to bear our cross with patience along the strait and painful path that leads to ultimate salvation. Radical pessimism (*quoad ens*), on the other hand, is un-Christian. It is the conviction that "human paths lead nowhere," [9] that mankind lives out

---

7. *Obras en prosa*, ed. L. Astrana Marín (Madrid, 1932), p. 1056a.
8. *Obras completas*, trans. Lorenzo Riber (Madrid, 1947–48), I, 604b.
9. Américo Castro attributes — wrongly, I feel — this conviction to Quevedo; see

its absurd life in a universe of absurdity. This no Christian can believe: Fray Francisco Ortiz (*fl. ca.* 1525) speaks of "the only wisdom worthy of the name [*toda buena filosofía*], which denies the name of unmitigated evil to everything except sin." [10] Even the embittered Mateo Alemán — another writer habitually listed among the pessimists [11] — wrote his *Guzmán de Alfarache* (1599) with a constructive, a melioristic end in view. His rogue-protagonist makes this clear: "But, since my purpose is to build a perfect man, whenever I find stones suitable for the edifice, I set about collecting them and heaping them up." [12] A writer who entertains such a purpose cannot be designated by the unqualified word "pessimist."

Spaniards during the five centuries under study here — they could not anticipate the eighteenth-century effects of the seventeenth-century scientific revolution — regarded the universe as good; its Creator could have said of it, as He did say of His Word: "it shall accomplish that which I please and it shall prosper in the thing whereto I sent it" (Is. 55:11). Of this point — to my knowledge — there was no doubt: the Divine handiwork, shown forth by the Psalmist's firmament, is perfect. In their attitude toward man and the effects of man's first disobedience, Spaniards differ widely, some of them approaching the extreme Augustinian view of utter human helplessness without God's uplifting (though unmerited) grace; but what the nation as a whole subscribed to is well expressed in these words of Herschel Baker: "If everything that happens . . . can be referred to God for causality . . . then everything assumes a dimension in infinity. The dignity of man and the patterned significance of all temporal affairs were immediate corollaries of the conviction that God manipulates all events to the consummation of his great design." [13] It was for this reason that the Society of

his "Escepticismo y contradicción en Quevedo," *Humanidades*, XIII (1928), 12–13. Castro elsewhere speaks of Quevedo's "radical pessimism."

10. *Epístolas familiares*, *BAE*, XIII, 262a. Cf. St. Thomas, *Summa*, II–II, 18, 4: "De omnipotentia autem Dei et misericordia eius certus est quicumque fidem habet." See also E. Gilson, "L'optimisme chrétien," in *L'esprit de la philosophie médiévale* (Paris, 1944).

11. "Alemán in the throes of his personal turmoil visualizes man in the generic sense as hopelessly victimized by a materialist world ruled by social evils and sinfulness inherited from Adam" (Sherman Eoff, *The Novels of Pérez Galdós* [St. Louis, Missouri, 1954], p. 38). The only error here is the use of the adverb *hopelessly*.

12. Ed. S. Gili Gaya (Madrid, 1926–36), III, 187.

13. *The Wars of Truth: Studies in the Decay of Christian Humanism in the*

Jesus was so successful in the land of its birth: the sons of St. Ignatius proclaimed the possibility of an accord between reason and faith, the essential soundness of human nature, the value of good works.[14] In this fundamental attitude the Jesuits were joined by practically the entirety of the nation. St. John of the Cross (d. 1591) — proponent of the *via negativa* of approaching the Godhead — declared that "a single human thought is of greater value than the entire world." [15]

Evil — the cause of pessimism — is a by-product of God-given free will, either in angels (Lucifer and his cohorts) or in man: "The first evil is intellectual, voluntary, and spiritual; bodily evil is therefore not the first in point of time," wrote the Catalan Raimundo Sabunde (d. 1436?); both types — spiritual and bodily, voluntary and involuntary — "are present in human nature, but the bodily-involuntary type was engendered by the spiritual." [16] Rare and very lonely, even among heretics, would have been the Spaniard who would or could have called this doctrine into question. I know of none who held that evil exists in the world in a primary, substantial, predominant way, or that the elimination of evil would involve the elimination of all existence. Beneath the bitterest outpourings of a Quevedo, the most disconsolate disenchantment (*desengaño*)[17] of a Gracián (d. 1658), or the revilings of the most life-denying ascetic, there existed always a bedrock of meliorism — not the typically nineteenth-century belief that the light of reason would improve the human condition, but the conviction that man

Earlier Seventeenth Century (Cambridge, Massachusetts, 1952), p. 14.

14. François de Dainville, *Les jésuites et l'éducation de la société française* (Paris, 1940), I, 242.

15. Cited by José Corts Grau in an essay, "La dignidad humana en Juan Luis Vives," in his *Estudios filosóficos y literarios* (Madrid, 1954), p. 84.

16. *Theologia naturalis*, trans. Michel de Montaigne, ed. A. Armaingaud (Paris, 1932), II, 131 (this is vol. X of Armaingaud's edition of the *Oeuvres complètes de Michel de Montaigne* [Paris, 1924–41]).

17. This disenchantment has been declared by many to be one of the most profound characteristics of "Castilian man." See J. M. de Semprún Gurrea, "El desengaño en la historia del pensamiento español," *Cuadernos del Congreso por la libertad de la cultura*, núm. 10 (1955), pp. 53–58. But the attitude is not confined to Spain. Even Spenser wrote: "If any strength we have, it is to ill" (cited by Lewis, *op. cit.*, p. 385); and J. B. Chassignet published his *Mépris de la vie et consolation de la mort* at Besançon in 1594. See Jean Rousset, *La littérature de l'âge baroque en France: Circé et le Paon* (Paris, 1953), for his account of the "baroque" view of life and of the world as a "mirage volatile, un jeu flottant d'apparances qui passent et se transforment." There will be a chapter on *desengaño* in our Volume IV.

long since had been liberated from the weight of original sin by the coming of the Redeemer.[18] When, therefore, mention is made in the present chapter of "pessimism," it must be borne in mind that we are normally speaking of a relative pessimism *quoad vitam*, tempered by meliorism: even Alemán seeks "to build a perfect man."

Concerning the goodness of the creation and the efficacy of the redemption, there existed no doubt (except in the dimly glimpsed consciousness of some few persons mentioned in the section on skepticism in our preceding chapter). Nor was there any doubt — any room for individual opinion — but that the Gospel was what its name implies: good news. Consequently the national belief was, in the last analysis, optimistic: The Christian life led — through tribulation to be sure, but none the less certainly — to ultimate Christian joy. Where opinion regarding goodness and badness did assume importance was in relation to the individual's estimate of the world of men as altered by human folly. Stated in more theological terms, doubt concerned the extent of the damage accomplished — through diabolical intervention — in Eden. This we have already noted in the chapter of Volume II on "The Nature and Destiny of Man." The world was either a theater in which the Christian could, by lifting his hand to God's, aspire to joys which (in the state of union of the mystics) were actual foretastes of divine glory; or the world was a vale of tears in which labor — the sweat-producing labor of Adam or the puerperal labor of Eve — was the all but overwhelming punishment of our depraved humanity, a sort of purgatory before Purgatory.[19] The party of Aquinas (and of Erasmus after him) was "unable to accept the notion that God imposed punishment for sins beyond man's control.[20] The party of Augustine was more conscious of all-enveloping evil, but even

18. See J. Ferrater Mora, *Diccionario de filosofía* (Buenos Aires, 1951), *s. v. pesimismo*. The problem of pessimism, though abundantly studied, "is still one of the 'virgin' problems," says Ferrater Mora (p. 728c).

19. When one says that Christ's kingdom "is not of this world," the reference is not to the "created world," but to "the form and shape and manner in which men live in the world"; and when one says that Satan is "the prince of this world," one refers, not to his power over the world (which is God's), but to the superhuman power of the Devil who, if God permitted, "would do what Job says of him in the forty-first chapter" (see Alejo Venegas, *Agonía del tránsito de la muerte, NBAE*, XVI, 260ab).

20. Herschel Baker, *The Dignity of Man: Studies in the Persistence of an Idea* (Cambridge, Massachusetts, 1947), p. 267.

Augustine in *The City of God* had written his theodicy — "both his answer to the problem of evil and his affirmation of an omnipotent deity by whose will even the wicked world and sinful men are put to glorious uses" (*ibid.*, p. 163).

The world of men was, along with the flesh and the Devil, one of the three enemies of the soul. Had not the Devil himself declared, during the temptation of Jesus, that "all the kingdoms of the world and the glory of them" were in his power to bestow "if thou wilt fall down and worship me" (Matt. 4:8–10)? These things being so, it was possible to entertain a wide variety of attitudes toward the exterior world, which indeed had a double character: on the one hand, the earth seen as God's footstool, a divinely organized mechanism in which the great chain of interlocking genera of creatures still showed — in spite of the creatures' enmity towards man for having broken the peace of Eden — traces of the shaping Hands; over against this, the world of relative or near-absolute human folly and downright evil intention.

MEANS AND EXTREMES OF ATTITUDE

The variety of attitudes was wide and impressive. In 1524 Vives wrote in his *Introductio ad sapientiam*: "Our life, what can it be called other than a certain pilgrimage and exile, exposed to a thousand shifts of fortune, combated by thousands of unforeseen events that befall us every day, a state the end of which hangs ever as by a thread . . . ? This being so, what greater madness can there be than to commit any unbecoming or evil act, knowing that our desire for life is so uncertain?" [21] The rules of St. Ignatius' *Exercitia Spiritualia* were published in 1548. The first rule of the *Segundas reglas de discreción* is, rather than a rule of ascetic conduct, a statement of something quite different — of the naturalness of Christian joy (which the Devil ever seeks to destroy): "It is characteristic of God and of his angels, when they stir the soul, to give true happiness and spiritual joy, removing all sadness and perturbation induced by the Devil; the latter naturally fights

21. *Introducción a la sabiduría* (Madrid, 1944), p. 28. See B. G. Monsegú, *Filosofía del humanismo de Juan Luis Vives* (Madrid, 1961). The author sets Vives in the Renaissance world and details his solutions of the problems of the period.

against that joy and consolation by means of false reasons, subtleties and fallacious trickery." [22]

Moving forward thirty-four years, we find a similar insistence on joy in Fray Luis de Granada's *Introduction to the Creed* (1582): "All men who ever were, have been, or shall be, are born with a natural appetite and desire to reach a state wherein they shall be so abundantly supplied with good things that they could desire nothing more. . . . This state they call happiness and blessedness, the highest good of man and his chief end. And men believe it possible to attain unto it, inasmuch as it would not have been reasonable for the author of all Nature to implant in our hearts this desire, this natural appetite, if its satisfaction were impossible: for verily nothing is done in vain and without purpose." [23]

Nearly half a century later (1618), when Trent's decrees had long since become the law of the Spanish nation, the world of the physical creation is viewed with Franciscan love by Fray Pedro Núñez de Castro: "No matter how one considers the works of God, one will find that they are complete and perfect in a thousand exquisite details. The tiniest water worm in a pool, the snail that flourishes amid flagstones and grass and which seems so superfluous, the shrub that blossoms in the cleft of the rocks — all this has its reason for being, all these things together have their harmony and consonance, and their totality is governed by the all-disposing art of Divine Providence." [24]

Quevedo, so often considered a radical pessimist, provides our final example of the optimistic view of human life. In *The Cradle and the Grave* (printed in 1635) he declares that man alone among all the animals is the fabricator of his own misery; yet what great things can have their seat in his mind! How great his dignity, since he bears God's image! His sad mistake is that he so often compels

22. In opposition to Luther and Calvin, "the Jesuits, with the Church Fathers and the Fathers of Trent [1563], maintain that Christianity does not destroy natural virtues but rather hierarchizes them and harmonizes them; it does not abolish Nature, it corrects Nature's deviations and fulfills her promise. There is no schism between reason and revelation . . ." (Dainville, *op. cit.*, I, 226).

23. *Obras*, V (Madrid, 1769), 433–34; the last statement was everywhere regarded as axiomatic.

24. *Santoral seráfico de las festividades y santos que se celebran en la seráfica religión de Nuestro Padre San Francisco*, cited by M. Herrero García (comp.), *Sermonario clásico* (Madrid, 1942), p. lxi.

his soul to follow its body, neglecting its health for the sake of assuaging a worthless appetite.[25]

The multiplicity of expressions of this life's worthlessness was made clear in Chapter IV of our Volume II. The "virginal light" of the Renaissance[26] was obviously offset at all times by another light that revealed the darker side of human existence. It would be idle to insist on the theme *De contemptu mundi* as it was treated across the centuries; what needs to be made clear is that we are not dealing with an epochal shift from gloom to brightness and back to gloom. Both the brightness and the gloom were present in Spanish thought in the same proportion as joy and misery are experienced in life.

In 1543 the Franciscan Friar Juan de Dueñas issued his *Mirror of Consolation for the Depressed, Wherein It Is Shown That Life's Calamities Are More Beneficial Than Its Blessings*. This edition, unknown to modern bibliographers but reported by Nicolás Antonio in his *Bibliotheca Hispana Nova*, was followed by another printed at Burgos in 1546. And the author also issued five additional "Parts," the last of which appeared at Medina del Campo in 1570. Fray Juan belonged to the same Franciscan Order as Fray Pedro Nuñez de Castro, whose joyous meditation on water worms and snails has just been quoted.

Fray Diego de Estella, another Franciscan (d. 1578), was the author of a work of devotion entitled *Treatise on the Vanity of the World*, which was translated into many languages. Pierre Jobit has studied Estella as a predecessor of St. Francis de Sales; the system of asceticism which he expounded is perfectly "classical": the consideration of the worthlessness of the human world is the traditionally normal first step for any soul that aspires to mystical union.[27]

The Dominican Fray Alonso de Cabrera, who toward the end of his own life and that of Philip II was preacher in the royal chapel,

25. See Robert Ricard, "Notes et matériaux pour l'étude du 'socratisme chrétien' chez Sainte Thérèse et les spirituels espagnols," II, *BHi*, XLIX (1957), 200–20, especially 201.

26. The phrase is Dámaso Alonso's. He used it (with safeguards) in a prologue written for J. M. de Cossío's *Fábulas mitológicas en España* and reproduced in his collective volume, *De los siglos oscuros al de oro* (Madrid, 1958), p. 197.

27. See Ricard's review of P. Jobit, *Un prédécesseur de saint François de Sales, Fray Diego de Estella (1524–1578)* (which appeared in serial form in *Cahiers de l'éducateur* [1950–55]), *BHi*, LIII (1951), 441.

is famous for the elegance of his sermons. True to a tradition centuries old, he declaims against this world of our making, wherein life is death. "Everything has a false foundation"; "everything advances over paths of trickery and deceit"; "the fruits of the world are tears and sighs, pain and sickness and death" — *Spinas et tribulos germinabit tibi*, as God said to Adam at the moment of expulsion from Eden (Gen. 3:18).[28]

Turning from doctrinal works to works of pure literature, we find the same contrast in the picaresque worlds of Cervantes and of Quevedo. The two young scamps who give their respective names to Cervantes' tale *Rinconete y Cortadillo* (published 1613) pass temporarily through the gay underworld of Seville without being contaminated by it. In Quevedo's *Historia de la vida del Buscón llamado Don Pablos* (printed 1626) there is much contamination and no gaiety. Professor Alexander Parker has said of the hero: "Pablos' refusal to adapt himself to society is a free choice, excusable on many grounds, but its motive is the *sin* of pride. That, surely, is the lesson his fate drives home"[29] — free choice, not social determinism.

It thus appears that each friar, each novelist, plays up or plays down one side or the other of the "medallion" — Divine Providence and the obedient snail, thorns and tribulation for erring man — as his immediate purpose dictates. Both sides of the medallion have a Scriptural basis and both are perfectly normal — at any time — in a Catholic society. The division into separate periods coupled with specific traits to which we have been long accustomed (light-heartedness under the Catholic Sovereigns and Charles V, gloom punctuated by frivolous pleasure seeking in the baroque age of the Philips and Charles II) is simplistic. The deepening gloom of the later reigns corresponds, not with a changed attitude toward man's destiny, but with general frustration and failure — the revelation of the emptiness of a once-cherished dream and strength-giving myth.[30] As we proceed we shall see that the changes in attitude

28. See his *Sermones*, ed. Miguel Mir, *NBAE*, III, 282a–83a.
29. "The Psychology of the *picaro* in *El Buscón*," *MLR*, XLII (1947), 58–69; see especially p. 68 (emphasis mine).
30. This was so even though there was a period between the battle of Lepanto (1571) and the defeat of the Armada (1588) during which that dream gave promise

revealed by our Spanish texts are determined by: individual temperament (ascetic or the opposite); philosophico-religious orientation (e.g. Pauline, Erasmian, Loyolan); [31] expansion or contraction of the political horizon (the state of the national hope) — all factors which color or alter every position taken with respect to the frailty or solidity of the basis for aspiration to a satisfying existence in the here-and-now. As we review these positions we must at all times remember that the here-and-now was universally regarded as a place and time of testing, a crucible for developing and showing forth human worth.[32] Happiness was either a by-product or a special gift from God — grace mysteriously granted.

CIRCUMSTANTIAL OPTIMISM-PESSIMISM

This is the least important of our subdivisions. National success or the lack of it is a matter so relative, within the wider framework of God's ultimate purposes and the Spaniards' deepest axiological convictions, that we shall trace but briefly the waxing and waning of the nation's enthusiasm as its fortunes appeared — or did not appear — in the ascendant. What is important is for us to understand the spirit with which these political successes and failures were enjoyed or endured.

That spirit was determined by belief. In all periods Spaniards felt themselves to be living in a universe of rational order in which chaos is controlled by Divine Reason and Love, and human appe-

---

of fulfillment. "The generation of Erasmus . . . could not have anticipated that their expectations would go down to disappointment in the wars of religion, as those of a later age were doomed by the wars of nationalism" (Myron P. Gilmore, *The World of Humanism* [New York, 1952], p. 207).

31. Loyola viewed the world as the scene of a continuous active combat (the Order he founded had a military discipline) between God and Satan. His *Meditation on Hell* was built on concepts centuries-old, held by Protestants and Catholics alike even to the time of our own Jonathan Edwards (d. 1758). See Paul Van Dyke, *Ignatius de Loyola, the Founder of the Jesuits* (New York, 1927), pp. 273–74, 285. On the joy of Loyola's followers, see F. Cereceda, *Diego Laínez en la Europa religiosa de su tiempo, 1512–1565* (Madrid, 1945–46), I, 82.

32. The New Testament regards calamity and suffering as necessary means for spiritual uplifting and the life of the individual and of mankind as opportunity for such development; it discerns divine love in the greatest sorrows that befall man and regards the activities of the powers of evil on earth from the same point of view. See A. Guttmacher, *Optimism and Pessimism in the Old and New Testaments* (Baltimore, 1903), p. 181.

tite is subject to human reason in the soul.³³ Juan de Mariana (d. 1623) defined law as "reason, permanent and invariable, which emanates from the mind of the Deity and enjoins things good and salutary, prohibiting their opposites."³⁴ This was, fundamentally, the definition of Aquinas and it was the measure by which those of Mariana's contemporaries who were concerned with the "problem of Spain" made their assessments of national weal or woe.

The Fifteenth Century ³⁵

In the fifteenth century we find, principally, expressions of woe, especially during the shameful reigns of Juan II and Enrique IV of Castile.³⁶ The anonymous *Libro de los pensamientos variables*, for example, is a harsh denunciation of the tyranny of the nobles and their oppression of the peasants.³⁷ The Marqués de Santillana even composed a *Lamentation Foretelling the Second Destruction of Spain*, i.e., a new calamity no less terrible than the invasion of the Moors in 711 A.D. It is difficult to tell how greatly he was moved by patriotic motives (as against the desire to imitate Petrarch's *Canzone* XVI, *Italia mia*) when he composed the sonnet al *itálico modo*:

> What shall I say of thee, sad western land,
> My country! ³⁸

33. Jorge de Montemayor (d. 1561) wrote: "If the world were bad, our God would not have created it; and if He had found it to be evil, He would not have been born of woman in it, nor would He have had dealings with men" — "Que si el mundo malo fuera, / nuestro Dios no lo criara; / y si malo lo hallara, / ni en él de muger nasciera, / ni con hombres conversara" (cited by Américo Castro, "Lo hispánico y el erasmismo," *RFH*, IV [1942], 61).

34. Cited by J. M. Gallegos Rocafull, *El hombre y el mundo de los teólogos españoles de los siglos de oro* (Mexico City, 1946), p. 121.

35. "Institutions in general are considered [at the end of the Middle Ages] as good or as bad as they can be: having been ordained by God, they are intrinsically good, only the sins of men pervert them. What therefore is in need of remedy is the individual soul. . . . We will have to wait until the eighteenth century . . . before men resolutely enter the path of social optimism; only then the perfectability of man and society is raised to the rank of a central dogma" (J. Huizinga, *The Waning of the Middle Ages: A Study of the Forms of Life, Thought and Art in France and the Netherlands in the XIVth and XVth Centuries* [London, 1924], p. 28).

36. On the calamitous nature of the times — immorality in high and low places — see the introductory remarks that preface Agapito Rey's edition of the brief fifteenth-century text, *Libro de la consolación de España*, in *Symposium*, IX (1955), 236–46.

37. See M. Menéndez y Pelayo, *Historia de la poesía castellana en la Edad Media* (Madrid, 1911–16), III, ch. XXI, especially p. 38.

38. "¿Oy qué diré de ti, triste empisperio?/ ¡ Patria mía!" Cited by Rafael Lapesa, *La*

Yet an act of literary imitation does not by itself exclude sincerity; any more than the rhetoric in Santillana's *Lamentación* necessarily excludes it. We have already discussed Santillana's revival, in times of political upheaval, of visions of national greatness (see Chapter IV above).

A very special interest attaches to the *Libro de la consolación de España* (see note 36 above), which is presented in the form of an allegorical dialogue between Gracia and España. After a prologue in which the unknown writer asserts that his country's sufferings are divinely visited upon her because of her wickedness, the dialogue opens with an invitation to España to set forth the causes of her unhappiness. As España voices her complaints, Gracia interrupts to remind her that lamentations avail nothing. If she will but take courage, her ills will abate; let her weep for her sins, and she will be cured. The patient answers that her troubles are internal; there is no health in her. Again she is rebuked and told to turn to God: a great good is in store for her. Contrite at last, España promises to follow God's path. Gracia's comforting words — "a great good awaits you" — constitute a prophecy that subsequent writers will repeat with increasing eloquence. The one thing needful is to be in tune with the Infinite. It is a doctrine of optimism.

Other foreshadowings of relief and of approaching greatness are not lacking. When Juan II ascended the throne, Gonzalo Martínez de Medina wrote in a *dezir*:

> Rejoice now, rejoice, oh most noble Spain,
> And behold in your King the one you've desired

— visualizing the new monarch as receiving in Jerusalem the crown of Emperor.[39] The imperial crown? And in Jerusalem? One is tempted to dismiss Martínez de Medina as a self-seeking flatterer. And yet he would hardly have chosen to raise his voice if there were no ears to hear. The dream, the myth, must have had emotional

obra literaria del Marqués de Santillana (Madrid, 1957), p. 190. I am at a loss to understand why Santillana used the word *emisperio* as a designation for Spain. In what follows I utilize the findings of Lapesa, *loc. cit.*

39. "Alégrate agora, la muy noble España, / e mira tu Rrey tan muy deseado" (cited by María Rosa Lida de Malkiel, *Juan de Mena, poeta del prerrenacimiento español* [Mexico City, 1950], p. 541; see also the review by J. E. Gillet, *HR*, XX [1952], 165).

value. Some day, some other Spanish king would be emperor; some day the Holy Land would be governed by Spaniards.

The aspiration to national unification and power is substantial to the great poem of Juan de Mena, *Laberinto de Fortuna* (see Chapter IV above). Indeed, Mena's high place of honor in the literary opinion of the Siglo de Oro has its basis, in no small measure, in his heroic quality: "Juan de Mena may be called heroic, because he celebrates . . . the deeds of many famous men" — so wrote his first commentator, Hernán Núñez, in the year 1499.[40]

National success, seeds of failure. The "comfort" longed for by so many poets and prose writers of the fifteenth century was at last provided by the strong and effective government of Ferdinand and Isabella, and this comfort became increasingly available to a newly rising social class — the *cristianos viejos* or "old Christians," whose dignity and status depended on their freedom, not from a former condition of servitude as in our own South, but from the slightest taint of any familial connection with the adherents of Judaism or Mohammedanism. This increasingly powerful class, whose rise was to take place at the expense of the formerly successful Jews and converted Jews, would seek to strengthen its position still further by insisting on the religious "unification" of the country — by force of arms and by acts of expulsion. In such "unification," however, lay the seeds of failure: recent studies are showing with cogency that the Inquisition, introduced "officially" to prevent religious backsliding (by forceably converted Jews especially), was utilized very early to achieve purely political ends. The "calvary" of the saintly Archbishop of Granada, Fray Hernando de Talavera (so often quoted in the course of this study), began in 1499.[41] Indeed, according to an increasing number of historians, Spain's ultimate loss of leadership in European politics and culture hinges on her refusal

40. See O. H. Green, "Juan de Mena in the Sixteenth Century: Additional Data," *HR*, XXI (1953), 138; W. J. Entwistle, "The Search for the Heroic Poem," in the University of Pennsylvania Bicentennial Conference volume, *Studies in Civilization* (Philadelphia, 1941), pp. 89–103.

41. See Francisco Márquez in the *Estudio Preliminar* which prefaces the edition by Francisco Martín Hernández of Talavera's *Católica Impugnación . . .* (Barcelona, 1961), p. 7; see also the earlier study by Eugenio Asensio, "El erasmismo y las corrientes espirituales afines (conversos, franciscanos, italianizantes)," *RFE*, XXXVI (1952), 31–99.

to avail herself of the constructive ability of many of the best men of the nation solely on the basis of this unreasoning prejudice (a prejudice which it is easy to compare with the attitudes that are producing upheavals in the United States in the 1960's).

Some writers go to extremes in attributing every unusual feature of the Spanish culture pattern to this suppression of the civil rights of an important part of the population.[42] I recognize the weight of this special factor, but must deny the thesis. That an attitude of general despair is to be traced in the works of converted Jews beginning with *La Celestina* (1499?) has been disproved by the section of our Volume II that deals with the theme of cosmic harmony and discord. If Pleberio's "world" in *La Celestina* is "treacherous," it is because he has placed his trust *in the deceitful world of men*, not because the world as universe is in itself deceitful. Furthermore, that a Spanish attitude of willful anti-intellectualism ("it is better to be ignorant, since the Jews are learned") stunted Spain's growth by inducing her best minds to renounce learning, thus depriving Spain of her chance to contribute to European culture a Hobbes, a Locke, a Leibnitz — this thesis has been disproved in the present volume (see Chapters IX and X). Many indeed were the Spaniards who desired intellectual eminence for themselves and for their country, who could not bear the thought that their culture was accused of being a military cast able to achieve distinction only in exploration, conquest, and colonial organization. Spain neither was a "know-nothing" nation nor desired to be one.[43]

And yet the national effort did fail, and the failure may in part be attributed to internal disharmony based on racio-religious injustice, as well as to thought control. In earlier chapters we have admired the constructive work of Cardinal Cisneros in building a new and revitalized Spain. The negative side of his activity is presented in the study by Francisco Márquez (cited above, see note 41). The great Cardinal employed force to convert mosques into churches, and he compelled multitudes to accept baptism. When mass revolt threatened his life, he escaped from the violence of the mob because he promised retention of the *status quo* and royal clemency — a promise he was unable to keep (Márquez, *op. cit.*,

42. See especially Américo Castro, *De la edad conflictiva* (Madrid, 1961).
43. This subject will be further treated in Volume IV.

p. 14). Later there would come the decree that only "old Christians" could hold various civil and religious posts of honor,[44] and the senseless struggles would begin over whether to utilize or reject the fruits of Hebrew scholarship in the field of Biblical studies. But we are getting ahead of our story.

We close our account of the fifteenth century by insisting once again that it was a period characterized by rising hopes and ever more reasonable expectations.

The Reign of Charles V

The positive aspect of national affairs was there for all to see, whereas the results of mistaken policies are only now being duly appreciated. An anonymous poet wrote, on the occasion of the fall of Gaeta in Italy in the year 1504:

> Gaeta at last is ours,
> And should our captain so wish it,
> Milan will soon follow suit.
> If the powerful Lord of Heaven
> Is the wager of this war,
> Who, I ask, can stand against us?
> If the Lord's favor is with us,
> What can the Frenchman do?
> Let the noble Spanish lions,
> Kings of their great estate,
> Cast away the final care
> From their royal heart and bosom;
> We see an end to their sufferings
> As they move from strength to strength,
> Winning all that lies before them.[45]

Some thirty years later, in his *Ingenious Comparison between Ancient and Modern Times* (1539),[46] Cristóbal de Villalón seems to

44. A. A. Sicroff, *Les controverses des statuts de "pureté de sang" en Espagne du XVe au XVIIe siècle* (Paris, 1960).

45. "Gaeta nos es sujeta, / y si quiere el Capitán, / también lo será Milán. / Si el poderoso Señor, / rey de los cielos y tierra, / quiere hacer esta guerra, / ¿quién será defendedor? / Si su favor da favor / a nuestro gran Capitán, / los franceses ¿qué harán? / Los poderosos Leones, / reyes de muy grand estado, / descuiden de su cuydado, / descansen sus corazones; / passados son sus pasiones, / y de bien en bien irán, / que todo lo ganarán" (cited by Benedetto Croce, *La Spagna nella vita italiana durante la Rinascenza* [Bari, 1917], pp. 99–100).

46. *Ingeniosa comparación entre lo antiguo y lo moderno*, ed. M. Serrano y Sanz (Madrid, 1898).

bear out the prediction that Nebrija had made in 1492 (see above, Chapter I) that there would come an age devoted to the arts of peace (though Villalón cannot avoid the temptation to exult in the accomplishments of Spanish arms as well as Spanish arts). Principally interested in the glories of modern painting, sculpture, architecture, and music, Villalón also has an eye for the practical: the ease of trade and communication between nations, with the attendant banking operations, and the ease of travel—especially travel exemplified by the endless journeys of Charles V. No Scipio can be compared to Charles. The great general admittedly defeated Carthage, but only with all the power of Rome behind him, and over a span of two years. Charles, on the other hand, with only 50,000 knights, the cream and flower of the most venerable houses in Spain, defeated Barbarossa in the short space of six weeks. The campaigns and the travels of 1535, 1536, and 1539 are recorded. A peace with France has recently been signed and has been confirmed as "perpetual" by both kings—clear evidence of God's desire to show favor to the Spaniards. No prince of ancient times, not a thousand of them together, could have accomplished such wonders (pp. 165–168). Villalón is no less pleased with Spain's position of political strength: "If I were to go into particulars and were to speak of the judgment, the prudence, the skill and the knowledge of the great men who govern in Spain, I would never end" (p. 164).

In 1553 Alfonso García de Matamoros published his *Pro adserenda hispanorum eruditione*. The University of Alcalá, with her "laureate theologians . . . who there seek to decipher the secret of the development of human life," is to him "the public oracle of all Spain." Spain could be filled from end to end, he says, with the wise men who yearly leave those learned halls, and he proceeds to list the greatest poets, musicians, astronomers, philosophers, physicians, and other intellectual torch bearers.[47]

This optimistic faith in the goodness—for the nation—of the wise men who inhabit halls of learning, or who emerge from them into the world of public affairs, finds an echo in a book published in the following year, the *Institutiones Rhetoricae* of Fadrique Furió Ceriol. He ascribes great power to the art of the rhetorician. The well-prepared orator, he says, is a man of magnificence, an

47. Ed. J. López de Toro (Madrid, 1943), p. 207.

excellent prince, a most powerful king who governs his nation by the cogency of his wise counsel, who establishes the order of urban life in great cities, who controls men with his elegant and refined eloquence. The man who, by the power of his oratory, can dominate a rebellious mob or expose the weakness of old men's decisions and the foolish ardor of the impulses of the young, is a man who possesses power. Such a man deserves the title of king.[48]

The most eloquent expression of patriotic optimism in the reign of the Emperor has been cited earlier in the present volume (Chapter IV). It is Hernando de Acuña's call for one King, one Empire, and a single sword: *fiet unum ovile et unus pastor*—"there shall be one sheepfold and one shepherd." In the poet's vision, the imperial standard bearer of the Crucified was destined to receive from God two gifts: the banner itself, and universal dominion.

Not all was optimism, however. If in 1527 the royal court was more Erasmian than ever;[49] if in 1528 religious liberty scattered its seed, protected by the indulgence of the supreme authorities, some thirty years later there would arise a new Inquisitor General (Quiroga) who would judge the leniency of his predecessor to have been weak and blameworthy (*ibid.*, p. 396). In 1529 the persecution of the mystical devotees of *iluminismo* entered a new phase, "incalculably dangerous in its threat to the Erasmian cause," as the former enemy (the practice of inner prayer which tended to make every man his own priest) yielded the foreground to an enemy vastly more powerful: Martin Luther himself (p. 424). Things also went badly in the broader European theater. In 1553 Charles retreated from Metz, his army decimated by enemy action, by typhus, by cold and hunger. In 1556 Fray Cipriano de Huerga, in a sermon preached on the day that Philip II took over the monarchy from his abdicating father, stressed the sacrificial role of the old

---

48. In 1589 it was possible to hold a very different view. Pedro Simón Abril, in his *Apuntamientos de cómo se deben reformar las doctrinas* . . . , declared eloquence to be of interest only to preachers, since government does not depend on swaying the populace in the Agora or in the Forum. Even lawsuits are decided on the basis of written briefs. He therefore recommends (since there is no need for oratory in assemblies or courtrooms) that the forensic style be learned from printed models (Cicero, Demosthenes, the best sermons of St. Basil, St. Cyril, etc.). See my article, "*Se acicalaron los auditorios*: An Aspect of the Spanish Literary Baroque," *HR*, XXVII (1959), 417, and D. W. Bleznick, "Las *Institutiones Rhetoricae* de Fadrique Furió," *NRFH*, XIII (1959), 339.

49. M. Bataillon, *Erasmo y España* (Mexico City–Buenos Aires, 1950), I, 313.

Monarch — Charles, the good shepherd who had shed his blood for his sheep. It was a moment of sadness and of pessimism: Charles had failed to heal the religious schism, had given up, after thirty years of struggle, his effort to act as arbiter between Rome and Protestant Germany.[50]

It is possible to point to three interesting statements of attitude toward Spain, her condition, and her probable future which were made at approximately this same time. Written from different points of view, they voice our age-old *Sic et Non*. The first is an out-and-out affirmation of confidence and satisfaction, with only an indirect allusion to the presence of trouble beyond the nation's borders, to the failure of the national purpose to achieve world-wide preponderance: Diego Gracián, in the preface to his translation of Xenophon (1552), speaks of Spain "where through God's mercy . . . the Christian religion flourishes without stain of evil sect, where [our] armies are more prosperous than in any other kingdom, and where letters find more favor than ever they did among the ancients."[51]

On the other hand, Fray Felipe de Meneses, a man in close touch with semi-Lutheran circles in Seville (whose tribulations he also suffered), wrote in his *Luz del alma* (1554): "We have been through two Councils and yet the heretics are more arrogant and proud than before." His pessimism is so great that he sees Spain as a *Festung Hispania*, toward which the Church is retreating; yet even Spain is bled white and hesitant, because of the general immorality. The people in their ignorance readily receive false doctrine. Were the "drum of Lutheran liberty" to be sounded in Spain, its effect might be no less startling than in Germany. The remedy? Propagation of good doctrine to combat the ignorance of God's law and the blindness of men's souls (Bataillon, *op. cit.*, II, 134).

On July 5, 1554, Dr. Andrés Laguna arrived at Augsburg just in time to witness the collapse of the Emperor's authority. In a letter to the Ambassador Francisco de Vargas he states that the policy of the Empire is going to ruin, while the king of France

---

50. *Ibid.*, II, 313 and bibliography provided in n. 9.

51. "[España]: donde por la bondad de Dios florece . . . la religión Christiana sin mácula de secta mala, y las armas más que en otro ningún reyno: y las letras mucho más que en los tiempos pasados . . ." (cited by Henry Thomas, *Spanish and Portuguese Romances of Chivalry* [Cambridge, 1920], p. 161).

threatens the Low Countries. In such troubled times — he continues — "our master has taken up sketching and clock repairing, while his heir relaxes [in] the royal pleasance at Aranjuez" (*ibid.*).

In view of this brief outline of ups and downs, of certainties and haunting doubts regarding Spain, we have an indication (which will be greatly fortified as we consider more fundamental aspects of optimism and pessimism) of the complexity of Spain's intellectual and emotional history. Accompanying every advance, there is at least the possibility of retrogression. Success implies the existence of its opposite.

The Reign of Philip II

The years 1555–1598 encompassed the reign of Philip II — a king often charged with having brought about, personally, a marked change of mood and temper — "light" of the Renaissance, "shadows" of the Counter Reformation [52] — as Spain strives to conserve her values and achieve her ends in an increasingly hostile Europe:

> A terror in the atmosphere
> As if King Philip listened near,

as Longfellow expressed it in his poem *Castles in Spain*. And yet. . . .

In our preceding section we saw how Villalón, comparing antiquity with modern times, was able to think of a Spain that seemed to fulfill Nebrija's joyous prognostications of 1492. We can find a similar example in the present reign. In 1591 Vicente Espinel published his collected poems, prefaced by a "Prologue in Praise of Poetry" by Alonso de Valdés, a gentleman of the king's bedchamber, who felt that not all was lost (even three years after the Armada) "in our Spain in this happy time of Philip the Second, our Lord," —

52. "There is something symbolic . . . in Philip's return to Spain in September 1559. From now on the king of Spain remained in the Iberian peninsula. . . . Henceforth, events were to be seen and judged from Spain, in a Spanish ambience, by Spanish personnel, and in Spanish interests. . . . Social and political tensions were aggravated by a religious crisis . . . but his greatest problem was . . . the effects of prolonged warfare. . . . Philip II was handicapped . . . less by his personality than by the nature of his task; it was this which imposed most of his attitudes upon him. More impressive than his weakness was the way in which he faced up to his vast responsibilities" (John Lynch, *Spain under the Habsburgs* [New York, 1964], pp. 168–75).

a time in which His Majesty has exalted both arms and letters "with so many conquests, so many triumphs, so many victories." Never in history have letters been so honored: through Philip "all the academies and republics of antiquity" are consigned to oblivion, "to the marvel and amazement of the world."[53]

It is hard to believe that what Espinel's prologuist says here should have been considered ridiculous by his contemporaries. Certainly not all was lost — at least not all could be viewed as lost — after 1588. The English still regarded Spain as a redoubtable power, even after the naval disaster.[54] In the body of the book prefaced so optimistically by Valdés there is a poem, *The House of Memory*, which is a register of, and a tribute to, the leading musicians and men of letters of the author's time. Yet in it the more militant glories of Spain are not forgotten. Memory (an allegorical personage) identifies past and present heroes: Hernán Cortés, Don John of Austria, the Marqués de Santa Cruz, and various others, all of whom

> in your time have been
> The honor and increase of this powerful land.[55]

The idea that Spain was a powerful and happy land was a familiar one in the reign of Philip II. Juan de Mal Lara had voiced it years before (1568) in his tribute — as a humanist — to the *Pax hispanica* enjoyed by the world under Spanish hegemony: "Spain, wherein Your Majesty reigns prosperously, with such admirable prudence that neither war dares disturb (by action of outside enemies or by revolt of vassals) the benignity and calm enjoyed in general happiness by the entire Kingdom, nor the calm of peace causes our enemies to lose the fear and awe in which they always hold you, seeing you armed with foresight and with all things needful for the defense of a happy nation."[56]

Where does the truth lie? How blind to the course of events were the authors of these testimonies? There were some who had

53. *Diversas rimas*, ed. Dorothy C. Clarke (New York, 1956), pp. 35–36.
54. "Philip was a stubborn man. The war might go on for years." So wrote Garrett Mattingly in ch. XXXIV of his book *The Armada* (Boston, 1959), p. 396; the chapter has the subheading: "Richmond, New Year's, 1589."
55. "en tu tiempo han sido / honra y aumento de la fuerte España" (*ed. cit.*, p. 88).
56. *Filosofía vulgar*, ed. Antonio Vilanova (Barcelona, 1958–59), I, 55.

their eyes open. The theologian Melchor Cano died in 1560; yet he lived long enough to perceive that the concept of a universal Christendom was disappearing, making way for a congeries of modern nations that were unwilling to accept St. Thomas' determination of the subordination of state to Church. Men were being called upon to serve two masters. The service of the state, as Cano saw clearly, might be injurious to the welfare of the Church, or vice versa. To avoid such injury, it was imperative to recognize for each separate spheres of legitimate action. The emperor, said Cano, may forcibly oppose interference in the governing of his lands, even by the pope. To put a stop to the abuses of Rome was a necessary step, for the good of Christianity and of the Holy See.[57] While this bowing to the force of reality could arouse pessimism in many theologians, it was, from the standpoint of the Spanish state in its opposition to the pope, a doctrine of optimism.

In 1565 Baltasar de Sotomayor, a grammarian, in the dedicatory letter of his *Grammar for Learning the French Language*, could regard the presence at the Spanish Court of a polyglot company of foreigners as a sign of his nation's hegemony: "The greatness of Spain (because of the happy star of our noble King Philip) has reached so high a point that any man who would dwell in his Court city must know most of the languages spoken in Europe; for (now that the diversity of the kingdoms that owe him allegiance causes men of so many nations to flock to it) communication becomes unpleasant, and often harmful, if knowledge of the various languages is lacking."[58]

At this time (1571) there occurred in the history of the sixteenth century an event of such good omen, not only for Spain but for the whole of Europe, that the waves of exultation stirred by it have been felt down to our day. "Long live Spain! Glory to God! Don John of Austria has set his people free," wrote the modern poet G. K. Chesterton; and to express the power of an emotion felt across more than three hundred years he chose the majestic language of Roman Catholicism, at length victorious in its age-long struggle against Islam:

57. Gallegos Rocafull, *op. cit.*, pp. 46–47.
58. Baltasar de Sotomayor, *Gramática . . . para aprender . . . la lengua francesa* (Alcalá, 1565), cited by Gallardo, *Ensayo*, IV, cols. 639–40.

> *Vivat Hispania!*
> *Domino gloria!*
> Don John of Austria
> Has set his people free.

The freedom involved was freedom from fear — from the terror inspired by the Turkish fleets that plied the Mediterranean threatening destruction, death, and unendurable captivity.

The story is simple. A Christian league, which included the Republic of Venice, the Papal State, and Spain, assembled overwhelming power and in 1571 broke the back of the Turkish navy in the battle of Lepanto in the Gulf of Corinth. This victory produced an almost unbelievable enthusiasm. It was celebrated in music by Juan Brudieu (d. 1591), chapelmaster of the cathedral of the Seo de Urgel, and by Don Fernando de los Infantes (d. 1600?), a Cordovan cleric and musician residing at Rome. Tintoretto (d. 1594) sought to eternalize it in painting; in this effort he was followed by Titian (d. 1576). There were statues, medallions, friezes; and in Rome the ceiling of a church was adorned with an inscription in gold leaf — gold taken as booty in the battle.

The event was sung in epics and in portions of epics, in poems in many forms and in many languages. Here at last was the heroic theme for that most "sublime" of all literary genres, heroic poetry. Amid the overwhelming quantity of this poetic production, quality was not always lacking. Fernando de Herrera (d. 1597), in his *Canción por la victoria de Lepanto*, imitating the song of Moses on the crossing the Red Sea by the children of Israel as well as the twenty-third chapter of the Book of Isaiah (following French and Italian predecessors), unquestionably gave to his verse the sweep of majesty:

> Thou hast shattered his strength, thou hast humbled
> Fierce Pharaoh, and the force of his warriors;
> Thou has covered with armor and corpses
> The depths of the sea's great abysses.
>
> . . . .
>
> Oh God, Lord of Battles, thy right arm
> Is the glory and health of thy people [59]

59. "Tú rompiste las fuerzas y la dura / frente de Faraón, feroz guerrero. / Sus escogidos príncipes cubrieron / los abismos del mar, y descendieron / cual piedra en el profundo. . . . / Tú (Dios de las batallas), tú eres diestra / salud y gloria nuestra" (cited by José López de Toro, *Los poetas de Lepanto* [Madrid, 1950], pp. 239–40).

Forty-four years after Lepanto, Cervantes, who fought with distinction in one of the Spanish galleys, said of this battle that it was the most glorious occasion ever seen in the course of the centuries, more glorious than any that future ages might hope to see (*Don Quijote*, II, Prologue). This victory would outweigh the loss of King Sebastian of Portugal in the battle of Alcazarquivir (1578); it would sustain the Spaniards during the dark days of the defeat of the Armada (1588) and the sack of Cadiz by the Earl of Essex (1596). The eventual triumph of Catholic Christianity would be regarded by Spaniards as certain for many years to come. Had not Job suffered calamities?

Over against the contention that Spain in the second half of the sixteenth century turned her back on culture to find nobility in ignorance (see above), we have the declaration of Fernando de Herrera in his commentary (1580) on the Second Eclogue of Garcilaso de la Vega: "There are never lacking, nor will there ever be lacking in Spain, learned men of outstanding erudition." [60] Herrera's prologuist, Francisco de Medina, though he dwells on Spain's role in humbling the pride of powerful nations, insists that Spain's conquests were accomplished with an all-but-superhuman prudence that raised the majesty of the nation to the greatest heights ever attained by human effort.

Yet there is always the *Non*. Juan Huarte de San Juan was an innovator who in his *Examen de ingenios para las ciencias* (1575) sought to initiate a new methodology. His book is full of imprecations against routine and stagnation, of plans for an authentic renovation of teaching methods, of projects for the realization of new possibilities. [61] And Fray Luis de León, lamenting in 1583 the general ignorance — which had resulted from the official denying of access to the Scriptures in translation — of things needful for salvation, offered his treatise *On the Names of Christ* as an example of the type of book, composed in the vernacular, which could most profitably fill this void. [62]

60. Cited by Ricardo del Arco, *La erudición española en el siglo XVII* (Madrid, 1950), I, 1.

61. See Mauricio de Iriarte, S. J., *El Doctor Huarte de San Juan y su "Examen de ingenios"* (Madrid, 1948), p. 158.

62. See Bataillon, *op. cit.*, II, 383–86. Fray Luis' much quoted line, "a toda la es-

This question of ignorance is viewed more optimistically by Pedro Malón de Chaide in *La conversión de la Magdalena* (1588). Making no reference to the inaccessibility of the Bible to those who knew no Latin (a point on which it may well have seemed profitless to express himself), he optimistically hopes that "the diligence and concern of men zealous for the honor of Spain" will bring it about that "we shall very soon see all serious texts [*cosas curiosas y graves*] available in our vernacular, and the Spanish tongue brought to such perfection that it shall need to envy no other language and shall be as far-flung as our national banners which are carrying it from pole to pole."[63]

In the following year (1589) the Jesuit Juan Bonifacio is more optimistic still. He wrote in his *De Sapiente fructuoso*: "Our age, having profited by the calamities suffered by the Church, no longer tolerates jocular and jesting preachers. The masses are not displeased by fictions and adornments, but wise men are; and . . . the number of these latter is today much greater than it was in the time of our grandfathers." If only, in those days when Luther started the great revolt, Italy had had the religious culture that it has today (after Trent)! If Germany had developed, as it has since, its piety and its erudition! If France had been able to muster and send into the lists the famous theologians of Paris (at that time given over to scholastic disputes)! Spain, alas, in those early years of the century had had enough to do in expelling Moors and Jews from her territory. But evils may bring blessings in their train: discord brought about what concord had been unable to do. Embattled Spain is wiser than before. German Catholics are making real thrusts at the enemies of the Faith; Italy has rejected her former barbarism (i.e., neopaganism); France, in those provinces that remain Catholic, is making more progress each day; while the Spaniards are working with enthusiasm and valor to achieve a learned virtue, capable of defending the religion they profess and improving the quality of public morality.[64]

paciosa y triste España" — "throughout the length and breadth of our sad Spain" — may not be cited as an indication of the national mood in the 1580's. The line is from the poem *Profecía del Tajo*, and the reference is to Spain's "destruction" by the Moorish invaders in A. D. 711.

63. Ed. P. Félix García (Madrid, 1947), II, 37–38.

64. Cited by Félix G. Olmedo in his edition of Don Francisco Terrones del Caño's *Instrucción de predicadores* (Madrid, 1946), pp. cxxxi–cxxxii.

Perhaps Father Bonifacio was carried away by his awareness of the successes of the Society of Jesus in various lands, but his conclusion appears to be in accord with that of a modern church historian: although the unity of the Church was shattered in the age of the Reformation, "the Christian consciousness of Europe was restored."[65]

Reverting to things military (the waging of war as a means of implementing national policy and maintaining national power), the year 1588 brought with it a new test, of an entirely different order of magnitude, of Spanish organizational competence, naval strength, and spiritual confidence. The failure of the Armada was as difficult to explain as the 1527 sack of Rome had been — but with this difference: it was Spain, not her opposition, that had gone down to defeat. The explanation arrived at was consistent with Spanish thinking in the past.

Alfonso García Valdecasas, in his study of the Spanish sense of honor, has written perceptively that throughout the history of Spanish literature one observes an evolution which, for all its forward movement, leaves intact one fundamental thought: the works of the life of action have a very real importance as fruits of human existence; yet failure or success is not directly proportional to the virtue displayed in such works, because Fortune often intervenes. One cannot assess the results of one's efforts by the criterion of success; anyone who does so is a lightweight.[66] It is Fortune's hand, as we soon shall see, that is regarded by Cervantes[67] as the determining factor in the defeat of the Armada — the *serious* Fortune that is none other than the Providence of God.[68]

Two odes on the defeat of the Armada, attributable to Cervantes though not with certainty, may be taken as typical of the spirit in which the Spanish nation accepted the ruin of its fleet. The first

65. Roland H. Bainton, "Man, God, and the Church in the Age of the Renaissance," in *The Renaissance: A Symposium* (Metropolitan Museum of Art; New York, 1952), p. 62.

66. *El hidalgo y el honor* (Madrid, 1948), pp. 39–40.

67. If we may believe the attribution to him of two odes on the Armada, preserved in a single manuscript; see his *Obras completas*, ed. A. Valbuena Prat (Madrid, 1956), pp. 60–63.

68. See the final chapter of Volume II ("Fortune and Fate") and my article, "Sobre las dos Fortunas: de tejas arriba y de tejas abajo," *Studia Philologica: Homenaje ofrecido a Dámaso Alonso*, II (Madrid, 1961), 143–54.

Canción is addressed to Fame (the spreader of rumors); it asks in anguished tones if the reports of disaster can be true. The second admits the inevitable and seeks such balm as religious faith and patriotic devotion can provide. We shall limit our following analysis to the second.

Addressing Spain, the poet begs her not to be dismayed as she sees her sons returning to her bosom, leaving the sea bestrewn with the relics of their hope. Those sons, as they return, are not driven by enemy action, but by the force of wind and sea and by the design of Heaven: if the enemy is permitted to rise, it is because the Divine Purpose intends his eventual downfall to be the greater. Heaven's action may be slow, but Heaven punishes the wicked. Then comes an exhortation to Philip to avenge piracy in the Indies, ships burned, and temples defiled. Let him only ask! The nation will give treasure and blood. Let him but raise his arm, as a Christian Moses, and "the Lutheran" will be struck down to the dust.

The appeal to the defeated heroes is really a vote of confidence: Spanish valor is strengthened by adversity. In the final stanza Spain, her king, and her great soldiers are reminded that they have but to offer, to command, and to obey (respectively). Heaven will assuredly aid the just.

In 1596 there came an even more galling defeat. The Earl of Essex sailed into the harbor of Cádiz, shot up the town and held it for twenty-four days, after which the Duke of Medina Sidonia (responsible for the defense) entered at the head of his troops together with a special auxiliary contingent that had been recruited in Seville by a certain Captain Becerra. The enemy had already withdrawn, and Cervantes was inspired to write a sonnet of contempt:

> We saw in July a second Holy Week,
> With surging crowds that pose as companies
> Of men at arms, of soldiers who impressed
> Our yokels with their valor, not the English!
> White plumes on helmets bright, yet not so bright
> But that they faded, as the swaggering figures —
> Striding Goliaths and their marching pals —
> And the apparatus of that weird procession
> Collapsed and fell to earth. Then came the rescue.
> The great Calf roared,[69] earth trembled, and the sky

69. *Becerro* means calf in Spanish.

> Grew dark with threat of all-avenging ruin.
> 'Twas at that moment (when the Earl had sailed
> From Cádiz with impunity) that our
> Medina, our great Duke, marched in in triumph.[70]

This sonnet rounds out our consideration of national optimism-pessimism in the reign of Philip II (d. 1598). The "evolution" in sixteenth-century Spanish attitudes suggested by Alfonso García Valdecasas (see above) in no way altered the basic axiom: the Spanish are God's chosen people and God's purposes will prevail — late or soon. The evolution, strictly speaking, consisted of an increasing sense of melancholy as the day of fulfillment receded into a future ever more remote. We shall reserve the pith of the testimony of Mateo Alemán and his picaresque novel, *Guzmán de Alfarache* (1599), for our survey of the *Sic et Non* of optimism-pessimism in the baroque in Volume IV. We must, however, anticipate slightly at this point. Alemán perceived that: "The name Spaniard, which in other days was a weapon of offense so effective that the whole world trembled before it, is now — as a result of our sins — a thing lost and almost of no consequence. We have come to such sore straits that the strength we have is not sufficient" (*ed. cit.*, II, 144–45). Here is the melancholy referred to by García Valdecasas, and it will be voiced many times in the baroque. But not even the seventeenth century has an atmosphere of all-pervading gloom; the rays of hope are more numerous, and brighter, than one would think.

OPTIMISM–PESSIMISM *QUOAD VITAM*

"A gust of pessimism spreads and becomes a noteworthy driving force in the cultural attitude of the second half of the sixteenth

---

70. The sonnet bears this heading: "A la Entrada del Duque de Medina Sidonia en Cádiz en julio de 1596, con socorro de tropas enseñadas en Sevilla por el Capitán Becerra, después de haber evacuado aquella ciudad las tropas inglesas y saqueádola por espacio de veinticuatro días al mando del Conde de Essex." Here is the text: "Vimos en julio otra Semana Santa / atestada de ciertas cofradías, / que los soldados llaman compañías, / de quien el vulgo, no el inglés, se espanta. / Hubo de plumas muchedumbre tanta, / que en menos de catorce o quince días / volaron sus pigmeos y Golías, / y cayó su edificio por la planta. / Bramó el Becerro, y púsoles en sarta; / tronó la tierra, oscurecióse el cielo, / amenazando una total ruina; / y al cabo, en Cádiz, con mesura harta, / ido ya el conde sin ningún recelo, / triunfando entró el duque de Medina" (*Obras completas, ed. cit.*, p. 51).

century." So wrote Werner Weisbach in his book on the baroque and the Counter Reformation.[71] Theodore Spencer, on the other hand, portrays Shakespeare's generation as sustained by essentially optimistic convictions, among them the belief that "there was an eternal law, a general order — in the universe, in the ranks of created things, in the institution of government — and it was the business of thoughtful men to discover it and describe it so that through knowledge of it they could fulfill the end for which God had made them."[72] It will be difficult, in our search for the truth in these matters with respect to Spain, to separate attitudes which are essential and radical from those which are relative, difficult to distinguish between *quoad vitam* and *quoad ens*. In Spain, denigration of the here and now implies — one may dare to say — exaltation of the hereafter. Above and beyond the City of Satan is the City "that hath foundations, whose builder and maker is God" (Heb. 11:10).

In 1524 Juan Luis Vives wrote in his *Introduction to Wisdom* (in words already familiar to us) that man's life is, as it were, a pilgrimage and an exile; it hangs by a thread, beset by a thousand unexpected dangers. Its duration is so uncertain that it is the height of folly to commit any act that might endanger our soul's eternal health (*ed. cit.*, p. 28). Alejo Venegas in 1537 warned against placing one's trust in man: King David was punished by three days of pestilence for having counted his soldiers, instead of remembering Jeremiah's curse upon whoever trusts man, not God. King David should have confided, not in numbers, but in his own anointing by the hand of Samuel.[73]

The first half of the sixteenth century has, as Weisbach implies, its optimistic voices. In Alfonso de Valdés' *Dialogue on the Sack of Rome* (1527) one interlocutor remarks: "You, apparently, aspire to create a new world." The answer is revealing: "I would wish to leave in it the good it now has, and take from it all evil." In the

71. *Der Barock als Kunst der Gegenreformation* (Berlin, 1921), p. 4.

72. *Shakespeare and the Nature of Man* (New York–Cambridge, Massachusetts, 1945), p. 1.

73. *Agonía del tránsito de la muerte*, NBAE, XVI, 244a. The thought is repeated in 1592 by Fray Hernando de Zárate in his *Discursos de la paciencia cristiana* (*Discourse on Christian Patience*), BAE, XXVII, 438a: "thus they incur the curse of the Prophet, who says: Cursed is the man who trusts in man. These are they who, as St. Augustine says, think they have no need of God."

same author's *Dialogue between Mercury and Charon*, concerned with the same subject, Mercury says to one of the souls seeking transportation across the Styx, "We should like to know what profession you followed in the world." The soul replies: "I was a poor friar, and my profession was to serve Jesus Christ." Mercury: "Do you call yourself poor when you served such a Master?" And the soul: "I was poor in the eyes of the world, and poor in virtues; with respect to the estate and the gifts I received from my Master, I was more than rich, more than blessed." [74] This is the Erasmian *Philosophia Christi*.

Much more numerous are the voices of those who would debase and humiliate man in order to bring him to his senses. As will become apparent, this debasement has an optimistic purpose: to lift the sinner's thoughts and heart to God. In this respect, the attitude toward man and the world is the same from the fifteenth-century Raimundo Sabunde to the seventeenth-century Quevedo and Gracián; it is exemplified by the following listings by Fray Juan de Pineda, in the index of his *Agricultura christiana* (1589): "World, the temple of God"; "World, one of the enemies of God."

Thus Francisco de Osuna declared in his *Third Spiritual Alphabet* (1524): "This mortal body is more fit to serve as food for worms than to be seen by our fellow men." [75] Fray Francisco Ortiz wrote to his brother Juan (about 1537): "Our life is like a flower of the field, and we post along a road of no return. The post rider sets the days' journeys, and so fast that he covers more than a thousand million leagues in twenty-four hours; and I must needs ride post behind him; . . . and he leads me and will deliver me, when least I expect it, to that Judge who is terrible to those who on earth have failed to serve him. The time I have been allotted to win salvation slips through my hands, as I strive to acquire a slight portion of dung and obvious deceit, which will soon leave me when I leave it; and I set my eyes on the beauty of created creatures . . . soon to be reduced to unendurable corruption." The eloquent text is long. The author perceives himself as following after sirens' calls — the disturbing incitements of the flesh and of the world. He sees that

74. See *Diálogo de las cosas ocurridas en Roma*, ed. J. F. Montesinos (Madrid, 1928), p. 183, and *Diálogo de Mercurio y Carón*, ed. *idem* (Madrid, 1929), p. 253.
75. *Tercer abecedario espiritual*, NBAE, XVI, 325b.

all is "a fantastic dream . . . of unsettled brains." When the rich awaken in death they will find themselves empty, their repentance too long delayed. After the sleep of this life comes everlasting death. And yet, "perceiving this great deceit, I allow myself to be hoodwinked; having eyes I see not, having a nose I smell not, like the idols of the vain world that we love." [76] The tone of this passage is indeed gloomy, yet the same writer declared in a letter dated 1537 (op. cit., 276b–77a) that even in this earthly life, he who observes God's commandments has a foretaste of his heavenly reward.[77]

Man, by himself, is nothing. The voices that tell us so are legion. In 1561 Luis Pérez, an otherwise unknown prothonotary, composed a new gloss on Jorge Manrique's famous Coplas on the death of his father (15 c.). It is his hope, the glossator says in his Carta nuncupatoria, that his sententiae will serve as a mirror "in which we may see . . . what we are, . . . what we have been and what we shall be, to the end that, like Job, we may perceive our life to be unending warfare, a shadow that passes, a vanishing dream, a flower that falls to earth, a valley of tears full of bitterness." [78]

But man has resources outside himself. In the "pessimistic" second half of the century, as in the "optimistic" first half, the painters of grim pictures of man's folly and willful depravity portray also something else: there are things infinitely worthy of being known — the law of God and His commandments.[79] God's mercy is the greater and more enduring, we are told by Fray Luis de León, in proportion as man is bereft of strength. Men pass, but the mercy that God showers upon them endures from age to age, descending from father to son forever. Let all creatures bless the Lord! [80] Pedro Malón de Chaide, in La conversión de la Magdalena, reminds us that we should ever stand with our loins girded for, as Job well knew, man's life on earth is a struggle which ends only with death. The battle-

76. Epístolas familiares, BAE, XIII, letter vii.

77. In his Third Spiritual Alphabet Osuna talks of his practice of inner concentration and mental prayer: "What I have noticed in this exercise is that men naturally melancholy make little progress in it, whereas those who are by nature joyful and dedicate their joy to God progress marvelously" (cited by Bataillon, op. cit., I, 206).

78. Glosas a las Coplas de Jorge Manrique, III: Luis Pérez, ed. facsimile by Antonio Pérez y Gómez (Cieza, 1962), fol. 16.

79. Fray Luis de Granada in the prologue to his Guía de pecadores (Obras, I [Madrid, 1768], no pagination).

80. De los nombres de Cristo, ed. F. de Onís (Madrid, 1914–21), III, 209.

field is the world; the soldiers, we ourselves; the enemies, the world, the flesh, and the devil. But . . . the object of this conquest is Heaven (*ed. cit.*, II, 44–45)!

After having cited so many churchmen, it will be well to examine the position of a jurist, Jerónimo de Mondragón, who in 1598 published at Lérida in Aragon a remarkable imitation (for this date) of Erasmus' *In Praise of Folly*, with the title *Condemnation and Excellence of Human Folly*.[81] Here Erasmus has been made completely orthodox and acceptable to Spanish taste in the post-Tridentine period. The author's purpose is didactic, melioristic. All the praises of folly, he explains in his prologue "To the Christian Reader," are to be taken as irony; they are part of his didactic system; the reader thus enticed will readily pay heed to doctrines which, if presented undisguised, would never reach him.

Chapter XXXV is entitled: "Wherein is Shown the Blessedness of Folly." The treatment is noteworthy in that it preaches a doctrine of illusion that compels us to think of the nineteenth century and of Friedrich Nietzsche. How could human beings endure life on this terrestrial ball without folly? Folly in the pejorative sense is defined as vainglory (p. 180); in the favorable sense, it is that quality which causes some men to renounce vainglory, which enables a man to be content with himself and with his gifts, not to worry about his stature, his charm or his beauty, his keenness of intellect, his birth, his homeland, his lineage. Folly enables him, in short, to find satisfaction in what he does, thinks, and says without concerning himself over what others may think (*ibid.*). It is often sufficient merely to feign folly in order to accomplish great things:

How happy, how more than happy, how joyous and jocund is the state of folly! Because of it man ceases to feel the unendurable pains, no longer tastes the bitter pills that the "sane" men of the world know only too well! . . . What moment does life grant me that is not sad, melancholy, unpleasant, and full of discontent, unless some measure of folly is injected into it? . . . Tell me, . . . could a nation long endure its prince, a vassal his overlord, a slave his master, a husband his wife, . . . a neighbor his neighbor if into the whole relationship there were not stirred some admixture of that sweet nectar known

81. *Censura de la locura humana y excelencias della*, ed. Antonio Vilanova (Barcelona, 1953).

as folly? Even Seneca said it in his essay *On Tranquility of Spirit*: "To turn one's back on sanity is at times a great joy, an infinite delight" (pp. 179–80).

The author of these lines is a meliorist: things could, indeed may be, better: hence his book. He is an adherent of Erasmian optimism whose doctrine is freed — nearly three generations after the scrutiny of Erasmus' works at Valladolid in 1527 — of all those elements that could have been offensive to the most Catholic of readers. His message — by a layman and for laymen — was issued with the usual ecclesiastical approval.

Before closing this section I would overstep the limits of the sixteenth century and cite a passage from the semipicaresque *Vida del Escudero Marcos de Obregón*, printed in 1618 by the semi-layman (*beneficiado*) Vicente Espinel (ordained late, after a boisterous youth). I cite it, not because it bears directly on the problem of mankind's condition as a fortunate or an unfortunate inhabitant of this planet, but rather because it reflects what perhaps was less rare than has been assumed for this time and place (fifty-five years after Trent) — joy of life, experienced by a man sound in mind and body:

"Finally I reached Málaga, or rather, I stopped to view the city from Zambara hill. So great was the comfort I received from the sight, from the fragrance of the wind that played through those magnificent orchards, bright with orange and lemon blossoms all year long, that I seemed to be looking into a corner of Paradise." He continues his description with unrestrained joy: the view of earth and sea, the appearance and situation of the buildings, the cathedral. In this happiest of places "the ears are delighted with bird song, . . . a sweet harmonious confusion that lifts the spirit up to a contemplation of the Creator of all things." There is no note of dissonance — not even man is vile.[82]

The above soundings of opinion must suffice. They show that the extremes of glorification and denigration of the human state are present in our period, as they were four centuries earlier in the mind of Pope Innocent III (d. 1218), whose *De miseria humanae*

82. Part I, Descanso xvii. I extracted this passage in full in another context in Volume II (p. 95).

conditionis, so frequently cited as a typical utterance of a mordant and pessimistic medieval asceticism, was to have been followed (as we learn from the *Prologus*) by a second volume on the dignity of human nature aided by Divine Grace. The existence of these extremes faces us with a problem in the history of Christianity — a problem, much more profound than a supposed opposition between Renaissance and Counter Reformation, which has been analyzed with great clarity by Arthur O. Lovejoy.[83] "The most important and distinctive circumstance in the history of religion and moral philosophy in the Occident," Lovejoy writes, "is the fact that both later Platonism [84] and the accepted philosophy of the Church combined *otherworldliness* with a virtual, if not usually a literal or unqualified, *optimism*. Both were equally committed to the two contradictory theses that 'this' world is an essentially *evil* thing to be escaped from, and that its existence, with precisely the attributes it has, is a good so great that in the production of it the divinest of all the attributes of deity was manifested."

A consistent otherworldly (i.e., pessimistic) philosophy which wishes to turn men's thoughts and affections from the visible world may take any one of three forms: (1) it may teach that the world is pure illusion; (2) it may admit the world's reality, yet assert that its existence is "utter and inexplicable disaster"; (3) it may turn its back on the metaphysical state of the world and devote its energies to persuading men to escape from the world. Early Christian tendencies to accept the second alternative eventually were rejected as Manichean heresy, though this position had the merit of being free from contradiction. On the other hand, the significance of the victorious alternative, the decision in favor of a "fruitful inconsistency," [85] did not become apparent, according to Lovejoy, until modern times. As a result of this inconsistency there were kept

83. *The Great Chain of Being* (Cambridge, Massachusetts, 1936), p. 98 (emphasis mine).

84. "Aristotle does not call for a redeemer because he feels no need of redemption and is obsessed by no sense of sin. The world as he viewed it was essentially good (that is, rational and orderly), and if man exploited his inherent rationality he might come to very comfortable terms with it" (Baker, *The Dignity of Man*, p. 130).

85. The term is Lovejoy's. Augustine's conception was that of a theocratic universe, a universe "demonstrably filled with evil and stained by the wicked fruits of man's perverted will, but none the less a universe established and controlled, for His own inscrutable ends, by God" (Baker, *The Dignity of Man*, p. 165).

alive, in the predominantly other-worldly thought of the Middle Ages, "certain roots of a 'this-worldly' philosophy": existence in the here-and-now is a good; the translation of supersensible possibilities into sensible realities means an increase, not a loss, of value; the very essence of the good consists in the maximal actualization of variety. Temporal and sensible experience is good, the supreme manifestation of the divine (*op. cit.*, pp. 96–98).

We have seen this inconsistent doctrine at work in our Volume II (see the chapters on "The Creation and the Creatures," "The Nature and Destiny of Man"). It is independent of the ups and downs of history: any given Christian thinker may be influenced by what is happening around him; but his inclination to stress (or to deny the possibility of) human happiness in this world has deeper causes than the brightness of hope or the deepness of gloom in a given age.[86] Erasmus and Luther were contemporaries; the receptiveness of each to anthropological optimism and anthropological pessimism, respectively, had its origin in a personal choice between the two opposing emphases that had developed through the centuries that preceded them: should one magnify God at the expense of man? Or on the contrary should one elevate man at the risk of reducing the majesty and the awfulness of the Creator? What happened in Europe in the sixteenth century (not merely its second half) was that what might be called the "anti-man" party became suddenly vocal, violently unwilling to coexist with the opposing side, the party — victorious in Spain — of "fruitful inconsistency," as Lovejoy so aptly designated it.

OPTIMISM *QUOAD ENS*

In this section I drop the word "pessimism" from my heading. Pessimism *quoad ens* is simply not found in Spain. What we find is, in the last analysis, the all-embracing optimism of St. Thomas — a doctrine which holds that all existence is good, evil being merely

86. It would be interesting to make a comparison of the following two books (and others like them): Baltasar Pérez del Castillo, *El teatro del mundo . . . de las miserias y de la dinidad del hombre*, published (Alcalá, 1574), three years after the victory of Lepanto, and Ambrosio Bautista, *Breve discurso de las miserias de la vida humana* (published in 1635, ten years before the death of Quevedo). Neither book is accessible to me.

an appearance, a relative and restricted view of reality.[87] Some readers will object — as Alain Guy inconsistently does — that belief in the ultimate triumph of truth and right does not suffice to make one an optimist, the prophet Jeremiah being a case in point. I must overrule the objection. Plato, for all the pessimism present in his critical examination of empirical life, is an optimist in his religious thought,[88] and this is precisely the position of our sixteenth-century Spaniards. While the philosophical terminology might be more accurate were I to use other adjectives — *noumenal* or *theological* — I prefer the Latin *quoad ens*, or the English *essential*. We are dealing with essential optimism; the writers to be cited in this section go — or attempt to go — to the ultimate heart, to the inmost *essence* of existence.

Jean Cassou establishes this point quite clearly with respect to Cervantes — an author whose literary activity began in 1585 and ended in 1616: "The reader who is familiar with the diapason of ideas and attitudes of the Renaissance will find its echo throughout all Cervantes' work. The play of ideas and the hope they give the spirit, the challenge and irony they arouse in the face of the relativity of opinions and the reality of things . . . all these opposing elements are evoked at every turn and put to the test."[89] Cervantes believes in an inner harmony, of the individual within himself, and in a larger harmony, of men with one another and with Nature.[90] His optimism — noumenal, theological, essential — is both Platonic (when it stresses harmony)[91] and Thomistic (when it

87. See Alain Guy, *La pensée de Fray Luis de León* (Limoges, 1943), pp. 328–29. Guy derives his definition from Lalande's *Vocabulaire philosophique* (ed. 1932, II, 544); Guy's identification of this type of optimism with Aquinas' doctrine of good and evil is found on p. 328.

88. "Er ist bei allem Pessimismus in der Beurteilung des empirischen Lebens in seinem religiösen Denken Optimist" (Gustav Entz, *Pessimismus und Weltflucht bei Plato* [Tübingen, 1911], p. 183). See also the statement of James M. Dunham: "But there is another definition of reason which [Plato] cordially endorsed — the world can be understood by men of trained intelligence. This implies that the good exists in total nature and we can analyze it in the same way that we analyze the good in man" (see the chapter entitled "Platonism" in *A History of Philosophical Systems*, ed. Virgilius Ferm [New York, 1950]), p. 102.

89. "An Introduction to Cervantes," in *Cervantes Across the Centuries*, ed. Angel Flores and M. J. Benardete (New York, 1947), p. 11.

90. See W. C. Atkinson, "Cervantes, El Pinciano, and the *Novelas Ejemplares*," *HR*, XVI (1948), 198–99.

91. Juan Boscán (d. 1542) incorporated the harmonious Platonic ideal in the Renaissance heroine of his *Historia de Leandro y Hero* in the following passage (quoted also

emphasizes knowledge and self-knowledge).[92] And throughout his life he derives spiritual comfort from St. Augustine, whose pessimism *quoad vitam* leaves intact his essential optimism: God's creation is ultimately good; the human soul is restless till it rests in Him. From Cervantes' first printed book to his last, he gives evidence that he was deeply affected by this thought.[93]

The Problem of Evil

"The conviction of the utter purposelessness of things is one of [the modern mind's] main characteristics," writes W. T. Stace, a philosopher of our own day, finding the origin of this attitude in the fact that "the rise of science, by a process of psychological suggestion and not by logic," brought it into being (*op. cit.*, pp. 98–99). According to this radically pessimistic view, "the energies of our system will decay, the glory of the sun will be dimmed, and the earth, tideless and inert, will no longer tolerate the race which has for a moment disturbed its solitude. Man will go down into the pit, and all his thoughts will perish. . . . Imperishable monuments and immortal deeds, death itself, and love stronger than death, will be as if they had not been. Nor will anything that is be better or worse for all that the labor, genius, devotion and suffering of man have striven through countless ages to effect" (*ibid.*, p. 145). According to the scientific conception of the universe (philosophical natur-

in Volume I, Chapter IV): "Her walk, her glance, the quiet of her repose, / Were so harmonious that they revealed / An indescribable something that no man / Can find words to define, a force extended / Through each and every part of that fair frame, / Ruled and controlled by such an inner power / That 'twere impossible to show its fixed abode" — "El andar, el mirar, el estar queda, / andaban en tal son, que descubrían / un cierto no sé qué, tan admirable, / tan tendido por todo y por sus partes, / con tal orden y fuerza recogido, / que era imposible dalle lugar cierto" (*Obras*, ed. W. Knapp [Madrid, 1875], p. 294).

92. "The revolt against Scholasticism indicates that men were becoming impatient with the manifest corruptions of a methodology, but not that they were compelled toward a radical reconstruction of their view of the world. . . . If Scholasticism meant anything, it was that a rational God was the author of a rational universe, and that both were legitimate objects of man's rational knowledge. The prevailing optimism of the sixteenth century required no revision of this set of assumptions; indeed, such assumptions made such optimism possible" (Baker, *The Dignity of Man*, p. 205). See also A. D. Sertillanges, *Les grandes thèses de la philosophie Thomiste* (Paris, [1928]) pp. 32–34.

93. As I have shown in my "Realidad, voluntad y gracia en Cervantes," *Ibérida: Revista de filologia*, III (1961), 125–28. See also Paul Oskar Kristeller, "Augustine and the Early Renaissance," *Review of Religion* (May, 1944), 339–58 (first published in *International Science*, I [1941]), 7–14.

alism), the world is wholly governed by blind physical forces; it has no purpose but is entirely senseless and meaningless; it is not a moral order, being indifferent to values of any kind (p. 143).

Standing against these conceptions is the religious world-view. This holds that the world is ultimately governed by spiritual forces; and that the world *is* a moral order (*ibid.*).

The *Weltanschauung* of modern scientific naturalism, with its attendant essential pessimism, was of course absent from Golden Age Spain. Yet the problem of evil — the greatest of all philosophical and theological problems — was at all times present in men's minds. Its awfulness was emphasized or de-emphasized according to individual temperament, but it was always there. For Augustine — and beyond him no Spanish believer could go — evil was simply the absence of good. If things exist (as they obviously do), they participate in some degree in the excellence of their Creator: God created the universe "and saw that it was very good." This conviction, "developed so gigantically in *The City of God*, provided an answer for all of Augustine's problems. Given the transcendental and absolute goodness of God, and the potential goodness of all his creation, the world — wicked though it be — becomes the theatre wherein is enacted the majestic working out of God's purposes." [94]

According to Augustine, sin and grace are mutually dependent. Without sin there could be no occasion for grace, and without grace the human race would be simply lost: "the deserved penalty of sin would have hurled all headlong into the second death, of which there is no end, had not the undeserved grace of God saved some therefrom" (*ibid.*, p. 173). "Saved some" — these two words mark the doorway whereby a relative pessimism can enter in. St. Bernard could believe that the number of the damned exceeds that of the blest. No matter! God's action — its total result — is altogether very good.

We shall examine the problem of evil as it is treated by Fray Luis de León (d. 1591). In his commentary on the Book of Job, this Spanish Augustinian declares that the mere fact of our existence is proof of God's care: "Surely it is an argument for a marvelous providence that a life as frail as ours, encased in so weak and brittle a

94. Baker, *The Dignity of Man*, p. 164.

body, ever exposed to the many possibilities of breakage that beset us night and day, could live and maintain its integrity for many years." [95]

Luis de León shares with Bossuet a keen awareness of the bitterness which is man's lot in the world of phenomena (*ibid.*, p. 335, n. 1). Everywhere in his writings one finds the idea that not to suffer is contrary to human nature and would imply a deviation from the law which rules this globe: even in his university lectures Fray Luis speaks of "the miseries and cruel evils of human life" (pp. 308–9). Evil is not just a "mode"; it is a profound characteristic of the cosmos, omnipresent and constant: *Nullum tempus fuisse quod vitio vacaret* — there never was a time when evil did not exist. Man is ever the enemy of man; there was no golden age (p. 318). Like Unamuno, Luis de León shows constantly two opposing tendencies: the most authentic psychic expansion, and the most integral and effective rational bitterness (p. 321).

Yet Fray Luis believed and confided in the ultimate triumph of the True and the Good (p. 328). His pessimism remains always phenomenal and never extends to the noumenal — to the afterlife. It is indeed this very phenomenal pessimism which causes him to exalt the saving virtue of the Redemption. There is in his thought no trace of despair; on the contrary, Fray Luis invites mankind to turn to the only Saviour who can give beatitude. Without Him, all is sheer loss (p. 331). In a poem *On the World and Its Vanity* he wrote:

> Nor would I e'er condemn
> The structure of this world, for God has made it.
> Only the deeds of men —
> Human abuse and wickedness — degrade it.[96]

Here we see repeated a thought now quite familiar: the world is the image of God; the "world," God's enemy. The only evil is sin.[97]

---

95. Cited by A. Guy, *op. cit.*, p. 307; see also pp. 350, 610–11.

96. "No condeno del mundo / la máquina, pues es de Dios hechura, / en los abusos fundo / la presente escritura / cuya verdad el campo me asegura" (cited *ibid.*, p. 314).

97. On the joy inherent in the Christian act of scorning the "world," compare this text from the allegorical novel *Blanquerna* by the thoroughly medieval Ramón Lull (d. 1315): "The Abbot asked the cause of his being always so joyful and contented. 'Sir,' replied the monk, 'so great is the pleasure which I derive from what I learn in

The Universe as a Moral Order

In a magnificent passage from a sermon preached at the height of the baroque — Christmas day of 1621 — Sir Thomas Browne, author of the *Religio Medici*, evokes the wealth, the treasures of the humble but redeemed human creature.

> But if thou canst take this light of reason that is in thee, this poor snuffe, that is almost out in thee, thy faint and dimme knowledge of God, that riseth out of this light of nature, if thou canst in those embers, those cold ashes, finde out one small coale, and wilt take paines to kneel downe, and blow that coale with thy devout *prayers* . . . thou shalt never envy the lustre and glory of the great lights of worldly men . . . , but thou shalt finde, that however they magnifie their lights, their wit, their learning . . . , their fortune, their favour . . . yet thou shalt see, that thou by thy small light hast gathered *Pearle* and Amber, and they by their great lights nothing but shels and pebles. . . .98

This passage from Browne may serve as "golden text" 99 for the exposition that is to follow. It shows that the attitude toward man's unaided "light of reason" is not widely different, in 1621, from that of 1524 (the date of Vives' *Introductio ad sapientiam*). It shows also that man's ultimate hope — if he will but blow on the coal with his devout prayers — is the eternal hope of Christian believers. Beside this golden text I wish to place another — Spanish this time, and likewise composed at the height of the baroque. It is from the picaresque novel, *Guzmán de Alfarache* (1599), by the supposed "pessimist," Mateo Alemán. The author relates the anecdote of a painter who was asked by a Spanish gentleman to paint a picture of a beautiful horse, well caparisoned but running loose. The painter fulfilled the commission with all the skill at his command and then put the canvas out to dry, inadvertently setting it upside down upon a chair. The gentleman stopped by the studio and, concluding that that was not what he had ordered, remarked: "Maestro, the horse that I want pictured should be galloping, and

the science of philosophy which teaches me to know God, that I consider myself fortunate to be in religion and to have fled the world; with the result that night and day I continually rejoice, especially because my science persuades me to scorn the world and all vainglory, causing me to love God and humility' " (ed. L. Riber [Madrid, 1944], p. 284).

98. Cited by Margaret L. Wiley, *The Subtle Knot: Creative Scepticism in Seventeenth-century England* (Cambridge, Massachusetts, 1952), pp. 134–35.

99. That is, the Biblical text with which it has for centuries been the practice to begin, and set the keynote for, a sermon.

this one seems, on the contrary, to be rolling on his back." The painter explained that it simply happened to be upside down, and the owner was completely satisfied. Alemán draws the moral: "If we consider the works of God, they often give the impression of a horse rolling on the grass; but if we would set upright the picture formed by the Supreme Artist, we would find that there has been no mistake, that the work is perfect. Our afflictions seem to us heavy; the fact is that we know them not, because of our ignorance. But when He who sends them to us, reveals to us the mercy that they represent, and finally turns them right side up, they cease to be trials and become pure joy" (ed. cit., V, 157–58).

Trials and afflictions "become pure joy" — so the believer is told in 1599, exactly as in the 1520's when enthusiasm for the *Philosophia Christi* of Erasmus was flooding the Peninsula. Bataillon, in his account of this wave of enthusiasm, warns against thinking of the Reformation and Counter Reformation as two schools dominated by a gloomy asceticism: there was a time when they had in common an optimistic sense of the redeeming, the freeing power of Divine Grace (op. cit., I, 205). And I would sound another warning: however great the "gloomy asceticism" of any period, the sense of grace is — must always be — present. Christian man must at all times recognize both his littleness, when he stands unaided, and his glorious state as a redeemed son of God.

To the "Erasmian" 1520's belong the writings of Fray Alonso de Madrid, whose ascetic books had a remarkable vogue. His *Mirror for Illustrious Persons* (1524) offers in its final chapter an injunction to all men to keep the image of death ever before their eyes — to the end that the sinner may return from his wickedness and the just man take pleasure in the thought that the closer death is to him, the nearer he is to life eternal. Each day we die, Fray Alonso quotes Seneca as saying; each day the great shears cut away a piece of life. And much later St. Gregory said that our present life is but a death prolonged. He who has small children, says Fray Alonso, should be aware of the Saint's warning, detaching his heart from the love of his offspring and teaching them to seek the only life untouched by death. Still another saint, St. Bernard, reminds us of the slow degeneration that most men have to endure as they approach their end, along with remorse for a life misspent and fears that cause us to tremble. Then devils assault us more subtly than ever; even against the virtuous they struggle desperately; it is right that we should ponder the awfulness of those demonic faces arrayed against us. O day of necessity, which finds us so unprepared to meet it! O day desirous of life, life that will not be given. O sad and cursed day, for those who have pursued life's comforts and consolations! Sad death! Sad torment forever! But how different is the lot of those who have remembered, remembered and prepared! O day of true birth unto eternal life! Here death ends, and triumphant living begins! This day casts its radiance backwards on all the days that preceded it, cleansing them of all worldly contagion. O day of glory and gain, when we offer the life that we have held so dear to the great Lord who wishes to take it, who gave his own life to enrich ours! Precious day in the eyes of the Lord! Here the just will see the glorious wealth, the treasures for which they were created.

The work ends with an appeal to the "illustrious persons" for whom it was composed. Let them serve the Lord whose they are — they and all their possessions. Let them think on these things, that they may never sin, attaining at last to the universal blessedness prepared — *in aeternum* — for those who here below have deserved it.[100]

To these same early years of the century — not to the baroque — belongs a treatise of Sir Thomas More (d. 1535), *Four Last Things*, a work of the humanist-saint's maturity. The true Christian, says More, will think earnestly of the dance of death depicted on the walls of St. Paul's — "the loathly figure of our dead bodies, bitten away the flesh." The best death one can hope for is to be "lying in thy bed, thy head shooting, thy back aching, thy veins beating, thine heart panting, thy throat rattling, thy flesh trembling, thy mouth gaping, thy nose sharping, thy legs cooling, thy fingers fumbling, thy breath shortening, thy life vanishing, and thy death drawing on." Like that other luminary of the early Renaissance, Giovanni Pico della Mirandola (d. 1494), Thomas More ended his life in the manner of a third-century ascetic. To me this fact does not seem "odd," as it did in 1947 to Professor Herschel Baker, who cites the passage in his *The Dignity of Man* (pp. 264–65).

100. *NBAE*, XVI, 648b–49b.

Juan Luis Vives' *Introduction to Wisdom* was printed in 1524. It has been said of Vives that he represents a bitter and disillusioned view of life; that in him "there is no trace of Renaissance joy." [101] This view of Vives is based on incomplete knowledge of his writings. The Valencian humanist is aware of the *Sic* and the *Non* in human life: "In the human spirit knowledge and virtue have their dwelling, as do their opposites, ignorance and vice." [102] In proportion as man lifts up his spirit from bodily to spiritual things, his life becomes more Godlike: "Thus it will come to pass that God will perceive in you a relationship or a similarity to His own divine nature, and will take delight in it, and will dwell with you as in His own true temple, which will be more pleasing to Him than temples of stone or metal" (*ibid.*, p. 65).

And not only man, but the world is God's creation: "The world is as it were a possession of His, or rather, His temple; He brought it forth from nothingness, and shaped and formed it in the beauty that we behold . . . " (p. 61). "Look well," Vives tells us, "[for] there is nothing great or small in all the universe, which, if you consider its inner principle, its nature, its force and power, can fail to lead you to contemplate the marvels of God, who created all; there is nothing which will not give you cause to adore Him" (p. 68).

Vives was thirty-two years of age when he put down these thoughts. Was this youthful optimism lost? Quite the contrary. In his *De anima et vita*, printed in 1538, two years before his death, Vives contrasts the bitter and unendurable thought of personal annihilation with the Christian's assurance of immortality (Book II, ch. 19): What marvelous comfort to know that there awaits the wise and good man an abode of blessedness, prepared by a most just, a good and perfect God! Why are men so slow to believe in this wonderful gift, so slow to live in accordance with this assurance? Because there exists a force hostile to man, an Adversary

---

101. "La curiosidad intelectiva de la tradición hispano-judía se magnifica en Vives, a la vez que su visión amarga y desilusionada del mundo. En este 'renacentista' no hay nada de la alegría del Renacimiento" (Américo Castro, "Un aspecto del pensar hispano-judío," *Hispania*, XXXV [1952], 166; see also p. 172). Castro has repeated this thought many times since he first expounded it in *España en su historia* (Buenos Aires, 1948).

102. *Introducción a la sabiduría*, ed. cit., p. 25.

whose purpose it is to controvert this truth, so necessary for our existence. "From the darkness of this enemy may God (the true, the immense Light) protect us." [103]

Vives taught a doctrine of pure joy: the end toward which Christian doctrine strives is a pure, a gentle and calm serenity (when once the passions have been brought under control) [104] — a serenity which shall make glad, delight, and expand the human spirit so that we may become like unto God and his angels.[105] All joy becomes impossible, however, when men reject the divine tutelage. They then have recourse to countless substitutes, but it is like trying to hold up a falling column with props. All such defenses cannot free them from the assaults and violence to which their flesh is heir, and which attack and undermine them continually and everywhere (Corts Grau, op. cit., p. 97). It appears to have been this vivid portrayal of the desperate lot of the godless — utterly rejected by Vives as the inevitable human lot — that has led to the mistaken idea of a pessimistic Vives.

The Erasmian Juan de Valdés (a layman, brother of Charles V's Latin secretary Alfonso) in 1525 printed his *Diálogo de doctrina cristiana*. In it he presents a dilemma: man must choose between the love of God, and self-love. He who chooses self will refer all things to his own person; the lover of God will love all things in and through, and to the glory of, God. When once the soul has been won over to the love of God, it feels itself lifted up by a great joy: Christ's yoke is gentle, and his burden light.[106]

We pass from Valdés to another layman, Hernán Pérez de Oliva (d. 1531). A man of wide learning, Pérez de Oliva took part in the theological scrutiny of the works of Erasmus at Valladolid in 1527. Had he lived he would have served as tutor and mentor to young

103. Cited by Julián Marías, *El tema del hombre* (Madrid, 1943), p. 175.

104. One must not condemn, as the Stoics did, the lower portion of man's nature (where the passions seethe), nor should one dream of converting human beings into senseless stones, disdaining all that pertains to the body; the outward case of the soul cannot be contemptible. What is important is to understand that the body must obey, the soul command (see José Corts Grau, *op. cit.*, p. 92). Corts Grau refers to Vives' *De anima* (III, 2) and *De tradendis disciplinis* (V, 3).

105. See *Introducción a la sabiduría*, p. 54.

106. Bataillon, *op. cit.*, I, 406. This catechism was too Erasmian in tone for the authorities of the Inquisition, and Valdés thought it prudent to leave the country. He became a religious leader in Italy. See Domingo Ricart, *Juan de Valdés y el pensamiento religioso europeo en los siglos XVI y XVII* (Mexico City, 1958).

Prince Philip, later Philip II — a post to which the emperor had appointed him. His *Diálogo de la dignidad del hombre*, modeled on Pico della Mirandola's *Oration on the Dignity of Man*, is a debate between two interlocutors, one of whom defends the position of the pagan philosophers that man is the most unfortunate of animals and the other, the Christian assumption of the goodness of the universe and of man's place in it. The scholar's life is not to be compared with the labors of Sisyphus, but rather with divine contemplation. Reason and wisdom place us in touch with God. Death is not terrible; it is a transition. Not fame, but to be forever present with our Creator is the chief end of man — the only *dignidad del hombre*. One sentence must suffice as illustration of his position: "The man who chooses an estate wherein to dwell with his own thoughts, intending to fulfill its obligations as these are revealed by Reason, lives happily and possesses delight." [107]

We pass to the year 1535. The purity of the ideal of rejecting all that (even unobtrusively or secretly) militates against satisfying the true hunger of the soul at times leads to expressions that may be interpreted — carelessly — as manifestations of pessimism. A thoughtful reading always reveals the presence in such expressions of the same burning desire for Christian perfection that we saw in Vives. I cite, for example, the *Letters* of Fray Francisco Ortiz: "Do not think that I condemn only gross sins: a blind man is aware of them. I go farther and condemn all appetites, all 'points of honor' and all feelings which, when judged by the rule of life established by God the Father and . . . Jesus Christ, carry with them a sense of discord and the 'odor of the world'; for though they be concealed and covered over with zeal, and with the false lights of the devil, be assured that they are full of baseness and keep us from satisfying the true hunger of the soul." [108] Belief in a higher hunger which can be satisfied is an optimistic belief. Indeed, in another letter, Fray Francisco, remembering Cicero's *Somnium Scipionis* and voicing what seems to be an awareness of sidereal infinity, declares that the earth, if set among the stars, would scarcely be more than a tiny

107. "El hombre que escoge estado en que vivir él y sus pensamientos, con voluntad de tratarlo como le mostrare la Razón, vive contento y tiene deleite" (*BAE*, LXV, 395a).

108. *Epístolas familiares*, *BAE*, XIII, 252ab.

point of light. When he considers the royal dwelling that God reserves for his elect, he can only "abominate" those who lose so great a future good for so insignificant a thing as our earthly life. This consideration, he says, gives him wings and breath to seek the higher Kingdom, to which God has given him every right to aspire (*ibid.*, p. 255b).

Fray Bernardino de Laredo, whose *Ascent of Mt. Zion by the Via Contemplativa* (1535) contains descriptions of nature proving him worthy of his Franciscan habit, sees the Great Chain of Being as a ladder that leads man to his Maker: "Since the creation is a ladder that leads to God, the senses should aid and serve man's higher faculties." Fray Bernardino leads the aspiring soul through and beyond the awareness of its own nothingness to the third "stage," which is a purely intellectual contemplation of the Divine. This contemplation is as possible to us, Fray Bernardino states, as it was to Adam before the Fall; it constitutes the dignity of our intelligence, though the wounds of original sin prevent us from giving ourselves over to it without intermission. The creatures, even the meanest herb, form a vast tableau, or a shop in which the Great Engineer of the Universe guides His subordinates (the whirling heavens, the four elements) in activities directed toward the service and the testing of mankind; the most delicate task, the insertion of the soul into each human being, God reserves for himself. That soul is a beautiful medallion upon which the Creator impresses His own image. This medallion, stolen by Satan, was recovered through the Incarnation and the redemption.[109]

Alejo Venegas was a layman, a pedagogue beset by poverty. In Chapter IV of our Volume II we saw how, in his *Diferencias de libros que ay en el vniuerso*, Venegas related Nature's occasional cruelty to man to the action of Divine Providence: our souls must ever be restless till they rest in God, and it is Nature that produces this restlessness — an evidence of the soul's immortality which can be placed beside the articles of faith. Man's striving must have a goal: otherwise there would be disorder in the universe. In Chapter IV of his *Agonía del tránsito de la muerte* — a treatise on dying well,

109. Fidèle de Ros, *Le Frère Bernardin de Laredo* (Paris, 1948), pp. 106, 115, 118, 222. Laredo's book, completed in 1529, was gone over by theologians and finally published in 1535.

which was completed in 1537 — Venegas declares that "in a certain sense the life of the Christian is a concatenation of miracles: baptism, confirmation, the sacrament of the Eucharist, extreme unction, and — in the after life — the light of glory" (*ed. cit.*, p. 115).

We may consider as attributable to the period after 1550 an anonymous allegorical religious play, *Auto de quando Abrahán se fue a tierra de Canaan*. In it the patriarch Abraham, on the way to the Land of Canaan, exclaims: "Oh great God, how marvelous are the works of thy hands! How terrible and awe-inspiring! For thou dost create all things for the good of man." [110] The theme is endlessly repeated: "Don't you see the new Jerusalem which awaits you, so full of every blessing?" [111]

Fray Luis de Granada's principal works of devotion were printed between 1554 and 1582–85. In all of his pages he sets forth the Christian idea of man, but in a complex manner. In his earlier writings there is more anthropological pessimism ("learn to die well") than in his later ones ("learn to live gloriously"). It is thus obvious that he cannot properly be quoted (as is often done) in support of a progression from "Renaissance light" to "baroque darkness." Indeed, the definitive edition of his *Sinners' Guide* (1567) is more optimistic — *quoad vitam* — than the first (1556), which the Inquisition required him to revise.[112] However, at the present moment we are concerned only with his attitudes *quoad ens*.

Inseparable from man's life are "both of these things: difficulty and gentleness [*suavidad*]: the one comes to us from the law of Nature, the other from the law of Grace" (*Obras, ed. cit.*, I, 383). "Grace is more powerful than Nature, God more powerful than Satan, the good angels more powerful than the bad" (*ibid.*, p. 431). Fray Luis, naturally, takes full account of suffering: Christ bids the Christian take up his cross and follow Him (p. 618). But "grace frees us from all . . . evils" (pp. 52–53), and the Creator has placed all the universe in man's hand: "Tell me, what good thing does God possess that he has not given to you? The heavens and the earth,

---

110. In *Colección de autos, farsas y coloquios del siglo XVI*, ed. Léo Rouanet (Barcelona, 1901), I, 37.

111. Luis Hurtado de Toledo and Micael de Carvajal, *Auto de las Cortes de la Muerte* (1557), *BAE*, XXXV, 6a.

112. See my review of Pedro Laín Entralgo, *La antropología en la obra de Fray Luis de Granada* (Madrid, 1946), in *HR*, XVI (1948), 180.

the sun and the moon, the stars, the rivers, the seas, birds and fishes, trees and animals, everything under heaven is in your hands. And not only what is beneath the sun, but also what is above the starry heavens: that is to say, the glory of the Empyrean, its treasures and its blessings are yours" (pp. 44–45). As for the here-and-now, Fray Luis wrote this in his *Introduction to the Creed* (1582): "When in this way the light of reason joins hands with faith, the soul receives a great joy and consolation" (cited by Lain Entralgo, *op. cit.*, p. 271).

Some five years prior to the issuing of Luis de Granada's *Introduction to the Creed*, Fray Diego de Estella published his popular *Devout Meditations on the Love of God* (1578). Though the work of this Franciscan is strongly Augustinian in tone, it stresses the existence of human dignity, of which self-examination must of necessity convince us. The soul addresses its Maker: "I shall open my eyes and behold the heavens, the work of Thy fingers, and the moon and the stars which Thou didst create. All the things that my eyes perceive command me to love Thee. And if I look at the 'little world' of man, turning my gaze inward upon myself, I find still greater cause to adore Thee, since everything I have enumerated was created by Thee for my service and benefit. If I open my ears I shall hear the Psalmist saying: 'In myself I behold thy wisdom.' "[113]

Another five years pass, and the Augustinian Fray Alonso de Orozco brings out a work entitled *Death's Victory*, in which he seems to soften, though he does not controvert (unless by the use of the word "many"), St. Augustine's interpretation of the consequences of the Fall: "Here it will be well to point out," he writes, "that the sweeping propositions of the Scriptures are not to be understood as rigorously as the words sound. The prophet David asserts: *All have fallen, there is none who performs the good.* This gives us to understand that through the sin of Adam we all are unable to act virtuously, and that our human efforts cannot enable us to serve God in such wise that He might grant us His glory. But David does not deny that through the grace of God there are many just men, now and always, because God was never without His Church, either under the natural law, the written law, or the holy

113. Cited by Robert Ricard, "Notes et matériaux . . . ," II, 177.

law of grace that we now enjoy. . . . " [114] Here Fray Alonso implies man's dignity, though he does not use the word *dignidad* as Fray Diego de Estella did in 1578.

It is curious that so many of our witnesses are Augustinians. In 1588 yet another Augustinian, Pedro Malón de Chaide, gave to the public his *Conversión de la Magdalena*. His doctrine is clearly that of the Bishop of Hippo: all creatures long for the beauty of God and find their rest when they possess it. [115] Man's dearest possession is life, and, being reasonable, he must desire the most perfect life, which is that of God. Since this cannot be had except by loving Him, our first duty is to love Him, since only He is superior to our will. This we can learn from the order of nature, inasmuch as lower creatures are converted into the substance of creatures superior to and more worthy than themselves: the substance of the elements is transformed into plants; these, by surrendering their fruits, "become" animals; and the latter, as their flesh is eaten by man and becomes his flesh, are perfected and ennobled. In order that this series of ascents may be brought to fruition, it is first of all necessary that man love God. All nature cries aloud that our first love must be the love of God; when this is lacking, all that remains is "evil love" and the undoing of the divine order (*ibid.*, 76). Mary Magdalene, as she hears the words of Jesus: "Neither do I condemn thee," enjoys, here on earth, the "peace that passeth all understanding." Even before Christ's own Ascension, her heart is in possession of the glory of heaven: "Oh miracle of penitence!" (*ibid.*, III, 159–60).

We approach the end of the century. The theologian Francisco Suárez flourished around 1597. The theme of his *De ultimo fine hominis* is that man's existence on earth is neither the product of chance nor purposeless. [116] As a special gift from his Creator, man is able to be a participator in the Divine Nature, to be God's friend and to behold the beatific vision of His Essence. It is an old doctrine, affirmed and reaffirmed by many Spaniards. In 1575 the layman Huarte de San Juan, in his *Examen de ingenios para las ciencias* and again in the "corrected" edition of 1594, insisted upon it: God and

---

114. *Victoria de la muerte* (Madrid, 1921), p. 40.
115. *Conversión de la Magdalena* (Madrid, 1947), I, 64.
116. "Homo nec frustra nec casu est in mundo" (Bk. III, ch. I, § I). See Mauricio de Iriarte, S. J., *El hombre Suárez y el hombre en Suárez* (Madrid, 1950), pp. 36–37.

Nature do nothing uselessly or in vain.[117] This teleological principle was, in the sixteenth century and throughout our period, regarded as an axiom "in every treatise on philosophy" (ibid.). Beside this doctrine of essential optimism we may well place another, that of the Jesuit theologian Luis de Molina (d. 1600): it is in man's power to be godlike; we are the masters of our destiny. This Spanish optimism was to brighten and gladden the optimism of St. Francis de Sales (d. 1622).[118]

SUMMARY

It is not necessary here to repeat our definition of terms. We have regarded as essentially optimistic every doctrine that considers the universe to be a moral order wherein all things serve a divine purpose that is altogether good. This belief is stated or is implicit in all the texts examined, even in those whose anthropological pessimism is most pronounced. Within this moral order, man is the measure of all things. As all creation has its center in the Creator (Augustine), so the creatures below the Empyrean have their center in man. As the lord of this lower creation, man finds himself in a position of tremendous responsibility. This responsibility involves self-knowledge and self-perfection and requires the passing upward along the ladder of ascents (the Great Chain of Being) of the praise and obeisance of all the creatures placed below him. Man is — if we may employ a figure of speech — a focusing device, a lens that concentrates and directs the rays of meaning and goodness of the entire creation, transmitting them back to their Center.

This doctrine remains intact in the baroque; it is not challenged during the lifetime of Calderón. To say that in the latter's time "man's greatest crime is to have been born" is to mistake the groaning of the as yet unenlightened dramatic personage Segismundo

117. "Dios y la naturaleza nunca hacen cosa baldía y sin fin"; see Iriarte, El doctor Huarte de San Juan . . . , p. 267.

118. "Ce dogme . . . c'est celui qui fonde la doctrine de Molina, d'après quoi [Saint François de Sales] conclut avec joie: 'Il est en nous d'être Dieu, nous sommes les maîtres de notre destinée.' François s'est livré à Dieu, et il sait que cela lui assure indubitablement son salut. Ainsi, nous pouvons dire que le molinisme épanouit l'optimisme salésien" (Francis Hermans, Histoire doctrinale de humanisme chrétien [Tournai–Paris, 1948], III, 41–42).

(*Life is a Dream*) for the conviction of the playwright,[119] and to overlook the teaching of Calderón's allegorical drama.[120] Similarly, to consider Quevedo's tragic sense of life as a denial of the teleological interpretation of existence as a whole, is not to know Quevedo, who wrote in a private letter that "by different roads both vice and virtue attenuate the fear of death: vice, by inspiring loathing and contempt for a misspent life; virtue, with the hope of future blessedness."[121] The essence of Gracián's *Lebenslehre* is that man is destined to enjoy blessedness in heaven: Nature is wise and beneficent, the world is good.[122]

We must content ourselves with this anticipatory glimpse (see Volume IV) of the complexities of thought in the great writers of the baroque, and must draw now to our conclusion. In her Mil-

119. For Calderón, that which passes like a dream is human happiness — *que toda la dicha humana / en fin pasa como sueño* (Act III, lines 1122–23); "Who for the sake of human vainglory / would lose a glory divine?" (lines 779–80); "Since pleasure is a beautiful flame / Whose brightness gives way to ashes / At the touch of the slightest wind, / Let us turn to things eternal" (lines 788–90). This is no more pessimistic than the Psalmist: "As for man, his days are as grass; as a flower of the field so he flourisheth; for the wind passeth over it and it is gone . . ." (Ps. 103:15).

120. "Calderón's quest for unity in dramatic structure springs from his 'view of man's moral responsibility which imposed a strict causal sequence upon different incidents. Man is shown to be responsible for his own fate'. . . . Calderón's 'serious plays have, at bottom, but one subject and one theme: man, subverting the order of natural values by his moral error and human frailty, or in the labyrinthine confusion of life groping towards the light by the aid of reason and discretion.'" See A. G. Reichenberger's review of Albert E. Sloman, *The Dramatic Craftsmanship of Calderón: His Use of Earlier Plays* (Oxford, 1958), in *HR*, XXIX (1961), 254. The light toward which Calderón's man gropes is the light of salvation. See Alexander A. Parker, *The Allegorical Drama of Calderón (An Introduction to the "Autos Sacramentales")* (Oxford–London, 1943); also Parker's edition of Calderón's *No hay más Fortuna que Dios* (Manchester, 1949).

121. "Ya que no puedo valer por el acierto de la perfección de la vida, que inculpable en los buenos hace hermosa la muerte, me valdré de las miserias que en los distraídos y delincuentes hacen aborrecible la vida. Por diferentes caminos el pecado y la virtud alivian el temor de la muerte; aquél con el fastidio del presente, ésta con la esperanza de lo futuro" (*Epistolario completo de D. Francisco de Quevedo*, ed. L. Astrana Marín [Madrid, 1946], p. 314).

122. See *El Criticón*, ed. M. Romera-Navarro (Philadelphia, 1938–40), I, 109: "Participa el hablar de lo necessario y de lo gustoso, que siempre atendió la sabia naturaleza a hermanar ambas cosas en todas las funciones de la vida." See also p. 119: "¡O lo que te enbidio — exclamó Critilo — tanta felicidad no imaginada, privilegio único del primer hombre y tuyo!: llegar a ver con novedad y con advertencia la grandeza, la hermosura, el concierto, la firmeza y la variedad desta gran máquina criada." And p. 121: " — ¡O qué será . . . aquella inmortal y gloriosa vista de aquel infinito Sol divino, aquel llegar a ver su infinitamente perfectíssima hermosura! ¡qué gozo, qué fruición, qué dicha, qué felicidad, qué gloria!"

tonian commitment to a world view which will not lead to Newton's, we see in Spain a collective state of mind — won at great cost, as we are now aware — which appears to have determined the nation's disregard for "numbering the hairs of the lion's mane," for the science that counts and measures and weighs things. This collective state of mind suggests strongly what Oswald Spengler in *The Decline of the West* called "the second religiousness" — with the difference that in Spain it was not "second." It was present during the expansion as well as during the decline and fall of Spanish culture.

XII · Literature and Society[1]

And when he shall have eaten and
drunk at table fittingly and with
temperance, he should (if he so
wishes) hear minstrels sing and
play their instruments, repeating
good songs and good accounts of
chivalrous deeds capable of stirring the hearts of those who hear
them to act nobly.

Don Juan Manuel[2]

That poetry is a divine art is
proved by many passages in many
books; Solomon uses it in his
Song of Songs, and the holy
Doctor Friar Thomas Aquinas in
that great and devout hymn that
the Church sets such store by;
therefore if I myself take
pleasure in this art, I do so
with full justification.

Fernán Pérez de Guzmán[3]

The idea of poetry in the minds
of men is surely God-inspired, to
the end that by its movement and
spirit we might be directed
toward Heaven, whence poetry
came; for poetry is nothing
if not a sharing in the
celestial, the divine breath.

Fray Luis de León[4]

1. In this chapter I intend to limit myself to the literal meaning of the chapter heading. An exposition of all aspects of poetic theory in our period would require a book in itself. We shall here discuss only the social responsibility of the writer.

2. *Libro de los estados, BAE,* LI, 311a.

3. "Que el trobar sea un saber diuino / asaz se demuestra en muchos lugares; / Salamón lo vsa en los sus Cantares, / e el doctor santo fray Tomás de Aquino / en aquel deuoto e notable hyno / del qual la Yglesia tanta mención faze; / por ende, sy a mí esta arte aplaze, / con rrazón muy justa a ello me inclino" (*Cancionero castellano del siglo XV,* ed. R. Foulché Delbosc [Madrid, 1912–15], I, 683).

4. Cited by Karl Vossler, *La poesía de la soledad en España,* trans. Ramón de la Serna (Buenos Aires, 1946), p. 165, n. 7.

POETRY: ITS DIVINITY AND ITS CORRUPTION

From ancient times it was recognized that poetry — and literature in the broader sense, especially eloquence — was an instrument of power. Whether that power was regarded as having had its source in some pagan supernatural force (Ovid's *est deus in nobis*) or as bestowed by the Hebrew-Christian Holy Ghost (Moses and his song of triumph, David and his Psalms), it was exercised for social, for civilizing ends: to induce men to live in harmonious secular association, or to educate them in the ways of holiness and salvation.

The divinity of poetry was asserted throughout all the centuries covered by our study — and that divinity was both pagan and Christian in origin. But there were other and more complex points of view. According to an anonymous Carolingian commentator on Horace's *Ars Poetica*, art is subject to an historical relativism which parallels the relative purity or impurity of human customs. Amphion did indeed cause men to live in peaceful communities; but later, as cities grew, discord grew with them, and a new type of poet — Homer, Tyrtaeus — came forward to create the heroic poetry of war. Still later, with the return of peaceful conditions, men became morally lax, and poetry and music degenerated and pandered to the new craving for luxury, with the result that additional genres came into existence: alongside the poet-theologians there appeared the writers of tragedy and comedy.

Theorists favored the simple or the complex view of poetry — that is to say, they focused their attention entirely on its sacred origin or recognized also the ease of its fall from grace — according to their individual temperaments. Three and a half centuries after our Carolingian commentator, Thomas Aquinas — following Augustine who followed Varro — saw in the mythical Orpheus, Musaeus, and Linus the first creators of theological songs, the first great poets. (These legendary Greeks supposedly lived at the time when the Judges ruled in Israel.) [5] Nearly half a millenium later John Milton (d. 1674), writing on the poet's function, recognized both its divinity and its frequent corruption: "These abilities,

5. Edgar de Bruyne, *Estudios de estética medieval*, trans. Fr. A. Suárez (Madrid, 1958–59), I, 225–28, especially 228. St. Thomas defined poetry as "the humblest branch of knowledge." See Allan H. Gilbert, *Literary Criticism from Plato to Dryden* (New York, 1940), p. 476 and n. 33.

wheresoever they be found, are the inspired gift of God rarely bestowed, but yet to some (though most abuse) [6] in every nation; and are of power, beside the office of the pulpit, to inbreed and cherish in a great people the seeds of virtue and . . . to celebrate in glorious and lofty hymns the throne and equipage of God's almightiness . . . " (cited by Gilbert, *op. cit.*, p. 590).

This sense of relativism (poetry is a divine gift, though most abuse it) appeared very early. All Antiquity saw the poet as sage, teacher, educator. Homer was, of course, an unconscious teacher; but the Ancients almost unanimously insisted on the pedagogical aim of poetry. Horace, bringing much previous discussion to a focus, declared that it was not sufficient for the poet to hold his audience spellbound as Homer did; poetry should be "useful" as well. On the other hand, philosophy invades the Greek mind and takes by storm one position after another. It is the rebellion of Logos against myth — but also against poetry. Hesiod denounced the epic in the name of truth.[7] The revolt was never fully successful, however, and myth lived on: *Sic et Non*.

For a medieval example of the relativism we cite John of Salisbury (12 c.). It may be assumed, he argues, that all writings except those disapproved [8] should be read by the Christian humanist, inasmuch as "all that has been written has been ordained for man's utility — although at times he makes bad use of it." In books there is something profitable for everyone, provided the reading is done with discrimination. It is somewhat dangerous, John of Salisbury admits, to expose the unsophisticated to pagan literature; but training in it is very useful for those safe in the faith: wide reading makes the scholar; careful selection, the saint.[9] Thus the "divinity"

6. Somewhat earlier than Milton, Cristóbal Suárez de Figueroa (d. 1639?) wrote in *Discurso LXXII* (On Pimps) of his encyclopedic work *Plaza universal de todas las ciencias y artes* (Madrid, 1615): "[The pimp], like the poet, uses fables as subject matter, verses as means, love as objective, song as instrument. . . . He is always devising verses for the client for whom he seeks opportunities. The Muses assist him in the singing of some new and agreeable event; the Graces help him to adorn this so that it will be believed. He goes about just 'happening' to have in his bosom pocket a sonnet, a ballad, a dozen *redondilla* stanzas, a *canzon* in sonorous and elevated style, which he recites with facility, eloquence, and elegance . . ." (fol. 276).

7. E. R. Curtius, *European Literature and the Latin Middle Ages*, trans. Willard R. Trask (New York, 1953), pp. 203–4.

8. See below, our section entitled "Social Control."

9. James D. Ross and Mary M. McLaughlin (eds.), *The Portable Medieval Reader* (New York, 1953), pp. 601–2.

of poetry is a corruptible divinity; its sacredness is subject to abuse. The question is never resolved in the minds of the theorists: rigorists condemn poetry; Christian humanists insist that it is essentially divine; conciliators of the extremes will advise that it be used with caution. Our Spanish critics, like those who preceded them or were their contemporaries in other countries, will both exalt and denounce literature of the imagination.

Not a Matter of Chronology

Karl Vossler, writing of Luis de León's (d. 1591) concept of the poet, erroneously declared it to be "the medieval and pre-humanistic concept of the *vates*, the poet as seer, which had been held centuries earlier by Dante and Albertino Mussato." [10] This implies a simplistic chronology, the inaccuracy of which is illustrated by the three quotations that serve as our epigraphs.

Our first epigraph is from Don Juan Manuel, who died *circa* 1348. The *juglares* — the minstrels — that he mentions are expected to sing heroic poetry, very much as Homer did, in the presence of a lord who has wined and dined wisely and well: the *social justification* of their art resides in its power to inspire noble listeners to *fazer bien* — to acquit themselves well, as a Spanish knight understood this.[11] Fernán Pérez de Guzmán (d. 1460?), who furnishes our second epigraph, was a lay moralist, a pre-humanistic translator of Seneca and compiler of Senecan *sententiae*; the first, indeed, to write a collection of modern biographies after the manner of Sallust. There is nothing in his pre-humanistic conception of poetry — its uplifting power, its divine origin — to set off this fifteenth-century moralist and poet from the sixteenth-century poet and moralist Luis de León, or from any number of other writers who expressed themselves on this subject after humanism had flowered in Spain. Fray Luis' idea of poetry as God-inspired (see our third epigraph) is not "medieval" in any distinctive or privative sense.

10. *Poetische Theorien in der italienischen Frührenaissance* (Berlin, 1900), pp. 3–4.

11. Minstrels sang their songs for the benefit of the army of Ferdinand III of Castile on the Adalusian frontier, and for the troops of Alfonso VII, "to give courage to the men at arms." They had also a different function: the law code of Alfonso X allowed the king "at times" to take comfort from the unpleasantness and the weariness of his royal duties as he listened to songs and instrumental music, and the same privilege was granted to prelates. See Ramón Menéndez Pidal, *Poesía juglaresca y orígenes de las literaturas románicas* (Madrid, 1957), pp. 54, 74.

At the midpoint of the eighteenth century, Robert Lowth, professor of poetry at Oxford and bishop of London, published his *De Sacra Poesi Hebraeorum* (1753), according to which the old Greek view of poetry as a sacred gift from heaven is a "memory" of the primitive concept of poetry which was once common to all mankind. The Greeks lost it in practice, the Old Testament has preserved it for modern Europe.[12]

As we proceed it will become more and more apparent that it is inaccurate to believe that the medieval concept is always "Dantesque," the humanist concept necessarily more "human," less "divine."

Before turning to our special section on the divine origin of poetry, let us examine two additional Spanish texts that represent the first and the declining years of the sixteenth century. The earlier text is from an anonymous manuscript entitled *Vida del soberbio y de la muerte*: "How lofty and how noble the art of poetry is and has always been among all nations, is a matter known to everyone, for surely it exceeds other forms of writing by the same degree of excellence that things divine exceed things simply human."[13] The later of our two texts is by Gabriel López Maldonado, a friend of Cervantes, who published his *Cancionero* at Madrid in 1586. In the prologue he speaks of "this divine art." That he is well within the humanistic tradition[14] is shown by what he says of licentious poets: "Some would wish verse to be not only well measured and full of wisdom [*sentencioso*], as indeed it should be, but also clean and chaste and proper. Others hold with Catullus, who says that provided the poet live chastely, it matters little how unchaste his verses are, and these even assert that poetry has more appeal and

---

12. Curtius, *op. cit.*, p. 237. Lowth's book created a sensation because in the eighteenth century everyone was looking for primitive poetry. Lowth stimulated Herder.

13. Gallardo, *Ensayo*, I, col. 1228.

14. Dante and Tasso figuratively clasp hands across two centuries. The former wrote in *Inferno*, XI, 104: *vostr' arte a Dio quasi è nipote* — "Your art is grandchild, as it were, to God." Tasso (d. 1595) declared: "Only God and the poet deserve the name of *creator*" (cited by Arthur O. Lovejoy, *The Great Chain of Being* [Cambridge, Massachusetts, 1936], p. 96. Lovejoy remarks: "In the Renaissance this aspect of the medieval conception comes fully into its own" (*ibid.*). See also Benedetto Croce: "The Renaissance rightly refrained from distinguishing, among the various types of poetry, a separate type that was didactic, because, for the Renaissance, all poetry was always didactic" (cited by Jean Seznec, *La survivance des dieux antiques* [London, 1940], p. 126, n. 2).

more wit in proportion as it is less chaste, as if one can peradventure be chaste though he deals in filth . . . and sings things filthy" (*ibid.*).

With all of these complexities in mind — heavenly origin, human abuse; identity (or similarity) of attitude in the medieval, the pre-humanistic, the humanistic, and the later periods — we may proceed to document with some thoroughness the idea of poetry as a gift of God (or of the gods).

THE DIVINITY OF POETRY

The Judaeo-Christian Tradition

Since Hebrew antiquity was thought to have preceded the culture of the Greeks, everything which was admired in the Hellenic past was believed to have been discovered much earlier by the Israelites. This doctrine of St. Jerome, propagated in the West by Isidore of Seville and by the Venerable Bede, was made to include all the arts. It was a theory of double inheritance — directly from the Scriptures, and indirectly from Greece and Rome. Each element — the pagan and the Judaeo-Christian — strengthened the other (De Bruyne, *op. cit.*, I, 225).

The Scriptural Tradition

St. Jerome was the "celestial patron" of poetry. It was he who first pointed out that poetry is present in Holy Writ, he who became the advocate of Christian humanism, the "saviour" of the poetry of the pagans, now purified and adapted to Christian purposes.[15] References to the Scriptural origin of poetry are numerous in Spain.

Juan Alfonso de Baena compiled his *Cancionero*, the first general anthology of lyric poems that has come down to us, about the year 1445. The section which he filled with poems by Alfonso Alvarez de Villasandino (d. 1428?) is headed by this introductory

---

15. María Rosa Lida de Malkiel, *Juan de Mena: Poeta del prerrenacimiento español* (Mexico City, 1950), p. 49. See also E. K. Rand, *Founders of the Middle Ages* (New York, 1928), chapters entitled "The Church and Pagan Culture: The Problem"; "The Church and Pagan Culture: The Solution"; "St. Jerome the Humanist." Even after his warning dream, Jerome continued to use classical allusions to a surprising degree, as Rand's statistics demonstrate.

statement: "Here begin the songs, the questions and answers (very subtle and well contrived), and the very elegant longer poems composed by the learned and intelligent . . . Alfonso Alvarez . . . who by infused grace that God granted him became the crown and monarch of all the poets and troubadours who until now have existed in Spain." [16]

Next in time, Iñigo López de Mendoza, Marqués de Santillana (d. 1458), in the *Prohemio* which he prepared as a preface to his collected works, states, on the authority of Isidore of Seville, that Moses, Joshua, and David were the first to compose in rhyme and to sing in metre; and he concludes that "this science of poetry is especially pleasing to God, as indicated by Cassiodorus [d. 583] in his *De Variis Causis*: 'All the splendor of eloquence, and every mode of . . . poetic utterance . . . had their beginning in the Divine Scriptures. Poetry is sung in holy temples, in the courts and palaces of emperors and kings, and all festivities whatsoever are, without this added grace, mute and deaf and silent.' " [17]

Gómez Manrique (d. 1490?) mentions St. Jerome as having pointed out the Mosaic origin of verse: "It appears that Moses was the first . . . to use metre and the poetic art in the Scriptures, as St. Jerome says. . . . Likewise David in the Psalms . . . as well as Solomon in the Proverbs . . . and in the Song of Songs" (*Cancionero castellano* . . . , II, 131).

This Biblical or Jehovistic concept of poetics extends into the sixteenth and seventeenth centuries. Juan Luis Vives was sufficiently puritanical to condemn secular poetry as a whole, yet even he recognized that it possessed charms which could be made to serve holy purposes. "The invention of measure, of rhyme, of harmony, answered a human need: to impress on men's minds certain truths by means of a phonetic enchantment which falls on the ear and touches the spirit. The most ancient use of poetry is sacred: Moses and David sang praises to the one God; the pagans gave poetic form to the oracles of their deities. But poetry has progressively fallen on evil times," Vives says in his *De Ratione Dicendi*. It is necessary that it be restored to its holy status: let it sing hymns to God and the angels, let it celebrate the triumphs of the saints, to

16. *Cancionero de Baena*, ed. F. Michel (Leipzig, 1860), I, 9–10.
17. *Obras*, ed. José Amador de los Ríos (Madrid, 1852), pp. 4–5.

the end that we may love them and be inspired to imitate them.[18]

We pass to the year 1553, which sees the publication of Antonio de Torquemada's *Coloquios satíricos*, the work of an Erasmian moralist (Bataillon, *op. cit.*, II, 259). The third dialogue is a *Colloquy Between Two Gentlemen . . . and a Shepherd, Amintas*, "in which there is a discussion of the excellencies and the perfection of the pastoral life, written for those who wish to live it, each argument being proved with natural reasons and with authoritative statements, and examples from Holy Scripture. . . . Its perusal is most profitable, in order that people may not live in discontent with their poverty and may not center happiness in the possession of great wealth or large estates." [19] The seventh and last of the *Coloquios* is a short pastoral novel in its own right. Torquemada justifies the pastoral life by the fact that Abraham, Jacob, David, and Moses were shepherds after the expulsion from Eden; and he justifies poetry, as so many had done before him, by its presence in the Bible.[20]

In the year 1580 Miguel Sánchez de Lima, a Portuguese employed in the service of the Castilian Marqués de Villena, published at Alcalá *El arte poética en romance castellano*, a work of humble pretensions and slight value, yet not without interest here. The first of its *Diálogos* "defines poetry and declares its excellence." [21] Both in the Old and in the New Testament, the author tells us (*ed. cit.*, p. 41), God has shown his delight in poetry. "Sing unto the Lord a new song," said the Psalmist — a command that every priest must obey daily. Poetry is the vehicle of excellent theology — *muy fina Theologia* (p. 43).

We move to the year 1587, date of the official *Aprovación* which prefaces the *Diversas Rimas* (1591) of Vincente Espinel. Espinel's prologuist, Alonso de Valdés, after relating all the conceivable excellencies of poetry, asks rhetorically if the Holy Ghost disdained to speak in verse through the mouth of the prophet David, and

18. Marcel Bataillon, *Erasmo y España* (Mexico City–Buenos Aires, 1950), II, 217–18; see also p. 219.

19. Cited by J. B. Avalle-Arce, *La novela pastoril española* (Madrid, 1959), pp. 9–10, n. 19.

20. See the text in M. Menéndez y Pelayo (ed.), *Orígenes de la novela* (Madrid, 1905–15), II, 514a.

21. Ed. Rafael de Balbín Lucas (Madrid, 1944), p. 15.

cites as further examples the Song of Songs, Jeremiah, the Blessed Virgin in the Magnificat, and the Gospels, where we read: "And after they had sung a hymn, they went out."

In 1589 Fray Juan de Pineda causes an interlocutor to remark: "You are quite right in observing that humane letters are often a handmaiden of letters divine." [22] And in the same year Pedro Sánchez de Viana published at Valladolid his translation of Ovid's *Metamorphoses*. We have here yet another Renaissance version of the medieval *Ovide moralisé*: [23] with a knowledge of this poetry, the translator declares, one has the key to all poetic writing. Indeed, the great doctors and saints of the Church of God — St. Jerome, St. Basil, St. Augustine — stress the need to "make use of the doctrine of the gentiles." All poets, Sánchez de Viana insists "are divine." [24]

In 1602 Luis Alfonso de Carballo (or Carvallo) issued at Medina del Campo his *Cisne de Apolo: De las excelencias y dignidad y todo lo que al arte poética y versificatoria pertenece*. The final dialogue bears this heading: "Wherein Is Explained How the Swan, Singing Sweetly in Old Age, Symbolizes the Protracted Experience which the Poet Requires, and How the Poet Imitates God." The imitation consists in the creation, by the human maker (*poeta faber*), of a poetic artifact — an argument, a fiction — *ex nihilo*, out of nothing, exactly as the Supreme Creator brought out from the void all the things that constitute the universe: *poeta*, in Greek, means *creator*. The Apostle's Creed, in the Greek, uses the word *Poetam* where the Latin ritual employs *Creatorem*. Christ said that his yoke is easy; easy, also, is the yoke of learning — any learning — when the poet has lightened it. [25]

On the eve of Góngora's great achievement — the creation of a body of poetry that is purely (or all but purely) poetic — Luis Carrillo y Sotomayor published at Madrid his *Obras* (1601), which in-

22. *Primera Parte de los Treynta y cinco Diálogos familiares de la Agricultura Christiana* (Salamanca, 1589), I, fol. 45.

23. See Davis P. Harding, *Milton and the Renaissance Ovid* (Urbana, Illinois, 1946); Georges May, *D'Ovide à Racine* (New Haven, 1944). Ovid is listed among the theological poets by Pineda, *op. cit.*, I, fol. 21v.

24. *Las Transformaciones de Ouidio, traduzidas del verso latino en tercetos y octauas rimas por el Licenciado Viana en lengua vulgar Castellana. Con el Comento y explicación de las fábulas; reduziéndolas a philosophia natural y moral y astrología e historia* (Valladolid, 1589).

25. Ed. A. Porqueras Mayo (Madrid, 1958), II, 226–30.

clude a *Liber unus* entitled *The Book of Poetic Erudition, or Lances of the Muses Directed against the Unlearned, Who Are Exiled from the Protection of Their Divinity.*[26] The margins are crowded with references: Julius Caesar, the theologian El Tostado; Saints Jerome, Isidore, and Cyprian; Plutarch, Scaliger. And not these authorities alone, but also Moses, the "father of history" and the "great general of divine letters"; King David, the strong-armed soldier and prudent captain; those martyrs who sang, with joy and love, amid the flames that consumed their bodies — all these illustrious dead and various others are cited as proof of the nobility and the divinity of the poet's art, of his ability to inspire. The Muses not only sing, they are potent in warfare; they waken valor and grant eternal fame (pp. 52–54).

Four years later, in 1615, Cristóbal Suárez de Figueroa brought out at Madrid his adaptation and enlargement of Tommaso Garzoni's encyclopedia, *Piazza universale*, with the title *Plaza universal de todas ciencias y artes.* The first subsection of *Discurso X* bears the title *De la Poesía.* After discussing the origins of the art among the Greeks, the compiler-translator speaks of the Hebrews, "much more ancient than the Greeks, as Josephus observes and Eusebius notes." [27] The well-known examples are present: Moses exulting over the drowning of the pursuing Egyptians, David and his hymns, and "all manner of metrical harmony" in the Bible, "whence the gentiles took it" (p. 628).

Long past the mid-century mark, the theorists still are repeating the old arguments set forth by Sánchez de Lima almost a hundred years earlier. In an unpublished work entitled *Apologético historial: Antigüedad y fundadores de la ciudad de Granada . . . ,* Francisco de Trillo y Figueroa makes complaint against a critic who had called him a mere poet, ignoring his efforts in the historical field: "If my adversary knew his Bible, he would not blame me for writing poetry. God was the first in the world to dictate verses; almost all of the Old Testament is in verse — Jeremiah and the prophets, the Psalms, Job, the Book of Proverbs, the Song of Solomon, and many other books. . . . Eusebius even discusses the

26. *Obras de Don Luis Carrillo y Sotomayor*, ed. M. Cardenal Iracheta (Madrid, 1946), pp. 50–109.
27. Ed. Madrid (1733), pp. 627b–28a.

various types of versification. . . . Let all blame be heaped on the head of the bad poet, never on his profession." [28]

Since verses were "first dictated" by the Holy Ghost to the transcribers of the Divine Message to mankind, not only are those who compose verses in modern times in tune with the Infinite; even a Maecenas may be considered as imitating, at one remove, the Godlike process of creation by the mere granting of his protection to the poet's creation — a conceit which may well serve as conclusion to our present section. Don Gabriel Bocángel y Unzueta published at Madrid in 1627 his *Rimas y prosas, junto con la Fábula de Leandro y Ero.* In the dedication to the Marqués de Camarasa he excuses his daring:

> Sir: great princes like yourself are the representatives of God on earth, and they are the more princely in proportion as they imitate Him the more closely. One of God's greatest acts is to create, and whosoever imitates Him in this act deserves to hear God say of him, as He said of David: "I have found a man after my own heart." Such imitation one may observe in your lordship, since you will be endowing with form — and shaping with your hands — this bit of nothingness which I offer you. . . . It is noble indeed, and the greatest achievement within man's power, to operate without operation. . . . He who offers least comes closest to attributing deity to the receiver. . . . God honors a humble and a contrite heart. . . . This humble shepherd's flute will someday become a clarion of glory and will then dare to do what it now fears to undertake. . . .[29]

PLATONIC "FURY"

"If Ariosto and our own [Juan de] Mena had not had each his own generous portion of madness, they could never have intoned such lofty, elegant, and polished verses." So wrote Jerónimo de

28. Antonio Gallego Morell, *Francisco y Juan de Trillo y Figueroa* (Granada, 1950), p. 59; see also p. 100.

29. Ed. Rafael Benítez Claros (Madrid, 1946), I, 9. This dedication would not have been written in the simpler age of Garcilaso; but it is not sacreligious in its handling of conceits. See the preface to the same poet's *Christian Temple Dedicated to the Undying Memory of the Serene and August Lady Doña Isabel de Borbón, Queen of Spain*: "The correctness of the doctrine in this work is vouched for by the custodians of Sacred Letters; but the arrangement and structure is the result of personal study, which perhaps will find some favor with Learned and Well-Intentioned Readers . . ." (*ed. cit.,* II, 73). The reference to the clarion of glory is a commonplace: the noblest poetry is that which sings of heroes. The implication is that Bocángel hopes to write of Camarasa in heroic vein.

Mondragón in his book *Censure of Human Folly* (1598).[30] The theory of the poet's divine frenzy set forth in Plato's *Ion* and *Phaedrus* was found "in diluted form" throughout antiquity and passed to the Middle Ages as a commonplace, the important transmitters being the fourth-century grammarian Marius Victorinus and Isidore of Seville (Curtius, *op. cit.*, pp. 442, 451, 474). In the Renaissance the idea of divine frenzy appears on every hand, even in so prosaic a place as a Latin dictionary: "The poets tell the fable of Minerva springing from the forehead of Jupiter, by which remark [*commento*] they wish to signify that the disciplines of humane letters are not the invention of the human mind, but have come from the brain of Jupiter, that is to say, from the inexhaustible fountain of divine wisdom, for human use." [31] Plato had, of course, given two very different solutions to the problem of literary inspiration. In the *Ion* and the *Phaedrus* he declared inspiration to be a divine alienation of the mind: poetry was not an art but was produced by men who did not know what they were doing. On the other hand, in the *Republic* he condemned poetry along with all other "mimetic" arts.[32] This Platonic *Sic et Non* had a cat-like tenacity of life. Sir Philip Sidney's *Defence of Poesie* (composed 1585?) contains a preliminary double definition of poetry from Aristotle and from Horace, an adaptation of Aristotelian doctrine making poetry a union of philosophy and history, and an invocation of Plato as a witness for poetry wherein the Socratic concessions to the poetic frenzy of the *Ion* are overrated.[33] Frequently, in the confusion, theorists cite Moses, Job, and Jeremiah, alongside Orpheus, Linus, Amphion, and Musaeus, as distinguished theological poets.[34] All of the confusions are found in Spain, but they are "confusions" only to us; the men who expressed them were not aware of them as such.[35] What was important to them was to glean,

30. Ed. A. Vilanova (Barcelona, 1953), pp. 177–78.

31. A. Calepinus, *Dictionarium* (Antwerp, 1572), *s. v. Minerva*.

32. C. S. Lewis, *English Literature in the Sixteenth Century Excluding Drama* (Oxford, 1954), p. 319.

33. William K. Wimsatt, Jr., and Cleanth Brooks, *Literary Criticism: A Short History* (New York, 1957), p. 169.

34. Charles Trinkaus, "A Humanist's Image of Humanism: The Inaugural Orations of Bartolommeo della Fonte" (d. 1513), *Studies in the Renaissance*, VII (1960), 113.

35. Fray Luis de León was a Thomist in his theology, a Platonist when he wrote

from every possible source, statements which could be considered as proof of poetry's divinity, antiquity, and nobility. They passed with ease, as did Sánchez de Lima in 1580 (see above, note 21), from Ovid's *est deus in nobis* to the canticles of Solomon and the Psalms of David. Thus the Marqués de Santillana in the fifteenth century had written in the *Prohemio* to his collected works: "And so, following the path of the Stoics . . . I make bold to say that metre is older and more perfect and of greater authority than prose. Isidore, the sainted bishop of Seville, approves this finding and declares that he who first . . . sang in metre was Moses . . . " (*ed. cit.*, p. 4).

Alfonso García de Matamoros, discussing early Roman poetry in his *Pro adserenda hispanorum eruditione* (1553) makes a statement which is of interest here because of a parenthetical remark: "Comrades in the literary efforts of those days were the poets (or, as Plato calls them, the messengers and interpreters of the gods) Decianus, Licianus, and Canius Rufus of Cadiz." [36]

In 1575 Juan Huarte de San Juan was more specific, writing in his *Examen de ingenios para las ciencias*: "There is a third sort of *ingenium* . . . : Plato calls it 'outstanding talent affected by a mania' [*ingenium excellens cum mania*]. Possessing it, poets utter words and *sententiae* so lofty that, unless it be by divine revelation (as Plato says), it is impossible to reach such heights; and thus he said: 'For the poet is an airlike, volatile and sacred thing, nor can he sing except when he is god-filled [*deo plenus*] and beside himself, and mentally alienated." [37] Huarte, ever naturalistically inclined, rejects Plato's supernatural explanation — but not absolutely. In another place, in his endeavor to explain the amazing popularity of the Spanish romances of chivalry, he relates this aberration of taste to the *furor poético* of young persons touched by the artistic temperament, which seems allied to "divine revelations." A man in full possession of his wits — he insists — can not be a poet.[38]

poetry. See Ludwig Pfandl, *Historia de la literatura nacional española en la Edad de Oro*, trans. J. Rubió Balaguer (Barcelona, 1933), p. 33.

36. Ed. José López de Toro (Madrid, 1943), p. 183.

37. Ed. R. Sanz (Madrid, 1930), I, 48.

38. See Angel Valbuena Prat, *La vida española en la edad de oro* (Barcelona, 1943), p. 64. Huarte would expel poets, not from the Republic as Plato suggested, but from the universities, for he considered the poetic imagination as unsuited for serious

There exists in Spanish literature of the Golden Age, according to Antonio Vilanova, no literary doctrine comparable to that expounded by Fernando de Herrera, in his *Anotaciones* (1580) to the poems of Garcilaso de la Vega, with respect to its deep perception of the impenetrable mystery of poetic creation; no doctrine that evaluates with more enthusiasm the supernatural and divine character of the subjective inspiration and sensibility of the poet.[39] Poetry, says Herrera,

is abundant and exuberant and rich in everything; free, possessing its own right and its own jurisdiction without let or hinderance of any kind; marvellously able . . . to exteriorize all the thoughts of the spirit . . . and all that is contained in human emotion (cited *ibid.*).

Making his own the concepts of the *Ion* and the *Phaedrus*, Herrera accepts the idea that the poet's subconscious operation is a divine frenzy:

One would not be far wrong in assuming that the "active reason" of Aristotle is the same as Plato's "genius." This it is that offers itself to men of supreme talent, that enters into them, to the end that in their writings they may reveal by means of its light their perception of secret things. For it often happens that, when the heavenly heat has cooled, the writers themselves are amazed at, or do not recognize, their own productions . . ." (*ibid.*).

It must not be supposed that we have to do here with Renaissance "paganism." Herrera was as impressed by the majesty of the Psalms as by the luminous thought world of Plato and Aristotle. Oreste Macrí has said of him: "On this 'Aristotelian' base operate the tendencies and meanings of the Stoicism and the Judaeo-Christian Neoplatonism which constitute the 'romantic' element of his system." [40] Herrera's syncretism is typical of that of his culture.

We have already mentioned Pedro Sánchez de Viana and his 1589 translation of the *Metapmorphoses* of Ovid — the poet whom he

study: "If the authorities would but pay attention to these [physical] signs, they would exile from the universities students who are aggresive and inclined to the use of weapons, who are lovers, and who are poets, as well as those who are concerned with the adornment of their person; for they do not have the gift or the ability for any [serious] study of letters" (cited by Mauricio de Iriarte, *El Doctor Huarte de San Juan y su "Examen de ingenios"* [Madrid, 1948], p. 36).

39. "Preceptistas españoles de los siglos XVI y XVII," in *Historia general de las literaturas hispánicas*, ed. Guillermo Díaz-Plaja (Barcelona 1949–58), III, 579.

40. *Fernando de Herrera* (Madrid, 1959), p. 103. Herrera gives naturalistic (i.e., Aristotelian and Huartean) interpretations of such poetic phenomena as tears and dreams (*ibid.*, pp. 103–5).

considers to be the sum total of all poetry. Poets partake of the divine, Sánchez de Viana says in his prologue; and he continues: "Human wisdom is a reflection of the Divine, and the music of our instruments is a replica of the harmony of the spheres." Even the "blind philosophers" of antiquity were aware of this wonderful correspondence. Our spirit longs to recover its wings, to soar to Heaven which is its home; unable to do so, it listens with joy to earthly music, all the while striving to imitate the divine. Not all men, obviously, are thus sensitive; but others, whose frame of mind is graver, by means of measured verses express the intimate concepts of their understanding: these are they who, stirred by the divine spirit, compose serious and philosophical [*sentenciosas*] poems and by the Divine Philosopher [Plato] are called poets, and what they write is poetry, which not only delights the ear like common music, but feeds the understanding with heavenly ambrosia. And this divine fury is bestowed by the Muses; without this gift and this grace he who would be a poet labors in vain. It is what in everyday Spanish we call *vena* [inspiration].[41]

Alonso López Pinciano's *Philosophia antigua poética* (1596) is generally regarded as the best Renaissance exposition of Aristotle's *Poetics* produced anywhere. One of the book's interlocutors, Fadrique, remarks that "this idea of Plato's divine frenzy does not satisfy me; for he said there were four types of it: prophetic, erotic, Bacchic, and poetic." [42] If one can find natural causes for a phenomenon, Fadrique continues, why should he seek a supernatural explanation? Aristotle is the one who understood this business: "manly [or male] poetry is the product of a versatile and furious mind" (*ibid.*, p. 224). In the discussion that follows Fadrique gives his own explanation:

Furious means possessed of a temperament which is easily stimulated and rises above the material things of the world below to lofty considerations and to contemplation; such stimulation and elevation can occur *humanamente*, without divine intervention or any special *furor*. Poetry is therefore, as Aristotle correctly defined it, the work of a versatile mind, because such a mind receives readily the idea or the form of things; or it can be something more: the work of a "furious" mind, because such a mind is capable of invention. Thus the man who has a well endowed and a trained mind is well fitted to be a poet;

41. *Ed. cit.*; in this paraphrasing I have compressed the original.
42. Ed. A. Carballo Picazo (Madrid, 1953), I, 222–23.

and he who has, in addition, the element of fury, will be a still more perfect poet.

The best poet is the man who, with all his natural endowments, is aided on occasion by the Divine Spirit, as were King David and others like him. And in such cases "the poet is usually assisted also by a different, a more lowly, a more natural 'fury,' which is the result of aroused emotion, of passion" (pp. 224–27). In an earlier section of Pinciano's work we read:

> The imagination does not give heed to the objects of sensory cognition [*especies verdaderas*], but invents new ones [such as a mountain of gold]. . . . The instrument of this faculty requires bodily heat and bodily dryness which are companions of furor, for which reason this faculty [*sentido*] is very useful in poetics (pp. 48–49).

Here López Pinciano appears to have been influenced by Huarte de San Juan and his humoral (Galenic) psychology.[43]

Each of the dialogues in Luis Alfonso de Carballo's *Cisne de Apolo* is summed up at its end in an octave of execrable didactic verse, for easy memorization. The octave on page 47 of volume I (*ed. cit.*) is a clear statement of the Platonic position in the *Ion* and in the *Phaedrus*. On page 193 of volume II, the author's spokesman declares that no one can become a poet unless by inspiration he be lifted out of himself and endowed with a new perceptiveness and awareness. Those who have never had this experience call it madness, and are unable to understand's Virgil's *insanire libet* (*insanire = hacer versos, componer*, i.e., to compose poetry). On pages 216 and following, Carballo discusses the question of whether this poetic frenzy is permanent or a mere transitory state. The answer is that the soul is at certain times less encumbered by its material frame than at others. When his soul feels free and untrammeled, the poet can dictate verses faster than a scribe can take them down, whereas at other times he cannot form a single verse; which is to say that, after the spirit and the afflatus have become calm and cold, after the sacred impetus and fury have ceased, the mind of the speaker becomes darkened, his tongue heavy (pp. 219–20).

"Among the defenders of poetry," writes Ernst Robert Curtius (*op. cit.*, p. 550), "Lope de Vega is not sought in vain." Prior to 1623,

---

43. See my article, "El *ingenioso* hidalgo," *HR*, XXV (1957), 175–93, especially 193.

the date of the death of the Maecenas and poet Juan de Arguijo, Lope dedicated to him a short essay *On the Honor Due to Poetry*, in which he set down his thoughts on this subject "in careless succession." Among the arguments are: Plato called poetry "sacred," as Ovid did poets, "with which both Cicero and Aristotle agree." Among barbarians, pagans, and Christians there has always existed ritual poetry "as I have pointed out in my *Isidro*." Chaste and innocent poetry — including the erotic — "is irreproachable" (cited *ibid.*).

The same year of 1623 saw the publication at Madrid of Pedro Soto de Rojas' *Desengaño de amor en rimas*, which contains a *Discourse on Poetics*. It is a principle of philosophy, the author states, that all things have two *internal causes*: formal and material; and two *external causes*: efficient and final. Passing over the first two, we find that for him the efficient cause of poetry is a certain natural ardor, the *quid divinum*, the *est deus in nobis* of the ancients, aided by training. The final cause is delight, the enticing of the reader or hearer to follow after the good.[44]

About the year 1624 the dramatist Tirso de Molina published a collection of tales and plays under the title *Cigarrales de Toledo* — a famous book. Tirso, in various of his other works, shows the influence of Ariosto's *Orlando furioso* in episodes in which disappointment in love is the cause of furor. In one of the tales a character loses his power of endurance, and with it his wits, and throws to the winds both wits and endurance. "The rustic servants of the house grappled with him, those of the neighborhood surrounded him, and he, at the top of his voice, spoke these verses, whereby he confirmed the opinion of those who say that poetry is 'fury,' since when his grief was most overwhelming, his disappointment exhaled its complaints in this fashion. . . ."[45]

A Portuguese critic, Manuel de Faria y Souza, in his commentary on the *Rimas* (1639) of Luis de Camoëns, expresses regret that the fifteenth-century Spanish poet Juan de Padilla, el Cartujano (a

---

44. *Obras*, ed. A. Gallego Morell (Madrid, 1950), pp. 25–26. It is somewhat startling to note that the *Desengaño de amor en rimas* is prefaced by a eulogy of the author by Lope de Vega, in which the great dramatist quotes Savonarola (d. at the stake, 1498) to the effect that poetry is a part of rational philosophy; see *ed. cit.*, p. 13.

45. Ed. V. Said Armesto (Madrid, 1913), p. 279.

primitive), should have fallen into near oblivion, declaring that Padilla exceeds all those who then wrote poems "learnedly and successfully" both in Castile and in Portugal. Describing this poet's principal work, *The Twelve Triumphs of the Twelve Apostles*, he declares that "the poetic fury is great, the erudition abundant and exquisite, the style excellent." [46]

We shall end our survey with Quevedo, who analyzes the various Platonic frenzies in this fashion: "Whether or not poetry is 'fury' is a question that must be examined. Cicero settles it saying: No one can be a good poet without inflammation of the spirits, without a certain afflatus almost of madness. And poets normally call their own 'fury' divine." After repeating Plato's contention that no one can approach the Muses aided only by human "art," Quevedo continues:

Therefore these frenzies are to be differentiated in this way, that in the *lover* the cause of fury is the will [the appetitive faculty of the soul] inflamed by desire; in the *poet*, the cause is the mind inflamed by the imagination; in the *drinker*, the cause is wine and heated blood. The lover is beside himself, being centered in the object of his love; the poet is possessed by his imagination. . . . The fury of the poet is divine . . . ; that of the lover is human, born of our nature; that of the drunken man is bestial. The first deserves praise; the second, envy; and the third, pity.[47]

POETA NASCITUR NON FIT

Closely related to the idea that poetic inspiration is a divine frenzy is the endlessly debated question of Nature versus Art. An art, supposedly, can be learned: practice makes perfect. But to what extent is the ability to master the poetic (or literary) art through study and diligence determined by the would-be artist's heredity?[48] In his posthumous romance, *Los Trabajos de Persiles y Segismunda* (1617), Cervantes grants to tailors the right to exercise the art of poetry and to be known as poets: "It is possible for an artisan to be a poet, because poetry is not of the hands but of the mind, and the soul of a tailor is no less capable of poetic composition than the soul

46. See Joaquín Gimeno, "Sobre el Cartujano y sus críticos," *HR*, XXIX (1961), 8–9.
47. *Obras en verso*, ed. L. Astrana Marín (Madrid, 1932) p. 689b.
48. See William Ringler, "*Poeta nascitur non fit*: Some Notes on the History of an Aphorism," *JHI*, II (1941) 497–504.

of a field marshal" (Bk. I, ch. xviii). Cervantes is speaking, of course, only of possibilities: the soul of a tailor is capable of poetic expression. He proceeds to expound the doctrine of the equality of all souls — stoutly defended by Spanish theologians of the Counter Reformation — in perfectly serious language. There may well have been present in Cervantes' mind an element of irony, for he resented a certain "Tailor of Toledo" — a protegé of Lope de Vega — who could sell the plays he composed, though Cervantes could not market his own. This much seems incontestable: Cervantes held that poets are born — *poetae nascuntur* — and he regarded himself as a born cultivator of the Muses "who exceeded most in inventiveness" without benefit of university training. Cervantes in various passages of his works endows the *vulgo*, the common and least noble mass of men, or at least certain parts or individuals of the *vulgo*, with the possibility of intellectual and artistic creativeness. He wrote:

> For in Madrid the mass knows sweet discretion.

The word *discreción* signified, in Cervantes' day, a highly intellectual quality.[49] It will be profitable to trace the history of this new *Sic et Non* (Nature vs. Art) in the literary theorizing of our period.

Though Aristotle says (*Rhetoric, III*) that "poetry is a thing inspired by the god," in another place (*Poetics, XVII*) he decides that "poetic art is the affair of the gifted rather than of the madman." Allan Gilbert, commenting on the second passage, says that it "does not suggest that the poet can succeed by art alone, as might be inferred from *Poetics*, VIII, and as Aristotle's analytic habits might influence us to suppose; natural endowment at least is needed" (*op. cit.*, pp. 94, 118). Longinus in *On the Sublime* wrote that "greatness is innate and not teachable, and only one art leads it: Nature" (Curtius, *op. cit.*, p. 398).

Boethius (d. 524), after discussing composers in *De Musica*, says that "poets, by instinct, under the influence of inspiration rather than by reason and reflexion, compose their songs" (De Bruyne, *op. cit.*, I, 43).

49. See Margaret Bates, *"Discreción" in the Works of Cervantes: A Semantic Study* (Washington, D.C., 1945), pp. 1–4; O. H. Green, "On the Attitude toward the *Vulgo* in the Spanish *Siglo de Oro*," *Studies in the Renaissance*, IV (1957), 190–200, especially 194–96.

In an oration *In Praise of Poetic Art*, delivered in 1485 or 1486, Bartolommeo della Fonte finds poetry to be a "divine madness": "he who comes to the doorposts of the poets without the inspiration of the muses, thinking he can make himself a bard by technique and learning, is vain and puerile in his poetizing" (Trinkaus, *op. cit.*, p. 105).

In *La Poetica* of Bernardino Daniello (1536) there is a discussion of Art versus Nature: "Replying to those who hold that only nature or genius or talent is required of the poet, he argues that if this were so, if nature were merely imitated by the nature of the poet, then the imitation would of necessity be inferior to nature itself. . . . But if art be added to the poet's nature — art which proceeds from the intellect and hence from man's divine component — what results is better than Nature herself." [50]

Torcuato Tasso, in a *Raggionamento della poesia* published in 1562, claims that the poet excels other men by reason of his divine furor and the universality of his knowledge: "without this extraordinary gift of nature [poetic frenzy], even though a man may have knowledge of all doctrines . . . still it will be impossible that he should turn out to be a good poet." The authorities cited are Plato and Cicero (cited *ibid.*, I, 283).

Somewhat later (1583) Sir Philip Sidney repeated the refrain in his *Defense of Poesie*: "a poet no industry can make, if his own genius be not carried into it; and therefore is an old proverb: *Orator fit, poeta nascitur*" (cited by Gilbert, *op. cit.*, p. 448).

In Spain, as we saw above, the compiler of the *Cancionero de Baena* (*ca.* 1445) prefaced the poems which he selected as representative of the work of Alfonso Alvarez de Villasandino with the statement that this poet (d. 1425?) wrote them "by the infused grace which God placed in him." Indeed, Alvarez de Villasandino makes the claim for himself and for all "good" poets:

> Let the law muzzle all poets who don't
> Possess the Divine Gift, and all babblers who won't
> Keep still when they should. . . .[51]

50. Bernard Weinberg, *A History of Literary Criticism in the Italian Renaissance* (Chicago, 1961), II, 721.

51. "manden que callen[n] aquellos que non / resciben por graçia divina este don / de la poetría . . . (*ed. cit.*, I, 80).

The date of Pedro Manuel Ximénez de Urrea's *Cancionero* is 1513. In the preface he insists that "assuredly . . . this poetic pow-er is in some men a gift of Nature, inasmuch as we see other men utterly unfitted for it, just as in the natural world certain birds — thrushes, parrots, magpies — are trained to talk, but not eagles or . . . kites." [52]

Juan del Encina, father of the Spanish drama (d. 1529?), in his *Arte de poesía castellana* first questions whether the art of poetry can be taught: "I, therefore, considering all these things, decided to write a *Manual of Castilian Poetry* which would make it possible, with greater success than heretofore, to teach how poetry should be written in our language, if such a thing can be taught." Further on in his work, he advises all men lacking in native endowment to avoid wasting time reading his precepts: "And let them take unto themselves the words of Quintilian in the first book of his *Insti-tutiones*, to the effect that neither instructions nor precepts avail anything if Nature deny her gifts; for one who lacks *ingenium*, these rules and precepts are as useless as are precepts of agriculture for the tilling of sterile lands." [53]

The festive poet Sebastián de Horozco's *Cancionero* (1550?) con-tains a similar statement in verse:

> And yet 'tis not everyone, candidly speaking,
> Can be called a poet, though rhymester he be;
> For a poet — true poet — is none other than he
> Whose verses flow with a facility
> That's always inborn; all others call we
> Poetasters. . . . .[54]

Alfonso García de Matamoros, in his *Pro adserenda hispanorum eruditione,* so frequently cited in the course of our study, tells how the eloquence of Constantino de la Fuente, court preacher to Charles V and to his son Philip, convinced him that the orator, no

52. Ed. Martín Villar (Zaragoza, 1878), pp. 7–8.

53. Reproduced in Juan del Encina, *Canciones,* ed. Angel J. Battistessa (Buenos Aires, 1941), pp. 135, 147–48.

54. "E aunque no todos, hablando verdad, / pueden trobando llamarse poetas, / sino quien tiene el habilidad / de su natural con facilidad, / porque a los otros llamanos porretas" (*Cancionero,* ed. Sociedad de Bibliófilos Andaluces [Seville, 1874], p. 95).

less than the poet, is born, and unless genius inspires him is inefficient and useless in his profession (*ed. cit.*, pp. 126–27).

A dissenting voice is heard in 1574: that of Francisco Sánchez de las Brozas, who preceded Herrera in issuing an annotated edition of the poems of Garcilaso de la Vega. In his commentary Sánchez states that he does not regard as a good poet the man who fails to imitate (Renaissance *imitatio*) the great poets of antiquity. The reason, he continues, that there are so few real poets among the thousands who write verses is simply that all inadequate poets lack the culture, the knowledge of languages, and the intellectual furniture [*doctrina*] which would enable them to "imitate." [55]

Juan Huarte de San Juan, the authority on vocational guidance, in his *Examen de ingenios para las ciencias* (1575) quotes "all the philosophers of the ancient world" as insisting that where natural ability is lacking as a force inclining a man toward learning, all effort expended on "rules of art" is wasted (*Proemio al Rey*). In the body of his work he declares that the poetic faculty is physical, offering by way of illustration the case of a man who, before he became suddenly irrational, never composed verses but who, when an attack of actual madness came upon him, spoke with rhythm and rhyme. Huarte explains the phenomenon on the basis of his theory of the bodily humors: the "temperament" or admixture of the humors that enables a sane man to write poetry is upset when that man becomes mentally ill; contrary effects are produced when the process is reversed. Huarte cites as his sources Aristotle's *Problems* and lines 301–5 of Horace's *Ars Poetica* (*ed. cit.*, I, 119–21). All arts that are based on a sense of form, of correspondence, of harmony and proportion, says Huarte, require a highly developed imagination. These arts are: poetry, eloquence, music, preaching, designing — and even the art of wit and repartee (Iriarte, *op. cit.*, p. 211).

We pass on to the year 1580 and to the now familiar *Arte poética en romance castellano* of Miguel Sánchez de Lima. In his preface to the reader he explains that in his opinion there are talented men in Spain who could write good things if they but had a book of instructions to guide them: the *raison d'être* of precepts is to make good the deficiencies of natural endowment. Recognizing that

55. *Opera Omnia* (Geneva, 1766), IV, 36.

Nature is superior to art, and that perfection can be achieved only by the harmonizing of the two, the author yet insists that one can be a poet though he have less than perfect endowment, "for art is merely a supplementary means whereby one artificially acquires what nature failed to give." By the mere issuing of his book, Sánchez shows at least his partial disagreement with those who hold "that this is a thing to be learned by Nature, not by art" (ed. cit., p. 11).

Luis Gálvez de Montalvo published in 1582 El pastor de Fílida, a minor yet estimable pastoral novel in the manner of Montemayor's Diana (1559). In the Carta dedicatoria he speaks of his own enjoyment of idle hours devoted "to the practice of the divine art of lofty poetry, to which so many feel called though so few are chosen. . . . "

This leads us to a pastoral by one greater than Montalvo — La Galatea (1585) of Miguel de Cervantes Saavedra. In Book IV of La Galatea the shepherd Lenio excuses himself for daring to address a discreet gathering since he possesses merely the talent and the experience which a rustic environment has given him; and for making bold to take issue with "the famous Tirsi," who has to his credit "solid studies in famous academies." In spite of these handicaps, Lenio nonetheless relies on the assurance that at times the force of natural talent, augmented by a limited experience, can open new paths in fields of learning long considered to be thoroughly known (por largos años sabidas). It is the old principle of Natura facit habilem. Cervantes has more to say on this subject in later works (to be discussed shortly).

Fray Juan de Pineda, in Part II of his Agricultura christiana, cites Ovid's Fasti, Horace's Ars Poetica, and Plato's Ion and Lysis on poetic frenzy, arriving finally at Cicero's accommodation (Pro Archia): native endowment without training is better than training without talent. Better still: Horace would intertwine talent and training to make a perfect man. What the ancients called divine fury, or rapture, "should really apply to the imagination." [56] This last statement may indicate influence of Huarte de San Juan (see above).

56. Segunda Parte de los treynta y cinco Diálogos familiares de la Agricultura christiana (Salamanca, 1589), fol. 19 [i.e., 18].

Emblem writers, as a group, hesitated to give the primacy to Nature. Two Spanish emblematists — each the author of a work entitled *Emblemas morales* — Juan de Horozco y Covarrubias (1601) and Sebastián de Covarrubias y Horozco (1610) prefer the compromise: *Ars naturam juvat* — Art comes to the aid of Nature. Each cites the example of the she-bear that with her tongue licks into shape the formless cub that she has just born.[57]

Of the greatest interest is the discussion of the nature of inspiration in Carballo's *Cisne de Apolo*. The author accepts the natural and "scientific" explanation offered by Huarte de San Juan, citing Huarte by name (*ed. cit.*, I, 70). Success in poetry is impossible without imagination, a faculty dependent on the degree of bodily heat characteristic of the individual. Bodily heat, in man, appears in three "degrees"; it is the third and highest degree that makes the poet.[58] The poet must be of choleric (as against sanguine, melancholy, or phlegmatic) temperament. Did not the satirist Juvenal write: *facit indignatio versus* — indignation produces verse? Carballo enumerates Huarte's *signa* — outward and inward signs — of "the third degree of heat," i.e., of the poet. They are the same as those of Don Quijote, no poet but none the less a dreamer of extraordinary dreams, a seer of amazing visions. Such a choleric man shows courage, liberality, inclination to enjoy women (present but well controlled in Don Quijote); his walk is graceful, catching the eye. His speech is rough-sounding; he is thin and hard, with prominent muscles and veins. His complexion is dark and olive-colored; his hair thick and stiff; his face not especially handsome. If this "heat" be not accompanied by a high degree of dryness (the second quality of the choleric man), the individual may still possess imagination and hence may still be a poet, though in lesser degree; he will in such case be merry, pleasant, fond of pastimes, affable, modest, and not especially attracted to the opposite sex; his voice will be well-rounded, gentle, and sonorous, not rough; his hair and his flesh will be softer (pp. 72–73). The man who lacks either one

57. Robert J. Clements, *Picta Poesis: Literary and Humanistic Theory in Renaissance Emblem Books* (Rome, 1960), pp. 48–49.

58. The poet is even said to compose better in summer than in winter, the former being a *tiempo caliente y seco* — a hot, dry time (*ibid.*, p. 71).

of these degrees of imagination cannot be an elegant poet though he know the precepts of the art (as Cicero did). He who possesses imagination will invent subtle, lofty, rare, and admirable things, in proportion to its degree.[59]

In the first part of Don Quijote (1605) Cervantes, whom we have already quoted on the equality of souls and the consequent possibility of poetic inspiration in artisans as well as field marshals, argues that the poet is born a poet "from his mother's womb, able to compose, without art or study, things which justify Ovid's *est deus in nobis.*" He adds, however, that he who avails himself of training will be a still better poet, the reason being that art does not surpass but does perfect Nature. Yet Cervantes is always aware of the problem of reconciling the rational and the vital, the poetic and the real.[60]

In 1617 Francisco Cascales published his Aristotelian *Tablas poéticas* in the city of Murcia. His treatise, he says, will be most useful to poets since poetry is an art and its essence is precepts. Citing the Italian theorist Francesco Robortello, he stresses the imagination much less than his predecessors.[61]

Juan de Jáuregui's *Rimas* were published in 1618. In the prologue the author grants supremacy (*imperio*) to inborn talent, to the poetic gift properly so called, indispensable always; "but let it not be thought," he adds, "that this is sufficient unto itself, because the splendor which good literary training [*buenas letras*] adds to native aptitude is incomparable and irresistible [*incomparable y forzoso*]." Lacking such good training, countless men of talent (*ingenios*) are like persons feeling their way in the dark.[62]

In or about the year 1632 Jusepe Antonio González de Salas published at Madrid his *New Idea of Ancient Tragedy*, a commentary on "the singular book of *Poetics* by Aristotle the Stagirite." In it he holds art to be "not only an imitation of Nature but an improve-

59. *Ibid.*, p. 74; see also pp. 171, 184, 205, and II, 192. I have studied all these physical and mental attributes in "El *ingenioso* hidalgo," cited above.

60. A. Castro, *El pensamiento de Cervantes* (Madrid, 1925), pp. 181–82.

61. Alberto Porqueras Mayo, *El problema de la verdad poética en el siglo de oro* (Madrid, 1961), pp. 21–22.

62. Cited by Adolfo de Castro (ed.) in the general preface to *Poetas líricos de los siglos XVI y XVII (BAE, XLII)*, p. xciii.

ment on it. Natural aptitude, the *vena poética*, is something distinct from art. Both are complementary to perfection." He gives primacy to the natural poet.[63]

As in the other sections of the present chapter, we have seen also in this one that much depends on the personal inclination of any individual theorizer as he considers the problem of native poetic gift versus instruction. To some, poetic (and general literary) power is a Platonic frenzy; to others, it is a matter of much study, of stern discipline, of trial and error leading to final success. Still others are scientifically minded in an almost modern way, regarding the imagination — a hereditary factor — as all-important. On balance, the syncretic tendency prevails.[64]

To all these theorists, however, the end product of native aptitude and poetic apprenticeship is a social value (despite the Plato of *The Republic*). The cities of Greece contended for the honor of having been Homer's birthplace (see Covarrubias' *Tesoro de la lengua castellana o española, s. v. Homero*). Every great poet brings honor to his village or his city, his country, and mankind. The how of his achievement is less important than its splendor, as Don Juan de Jáuregui was well aware.

DEFINITIONS OF POETRY: *SUB VELAMINE*

"And what is poetry," wrote the Marqués de Santillana in the fifteenth century, "but a feigning of useful things,[65] covered or veiled by a most beautiful covering, composed, set off, and scanned in accordance with a certain number, weight, and measure?" (*Obras, ed. cit.*, p. 4). Menéndez y Pelayo pointed out the aesthetic elements (beauty, creative imagination), and the idea of social usefulness which are contained in this definition.[66] Its primary source is Boccaccio's *De genealogia deorum*, the Magna Charta of the dig-

63. Edward C. Riley, "The Dramatic Theories of Don Jusepe González de Salas," *HR*, XIX (1951), 183–203; see section III of the article, especially pp. 196–99.

64. *Natura facit habilem, ars vero facilem, ususque potentem*, according to the adage. See Iriarte, *op. cit.*, p. 204.

65. See below, the sections entitled "Poetry and Religion: The Ancient Gods" and "Delightful Instruction."

66. *Antología de poetas líricos castellanos* (new ed.; Santander, 1944–45), II, 82.

nity of letters.[67] But Boccaccio did not originate the idea of the veil, which had both a religious and a secular aspect. St. Augustine had been intrigued by the appearance of symbols in the Bible. "Why was it pleasant to linger in symbols? Was it commendable? The more . . . difficult the divine symbol . . . , the more difficult perhaps the problem" (Wimsatt and Brooks, op. cit., p. 125). Rabanus Maurus (d. 856), in his encyclopedic De Universitate sought, precisely, to determine both the literal and the symbolic meaning of the words of the Scriptures, to solve the problem of the Bible's obscurity. This obscurity, he says, is willed by God for two reasons, one moral and the other aesthetic. It humbles human pride by imposing upon it the task of searching out deep meanings; it delights the poetic imagination by renewing ceaselessly man's interest (De Bruyne, op. cit., I, 356–57). St. Augustine had remarked that beauty cannot bear scrutiny in isolation (Wimsatt and Brooks, loc. cit.).

The persistence of these thoughts in the Middle Ages is traced by Aldo S. Bernardo.[68] In the Renaissance, Roger Ascham's (d. 1568) general theory of poetry is that poets "under the covering of a fable do hide . . . goodly precepts of philosophy" (cited in Lewis, op. cit., p. 281). Thomas Lodge's defense of poetry (1579?) is essentially the same as Boccaccio's (ibid., p. 396). Sir Philip Sidney (d. 1586) calls upon his readers "to believe . . . that it pleased the heavenly Deity, by Hesiod and Homer, under the veil of fables, to give us all knowledge . . . ; that there are many mysteries contained in poetry which of purpose were written darkly lest by profane wits it should be abused" (cited by Gilbert, op. cit., p. 458). In Lodovico Dolce's Dialogue on Painting one interlocutor recalls having heard it said that in Michelangelo's stupendous Judgment "are contained several very deep allegorical meanings which are understood by few," and another speaker adds: "In this he would deserve praise, since it would appear that he had imitated those great philosophers who hid under the veil of poetry the greatest mysteries of philosophy." [69]

67. So called by Vittore Branca, "Motivi preumanistici nell'opera del Boccaccio" in Pensée humaniste et tradition chrétienne aux XVᵉ e XVIᵉ siècles (Paris, 1950), p. 81. See also Charles G. Osgood, Boccaccio on Poetry (Princeton, 1930), pp. 121 ff.

68. "Petrarch's Attitude toward Dante," PMLA, LXX (1955), 494–95.

69. Cited in R. J. Clements, Michelangelo's Theory of Art (New York, 1961), p. 228.

In the theory of the "beautiful veil" there is, therefore, something of the spirit of the Hebrew holy of holies; of the Psalmist's "such knowledge is too wonderful for me" (Ps. 139:6); something also of Horace's *procul profani* — "keep your distance, hateful crowd"; as well as something of the psychological principle of difficult, of hermetic, art: beneath the deceptively apprehensible surface there lies something far more deeply interfused, something reserved for the truly perceptive eye, the knowing heart.

Readers of the chapter on "Medieval Laughter" in Volume I will remember the insistence with which the Archpriest of Hita warns his readers to look beneath the surface, to avoid being misled by unattractive exteriors, to dig for the hidden meaning, that is to say, to lift the shrouding veil:

> Beneath the bush's threatening thorn smiles
> many a lovely rose;
> A learned doctor's crabbed hand makes
> illegible wondrous prose;
> A torn cape hides a merry soul, and my
> book — where'er it goes —
> Carries between torn covers what only a
> wise man knows.[70]

These lines, with their joyous parody of the idea of deeply significant obscurity, were composed some hundred years earlier than Santillana's definition of poetry as useful doctrine, beautifully veiled. A century later Feliciano de Silva (whose involved conceits were the delight of Don Quijote) prefaced his continuation (1534) of Rojas' *Celestina* with a *Carta Proemial* in which he complains — already! — of the oversophistication of his age (*como ya los hombres tengan el gusto tan dañado para recebir las virtudes*) and explains that he seeks to succeed in his didactic purpose "by covering with the gilt coating of jokes and pleasant matters the bitter pill of truth." [71]

The anonymous *El Crotalón* was composed about the year 1552.

70. "So la espina está la noble rosa flor, / en fea letra está saber de grand dotor; / como so mala capa yaze buen bebedor, / ansí so el mal tabardo yaze el buen amor" (*Libro de buen amor*, ed. J. Ducamin [Toulouse, 1901], stanza 18). I have chosen variant readings from different MSS in order to make the best text.

71. *Segunda comedia de la famosa Celestina*, ed. J. A. de Balenchana (Madrid, 1874), p. 1.

In the prologue the author explains how, having idle time on his hands, he determined to write something that could convey good doctrine "in pleasant style." He therefore conceived the idea of revealing the wickedness of contemporary daily life "beneath a pleasing cortex, so as to purvey pleasure." In this, he says, he has glorious predecessors — Aesop, Cato, Aulus Gellius, Boccaccio (greatly esteemed as a moralist because of his serious works in Latin), Poggio Bracciolini, Aristotle, Plutarch, Plato, and even Christ himself, who taught by means of parables.[72]

The decades pass, and Fray Juan de Pineda writes in the first part of his *Agricultura christiana*:

> Lactantius, Palephatus, and St. Fulgentius tell us that the poets never intended to be feigners of lies, but rather to veil truths, in order that by means of those veils they might entice the masses of men to worship God and to do good; for the "lying" of the poets is only word-deep and does not extend to the meaning which their words are intended to convey; if it were not so, the poets would not deserve the name of great wisemen which we give them, but would be time-wasters, as the composers of novels of chivalry really are (*ed. cit.*, fol. 22).

The idea is still very much alive when the Spanish emblematists take it over, at the end of the century. The cryptic veiling of moral truths is the very essence of their art, as shown in the *Emblemas morales* of Hernando de Soto, published at Madrid in 1599 (Clements, *Picta Poesis* . . . , p. 100).

We encounter again the *Cisne de Apolo* of the theorist Luis Alfonso de Carballo, who quotes Badius Ascensius and Battista Mantuano to the effect that meadows do not really smile or laugh, that love is not really a blindfolded child: *Sub poetico figmento semper res diuinae latent* — beneath the poetic covering lie meanings which are divine (*ed. cit.*, I, 99). Farther on in the dialogue, the author's spokesman cites Lactantius: the poet's duty is to expound great truths in darkly symbolic language — *embueltas con obscuras figuras* (ibid., p. 111). Only those of no understanding consider the poet a liar. What poets do is to teach by means of difficulty, for the purpose of retaining the attention; the reconditeness of their style incites the learner: *difficultas attentionem excitat, quam fastidium expellit* (pp. 113–14).

72. Text in Menéndez y Pelayo, *Orígenes* . . . , *ed. cit.*, II, 119a.

Lope de Vega goes so far as to apply the principle of the veil to the generally condemned romances of chivalry, saying in the dedication of his play *El Desconfiado*, published in Part XIII of his *Comedias* (1620): "Many laugh at the novels of derring-do . . . and they are right if they consider merely the outward surface, exactly as one would be right in condemning certain works of Antiquity no less vain and fruitless than the *Ass of Gold* . . . ; but when one penetrates beneath their cortex and finds the heart of these books, one encounters all the parts of philosophy." We quote this text because Lope would scarcely have wished to be laughed out of court for saying something without a foundation in fact. Indeed, the best novels of chivalry, such as *Amadís*, and others less good, such as the *Florisando*, did indeed contain much interspersed "good doctrine." But it should be remembered that Lope here makes a very special application of his reference to the *libros de caballerías*. The normal action in such novels is the defense of some lady in distress. *Ergo*, Lope's patrons should defend him from the malice of the ignorant.[73]

We shall conclude our survey with the year 1646, which saw the publication of Gracián's *El Héroe*. In its prologue Vicencio Juan de Lastanosa reports having heard complaints that Gracián's prose style "destroyed the clarity of the Castilian language," to which he replies: "I say that one does not compose his works for all men, and that obscurity of style is intended to increase veneration for the sublimity of the matter treated, since the mysterious way of expressing it causes it to be the more greatly revered."[74]

THE POET AS CIVILIZER

That the poets were mankind's first teachers — of theology, science, and civics — is an idea so pervasive in classical literature that it is unnecessary to quote ancient texts. Nor is it necessary to compile an anthology of pertinent passages from Spanish writers. We shall limit ourselves to three examples: one from Vincente Espinel's prologuist, Alonso de Valdés, one from Lope de Vega, and one from Cervantes.

73. A. de Castro (ed.), *Curiosidades bibliográficas* (*BAE*, XXXVI), p. xviii.
74. Cited by M. Romera-Navarro (ed.), *El Criticón* (Philadelphia, 1938–40), I, 29.

The preliminaries of Espinel's *Diversas Rimas* (Madrid, 1591) are dated 1587. In the *Prólogo* Valdés set forth the excellencies of poetry in impressive fashion:

Poetry in her flight penetrates Heaven, revealing the glory of the Most High, the penalties of Purgatory, the eternal death of Hell; she unveils the secrets of astronomy, the courses of the stars, the movements of the celestial spheres, the influences of the planets; the opposition each to each of the elements, the nature of things, the properties of plants, animals, herbs, juices; tastes, odors; the literary function of invention and of history; the ugliness of vice, the beauty of virtue, the scales of justice and its distortion; the vanity of the world, the contempt of wealth; chastity and goodness; the reward of right conduct; laws and rites, peace and war; serenity of spirit and repose of life; natural and moral philosophy; the truth of the Faith, the marvels of the Old and New Testament, and the Prophecies. In short: there is no department in which poetry has not shed revealing light on all things spiritual, natural and supernatural. Poetry contains within herself the congruities of geometry, the subtlety of philosophy, the elegance of rhetoric, the secrets of astrology, the admirable truths of theology. As the bestower of all that is sublime and lofty in human knowledge she should be esteemed, favored, and supported by the powerful of the earth.

Lope de Vega's *La Arcadia* came out in 1598, and it too contains a statement of the greatness of the domain in which poetry is queen:

The poet must not only know all the sciences, or at least the principles of all of them, but he must have very great experience of all that happens on land and sea, so that if the occasion to dispose an army or describe a fleet arises, he will not talk blindly and be censured and taken for an ignoramus by those who have seen such things. No more, no less, he must know the usages, customs, and manner of life of all sorts of people; and finally, all the things that are talked of, dealt with and lived by, because there is nothing in the world so exalted or base that there is not occasion for dealing with it some time, from the Creator himself down to the lowest worm or creature of the earth.[75]

"Poetry appears in Cervantes' *Viaje del Parnaso* (1615) with the liberal arts and sciences all ministering to her and treating her with 'loving affection' and 'most holy respect,' enhancing thereby their own prestige," writes E. C. Riley. "This beauteous, blessed maiden Poetry knows all; she locks up and unlocks secrets; she lodges with divine and moral philosophy, is herself incomparably the most learned and universal of all sciences, and knows no limits. The whole time-honoured idea obviously appeals to the idealistic imagination of Cervantes. It is repeated by Don Quixote in another

75. *BAE*, XXXVIII, 93.

eulogy of poetry and again by the Licenciado Vidriera." [76] We quote
Don Quijote's words (II, 16):

> Poetry, my dear sir, seems to me like a tender damsel of few years and ex-
> tremely beautiful, in whose service are many other damsels which are the other
> sciences; and the duty of these is to enrich, enhance, and adorn her, and her
> obligation is to make use of them and at the same time elevate them by the
> power of her authority; but this damsel will not be touched or handled, nor
> led through the streets, nor made public on corners or in plazas or in the dark
> corners of palaces. Her alchemy is of such virtue that he who cultivates her
> will convert her into purest gold of inestimable price. . . .

And by the word poetry Cervantes did not mean merely verse;
the same spiritual wealth is available to the novelist: "The varie-
gated items enumerated by the Canon in his recipe for the ideal
romance [Don Quijote, II, 48] reflect something of the idea. Cervantes' claim that he has the 'ability, sufficiency, and wit' to deal
with the whole universe is also a probable reminiscence of the vast
range permitted to the poet . . ." (ibid., p. 61).

POETRY AS THE GIVER OF FAME

It is not the purpose of this section to document the existence of
the desire for fame in the Middle Ages and its growth in the Renaissance.[77] My aim is, rather, to show that the man of letters possessed
in those centuries something akin to the modern "power of the
press" — a power which was highly respected. In view of the generally ethical character of Spanish literature, it will be well first to
quote two "other-worldly" authorities on the idea of fame as held
by the highly devout. Luis Vives wrote in his Introductio ad sapientiam: "Even though you may never do anything for which men
in general may see and esteem you, one's fame is a thing very properly to be kept clean and uninjured, because our concern over it
on many occasions restrains us from doing things which are unseemly; and we should concern ourselves with it very especially to
the end that our good example may shine forth for the good of

76. Cervantes's Theory of the Novel (Oxford, 1962), pp. 74–95.

77. This task has already been well begun by María Rosa Lida de Malkiel's La
idea de la fama en la Edad Media castellana (Mexico City, 1952).

others." [78] Two generations later Fray Juan de Pineda stated in his *Agricultura christiana*: "He who strives after virtue in order to serve God will acquire a fame more honorable than that won by Hercules when he chained Cerberus." [79]

The desire to be immortalized in a book is common enough in the Middle Ages: "Our achievement will be recorded in chronicles," says a personage in the *Libro de Alexandre* (cited *ibid.*, p. 184). Much slower in making its appearance is the eagerness to be immortalized by the magic of poetry. Appreciation of the force of this magic is first manifested in the anonymous *Chronicle of Don Alvaro de Luna*. As the historian puts down his record of a battle in which Don Alvaro was wounded by an arrow, he inserts certain lines by the poet Juan de Mena, introduced with a degree of respect hitherto never shown to a mere man of letters: "It seems proper to place here certain couplets of a great and most famous poet named Juan de Mena." And in like manner the author of the chronicle cites also a poem of the Marqués de Santillana, whom he describes as "a gentleman of inventive mind and great mental power, and a fine poet" (cited *ibid.*, pp. 242, 243).

Juan de Mena himself, in his masterpiece *El Laberinto de Fortuna*, proclaims his intention to save from oblivion the glories of Spanish arms. In his initial invocation he claims for himself and for his colleagues the function exercised by the poets of old. The great deeds of the Spaniards have hitherto lain in neglect, forgotten *por falta de autores* — for lack of authors — but now:

> Let Fame raise to heaven her incomparable voice,
> To the end that the deeds performed in our time
> May be spread abroad from nation to nation —
> Let oblivion be thwarted and memory live on.[80]

The attitude persists in the sixteenth and seventeenth centuries. In 1582 Lupercio Leonardo de Argensola writes a poetic epistle to

---

78. *Introducción a la sabiduría* (Madrid, 1944), p. 35.

79. *Ed. cit.*, Part I, fol. 202. See also Edwin B. Benjamin, "Fame, Poetry, and the Order of History in the Literature of the English Renaissance," *Studies in the Renaissance*, VI (1959), 64–84. St. Thomas ruled that anything which impels men to do good is not a sin; the desire for glory is such an impulse; therefore the desire for glory is not a sin (Mrs. Malkiel, *La idea de la fama* . . . , p. 119, n. 14).

80. "Leuante la Fama su boz ynefable, / porque los fechos que son al presente /

Don Juan de Albión from the Catalan city of Lérida, where he finds himself a prisoner of the confusion apparently inseparable from the royal court — or portions thereof — whether at Madrid or traveling through the provinces. Complaining of his inability to write serious verse under such harassing conditions, Lupercio indulges in dreaming of the happy day when a more favorable future will permit him to do serious poetic work. He even imagines the heroic poem he will then compose. His theme will be the turning back of the invading Moors in his native Pyrenean region of Aragon, in the days of the reconquest of the Peninsula, and — more precisely — the valor and the virtue of many heroes, alas! long since forgotten:

> I'll bring the blush of shame to downy cheeks,
> To smug youths all too happy and well fed,
> Whose ancestors were valiant as the Greeks;
> Perhaps by my rude verses they'll be led
> To tread once more the hard, steep paths of glory
> And emulate their great, illustrious dead.[81]

Similar hopes were expressed by scores of poets. Aristotle's exaltation of the epic in his *Poetics* unquestionably had much to do with the preference for the heroic; but there was more than that: Spain's poets wished to immortalize her politico-religious ideals in the most austere literary form that the times could offer. Many religious epics were dedicated to personages high in rank and in government, and in terms of glowing patriotism and burning faith.[82] "The poet's task in life," wrote our theorist Luis Alfonso de Carballo in his *Cisne de Apolo (ed. cit.*, II, 7), "is like unto that of a king, who rewards the good and punishes the bad. In this he imitates not only the king, but God (who rewards and punishes with infinite justice and mercy); and let this be proof of what I said in my definition of the poet, namely that in his activity he comes close to the divine scheme of things [*artificio*]."

vayan de gente sabidos en gente, / oluido non priue lo que es memorable" (cited *ibid.*, p. 285).

81. "Haré ver con vergüenza a mil mozuelos, / que viven de sí mismos satisfechos, / cuán diferentes eran sus abuelos; / quizá daré calor assí a sus pechos / i aspirarán a la heredada gloria, / émulos dignamente de sus hechos" (*Rimas de Lupercio y Bartolomé L. de Argensola*, ed. J. M. Blecua [Zaragoza, 1950–51], I, 102).

82. Frank Pierce, "Some Aspects of the Spanish 'Religious Epic' of the Golden Age," *HR*, XII (1944), 1–10; see especially p. 3.

POETRY AND RELIGION: THE ANCIENT GODS

Manuel de Faría y Souza wrote of Luis de Camoëns, the author of the Portuguese national epic: "The poet uses these gods as a great philosopher," to reveal "divine mysteries and teachings." All worthy poetry, the men of this age believed, "bears some witness to Truth," and "authentic revelations have been made to the epic poets especially." There was no antinomy between pagan and Christian elements: the "pagan marvelous" was regarded as a devout, Catholic, and true allegory. Camoëns identifies Jupiter with Divine Providence.[83] Edgar Wind, writing of Jacopo Sannazaro's poem *De partu Virginis*, observes that "the Virgilian tone has acquired a twist of mystical ardor which is unmistakably Christian; and Renaissance art produced many images of Venus which resemble a Madonna or a Magdalen. . . . Unquestionably, once the transference of types became a universal practice, it was applied by inferior artists without much thought." One must not look for a mystery behind every hybrid image of the Renaissance. Yet in principle "the artistic habit of exploring and playing with these oscillations, was sanctioned by a theory of concordance which discovered a sacred mystery in pagan beauty, conceiving it to be a poetic medium through which the divine splendour had been transmitted." [84]

Quevedo made the following defense:

There will surely be some who will call me to task for having cited, in a work of sacred subject, verses of Claudian, a Latin poet. I do not raise the point that by some he is said to have been a Christian: I have no means of knowing and, out of respect for so great a genius, I do not wish to deny him such a blessing. . . . Even if he was a pagan, let my action be justified by the example of St. Augustine in his Sermon *De resurrectione corporum contra infideles*. The subject matter could not be more grave, more important; yet the Saint cites two verses of Virgil, from *Aeneid*, VI.[85]

Quevedo was perhaps excessively scrupulous. The use of pagan mythology as a decorative element to enhance the connotative pow-

83. See Edward Glaser, "Manuel de Faría e Sousa and the Mythology of *Os Lusiadas*," *Miscelánea de Estudos a Joaquim de Carvalho*, VI (1961), 614 ff., especially 615–19.

84. *Pagan Mysteries in the Renaissance* (New Haven, 1958), p. 29; see also p. 49; Weinberg, *op. cit.*, II, 886; Charles Norris Cochrane, *Christianity and Classical Literature* (New York, 1957).

85. *Obras en prosa*, ed. L. Astrana Marín (Madrid, 1932), pp. 1009b–10a.

er of a poem was common practice, even when the poem was sacred. Alonso de Acevedo, in his religious epic *La creación del mundo* (1617), recounting the events of the First Day of creation as recorded in Genesis, composes an apostrophe to Night:

> The lovely dell-nymphs in the quiet glades,
> Joyous and happy in the forest's depths,
> Renew the rhythms of their rounds and dances,
> Mingling with dryads, no less fair than they.
> The naiads, fording streams with splashing step —
> Ever alert for spying fawn or satyr —
> Guard their bare bodies from all prying eyes
> And make the fountain flash with foamy waters.[86]

In seeking an explanation of this decorative use, we must go beyond the fact that the poetry of the ancients was too closely intertwined with contemporary culture to be ignored and search for a cause closer to the wellsprings of human nature. This has been done by C. S. Lewis. "No religion, so long as it is believed," he writes, "can have that kind of beauty which we find in the gods of Titian, of Botticelli, or of our own romantic poets." [87] And he continues (in texts already familiar):

> For poetry to spread its wings fully, there must be, besides the believed religion, a marvellous that knows itself as myth. For this to come about, the old marvellous, which was once taken as fact, must be stored up somewhere, not wholly dead, but in a winter sleep, waiting its time (p. 83). The decline of the gods, from deity to hypostasis and from hypostasis to decoration, was not, for them nor for us, a history of sheer loss. For decoration may let romance in. The poet is free to invent, beyond the limits of the possible, regions of strangeness and beauty for their own sake (p. 75).

Mythology and the pagan Parnassus were thus a part, an increasingly important part, of the "very beautiful covering" which the Marqués de Santillana regarded as the essence of poetry.[88] Seznec's *La survivance des dieux antiques* is, from beginning to end, a his-

---

86. "Entonces las napeas por los prados / de los bosques alegres y gozosas, / renovando los bailes concertados, / se mezclan con las dríadas hermosas; / las náyades, saltando por los vados / de las fuentes y ríos, vergonzosas / del sátiro y del fauno se recelan, / que por ver sus desnudos cuerpos velan" (*BAE*, XXIX, 249a).

87. *The Allegory of Love: A Study in Medieval Tradition* (Oxford, 1936), p. 83.

88. In the following discussion I condense my article, "*Fingen los poetas*: Notes on the Spanish Attitude Toward Pagan Mythology," *Estudios dedicados a Menéndez Pidal*, I (Madrid, 1950), 276–88.

tory of this adaptation, whereby the "feignings of the poets" were converted into allegories and symbols. The adaptation was not, however, perfect: it produced a certain *gêne*. Yet this uneasiness is not so great as might be assumed from a reading, in the fifteenth-century *cancioneros*, of various renunciations of the pagan invocation (as against Milton's "Sing, heavenly Muse"). In his *Arte de la poesía castellana* Juan del Encina (d. 1529?) uses the words *fiction* and *feigned* to explain the common use by poets of the pseudo-pagan invocation, e.g.: *O bright and shining Jupiter* (Santillana); *O Jupiter high and mighty* (Gerónimo de Artés); *Powerful Jupiter* (Johan de Andújar). Encina, speaking of the dignity of poetry, says that its origin was attributed by the ancients to their gods and to the Muses,

as we gather from the invocations of the ancient poets, from whom we ourselves have taken them over, not because we believe as they did or regard them as gods when we invoke them (which would be the worst possible error and heresy); but to avail ourselves of their elegance and poetic order, so that when we propose, invoke, narrate, or tell great and imposing fictions, we may very well use these devices because, the work itself being but a figment of the imagination, it is fitting that the invocation be in like manner fictitious. But when we compose a serious work of devotion or one that touches upon matters of our Faith, we invoke God himself, or his blessed Mother, or some saint to be our intercessor and mediator, to the end that we may obtain grace.

This method was perfectly described, in eight words, by Fray Luis de León: "to work the pagan marble with Christian hands." The precept was quite generally followed. Quevedo's *canto épico*, entitled *Cristo resucitado*, begins, as does *Paradise Lost*, with a Christian invocation: *christiana Musa mía*. Calderón makes the amplest use of mythology in his allegorical Eucharist plays. The religion of the ancients — like all other aspects of their culture — was considered a way station, a preparation, a *figura* of the coming Law of Grace.

COMEDY AND SOCRATIC SELF-KNOWLEDGE [89]

"Only in antique Athens and in the London of Queen Elizabeth has there ever existed a drama as national and as popular as that of

89. We shall discuss comedy again in this chapter when we consider literature as entertainment.

the Spanish period of florescence" (Curtius, *op. cit.*, p. 345). In the main, the Spanish *comedia* is a denial of classical precepts and practice, especially with regard to the separation of the dramatic into comedy and tragedy. Like Elizabethan drama, indeed like nearly all modern drama, it aims at presenting a complete and integrated view of life.[90]

Bartolomé de Torres Naharro, the first Spaniard to write dramatic criticism (in the preface of his *Propalladia,* 1517), appears to take dramatic entertainment for granted: "Seeing all the world given over to fiestas of comedies and similar things." [91] In the *Prohemio* of his book he quotes Cicero's dictum that "comedy is an imitation of life, a mirror of customs, the image of truth." He himself makes a remarkable distinction between *comedia a noticia,* realistic comedy, and *comedia a fantasia,* romantic comedy. Indeed, two of his plays, the *Comedia Tinellaria* and the *Comedia Soldadesca,* are outstanding examples of dramatic realism *avant la lettre.*

The holding up of a mirror to human life may (or may not) have a value beyond that of satisfying our amused curiosity and interest. It may have the negative value of satire — *castigat ridendo mores* — or the positive value of an object lesson, as a speech in Lope de Vega's *El Castigo sin venganza* makes clear:

> Know you not, friend Richard,
> That a comedy's a mirror,
> Wherein the fool and the wise man,
> The old, the young, the strong, the gallant,
> The governor, the king, the damsel,
> And the mistress of her household
> Form a picture of our customs
> That can serve us as a model
> Of life and honor . . . ?[92]

90. *Torres Naharro and the Drama of the Renaissance,* by J. E. Gillet, ed., transcribed, and completed by O. H. Green (Philadelphia, 1961), p. 572. (This is volume IV of *Propalladia and Other Works of Bartolomé de Torres Naharro,* ed. Gillet; it will be cited as Gillet-Green.)

91. *Propalladia* . . . (Bryn Mawr, Pennsylvania, 1943–51) I, 137.

92. "¿Ahora sabes, Ricardo, / que es la comedia un espejo, / en que el necio, el sabio, el viejo, / el mozo, el fuerte, el gallardo, / el rey, el gobernador, / la doncella, las casada / seindo al ejemplo escuchada / de la vida y del honor, / retrata[n] nuestras costumbres . . . ?" See Lope de Vega, *Teatro,* I, ed. Alfonso Reyes (Madrid, 1919), 190–91.

The assumption is, of course, that each estate will be led to self-improvement by seeing itself revealed "with jokes and jests and witticisms, involved in its characteristic troubles" (*ibid.*). In Carballo's theoretic analysis of comedy, a character appropriately named Zoylo (i.e., "carping critic") objects even to the discussion of such frivolous matters: "If to see the acting of a comedy is to waste time badly, it will be no less bad to hear comedy discussed." This charge the author's spokesman immediately denies: "You err, inasmuch as comedy is the imitation of life, the mirror of customs, the image of the truth" (*Cisne de Apolo, ed. cit.*, II, 14). The idea was not merely Ciceronian. Seneca (Ad Lucilium, Ep. 76,31) and Epictetus (El Brocense's translation, 1612) had seen the totality of human life as a comedy whose parts are distributed by God: "Life is a comedy, and God the one who gives out the roles and assigns the speeches" (Bataillon, *op. cit.*, II, 426, n. 103).

Although theatrical representations of sacred themes were a firmly established element of Spanish culture, the other two types of theater, the historical and the descriptive of manners,[93] were approved (or condemned) by an impressive number of writers, with a few taking a middle ground — that the theater in itself is morally indifferent (see Cotarelo, *op. cit.*, pp. 130, 237, 466). With the exception of the definitive suppression of the Eucharistic *autos sacramentales* in 1765, the rigorists were never able to carry the day for long.[94] The story of the pros and cons is much too complex for full development except in a treatise of book length. A complete account is not needed here, but rather a summing up of the argument in favor of the "mirror of life" theory: "each one goes [to the theater] to see portrayed his personal character, his trade, or his occupation, imitated so vividly by the talent of the poet that it appears as it ought to be, not as it is; he goes to learn the perfection of his own estate in life," so much so that "the nation has every right to resent being deprived [by official action] of a source of so much delight, of such great profit . . ." (*ibid.*, p. 237b).

To learn perfection, to become aware of the ideal to which one

93. See Fray Francisco de Alcocer's analysis (1559) in Emilio Cotarelo y Mori, *Bibliografía de las controversias sobre la licitud del teatro en España* (Madrid, 1904), p. 55a.

94. We shall return to this subject when we discuss social control of literature.

should aspire in life, to apprehend it by seeing men and women acting out upon the stage a figment of the poet's imagination and creative power — this, much more than the relaxing entertainment or
the satirical reproof which we shall study in later sections, is the
true end of comedy.[95] It is an extension of the Socratic (and Christian) "Know thyself."

Satire: castigat ridendo mores

"The artist has two roles: to excite to happiness and vitality, and
to destroy misery and deadening oppression. He does this, not didac-
tically but by the expression of values. Although his function is
often to reveal a deeper harmony, he has another function scarcely
less important: to shatter the hard shell of an outworn order in
which the spirit turns emptily in a vacuum. . . . There is a process
of creative dying, a continual sloughing off of diseased members."[96]
This function of the poet is that which makes the satirist a *censor de
vicios*, a censor of vice, so that Badius Ascensius could write in the
early sixteenth century that "the true task of the satiric poet is today
the same as that of the preacher" (cited by Carballo, *op. cit.*, II, 62).
But satire also has a tendency to exist for its own sake, so that concern for the public weal is often little more than a side effect: "Satire
has always exploited the opportunity to satisfy an interest in vice by
attacking it."[97] One can hardly deny that Quevedo attacked in
satirical prose and verse things he hated; but that is not the entire
story. He exploited the general interest in vice as a means of realizing himself artistically. His keenest satisfaction came from his delight as an artist — a word artist who often shaped his satires so as
to achieve a brilliant word play. When one reads Quevedo's satires
on womankind, for example, and then turns to his private correspondence, one finds two different sets of values, often diametrically

95. Tragedy in the Sophoclean or Shakespearian sense did not flourish in Spain,
quite possibly because the nation's hard-won doctrinal unanimity practically eliminated every moral dilemma. Truth was as near as the nearest parish church. The
solutions of the prophet and of the tragedian are mutually incompatible. "Tragedy
. . . cannot exist where there is no faith; conversely, it cannot exist where there is
doubt; it can exist only in an atmosphere of skeptical faith" (Herbert Weisinger,
Tragedy and the Paradox of the Fortunate Fall [London, 1953], pp. 227–28).

96. Melvin A. Rader, *A Modern Book of Esthetics* (New York, 1935), p. xx.

97. Alfred Harbage, *As They Liked It: An Essay on Shakespeare and Morality* (New
York, 1947), p. 194.

opposed.[98] It is therefore unsafe to take satirical writings as social documents; Juvenal's satires must be verified in Tacitus' histories.

Our purpose here is neither to write a history of Spanish satire, nor to derive from satires written by Spaniards a picture of what contemporary life must have been like. It is, rather, to acquire some understanding of how the Spaniards of our period regarded, theoretically, the satirist's task. The answer may be anticipated at this point: they held that the satirist should be a corrector of social vices, but they knew that he was often something quite different — a man who made artistic constructs for the sake of the art with which he made them. The satire of the *gracioso*, the funnyman, in the plays of Lope de Vega and his school, existed not as a social corrective, but as a vehicle for literary humor, a winner of gate receipts. In the wide field of satire it is constantly a question "of self-conscious art, of traditions, conventions, considerations of poetic means in terms of poetic ends."[99]

Carballo recognized that satire is "poetry of reprehension," whether "just or unjust": "this exercise that draws blood, was called satire" (*op. cit.*, II, 62–63). It was a type of unofficial punishment and as such was, in ancient times, "allowed": Alcaeus was even given a gold plectrum because he had written against tyrants; in Rome, Lucilius cried out against vices as passionately as if he were attacking them with the sword. Yet this activity became subject to abuse: Horace's *carmina mala*. The same thing happened, centuries later, in Spain. Juan de Lucena (15 c.) wrote in his *Libro de vida beata*: "If the Athenians trained their sons for letters, and the Romans for arms, we train ours for insults [*pullas*]."[100]

The medieval *cantigas de escarnio* (songs of contempt) may well have been holdovers from a simpler day when abuse was ritualistic, accompanying, as the reverse of the medallion, rites intended to please the supernaturals.[101] The same origin may be posited for the

98. I am here following my review-article, "A Hispanist's Thoughts on [Gilbert Highet's] *The Anatomy of Satire*," *RPh*, XVII (1963), 122–33; see p. 125.

99. A. Kernan, *The Cankered Muse: Satire of the English Renaissance* (New Haven, 1959), pp. 247–48.

100. A. Paz y Melia (ed.), *Opúsculos literarios de los siglos XIV a XVI* (Madrid, 1892), p. 199.

101. See O. H. Green, "On Juan Ruiz's Parody of the Canonical Hours," *HR*, XXVI (1958), 12–34.

pullas, or contests of abuse, which appear as literature of entertainment in Spanish sixteenth-century comedy, before Lope de Vega. At the Renaissance satire became humanistic, bookish:

> Satire as a literary form must be distinguished from the satiric, an element which can occur (like the pathetic, or the heroic) in almost any composition. It had been frequent in our medieval literature. What is new [in the Renaissance] is the crop of satires imitated, on humanistic principles, from the satires of the Romans. Whether Roman satire is a true literary kind at all may be questioned. It has no structural characteristic peculiar to it; by writing a "satire" one is committed to nothing except to a continuous use of the satiric element, so that to have a book called a "satire" is as odd, and as suspect, as it would be if we had a book called "A pathos." . . . The great works in the modern vernaculars which we usually call "satires" do not descend from the *Satira* of the Romans. . . . They are all fantastic narratives, and their true ancestors are Rabelais, Cervantes, the *Apocolocyntosis*, Lucian, and the *Frogs and Mice*. It was, therefore, arguably, in an evil hour that the humanistic passion for reviving all ancient kinds led certain Elizabethans to express their satiric impulses in formal satire. It was much more fruitfully expressed in their comedies and pamphlets.[102]

In the Renaissance, satire — as distinct from invective, which flourished mightily, especially in Italy — was defined by the theorists as an impersonal genre, attacking, not the vicious, but vice itself. Alonso López Pinciano, in his *Philosophía antigua poética* (1596), points out that the cruelty of the "old" satire of Greece was banished by the gentler language of the new (i.e., Roman); for his own day he prescribes that the satirist use "paraphrases and dark circumlocutions . . . in such a manner that the meaning could be interpreted in various ways." [103] Another Spanish theorist, Bartolomé Leonardo de Argensola, in an essay, "Del estilo propio de la sátira," [104] points out that in modern times Ariosto had properly led the way to a "graver" style in satirical writing. With Horace, he avers, satire became an authoritative voice of great value to the state: "Laughter was tempered by grave locutions and reproof was administered majestically." Satire, like Terentian comedy (which Argensola admired), came "to adorn itself with art." Thus satire became abstract, grave, and serious — in theory. In practice there remained the nasti-

---

102. Lewis, *English Literature* . . . , pp. 468–69.

103. Cited by S. Shepard, *El Pinciano y las teorías literarias del Siglo de Oro* (Madrid, 1962), p. 151.

104. *Obras sueltas*, ed. El Conde de la Viñaza (Madrid, 1889), II, 295–301.

ness of Quevedo, the unveiled personal attacks on the humpbacked
dramatist Juan Ruiz de Alarcón,[105] and endless compositions (some
by Argensola himself, e.g. the sonnet *En la manchada holanda del
tributo*) whose reason for existence was the pleasure derived from
showing off one's cleverness, one's ability to be a Spanish Martial.
In practice, also, there were produced serious works expressive of
the national conscience, prominent among them being the anonymous picaresque novel *Lazarillo de Tormes*[106] and the moralizing
dramas of Juan Ruiz de Alarcón (whose *La verdad sospechosa* provided inspiration for Corneille's *Le Menteur*, the liar). Cervantes,
though he surely wrote satire, claimed that he did not — supposedly
holding to the definition of the term as invective and abuse. His
great novel is a parody full of satiric elements; but its proclaimed
purpose — to banish the romances of chivalry — must be understood
in a very limited sense. What he sought to do, and did, was to elevate that genre and convert it into something new — the modern
novel — wherein the treatment of the fabulous and of the vagaries
of a diseased imagination could lead to the highest pinnacles of
art.[107] The novels of chivalry were more than "smiled away"; they
were eclipsed by the brilliance of a new creation.

The abstract and literary character of much Renaissance satire
is shown by the following text, written by Jusepe González de Salas,
Quevedo's literary heir and editor, to explain his alteration of a
poem by Quevedo entitled "On the Risks of Matrimony, and
Worthless Spouses":

> I found that the original manuscript shows improprieties and things un-
> seemly, to such an extent that at first glance they might have persuaded me
> not to admit the poem in this *Parnassus*. The imitation of Juvenal was very
> close, with the result that Venus appeared naked and repulsive to our eyes,
> which do not tolerate the portrayal of her lascivious incontinence except
> with veils and coverings. Nor is one persuaded otherwise (indeed he should
> not be) by the fact that the same license, the same shock-method of censuring
> customs, was used not only by gentile Greek and Roman writers of all pro-
> fessions, but likewise by Catholics and even saints, as I proved in my *Apology
> for the Satyricon of Petronius Arbiter*.

105. O. H. Green, "Juan Ruiz de Alarcón and the *Topos 'Homo Deformis et
Pravus,'*" *BHS*, XXXIII (1956), 99–103.
106. Manuel J. Asensio, "La intención religiosa del *Lazarillo* y Juan de Valdés,"
HR, XXVII (1959), 397–412.
107. See my "A Hispanist's Thoughts...," p. 131–32.

The scrupulous editor admits that he "corrected" his poet's text: "Corrigióse, pues, aquella malicia. . . ." [108]

It is well to recall at all times Luigi Settembrini's definition of satire as "the aesthetic depiction of evil." [109]

DELIGHTFUL INSTRUCTION

Though the present chapter will have a section on the autonomy (or rather on the growing sense of autonomy) of literature, the material on which that section will be based is scarcely one fourth as ample as the material that forms the basis of the present subdivision. This statistic is significant: the sheer mass of the testimony shows the importance which the theorists at all times attached to the Aristotelian-Horatian principle that literary works should do more than give men pleasure — that they should, over and above the delight, provide indirect instruction intended to make men better. What is most impressive about the statements of didactic purpose — a "disastrous" doctrine, according to C. S. Lewis — is not so much their impressive number as their predominance throughout the whole period of our study. The idea that literature should teach was not born at the Council of Trent.

When, in the preface of his own version of the *Amadís de Gaula* (1508), Garci Rodríguez de Montalvo indicates that a work of fiction of this sort can have virtue only by reason of the moralizing matter which he has interpolated in the story, he is echoing a commonplace of medieval aesthetics.[110] When Sir Philip Sidney (d.

---

108. In Quevedo, *Obras en verso, ed. cit.*, pp. 1275b–76a.

109. Vittorio Cian, *La Satira* (Milan, 1923–39), I, 2.

110. Hugh of St. Victor taught that poetry prepares the way to philosophy and is desirable for that purpose and no other; if there is time, the playful mingled with the serious "is wont to delight more." See Ross and McLaughlin (eds.), *op. cit.*, pp. 576–77, and De Bruyne, *op. cit.* A text of capital importance was St. Basil's *To the Young Men, on the Way in Which They May Get Profit from Heathen Books* (available in Migne, *Patrologia Graeca*, XXXI), which was published in Latin at Salamanca in the year 1496: *De legendis libris gentilium* (the Hispanic Society of America has a copy). In 1587 Jacopo Mazzoni in his *Difesa* of Dante's *Commedia* still advised the poet to "give attention and care to being understood by the common people, and at the same time . . . embellish his poem . . . with some worthy concept taken from the schools of philosophers" (Weinberg, *op. cit.*, II, 642). In 1626 Juan Lerín y García published at Paris a work entitled *The Good and the Evil of Human Sciences, Wherein Is Shown How One Should Make Use of the Doctrine of the Philosophers and*

1586) in his first definition names the purpose of poetry explicitly
as teaching, he is advocating the commonly accepted formula of
Italian Renaissance criticism — the Horatio-Aristotelian admixture
of instruction and pleasure (Wimsatt and Brooks, *op. cit.*, p. 167).
The Erasmists, with their concern for a purer way of life, for a
Christianity more worthy of its Founder, naturally argued for the
production of a literature of truth and reason. Their influence on
literary ideas was great, reinforcing the tendencies just enumerated;
restricting the book to nobly utilitarian ends, they tended to negate
literary art [111] rather than to contribute to its flourishing (Bataillon,
op. cit., II, 248). Art was thus considered, by the theorizers and by
most practitioners, as "an inferior form of philosophy . . . philosophy for children or for the childlike public, or for those who
were deficient and immature in philosophy proper." [112] This was in
line with theological thinking. Fray Luis de Granada (d. 1588) held
that the visible world exists for the use, for the recreation, and for
the instruction of mankind, and that art, insofar as it is able, imitates nature, creating artifical objects which are not only useful but
beautiful. Man, created in the Divine image, imitates the Creator
by serving the two ends of usefulness and loveliness: "just as God
created the world full of natural works, so art has, as it were, created another new world of artificial things." [113]

The degree of appreciation of the aesthetic, or of its reduction to
a mere primer for the ignorant and frivolous, depended — as such
things always do — on individual temperament. Granada, an aesthet-
ically sensitive and perceptive man, gives due weight to the beautiful. More forbidding temperaments, like the secular-minded Huarte, would banish poets from the universities as unfit for stern
intellectual endeavor, i.e., philosophy and theology. Marsilio Ficino's (d. 1499) chief contribution, on the other hand, was his new

Fables of the Poets. On instructional delight in medieval literature see Curtius, *op.
cit.*, pp. 224, 243, 437–38, 444, 554.

111. J. C. Scaliger maintained that Latin tragedy (Seneca) was superior to Greek
simply because the former was full of moral maxims. See the first *Apéndice* to Astrana
Marín's edition of the *Obras en verso* of Quevedo, p. 1175a.

112. Benedetto Croce, "La teoria poetica del Cinquecento," in his *Poeti e scrittori
del pieno e del tardo Rinascimento* (Bari, 1945), pp. 103–7.

113. Pedro Laín Entralgo, *La antropología en la obra de Fray Luis de Granada*
(Madrid, 1946), pp. 67, 91, 269. See also De Bruyne, *op. cit.*, II, 243.

emphasis on *poesis* rather than on *mimesis*, on creative imagination rather than decorous imitation, on the responsibility of the artist to cause wonder rather than to teach.[114] Perhaps no great work of the Renaissance is more committed to sheer exultation in the poet's power of wizardry than is Ariosto's *Orlando Furioso*. This poem was translated into Castilian verse in 1550 (Toledo), with this long and moralizing title: *Orlando Furioso . . . Translated . . . by Hernando Alcocer . . . with a Moral Exposition of Each Canto, and a Brief Declaration in Prose at the Beginning Indicating the Source of the Work.*

And not only was Ariosto's great poem translated; it was imitated in various Spanish sequels, one of which — Luis Barahona de Soto's *Las lágrimas de Angélica* (1586) — should detain our attention for a moment. This romantic epic is accompanied by *advertimientos y sumarios* (forewords and summaries), composed by Fray Pedro Verdugo de Sarria, to begin each canto; there is also a preface by Gregorio López de Benavente the purpose of which is to reveal "the many secrets and mysteries that the author chose to conceal beneath the covering of such pleasant and easily understandable subject-matter." "Secrets and mysteries" beneath a veil of loveliness — this was the poetic and literary ideal which held the center of the stage from the Middle Ages through the baroque. Let us proceed to validate this statement.

It was made clear in the first three chapters of Volume I that literature in the Middle Ages and the early Renaissance was not free; that the man who felt the need for self-expression through the medium of creative writing could satisfy this drive only by making concessions: his tale or poem must have instrumental value — at least some instrumental value in its subordinate parts, e.g. as when the narrator of a novel of chivalry [115] made a break in the action in

114. Sears Jane reviewing André Chastel, *Marsile Ficin et l'art* (Geneva, 1954) in *Renaissance News*, XI (1958), 145. Ficino did not carry the day. "Sidney in the *Apologie* and Spenser in the letter to Raleigh prefixed to the *Fairie Queene* say . . . that the story of a noble person gives more pleasure than a book of moral philosophy and is therefore more effective. More effective for what? For the teaching of morals. The element of aesthetic pleasure is recognized but is not conceived of apart from morals" (Hardin Craig, *The Enchanted Glass: The Elizabethan Mind in Literature* [New York, 1950], p. 228).

115. See Maxime Chevalier, "Le roman de chevalerie morigéné: le *Florisando*," *BHi*, LXXX (1958), 441–49.

order to bring in the often-repeated "morality." Juan Ruiz, a highly creative spirit, was constantly aware of the need to insert various sorts of grave "considerations" into his *Libro de buen amor* to serve as "payers of freight." And there were other devices, such as the warning call to all readers to avoid the author's "errors"; the palinode or recantation; or, at the very least, the insistence that a literary "toy" was precisely that — a socially useful means of keeping idle hands (and minds) from the Devil's employ, or simply a device for relaxing the taut nerves of the weary feudal administrator-warrior. We shall have a separate section on literature as relaxation; in the remainder of this section we shall offer a number of testimonies that literature did not become really autonomous in the Renaissance or the post-Renaissance.

The fifteenth century produced two famous satires: the *Coplas del Provincial* (passed over here because it is invective of the lowest type) and the *Coplas de Mingo Revulgo*, in which the serious social purpose is clear. Hernando del Pulgar, the most ancient of the commentators on the *Mingo Revulgo* (he may have written it), insists on the hidden "doctrine" — and on the pleasure that the capable reader will derive from discovering that doctrine for himself, beneath its disguise of a feigned rustic speech and a pastoral setting.[116]

The moral purpose of Fernando de Rojas in *La Celestina* (1499?) is unquestionable: he offers his play as a service, both to his patron and to his country.[117]

Juan Luis Vives (d. 1540) had no regard for literature as such, yet he eagerly assimilated the beauty of the classical literary heritage in order (as he said) "to wrap in ancient elegance, as in a white and delicate drapery, the truth" — the constant and consuming passion of his life.[118]

The first picaresque novel, *La vida de Lazarillo de Tormes*, may have been written as early as 1525 (or, as some contend, 1539). The

116. Menéndez y Pelayo, *Antología de poetas . . .* , ed. cit., II, 296–97.

117. The question of the work's moral intention may be considered settled; see my review-article on María Rosa Lida de Malkiel, *La originalidad artística de La Celestina* (Buenos Aires, 1962) in *HR*, XXXII (1964). Mrs. Malkiel has settled the problem of *La Celestina's* classification; in spite of its length, it is a dramatic work, not a novel in dialogue.

118. Mariano Puigdollers, *La filosofía española de Luis Vives* (Barcelona, 1940), p. 79.

anonymous author admits in his prologue that he expects praise for his accomplishment and expresses the hope that his book may give pleasure, either deep (*agrado*) or superficial (*deleyte*). In the first chapter (*Tratado*) he makes clear his didactic purpose: "I take pleasure in reporting to you these childish adventures to the end that all may see how great is a man's virtue when he rises from a low estate; and on the contrary, what great vice it is to allow oneself to slip from the heights to the depths." [119]

The testimonies are so numerous that our selection must be rigorous. In 1551 Lorenzo de Sepúlveda published at Antwerp a volume of historical ballads based on the old chronicles of Spain. In the preface, addressed to a friend, Sepúlveda stresses the value of history both as inspiration to noble deeds and as recreation for the mind: "if the non-sacred histories of the gentiles find such favor with readers, though their contents are often mere fiction and beautiful lies, how much greater will be the delight provided by the present work, which is not only . . . based on the truest history I could find, but is presented . . . in the Castilian metre of our traditional ballads, now so popular." [120]

In 1552 Alonso Núñez de Reinoso published at Venice an imitation of a Greek novel by Achilles Tatius and entitled it *Historia de los amores de Clareo y Florisea*. In its prefatory material there is a sonnet "by a gentleman whose name is reserved for greater things" — rightly so, for the sonnet merits translation only into prose: "He who would see joined together utility and sweetness, virtue, discretion, and courtesy, and a chaste habit of life; he who would enjoy subtle invention, together with an epitome of moral philosophy; he who would see harmonized [Aristotle's] concepts of history and poetry, will find the perfect model here. . . ." [121]

Diego Sánchez de Badajoz's dramatic works were composed between 1525 and 1547. His *Recopilación en metro* was published by his nephew in 1554 with a dedicatory letter to the Conde de Feria. The nephew, after speaking of the desire of all men to live on after death either in their children or in their literary works, says that he

119. Ed. J. Cejador (Madrid, 1914), p. 91.
120. *Romances nuevamente sacados de historias antiguas de la crónica de España* (Antwerp, 1551), *Prólogo*.
121. See Gallardo, *Ensayo*, III, col. 986; see also Menéndez y Pelayo, *Orígenes . . .* , (new ed.; Santander, 1943), II, 74 ff.

has decided to give to his uncle the latter type of immortality, finding his writings to be "of no little profit, nor worthy of oblivion." The matter is set forth "in a style so clear and palpable that it would seem that the listeners themselves had thought it up, though much study and good teachers were necessary to acquire it; nor is the matter dry . . . ; rather do these 'representations' show discretion and artful artlessness, for the author was a man not only learned but also of great wit and solid judgment." [122]

After the publication of the decrees of the Council of Trent (1563) one does not find, in any pronounced measure, the expected change in tone. In Spain as in the rest of Europe, including Protestant England, instruction and delight simply remain (as they had always been) the great pillars of the literary edifice.

In 1582 the humanist Francisco Sánchez de las Brozas — a very independent humanist indeed — issued at Salamanca his commentary on the fifteenth-century Juan de Mena. In his preface he states as his motive the old Aristotelian-Horatian principle: Mena's matter is "moral philosophy"; his poetry is "chaste and clean and edifying." Mena is "the first man to elevate and ennoble the Castilian language." "Heroic poetry such as this needs, in order to achieve its effect of gravity, to employ words and statements which are both grave and archaic, to achieve elevation of the style." The heroic, to which Aristotle in the *Poetics* had given the highest value, was in itself a noble thing, needful in any cultured society.

On a much humbler level is the *Cancionero* (Madrid, 1586) of Gabriel López Maldonado, who says in his foreword: "In this small work I have tried to do what the planter of a garden does who enriches his plot of ground with fragrant and showy flowers, but, not content with that, includes also some medicinal herbs, less agreeable to the senses of sight and smell, yet very important for other needs."

In 1589 Fray Juan de Pineda said in the preface to his *Agricultura christiana*: "and because humane letters have a certain enticing taste, I have given a generous admixture thereof to what is otherwise Christian doctrine; [but] I make all the fables here included speak in a language which is doctrinal and useful for the furtherance of virtue."

122. Ed. J. López Prudencio (Badajoz, 1910), I, 2–3.

There is simply no end to such statements. The theory of the matter is treated many times in López Pinciano's *Philosophía antigua poética* (1596): literature should include "both philosophies, natural and moral" (*ed. cit.*, I, 215). Even frivolous comedy must teach: "laughter is the main thing to be sought, after doctrine" (*ibid.*, II, 24).

In 1598 Agustín de Almazán prefaced his translation of Leon Battista Alberti's *Momus* (Madrid) with these important *conclusiones*: (1) poetry is not a "vain fiction," as the ignorant believe it to be; (2) poetry is a "rational fiction" which serves as a "cipher" of some natural, historical, or moral truth; (3) the principal end of poetry has always been to direct men's attention to the precepts of moral philosophy by a very special means — the exciting of wonder and admiration.

In 1599 Mateo Alemán states in the *Prólogo* of his picaresque *Guzmán de Alfarache*: "not all of this came from my quiver; rather did I select it from learned and holy writers: this part I am able to praise and to 'sell' [*vendo*] to the reader."

Rinaldo Froldi has thought that he perceived in Tirso de Molina's miscellany, *Cigarrales de Toledo* (first ed. 1624), a predominantly hedonistic aesthetics.[123] Yet in the very last *Cigarral* one of the guests remarks, after witnessing the performance of Tirso's play *El celoso prudente* (included in the text), that not a single detail is worthy of reproof, nor will chaste persons be tempted to forget their chasteness; here the jealous will learn not to judge by appearance; husbands will learn prudence; ladies will see an example of constancy; princes will learn to keep their promises, fathers to guard the honor of their daughters; and all the spectators to esteem the excellence of the "new comedy" of Lope de Vega and his followers, which has eliminated earlier imperfections and now appears "clean and free of any questionable action, giving delight as it teaches and teaching as it delights." [124]

The whole question of Quevedo's numerous prologues is complex. In the dedication of his *Sueño de la Muerte* (*Dream of Death*)

123. See the *Introduzione* of his edition of Tirso's *La Patrona de las Musas* (Milan, 1959), p. 6.
124. *Ed. cit.*, pp. 380–81. Tirso published in 1635 another miscellany entitled precisely *Deleitar aprovechando*. Here, as Froldi says (*loc. cit.*) "literature is thought of as a means of persuading to the truth."

he writes to Doña María Enríquez, Marchioness of Villamagna: "Nor, amid all the laughter, have I neglected doctrine, unless my style and my diligence have failed me" (*Obras en prosa, ed. cit.*, p. 175). In his "Approbation" (dated 1630) of Quevedo's *The Cradle and the Grave*, Dr. Vito de Vera observes that the author's *doctrina moral* appears here to better advantage than ever before: "the author has mingled together the sweetness of earlier productions and the utility of a Christian philosophy" (*ibid.*, p. 898).

In his *Paradoxas racionales* of 1635 Antonio López de Vega introduces a new note: he has written to give himself psychological relief; any "disillusionment" can provide a useful lesson in this weary world; but the author has really very little hope that the abuses will be remedied. Wise men of necessity disregard them; politicians, on the other hand, approve them, and the citizenry tends to approve them too.[125]

Passing over numerous writers we shall end this survey with Baltasar Gracián, the high priest of literature as wit (see below). Juan Francisco Andrés de Uztarroz, in his *censura* of the second part of Gracián's *El Criticón* (1635), observes: "under the disguise of most ingenious metaphors, he both teaches and delights his readers" (*ed. cit.*, II, 3). In the *censura* of the third part (1657), Fray Estevan Sanz speaks of the author's metaphors, similes, examples, metamorphoses, moralities, and allusions "for the reprehension of vice and the inculcation of virtue," whereby he "teaches with sweetness" (*ibid.*, III, 6). In the *Segunda Parte* (Crisi IV), the Nymph in the Palace of Understanding makes this criticism of the great poet of art-for-art's-sake, Luis de Góngora: "If this learned Cordovan plectrum had raised moral teaching to the height of his cultured style, if he had chosen matter worthy of the gallantry of his verse and the subtlety of his concepts, I assure you that his shell would need to be made not of marble but of the finest diamond" (*ibid.*, II, 132–33).

LITERATURE AS ENTERTAINMENT

In the first paragraph of the *Prohemio e Carta* (letter-introduction) which the Marqués de Santillana wrote to accompany the

125. Ed. E. Buceta (Madrid, 1935), p. 6.

copy of his works requested by Don Pedro de Portugal, the Marqués protests that he would have preferred to offer to the Constable of Portugal something more serious than his "songs and longer poems," most of which he finds unworthy of "memorable registro" — of being eternalized in a book. These trifles were composed in his youth when, like St. Paul, he "thought as a child." And indeed it is a young man who now asks for a copy of them. Youth is the time when a man gives thought to inconsequential things: to the ostentation of his costume, to jousting, to dancing and other courtly exercises, as well as to more or less frivolous poetry. Let youth, then, have its way; the Constable's polite command shall be carried out. From his own and from other people's notebooks, Santillana has caused his poems to be sought out and copied "as I wrote them." [126]

Santillana speaks of "cosas alegres e jocosas" — of merry and jocose trifles, such as a young man may take delight in (though the book contains much more than that). Thus to take delight is — in one's youth — considered to be entirely normal and fitting; and perhaps not only in youth: all of Chapter II of our Volume I ("Medieval Laughter") is a demonstration that the literature of entertainment had, in the Spain of the Middle Ages as elsewhere, its *raison d'être*. There is no deviation from this principle as the centuries advance. In 1531 a novel of chivalry, *Los quatro libro del valerosíssimo cauallero Felix Magno*, was dedicated to the Bishop of Sigüenza and was probably printed at the expense of the viceroy of the principality of Catalonia.[127] In 1605 we find the following statement in the approbation of Miguel de Madrigal's *Segunda Parte del Romancero general y Flor de diversa poesía* (Valladolid): "My view is that, just as the public is permitted to enjoy comedies and things of like character for its entertainment, it is proper that it find amusement reading ballads and poems that are not obscene,[128] as these are not, nor do they contain anything that would militate against our Faith and good customs." [129]

126. *Obras*, ed. J. Amador de los Ríos (Madrid, 1852), pp. 1–2.

127. Gallardo, *Ensayo*, I, 759. Attempts to suppress the secular theater were never successful for long. The Inquisition did not object to literature as entertainment: what it suppressed was any suspicion of non-Catholic doctrine; it also wished to suppress irreverence. See below, the section on "Social Control."

128. Censorship by no means eliminated obscenity; it both overlooked it and allowed it to pass.

129. See Curtius, *op. cit.*, Excursuses IV and X. For the Renaissance (1561): J. C.

In 1658 there appeared at Zaragoza a *New Dish of Mixed Viands to Provide Diversion for Idle Moments,* by a certain Luis Antonio, self-styled as a *lego del Parnaso* — "a man untrained in poetry."

The Spanish theorists agree. In a work written in 1550, Juan Arce de Otálora suggests that the popularity of the romances of chivalry is perhaps a good thing, in that it keeps readers from pursuits more harmful than the enjoyment of fiction — even irresponsible fiction; and he points to the practice of reading such novels (aloud) from the steps of the cathedral of Seville as a wise measure for keeping boys off the streets and men away from the taverns.[130]

Luis Alfonso de Carballo in 1602 ruled that comedies are to be classified as entertainment: "and since this is so licit and decent, it is permitted by human and divine law as a means of repose, inasmuch as men cannot unrelentingly concentrate on work" (*op. cit.,* II, 25). And in another place: "Satires composed in a spirit of fun and play, especially when exchanged between friends in order to amuse themselves, . . . are permitted . . . if their purpose is only to . . . show cleverness and give pleasure" (*ibid.,* p. 67).

Pedro de Valencia, the writer of the *Aprobación* of Carrillo y Sotomayor's *Libro de la erudición poética* (published posthumously in 1611), declares that the author "gives a fine account in this treatise of how he employed his idle moments . . . occupying them with such pure and praiseworthy entertainment."

The Aragonese historian Jerónimo Zurita (d. 1580), as consultant to the Holy Office of the Inquisition, prepared a report on the permitting and the prohibiting of books in which he shows himself to be remarkably liberal. Works like *La Celestina,* the *Cárcel de amor,* and their congeners he considers *escritos con honestidad* — written with moral integrity; these he permits. Others, written in the same style but with less decency, he would forbid. As for works

Scaliger in his *Poetices libri septem,* discussing pleasure as an end in literature, says that "the need for pleasure has been responsible for the rise of certain minor genres; the mind of the auditor has sought relaxation or relief in serious or noble spectacles, and such relief has been provided by less pretentious interludes" (cited by Weinberg, *op. cit.,* II, 749). For the seventeenth century: Johannes Senftleben in his *Philosophia moralis* admits that even such a hedonistic form as the *nuga* or the *facetia* has a justification: it relaxes one after work or study (Clements, *Picta Poesis . . . ,* p. 192).

130. See *Coloquios de Palatino y Pinciano, an Erasmian Dialogue of the Sixteenth Century: A Critical Analysis of the Unpublished Manuscript* by Patricia Norene O'Connor (University of Texas, unpublished dissertation, 1952), p. 128.

in Latin, he holds that even schoolboys may properly read Plautus and most of Terence. And since racy and spicy literature will in any case be read by the young, they might better read it in the works of good authors from which they can absorb "elegance and the virtues of poetry, and a distaste for the other type." [131]

The Jesuit Juan Eusebio Nieremberg (d. 1658) in one of the letters of his *Epistolario* analyzes the pleasure which men receive from seeing or hearing a thing — any thing — well imitated. His thought is Aristotelian. The "great master of those who know" taught in the *Poetics* that the poet is like the Creator in giving to a work of art the organic quality we find in the works of nature, and this is why rational man takes pleasure in being made aware of the harmony of the rational universe. The artist, with creative vision, seeks the end toward which nature is striving, "and completes that effort in a rounded whole." [132] Father Nieremberg, interestingly, applies all this to the needs of a friend whose son-in-law has been "mocked," and his discussion goes to the heart of the whole question of Aristotelian *imitatio* in art and literature:

Human meanness [Nieremberg says] cannot be the general cause of our pleasure in the art of mockery, since men take pleasure in it even when the object mocked is not (or is not considered) contemptible: it gives us pleasure to hear the skillful imitation of bird song, of the barking of dogs, or the neighing of horses. . . . And thus my speculation concerns itself with the general cause of the enjoyment produced by seeing one person imitate another, because the pleasure is no less there when the thing imitated is in itself unpleasant. One derives no pleasure at all from hearing wolves howl, or a man speak with a nasal twang; yet even so, when these things are imitated properly they provide entertainment. The great cause of this, in my opinion, is the order, propriety, and harmony which are shown to exist between the action imitated and its representation, because all of this is characteristic of rational nature. In everything there is an order and adjustment, and by reason of a secret sympathy we take pleasure in perceiving it — so related is it to universal order and proportion. This is the cause of our pleasure in music and beauty — the order which we apprehend in the harmony and proportion of the parts — a thing enjoyed by men and not by animals lacking the gift of reason.[133]

Entertainment of the sort analyzed by Father Nieremberg — on every level of dignity or the lack of it — was always enjoyed in Spain.

131. Menéndez y Pelayo, *Orígenes* . . . (old ed.), IV, 390.
132. Cited by Lane Cooper, *The Poetics of Aristotle: Its Meaning and Influence* (Ithaca, New York, 1956), p. 76.
133. Ed. N. Alonso Cortés, *BAE*, XXX (Madrid, 1915), 263–64.

I offer a few examples of defensive — or self-assertive — criticism and auto-criticism. An early one (15 c.) is a *pregunta* proposed by Gómez Manrique to his fellow poet Francisco de Bocanegra (*Cancionero castellano* . . . , poem no. 311).

Por quanto la ociosidad, amado mucho de my, es causa, segun oy, de pensar mucha maldad; e solo por esquivar aquesto, consideré esta quistyón que no sé por trobas vos preguntar. . . .	Inasmuch as idleness, my dearly beloved friend, is the cause (as I have heard) of many an evil thought; and in order to forestall such an eventuality, it has occurred to me to address to you this question for which I am unable to provide an answer. . . .

In the following century (1566) Juan de Timoneda prefaced his *El Patrañuelo* with these words addressed to the "Most Devoted Reader": "Inasmuch as the present work has no other pretension than that of providing a certain amount of pastime and secular recreation. . . . " At the end of the century (1599), the moralist Mateo Alemán presented the reader of his *Guzmán de Alfarache* with an invitation to enjoy the picaresque adventures as such:

I am persuaded that things which can cause no harm are many times of actual value. In the course of this tale you may "moralize" as you wish: you will have plenty of occasion to do so. Whatever you find to be insufficiently grave or proper, you should attribute to the fact that a picaro, a rogue, is the subject of the book. When you encounter such things (they are few in number) enjoy them like a picaro, remembering that on splendidly set tables there should be viands for all tastes, wines dry and sweet to help with the digestion, and music to entertain.

In the early years of the seventeenth century Juan Hidalgo printed his *Ballads in Thieves' Jargon*, assuring the reader that they would profit both good and wicked readers by providing a warning to the former, a horrible example to the latter; furthermore, "the most learned and self-respecting man, without thinking it beneath him, may well occupy an idle moment by reading about these people and learning their vocabulary and style." [134] A character encountered by Don Quijote in his wanderings, Don Diego de Miranda, tells of his reading habits (in words already cited in an-

---

134. "El más honesto y más sabio, / sin tenerlo en menosprecio, / se puede ocupar un rato / en leer de aquesta gente / sus términos y vocablos." Cited by Ernest Mérimée, *Essai sur la vie et les oeuvres de Francisco de Quevedo* (Paris, 1886), p. 388.

other context): "I own more than six dozens of books. . . . I give more attention to those on secular than to those on sacred subjects, provided that the former be books of honest entertainment, and written so as to delight me with their language and to uplift my spirit with a sense of wonder" (Part II, ch. 16). In his *Cigarrales de Toledo* Tirso de Molina reports that the part of the timid man in his own play, *El vergonzoso en palacio*, was performed by one of the noblest grandees of Castile, and so well that the professionals of the theater were shamed by seeing this amateur surpass, in a brief hour of licit entertainment, the result of their own best efforts (*ed. cit.*, p. 118). In his address to the "Well-intentioned Reader" of his volume, Tirso informs the public of the printing of the corpus of his *comedias*: the first *Parte* will soon be out, the first of many which he hopes to publish — plays selected from the more than three hundred "which during fourteen years have relieved melancholy and provided honest diversion for idle moments." [135]

And we return once more to the greatest: in his *Viaje del Parnaso* (1615) Cervantes claimed that

> In Don Quijote I've provided pastime
> For every sad and melancholy breast.[136]

LITERATURE AS WIT

It will be remembered that C. S. Lewis, in his book on the literature of the Renaissance in England, speaks of the early sixteenth century as characteristically "drab," of the period of Sidney and Spenser as "golden" (when one had only "to play out again and again the strong simple music of the uncontorted line"), after

---

135. The defenders of the *comedia*, being on the defensive, were wont to stress the value of comedy as a "mirror of the truth"; but the *comedia* could not escape the fact that it was essentially entertainment. In 1598 the city of Madrid appealed to the king to reopen the theaters, which for some time had been closed by royal order. Actors should be allowed to dress in silk and gold, it was claimed, because "their acts are festive, and the dress should match the spirit of the occasion." Furthermore, "not all men can be occupied on the high level of great tasks, for God did not make us all prophets nor doctors [of the Church]." See Cristóbal Pérez Pastor, *Bibliografía madrileña* (Madrid, 1899–1907), I, 304–7. On the *comedia* as sheer entertainment, see my article, "On the Literary Court of the Conde de Lemos at Naples, 1610–1616," *HR*, I (1933), 305–6, especially n. 78.

136. "Yo he dado en el *Quijote* pasatiempo / al pecho melancólico y mohino" (Ch. IV).

which he casts a glance at the period often called "baroque": [137] "Only later, when the ingenuous taste has been satisfied, will it become necessary to seek for novelty, to set oneself difficult tasks, to make beauty out of violence." These three measures of literary sophistication are usefully applicable to the Spanish sixteenth century, but we must make one reservation: the Spanish taste for wit, for the "conceit," is observable earlier, especially in the poetry of the fifteenth-century *cancioneros*. Mario Equicola, in his *Libro de natura d'amore* (Venice, 1525), endeavors to analyze all the existing literature on his subject. His source for the Spanish contribution to the corpus of amatory literature is obviously the *Cancionero General* of 1511, in which ingenuity is, as he observes, the outstanding characteristic: "gli ingeniosissimi spagnuoli." Juan de Valdés in his *Diálogo de la lengua*, composed at Naples about 1535, observes that "we Spaniards have many equivocal words, and I say further that whereas in other languages punning is a defect, in Castilian it is an ornamentation, because with these equivocal words it is possible to say many ingenious, subtle, and gallant things." [138] Asked to provide an example, Valdés quotes an old epigram attributed to the Comendador de la Magdalena de Salamanca, who apparently composed it while riding with a gentleman so thin and emaciated that, as our own limerick has it, "sidewise he couldn't be seen." He was also riding a horse with ribs no less visible than those of Rocinante. The poem follows, a fine example of the ancient lineage of Spanish *conceptismo*:

Vuestro rocín, bien mirado,	Your nag, sir, if one considers
por compás y por nivel,	everything in due proportion,
os es tan pintiparado	suits your person so exactly —
en lo flaco y descarnado	fleshless bones, the two of you —
que él es vos y vos sois él;	that you're interchangeable. Yet
mas una cosa os socorre	in all this there's a contrast that
en que no le parecéis:	avoids such sad confusion: he's
que él de flaco *no corre*	too thin for locomotion, while
y vos de flaco *os corréis*.	thinness for you is a bitter potion.[139]

137. But not by Lewis; see his *English Literature* . . . , pp. 64–65, and my Volume I, pp. 138–39.

138. Ed. J. F. Montesinos (Madrid, 1928), p. 122.

139. *Ibid.*, p. 123 (italics mine). See Antony A. Giulian, *Martial and the Epigram in Spain in the Sixteenth and Seventeenth Centuries* (Philadelphia, 1930); F. C. Sainz

The pun is untranslatable: *no corre* means "does not run"; *os corréis*, while suggesting "you do run," means something altogether different: "you are ashamed."

The theory which justifies such exercises of ingenuity is expressed by a letter which Roberto Duport, the Maecenas who paid the cost of printing Quevedo's *La vida del Buscón llamado don Pablos* (Zaragoza, 1626), included in the preliminary pages of that picaresque novel. Addressed to Fray Juan Agustín de Funes, a Knight of the Order of St. John, it says: "inasmuch as the wise man at times takes more pleasure reading the thoughtless malice of Martial than perusing the maxims of Seneca, I place this book in your hands in the hope that you may amuse yourself with its conceits [*agudezas*]." Quevedo himself in 1634 wrote an approbation for Lope de Vega's book of poems entitled *Rimas del Licenciado Tomé de Burguillos*, describing it as a book "written with shrewdness of mind and wit, exceedingly entertaining, without allowing the wit to descend to malice or ruining it with a debased and disgusting vocabulary — a claim no other book of Attic salt that I have seen can properly make."

The significance of all this is that we are tracing tendencies, both ancient and honorable, which will lead us to our next section on the growing (but still relative) autonomy of literature: clever nonsense, or just plain cleverness, is worthwhile and — more than that — it can bring honor to a writer. As the next step, I cite critical estimates in which there is a balance, more or less weighted in favor of ingenuity as against "useful" doctrine, following these with other examples wherein, though the final step of emancipation is not taken, the interest of the critic seems more obviously centered on the element of wit in the Martialesque sense.

In 1609 L. Gaspar Escolano, Rector of San Esteban, wrote in his approbation of *La Constante Amarilis* of Cristóbal Suárez de Figueroa: "Beneath the pastoral disguise [are] many useful discourses and grave maxims, accompanied by keenness of wit, eloquence of expression, and suavity of style." Various social groups can here learn how to conduct their lives wisely, we are told, "and those fond

de Robles (ed.), *El epigrama español del siglo I al XX* (Madrid, 1946); Hoyt Hopewell Hudson, *The Epigram in the English Renaissance* (Princeton, 1947).

of poetry can take lessons on how to practice this art with the purity that it deserves" (Gallardo, *Ensayo*, IV, col. 650). Eight years later Suárez de Figueroa himself wrote in the text of *El Passagero* (Madrid, 1617, p. 94): "Novels, when written with due rigor, are a most ingenius genre, whose examples call on the reader to imitate them or to avoid them. It should not be a bare narration, but rather clever, adorned with *sententiae* full of wise teaching, and all the other elements which prudent philosophy can provide." The words to be noticed especially here are *composición ingeniosísima*. In 1629 the Dominican Fray Vicente Gómez approved Alonso de Castillo Solórzano's *La huerta de Valencia*: "it is a book of good taste, since the taste of the author is exquisite, as he brings together in a work of honest entertainment subtle and ingenious concepts . . . expressed in chaste language, and appropriate stories . . . which could be regarded as true. . . . The entire book is curious, providing much pleasure and no little profit" (Gallardo, *Ensayo*, II, col. 303). *Los rayos del Faetón* of Pedro Soto de Rojas came out in 1639. It had four *Aprobaciones*, and I cite from each: "sweet and gallant style, full of eloquence and erudition" — plus doctrine; "such great eloquence and erudition, and such good doctrine in so far as poetry allows"; "gallant phrases and concepts treated with much elegance and, insofar as poetry allows, good doctrine"; "much erudition, elegance, clear concepts" — plus doctrine (*Obras, ed. cit.*, p. 287).

We move now closer to the borderline between semididactic and "free" literary composition. Juan de Jáuregui wrote this opinion of the poems of Baltasar del Alcázar (d. 1606), who was known to his contemporaries as the Andalusian Martial: "His verses show such grace and subtlety that I judge him . . . to be unique among all others. . . . And what I most admire is that at times, with a simple *sententia* or none at all, he creates a savory dish out of what otherwise would fall flat [*lo más frío*], and he develops in his jesting trifles a style so well wrought that the mere flowing of his verses is engaging, and with the most artful artlessness he stimulates our taste. In short: his manner of composition, by the same token that it is inimitable, can scarcely be described" (Gallardo, *Ensayo*, I, col. 74). In 1624 Tomás Tamayo de Vargas finished his bibliographical work, *Junta de libros la mayor que España ha visto en su lengua* (which was never printed but was incorporated into the great *Bibliotheca Hispana Nova* of Nicolás Antonio). In it he says of the picaresque novel *Lazarillo de Tormes*: "Spain's most ingenious book; and I know not if in foreign nations there is another that can match the festive quality of its subject" (fol. 136v).

The literature of the *concepto*, of the conceit, had its two high priests, Quevedo and Gracián. A discussion of their effect on Spanish literature must await our treatment of the baroque in Volume IV. Both of them held that the display of festive wit should have as its ultimate goal moral teaching; but we see each of them given over, frequently, to the purely recreational activity of jest for jest's sake, of dazzling wit for the sake of dazzling wit, of word-play for the sake of what Romera-Navarro has called "gracioso humor," perhaps best translated as the will to achieve startling humorous effects — effects which often had their moral implication and, biting deep, could "slap the face to strike the heart." [140]

TOWARD THE AUTONOMY OF LITERATURE

The act of taking delight in beautiful painting or melodious songs without referring the pleasure to God was sinful, John Scotus Erigena (d. 877?) asserted (De Bruyne, *op. cit.*, I, 386). Indeed, if we may believe Ernst Robert Curtius (*op. cit.*, p. 147), the concept of poetics as an autonomous discipline was lost in the West for a millenium and only reappeared around 1150 in Dominicus Gundissalinus' treatise *De divisione philosophiae*. Among Renaissance theorists, Lodovico Castelvetro was one of the earliest to make a disavowal (*Poetica*, 1570) of the didactic view — a disavowal that would gain ground with the French seventeenth-century critics (Wimsatt and Brooks, *op. cit.*, pp. 167–68). Michelangelo (d. 1564) "gave the classical ideal of nobility or sublimity a triple value: Art is couched in a lofty style; it treats of lofty subjects; it is the indulgence of noble people." [141] Giambattista Marino (d. 1625), an Italian contemporary of Lope de Vega, boldly expressed what

140. See A. A. Parker, "La 'agudeza' en algunos sonetos de Quevedo," *Estudios dedicados a Menéndez Pidal*, III (Madrid, 1952), p. 359: M. Romera-Navarro, *Estudios sobre Gracián* (Austin, Texas, 1950), p. 45.

141. Clements, *Michelangelo's Theory of Art*, p. 234.

Ficino (1499) had adumbrated in the fifteenth century (see also Volume I, p. 126):

> The poet's only task is to create wonder;
> Who can't, or won't, should go and curry mules.[142]

Yet a purely hedonistic, or even a purely independent, theory of literary art is hard to find. When Góngora writes his panegyric, *La toma de Larache* (1610?), he is consciously cultivating a "sublime" genre. In Góngora's age the "heroic" was synonymous with Matthew Arnold's "high seriousness," and — whatever the genre might be — the choice of a famous Ovidian fable as the theme of his *Soledades* was advertisement that the poet meant to attempt an important aesthetic achievement.[143] This cultivation of the sublime was an ennoblement of both poet and reader; was, in a way, a very special type of *deleitar aprovechando,* of instructional delight, of uplift.

Alfonso Alvarez de Villasandino, in a poem collected by Baena and presented in his fifteenth-century *Cancionero (ed. cit.,* I, 152), says simply that the complex poetic forms he uses are a source of boundless joy: "los desires encadenados / sson alegria sobeja" (*ed. cit.,* I, 152). Baena himself, in the "Prologus Baenensis" with which he prefaced his anthology, says that kings and great princes "should have and read and understand many books and writings," giving due attention to their saintly and profitable subject matter; but he stresses with noticeably greater eloquence the joy of the aesthetic emotion: "the said books and other writings, treating as they do new and diverse matters, are comparable to the variety of noble and precious garments and draperies" which one finds in palaces: "since they display many colors and new styles never before seen, they please and greatly satisfy the minds of great lords" (*ibid.,* pp.7–8).

Santillana in his *Sueño* takes as his theme a brief moment of Virgil's *Aeneid* (Ascanius inspiring love in the bosom of Dido) and proclaims his unconcern for any who may not understand:

142. "E del poeta il fin la meraviglia; / Chi non sa far stupir vada alla striglia" (cited by A. Graf, *Attraverso il Cinquecento* [Turin, 1888], p. 85).

143. William J. Entwistle, "A Meditation on the *Primera Soledad,*" *Estudios Hispánicos: Homenaje a Archer M. Huntington* (Wellesley, Massachusetts, 1952), p. 126.

> If my lowly style be not as lowly
> As certain unread readers would prefer,
> The blame is theirs, not mine; they never studied
> The ancient tales, which I will not explain.[144]

The same regard for erudite poetry and for nobility of style is expressed in Hernán Núñez's commentary (1499) on Juan de Mena's *Laberinto de Fortuna*: "[The poet] now proceeds to record the deeds of various leading knights of these kingdoms, among whom he chose as being most illustrious and memorable . . . the Conde de Niebla; . . . to whom he attributes and ascribes such glory that in the mere relating of his death at the siege of Gibraltar he uses one tenth of the space of his poem. In these stanzas he outdid himself, so that in no other portion of this poem does he appear so erudite, so eloquent and lofty, nor shows such learning and excellence of expression" (commentary on *Copla* CLIX).

The brief prologue of *Lazarillo de Tormes*, Marcel Bataillon points out, is an unostentatiously triumphal glorification of art and the artist, an expression of the satisfaction of having inaugurated in the Castilian language an amusing and true type of fiction, of having competed successfully with the ancients, of having discovered new lands in that world which is the literary representation of human life; yet with the strange circumstance that the work is issued anonymously.[145] "I deem it proper," the unknown author writes, "that things so remarkable, and perhaps never heard or seen before, should come to the notice of many and not remain buried in oblivion, since it might be that someone, reading them, would find them to his liking." He expects honor for what he has done. Has not Cicero said that honor causes the arts to flourish? It will not grieve him if all who are so inclined should find pleasure in the perusal of the work he is offering and should see how a man lives with so many turns of fortune, so many perils and adversities.

On the occasion of the death in 1549 of Juan Fernández de Heredia, a poet of Valencia, Pedro Rhoda, composed these four lines in the still newly naturalized Italian hendecasyllabic metre of Boscán and Garcilaso:

---

144. Cited by R. Lapesa, *Los decires narrativos del Marqués de Santillana* (Madrid, 1954), p. 76.
145. *El sentido del Lazarillo de Tormes* (Paris–Toulouse, 1954), p. 29.

Who now will dwell on Helicon's bright summit?
Who now will sing of love with delicate art
And tell the thousand joys that love bestows?
Don Juan has taken with him art and joy! [146]

Antonio de Torquemada's *Coloquios satíricos* were published in 1553. The seventh and last dialogue differs from the others in being free fiction, as J. B. Avalle-Arce has explained. But the author is uneasy because of this freedom, and he invites the reader to look for a "deeper meaning." Even so, the pastoral tale is not made subordinate to a non-literary moral. Indeed, the moralists of the sixteenth century attack with growing aggressiveness (but without success) free fiction of this type. [147]

Cervantes' own pastoral, *La Galatea,* saw the light thirty-two years later. Lucas Gracián Dantisco in his approbation recommends the book as "a pleasant work of great inventiveness, of chaste style, authentic in its use of the Spanish language, of clever and delightful plot." He mentions *provecho,* profit, but in a minor key. [148]

Cervantes always sees himself as overshadowed by supernal forces: the artist Cervantes never denies God, or His institutions, the king and the state. [149] Yet Cervantes knows that he possesses his own kind of kingship, his own unique excellence as an unrivaled creator. He knows, in short, that his art is valid and independent as art, that he, as artist, is a "raro inventor," uniquely original (see his *Viaje del Parnaso,* ch. IV).

It is a historical miracle [writes Spitzer] that, in Spain of the Counter-Reformation, when the trend was toward the reestablishment of authoritarian discipline, an artist should have arisen who . . . was to give us a narrative which

146. "¿Quién hará en Helicón digna morada? / ¿quién cantará de amor con gentil arte / la gala y gracias mil que amor reparte? / ¡Se parten con don Ioan esta jornada!" (*Obras de D. Juan Fernández de Heredia,* ed. F. Martí Grajales [Valencia, 1913], p. 270).

147. *La novela pastoril española* (Madrid, 1959), p. 39.

148. Somewhat earlier Alonso de Ercilla, author of Spain's principal learned epic, *La Araucana,* wrote an approbation of Pedro de Padilla's *Tesoro de varias poesías* (Madrid, 1580) which is exceptional, making no mention of profit, of conformity to customs, etc.: "and in addition to the excellent concepts with which it is filled, there are matters of great imagination, keenly and charmingly expressed; therefore it is my opinion that Pedro de Padilla deserves for his work the reward of publication which he requests."

149. In this and in what follows I am indebted to Leo Spitzer's essay, "Linguistic Perspectivism in *Don Quijote,*" in his *Linguistics and Literary History: Essays in Stylistics* (Princeton, 1948); see p. 61.

is simply one exaltation of the independent mind of man — and of a particularly powerful type of man: of the artist. . . . For let us not be mistaken: the real protagonist of this novel is not Quijote, with his continual misrepresentation of reality, or Sancho with his skeptical half-endorsement of quixotism . . . the hero is Cervantes, the artist himself, who combines a critical and illusionist art according to his free will. From the moment we open the book . . . we are given to understand that an almighty power is directing us, who leads us where he pleases. . . . In the speech from the pen of the pseudo-chronicler [at the very end] we have the most discreet and the most powerful self-glorification of the artist which has ever been written (*op. cit.*, pp. 69–70).

Cervantes willingly destroys his artistic illusions: "he, the puppeteer, lets us see the strings of his puppet-show: see, reader, this is not life, but a stage, a book; art; recognize the life-giving power of the artist as a thing distinct from life. By multiplying his masks . . . Cervantes seems to strengthen his grip on [the] whole artistic cosmos" (*ibid.*, pp. 70–71).[150]

This autonomy of Cervantes' art is not esoteric, nor did Cervantes write for the few only, though he knew that only select spirits could appreciate his efforts — and not a sufficiently large number of these, as he complains to Apollo in the *Viaje del Parnaso*. His conception of poetry, though noble, was conventional.[151] Very different is the position of Luis de Góngora, who wrote in a letter in reply to one sent to him:

That is what you will find in my *Soledades*, if you have the capacity to remove the husk and discover the mystery within. . . . In two ways, it seems to me, this poem has brought me honor: if it is understood by the learned, it will confer upon me authority, since inevitably one must venerate my having raised, by my efforts, our language to the level and the perfection of the Latin tongue. . . . And another source of honor is that I have made myself obscure and unintelligible to the ignorant (which is the distinction of the learned), that I have written in such a way that my writings appear to them as so much Greek, for precious stones are not to be cast before bristled animals.[152]

His contemporaries accepted this self-analysis: "No ancient formula of expression was hidden from him"; "he was one of those

150. See also Joseph E. Gillet, "The Autonomous Character in Spanish and European Literature," *HR*, XXIV (1956), 179–90; and Riley, *Cervantes's Theory*. . . .

151. "Within her dwelling live her two companions, / Moral philosophy and theology" — *Moran con ella en una misma estancia / la divina y moral filosofía* (*Viaje del Parnaso*, ch. IV).

152. Cited in Eunice Joiner Gates, "Sidelights on Contemporary Criticism of Góngora's *Polifemo*,"*PMLA*, LXXV (1960), 508.

who most adorned our language with figures never before used in Castilian"; "he can be called the father of our language"; "his greatest authority is having been a Poet" (cited *ibid.*).

The other high priest of art for art's sake in the seventeenth century is Baltasar Gracián (d. 1658).[153] He claimed (see above) that his cult of the conceit — of the intellectual bridge between concepts that could be associated in the mind only by an effort which, when successful, gave pleasure — was a source of "profit," but in practice the difficulty of his style could only repel unlearned readers; in the sophisticated, it produced a sort of painful pleasure, a pleasure perhaps akin to that derived from the stern physical effort of the chase. He gave to this effort a name: *empleo de querubines*, an occupation worthy of the cherubim, those spirits who, in the hierarchy of the orders of angels, were pure intelligence (as the seraphim were pure love).[154] On September 2, 1637, the Aragonese historian and critic Juan Francisco Andrés de Uztarroz wrote to the great scholar and antiquarian Vicencio Juan de Lastanosa: "Some days ago . . . my friend Juan de Gárriz gave me . . . Gracián's *El Héroe*. . . . In it there is much to see and much to admire — the concision of its style and the mysteries that are to be found in it. It is a book of few pages but of much substance requiring comprehension; worthy of being read by all intellectuals with the greatest attention because of the danger of missing the sense, for a laconic style inevitably is shrouded by mists of obscurity." [155] Lastanosa himself wrote in his preface to Gracián's *El Discreto* (in answer to readers' complaints of obscurity): "One does not write for everybody. . . . The darkness of the style should increase one's veneration for the sublimity of the matter treated . . . " (cited *ibid.*). Gracián wrote his own *retórica conceptista*, his manual for the forger of conceits, first with the title *Art of Invention (El arte ingenio*, 1642) and, in a revised edition, *Keenness of Wit and Art of Invention (Agudeza y arte de ingenio*, 1648).

153. I am unable to isolate Quevedo's literary passion — his cult of the power of the word — from the idea of profit. Fray Tomás Roca's approbation of his *Sueños y discursos* (1627) praises his shrewdness of intellect and varied erudition and adds: "and even those who are highly informed will learn many profitable things" (*Obras en verso*, ed. *cit.*, p. 899ab).

154. See my article, "On the Meaning of *Crisi(s)* before *El Criticón*," *HR*, XXI (1953), 218–19.

155. Cited by Romera-Navarro in his ed. of *El Criticón*, I, 29.

The two movements — that of Góngora and that of Gracián — really had one aim, and otherwise showed many traits in common: the poet should be a Poet; style should be grandiloquent, charged with meaning, suitable and decorous, in no way and at no time humble. We have come far from the simple music of the uncontorted line of Garcilaso, the simply flowing prose of *Lazarillo de Tormes*. Modern criticism has learned to read these difficult authors with empathy. The best among them, in prose or verse, are honored as great writers. Góngora is closer to contemporary poetry than is Lope de Vega, just as El Greco is closer to the painters of our day than is Velazquez.

VOICES OF PROTEST

The conflicting views of the various generations of Church Fathers regarding the legitimacy and the uses of literature have been recorded and analyzed by Curtius.[156] Medieval vacillations have been reviewed in our Volume I. In the Renaissance, the Christian humanists adopted a view of the responsibility of the individual to society that ruled out (theoretically) all areas of intellectual activity which did not have the betterment of man's estate in the world as the ultimate point of reference.[157] From the standpoint of Renaissance Platonic philosophy, the position is well stated by León Hebreo, as translated (1590) by Garcilaso de la Vega (the Inca): "how many men of good ear fail to enjoy music, and neither find it beautiful nor love it; and how many others exist, to whom beautiful verse and prose appear useless! It would seem that the perception of corporeal beauty, and delight in it and love of it, depend not on the eyes and ears through which these things pass, but on the soul which is their destination."[158] To illustrate the point of view of Renaissance theology, we have a statement by Fray Juan de Pineda in his *Agricultura Christiana* (1589). Various authorities, he says, have told us how to interpret the allegories of the

156. *Op. cit.*, Excursus XXII ("Theological Art-Theory in the Spanish Literature of the Seventeenth Century"), especially pp. 551 ff.

157. E. L. Marilla, "Milton on 'Vain Wisdom' and 'False Philosophie,'" *Studia Neophilologica*, XXV (1953), 3.

158. *Diálogos de amor*, NBAE, XXI, 428a.

poets — naturally, morally, theologically. For the last method he has scant sympathy: "I pay little attention to allegories *in divinis* which have been composed by poets, having . . . the Holy Scriptures to teach me in Catholic language" (Part II, fol. 20.).

The subject matter and the artistic form of literature thus appear to be matters which affect the soul. The great majority of Spaniards at all times accepted them as unquestioned values, supplementary to Holy Writ, to theology, and to philosophy — though they recognized that many (or "most" as Milton claimed; see above) abused them. In addition to inveighing against these values, the minority of dissenters had at their disposal two avenues of attack. One was to reach out and adapt the beauty of sensuously appealing imagery to the inculcation of spiritual truths. There thus grew up, in Spain as in all of Europe, a large body of *contrafacta*, of literature *a lo divino*.[159] Luis Alfonso de Carballo in his *Cisne de Apolo* finds that this manner of revamping popular material and making it serve Christian uses is "very important, because there are unseemly and obscene ditties so popular with the mass of people that one must have divine help to exterminate them; and, since their tunes are charming and catching, it is very necessary to reconstruct them *a lo divino*, to the end that at least the vain words may be banished and the tune converted to a good use. . . . Poets who claim to be Christians, and yet employ their talent in the service of the Evil One, should be ashamed of themselves" (*ed. cit.*, II, 174). The other avenue of attack lay through official suppression of the offending literature. But before proceeding to a consideration of social control, it will be well to record a few early voices of protest, ending with the year 1545 when the Council of Trent was opened.

The first voice of protest raised against literary frivolity is that of Ferrant Sánchez Calavera in the *Cancionero de Baena* in 1445, one hundred years before Trent (*ed. cit.*, II, 235):

Todo es sueño e sonbra de luna,
salvo el tienpo en que a Dios loamos,
e todo lo al es burla en que andamos
enbueltos en calma, syguyendo fortuna.

All time not given to praising God is like a shadow cast by the moon; all else is mere chaff, a boat on a becalmed sea at the mercy of life's vicissitudes.

159. Bruce W. Wardropper, *Historia de la poesía lírica a lo divino en la cristiandad occidental* (Madrid, 1958).

Next in time is the voice of the tremendously popular Fray Antonio de Guevara, who in the prologue of his *Dial of Princes* (1529) observes that "not without cause . . . ought many books to be torn to shreds and burned." He refers to the romances of chivalry and others tales of love which, in his opinion, are dangerous in proportion as they are delightful.[160]

Francisco de Osuna, the pioneer of Spanish mystical writing, published in 1531 his *Norte de los estados* (*Guide for Men in Every Walk of Life*), in which he quotes, without adopting it, the opinion of some persons who claim that it would be better if women did not learn to read. "Our married people are Christians," he says, "yet they read *La Celestina* and similar books more avidly than other works which could do them good, and men more readily read things un-Christlike than things Christlike. Alas for the husband who has such books in his home! If his wife commits adultery or enjoys the dallying of courtly love, it is because she reads, or hears read, romances of love and chivalry." [161]

In 1537 an anonymous writer published a book entitled *Withdrawal of the Soul* in which he states that his intention is the opposite of that of those pious persons who rewrite pretty poems adapting them to divine subjects. His work shall be in sober prose. The "showy flowers and fruitless herbs of verse" can appeal to the eye, but they totally suppress the truth. Let the vain and sensuous literary "flowers" which he himself produced in his youthful years "wither and die" (Gallardo, *Ensayo*, I, col. 1110).

Juan Luis Vives (d. 1540), in many of his books but most notably in his *Christi Jesu Triumphus*, speaking of authors that should not be read, mentions those who can foment and nourish vices that may affect the reader: Ovid is sensual, Martial a trifler, Lucian a slanderer, Lucretius inclined to impiety along with most of the philosophers, especially the Epicureans. Even Cicero is given to boasting. [162]

160. See F. de Ros, "Guevara, auteur ascétique," one of the studies in memory of Guevara on the fourth centenary of his death in *Archivo ibero-americano*, VI (1946), 339–404, especially 365 ff., 387, 393, for the arbitrary expurgation of Guevara's own writings.

161. Fidèle Alonso, "Le *Norte de los estados* du P. Francisco de Osuna," *BHi*, XXXVII (1935), 470, n. 29.

162. Puigdollers, *op. cit.*, p. 78. On Vives' attitude toward literature, see Bataillon, *Erasmo y España*, II, 217, 219. Vives' puritanical stand is hard to reconcile with his

In 1545, fourteen years before the first Spanish Index of forbidden books was published, the theologian Alonso Cedillo, in words "To the Reader" that were reproduced in the Salamanca (1572) edition of Venegas' *Differencias de libros que ay en el uniuerso*, warns the Christian to "abhor injurious books, whose soft words damage the conscience . . . especially works of poets who write lasciviously; they delight the ears of persons easily attracted to vanities, and so infect their souls."

All of these expressions are typical of a certain sector of Spanish thought both before and after Trent. So widespread was the feeling of protest that there existed a system whereby outraged or offended citizens could send in to the Holy Office of the Inquisition their private objections and denunciations of works of literature — denunciations which could be simply filed, to become a dead letter.[163]

SOCIAL CONTROL

It will be possible here to give only the briefest indication of the nature of literary censorship in sixteenth- and seventeenth-century Spain. Perhaps we can do no better than to begin with the significant fact that, although the moralists inveighed against them ceasely as "books of lies" and "false flowers of sensuous enticement," scarcely a novel of chivalry was banned by the Inquisition.[164] It will be well to point out also that the banning and the burning of books was an act of social discipline not limited to Spain. As early as 1532 inquisitorial action in France is reflected in a work of literature: in Rabelais' *Pantagruel* (II, 5) the giant leaves Poitiers determined to visit the other universities of France and arrives at Toulouse, "where he learned to dance well . . .; but he did not stay there long, when he saw that they burned alive their Regents like Red-Herrings. . . ."[165] The colonial regimes of Spain and of France

very great contributions to humanistic culture in England and the Low Countries as well as in Spain. For him the *summum bonum* is virtue and virtue only.

163. The nature of such protests can be determined by looking into A. Paz y Melia's *Catálogo abreviado de papeles de Inquisición* (Madrid, 1914). And see my article, "Additional Note on the *Celestina* and the Inquisition," *HR*, XVI (1948), 70–71.

164. Riley, *Cervantes's Theory* . . . , p. 98.

165. Trans. W. F. Smith (London, 1893), I, 230. For England, one should consult Charles R. Gillett, *Burned Books: Neglected Chapters in British History and Literature* (New York, 1932).

have already been contrasted in regard to thought control (Chapter III of the present volume), with the advantage seen to be all on the side of Spain. Even in the age of the Enlightenment in France Jean François, chevalier de la Barre, was barbarously executed for free thinking and for the alleged crime of having mutilated a crucifix.[166] With respect to the Spanish Peninsula, the records of trials of scholars before the tribunal of the Inquisition have added greatly to our knowledge and will continue to do so.[167]

A few statistics, briefly given, will help our understanding of the problem both for Spain and for her colonies. The Inquisition was established in Mexico only in 1571. During the years 1536–43 Bishop Juan de Zumárraga served as Inquisitor General. In those seven years he acted in 152 cases, of which 66 had to do with blasphemy, 5 with Lutheranism, 14 with native idolatry and human sacrifice, 19 with relapses into Judaism, 23 with witchcraft and superstition, 8 with heretical propositions, 20 with bigamy, 5 with crimes committed by ecclesiastics.[168] It would thus appear that only a very small part of the Bishop's total inquisitorial activity had to do with matters related to censorship. More than a century later, in 1682, all forms of expression were vigilantly scrutinized in Mexico. Books and pamphlets with some frequency were subject to slight expurgation or emendation but were seldom barred from circulation. The theater was consistently watched, but only exceptionally was a play regarded as in such bad taste and so irreverent that the Holy Office banished it from the stage. On one occasion the official machinery worked so slowly that the formal decree against a play was not issued until nearly a year after its first denunciation, during which time the offending work had been quietly dropped from the

166. See Voltaire, Oeuvres (Paris, 1883–85), LII (Table Générale), s.v. La Barre.

167. A study of the Spanish Indices of forbidden books from 1547 to 1559, promised by I. S. Révah, is eagerly awaited. Meanwhile, consult A. Sierra Corella, La censura de libros y papeles en España y los Indices y catálogos de los prohibidos y expurgados (Madrid, 1947); A. Tovar and M. de la Pinta Llorente, Procesos inquisitoriales contra Francisco Sánchez de las Brozas (Madrid, 1941) and the review by M. Herrerro García in RFE, XXV (1941), 533; M. de la Pinta Llorente, La Inquisición española y los problemas de la cultura y de la intolerancia (Madrid, 1953). For continental France, we have the recent work of Joseph Lecler, Histoire de la tolérance au siècle de la Réforme (Paris, 1955), especially Bk. VI, ch. vi, on literary works.

168. See the review by Pedro Borgues of Richard E. Greenleaf, Zumárraga and the Mexican Inquisition, 1536–1543 (Washington, D.C., 1961), Archivo ibero-americano, XXIII (1963), 320–21.

extensive repertory of the actors and impresario concerned.[169] This slowness of action was consistent with the general laxness of enforcement which in the year 1600 allowed works actually on the Index to be shipped from Spain to Mexico for sale to the trade.[170]

Returning to the mother country, we offer a cross-section of materials showing that action — or the fear of action — on the part of persons or of institutions could interfere with the success of an author. In the fifteenth century Juan de Padilla issued his *Twelve Triumphs of the Twelve Apostles* with considerable misgiving, although it was well into the sixteenth century (*ca.* 1525) before the Inquisition assumed responsibility for determining what reading matter should circulate. "Great histories, both easy and difficult to decipher," Fray Juan explains in his preface, "and other intricate matters are contained in this contemplative work," which its author submits to the correction of Catholic theologians *in divinis*, and to competent poets and prose writers in matters not touching on the faith. The reader should bear in mind, he insists, three stanzas of the final canto of another work of his, *Retable of the Life of Christ* (which he here reproduces for convenience). Their purport is that the author has written on so sacred a subject "with trembling hand"; let no one criticize it who has read it only in haste, for God's grace enables the simple-minded and even the mute to utter great truths and at times throws into confusion the wisdom of the learned. Apelles long ago said that the shoemaker should stick to his last; only tillers of the soil may speak out on matters agricultural. Yet false "doctors" seek to show off their learning though they have none; they praise where no praise is due and fail to see obvious errors. Such critics are sinners; they should hold their peace (*Cancionero castellano* . . . , I, 290a).

This is essentially the situation faced by Fernando de Rojas when he launched the primitive *Celestina* about the year 1499. He shows fear not of punishment but of censure by those who do not read with sufficient care to perceive his higher purposes.[171]

The publication and distribution of books was controlled by leg-

169. Irving A. Leonard, "Montalbán's *El valor perseguido* and the Mexican Inquisition, 1682," *HR*, XI (1943), 47–56.

170. Irving A. Leonard and O. H. Green, "On the Mexican Book Trade in 1600: A Chapter in Cultural History," *HR*, IX (1941), 1–40; see also above, Chapter III.

171. See the section on cosmic harmony and discord in Volume II, Chapter III.

islation from 1502 onward, and what John Milton called "the narrow bridge of licensing" was a long one. An author had to obtain the *licencia* of the Consejo de la Cámara; the *privilegio* or copyright, which the author frequently sold outright to some printer-dealer to meet the cost of publication or to obtain ready cash; and the *licencia eclesiástica* (which, strangely enough, was not always required). He usually sought a patron, or a grant-in-aid from the Cortes de Castilla or from a municipality (in some cases merely a loan); this done, he made his deal with his *librero*, stipulating quality of paper, format, type face, publication deadline, size of edition, and cost. Questions of "the faith" and "good customs" were not the only ones that might constitute a barrier; there were also problems of national security, and difficulties arising from the resentment of persons in power.[172] In the cases in which the Inquisition raised limited objections, special broadsides in the nature of *ad hoc* expurgatorial indices were issued from time to time.[173]

We have already had more than one hint that the treatment of literary texts was in general lenient. We have observed that the much berated romances of chivalry circulated with scarcely any impediment (see above). Gerhard Moldenhauer found the same leniency in the treatment accorded the picaresque novels.[174] Professor Gillet, after collating the original editions and the expurgated edition (1573) of Torres Naharro's *Propalladia*, arrived at a similar conclusion: the alterations were not substantial (see our Volume I, 115, n. 153). I have shown that *La Celestina*, for all the unfavorable aspersions it cast on the moral habits of the clergy, was expurgated only in 1640, and that the resulting text is surprising for its permissiveness: the inquisitor was interested only in things considered dangerous to the Church as an institution. After

172. The Conde de Villamediana was assassinated in 1622 — by royal order, many thought. In 1629 Dionisio Hipólito de los Valles collected and edited the dead man's works, remarking in the preface: "Do not seek herein satires, and do not complain that certain papers are lacking; for the first was not permitted, and as for the second, all possible diligence has been exercised" — *que lo primero no se ha permitido; y para lo segundo, no ha sido poca la mayor diligencia* (Gallardo, *Ensayo*, IV, 685). The implication is clear: powerful persons suppressed the satires.

173. The above is taken from my review of Augustín G. de Amezúa y Mayo, *Cómo se hacía un libro en nuestro siglo de oro* (Madrid, 1946) in *HR*, XV (1947), 405–6.

174. "Spanische Zensur und Schelmenroman," *Estudios eruditos in memoriam de Adolfo Bonilla y San Martín* (Madrid, 1927), I, 223–39. Of over one hundred picaresque novels, only two were permanently forbidden, four expurgated (p. 239).

the publication of Alfonso de Valdés' *Diálogo de las cosas ocurridas en Roma* (anonymously, 1528?), the Inquisition had it examined by Pedro Olivar, who found nothing heretical in it but recommended that it be kept from circulation as being too outspoken: it would tend to stir up the ignorant.[175]

Jorge de Montemayor, on the other hand, encountered doctrinal objections when he sought to publish his *Cancionero espiritual*. He was said to be "ill prepared to write books of spirituality and theology." [176] Poetic works of Fray Pedro de Padilla and Fray Hernando de Castillo were ordered out of circulation by the Inquisition of Toledo. In one case it is specified why: the author "tends to present the Canonical Hours in the vernacular." Padilla drew up a petition requesting that a commission be appointed to determine what should be changed.[177]

The most famous sixteenth-century case of inquisitorial injustice against a man of letters is that of Fray Luis de León, who spent nearly five years in prison as its result. The accusation was that he preferred rabbinical interpretations to those of the Vulgate text of the Bible, that he showed slight respect for the Vulgate, and that he had translated the *Song of Solomon* into Spanish. He was finally declared innocent of any act dangerous to orthodoxy and returned to his University chair at Salamanca.

Francisco Sánchez de las Brozas, another prominent man of letters, likewise had difficulties in 1584 with the Holy Office and was reprimanded and warned. Yet in 1587 the Inquisition had sufficient confidence in his orthodoxy to charge him with helping a commission entrusted with the task of revising the *Index Expurgatorius*. From 1593 to 1600 he was again under a cloud, his books and papers being confiscated in the latter year. He died (December 5, 1600) before he was cleared.[178]

Several times in the course of the present work mention has been made of the ineffectualness of the efforts that were made to suppress the theater. A chronological list of texts for and against the theater

175. Ed. J. F. Montesinos (Madrid, 1928), pp. 63–64. The text of the *censura* is reproduced as an appendix.

176. Francisco López Estrada, "La epístola de Jorge de Montemayor a Diego Ramírez Pagán," *Estudios dedicados a Menéndez Pidal*, VI, (1956), 402.

177. Paz y Melia, *Catálogo . . .*, nos. 1077, 1081, 1084.

178. Bataillon, *Erasmo y España*, II, 351–55.

as summarized, and in part reproduced, by Emilio Cotarelo y Mori [179] shows twenty-eight items belonging to the sixteenth century; in his section entitled *Legislación* (pp. 617 ff.) only the first five items are dated before 1600. This is natural, inasmuch as Lope de Vega's "new comedy" became a national genre only about the year 1588. Luis Alfonso de Carballo in his much quoted *Cisne de Apolo* (1602) makes a spirited defense of the *comedia*, concluding: "And in our own time, because they went too far in admitting dances invented (we may suppose) by the Adversary of mankind, and for many other reasons that apparently existed, they were banned; but when it was recognized how necessary they are, they were justly and properly reintroduced" (cited *ibid.*, p. 142b).

Cervantes marks the turn of the century. In spite of his unquestionably devout spirit, he was not the most respectful of authors; yet the Inquisition scarcely disturbed him. It objected to a passage in *Don Quijote* (1615) wherein it appears that works without charity are useless (II, 36) — an idea that had come to be associated with the persecuted *alumbrados* and with Protestantism, though to Cervantes it was merely an expression of the essentially Erasmian character of his religious experience. In chapter VI of Part I (the famous "scrutiny" of Don Quijote's library) there is a passage which seems to show that Cervantes was aware of the growing disfavor with which the authorities regarded Ariosto, though the *Orlando Furioso* is not actually found with the other books of the library. "If I find him here in any other language than his original Tuscan, I shall have no mercy on him," says the Curate, "but I shall show him all possible honor if he speaks in Italian." When the Barber remarks that he owns a copy of Ariosto's poem in Italian but is unable to understand it, the Curate observes cryptically: "Nor would it be well if you could."

The effect of social control of polite literature in the sixteenth century is thus seen to have been slight. With respect to the theater, control is stepped up sharply from the year 1600 (Cotarelo, *op. cit.*, pp. 20, 621 ff.). Great writers like Quevedo and Tirso de Molina have their brushes with the Inquisition, but the concern is over matters of seemliness, not of faith. As a typical objection to creative

179. *Bibliografía de las controversias sobre la licitud del teatro en España* (Madrid, 1914), pp. 611 ff.

literature in general, we may take that of the moralist Alejo Venegas: reporting on Antonio de Torquemeda's *Coloquios satíricos*, he finds that the pastoral dialogue is more characteristic of well-read urban dwellers than of shepherds, and that its warnings against love "contain many snares which actually teach the ignorant how to make love." Such persons should not, Venegas contends, be so instructed by their reading that they will dare to undertake what in their ignorance they would not otherwise embark upon; if Torquemada's work is to be printed, it should be altered in accordance with the observations made on the manuscript. Thus the censor does not prohibit publication, but he does disapprove. The corrections are not many, he says, though "some are substantial"—which I take to mean that there must have been a certain number of points of theological doctrine that were unacceptable.[180]

In the field of scholarship the action of the Inquisition was much more deleterious. In 1556 the Valencian Pedro Juan Núñez wrote to the historian Jerónimo Zurita:

Your approval of my studies gives me great encouragement to go on with them; otherwise I would despair, having no one here with whom to discuss a good textual emendation or explication, not because there is a dearth of learned men in this city, but because their interests are different; and the worst of all is that they would prefer that no one should study humanities at all, because of the dangers (as they claim) which beset them: the danger that, just as a humanist may emend a passage in Cicero, he may make bold to alter a passage in the Bible; and just as he may speak ill of Aristotle's commentators, he may do the same with the Doctors of the Church. This and other foolishness has me so beside myself that I often feel like giving up.[181]

We have just noticed that Fray Luis de León's five-year imprisonment had as its cause his activity as a textual critic of the Scriptures and his supposed "slight respect" for the Vulgate version of St. Jerome — a difficulty and a bone of contention between modernists and conservatives since the early days of Nebrija.[182] As the sixteenth

180. Venegas appears not to have eliminated all of the "many snares," if one may judge by the passages of heightened erotic tone, pp. 558–59 of Menéndez y Pelayo's reprint in *Orígenes* . . . , (old ed.) II; see also p. 486a.

181. Letter reproduced by J. F. Andrés de Uztarroz and D. J. Dormer, *Progresos de la historia en el reino de Aragón* (2d. ed.; Zaragoza, 1878), p. 594. (This letter was cited in another connection in Chapter VIII, above.) See also Bataillon, *Erasmo y España*, II, 342–45.

182. Among conservatives, even when they were persons of intellectual power, there was a hostility to "novelty," and scholars who engaged in textual criticism of

century advanced it became a matter of considerable danger to advocate the use of rabbinical textual science in Biblical studies: witness the *Proceso criminal contra el hebraísta salmantino Martin Martínez de Cantalapiedra*.[183] A much greater scholar than Martínez de Cantalapiedra was Benito Arias Montano (d. 1598), himself the author of an *Index Expurgatorius* (1571) in which he endeavored to save for scholarship as many works as possible (Bataillon, *Erasmo y España*, II, 336–39). It was Arias Montano who had the principal part in bringing out the second Spanish polyglot Bible, the *Biblia poliglota de Amberes*. He corrected the text of the Latin version of the Old Testament as given by Santes Pagnini, and his Latin version of the Greek text of the New Testament was so good that it was frequently reproduced by later editors. This "bel ouvrage" (as it is called in Vigouroux's *Dictionnaire de la Bible*) did honor to Arias Montano — but it also produced an enemy in the person of León de Castro, professor of Oriental languages at Salamanca, who denounced it to the Inquisition. Arias was forced to go to Rome to defend his cause; he was absolved in 1580. It is certain, says the *Dictionnaire de la Bible*, that Arias Montano contributed to the progress of Oriental studies.[184]

The terror that the possibility of such episodes could cause in the learned is documented for us by Juan de Mal Lara in his poem *La Psyche*. In 1561 suspicion fell upon him when there occurred in Seville an episode that recalls the "affaire des Placards" at Paris in 1534: broadsides hostile to the Church, and especially to the clergy, were released. On purely circumstantial evidence Mal Lara was suspected: he had, in the past, written verses in praise of Constantino Ponce de la Fuente, an Erasmian theologian accused of Lutheran tendencies who had died in the dungeons of the Inquisi-

---

Biblical texts were especially open to the charge of being dissatisfied with a hallowed tradition (that of the Vulgate). Quevedo wrote: "Novelty is so dissatisfied with itself that, having tired of what was, it wearies also of what is. And to maintain itself as novelty, it must forever cease to be the novelty that it was; likewise the innovator's life is nothing but an unending succession of deaths; so that it is necessary either that he cease to be an innovator or that his main occupation be the business of ceasing to be" (*Obras en prosa, ed. cit.*, p. 589b).

183. Ed. and analyzed by Miguel de la Pinta Llorente (Madrid–Barcelona, 1946).

184. See Aubrey F. G. Bell, *Benito Arias Montano* (New York, 1922); M. de la Pinta Llorente (ed.), *Causa criminal contra el biblista Alonso Gudiel, catedrático de Osuna* (Madrid, 1944).

tion at Triana. Between February 7, 1561, and the following May 14 when he was absolved, Mal Lara knew the depths of human dejection and despair. In the poem in question he praises his wife María for her faith and constancy during that trial, when Mal Lara saw himself

> Bereft of property, bereft of soul,
> Honorless and with no name among men.[185]

In the secular field, the Inquisition's *Index expurgatorius* of 1584 suppressed chapter VII of Huarte de San Juan's *Examen de ingenios para las ciencias*, and did so, as his modern editor Rodrigo Sanz has put it, "terrified by the scientific novelty of his teaching." [186] As Diego Alvarez explained to Huarte, all theologians believed, and taught as a thing known and unshakable, that the soul does not die because it is independent of the body. If this door were closed, as it appeared to be by Huarte's insistence on bodily influences on the memory and understanding (which are faculties of the soul), it would be necessary to rewrite all the Scholastic treatises *De Anima* and the whole of Scholastic psychology; even the catechism would require revamping — this in spite of the fact that the first edition (1575) had had warm ecclesiastical approval! The revised edition came out in 1594.

There were other cases. The historian Juan de Mariana, though he had been the judge who vindicated Arias Montano (see above), was himself accused in 1609, suffering imprisonment for more than a year. He complains of the "tempests that threaten those who maintain publicly and freely what they think." [187]

We are thus brought to a point where it is well to repeat what was said in an earlier chapter: Spain's "unanimity" was purchased at a great cost in suffering, in liberty, and — in non-literary fields — in achievement. It has been claimed that the Inquisition was a political necessity in an ill-united country and that, by maintaining domestic tranquility, it actually favored — indirectly — the develop-

---

185. "estuve en aquel término de verme/ sin hazienda, sin vida, ni honor y alma,/ de no ser ya en el mundo más entre hombres" (cited by A. Vilanova in the *Prólogo* to his edition of Mal Lara's *Filosofía vulgar* [Barcelona, 1958–59], I, 290). See also F. Sánchez y Escribano, *Juan de Mal Lara: Su vida y sus obras* (New York, 1941), ch. V: "Incidente con la Inquisición."

186. See vol. I, pp. xix–xx, of his edition, already cited.

187. Georges Cirot, "Chronique," *BHi*, XXV (1933), 473.

ment of a *Blütezeit*, a Golden Age, and made possible the extension of the life of the empire for many years.[188] The evidence we have marshaled makes it difficult to agree with that view. We can agree, rather, with Father Pedro M. Vélez when he considers the debit side of the balance sheet (*op. cit.*, p. 342; see also p. 332): harsh and cruel in individual cases, remarkably lenient in others, the Inquisition was always there. It did not stifle originality: *Don Quijote* proves the contrary. By guaranteeing, after long struggle, a unified Catholic background of belief, it may well have determined the character of the Spanish national theater, with its absence of tragic conflict. Similarly the leveling effect of its thought control may have placed a check on Quevedo — an admirer of Montaigne, whom he called, "el señor de la Montaña" — with the result that Quevedo did not regard life as an experiment, an *essai*: no life is an experiment when he who lives it feels himself contained in the palm of the Creator's hand. But conjectures such as these cannot be scientific, nor are they part of the historian's task. The historian can only say — as Father Vélez admits — that, in the scientific realm, the Holy Office of the Inquisition restricted thought — not "totally," but in part and indirectly — and that even the partial restraint had serious, that is to say, unfavorable, results. One can not agree with Aubrey Bell that the Inquisition had no part in Spain's national decline.

The credit side of the balance sheet can only be suggested in the present volume. Spain in the baroque age — its greatness and its miseries and its final retreat into the never-never land of the great powers that failed to meet life's challenge — will be the subject of our final volume.

As we look backward over the ground traversed in this volume, let us remember that Cristóbal de Castillejo's (d. 1550) dedication of his translation of Cicero's *De Senectute* and *De Amicitia* has all the optimism of Nebrija's famous prologue to his *Gramática castellana* (1942); that Cristóbal de Villalón's (d. 1581?) *Ingeniosa*

188. Aubrey F. G. Bell, *Fray Luis de León: A Study of the Spanish Renaissance* (Oxford, 1925); Pedro M. Vélez, *Observaciones al libro de Aubrey F. G. Bell sobre Fray Luis de León: Contribución a la historia del Renacimiento y de la Inquisición española* (El Escorial, 1931).

comparación entre lo antiguo y lo presente (1559) is a hymn of praise to the present; that Hernán Pérez de Oliva, who died (much too young) about 1531, declared that the man who directs his life according to reason "lives content and possesses happiness"; that Vives, who died before his time in 1540, proclaimed that there is nothing in the whole breadth of the universe which, if we but consider its origin, its nature, its property and the force it exerts, will not impel us to consider the marvels of God and to adore Him. Though it is impossible and undesirable to formulate a *leyenda blanca*—a white legend to offset the "black legend" of Spain— fidelity to historical truth requires that we recognize the human values of the cultural creation that the Spaniards worked out for themselves on their harsh and demanding peninsula. This creation took place during the Spanish Renaissance between the date of Nebrija's return from Italy in 1473 and a terminal date which we may place, for the present, at the turn of the century, when Cervantes was bringing forth the two parts of his magnificent book— the book that revealed his glimpse into human reality from the Catholic point of view [189] — in the years 1605 and 1615.

189. See O. H. Green, "Realidad, voluntad y gracia en Cervantes," *Ibérida*, III (1961), 113–28. Cervantes' Augustinianism is impressive: "Thou hast made us for thyself and our hearts are restless till they rest in Thee."

Bibliography
Index

PERIODICAL ABBREVIATIONS
USED IN FOOTNOTES

Boletín de la Real Academia Española (BRAE)
    Boletín de la Academia Española is the same publication; "Real" was dropped from the title for a short time.
Bulletin Hispanique (BHi)
Bulletin of Spanish Studies (BSS)
    The current name of this publication is *Bulletin of Hispanic Studies.*
Hispania (Hisp.)
Hispanic Review (HR)
Journal of the History of Ideas (JHI)
Modern Language Quarterly (MLQ)
Modern Language Review (MLR)
Nueva revista de filología hispánica (NRFH)
    The earlier name of this publication was *Revista de filología hispánica, (RFH)*
Publications of the Modern Language Association of America (PMLA)
Revista de filología española (RFE)
Revista de filosofía (Rev. de filosofía)
Revue de littérature comparée (RLC)
Revue Hispanique (RHi)
Romance Philology (RPh)
Romanische Forschungen (RF)
Studies in Philology (SP)
    Also abbreviated throughout the notes are Biblioteca de autores españoles *(BAE)* and Nueva biblioteca de autores españoles *(NBAE)*, which are series of editions of older Spanish texts.

NOTE: Items included in the Bibliography of Volumes I and II are omitted from this Bibliography.

Bibliography

ARTICLES

Allen, Don Cameron. "The Rehabilitation of Epicurus and His Theory of Pleasure in the Early Renaissance," *Studies in Philology*, XLI (1944), 1–15.

Alonso, Fidèle. "Le *Norte de los estados* du P. Francisco de Osuna," *Bulletin Hispanique*, XXXVII (1935), 460–72.

Asensio, Eugenio. "El erasmismo y las corrientes espirituales afines (conversos, franciscanos, italianizantes)," *Revista de filología española*, XXXVI (1952), 31–99.

————. "La lengua compañera del imperio: Historia de una idea de Nebrija en España y Portugal," *ibid.*, XLIII (1960), 399–413.

Asensio, Manuel J. "La intención religiosa del *Lazarillo de Tormes* y Juan de Valdés," *Hispanic Review*, XXVII (1959), 397–412.

Atkinson, W. C. "Cervantes, El Pinciano, and the *Novelas Ejemplares*," *Hispanic Review*, XVI (1948), 189–208.

————. "Medieval and Renaissance: A Footnote to Spanish Literary History," *Bulletin of Spanish Studies*, XXV (1948), 213–21.

Baron, Hans. "The *Querelle* of the Ancients and the Moderns as a Problem for Renaissance Scholarship," *Journal of the History of Ideas*, XX (1959), 3–22.

Bataillon, Marcel. "Andrés Laguna, auteur du *Viaje de Turquía*, à la lumière de recherches récentes," *Bulletin Hispanique*, LVIII (1956), 121–81.

————. "Charles-Quint bon pasteur, selon Fray Cipriano de Huerga," *ibid.*, L (1948), 398–406.

————. "Sur l'humanisme du Docteur Laguna: Deux petits livres latins de 1543," *Romance Philology*, XVII (1963), 207–34.

————. "L'idée de la découverte de l'Amérique chez les Espagnols du XVIe siècle (d'apres un livre récent)," *Bulletin Hispanique*, LV (1953), 25–55.

————. "De Savonarole à Luis de Grenade," *Revue de littérature comparée*, XVI (1936), 23–39.

Bell, Aubrey F. G. "Notes on the Spanish Renaissance," *Revue Hispanique*, LXXX (1930), 319–652.

Beltrán de Heredia, V. "Accidental y efímera aparición del nominalismo en Salamanca," *Ciencia tomista*, LX (1942), 62–101.

Bleznick, D. W. "Las *Institutiones Rhetoricae* de Fadrique Furió," *Nueva revista de filología hispánica*, XIII (1959), 334–39.

Bonilla y San Martín, Adolfo. "Un aristotélico del Renacimiento: Hernando Alonso de Herrera," *Revue Hispanique*, L (1920), 61–196.

Buceta, Erasmo. "Ensayo de interpretación de la poesía de Villasandino, número 199 del *Cancionero de Baena*," *Revista de filología española*, XV (1928), 354–74.

Buchanan, Milton A. "Annotations, III: Hernando de Acuña's Sonnet Addressed to Charles V," *Hispanic Review*, XV (1947), 466–67.

Bulatkin, Eleanor Webster. "La Introducción al *Poema Heroico* de Hernando Domínguez Camargo," *Thesaurus*, XVII (1962), 51–109.

Campos, Jorge. "Letras de América: La protesta del petrarquista Francisco de Terrazas," *Insula*, núm. 185 (April, 1962).

———. "Presencia de América en la obra de Cervantes," *Revista de Indias*, VIII (1947), 371–404.

Capote, H. "Las Indias en la poesía española del Siglo de Oro," *Estudios americanos*, VI (1953), 5–36.

Castro, Américo. "El enfoque histórico y la no hispanidad de los visigodos," *Nueva revista de filología hispánica*, III (1949), 217–63.

———. "Escepticismo y contradicción en Quevedo," *Humanidades*, XIII (1928), 12–13.

———. "Lo hispánico y el erasmismo" (Part II), *Revista de filología hispánica*, IV (1942), 1–66.

———. "Los prólogos al Quijote," *ibid.*, III (1941), 314–38.

Chacón y Calvo, J. M. "Quevedo y la tradición senequista," *Realidad*, III (1948), 318–42.

Cidade, H. "La literatura portuguesa y la expansión ultramarina," *Estudios americanos*, XX (1960), 219–40.

Davis, Gifford. "The Development of a National Theme in Medieval Castilian Literature," *Hispanic Review*, III (1935), 149–61.

Delacroix, Pierre. "Quevedo et Sénèque," *Bulletin Hispanique*, LVI (1954), 305–7.

Farinelli, Arturo. "Consideraciones sobre los caracteres fundamentales de la literatura española," *Archivum Romanicum*, VII (1923), 249–74.

Ferrater Mora, José. "Is there a Spanish Philosophy?" *Hispanic Review*, XIX (1951), 1–10.

———. "Suárez y la filosofía moderna," *Notas y estudios de filosofía*, II (1951), 269–94.

Frankl, Victor. "Augustinismo y nominalismo en la filosofía de la historia según Gonzalo Jiménez de Quesada," *Estudios americanos*, XVI (1958), 1–32.

Gilbert, Felix. "Political Thought of the Renaissance and Reformation: A Report of Recent Scholarship," *Huntington Library Quarterly*, IV (1941), 433–68.

Gilman, Stephen. "Fernando de Rojas as Author," *Romanische Forschungen,* LXXVI (1964), 255–90.

Gimeno, Joaquín. "Sobre el Cartujano y sus críticos," *Hispanic Review,* XXIX (1961), 1–14.

Glaser, Edward. "Manuel de Faría e Sousa and the Mythology of *Os Lusíadas,*" *Miscelánea de Estudos a Joaquim de Carvalho,* No. 6 (1961), 614–27.

González de la Calle, P. U. "Francisco de Vergara y la pronunciación de la z griega," *Boletín del Instituto Caro y Cuervo,* IV (1948), 249–320.

González-Haba, María Josefa. "Séneca en la espiritualidad española de los siglos XVI y XVII," *Revista de filosofía,* XI (1952), 287–302.

Green, Otis H. "Additional Data on Erasmus in Spain," *Modern Language Quarterly,* X (1949), 47–48.

———. "The Artistic Originality of *La Celestina,*" *Hispanic Review,* XXXIII (1965), 15–31.

———. "On the Attitude toward the *Vulgo* in the Spanish *Siglo de Oro,*" *Studies in the Renaissance,* IV (1957), 190–200.

———. "A Critical Survey of Scholarship in the Field of Spanish Renaissance Literature, 1914–1944," *Studies in Philology,* XLIV (1947), 228–64.

———. "Did the 'World' 'Create' Pleberio?" *Romanische Forschungen,* LXXVII (1965), 108–10.

———. "Juan de Mena in the Sixteenth Century: Additional Data," *Hispanic Review,* XXI (1953), 138–40.

———. "The Literary Court of the Conde de Lemos at Naples, 1610–1616," *ibid.,* I (1933), 290–308.

———. "On the Meaning of *Crisi(s)* before *El Criticón,*" *ibid.,* XXI (1953), 218–20.

———. "New Documents for the Biography of Guillén de Castro y Bellvís," *Revue Hispanique,* LXXXI (1933), 248–60.

———. "A Note on Spanish Humanism: Sepúlveda and His Translation of Aristotle's *Politics,*" *Hispanic Review,* VIII (1940), 339–42.

———. "Notes on the Pizarro Trilogy of Tirso de Molina," *ibid.,* IV (1936), 201–25.

Guillaume, Pierre. "Un précurseur de la Réforme Catholique. Alonso de Madrid: *L'Arte para servir a Dios,*" *Revue d'histoire ecclésiastique,* XXV (1929), 260–74.

Hanke, Lewis. "The Dawn of Conscience in America: Spanish Experiences with Indians in the New World," *Proceedings of the American Philosophical Society,* CVII (1963), 83–92.

Henríquez Ureña, Pedro. "El humanista Hernán Pérez de Oliva," *Cuba contemporánea,* VI (1914), 19–55.

Jungkuntz, Richard P. "Christian Approval of Epicureanism," *Church History,* XXX (1962), 279–93.

Krauss, Werner. "Wege der spanischen Renaissancelyrik," *Romanische Forschungen,* XLIX (1935), 119–25.

Kristeller, Paul Oskar. "Augustine and the Early Renaissance," *Review of Religion* (May, 1944), 339–58. (First pub. in *International Science*, I [1941], 7–14.)

——. "Humanism and Scholasticism in the Italian Renaissance," *Byzantion*, XVII (1944–45), 346–74.

——. El mito del ateísmo renacentista y la tradición francesa del libre pensamiento," *Notas y estudios de filosofía*, IV (1953), 1–14.

——. "Studies on Renaissance Humanism during the Last Twenty Years," *Studies in the Renaissance*, IX (1962), 7–30.

La Granda, Antonio de. "Huarte de San Juan y Francisco Villarino," *Estudios de historia social de España* (of the Instituto Balmes de Sociología, Madrid), I (1949), 655–69.

Láscaris Comneno, Constantino. "Senequismo y augustinismo en Quevedo," *Revista de filosofía*, IX (1950), 461–85.

Leonard, Irving A. "The *Encontradas correspondencias* of Sor Juana Inés: An Interpretation," *Hispanic Review*, XXIII (1955), 33–47.

——. "Montalbán's *El valor perseguido* and the Mexican Inquisition, 1682," *ibid.*, XI (1943), 47–56.

Lida, Raimundo. "Cartas de Quevedo," *Cuadernos americanos*, XII (1935), 193–210.

——. "Quevedo y la *Introducción a la vida devota*," *Nueva revista de filología hispánica*, VII (1953), 638–56.

Lockwood, Dean P., and Roland H. Bainton. "Classical and Biblical Scholarship in the Age of the Renaissance and Reformation," *Church History*, X (1941), 3–21.

Luttrell, Anthony. "Greek Histories Translated and Compiled for Juan Fernández de Heredia, Master of Rhodes, 1377–1396," *Speculum*, XXXV (1960), 401–7.

Malkiel, María Rosa Lida de. "La *Garcineida* de García de Toledo," *Nueva revista de filología hispánica*, VII (1953), 246–58.

Marilla, E. L. "Milton on 'Vain Wisdom' and 'False Philosophie,'" *Studia Neophilologica*, XXV (1953), 1–5.

Martinengo, Alessandro. "La cultura letteraria di Juan Rodríguez Freyle: Saggio sulle fonti di una cronaca bogotana del Seicento," *Annali* (of the Istituto Universitario Orientale, Naples), *Sezione Romanza*, IV, 1 (1962), 57–81.

May, T. E. "Fray Luis de León and Boethius," *Modern Language Review*, IX (1954), 183–92.

Meregalli, Franco. "Las relaciones literarias entre Italia y España en el Renacimiento," *Thesaurus*, XVII (1962), 606–24.

Mesnard, P. "Erasme et l'Espagne," *Revue de la Méditerranée*, III (1946), 57–77.

Morley, S. G. "Juliana Morell: Postscript," *Hispanic Review*, IX (1941), 399–402.

————. "Juliana Morell: Problems," *ibid.*, 137–50.

Morreale, Margherita. "Carlos V Rex Bonus, Felix Imperator," *Estudios y documentos: Cuadernos de historia moderna*, núm. 3 (1954), 7–20.

————. "El tratado de Juan de Lucena sobre la felicidad," *Nueva revista de filología hispánica*, IX (1955), 1–21.

Oettel, Thérèse. "Una catedrática en el siglo de Isabel la Católica: Luisa (Lucía) de Medrano," *Boletín de la Academia de la Historia*, CVII (1935), 289–368.

Parker, Alexander. "The Psychology of the *Pícaro* in *El Buscón*," *Modern Language Review*, XLII (1947), 58–69.

Pierce, Frank. "The *Canto Épico* of the Seventeenth and Eighteenth Centuries," *Hispanic Review*, XV (1957), 1–48.

————. "Some Aspects of the Spanish 'Religious Epic' of the Golden Age," *ibid.*, XII (1944), 1–10.

Pons, Joseph-S. "Le *Spill* de Jaume Roig," *Bulletin Hispanique*, LIV (1952), 5–14.

Post, Gaines. "*Blessed Lady Spain* — Vincentius Hispanus and Spanish Nationalism in the Thirteenth Century," *Speculum*, XXIX (1954), 198–209.

Reichenberger, Arnold. "The Uniqueness of the *Comedia*," *Hispanic Review*, XXVII (1959), 303–16.

Reynolds, Winston A. "Gonzalo de Illescas and the Cortés-Luther Confrontation," *Hispania*, XLV (1962), 402–4.

Ricard, R. "L'Infant D. Pedro de Portugal et *O livro da virtuosa bemfeitoria*," *Bulletin des études portugaises*, XVII (1953), 1–65.

Richter, B. L. O. "The Thought of Louis Le Roy according to His Early Pamphlets," *Studies in the Renaissance*, VIII (1961), 173–96.

Riley, Edward C. "The Dramatic Theories of Don Jusepe González de Salas," *Hispanic Review*, XIX (1951), 183–203.

Ringler, William. "*Poeta nascitur non fit*: Some Notes on the History of an Aphorism," *Journal of the History of Ideas*, II (1941), 497–504.

Romera-Navarro, M. "La defensa de la lengua española en el siglo XVI," *Bulletin Hispanique*, XXXI (1929), 204–55.

Ros, Fidèle de. "Guevara, auteur ascétique," *Archivo ibero-americano*, IV (1946), 339–404.

Round, Nicholas G. "Renaissance Culture and Its Opponents in Fifteenth-century Castile," *Modern Language Review*, LVII (1962), 204–15.

Sánchez Montes, Juan. "Actitudes del español en la epoca de Carlos V," *Estudios americanos*, III (1951), 169–99.

Schevill, R. "The *Comedias* of Diego Ximénez de Enciso," *Publications of the Modern Language Association of America*, XVII (1903), 194–210.

Sciacca, Michele F. "La opera philosophica de Francisco Sanches," *Miscelánea de Estudos a Joaquim de Carvalho*, No. 2 (1959), 173–75.

Selke de Sánchez, Angela. "El caso del Bachiller Antonio de Medrano, iluminado epicúreo del siglo XVI," *Bulletin Hispanique*, LVIII (1956), 393–420.

Semprún Gurrea, J. M. de. "El desengaño en la historia del pensamiento español," *Cuadernos del Congreso por la libertad de la cultura*, núm. 10 (1955), 53–58.

Setton, Kenneth M. "The Byzantine Background to the Italian Renaissance," *Proceedings of the American Philosophical Society*, C (1956), 1–76.

Spitzer, Leo. "Soy quien soy," *Nueva revista de filología hispánica*, I (1947), 113–27.

Swaen, A. E. H. "Sidelights on *Amphitryon*," *Studia Neophilologica*, XIX (1946), 93–118.

Tate, Robert B. "Italian Humanism and Spanish Historiography in the Fifteenth Century," *Bulletin of the John Rylands Library* (Manchester), XXXIV (1951), 137–65.

Vega Díaz, Francisco. "Miguel Servet entre la condenación y la gloria," *Clavileño*, núm. 34 (1955), 6–19.

Vendrell Gallostra, Francisca. "La corte literaria de Alfonso V de Aragón y tres poetas de la misma," *Boletín de la Real Academia Española*, XIX (1932), 85–100, 388–405, 468–84, 733–47, and XX (1933), 69–91.

Wardropper, Bruce W. "Metamorphosis in the Theater of Juan del Encina," *Studies in Philology*, LIX (1962), 41–51.

Williams, John D. "Notes on the Legend of the Eaten Heart in Spain," *Hispanic Review*, XXVI (1958), 91–98.

BOOKS

Alonso, Dámaso. *Góngora y el "Polifemo,"* 2 vols. Madrid, 1961.

———. *De los siglos oscuros al de oro.* Madrid, 1958.

Amezúa y Mayo, Augustín G. de. *Cómo se hacía un libro en nuestro siglo de oro.* Madrid, 1946.

Anderson Imbert, Enrique. *Historia de la literatura hispanoamericana.* Mexico City–Buenos Aires, 1954.

Andrés de Uztarroz, J. F., and D. J. Dormer. *Progresos de la historia en el reino de Aragón.* 2d ed.; Zaragoza, 1878.

Andrés Marcos, Teodoro. *Los imperialismos de J. D. de Sepúlveda en su "Democrates alter."* Madrid, 1948.

Asensio, Eugenio. "Juan de Valdés contra Delicado: Fondo de una polémica," in *Studia Philologica: Homenaje ofrecido a Dámaso Alonso por sus amigos y discípulos con ocasión de su 60.° aniversario,* I. Madrid, 1960. Pp. 101–13.

Atkinson, William C. "On Aristotle and the Concept of Lyric Poetry in Early Spanish Criticism," in *Estudios dedicados a Menéndez Pidal,* VI. Madrid, 1956. Pp. 189–213.

Bainton, Roland H. *Hunted Heretic: The Life and Death of Michael Servetus, 1511–1553.* Boston, 1960.

———. *The Reformation of the Sixteenth Century.* Boston, 1952.

Bataillon, Marcel. "¿Melancolía renacentista o melancolía judía?" in *Estudios Hispánicos: Homenaje a Archer M. Huntington.* Wellesley, Massachusetts, 1952. Pp. 39–50.

———. "Plus Oultre: La cour découvre le Nouveau Monde," in *Fêtes et cérémonies au temps de Charles Quint,* ed. Jean Jacquot. Paris, 1960. Pp. 13–27.

———. *El sentido del Lazarillo de Tormes.* Paris–Toulouse, 1954.

Bell, Aubrey F. G. *Benito Arias Montano.* New York, 1922.

———. *Fray Luis de León: A Study of the Spanish Renaissance.* Oxford, 1925. Spanish translation by Celso García. Barcelona, *ca.* 1928.

———. *Juan Ginés de Sepúlveda.* Oxford, 1925.

Belloni, Antonio. *Il poema epico e mitologico.* Milan, n.d.

Beneyto Pérez, Juan. *Espíritu y estado en el siglo XVI.* Madrid, 1952.

Bonilla y San Martín, Adolfo. *Fernando de Córdoba, 1425?–1486?, y los orígenes del Renacimiento filosófico en España.* Madrid, 1911.

———. *Luis Vives y la filosofía del Renacimiento.* Madrid, 1903.

Bullón y Fernández, Eloy. *Los precursores españoles de Bacon y Descartes.* Salamanca, 1905.

Burckhardt, Jacob. *The Civilization of the Renaissance in Italy,* trans. S. G. C. Middlemore. 2 vols. ("Harper Torchbooks," TB40–41.) New York, 1958.

Castro, Américo. *Aspectos del vivir hispánico.* Santiago, Chile, 1949.

———. *De la edad conflictiva.* Madrid, 1961.

———. "Gracián y España," in his *Santa Teresa y otros ensayos.* Madrid, 1929. Pp. 253–64.

———. "Juan de Mal Lara y su *Filosofía vulgar,*" in *Homenaje ofrecido a Menéndez Pidal: Miscelánea de estudios lingüísticos, literarios e históricos,* III. Madrid, 1925. Pp. 563–92.

Chevalier, Jacques. "Y a-t-il une philosophie espagnole?" in *Estudios eruditos in memoriam de Adolfo Bonilla y San Martín,* I. Madrid, 1927. Pp. 1–4.

Clements, Robert J. *Picta Poesis: Literary and Humanistic Theory in Renaissance Emblem Books.* Rome, 1960.

Cochrane, Charles Norris. *Christianity and Classical Literature.* New York, 1957.

Cohn, Norman. *The Pursuit of the Milennium.* ("Essential Books.") Fairlawn, New Jersey, 1957.

Corominas, Juan. *Diccionario crítico etimológico de la lengua castellana.* 4 vols. Bern, 1954.

Coster, Adolphe. *Fernando de Herrera (El Divino), 1534–1597.* Paris, 1908.

Cotarelo y Mori, Emilio. *Bibliografía de las controversias sobre la licitud del teatro en España.* Madrid, 1904.

Cuervo, Fray Justo. "Fray Luis de Granada y la Inquisición," in *Homenaje á Menéndez y Pelayo en el año vigésimo de su profesorado: Estudios de erudición española con un prólogo de D. Juan Valera,* I. Madrid, 1899. Pp. 733–43.

Dainville, François de. *Les jésuites et l'éducation de la société française.* 2 vols. Paris, 1940.

Del Arco, Ricardo. *La erudición española en el siglo XVII.* 2 vols. Madrid, 1950.

―――. *La idea de imperio en la política y la literatura españolas.* Madrid, 1944.

Dempf, Alois. *La concepción del mundo en la Edad Media,* trans. José Pérez Riesco. Madrid, 1958.

Dubler, César E. *D. Andrés Laguna y su época.* Barcelona, 1955.

Durán, Manuel. *La ambigüedad en el Quijote.* Xalapa, Mexico, 1960.

Entwistle, William J. *Cervantes.* Oxford, 1940.

―――. "A Meditation on the *Primera Soledad,*" in *Estudios Hispánicos: Homenaje a Archer M. Huntington.* Wellesley, Massachusetts, 1952. Pp. 125–30.

Estelrich, Joan. "Coup d'oeil sur le platonisme en Espagne" (Résumé) in Association Guillaume Budé, *Congrès de Tours et Poitiers, 3–9 Septembre 1953: Actes du Congrès.* Paris, 1954. Pp. 382–83.

Farinelli, Arturo. *Italia e Spagna.* 2 vols. Turin, 1929.

Febvre, Lucien. *Autour de l'Heptaméron.* Paris, 1944.

Ferrater Mora, José. *Diccionario de filosofía.* Buenos Aires, 1951.

Fitzmaurice-Kelly, James. *Chapters on Spanish Literature.* London, 1908.

Fucilla, J. G. *Estudios sobre el petrarquismo en España.* Madrid, 1960.

―――. *Studies and Notes (Literary and Historical).* Naples–Rome, 1953.

―――. *Relaciones hispanoitalianas.* Madrid, 1953.

Gallego Morell, Antonio. *Francisco y Juan de Trillo y Figueroa.* Granada, 1950.

García Icazbalceta, J. *Francisco de Terrazas y otros poetas del siglo XVI.* Madrid, 1962.

Gilson, Etienne. "La doctrine de la double vérité," in *Etudes de philosophie médiévale.* ("Pub. de la Faculté des lettres de l'Université de Strasbourg," fasc. 3.) Strasbourg, 1921. Pp. 51–75.

―――. *La philosophie au moyen âge.* Paris, 1947.

Giulian, Antony A. *Martial and the Epigram in Spain in the Sixteenth and Seventeenth Centuries.* Philadelphia, 1930.

González Palencia, A. *Gonzalo Pérez, Secretario de Felipe Segundo.* 2 vols. Madrid, 1946.

Gossart, E. *Les Espagnols en Flandre.* Brussels, 1914.

Greenleaf, Richard E. *Zumárraga and the Mexican Inquisition, 1536–1543.* Washington, D.C., 1961.

Guy, Alain. *Les philosophes espagnols d'hier et d'aujourd'hui.* 2 vols. Toulouse, 1956.

Henríquez Ureña, Pedro. *Literary Currents in Hispanic America.* Cambridge, Massachusetts, 1945.

Iriarte, Mauricio de. *Genio y figura del iluminado Maestro B. Ramón Lull.* Madrid, 1945.

Kelso, Ruth. *Doctrine for the Lady of the Renaissance.* Urbana, Illinois, 1956.

Keniston, Hayward. *Francisco de los Cobos, Secretary to the Emperor Charles V.* Pittsburgh, *ca.* 1959.

―――. "Notes on the *De liberis educandis* of Antonio de Lebrija," in *Homenaje ofrecido a Menéndez Pidal: Miscelánea de estudios lingüísticos, literarios e históricos*, III. Madrid, 1925. Pp. 127–41.

Kennedy, Ruth Lee. "The Madrid of 1617–1625: Certain Aspects of Social, Moral, and Educational Reform," in *Estudios Hispánicos: Homenaje a Archer M. Huntington.* Wellesley, Massachusetts, 1952. Pp. 275–309.

Lanning, John Tate. *Academic Culture in the Spanish Colonies.* London–New York–Toronto, 1949.

―――. *The University in the Kingdom of Guatemala.* Ithaca, New York, 1955.

Lapesa, Rafael. *Los decires narrativos del Marqués de Santillana.* Madrid, 1954.

―――. "Gutierre de Cetina: Disquisiciones biográficas," in *Estudios Hispánicos: Homenaje a Archer M. Huntington.* Wellesley, Massachusetts, 1952. Pp. 311–26.

La Pinta Llorente, Miguel de. *La Inquisición española y los problemas de la cultura y de la tolerancia.* Madrid, 1953.

Lea, Henry C. *Chapters from the Religious History of Spain Connected with the Inquisition.* Philadelphia, 1890.

―――. *The Moriscos of Spain.* Philadelphia, 1901.

Lecler, Joseph. *Histoire de la tolérance au siècle de la Réforme.* 2 vols. Paris, 1955.

Legrand, Emile. *Bibliographie hispano-grecque.* 3 vols. New York–Paris, 1915–17. (These are vols. XI–XIII of the *Bibliographie hispanique*, comp. R. Foulché-Delbosc. 13 vols. New York–Paris, 1905–17.)

Leonard, Irving A. *Baroque Times in Old Mexico: Seventeenth-century Persons, Places, and Practices.* Ann Arbor, Michigan, 1959.

―――. *Books of the Brave: Being an Account of Books and Men in the Spanish Conquest and Settlement of the Sixteenth-century New World.* Cambridge, Massachusetts, 1949.

Levin, Harry. "English Literature of the Renaissance," in *The Renaissance: A Reconsideration of the Theories and Interpretations of the Age*, ed. Tinsley Helton. Madison, Wisconsin, 1961. Pp. 125–51.

Lida, Raimundo. "La *España defendida* y la síntesis pagano-cristiana," in his *Letras hispánicas: Estudios, esquemas.* Mexico City–Buenos Aires, 1958. Pp. 142–48. (Reprinted from *Imago mundi*, II [1955], 3–8.)

López de Toro, José. *Los poetas de Lepanto.* Madrid, 1950.

López Estrada, Francisco. "La epístola de Jorge de Montemayor a Diego Ramírez Pagán," in *Estudios dedicados a Menéndez Pidal*, VI. Madrid, 1956. Pp. 387–406.

López Martínez, Nicolás. *Los judaizantes castellanos y la Inquisición en tiempo de Isabel la Católica.* Burgos, 1954.

Losada, Angel. *Juan Ginés de Sepúlveda.* Madrid, 1944.

Lynch, John. *Spain under the Habsburgs.* New York, 1964.

Lynn, Caro. *A College Professor of the Renaissance: Lucio Marineo Siculo among the Spanish Humanists*. Chicago, 1937.

Llanos y Torriglia, Félix de. *Una consejera de Estado: Doña Beatriz Galindo, "La Latina."* Madrid, 1920.

McDowell, Ernest W. *The Beguines and Beghards in Medieval Culture, with Special Emphasis on the Belgian Scene*. New Brunswick, New Jersey, 1954.

Malkiel, María Rosa Lida de. *La originalidad artística de la Celestina*. Buenos Aires, 1962.

————. *La visión de trasmundo en las literaturas hispánicas*, an *Apéndice* in Howard Patch, *El otro mundo en la literatura medieval*, trans. J. Hernández Campos. (English version [without appendix]: *The Other World according to Descriptions in Medieval Literature*. Cambridge, Massachusetts, 1950.)

Maravall, Juan Antonio. *Carlos V y el pensamiento político del Renacimiento*. Madrid, 1960.

————. *La philosophie politique espagnole au XVIIᵉ siècle dans ses rapports avec l'esprit de la Contre-Réforme*, trans. Louis Cazes and Pierre Mesnard. Paris, 1955.

Marichal, Juan. *La voluntad de estilo (Teoría e historia del ensayismo hispánico)*. Barcelona, 1957.

Marín Ocete, A. *El Negro Juan Latino*. Granada, 1925.

Mattingly, Garrett. "Changing Attitudes toward the State during the Renaissance," in *Facets of the Renaissance*, ed. William H. Werkmeister. Los Angeles, 1959.

Mecham, John Lloyd. *Church and State in Latin America: A History of Politico-ecclesiastical Relations*. Chapel Hill, North Carolina, 1934.

Méndez Plancarte, Gabriel (ed.). *Humanismo mexicano del siglo XVI*. Mexico City, 1946.

Menéndez Pidal, Ramón (ed.). *Antología de prosistas castellanos*. Madrid, 1920.

————. "Fray Antonio de Guevara y la idea imperial de Carlos V," in his *España y su historia*, II. Madrid, 1957. Pp. 108–13.

————. "La idea imperial de Carlos V," in his *Mis páginas preferidas: Estudios lingüísticos e históricos*. Madrid, 1957. Pp. 232–53.

————. "Los Reyes Católicos," *ibid*. Pp. 209–31.

Menéndez y Pelayo, Marcelino. *Bibliografía hispano-latina clásica*, ed. E. Sánchez Reyes. 10 vols. Santander, 1950–53. (These are vols. XLIV–LIII of the *Edición nacional de los obras completas de Menéndez y Pelayo*. 65 vols. Santander, 1940–58.)

————. *Ensayos de crítica filosófica*, ed. E. Sánchez Reyes. Santander, 1948. (This is vol. XLIII of the *Obras completas*; see above).

————. *Historia de la poesía castellana en la Edad Media*. 3 vols. Madrid, 1911–16.

Mérimée, Ernest. *Essai sur la vie et les oeuvres de Francisco de Quevedo*. Paris, 1886.

Merriman, Roger B. *The Rise of the Spanish Empire in the Old World and in the New.* 4 vols. New York, 1918–34.

Moldenhauer, Gerhard. "Spanische Zensur und Schelmenroman," in *Estudios eruditos in memoriam de Adolfo Bonilla y San Martín,* I. Madrid, 1927. Pp. 223–39.

Monsegú, B. G. *Filosofía del humanismo de Juan Luis Vives.* Madrid, 1961.

Montolíu, Manuel de. *El alma de España y sus reflejos en la literatura del siglo de oro.* Barcelona, n.d.

———. "Un tema estoico en la lírica de Fray Luis de León," in *Estudios dedicados a Menéndez Pidal,* IV. Madrid, 1953. Pp. 461–67.

Muñoz, Cipriano, Conde de la Viñaza. *Biblioteca histórica de la filología española.* Madrid, 1893.

O'Gorman, Edmundo. *La invención de América.* Mexico City, 1958.

Onís, F. de. "El concepto del Renacimiento aplicado a la literatura española," in his *Ensayos sobre el sentido de la cultura española.* Madrid, 1932. Pp. 195–223.

Parker, A. A. "La 'agudeza' en algunos sonetos de Quevedo," in *Estudios dedicados a Menéndez Pidal,* III. Madrid, 1952. Pp. 345–60.

Parry, J. H. *The Spanish Theory of Empire in the Sixteenth Century.* Cambridge, 1940.

Pastor, José F. *Las apologías de la lengua castellana en el siglo de oro.* Madrid, 1929.

Paz y Melia, A. *Catálogo abreviado de papeles de Inquisición.* Madrid, 1914.

Peeters-Fontainas, J. *Bibliographie des impressions espagnoles des Pays-Bas.* Louvain–Antwerp, 1933.

Pérez Pastor, Cristóbal. *Bibliografía madrileña.* 3 vols. Madrid, 1899–1907.

Porqueras Mayo, Alberto. *El problema de la verdad poética en el siglo de oro.* Madrid, 1961.

Pou, J. M. *Visionarios, beguinos y fraticellos catalanes (siglos XII–XIV).* Vich, Catalonia, 1930.

Puigdollers, Mariano. *La filosofía española de Luis Vives.* Barcelona, 1940.

Reusch, Franz Heinrich. *Der Index der verbotenen Bücher: Ein Beitrag zur Kirchen- und Literaturgeschichte.* 2 vols. Bonn, 1883–85.

Révah, I. S. *La censure inquisitoriale portugaise au XVI⁰ siècle.* Lisbon, 1960.

Ricart, Domingo. *Juan de Valdés y el pensamiento religioso europeo en los siglos XVI y XVII.* Mexico City, 1958.

Riley, E. C. *Cervantes's Theory of the Novel.* Oxford, 1962.

Romera-Navarro, M. *Estudios sobre Gracián.* ("University of Texas Hispanic Studies," 2.) Austin, 1950.

———. "Lope y su autoridad frente a los antiguos," in his *La preceptiva dramática de Lope de Vega y otros ensayos sobre el Fénix.* Madrid, 1935. Pp. 11–59.

Ros, Fidèle de. *Un maître de Sainte Thérèse, le Père François d'Osuna.* Paris, 1937.

Rubio, David. *Classical Scholarship in Spain.* Washington, D.C., 1934.

Salinas, Pedro. "En busca de Juana de Asbaje," in *Memoria del Segundo Congreso Internacional de Catedráticos de Literatura Iberoamericana.* Berkeley–Los Angeles, 1941. Pp. 173–91.

Sánchez Albornoz, Claudio. *España: Un enigma histórico.* 2 vols. Buenos Aires, 1956.

Sánchez y Escribano, Federico. *Juan de Mal Lara: Su vida y sus obras.* New York, 1941.

Sandys, J. E. *A History of Classical Scholarship.* 3 vols. Cambridge, 1903–8. (Reprint: New York, 1958.)

Sainz de Robles, F. C. (ed.). *El Epigrama español del siglo I al XX.* Madrid, 1946.

Saunders, Jason Lewis. *Justus Lipsius: The Philosophy of Renaissance Stoicism.* New York, 1955.

Schiff, Mario. *La bibliothèque du Marquis de Santillane.* ("Bibliothèque de l'Ecole des Hautes Etudes," fasc. 153.) Paris, 1905.

Schumacher, Hermann. *Petrus Martyr, der Geschichtsschreiber des Weltmeers.* New York–Leipzig–London, 1879.

Seidlmayer, Michael. *Currents of Medieval Thought with Special Reference to Germany,* trans. D. Barker. Oxford, 1960.

Serrano y Sanz, Manuel. *Apuntes para una Biblioteca de escritoras españolas desde el año 1401 al 1883.* 2 vols. Madrid, 1905.

Seznec, Jean. *La survivance des dieux antiques.* London, 1940.

Shepard, S. *El Pinciano y las teorías literarias del Siglo de Oro.* Madrid, 1962.

Sierra Corella, A. *La censura de libros y papeles en España y los Indices y catálogos de los prohibidos y expurgados.* Madrid, 1947.

Simón Díaz, José. *Bibliografía de la literatura hispánica.* 6 vols. Madrid, 1950–61.

Solana, Marcial. *Los grandes escolásticos españoles de los siglos XVI y XVII: Sus doctrinas filosóficas y su significación en la historia de la filosofía.* Madrid, n.d.

————. *Historia de la filosofía española: Época del Renacimiento (siglo XVI).* 3 vols. Madrid, 1941.

Spitzer, Leo. "Linguistic Perspectivism in *Don Quijote*," in his *Linguistics and Literary History: Essays in Stylistics.* Princeton, 1948. Pp. 41–85.

Spratlin, V. B. *Juan Latino, Slave and Humanist.* New York, 1938.

Terlingen, Juan. *Los italianismos en español.* Amsterdam, 1943.

Toda y Güell, E. *Bibliografía espanyola d'Italia dels origines de la imprempta fins a l'any 1900.* 5 vols. Barcelona, 1927–31.

Torner, Florencio M. *Doña Oliva Sabuco de Nantes.* Madrid, 1935.

Valbuena Prat, Angel. *Literatura dramática española.* Barcelona–Buenos Aires, 1930.

————. *La vida española en la edad de oro.* Barcelona, 1943.

Van Dyke, Paul. *Ignatius Loyola, the Founder of the Jesuits.* New York, 1927.

Vélez, P. M. *Observaciones al libro de Aubrey F. G. Bell sobre Fray Luis de León.* El Escorial, 1931.

Vilanova, Antonio. *Las fuentes y los temas del Polifemo de Góngora.* (*Revista de filología española,* Anejo 66). 2 vols. Madrid, 1957.

Viñaza, Conde de. See Muñoz.

Vossler, Karl. *Introducción a la literatura española del siglo de oro.* Madrid, 1934.

Weinberg, Bernard. *A History of Literary Criticism in the Italian Renaissance.* 2 vols. Chicago, 1961.

Whitaker, Arthur (ed.). *Latin America and the Enlightenment.* 2d ed.; Ithaca, New York, 1961.

Wimsatt, W. K., Jr., and Cleanth Brooks. *Literary Criticism: A Short History.* New York, 1957.

Wolf, Eric R. *Sons of the Shaking Earth: The People of Mexico and Guatemala — Their Land, History, and Culture.* Chicago, 1962.

Woodward, William Harrison. *Studies in Education during the Age of the Renaissance.* Cambridge, 1906.

Yáñez, Augustín. *El contenido social de la literatura iberoamericana* (El Colegio de México, *Jornadas* 14). Mexico City, n.d.

Zaccaria, E. *Bibliografia italo-iberica.* Carpi, 1908.

Zavala, Silvio. *La filosofía política en la conquista de América.* Mexico City, ca. 1949.

———. *La "Utopía" de Tomás Moro en la Nueva España y otros estudios.* Mexico City, 1937.

MEDIEVAL AND RENAISSANCE TEXTS

Angeles, Fray Juan de los. *Diálogos de la conquista del espiritual y secreto reino de Dios.* ("Nueva biblioteca de autores españoles," XX.) Madrid, 1912.

Balbuena, Bernardo de. *Grandeza mexicana,* ed. Francisco Monterde. Mexico City, 1941.

Bocángel y Unzueta, Gabriel. *Rimas y prosas, junto con la Fábula de Leandro y Ero,* ed. Rafael Benítez Claros. 3 vols. Madrid, 1946.

Bonilla y San Martín, Adolfo (ed.). *Clarorum Hispaniensium epistolae ineditae,* in *Revue Hispanique,* VIII (1901), 181–308.

Cabrera, Fray Alonso de. *Sermones,* ed. Miguel Mir. ("Nueva biblioteca de autores españoles," III.) Madrid, 1906.

Calvete de Estrella, J. C. *El felicísimo viaje del muy alto y muy poderoso príncipe y señor nuestro Don Felipe, Príncipe de las Españas, a sus tierras de la Baja Alemania,* ed. La Sociedad de Bibliófilos Españoles. 2 vols. Madrid, 1930.

Carrillo y Sotomayor, Luis. *Obras de Don Luis Carrillo y Sotomayor,* ed. M. Cardenal de Iracheta. Madrid, 1946.

Cervantes de Salazar, Francisco. *México en 1554: Tres diálogos latinos*, trans. J. García Icazbalceta. Mexico City, 1937.

Fernández de Heredia, Juan. *Obras de D. Juan Fernández de Heredia*, ed. F. Martí Grajales. Valencia, 1913.

Figueroa, Francisco de. *Obras*, ed. facsimile by A. M. Huntington. New York, 1903.

Filosofía española y portuguesa de 1500 a 1650, ed. Biblioteca Nacional. Madrid, 1948. (Pub. by the Ministerio de Educación Nacional, Dirección General de Propaganda.)

García de Matamoros, Alfonso. *"Pro adserenda hispanorum eruditione,"* ed. and trans. José López de Toro. (*Revista de filología española*, Anejo XXVIII.) Madrid, 1943.

Horozco, Sebastián de. *Cancionero de Sebastián de Horozco, poeta toledano del siglo XVI*, ed. Antonio Martín Gamero. (Sociedad de Bibliófilos Andaluces, ser. I, vol. VII.) Seville, 1874.

La Pinta Llorente, Miguel de (ed.). *Causa criminal contra el biblista Alonso Gudiel, catedrático de la Universidad de Osuna*. Madrid, 1944.

———— (ed.). *Proceso criminal contra el hebraísta salmantino Martín Martínez de Cantalapiedra*. Madrid–Barcelona, 1946.

La Torre, Francisco de. *Poesías*, ed. A. Zamora Vicente. Madrid, 1944.

La Vega, Alonso de. *Tragedia llamada Seraphina*, ed. M. Menéndez y Pelayo in *Gesellschaft für Romanische Literatur*. Dresden, 1905. Pp. v–xxx, 39–70.

León, Fray Luis de. *De los nombres de Cristo*, ed. F. de Onís. 3 vols. Madrid, 1914–21.

Leonardo de Argensola, Bartolomé. *Conquista de las Islas Malucas*, ed. Miguel Mir. Zaragoza, 1891.

————, and Lupercio Leonardo de Argensola. *Obras sueltas*, ed. El Conde de la Viñaza. 2 vols. Madrid, 1889.

Libro de los Gatos, ed. John E. Keller. Madrid, 1958.

López de Gómara, Francisco. *Hispania Victrix: Primera y segunda parte de la historia general de las Indias*, in *Historiadores primitivos de Indias*. ("Biblioteca de autores españoles," XXII.) Madrid, 1852. Pp. 155–455.

López de Yanguas, Hernán. *Cuatro obras del Bachiller Hernán López de Yanguas, siglo XVI*, ed. facsimile by A. Pérez y Gómez. Cieza, 1960.

Madrid, Fray Alonso de. *Espejo para los personajes ilustres*, in *Escritores místicos españoles*, I ("Nueva biblioteca de autores españoles," XVI.) Madrid, 1911. Pp. 635–49.

Madrid, Francisco de. *Egloga*, ed. J. E. Gillet in *Hispanic Review*, XI (1943), 275–303.

Manrique, Jorge. *Glosas a las Coplas de Jorge Manrique, III: Luis Pérez*, ed. facsimile by A. Pérez y Gómez. Cieza, 1962.

Nebrija, Antonio de. *Gramática de la lengua castellana*, ed. Ignacio González Llubera. Oxford, 1926.

Núñez, Hernán (Fernando Núñez y Guzmán). *Refranes o proberbios en caste-*

llano por el orden alfabético que juntó y glosó el Comendador Hernán Núñez, revised and emended by León de Castro. 4 vols. Madrid, 1803–4.

Ortiz, Andrés. "A Spanish Play on the Battle of Pavia (1525)," ed. J. E. Gillet in *Publications of the Modern Language Association of America*, XLV (1930), 516–31.

Poesías barias y recreación de buenos ingenios, ed. John M. Hill. ("Indiana University Studies," vol. X, no. 60.) Bloomington, 1923.

Poetas líricos de los siglos XVI y XVII, ed. Adolfo de Castro. ("Biblioteca de autores españoles," XLII.) Madrid, 1923.

Rivadeneyra, Pedro de. *Tratado de la tribulación*. ("Joyas de la mística española," VII.) Madrid, n.d.

Rodríguez, Alonso. *Ejercicio de perfección y virtudes cristianas*. ("Joyas de la mística española," VIII.) Madrid, n.d.

Rodríguez del Padrón (de la Cámara), Juan. *Obras*, ed. A. Paz y Melia. Madrid, 1884.

Sánchez de Lima, Miguel. *El arte poética en romance castellano*, ed. Rafael de Balbín Lucas. Madrid, 1944.

Santillana, Iñigo López de Mendoza, Marqués de. *Obras*, ed. J. Amador de los Ríos. Madrid, 1852.

Spanish Poetry of the Golden Age, ed. M. A. Buchanan. Toronto, 1942.

Talavera, Fray Hernando de. *Católica impugnación del herético libelo maldito y descomulgado que en el año pasado del nacimiento de nuestro Señor Jesucristo de mil y cuatrocientos y ochenta años fué divulgado en la ciudad de Sevilla*, ed. Francisco Martín Hernández, with an *Estudio preliminar* by Francisco Márquez. Barcelona, 1961.

Tirso de Molina. *La Patrona de las Musas*, ed. Rinaldo Froldi. Milan, 1959.

Toledo y Godoy, Ignacio de. *Cancionero antequerano*, eds. Dámaso Alonso and Rafael Ferreres. Madrid, 1950.

Tovar, Antonio, and Miguel de la Pinta Llorente (eds.). *Procesos inquisitoriales contra Francisco Sánchez de las Brozas*. Madrid, 1941.

Valdés, Alfonso de. *Diálogo de las cosas ocurridas en Roma*, ed. J. F. Montesinos. Madrid, 1928.

———. *Diálogo de Mercurio y Carón*, ed. J. F. Montesinos. Madrid, 1929.

Valdés, Juan de. *Cartas inéditas de Juan de Valdés*, ed. J. F. Montesinos. Madrid, 1931.

———. *Diálogo de doctrina cristiana*, ed. M. Bataillon. Coimbra, 1925.

———. *Diálogo de la lengua*, ed. J. F. Montesinos. Madrid, 1928.

Vega, Lope de. *La Arcadia*, in *Colección escogida de obras no dramáticas*. ("Biblioteca de autores españoles," XXXVIII.) Madrid, 1872. Pp. 47–136.

———. *Lope de Vega's "El Brasil restituido," Together with a Study of Patriotism in His Theater*, ed. Gino de Solenni. New York, 1929.

———. *Carlos Quinto en Francia*, ed. Arnold G. Reichenberger, Philadelphia, 1962.

———. *La Dorotea*, ed. J. M. Blecua. Madrid, 1955.

————. *El Castigo sin venganza*, in *Teatro*, I, ed. Alfonso Reyes, Madrid, 1919. Pp. 185–258.

La Vida de Lazarillo de Tormes, ed. J. Cejador. Madrid, 1914.

Ximénez de Enciso, Diego. *El Encubierto y Juan Latino*, ed. Eduard Juliá Martínez. Madrid, 1951.

Index